ICT Adoption and Application in the Malaysian Public Sector

Abdul Raufu Ambali
Universiti Teknologi MARA, Malaysia & Kwara State University Malete, Nigeria

Ahmad Naqiyuddin Bakar
Universiti Teknologi MARA, Malaysia

A volume in the Advances in Public Policy and
Administration (APPA) Book Series

An Imprint of IGI Global

Managing Director:	Lindsay Johnston
Acquisitions Editor:	Kayla Wolfe
Production Editor:	Christina Henning
Development Editor:	Allison McGinniss
Typesetter:	Amanda Smith
Cover Design:	Jason Mull

Published in the United States of America by
Information Science Reference (an imprint of IGI Global)
701 E. Chocolate Avenue
Hershey PA, USA 17033
Tel: 717-533-8845
Fax: 717-533-8661
E-mail: cust@igi-global.com
Web site: http://www.igi-global.com

Library of Congress Cataloging-in-Publication Data

Ambal, Abdul Raufu, 1968-
ICT adoption and application in the Malaysian public sector / by Abdul Raufu
Ambali and Ahmad Naqiyuddin Bakar.
    pages cm
Includes bibliographical references and index.
  ISBN 978-1-4666-6579-8 (hardcover) -- ISBN 978-1-4666-6580-4 (ebook) -- ISBN 978-1-4666-6582-8 (print & perpetual access) 1. Internet in public administration--Malaysia. 2. Information technology--Government policy--Malaysia. 3. Municipal services--Malaysia. I. Bakar, Ahmad Naqiyuddin, 1970- II. Title.
  JQ1062.A56A83 2014
  352.3'802854678--dc23
                              2014029328

This book is published in the IGI Global book series Advances in Public Policy and Administration (APPA) (ISSN: pending; eISSN: pending)

British Cataloguing in Publication Data
A Cataloguing in Publication record for this book is available from the British Library.

For electronic access to this publication, please contact: eresources@igi-global.com.

Advances in Public Policy and Administration (APPA) Book Series

ISSN: pending

EISSN: pending

Mission

Proper management of the public sphere is necessary in order to maintain order in modern society. Research developments in the field of public policy and administration can assist in uncovering the latest tools, practices, and methodologies for governing societies around the world.

The **Advances in Public Policy and Administration (APPA) Book Series** aims to publish scholarly publications focused on topics pertaining to the governance of the public domain. APPA's focus on timely topics relating to government, public funding, politics, public safety, policy, and law enforcement is particularly relevant to academicians, government officials, and upper-level students seeking the most up-to-date research in their field.

Coverage

- Government
- Law Enforcement
- Political Economy
- Politics
- Public Administration
- Public Funding
- Public Policy
- Resource Allocation
- Urban Planning

IGI Global is currently accepting manuscripts for publication within this series. To submit a proposal for a volume in this series, please contact our Acquisition Editors at Acquisitions@igi-global.com or visit: http://www.igi-global.com/publish/.

Titles in this Series

For a list of additional titles in this series, please visit: www.igi-global.com

Human Rights and the Impact of ICT in the Public Sphere Participation, Democracy, and Political Autonomy
Christina M. Akrivopoulou (Hellenic Open University, Greece) and N. Garipidis (Aristotle University of Thessaloniki, Greece)
Information Science Reference • copyright 2014 • 371pp • H/C (ISBN: 9781466662483) • US $185.00 (our price)

Chaos and Complexity Theory in World Politics
Şefika Şule Erçetin (Hacettepe University, Turkey) and Santo Banerjee (University Putra Malaysia, Malaysia)
Information Science Reference • copyright 2014 • 374pp • H/C (ISBN: 9781466660700) • US $210.00 (our price)

Transforming Politics and Policy in the Digital Age
Jonathan Bishop (Centre for Research into Online Communities and E-Learning Systems, Belgium)
Information Science Reference • copyright 2014 • 312pp • H/C (ISBN: 9781466660380) • US $200.00 (our price)

www.igi-global.com

701 E. Chocolate Ave., Hershey, PA 17033
Order online at www.igi-global.com or call 717-533-8845 x100
To place a standing order for titles released in this series, contact: cust@igi-global.com
Mon-Fri 8:00 am - 5:00 pm (est) or fax 24 hours a day 717-533-8661

Table of Contents

Chapter 8

Section 3
Application and Practice of ICT in Malaysia: Empirical Impact of Human Reaction to ICT Adoption in the Public Sector

Chapter 9

Chapter 10

Chapter 15

Preface

The overall aim of this book is to examine the impact of new Information and Communication Technologies (ICTs), in particular the Internet and new media communications, upon Malaysian public service deliveries. Through multiple theories of ICT adoption, network, convergence, and ICT governance models, the writing addresses three important dimensions of the impact of the Internet and digital communications, namely the Asia experience and the theoretical underpinnings of the network theories within the context of the new technologies by providing the two lenses of the perspectives on the theoretical framework and empirical issues pertaining to the impact of ICT in government services delivery system. In brief, this book sets out to critically analyse the nature in which the policy-driven network practiced by Malaysia has constantly challenged the country's new ICT agenda, thereby posing some kind of dilemma to its complex internal ICT governance processes. This book generally deals with the transformation of the digital convergence model as a form of ICT policy adoption and the impacts it creates on the overall ICT and information governance framework in Malaysia. It also looks at the human attitudinal reactions to the use of ICT for public service delivery by assessing various theories of ICT adoption and to expose other challenges that might be hidden in application of ICT for delivering public services to the people.

The target audience of this book includes policymakers, academicians, ICT designers, Internet researchers, and postgraduate students of higher learning institutions.

OVERVIEW OF THE BOOK

The book first captures the general application of ICT in public sectors of the Asia continent to set the platform for the case study of Malaysia, which is the main focus. In the Malaysian context, this book begins with the period prior to the formation of Communication and Multimedia Act (CMA) in 1998 to its subsequent phase of development and the present. This area of assessment is of primary importance, since major decisions implemented by the government through regulatory/authority agencies like Malaysian Communication and Multimedia Commission (MCMC) and the Information and Energy Ministry, as well as the subsequent development of a new regime thereafter has special historical link during the early phase. More specifically, the central focus of this book is the new policy, regulatory, and institutional issues brought by the increasingly intensified trend of digital convergence. This arises from the fact that the initial focus on regulating bodies, such as the MCMC and the Ministry of Science, Technology, and Innovation (MoSTI), the Energy Ministry, are managed by new agencies, such as Ministry of Communication and Multimedia Malaysia (MCMM) and MoSTI, as the sole and most important entity in providing information in the area where advocating for new mode of ICT governance forms the most critical aspect of digital convergence in Malaysia. It illustrates the implications of these intersectional and fundamental issues surrounding the design, implementation, and policy processes as depicted from the development and subsequent implementation of convergence initiatives by the government to regulate digital information. In view of this, it is essential to point out several questions focusing on issues of self-regulatory, its mechanisms, and the actual strategic decisions and behaviour of various network actors[1] in the pursuit of a balanced achievement of good ICT governance and information processes in Malaysia.

The book shows that the practice of policy networks portrayed by various stakeholders and ministries contributes to creating a new dimension of ICT governance for effective service delivery (i.e., network governance at the national level). However, despite ICTs at the centre of the government's growth strategy to build a genuine knowledge-based economy and society through effective information dissemination, it is found that the link between the past series of ICT policy reforms and the present character of new regime or body, policy network initiatives, are constrained by complicated ICT governance issues of different stakeholders and service providers. The analysis of the new regime's framework as addressed by the book (convergence model) considers whether Malaysia's initiatives are compensating for the gap between the "ethos of network governance" and the existing capacity or reality to support the process of good ICT governance and effective information dissemination throughout the country. Given the above concern, this book finds that the most important ICT convergence measures are to be found in the impact it exerts on the development of ICT and the design of Information Society agenda, and in the way in which that proliferation of convergence affects policy participation and political discourse. In addition, as informed by first-hand empirical data about the evolving nature of digital convergence and its impact on new governance, this book looks at the perceptions and actions of network actors to examine whether they have indeed changed over the years and whether these practices were in fact related to the influence of convergence within a national policy context of Malaysia's New Regulatory Regime (MNRR).

In nutshell, the first section of the book confines its scope to analysing the stakeholder agenda on ICT adoption for controlling information, regulations, and institutional reforms that together illustrate the systems of networks and mechanisms of the ICT in line with the digital convergence model for Malaysia, in all the three converging sectors[2]: telecommunications, broadcasting, and the Internet in Malaysia. It is argued in the book that in all three sectors these components are undergoing fundamental changes, primarily through the application of digital technology, which has significant impact for convergence policy and regulation of ICT adoption for public sector in Malaysia.

Having given the policy frameworks and models of how information and ICT adoption in public sector are regulated and managed, the book addresses various theories of ICT application in the public sector with a focus on the acceptance of such technology by people in relation to the behaviour of the users towards the adoption as well as lessons or implications contained for the policymakers and ICT designers.

WHERE THIS BOOK FITS OR STANDS

This book stands at the core value of new public management of public organization via ICT adoption and implementation. Given that greater commitments are now being dispensed by both political and executive bodies of government to improve service delivery, administration of public enterprises is re-conceptualized and re-managed as business with special reference to service delivery by harnessing the opportunities brought by technology. The idea is to administer public organizations with quality, efficiency, and adequate satisfaction of the citizens. Reforming public sector through the adoption of ICT is not only to satisfy or meet the ever-increasing demands of the masses but also to help establish trust between the government, civil servants, and the people they serve. Hence, political leaders and bureaucrats believe that they can benefit from improvement of service delivery to people.

This book is devoted to policy initiatives for reforming public service delivery system in this era of information technology. The book firstly focuses on how governance in the new ICT is working compared to the traditional forms in this contemporary era of services delivery in Malaysia. It delves into the relationship between policy network strategies and/or models being practised and the impact they bring in the new mode of governance regarding ICT in Malaysia for better services delivery. As an essential area of investigation, the book also includes the role that the government is playing in the transition from the traditional ICT regime towards the new convergence regime in Malaysia as seen in the context of policy and network governance theories. As an important feature of new ICT governance, the value of widening the political participation was gaining a strong momentum in each pillar of the debates on government's achievement in the information age with special references to Malaysia context.

What and how policies are utilised to reconcile the underlying tension between regulatory as well as institutional discrepancies or challenges of governance impacted by agencies in Malaysia are equally addressed. To be more specific, the book covers the different features of convergence initiatives for the success of new ICT governance agenda for effective service delivery in the country. It is argued that although the initial strategic alliance and industrial collaboration could be traced back as early as in the 1980s when Privatisation Policy was first adopted by the government; yet it was not until the late 1990s that enactment of CMA has legally pushed forward the idea of multiple engagement and became a new emerging phenomenon for ICT network governance in Malaysia. This actually extends the concept of new model of ICT governance as envisaged in the National Information Technology Agenda (NITA) leading to the framework called model of convergence. Hence, what may be the motivating factors that pull together convergence actors into the term of political discourse is a fit that was addressed in this volume. In other words, the nature of collaboration between public and industrial sectors have been significantly changed by the new framework of legal and regulatory mechanisms were brought into discussions. In the discussion, the strategies, policies, and regulatory frameworks interface between what we termed "the old regimes and the laws concerning digital convergence" are thoroghly explained. To expantiate this perspective, the extent of the legal and regulatory framework influence, its complement, and/or even substitute for the new mode of collaboration and what brings about a different and more effective way of ICT governance model are covered. Furthermore, the book draws attention to human reactions or attitude, especially of the civil servants towards the technology provided along the line of theoretical frameworks of ICT in the literatures to investigate the reality in Malaysia. Thus, the book bridges the gap between theoretical assumptions and what is actually happening in practice with respect to technology adoption for service delivery in the Malaysian public sector.

ORGANISATION OF THE BOOK

Apart from the introduction, the book is organized into three sections with a total of 15 chapters. Section 1 is comprised of Chapters 1-5, while Section 2 is made up of Chapters 6 through 8. Section 3 of the book is comprised of Chapters 9 to 15, including conclusions and recommendations. A brief description of each chapter is as follows:

Chapter 1 of the book presents the general adoption and applications of ICT in public sector with special references to Asia experience. To set the scene, the chapter examines e-government application in public sector and how it provides interactive access of people to social services, employment assistance, tax and revenue services, corporate registration, licenses and permits or renewals, which are possible through a common entry point and shared portal services provided by government agencies around the world and Asia countries. Thus, the chapter explores interactive model several factors which are driving forces for the application of e-government in various government entities in Asia and anywhere else in the world. These include potential benefits, potential challenges particularly in the technology development, such as growing of computing power and telecommunications bandwidth, business investment in adoption of technology, and competitive pressures. However, the findings in the chapter also reveal that e-government application in public sector is associated with many issues, especially privacy and security of data information and many other related problems that can leave people reluctant to adopt or use the ICT system. It is therefore argued that e-government application in public sector should be value-driven and not technology-driven. Some future directions for coping with challenges in ICT applications in the public sector are also highlighted.

Chapter 2 discusses the wave of digital convergence on ICT adoption and application in Malaysia. The chapter examines how much Malaysian convergence policy has achieved, in response to global reform, since 1990s. The chapter discusses policy and regulatory implications as well as the nature of new mode of ICT governance with particular focus on digital convergence model. The analysis draws on the scope of collective action that has been compared with the widening of participation of different key players in ICT adoption in Malaysia. Thus, this chapter explores convergence model and how public policy, MNRR, and institutional reforms affect the continuous search for new mode of governing ICT, in consequence with the global march towards technology and knowledge society. The first section, in particular, gives general accounts of the early formation of convergence policy practices and its effect on the ICT governance processes, locating it at the centre of network model and policy network literatures. The second section gives special overview of the evolution of new private self-regulatory regime, which is of direct relevance to the new ICT governance model. Finally, a conceptual framework for the promotion of new mode of governance in ICT adoption is identified as a basis for evaluation as factor that unfold Malaysia's digital convergence schemes.

Chapter 3 sets a focus on model of digital convergence of ICT adoption within the framework of network governance policy. This chapter considers the literatures relevant to a study of the impact of digital convergence upon ICT governance policy that impinges the overall manifestation of ICTs in the public sector today including Malaysia. The central theme of this chapter has highlighted the proliferation of ICT agenda, with particular reference to digital convergence, and eventually show that the mode of ICT governance model is affected by three important factors: first, policy network; second, new legal or regulatory environment; and third, institutional reforms which does not only addressed the rise of the policy network perspectives but also showed that the representation in digital age is about innovation and participation of key ICT players or actors that dominate government service delivery system. The chapter opines that emergence and development of digital convergence will enrich ICT governance policy beyond technological factors only. Thus, the chapter concludes that the digital convergence that is believed to influence ICT policy network and growth does not occur in a vacuum. The key actors must be regulated and managed with effective legislation to achieve the goals ICT adoption.

Chapter 4 examines new society and ICT adoption with references to investigation on the link between policy network and network management by the government. Thus, following the proliferation of the new multimedia and ICTs, the chapter highlights a new emerged metaphor that impinged on modern societies: the network society. In this chapter, discussions about public actors and policy networks relationships are highlighted and it is asserted that network theory, by no means, presumes that governments are like other actors. The findings show that governments have access to considerable resources ranging from sizeable budgets and personnel, special powers, access to mass media, a monopoly on the use of force and democratic legitimisation, which bear impact on ICT adoption and management. However, these are not without limitations, especially when they enter the network games with other network actors. In explaining the theoretical framework as well as the practice of self-regulation, the concept of "power-dependence" is examined in the chapter in relation to the digital management. The chapter identified this as being instrumental in bringing some notable changes and achievements in numbers of areas such as policy orientation, market flexibility, industry initiatives, as well as the general attitudes and responses of the public or consumers at large and eventually to facilitate the formation of a networked society.

Chapter 5 of the book addresses models of political representation for ICT adoption in a networked society. This chapter is a complementary discussion to Chapter 4. It examines the role of parliament within contemporary democratic ICT governance by addressing discussion on political online communication from the perspective of four different models of political representation. The chapter concludes that online discussion is a symbol of a political representation in the networked society. In this context, the chapter finds technology as transformative agent such as the Internet that allow representations of different actors possible, whereas the Internet itself is seen as support to the existing relationships between parliamentarians and their constituents. The chapter concludes that online political representation should not be understood in a limited nature of political process such as electoral or referendum purposes but must be "outcome" based, for example, getting the "right" information into the space for discussions, promoting the Internet communication as the innovative conduit for quality participation towards sustained democracy.

Chapter 6 explains the Theory of Reasoned Action (TRA) and its relations to ICT adoption and application in public sector. The findings in the book have shown some generic issues related to human side of adopting technology system for accomplishing designated works in public sector. These include, according to theoretical underpinning of this framework: the attitude, subjective norms, and intention. It shows that sole intention to use the technology is a function of both attitude and influence of colleagues in the organizational environment. Actual use of such technology may not take place as expected if there is no strong intention and that strong intention can only happen when the bureaucrats or civil servants at large had developed a positive attitude towards its utilization for accomplishing tasks. However, the chapter highlighted some limitation of TRA, especially on the issues of its applicability to non-volitional behaviours for policymakers and technology designers.

Chapter 7 explained the Theory of Planned Behaviour (TPB) and its expansion in relations to ICT adoption and application. It is another fundamental theory that help explains human reaction to ICT adoption in public sector. The Theory of Planned Behaviour (TPB) was mainly developed to improve the predictive power of the earlier Theory of Reasoned Action (TRA). According to the findings in this chapter, the main message of TPB is the introduction of Perceived Behavioural Control (PBC) which is considered a critical aspect of technology acceptance among public workers. The chapter highlights that since PBC is the degree of difficulties in performing behaviour (i.e., response perceptual reaction to adopting ICT) would interactively predict a behavioural reaction of human being to technology whereby man's intentions become stronger predictors of behaviour as PBC increased favourably. However, the chapter highlights some arguments where PBC is assumed to unilaterally influence a particular behaviour, especially in the context of people's reactions to ICT utilization within the presence of favourable conditions organization settings.

Chapter 8 discusses the Technology Acceptance Model (TAM) with its expansion in relation to ICT adoption and application in public sector. The chapter explained the trends and huge changes in technology environment and its wider applications, with special reference to TAM2, which expands the original TAM framework. The aim was to equip the original TAM with other eliciting belief variables, which are external to the perceived usefulness component of the TAM1. In order to further complement the practical significant use of original TAM in assessing acceptance of technology by users, the chapter discuses TAM3 with main focus of attention on the determinants of perceived ease of use that was not addressed in TAM2. The chapter addresses more pressing issues from technology acceptance to adoption with special reference to individual differences, system characteristics, social influence, and facilitating conditions as the determinants of both perceived usefulness and perceived ease of use. The findings in this chapter have shown that the utility aspect of technology is important in terms of outcomes of using a technology to accomplish tasks, yet the ease of using it in terms of perceived facility is equally crucial for the end users. Therefore, in the context of public sector adoption and acceptance of ICT, it means effect of some external variables, such as the features of the technology systems, its development process, and even training, are crucial to address for making the technology usage easy for people by designers.

Chapter 9 addresses the empirical Investigation of ICT usage in Malaysian public sector using Extension of Theory of Reasoned Action. Based on the call for extension of theories and models in the part II of this book, the original Theory of Reasoned Action (TRA) has been extended to fit the context of ICT usage in one of the chosen public organisations as a case study. A preliminary focus group interview was used to underpin and identify the most pertinent issues related to usage of ICT in a particular public organization. Based on the result, prior experience was introduced into the original theoretical framework of TRA as antecedent of attitude towards use of ICT in that public organization. As a new variable of interest added to extend the TRA, the causal link between prior experience and attitude was found to be statistically and positively significant. The chapter also sought a new finding of significant relationship between the link direct link of subjective norm and attitude variable as part of TRA extended model. These two findings provide a new dimension for academic investigations that does not addressed earlier. Based on such findings, the chapter concludes that the practical significant contribution to the public sector is that adoption of ICT is one thing but technical know-how and/or the experience of how to use ICT successfully to accomplish the goal of adoption is the most important. In other words, experience of how to use ICT and the presence of important individuals such as colleagues to give motivation and positive impression would make a user form positive attitude towards using ICT to do work.

Chapter 10 of the book conducted empirical investigation of ICT usage in Malaysian public sector using extension of theory of planned behaviour to bridge the gap between theory and practice using a problem-based approach of perceived usefulness of ICT among the subjects of the study at one of the government agencies in Malaysia. Thus, the study has extended the original TPB model by inclusion of perceived usefulness as antecedent of attitude of the respondents in this chapter. Statistically, the result obtained has reflected the relative importance of this newly construct added to the original model. In this context, perceived usefulness was found to have highest structural correlation with behavioural attitude. The chapter highlights the practical significant of this finding and formally confirmed the call to modify theory of planned behaviour, which was earlier discussed in the book. Based on the findings, the chapter concludes that perceived usefulness of technology can make users form a positive attitude towards intention to use the ICT system. In addition, the findings also show that perceived usefulness would strengthen the positive attitude towards use of ICT or can help change negative perception of users to positively use technology system. Thus, the practical significance of such findings to both policymakers and industries is that technologies must be made useful in achieving the purpose of adopting them in any type of organisations.

Chapter 11 examines the empirical Investigation of ICT Usage in Malaysian public sector using extension of technology acceptance model using another extended variable that was based on a problem-based approach via the results of the focus group interview. The most important additional contribution of the chapter was the focus on the external variables to perceived usefulness and perceived ease of using i-class at university. The university has adopted e-learning using i-class system through which teaching and learning are facilitated as alternative method of delivering knowledge to students face-to-face. Since majority of targeted group of students learning through this mode are adults, perceived computer self-efficacy, perceived convenience, and subjective norm were confirmed during the interview section and used to extend the original model. The findings in this chapter show that the rate at which the targeted students are using the system was very poor. Only a minimal number per whole week devoted their time to access i-class system for their studies. The chapter concludes that poor participation could lead to failure of technology device in public sector. The findings show that ease of using the i-class is relatively different from one student to another and it all depends on individual level of technology savvy and computer self-efficacy.

Chapter 12 empirically investigates ICT usage in Malaysian public sector using extension of technology acceptance model with trust in technology system as moderator. The chapter examines the moderating effect of trust in technology system. The inclusion of pertinent variables such as system factors, self-efficacy, and trust make a different to original Technology Acceptance Model (TAM) in this chapter. Based on the new findings, this chapter concludes that system factor, self-efficacy in individual factors, word of mouth in social factor play important roles in the use of ICT by MPs to engage their electorates when these variables are moderated with trust in ICT adoption. The chapter concludes that provision of e-parliament system is not enough until the MPs are really trained for appropriate use of ICT; otherwise, they might be reluctant to use the system due to lack of skills and capability and issue of self-efficacy. In addition, there is a need to gain people's trust towards ICT in terms of perceived usefulness and ease of using it to achieve the primary goals of technology devices.

Chapter 13 is devoted to empirically examine ICT usage in Malaysian public sector using a modified-extended model of Unified Theory of Acceptance and Use of Technology. The chapter uses the background information gathered from one of the Malaysian agencies to modify and extend the model in the context of local and organizational culture. Thus, the modified-extended model used in this chapter has statistically examined the relationships between predictors such as performance expectancy, effort expectancy, social influence, facilitating condition, and behavioural intention to use ICT with moderating effect of gender difference at the organization. In addition, it has also examined the relationship between facilitating condition and actual use behaviour as well as the moderating effect of gender difference on each predictor and behavioural intention. The findings confirmed a positive and significant relationship between three predictors and behavioural intention as well as actual use behaviour of ICT device among the staff. However, the finding shows a negative and insignificant relation between social influence and behavioural intention. The chapter concludes with another interesting finding that there is a significant impact of gender on the various predictors and predicted variable as clearly discussed.

Chapter 14 addresses the general prospects and contending issues among the actors and/or players that can affect impede on effective implementation of the Malaysian ICT policy adoption. The chapter reflects that since the middle 1990s there was a gradual but systematic public and private sector initiatives towards ICT agenda with the prominent role of the state. A remarkable launch of the National Information-tion Technology Agenda (NITA) and the Multimedia Super Corridor (MSC), which sets forth the future agenda related to the Information Age, promises greater expansion of the ICT for the country's mode of service delivery to meet the public demands. While the liberalization of telecommunication sector which paves ways for the proliferation of the new Communication and Multimedia (C&M) industries could be regarded as Malaysia's response to deal with the ICT governance model in the innovation policies regarding ICT, the eventual development of MSC has not resolved the issue of digital divide, indigenous R&D, and employment opportunities. Although not financially, the state considers ICTs' strategic con-tribution through the provision of consultancy and technical advisory services and the deployment of MSCs' developmental and marketing programmers to realize the MSC Malaysia national rollout and MSC Malaysia agenda are highlighted. The chapter also highlights various issues associated with digital convergence and how they were affected by the three critical factors: the innovative policy, the regulatory, and the institutional reform, within the context of the Malaysian ICT agenda since the middle 1990s.

Chapter 15 summarises the overall findings and main results of the theoretical and empirical research. The analysis contains an assessment of the extent to which the Malaysian digital convergence have fol-lowed the practices of an ideal network governance to see if there are other practices or methods adopted in their efforts to manage conflicts. In addition, the chapter also incorporates some of the insights pro-vided by other theories or approaches to explain the Malaysian contextual model. This is an overview of alternative approaches used by various scholars to analyse Malaysian network governance develop-ment as well as its responsiveness, which may give different interpretation of the Malaysian model of ICT convergence. It focuses on qualitative data description and analysis in order to assess alternative governance strategies for Malaysian eAgenda. Some policy implications and recommendations on how to improve the current governance policy and strategy are also included in this chapter.

Abdul Raufu Ambali
Universiti Teknologi MARA, Malaysia & Kwara State University Malete, Nigeria

Ahmad Naqiyuddin Bakar
Universiti Teknologi MARA, Malaysia

ENDNOTES

[1] Network actors is used interchangeably with convergence actors to denote the parties involved in a policy discourse about ICT adoption.

[2] The focus on policy, regulatory, and institutional politics of reform ICT points to the digital conver-gence discourse, so much so to highlight the sectoral domains of convergence in the C&M sector, albeit largely from telecommunications and broadcasting perspectives.

Acknowledgment

We would like to express our gratitude to IGI Global for their support throughout the stages of preparing the book. We express our appreciation to UiTM and KWASU authorities for facilities and enabling the environment and space granted to us for writing the book. We equally appreciate all suggestions, observations, and input from all the unknown reviewers chosen by IGI Global for evaluation of the manuscripts. We are also indebted to our families for being patient with us, especially during the sleepless period of writing the book. Finally, we thank all our research assistants for their timeless efforts rendered in data collections. May God reward them abundantly and let this new volume be helpful and useful to them and enrich their knowledge of policy implications for ICT adoption in the public sector.

Abdul Raufu Ambali
Universiti Teknologi MARA, Malaysia & Kwara State University Malete, Nigeria

Ahmad Naqiyuddin Bakar
Universiti Teknologi MARA, Malaysia

Introduction

GENERAL INTRODUCTION ON GLOBAL INFORMATION AND DIGITAL COMMUNICATION REVOLUTION IN MALAYSIA

One of the fundamental questions concerning the future of Malaysia's national "e" agenda is how to reform the state institutions to achieve good ICT governance and better delivery of services. It is acknowledged that good ICT governance model depends critically on the state actors'—be it public, private, or civil society—abilities to utilise information and communication technologies (ICTs) by making use of networks, and engaging within a multiple level of interactions (Norris, 2005). The call by Government policymakers for widen and more direct involvement in improving network governance is coincided with the converging trend of multimedia, broadcasting and telecommunications industry, which affects virtually every single stakeholder of these sectors. Facilitated by the convergence scheme, all stakeholders are able to interact, collaborate, and practising of what is known as the self-regulatory regime, progressively evolving and come out from the traditional or old regime associated with unilateral policy directives from the Government. The fundamental principles of this new regulatory framework was based on the values of transparency, technology, neutral, and self-regulation, which covers the scope of economic, technical, consumer, and social regulation (MCMC, 2014).

The concept of 'policy community' involves the process which allow members to share resources and experience through the 'complex web of interactions as well as participate in the process of policy making and refinements (Humphreys, 1994). The outcome of this is the emergence of networked participatory interactions (Calista & Melitski, 2007) as well as a number of 'policy networks' domains. Such 'policy networks' may be defined as a (more or less) structured cluster of public and private actors as well as civil communities, who are stakeholders in a specific domain of policy and possess resources which allow them to affect policy outcomes. Theoretically, the workings of policy networks are critical for promoting the diffusion of policy innovations. There is a view (as argued some of the chapters) that Malaysia is fast becoming a 'network state' —where different parts of the policy processes are linked together with a high speed or converging multimedia and information infrastructure, and being further extended to a regional as well as global level. Consequently, network ICT governance is not based on government-like structures that operate on a rather authoritative basis, but the political power within the policy setting and processes is exercised by sharing and pooling resources through establishing policy networks. For Malaysia, through the new and self-regulatory regime, the practice of policy networks of multiple stakeholders are crucial because these are perceived to be better situated in understanding the local situation and local dynamics relevant to the promotion of ICT governance whilst propelling Malaysia as the global communication and multimedia (CM) hub. Thus, riding upon the convergence of ICT – particularly through the Internet and the World Wide Web, there shall be an ever expanding mode of engagement from different actors in the policy process, seeking more autonomy and participation.

CONTEXTUAL BACKGROUND

The ICT Evolution in Malaysia: Historical Overview of Malaysia's National IT Agenda

Malaysia's telecommunication infrastructure development can be traced back to the late 1970s when it was geared largely to support primary sources of basic telecommunications services – namely the telephone, telegraph, and telex service. The then Department of Telecommunication was the agency that managed the data communication services, i.e., approval of leasing, mainly for commercial or private sector use such as banks or airline system. The Fourth Malaysia Plan (1981-1985) precipitated the establishment of the Public Data Network (PDN) and gradual change of the communication network from an analogue to a digital base. Eventually, various services were introduced including MAYPAC (Malaysian Packet Switched Network) and MAYCIS (Malaysian Circuit Switched Network), Data Transmission on the Switched Telephone Network (DATEL) which were all oriented towards global access at greater speeds of data transmission capability (Wijasuriya, 1998). The 1980s also saw the establishment of Malaysian Institute of Microelectronic Systems (MIMOS) – a government R & D facility whose initial focus on stimulating the microelectronic industry has since expanded greatly in terms of providing the backbone network for access to the Internet or the information superhighways. MIMOS developed RangKoM (*Rangkaian Komputer Malaysia* - Malaysian Computer Network) in

1987, which paved the way for linking a number of institutions. In 1987, Telekom Malaysia (TM) was corporatized in respond to the rapid advances in telecommunications technology; however, at that time the Government was still influencing important policy decisions, i.e. the approval of *Dasar Telekomunikasi Negara* (DTN) in May 1994 which provides the blueprint for policy guidelines for the development of the telecommunications infrastructure of the country for the period 1994-2020. To exploit the most of information revolution, Malaysia's own MEASAT-1 (Malaysia East Asia Satellite) launched in January 1996 further marked an exciting journey which supplemented the already improved infrastructure such as a fiber optic cable network nation-wide, optical fiber cables (including those laid under the sea bed connecting Sarawak and Sabah), the introduction of the Integrated Services Digital Network (ISDN), the Asynchronous Transfer Mode (ATM), microwave, satellite and other key technologies.

The construct of the ICT-led agenda during the end of 1980s followed the political representation model, that is the activity of making citizen's voices, opinions, and perspectives "present" in the public policy making processes (Dovi, 2008) in which the members are not only politicians and political party members. In fact, this was encapsulated by the formation of the Association of the Computer Industry Malaysia (PIKOM[1]) in 1986 which facilitated the development of an IT culture through its programmes and activities. The establishment of the National Information Technology Council (NITC) chaired by the Prime Minister further underscores the importance of the entire IT industry in overall national development and government intent in guiding future directions in the interest of the nation (NITC, 2014). NITC, despite has been shrunken in size as well as solely represented by the key bureaucrats (as opposed to its diversified members in its early formation), functions as a think tank and advises government on IT development in the country. It has initiated the formulation of a national IT plan which will identify key programmes geared towards transforming the nation into a knowledge based society. While driving the agenda of ICT for the country, the NITC in its early formation comprises of members from industry and NGOs as well as prominent experts among academicians that reflect some semblance of Castell (2006; 2005)'s notion of "network society."

Government agencies and industry partners around the world are met with the challenge of developing effective governance framework identify new opportunities; create innovative solutions and most importantly keeping up with the ever changing technology innovations centred on digital convergence. Moreover, during the 1990s, the growth of the Internet and an increasingly awareness of the implications of convergence of ICT, new media and telecommunications, led to a new global policy discourse involving various countries led by the US and the European engaged in a scores of international agencies such as WTO, and its predecessor organisation - the General Agreement on Tariffs and Trade (GATT) (Humphreys & Simpson, 2005, pp. 149-169). Policymakers have come to the painful realisation that the governance issues associated with cyberspace are not merely academic but also affecting the political and policy processes. One of the fundamental issues concerning the future governance is how to reform its institutions and working mechanisms in order to boost effectiveness by concentrating on offering citizens more participatory roles as networked actors (Calista & Melitski, 2007) thereby achieve good ICT governance.

Malaysia has not been spared of this. The two initial overarching initiatives are the Malaysia's Multimedia Super Corridor (MSC) which began in 1994 and the National IT Agenda (NITA) which came immediately after, but is more encompassing as it envisages the entire nation (Azzman, 2000). The concept of an intelligent city has been intensely debated across various fields such as geography, urban planning, and sociology, usually in relation to debates on the knowledge economy (Agar, Green, & Harvey, 2002; Gad, et al., 2012; Komninos, 2011; Massey & Wield, 2003; Saxenien, 2006). The making of intelligent cities embraces different configurations of spatial and digital factors that are realized in various forms, such as business incubators, R&D centers, science parks, technopoles, and innovation centres (Castells & Hall, 1994; Komninos, 2011; Massey & Wield, 2003). From the state's viewpoint, the realization of the MSC project is akin to interpreting a vision for a new Malaysia. Interestingly, MSC – after a decade since its formation, has now evolved and expanded into a number of cybercities across few states in Malaysia, seeks consistently for dual role objectives of not just an intelligent city or property development but at the same time symbolizes the country's effort to embrace new future with the Malaysian's mould. Mahathir Mohamad (former Prime Minister) has summed this up in his speech at the opening of the Multimedia Conference on the Multimedia Super Corridor in Kuala Lumpur on August 1, 1996:

I see the MSC as a global facilitator of the information age, a carefully constructed mechanism to enable mutual enrichment of companies and countries using leading technologies and the borderless world. Other plans may sound similar because they use "IT," "Cyber," or "Multimedia" to market one development or another. But we are not adding new facilities to existing ones; we are building and installing the latest on a huge 15-by-50 km greenfield site. We are not just upgrading. We are talking here about something much more far-reaching. We are talking about changing the way we live and work within the MSC. This special area will be a global testbed for the new roles of government, new cyberlaws and guarantees, collaborations between government and companies, companies and companies, new delivery of healthcare, and applications of new technologies [italics added]. We are taking a single-minded approach to developing the country using the

xxii

new tools offered by the information age. The MSC will be the R&D centre for the information based industries, to develop new codes of ethics in a shrunken world when everyone is a neighbour to everyone else, where we have to live with each other without unnecessary tension and conflicts. (Mahathir, 1996, p. 2)

The officially stated goal in the setting up of Cyberjaya is to create an intelligent city, a "model" city for the other states in Malaysia. Underpinning this effort is the top-down approach of interweaving high-class ICT facilities and urban infrastructure with the aim of attracting the experts in a broad spectrum of fields—engineers, researchers, and professionals in ICT fields—to live and work in Cyberjaya. The transformative potential and consequent benefits of the MSC, as the nucleus for growth access is prevalent across all levels of development including information, knowledge and techno-preneurship initiatives in Malaysia, however, the MSC is seen not merely an infrastructure project, but rather as a living organism that would continue to evolve and innovate technology development to propel the country to the k-economy.

Azzman (1998a), in addition, argues that NITA and the MSC are the two key ICT instruments that are interrelated and complement each other. According to Mahathir Mohamad, the MSC will be a "... multicultural web of mutually dependent international and Malaysian companies collaborating to deliver new products and new services across an economically vibrant Asia and beyond..." (MDeC 2014)[2]. The NITC, chaired by the Prime Minister, functions "as the primary advisor and consultant to the Malaysian Government on matters pertaining to ICT in Malaysia's national development" (NITC, 2000). To be sure, the vision of NITC is in line with the aspirations of Vision 2020 (NITC, 2013):

To evolve a knowledge society in the Malaysian mould where the society is rich in information,

empowered by knowledge, infused with a distinctive value-system and is self-governing.

Arguably, network society has always been going further that the information society as it is not purely the technology that defines modern societies, but also cultural, economic and political factors that characterised the network society. As a matter of fact, Saloma-Akpedony (2008) has alluded to the foundation of "knowledge society" encapsulated by the philosophy of Malaysia's National Information Technology Agenda (NITA) when charting the development of MSC. Some seven years after the formation of the MSC, the Internet continues to challenge traditional governance concepts, and to redefine the boundaries of policy making. ICT as a key enabler has clearly been given great importance to improve Malaysia's competitiveness so much so it transpired in recent Malaysian Plans, the Outline Perspective Plan 3 (OPP3) as well as numerous sectoral master plans or blueprints. To date, some current policy initiatives eventually emerged include MyICMS886, National Broadband Plan, Critical National Information Infrastructure (CNII), National Cyber-Security Policy (NCSP), Malaysian Public Sector Open Source Software Programme, Intellectual Property (IP) Commercialisation Policy, Science and Technology (S&T) Policy, National Biotechnology Policy, National Creative Industry Policy etc (see NITC Website for more information). At the core, Malaysia's Vision 2020 visualize the creation of a civil society as the ultimate goal where all Malaysian will have access to learning through 'infostructure' for personal, organisational and national advancement by the year 2020 (Azzman, 1998a; Xue, 2005). Additionally, it should be noted that the liberalisation of the education sector in 1995 has seen the formation of the Multimedia University (MMU) in 1998 with a special mission to producing ICT-graduates as well as ICT-related research outputs. Apparently, there has been a surge in interest in the evolution experiences of Malaysia information technology

(IT) agenda with particular reference to its model of new regulatory environment (Ramasamy, 2010). Among significant initiatives are the 10-National Policy Objectives for the C&M industry, as one of the crucial strategies outlined to achieve the vision. This symbolise the proactive role of the Government to engage various stakeholders such as the regulator, industry players, consumers to form a civil society where behaviour is expected to be in the interest of the nation (Lim, 2004).

The most notable consultative mechanism created in 1997 is an International Advisory Panel (IAP) which one could argue that its mission is to enroll the world's telecommunications and computer powerhouses. Now, in its 16th year, the MSC Malaysia IAP advises the Prime Minister of Malaysia on technology and wealth creation strategies. The IAP is made up of an impressive line-up of high profile thought leaders that includes top industry luminaries; the IAP panel members have unrivalled access to the Malaysian Premier and other top Malaysian Government Officials to help design policies and programs that will shape the country for generations to come. In 2011, the state reaffirmed its commitment to the MSC with the creation of MSC Malaysia Local Advisory Panel (LAP) - held its first meeting to chart strategies for the further development of the country's MSC Malaysia initiative. LAP members discussed key issues on preparing the nation for the innovative digital economy, through three main initiatives. The objectives are Growing Domestic Direct Investment (DDI) by strengthening the local ICT industry, enhancing competitiveness through specialisation in niche areas, and boosting talent by harnessing the right skill sets. The LAP is one of the initiatives under the MSC Malaysia 2.0 strategic plan, which provides a framework for the third phase of the MSC Malaysia's development from 2011 to 2020. Mirroring IAP, LAP members comprise local ICT industry luminaries and thought leaders, as well as representatives from non-government organisations, institutions of higher learning, and the private and public

sectors; advises, counsels and provides input to the Government in setting the agenda for the way forward in the development and growth of the MSC Malaysia and ICT industry in general (The Star Online, 2010). The aim is to reach out the impact of intelligent cities as widest as possible across the country.

This initial schema for new governance could actually be traced back to the privatisation of the Telecommunications Department Malaysia (TDM) in 1987, and the formation of the National Telecommunication Policy (NTP) in 1994, which paved the way for the full liberalisation of the industry (Moggie, 1999). The liberalisation of the telecommunication sector indeed marked an important milestone to exploit the most of the digital convergence of ICTs (Ahmad, 2008). The enactment of Communication and Multimedia Act 1998 (CMA1998) legitimises the process of convergence between the telecommunications, broadcasting, and the Internet. This is in tandem with the theme envisaged by NITA's vision of K-Malaysia 2020; that is to transform the entire apparatuses of Government as well as the Malaysian society by means of ICT. Some educational scholars see it as the impact of globalisation 'across all sectors, into an information society, then a knowledge society, and finally a "value-based" knowledge society. This concept is analogues to the 'tidal wave' of change (Fariza, et al., 2011) has been clearly identified as the strategic desired end-state envisioned that have been made in a particular reference to the Strategic Agenda that highlights the need to address five areas critical to our migration to the E-World, namely E-Community, E-Public Services, E-Learning, E-Economy and E-Sovereignty (NITC website).

The creation of the new regulatory framework as an importance piece under the new regime would require, among others, a fresh mindset to understand the changing pattern of governance in the information age particularly the movement from a largely hierarchical power structure to an increasingly networked governance structure[3].

At the heart of convergence is interconnectivity and the exciting potential it offers for a dramatic transformation into a globalised economy and knowledge-driven society (Moggie, 1999). The new emphasis by the Malaysian Government is on creating a public policy environment that encourages the growth of the C&M industry and facilitates the development of an electronic marketplace where the possibilities for further growth are limitless. Perhaps, more importantly, there is an increasing need to cooperate locally amongst policymakers, regulators, and other industry players and consumers, in order to compete globally which is the key item in the new regime.

With a marked shift of movement towards digital convergence, Malaysia is now fast adapting itself to meet the demand of this converging landscape. A number of grassroots initiatives were spawned and listed in the NITC's website such as Digital Malaysia, New Economic Model, MSC Malaysia, MSC Flagship Applications, MSC's Cybercities, MyGovernment Portal, eKuala Lumpur, .My Domain Registry, Malaysian Communication and Multimedia Commission, Communication Content Infrastructure, Creative Industry Lifelong Learning Programme (NITC, 2014). As the technologies became progressively more sophisticated and broadly dispersed, from the policy network's viewpoint, it is found that one of the biggest challenges in designing a comprehensive national policy framework for the converging industries faced by the Government, is to commit the nation to the basic principles of transparency, fairness, healthy competition, and industry self-regulation (Moggie, 1999). These mainly theoretical points were elaborated in great details as in Chapters 2, 3, 4 and 5.

Digital Convergence, Policy Networks, and the Quest for New Mode of ICT Governance

From the turn of the twenty-first century, the immediate blurring of borders between telecom-munication, broadcasting and computing posed invariable challenge to the old legislative and regulatory infrastructure, and ultimately, raised the further quest for a new mode of governance. Conceptually, the outcome of this development resembles the creation of new synergies, new behaviours, new opportunities and innovations (Negroponte, 1996), which begins to crafting an indispensable role in a new governance dimension in most countries. Regarding this, the new ICT has played a pivotal role by opening up the potential for a shift away from rigid hierarchical forms of organisation, towards more flexible, adaptive and interactive systems and networks (Castells, 1996; 2005). It quickly becomes clear that the ability to raise up effectively to the challenge of new governance depends greatly on the manner in which the potential of ICT can be used to increase political participation and to address other "democratic deficits" in representative democracy (Pautz, 2010).

Surely, a state which is typically hierarchical and organised based on the structure of command and control will become the stumbling factor for new mode of governance. To be sure, ICT is high on the agenda for many countries in the world regardless their status of development. This is not to say other sectoral economies, such as agriculture, manufacturing, human resources training and development, or other subjective factors such as the social and cultural context, and the state-society relations, do not tap the most opportunity in the information age, but to stress the significance of the digital technology as the key dimension for new governance. Field scholars clearly emphasise that the proficiency with which ICT and digital technologies is conducted constitutes the most important aspect of the whole governance function and directly affects all other public policy activities (Castells, 1996; Axford & Huggins, 2001, Hendriks, 2009). Humphrey, (1994, p. 5), in his analysis of the perspective of the mass media as an area of 'public policy' for instance notes:

... the organisation of the mass media system in a liberal democracy involves, more than most areas, addressing the crucial and quintessentially 'political' question of the proper balance of public and private involvement in policy-making.

Certainly, no state can be presumed to be ahead in its "e" agenda if it lacks the capacity to govern its ICT policy effectively. As this process is increasingly inevitable, Castells (1996) argues, the network patterns of authority have become a salient feature which redefines governance and facilitates the shift away from rigid hierarchical forms of organisation, towards more flexible, adaptive and interactive systems of networks. The shift eventually, prompted a complete re-evaluation of the role of network actors.

Further, the nature of digital technology integrates multiple platforms into a single channel. The merging of content and carriage is made possible via various CM applications. As a case in point, the convergence policy is now fast becoming the primary driver of connectivity agenda to close the prevailing gap between the "have and have-nots" within the society, as opposed to one during the previous regime, where such efforts are less integrated. New governance issues are now being championed and being taken to a new height in correspondence with an ever expanding growth of digital technologies. Thereby, this corroborates the fashionable trend for people-centred agenda, commonly articulated in the national information infrastructure (NII)[4] scheme. Indeed, convergence policy is having a critical role, particularly in establishing a foundation for governance process of future information societies.

Meantime, for over three decades, the competition for new technologies has been escalated, and is not only confined within industrial players, who pioneered the major exploitation of new technology, but also the national governments worldwide whose policies and regulations gaining momentums with the information industry. This requires special attention, mainly because

the policies outcomes have greater impact to all citizens. A combination of academic debates and empirical gathering since 1970s has made an interesting discovery with regard to the changes in governance patterns, which appear to take the "form of relatively stable sets of private and public organisations that negotiate in a horizontal, coordinating manner" (Coleman & Perl, 1999, p. 693). According to Coleman and Perl (1999, p. 693), "public authorities increasingly deal with corporate actors possessing a well-developed power base rather than with an amorphous public or with broad groups like social classes." Ironically, in the developing countries, the relationship between the broad socio-economic development and governance are now more than ever, evident and critical, where there is limited political participation and where political-bureaucrat elites hold great power in directing the state's policies and action.

As it happened, one obvious fact is that convergence policy is directly linked to states's relationships with industry players and other stakeholders. Digital technology, such as the Internet, brings in itself the force that greatly affects the nature of this relationship to make representative institutions more transparently accessible and open to interactive discussion (Coleman, 2006). It is a kind of 'self-organising, inter-organisational networks' which have led to the State's sovereignty being compromised. Rhodes has coined out the term 'the hollowing out of the state' to describe this situation (Rhodes, 1996, in Davies, 2002). Within the larger perspective of network society, "the architecture of relationships between networks, enacted by light-speed operating information technologies, configure dominant processes, and functions in our societies" (Castells, 1996, p. 470).

Therefore, the digitalisation[5] process has progressively brought about an exponential impact throughout the world and in itself is challenging and complex. Digital convergence has emerged and proliferated as an influential global medium with two unique features - the coming about, or more accurately, the blend between telecommunications and other digital media technologies; and, the opening up of a new governance landscape. Coinciding with the dramatic impact of interconnected global network society on public policy making has been the debate on the nature and functions of the nation state. It has been established that the capabilities of the state, in terms of governance, is also determined by adopting governance system that attempts to boost effectiveness by concentrating on offering citizens more participatory roles as networked actors (Calista & Melitski, 2007). It is also commonly agreed by many practitioners that in order to realising the proper governance policy in the information age requires active and meaningful practices that can secure widening of political participation, thereby meeting social and political objectives (Calista & Melitski, 2007; Coleman, 2006; Nuraizah, 2003; Moggie, 1999).[6]

Governments, around the globe, declare in the information age agenda, that they seek for a better governance process. However, declaration is one thing and the practice is something else. Experience reveals that most government declare policies, vision and commitments but fail to lay down the practical implementation required to meet the intended objectives. Hence, what matters most is not so much the declared intention, rather the actual practice.

There also, have been a surge of interest and scholarly debates from various disciplines from political science to technological communication and international relations to government studies to decide the ideal model for new mode of governance suitable for the information age (Hendriks, 2010). Various concepts and models have already been generated in the literature that attempt to provide the best approach or to solve the issue of the lack of effective governance. For instance, Loughlin (2004) suggested the partnership replaces 'top-down' approach with 'bottom-up' and governance is understood as 'steering rather than directing' to the extent it supplements or even replaces government. In the context of policy network, policy communities form around policy problems that 'involve complex political, economic and technical task and resourced interdependencies' (Kenis & Schneider, 1991). The various constellations of actors will 'interact strategically, while engaging in exchanges involving the sharing of information, expertise, and political support' (Coleman & Perl, 1999). The context of policy deliberations subsequently emerged as the outcome of different patterns of public-private relationships, known as "policy networks," based on the sharing and distribution of resources among policy actors (Coleman & Skogstad, 1990; Atkinson & Coleman, 1992; Hendriks, 2010).

An early, wide ranging, and highly influential statement of a participatory model has been notably proposed by Yoneji Masuda back in 1980. This model basically stresses a more complex, horizontal, and multidirectional interactivity (Chadwick, et. al., 2003). It is contended that while states may facilitate political discussion and interaction, they are but one association among many with a presence in civil society. The opinion formulation and political action based on forums, groups, or new 'virtual communities' formed the development of civil society, the concept of interactivity is understood in the context of 'how message are related closely together in a sequence of message exchange.' What is important is that the model stresses the role of the state to protect liberal-democratic values of free speech and expression that might otherwise be disregarded, while also providing infrastructure and regulation (Masuda, 1980). So, rules (formal or informal), resource divisions and organised political action are treated as a complementary support to institutional setting. The concern on this model is basically on the view that the characteristic trends of post industrial democracies – fragmentation and single-issue politics – as being intensified under the weight of new information networks. It is the new and different ways by the Internet have opened up the possibility that even those without large, stable memberships of affiliation with established institutions, be possibly heard as their views develop and move more quicker in the cycle of mobilisation in the increasing pool of publicly available information. Because of this, civil society – broadly defined as a political realm of ideas and actors separate from state influences or control, is now generally recognized by many scholars as a necessary condition for the democratization process (Kalathil, 2003; Brown, 2006; Hendriks, 2006).

Each of the models or approaches presented has their own merits. With the progressive development towards digital convergence, there has been considerable debate within the academic as well as practitioner community about the relevancy of these approaches when compared with the traditional hierarchical, top down command and control system of the past. One can notice easily that much of the current governance in the digital age literature is written in a way that acknowledges the tremendous policy, regulatory and institutional impact of digital convergence. Nevertheless, at the same breadth, mostly share the fact that governments are often trapped in the framework of the old regime which dampens many governance efforts.

Despite the argument of the merit of new governance, the basic concept of a new mode of governance remained contending issues in the information age agenda. Governance in principle continues to hold a serious place in the putative march towards information age society and this is primarily because the digital technologies is the driving force that affect each other sectoral policies. When the new regulatory framework was instituted, Government assumed that this will enhance the values of "transparency, reflexivity, efficiency and accountability" which is commonly being associated with the core ethos or values of good governance. These principles continue to hold a serious place in the value system of public policy and this is largely because ICT policy is having a pervasive impact to many economic sectors. Governance in the digital age is considered as a greater necessity than in a policy application and dictates normative as well as instrumental roles.

Governance through policy network forms an important component of the information age and digital convergence, as such, may promise a remedy to reduce the gap between the old and the new regime. A closer look at the characteristics of the governance system reveals that this model differs little from the ideas suggested by Castells (2005; 2007) when he formulated his concept of the network state (see Humphreys, 1994).

The variety of concepts offered in the literature lead to different options of the course of action. It is also interesting to note that despite massive international scholarly work, the network approach can hardly be considered as a widely accepted theory (Klijn & Koppenjan, 2000; Hendriks, 2010). Link to this, the contribution of this research is therefore, to point out with empirical evidences that explain the discrepancies between the role of network governance and the practical challenges in converging phenomenon. It could be interesting to point out any significant implications of digital convergence on new governance. Although other examples of relationship can be found in which advising and monitoring co-exist, the relationship between these two is particularly interesting because we can observe an attempt to separate the new Government roles with traditional ones. Further, particularly in Malaysia, there has been almost no formal serious research focus on this particular subject area. Thus, this may contribute to the debate on the relative effectiveness and of various governance patterns as well as shed some new understanding on yet unknown and unidentified deficiencies in achieving the governance within the process of convergence.

STATEMENT OF THE PROBLEM SITUATION

Encroaching middle 2000s, with the convergent development of ICTs for service delivery in Malaysia, it was in 1998 the Government created two institutions to carry out policy and regulatory goals in telecommunications and multimedia – the Ministry of Energy, Communication and Multimedia (MECM) – as the executive body to implement laws and the Malaysian Communications and Multimedia Commission (MCMC) – a regulator for the CM sector (Ahmad, 2008). The Communication and Multimedia Act (CMA) 1998 was enacted based on these basic principles: transparency and clarity; more competition and less regulation; flexibility; bias towards generic rules; regulatory forbearance; emphasis on process rather than content; administrative and sector transparency; and industry self-regulation (MCMC, 2013). However, governance of ICT, which many observers found to be very complex and perplexing, often overshadow the role of the MCMC. Innovation agenda was very complicated - seats between these two institutional authorities (MCMC and Ministry). MCMC was then put under the ambit of MoSTI; currently under the newly rebranding Ministry of Communication and Multimedia (previously Ministry of Information, Communication and Culture), with the latest restructuring of the Ministerial Cabinet 2013. Corresponding to this, we can hypothesis that the latest policy and institutional propositions, as explicitly outlined in the post-General Election Ministerial Cabinet restructuring, are Malaysia's latest response to the increasing demand arising from globalization era and the rapid changes in the ICT revolution.

The successful implementation of ICT agenda and governance motives is contingent upon many factors. The true value of the digital convergence scheme is viewed not only in the potential the technology offers but equally important also, the system as well as the enabling environments

that advocate the proper governance of the process. Nowadays, with various strategic plans, and institutional mechanisms, the Government of Malaysia has demonstrated its commitment to provide necessary capacity to spearhead the country into the eWorld. The primary goal of the NITC Strategic Agenda is defined in this way: 'to effectively facilitate the migration of Malaysians and institutional structures into the eWorld. This migration must be "ipso facto a people-driven transformation." The key challenge is thus how to engender the requisite mindset in our people and institutions to successfully participate, develop and grow in this emerging networked global society of the 21st Century (NITC Website). At the outset, the emerging eWorld equates the rise of the network society, which is in correspondence with the outcome of the convergence of ICTs and has considerable impact on economic, social and political domains of people lives.

Yet, observers (Ramasamy, 2010; Hazman & Munirah, 2003; Sophiee, 2002; Azzman, 1998b) express their concern that while braving the future, Malaysia faces serious political and economic challenges. The economic challenges it faces is that its economy is driven mainly by production based, while the political challenge it face is the excessive concentration of authority in Government and the lack of meaningful political participation. Within the context of national competitiveness, Hazman and Munirah (2003, p.3):

At the national level, however, despite many innovative changes to improve the quality of public service, many schemes to widen training and educational opportunities and many fiscal and financial incentives to stimulate the businesses to adopt new ways especially through increasing use of IT, innovation and creativity has not truly become a source of mark of national strength.

Apart from the political and the economic challenges, there are serious worries that current public policy processes might lead to ineffective policy outcomes. In the context of ICT and convergence policy, what the country has now are sets of building blocks that do not fit together very well - if at all, i.e., infrastructure and service competition. Critiques argue about misalignments which are evident between broad policies, implementing strategies, and monitoring (Siddique, 2008). Furthermore in practice, delivering good governance has not been easy for public administrators in the country's typical hierarchical and pluralistic society such as Malaysia as political decision-making has always the need to be sensitive to preserve peace and stability. The challenge for governance in Malaysia therefore is to primarily manage this global age transition whilst reconciling it with such a complex account of the local socio-political reality.

As debated elsewhere, dilemma of ICT governance in the era of digital convergence is not a new issue altogether. The Malaysian Government has become aware of this challenge. The earliest bold effort towards convergence of the telecommunications and broadcasting industries was indeed marked by the enactment of the CMA 1998 which have paved ways for a more substantive initiative thereafter, slowly but significantly emerged itself out of the old regime. At the beginning of the last decade, this new regime raises the major issue of how the NITC, together with the Ministry of Energy, Water and Communication (MEWC) and the Malaysian Communications and Multimedia Commission (MCMC), as the central ICT policy making body, authority and regulator, should be able to address the new challenges of the new reality.

The change, however, was overshadowed by tremendous regulatory complications as the general framework is still embodied by separate laws mostly caused the dilemmas between the cyber laws and the traditional laws. Edappagath (2004), an expert in cyber laws, argues that there is a challenge the government faces in terms of to reconcile between the old and the new legislations:

The existing legislations and statutes need to be reviewed to determine whether they can address the issues arising out of the new ICT era. If the current laws are inadequate to deal with the problems, national governments and/or appropriate regional and international bodies need to either revise the existing laws or enact new laws to provide individual, corporate and government users with maximum trust and security.

Government awareness of the need to create a new environment for policy process, in furtherance to the people-centred agenda of NITA has been reflected by the establishment of a NRR through self-regulatory and voluntary compliance. Of paramount importance, the recreation of the Ministry of Energy, Communication and Multimedia (MECM) to become Ministry of Energy, Water and Communication (MEWC), from previously Ministry of Energy, Telecommunications and Post (METP) as well as the Malaysian Communication and Multimedia Commission (MCMC) is also assigned with the mission of developing and recommending convergence policies to cope with new challenges.

The challenge that arose at the initial stage includes the creation of the NITA's model of governance based on people. The National IT Framework which subsequently emerged is considered the most instrumental outcome in the governance development in modern Malaysia history. As transpired, the NITA devises broad aspects pointing out to what sort of governance model suitable for Malaysia's eAgenda scheme. The contemporary Malaysian ICT policy framework is expected to fulfill with the spirits of NITA and to make sure its provision are reflected in the convergence policies and procedures, particularly those relevant to ensure the growth of the sector. However, the extent of consistency between the current practice and the demands of the new mode of governance as required by NITA is highly political and requires close examination.

In Malaysia, typical of any modern state, the policy process is constantly being challenged with the unprecedented change in digital technology, compared with much lesser pressure for growth in the early stage of development. One direct result of this pressure for development was that bureaucracy or policy makers were seldom caught off guard and driven by the technological changes without sufficient account of guarantees on what could be the possible outcomes. Often the case, the Government would put some breaks when they finally realised that some of decisions were too much politically risk to pursue.

As found later in this research, during the early years of ICT development, there was a state of clumsiness in the way the policy and project implementation being organised, particularly by the NITC. To some extent, the failure of some projects, e.g., Smart School, PC Ownership Campaign, were awarded to some individuals/contractors and they were through their link with political leaders rather than based on their qualities. Favouritism was the direct result of the too much power centralisation at the hand of political masters without formalised or transparent procedures. In Malaysia, as reported in Chapter 14, the Ministers commonly enjoy greater power by the law and the law itself has many provisional exemptions in the hand of the Minister.

The widening of political participation in the past was far less ideal than what it is today, though this is subjected to more debates (Johnston, 2010). The nature of digital technology propels new kind of relationship since cyber-spacer is no respecter of any boundaries, and if anything, this is even greater with the 'killer applications' afforded by digitalisation. Government may see this as a threat; however, with the impending march towards 'globalisation and the convergence'[7], there is always a constant pressure for the Government to secure the principles of governance to ensure that the system works for all. To be sure, digital convergence has put pressure on Government to explore the most effective mechanism to encourage even more proactive roles of the private sector in overcoming the digital divide issue, particularly the basic connectivity—which was the Government's core business of the past.

Further, as the CMA1998 emerged, the obligation to enhance the value of new mode of governance is getting ever more prevalent and increasingly formidable. Unlike NITA which has no legal credentials, the CMA1998, by virtue of its existence, demands the review of administrative structures, policies and regulations which should be in conformity with the new mode of governance. Hence, combining NITA and CMA together, not only are the Government and its political institutions obliged to rule according to the requirements of the model, but the policy framework, regulatory structures, and institutional settings should be in conformity with this two overarching documents, as well.

Meantime, despite an exponential impact of technology and the Internet, there is very little field investigation to provide evidence on the determinants as well implications of policy networks and its constituents particularly in the case of Malaysia. Initially, there was a paucity of empirical reports devoted to categorising the influences of the "e" agenda development upon public administration and its services. As of current situation, much more research has been conducted mainly on eGovernment and eCommerce aspect, which falls short of concrete theoretical exposition particularly on the basis of detailed studies of digital convergence. While ad hoc actions have been initiated to adapt public administration with the values of network governance in correspondence with the eGovernment agenda, there seems to have been patchy effort directed at synthesising views of the implications for digital convergence or developing strategies for dealing with its implications. Almost certainly, this occurred against the midst of the call for better governance between the supporters of pro-governance development strategies and sceptic views on whether the NRR in Malaysia will 'work' to bring about the new image of government in the era of cyberspace.

While the principles of democracy were settled in many advanced countries decades ago, these are still a matter of great debate in developing countries, such as Malaysia. The Malaysian system relies heavily on the discretion of political masters and elite bureaucrats in public agencies to secure important policy decisions. Navaratnam (2003, p. 293), a distinguished Malaysian expert who served with the Malaysian Treasury for 27 years, opined:

The civil service is generally far too centralised. Most major policies governing service and establishment of policies and principles are controlled by the Public Service Department (PSD). On the other hand, all major approvals of a financial nature are referred to the Treasury. Furthermore, economic development issues are invariably controlled by the Economic Planning Unit (EPU) in the Prime Minister's Department.

He argues that in such situation, plus many other factors, current framework may explain the reason why the civil service has become slower and less effective, and so too, directly or indirectly, being put under the power of a few individual Ministers. Navaratnam's observation indeed gives a good reason for investigating the implications this institutional design has on digital convergence, and vice versa.

This is also very much related to the way the institutional policy making decision which is highly centralised especially when it is move towards the top. It might be useful in this chapter to quote what is written about the centralisation of power of the Prime Minister; BICA Report in 2002 (p. 153) states:

Policy capacity parallels state capacity in Malaysia's case. Much of the advice given to the Prime Minister emerges from his own office or from closely connected organisations and institutes. The

dangers are parallel as well, in the high exposure to political risk and the dangers to the budget of the expensive bailouts following 1997.

The topic becomes even more critical, bearing in mind that some published studies mentioned that nepotism and cronyism[8] are considered peculiar in Malaysia.

OBJECTIVES OF THE BOOK

The broad aims of the book are. First, is to examine the impact of the ICT and digital convergence and second, to delve into theoretical underpinning of the ICT adoption that explains human reactions to technology. Third, is to empirically evaluate the extent to which Malaysia is capable of embracing the opportunity brought by digital convergence and effectively addressing the challenges associated with new ICTs drawing upon a convergent conclusion between theory and practice of ICT policy adoption in the public sector.

More specifically, the objectives of the book can be summarised as follows:

- To utilise related theories of policy networks as well as theories of ICT adoption in an analysis of the formation and subsequent evolution of a new regime as encapsulated by the overall Malaysian initiatives of ICT and digital convergence, seen in the context of NITA;
- To apply and extend all the theoretical frameworks utilising theories such as Technology Acceptance Behaviour (TPB), Theories of Reasoned Action, and Technology Acceptance Models (TAM) in the context of Malaysian public services' ICT policy adoptions;
- To comprehend the Malaysian ICT agenda in the context of the application and practice of ICT in the country by explaining how such features affect the search of a

new mode of ICT governance and human behavioural reactions;

- To examine the extent to which the policies being adopted are practiced and influenced by the multiple network actors and how this process is related to digital convergence;
- To identify and build a framework explaining the determinants of ICT adoption in Malaysia, and to empirically evaluate the extent to which ICT values are transpired in the actual practices;
- To evaluate some generic issues pertaining to ICT and challenges from technology and human sides in the public sector;
- To suggest general policy recommendations that might lead to the improvement in the behaviour and strategic thinking towards harnessing the potential of ICTs for Malaysia in the digital age for public service delivery system.

Scope of this Section

In order to provide a comprehensive and detailed understanding of the issues outlined above, an analysis is made to a range of interrelated issues exponentially deliberated in the literature, together with a series of empirical studies. The former draws upon a wide range of academic literature, and the latter focuses on the Malaysian ICT environment, in which convergence policy as the nodes within larger setting of Malaysia's agenda for ICT will be specifically analysed through detailed case studies.

The formation of a new regime as argued in the book has followed a strategy based on policy networks in view of network governance approach. The book looks at relevant network theories since they are modeled upon these practices and appear to be most relevant in describing the working of the system. Besides, the theories also bear significant elements of determining the extent to which Malaysia raised up to the opportunities and challenges through its implementation of NRR. This analysis will try to establish a linkage be-

tween the practices of governance and the issues or complications that lie beneath, that have not been addressed by other studies.

In consistent with the key focus explained earlier, this can be broken up into three major strands of inquiry, explained together with its theoretical rationales and assumptions.

People-Centred Governance Agenda

The first area of research was to concern with the rationale and reasons for the adoption of an innovation agenda centred on 'people factor'[9] in Malaysia, as reflected in the formulation of Malaysia's Vision for eWorld—such as the Vision 2020, NITA Framework and subsequent series of the five-year Malaysia Plan, which demonstrates broad national strategies in creating the quantum leap for governance change. Within NITA itself, the role of information is very instrumental, as a critical node that link between three key elements, namely, people, infrastructure, and application, with "people" as the most important feature of all.

The widening of political participation has become one of a dominant, and perhaps the most debated issue to determine the successfulness of governance agenda today. In the case of Malaysia, an overarching Vision 2020 was perhaps the radical impetus for change which paved the stimulus for the utilisation of ICT as it will lay down the gauntlet for future's multimedia policy. Ultimately, this will spur the nation towards the creation of a civil society where Malaysian will have access to learning through "info structure for personal, organisational, and national advancement by the year 2020" (John, 1998, p. 5). In addition, the Eighth Malaysia Plan (8MP) is the guiding innovative policies to be implemented in line with the march towards the National Vision Policy. It was based on the notion that the 'technology' element provides impetus to improve and drive unparalleled productivity gains in the knowledge-based economy ('K-economy') as opposed to the production-based economy ('P-economy'). At the core of MSC flagship, in particular, eGovernment, there is a growing recognition that the of the social inclusion which is not merely an adoption of 'technology initiative' alone but seen as a major part of a wider Government-wide transformation service agenda which can radically transform the very nature of governance (Rais, 1999).

On another respect, however, the novel purpose of enhancing the legitimacy of political institutions through an increased accessibility, responsiveness, and comprehensibility will badly undermined if the shift to network governance reinforces a new 'digital divide' issues which can occur in various forms (Bellamy, 2003). The nature of society inclusion is analysed in order to attest how crucial the social agenda in promoting the good governance, measured through the principles of political participation (Masuda, 1980). The variation of societal dimension initiatives (so as to determine the relative and strengths and drawbacks of social inclusivity as against its intended NITA objectives) is compared with the convergence's national objectives for C&M sector.

The national policy objectives, which envisages the concept of industry self-regulation imply a "certain degree of discipline, cultural and ethical norms," is basically speak of a "civil society and national identity" (Lim, 2004). Of course, this in one of various differentiated views of a number of scholars over the nature of and the degree of political participation and its significance to governance motives. By studying the nature of convergence evolution, particularly the necessary strategies adopted, the book hopes to see the important role of political participation in determining the overall achievement of e Agenda.

Legal and Regulatory Framework

The second area of research was to evaluate the legal and regulatory mechanisms that have been derived to support and enhance the new mode of ICT governance model in the country in relation to digital convergence. This is to examine whether it was consistent with the development philosophy of NITA policy, against the phenomenon of convergence. Such an analysis would be relevant to ascertain whether Government adopted a consistent and dynamic regulatory mechanism to achieving its long term goals of eVision, thereby embracing new governance.

As argued, there was an increased tendency towards digital convergence since the end of 1990s. It is found, historically distinct legal and regulatory frameworks was due to the separation of the technologies and infrastructure. With convergence, there are calls for mechanisms established at an early stage which ensure much closer cooperation and the determination of common policy goals between distinct regulators, as well as the sharing of information and resources under "new frontiers" of representation (Urbinati & Warren, 2008). Focus in this area included a review of the present situation, with the specific purpose of identifying the appropriate policies adopted in a timely manner to achieve its desired intention. The regulatory framework laid a foundation for the conducing governance in seemingly the most realistic manner. The advent of digital convergence is certainly contributing towards a higher capability of new mode of governance and "through the Commission close working collaboration with the industry participants to develop or adopt relevant international, regional or industry standards for use by the industry" (Syed Hussein, 1999).

As such, digital convergence clearly sets forth the new barometer for ICT governance both in Malaysia and elsewhere in the world. What is important here is that it is being extended beyond the bigger scope which reveals the different boundaries of multiple levels of policy interactions for Malaysia. The study of the influence of legal and regulatory framework in determining the level of convergence evolution will provide us with an opportunity to understand the nature of a new regime, and most importantly, it will also enable us to see how the policy institutions transform and adapt themselves to the new technological environment in Malaysia context.

Institutional/Structural Framework

The third area of research was to trace the institutional changes and their implications on new mode of ICT governance in the country. This included the various attempt made towards the formation of various institution of convergence, e.g., notably with the creation on the then MEWC to become MCMM and MCMC, in developing the new regime. This review is particularly important to compare and evaluate the approach taken before and after the convergence scheme takes place.

Institutional reforms are incomplete without considering 'political' factors such as federalism and decentralisation mechanisms for wider engagement and participation of different stakeholders and providers. This is important because such factors bear considerable impact in determining the propagation and sustenance of the ICT governance values. As argued that the transformation of innovation agenda[10] towards the ultimatum point of convergence will be most likely possible with the incorporation of wider participation into the whole administrative structure, based on the active engagement of various network actors, reconciled with national and global conditions. Only from this kind of network governance model developed and expanded within the mutual political process resulting from the spirit of active engagement can provide an avenue which would trigger the governance paradigm the country aspires to be.

Studying the mechanisms and arrangement of institutional framework along those dimensions offers the opportunity to address the role played by network actors in deliberating policy networks, multimedia convergence, and widening political participation.

In sum, these theoretical models and assumptions are used as an anchor to further examine three substantial domains of the politics of digital convergence. They are; first, the extent through which the impending issues of social inclusion or political participation, and the dynamism of integration amongst different actors in the networks system has impact on overall setting of ICT agenda; second, the constitution of legislative and regulatory framework essential for new governing regime, against the backdrop of multimedia convergence towards the promotion of governance values; and, thirdly, the establishment of the necessary institutional or structural framework to support the national policies and strategic planning framework and to what extent policy goals and outcomes are shaped by the interactions between actors associated with each domain structural setting for the implementation and sustenance of the evolutionary stages of convergence.

Section 1 of the book focuses on adoption and governance models of implementation of ICT adoption in public sector. In this part some contextual background of ICT development in Malaysia are given, in relation to the general convergence-divergence and other related models, and snapshot of some impending issues facing the Malaysian ICT and digital initiatives, and a discussion of how they affect the overall Malaysian ICT agenda. The brief review to theories which are relevant to the study of network governance and related concepts are highlighted. This offers an introduction to the overall perspective of the Malaysian ICT agenda and digital convergence with brief overview on Malaysia's changing landscape of governance impacted by the digital convergence. It focuses on the Malaysian national ICT initiatives in terms of its initial development, subsequent evolution, and overall governance scheme being impacted by the global trend of ICT and convergence. The discussion argues that Malaysian ICT evolution is fast shaped by the digital convergence phenomenon.

Section 2 focuses on theoretical explanation of people's reactions to ICT adoption in public sector. In other words, Section 2 of this book is devoted to the theories which provide the ground to clarify the human reaction to adoption of ICT in public organizations where most of the tasks assigned are obligatory in nature. This further helps advance the empirical analysis to underpin human characteristic behaviour to ICT acceptance by civil servants to accomplish tasks. These theories are broken down into Chapter 6: Theories of Reasoned Action (TRA) and its relations to ICT adoption and application; Chapter 7: Theories of Planned Behaviour (TPB) and its expansion in relations to ICT adoption and application; Chapter 8: Technology Acceptance Model (TAM) with its expansion in relation to ICT adoption and application.

Section 3 focuses on application and practice of ICT in Malaysian public sector to draw out empirical impact of human reaction to ICT adoption in accomplishing tasks and to pinpoint pertinent issues that were earlier highlighted in various theories discussed in Section 2 of the book. As such, Section 3 encapsulates the empirical chapters' attempts to link various models and theories found in the chapters of Section 2 of the book with empirical findings from field research with new variables identified. This is an effort to build appropriate theoretical explanation incorporating various inputs that were found in Section 2 on awakening of a call for extension of models in tandem to research settings and cultural background of the participants. The lists of the chapters' title in this section are as follow: Chapter 9: Empirical Investigation of ICT Usage in Malaysian public sector using Extension of Theory of Reasoned Action. Chapter 10: Empirical Investigation of ICT Usage in Malaysian public sector using Extension of Theory of Planned Behaviour. Chapter 11: Empirical Investigation of ICT Usage in Malaysian public sector using Extension of Technology Acceptance Model. Chapter 12: Empirical Investigation of ICT Usage in Malaysian public sector using Extension of Technology Acceptance Model with Trust in Technology System as Moderator. Chapter 13: Empirical Investigation of ICT Usage in Malaysian public sector using Unified Theory of Acceptance and Use of Technology. References for all these chapters are mainly from the primary materials such as interviews and surveys.

REFERENCES

Agar, J. E., Harvey, P., & Green, S. (2002). Cotton to computers: From industrial to information revolutions. In S. Woolgar (Ed.), *Virtual society? Technology, cyberbole, reality*. Oxford, UK: Oxford University Press.

Ahmad, N. B. (2008). *Towards a new mode of governance in Malaysia: Policy, regulatory and institutional challenges of digital convergence.* (Unpublished PhD Thesis). University of Hull, Hull, UK.

Atkinson, M. M., & Coleman, W. D. (1992). Policy networks, policy communities and the problems of governance. *Governance: An International Journal of Policy, Administration and Institutions*, 5(2), 154–180. doi:10.1111/j.1468-0491.1992. tb00034.x

Axford, B., & Huggins, R. (Eds.). (2001). *New media and politics*. London: Sage.

Azzman, T. M. S. (1988). *Microelectronics, information technology and society*. Paper presented at First Raja Tan Sri Zainal Lecture, IEM/MIMOS. Kuala Lumpur, Malaysia.

Azzman, T. M. S. (1998). *Nurturing the development of dyber communities: Will Asia be in conflict with the West?* Paper presented at the Global Information Summit. Tokyo, Japan.

Azzman, T. M. S. (2000). The changing world: ICT and governance. In NITC, Access, Empowerment and Governance in the Information Age. NITC Malaysia Publication.

Bellamy, C. (2003). Moving to e-government. *Public Management and Governance, 113.*

Brown, M. B. (2006). Survey article: Citizen panels and the concept of representation. *Journal of Political Philosophy*, *14*(2), 203–225. doi:10.1111/j.1467-9760.2006.00245.x

Building Institutional Capacity in Asia Report (BICA). (2002). *Alleviating the digital divide: Policy recommendations–Malaysia, Thailand, the Philippines, Vietnam*. Research Institute for Asia and the Pacific, University of Sydney. Retrieved from http://www.riap.usyd.edu.my

Calista, D. J., & Melitski, J. (2007). E-government and e-governance: Converging constructs of public sector information and communications technologies. *Public Administration Quarterly*, 87–120.

Castells, M. (1996). *The rise of the network society*. Cambridge, MA: Blackwell Publishers.

Castells, M. (2005). Global governance and global politics. *Political Science and Politics*, *38*(1), 9–16. doi:10.1017/S1049096505055678

Castells, M. (2007). Communication, power and counter-power in the network society. *International Journal of Communication*, *1*(1), 29.

Castells, M., & Hall, P. (1994). Technopoles of the world. In *The making of 21st century industrial complexes*. London: Academic Press.

Chadwick, A., & May, C. (2003). Interaction between states and citizens in the age of the internet: "e-government" in the United States, Britain, and the European Union. *Governance: An International Journal of Policy, Administration and Institutions*, *16*(2), 271–300. doi:10.1111/1468-0491.00216

Coleman, S. (2006). Parliamentary communication in an age of digital interactivity. *Aslib Proceedings*, *58*(5), 371–388. doi:10.1108/00012530610692339

Coleman, W. D., & Perl, A. (1999). Internationalized policy environments and policy network analysis. *Political Studies*, *47*(4), 691–709. doi:10.1111/1467-9248.00225

Coleman, W. D., & Skogstad, G. (1990). Policy communities and policy networks: A structural approach. *Policy Communities and Public Policy*, 14-33.

Davies, A. (2002). Power, politics and networks: Shaping partnerships for sustainable communities. *Area*, *34*(2), 190–203. doi:10.1111/1475-4762.00071

Davies, J. S. (2002). The governance of urban regeneration: A critique of the 'governing without government' thesis. *Public Administration*, *80*(2), 301-322.

Dovi, S. (2008). Political representation. In *Stanford Encyclopedia of Philosophy*. Palo Alto, CA: Stanford University Press.

Edappagath, A. (2004). Cyber-laws and enforcements to optimize benefits of ICT. *I-Ways: The Journal of E-Government Policy and Regulation*, *27*(3), 167–173.

Gad, S., Ramakrishnan, N., Hampton, K. N., & Kavanaugh, A. (2012, December). Bridging the divide in democratic engagement: Studying conversation patterns in advantaged and disadvantaged communities. In Proceedings of Social Informatics (SocialInformatics), (pp. 165-176). IEEE.

Hazman, S. A., & Munirah, R. A. (2003). *Nurturing human capital for the new growth thrust*. Faculty of Administration and Law, Universiti Teknologi MARA.

Hendriks, B. (2010). *urban livelihoods, institutions and inclusive governance in Nairobi: 'Spaces' and their impacts on quality of life, influence and political rights*. Amsterdam University Press. Retrieved from http://iap-portal.mscmalaysia.my/iap2011

Hendriks, C. M. (2006). When the forum meets interest politics: Strategic uses of public deliberation. *Politics & Society*, *34*(4), 571–602. doi:10.1177/0032329206293641

Hendriks, C. M. (2009). The democratic soup: Mixed meanings of political representation in governance networks. *Governance: An International Journal of Policy, Administration and Institutions*, *22*(4), 689–715. doi:10.1111/j.1468-0491.2009.01459.x

Humphreys, P. (1994). *Media and media policy in Germany: The press and broadcasting since 1945*. Oxford, UK: Berg.

Humphreys, P., & Simpson, S. (2005). *Globalisation, convergence and European telecommunications regulation*. Edward Elgar Publishing.

Johnston, F. (2010). Governance infrastructures in 2020. *Public Administration Review*, *70*(1), 122–128. doi:10.1111/j.1540-6210.2010.02254.x

Kalathil, S. (2003). The internet and civil society in China and Southeast Asia. *Zhang/Woesler*, 31-46.

Kenis, P. N., & Schneider, V. (1991). Policy networks and policy analysis: Scrutinizing a new analytical toolbox. In B. Marin & R. Mayntz (Eds.), *Policy networks: Empirical evidence and thereotical considerations*. Frankfurt: Campus.

Klijn, E. H., & Koppenjan, J. F. (2000). Public management and policy networks: Foundations of a network approach to governance. *Public Management an International Journal of Research and Theory*, *2*(2), 135–158.

Komninos, N. (2011). Intelligent cities: Variable geometries of spatial intelligence. *Intelligent Buildings International*, *3*(3), 172–188. doi:10.1080/17508975.2011.579339

Lim, P. (2004). A structured approach to successful e-government transformation in Asia Pacific. *JARING Internet Magazine*. Retrieved from http://www.magazine.jaring.my/2004/August

Loughlin, J. (2004). The "transformation" of governance: New directions in policy and politics. *The Australian Journal of Politics and History*, *50*(1), 8–22. doi:10.1111/j.1467-8497.2004.00317.x

Mahathir, M. (1996). *Keynote address*. Paper presented at the INFOTECH Malaysia '96. Kuala Lumpur, Malaysia.

Malaysian Communication and Multimedia Commission (CMC). (2014). Retrieved from http://www.skmm.gov.my/

Massey, D., & Wield, D. (2003). *High-tech fantasies: Science parks in society, science and space*. New York: Routledge.

Masuda, Y. (1980). *The information society as post-industrial society*. Tokyo: Institute for Information Society.

Muggie, L. (1999). *Opening address*. Paper presented at the Industry Briefing and Workshop on the Communications and Multimedia Act 1998 (CMA) at PWTC. Kuala Lumpur, Malaysia.

Muhammad Rais, A. K. (Ed.). (1999). *Reengineering the public service: Leadership and change in an electronic age*. Malaysia: Pelanduk Publications.

National Information Technology Council (NITA). (2014). *NITC Malaysia*. Retrieved from http://www.nitc.org.my

Navaratnam, R. V. (2003). *Malaysia's economic challenges - A critical analysis of the Malaysian economy, governance and society*. London: ASEAN Academic Press.

Negroponte, N. (1995). *Being digital*. New York: Knopf.

Nor Fariza, M. N., Norizan, A. R., Abdullah, M. Y., Salman, A., Abdul Malek, J., & Hussin, S. (2011, October). Empowering the community through ICT innovation. In Proceedings of Communications (MICC), (pp. 13-17). IEEE.

Norris, P. (2005). The impact of the internet on political activism: Evidence from Europe. *International Journal of Electronic Government Research, 1*(1), 19–39. doi:10.4018/jegr.2005010102

Nuraizah, A. H. (2003a). *Keynote address.* Paper presented at Majlis Malam Perdana Komunikasi Universiti Kebangsaan Malaysia. Kuala Lumpur, Malaysia.

Nuraizah, A. H. (2003b). *Welcome address.* Paper presented at the MCMC - Next Generation Networks Workshop 2003. Kuala Lumpur, Malaysia.

Pautz, H. (2010). The internet, political participation and election turnout: A case study of Germany's www.abgeordnetenwatch.de. *German Politics & Society, 28*(3), 156-175.

Ramasamy, R. (2010). Benchmarking Malaysia in the global information society: Regressing or progressing? *Journal of CENTRUM Cathedra, 3*(1), 67–83. doi:10.7835/jcc-berj-2010-0039

Rhodes, R. A. W. (1996). The new governance: Governing without government. *Political Studies, 44*(4), 652–667. doi:10.1111/j.1467-9248.1996.tb01747.x

Saloma-Akpedonu, C. (2008). Malaysian technological elite: Specifics of a knowledge society in a developing country. *Perspectives on Global Development and Technology, 7*(1), 1–14. doi:10.1163/156914907X253233

Saxenien, A. L. (2006). *The new Argonauts: Regional advantage in the global economy.* Cambridge, MA: Harvard University Press.

Siddiquee, N. A. (2008). Service delivery innovations and governance: The Malaysian experience. *Transforming Government: People. Process and Policy, 2*(3), 194–213.

Sophiee, N. (2002, September 12). The k-economy challenge. *New Straits Times.*

Star Online. (2010, May 14). *MSC Malaysia local advisory panel holds inaugural meeting.* Retrieved from http:archives.thestar.com.my/news/story.asp

Syed Hussein, M. (1999). *Keynote address.* Paper presented at the Industry Briefing and Workshop on the Communications and Multimedia Act 1998. Kuala Lumpur, Malaysia.

Urbinati, N., & Warren, M. E. (2008). The concept of representation in contemporary democratic theory. *Annual Review of Political Science, 11*(1), 387–412. doi:10.1146/annurev.polisci.11.053006.190533

Wijasuriya, D. E. K. (1998). Towards an information society: The Malaysian experience. *Information Development, 14*(2), 61–68. doi:10.1177/0266666984239157

Xue, S. (2005). Internet policy and diffusion in China, Malaysia and Singapore. *Journal of Information Science, 31*(3), 238–250. doi:10.1177/0165551505052472

KEY TERMS AND DEFINITIONS

Civil Society: A group of people in society coming together to agitate for rights and collective activities. It includes the non-governmental organizations (NGO).

Computer Network: A group of computer systems and other computing hardware devices that are linked together through the Internet for exchange of information among users from various parts of the globe.

Governance Framework: How the information technology infrastructure should be functioning to achieve the primary objective of ICT adoption.

Healthy Competition: As delivering of a quality services and products by public service providers or industrial players to the people with continuous improvement that can achieve citizen satisfaction.

Information and Communication Technology (ICT): Integration of telecommunication devices and computers as well as other software, middleware, storage and audio-visual systems that help users gain access, store, and transmit information to others.

Multimedia: As the using of several forms of communication technologies such as combination of text, audio, still images, video, and animation contents.

Political Party: An organization of people who have similar political beliefs and ideas and who work together.

Public Policy: A course of actions taken by the government to tackle public socioeconomic and political matters in a country. The course of actions taken can be laws, regulatory measures, or funding priorities concerning a given topic promulgated by a governmental entity and/or its representatives.

Public Sector: One aspect of the national economy charged to provide the basic unit of life such as services that cannot be provided by the private sector.

Regulation: An official rule or law designed to control and govern how certain action must be done. In ICT adoption, it extends to monitoring and enforcement of the rules for operation.

Telecommunication: The exchange of information over significant distances by electronic means such as cable, telegraph, telephone, and/ or broadcasting.

Unilateral Policy: A policy that has been formulated by one side or party to reach out the administration's goals.

ENDNOTES

[1] PIKOM objectives, among others, aimed to spearhead, promote, and coordinate development of resources, professional skills, and programmes in the IT industry in Malaysia; represent the local IT industry to the government and other organizations both local and foreign; provide a forum for discussion; promote the use of computers and foster high standards of conduct and service.

[2] The Multimedia Super Corridor, which is the centerpiece of the country's Vision 2020, intended as a vehicle for attracting technology-led companies and developing local industries. It is to be an exemplar, an island of excellence with multimedia-specific capabilities, technologies, infrastructure, legislation, and policies. It is to provide an ideal test site for new inventions and research. When fully developed, it will be a Multimedia Utopia, providing a productive and intelligent environment for the production of high value multimedia goods and services for delivery across the globe. The corridor will comprise of a global community of smart homes, smart cities, smart schools, smart cards, and smart partnerships - right on the cutting edge of a global information society.

[3] Dai (2003) uses similar concept to describe the paradigm shift in European governance to describe changing scenario of governance in the information age, with particular reference to his research of two major transnational networks (i.e. eris@ and TeleCities).

[4] NII initiative found its root in the US, but more commonly known as the Information Society in the Europe, in Malaysia, it is known as National IT Agenda. The term 'scheme', 'agenda', 'initiatives,' and 'policy' are used interchangeably where relevant to provide a context of discussion in which the flow of discussions are deemed appropriate, within this book.

[5] Digitalisation meant that "data, sound, and images could all be transmitted over the same networks", a general phenomenon of which telecommunications liberalisation converge

with 'information' and 'broadcasting', and became a central feature of 'global information society' (Humphreys and Simpson, 2005, p. 93).

6   The phenomenal growth of digital technologies (statistical details with regard to Malaysia will appear in Chapter Four) and their consequent impact on information networks and systems over the last decade have led to unlimited enhancements to the human endeavour. This suggests that new technological convergence is not intended to be an end in itself. In other words, among others, it effects the way business is conducted, interaction between the Government and the public, and the operations of public utilities can be attributed to this phenomenon (Nuraizah, 2003b).

7   The concept of 'globalisation' is mentioned together with 'convergence' as there has been considerable research done on how the digital convergence was significantly impacted by the global political discourse (i.e. international arrangements) led to fundamental and constant refining of the latter.

8   Cronyism can be regarded as the practice of associating closely with influential leaders and gaining undue concessions or favour of any kind (e.g., large contracts) privilege licenses which lead to monopolies and oligopolies often inordinately large profits, through the relationship. This subject, nonetheless, is insignificant to the book.

9   'People factor' or 'people-based' agenda serves as a guiding philosophy involving a complex and highly political interrelationship between technological convergence and 'local' adaptation for the impact of governing of the new age.

10   Innovation agenda is more general term used to include ICT and digital convergence policy initiatives.

Section 1
Adoption, Governance, and Theoretical Models of Implementation of ICT in Public Sector

Chapter 1
General Adoption and Applications of ICT in Public Sector:
Asia Experience and Findings

ABSTRACT

The emergence of the Internet and concerns for effective service delivery in the public sector have called for adoption of ICT in processing capacity as well as data storage since the 1990s. This, to some extent, has significantly altered the environment for ICT utilizations across society and governmental institutions and agencies to meet the demand of their people. While the long-term effects of this digital revolution are likely to bring some challenges, the needs for fast delivery of services and information have drastically pressured the public sectors to improve performances, capitalize on external opportunities within the environment, and prepare to overcome both internal weaknesses as well as external threats. This chapter looks within the context of the Asian experience of technology adoption and highlights various benefits and challenges encountered in practice by different parts of the countries in the continent.

INTRODUCTION

For any country to survive and prosper in this competitive global economy, it must manage its human capital and material resources both efficiently and effectively. The world is moving towards more democratic and open forms of governance. Hence, governments are under increasing pressure to improve managerial performance of their public sectors. Electronic government application, with special reference to IT, lies at the heart of

any management process to build the interface between the government and its people. With the growing complexity of modern organisations, not to speak of the systems of public sector, information technology is playing greater role in providing integration, coordination in public sectors and in building the interface between the government and its services to the people.

In the light of the above, the chapter examines the application of electronic government in public sector focusing on benefits and challenges it poses

DOI: 10.4018/978-1-4666-6579-8.ch001

on developing countries. The chapter begins with driving forces that spearhead the application of e-government in public sector. It goes on to discuss the core areas of e-government interfaces in order to trace the root of benefits and challenges in e-government application. Finally, it puts forward some ways to "move-on" in implementations of e-government and overcoming the problematic issues in ICT adoptions and applications in public sector.

The emergence of the Internet and concerns for developments in processing capacity as well as data storage over the 1990s has significantly altered the environment for ICT use across society and governmental institutions and agencies. While the long-term effects of this digital revolution are likely to be profound, the needs for developments have drastically pressurized the public sectors to improve performances, capitalize on external opportunities within the environment and prepare to overcome both internal weaknesses as well as external threats (Bhatnagar, 2014).

Due to the differences in ideological lens and/ or perception of individuals, e-government means different things to different people. According to Stephen (2001), e-government is the use of Internet technology and protocols to transform agency effectiveness, efficiency, and service quality. In a different way, Gartner Group (2000, p.2) describes e-government as "the continuous optimization of service delivery, constituency participation and governance by transforming internal and external relationships through technology, the Internet and new media." Detlor and Finn (2002, p.101) define electronic government as "the delivery and administration of government products and services over an information technology infrastructure." According to Gronlund (2001, p.1), "e-Government generally refers certainly to more use of IT, but more importantly to attempts to achieve more strategic for the use of ICT in public sector." In a more comprehensive way, Kieley, *et al.* (2002, p.341) defines electronic government as "an IT-led reconfiguration of public sector governance-and

how knowledge, power and purpose are redistributed in light of new technological realities." In this chapter, electronic government is defined as the use of information and communications technology (ICT) to promote more efficient and cost-effective government, facilitate more convenient government services, allow greater public access to information and make government more accountable to its citizens.

ROLE OF INFORMATION-SOCIETY ON E-GOVERNMENT

The advent of Information Society is creating unprecedented conditions for access to, and exploitation of, public sector information and represents a potential turning point in the ways in which societies are governed, administered and public services delivered. In other words, Information and Communication Technologies can be argued to be a driving force and a powerful tool to help achieve the Millennium's developmental goals. Indeed, the Millennium declaration and its road map to globalisation campaigns have called on governments to pursue a strategic-management through the knowledge infrastructure, particularly ICTs, via a creative partnership. In fact, the mainstream of ICT, within planning and design of improving strategies in public sectors is pivotal, both at national, local and regional levels of government administrative bodies. Hence, e-government becomes a particularly important ICT application in public sector.

More importantly, the "World Summit on the Information Society," which took place in Geneva, December 2003 and Tunis, 2005, pointed out the international community's readiness to improve initiatives that enhance the role of ICT for political, cultural and economic development. The summit specifically explored the best practices in new ICT based modes of interaction between government and its citizens. As such, e-government can be considered a process, or a means to an end, rather than an end in itself. E-government is still in the earliest stages of development and promises to evolve with advances in technology and increased acceptance and trust in electronic communication (Fred, 1999; Bhatnagar, 2014).

DIMENSIONS OF E-GOVERNMENT APPLICATIONS IN PUBLIC SECTOR

The conceptual section of this chapter provides the basis for structural dimensions of application of e-Government in public sector. Some analysts sought e-government in terms of specific course of action to enhance job information. Others have broadly perceived e-government as automating the delivery of government services to people. In other words, e-government is seen as a means to enable citizens interact and receive services from the federal government, state, and local governments as shown in Figure 1.

On the basis of this different conceptualisation, one can identify three distinctive areas for application of e-government in public sector.

First, e-government application can be from government to government, second, from government to business, and third, from government to citizens as in the figure below. Some people may point to another area such as from government to employee. However, the chapter does not lose sight on that dimension, but is considered to be a subset or intra-agency activities of the government to government interface. Hence, it is not addressed as a separate entity.

Government to Government Dimension of E-Government Application

Government to government dimension application represents the corner stone of e-government. In fact, it has been argued by Atkinson and Ulevich that federal, state and local governments should enhance their own internal systems and procedures before electronic transactions with both citizens and business communities could be successful (Atkinson & Ulevich, 2000; Bhatnagar, 2008).

Figure 1. E-government interaction

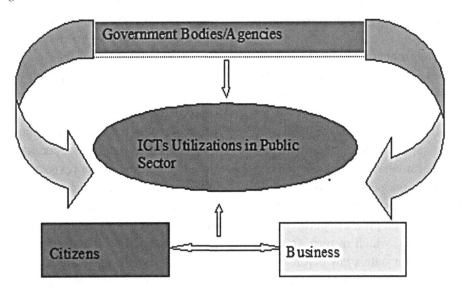

There are three levels of initiative forces that call for the application government to government dimension of e-government. First, in relations to laws and government regulations, the growing emphasis is on paperwork reduction in order to reduce the information collection efforts and reporting requirements of the federal government as well as to coordination of government-wide information management activities easier. In addition, the importance of computer security requires that the federal agencies need to adopt an information security plans. Second, the interest in improved efficiency, cost savings by increasing the speed of transactions, reducing the number of personnel necessary to complete a task and improving the consistency of outputs (Trattner, 2000; Asgarkhani, 2005). Third, according to Sprehe (2001), an attempt to apply 'best practices' in public sectors, as in private sectors, make it imperative for government to government electronic initiatives. He contends that state and local governments are often perceived as models for e-government initiatives due to their role in delivering services to citizens. Most of the policy-makers are now advocating for best approach to restructuring government-government relationships. In this context, e-government is often proposed as solution.

A glaring example of government to government application of e-government is the Northeast Gang Information System (NEGIS) in US. NEGIS is sponsored by Department of Justice and Services as a shared resource for street gang information for states in the northeast such as Rhode Island, Vermont and New York. NEGIS covers information on gang related activities, gang intelligence and even reference library. Hence, it connects state police departments of the participant-states, which in turn, transmit the information to the state's law enforcement agencies (The National Institute of Justice-NIJ, 2000).

Government to Business Dimension of E-Government Application

Another dimension of e-government application in public sector is the building of interface between government and business sector of a nation's economy. According to Gilbert, government to business initiatives receive a significant amount of attention in part because of the high enthusiasm of the business sector and the potential for reducing costs through improved procurement practices and increased competition (Gilbert, 2001). This dimension of e-government can reflect information about the sale of surplus government goods to the public as well as procurement of goods and services. Although not all are directly dependent on the use of information technology, however, performance-based contracting is a sound electronic method in which the payment that governments make to the contractors can be based on the actual goals and outcomes of the job done.

Another government to business e-method is Share-in-Savings contracts. This is a method in which the contractor pays for the up-front costs of a project, such as installation of a new computer system and receives payment passed on the savings generated (Langlois, 2001, p.44). The third e-government application to government-business interface is a reverse auction method that can be conducted over Internet. This method allows companies to openly bidding against each other in real time to win a government contract. The main objective of this method is to drive prices down to market levels. Hence, in a situation where major emphasis is on price, reverse auctions are the best-suited for both quality and expected performance. These are usually clear and easily assessed.

There are two primary motives for application of e-government in building the interface between government and business sector of any country. The first rationale and/or motive is the business community itself, whereby the use of electronic means to carry out various activities like procurement, sales and hiring can become an easy task for state industries. In addition, many companies would like to extend the cost savings realised in their business-to-business transactions to their business with federal, state and local governments. The second motive is the growing demand by policy-makers for cost cutting and more efficient procurement. The fact is that the government to business e-government initiatives is promoted on the potential to streamline and improve the consistency of personnel-intensive tasks, such as processing license renewals or employee benefit changes as in the Malaysian government proposal for e-government (see: MAMPU, 1997, Rais, 2003; Ambali, 2010).

In practice, one-stop example of government-to-business e-government application is Government Services Administration Auctions (GSAA) where GSAA sells federal surplus property via online Web site to the highest bidders. The items sold to industrial machinery and vehicles range from hand tools to furniture (GSAA). Another government-to-business initiative administered by GSA Federal Technology Service (FTS) is Buyers.gov. It is a business auction site that facilitates the purchase of information technology products by federal government agencies through the use of reverse auctions and aggregating demand for commonly purchased products (GSAA).

Government to Citizen Dimension of E-Government Application

The third application of e-government in public sector is to build interface between government and its citizens. It is a realistic initiative to facilitate citizen interaction with the government. As a public sector that is responsible for the needs of the people, government-to-citizen electronic application can provide transactions relating to renewal of licenses and certifications, tax-payments, applying for certain benefits by the citizens, such as government loans or houses in a lesser time consuming and easiness in carrying

out. More importantly, this structural dimension strives to enhance citizen access to public information through the use of dissemination tools like web sites and/or kiosks. In other words, it is a dimension purposefully meant to attenuate the agency-centric, and at times, process-laden nature of some government functions towards its citizens. In the same line of argument, some e-government advocates suggest that one of the goals of implementing this dimension should be to create a "one-stop shopping" site where citizens can carry out a variety of tasks, especially those of multiple agencies, without requiring the citizen to initiate contacts with each agency individually (Hasson, 2001; William, 2000). Another potential outcome from this dimension is that it may also lead to citizen-to-citizen interaction and increase their participations in government with more opportunities to overcome possible time consuming and geographical barriers.

The growing younger citizen demand is one of the driving motives for establishing this dimension by any administrative institutions of government. In fact, e-government application in public sector is expected to increase significantly in Asia within the next decade as the youths, who are now growing up with personal computers and the Internet as a routine presence in their lives, become adults (*The Economist*, 24th June, 2000, p.31). Another pressing factor for application of e-government in building government-citizen interface is time frame. The citizen may demand for ways to reduce time spent standing and queuing up in administrative departments for permits or any kinds of transactions.

Although, this dimension is yet to be developed or fully grown in Asia however, one can find a good example named FirstGov website in US and many other developed countries. The FirstGov website was established in September 1987 purposely for public-private partnership to serve as online portal but has changed the name to USA.gov in 2007. It contains about 51 million pages of government information, services and online transactions (United States' Government, 2007).

POTENTIAL BENEFITS OF E-GOVERNMENT APPLICATIONS IN PUBLIC SECTOR

Improved Efficiency

One of the overarching benefits of e-government application in public sectors is improved efficiency. In applying e-government, the efficiency can take different forms. For example, one form is to reduce errors and improve consistency of outcomes of governmental projects through automating standard tasks. The second form of efficiency improvement is to reduce costs and the many layers of organisational processes (the popular bureaucracy) by streamlining operating procedures through e-applications. Part of efficiency improvement is reduction in time spent on repetitive tasks. According to Breen, this will give the federal, state and local government employees ample opportunity to develop new skills and advance their carriers (Breen, 2000; Kunakorpaiboonsiri, 2013).

Services Improvement

Application of e-government in public sector provides opportunity and benefit to improve quality and accessibility of services to the citizens. In addition to efficiency enhancement, the quality of services may improve via quicker transactions, accountability and fast/better processes. The evolution of e-government can also create potential for new services. The potential benefit is to contribute to a qualitative change in how government agencies handle business functions and how citizens interact with government as the case in Malaysia and many other Asia countries of the world (Rashid, et al., 2010; Kunakorpaiboonsiri, 2013).

Increasing Citizen Participation in Government Activities

One potential benefit of e-government application is to increase citizens' participations in government activities. The citizens in remote areas can be easily connected through establishment of 'one-stop' flagship centre to send and receive information more easily from the government agencies and institutional bodies. Application of e-government in public sectors also allows citizen-to-citizen interaction by providing opportunities for people with similar interests, opinions and concerns, who may be geographically separated, to interact and share information affecting their daily lives and the country in general as envisioned in Indonesia and Cambodia (Kunakorpaiboonsiri, 2013, Parks, 2003).

Administrative Reform and Improvement

It is highly believed that no managerial reform can be materialised unless it is supported by ICT to improve effectiveness and efficiency of personnel management, procurements and many other government activities. Kaboolian (1988, p.190) has argued that "the opportunities presented by e-government for improved administration, among other things, are leading to a global convergence toward a standard reform model." Landsbergen and Wolken (2001) and Parks, (2003) have also pointed out that ICT-enabled reforms can yield many benefits, including lower administrative costs, faster and more accurate response to requests and queries of the citizen, especially after the normal office hours. It will also lead to direct access to transaction or customer accounts held in different parts of government. More so, it provides basis for ability to harvest data from operational systems, thus increasing the quality of feedback to manager and policymakers. However, the benefit can only be materialised if different offices and people are willing to share information.

BENEFITS OF E-GOVERNMENT: TRENDS IN ASIA PERSPECTIVE

Network Information Dissemination between Government Agencies

Application of network (as advocated by e-government) in government agencies typically supports basic administrative functions relating to payroll and accounts. Adopting such systems can deliver significant benefits such as reduction of information in handling costs and compliance costs. The net savings can also be realised from reduced labour costs and speeded up of processing tasks. E-government application can provide integration of all departments and function across public sector with one single computer system that can serve the needs of different departments. A living example of network application in government agencies in Asia context is Computer Crime Investigation Department (CCID) established in 2000 by the Republic of Korea Supreme Prosecutor's Office and the Seoul District Prosecutor's Office (Ho, 2012). This enables the prosecution of offences that become more technological tactical in nature easier to deal with (Paek, 2000; Ho, 2012).

In Pakistan, ICT systems have been introduced into entire tax department and had helped reduced contact between tax collectors and taxpayers (Maqbool, 2000; Rehman, et al. 2012). According to Parry, effective application of e-government is the new financial management systems designed for Sri Lanka government as a way to offer an attractive networking environment. The new systems provide opportunities to the public sector to effectively handle different financial managements, such as treasury cash management, human resources management relating payroll and records management within a one-stop computer system. Initially, the systems used to be a client-based, but the latest versions are increasingly Internet-based that allows information to be accessed independently by anyone (Parry, 1997; Hung, et al. 2005).

Inter-Organizational Benefits of E-Government

In relation to inter-organisation benefits, e-government application in public sector provides opportunities to manage workflow. Workflow refers to the ability to move images, files and documents from one workstation to another. This may include authorisation, data entry, and data editing. Hence, transaction procedures that are used to be accomplished by moving papers can now be electronically managed. This helps to solve the problem of delay often associated with paper hard-copy documents and manual processing. The workflow systems also entail claims processing and management, bid and proposal routine, and tracking. E-government also helps in handling people's complaints, grants and scholarship awards, as well as human resource recruitments and/or hiring. A glaring example is the National Tax Service Unit in the Republic of Korea. The unit has recently introduced a Tax Integrated system through a computerised system that accumulates tax-related information. This makes discriminative selection of taxpayers to be audited by tax officials reduced to some extent. Hence, a manual assessment of about 5 million cases on a yearly basis has been replaced by computer-assisted assessment. Thus, it closes all unnecessary face-to-face meetings between tax officials and taxpayers and helps to eliminate unfair influences of tax officials in selecting taxpayers for audit (Sang-Yool, 2000; Bertot, et al. 2008)

Another example is the Department of Budget and Management (DBM) in Philippines, which has been posting it major budgetary releases to government agencies on the Internet. This makes transactions more transparent to the public. The online system contains information on government's accounts payable and the amount released by the DBM. Thus, in part, it gives private contractors the ability to check the veracity of the department officials' procurements against the DBM budgetary releases. Therefore, the details of all accounts payable and releases for each government agency can be accessed every month along the line with the names of the contractors and the amount of payment they are supposed to receive monthly (Republic of Philippines, 2000; Iglesias, 2010).

Enhancing Government-Citizen Interface

One of the potential benefits of e-government application in public sector is enhancement of government-citizen interface through effective communication. In other words, e-government has been used to resolve the problem of communication gap between citizens and governments in Asia. In India state of Andhra Pradesh, Computer-aided Administration of Registration Department (CARD) is a good example of a successful e-government application to enhance the interface between government and citizens. According to World Bank report, about 214 registration offices have completely computerised in Andhra Pradesh since 1998. This facilitates deeds registration in less than an hour, while services like issue of encumbrance certificates and valuation certificates can be accomplished in just about 15 minutes. Thus, it brings the opaqueness of property valuation that used to force citizens to hire middlemen to an end. More importantly, the time frame always consumes by manual copying of documents and storage in paper-forms has been replaced by computer-aided system. In Hong Kong, an estimated 65% of amenable government services delivery to citizen is available online at (Worldbank.egov).

Enhancing Government to Business Transactions

Electronic government applications in public sector have supported the development of flexible and convenient ways for people to conduct business with government. In Asia, for example, the Philippines Custom Bureau has developed

systems for custom payments, processing of clearance documents and releasing of shipments from custom **control**. The benefit is sought to minimise the chance of fraud and corruption that always arise from contact between business people, officials and messengers (Parayno, 1999; Bertot, et al. 2008).

In addition, the Korea Republic Procurement service has developed an Electronic Data Interchange (EDI) to make the purchase of commodities and all accounting transactions be easily executed. Thus, cyber shopping is available for the procurement of office supplies, cultural products and cycled goods as well. In fact, the computerisation of contract data and the use of automation to supply procurements are also underway. This is aimed at reducing opportunities for officers to contact customers for illegal objectives. Databases are being set up for the pre-qualification and cost accounting process as well as storing information of supply firms. The expected benefit, among other things, is that documents from contractors will be obtained using computer networks of relevant organisations rather than receiving such documents directly from contractors in order to prevent submission of false documents (see: Byungtaa, 2000, The Republic of Korea, 2003; Ho, 2012).

POTENTIAL CHALLENGES FOR E-GOVERNMENT APPLICATIONS

Disparities in Computer Access (Digital Divide)

The disparities in computer access or the so-called digital divide is a potential challenge for e-government applications in public sector. It serves as a potential barrier because the poor and lower income groups who do not have access to the Internet will be unable to benefit from online services provided by government. Hence, the inability of government to provide online service to all citizens may cause set-back to e-government applications. Although it is beyond a reasonable doubt that, in Asia region, a growing number of people have access to the Internet however, there are still large numbers of people who do not. In addition, advocates for the disabled argue that computer can present new obstacles for citizens, ranging from the blind to physically impaired, who may require a very costly hardware or software (i.e., oral controls) for their computers to be able to access online information and services of the public sectors (see: *The Economist*, 24th June 2000, p.2; Bertot, 2003).

Privacy Challenge

Privacy issue poses a big challenge to application of e-government in managerial activities of public sector. Citizens are unlikely to use e-government services without a solid guarantee of their privacy protection. Various concerns about the issue of "cookies,"[1] information sharing between agencies and the disclosure of citizens' private information have become subjects of debate in society. Privacy issue in e-government is a crucial challenge that needs to be addressed for successful application even in the developed countries including USA, talk-less of Asia's developing countries. For example, in June 2000, it was reported that the National Drug Control Policy Office was using 'cookies' to track the Internet movement of visitors to its site (see: Harris & Schwartz, 2000, Hung, et al. 2005). Such breach of privacy jeopardises the citizens' trust in government Web sites and Web-based services provided. In the context of Asia, one may argue that addressing the issue of privacy challenge to e-government application would require both technical and careful policy responses.

Computer Security Challenge in E-Government

Computer security is another underpinning challenge for e-government application in public

sector. This challenge is not only in Asia region but is also throughout the globe. For example, in a series of evaluations published since July 1999, the General Accounting Office (GAO) in US has repeatedly alerted that the largest federal agencies "were not adequately protecting critical federal operations and assets from computer-based attacks" (GAO, 10th November, 1999, p.1).[2] In the same line of argument, another report in year 2001 by GAO has identified six crucial areas of weakness in application of e-government. These include: security programme management, access controls, software development and change controls, segregation of duties, operating systems control and service continuity. In other words, it can be inferred from such alert that effective service continuity in e-government application in public sector is not only for availability of services delivery, but also to build citizens' confidence and/or trust in government institutions or agencies (Bertot, et al. 2008, Matavire, et al. 2010).

Corruption Challenge to E-Government

It is a common belief that the application of e-government in public sector will reduce opportunities for corruption, but the reality is more complex (Gouscos, et al. 2007). While ICT does sometimes facilitate ways to combat corruption in the administration of public sector, it can also provide new avenues for corruption opportunities. It can provide new sources of corrupt income, especially for ICT professionals and removing opportunities from those without ICT skills. In addition, it should be admitted by Asia and global governments that computerisation of records often closes down access to some administrative staff members but opens up access to others who operate the ICT systems in e-government. One may argue that, with application of e-government in public sector, corruption may increase or decrease depending on the relative integrity of the staff members (Andersen, & Rand, 2006). In other words, data quality and the myth of computer omnipotence have made many government agency leaders to believe that ICT totally removes opportunities for corruption. Thus, they fail to institute controls on computerised systems used for service delivery to public masses. Yes, ICT advances, like other technological changes, can improve the productivity potential and services delivery of public sector to the people, however, Olson (2000) points out that only the top management of e-government knows the actual productivity and services improvement obtained. Hence, it is in the collective interest of the managers of public assets that service potential of the ICT advances be underestimated by their superiors. In such cases, agencies may receive more resources than they need, which can in turn be used to increase the income or leisure of staff or management. This form of corruption is widely practised in centrally planned economies.

FUTURE DIRECTION FOR COPING WITH CHALLENGES IN ICT APPLICATIONS IN PUBLIC SECTOR

Ensuring a Common Vision

A common vision is an integral part of a successful e-government implementation in administration of public sector. Common vision is essential to e-government as a means to manage and coordinate agency activities. A common vision is not a goal in itself, but a means to achieve the desired e-government objectives. A government-wide vision helps to tie e-government initiatives, in any country, with broader strategic reform objectives. It can promote inter-ministerial coordination, ensure balance and fairness and even help to stay the course of actions in service delivery to people forever. Having a clear vision of reforming public sector through application of e-government helps maintain consistency and a sense of purpose.

Towards this end, political leaders and government agency administrators are key supporters of e-government vision. Political leadership serves to diffuse the vision and give it added weight. While a clear vision statement is needed, however, it is not enough. The vision rationale and the validation for better change in public sector also need to be communicated throughout the government administrations that are implementing e-government.

The Need for Effective Coordination of E-Government Implementation

The nature of e-government requires a level of cooperative action to ensure interoperability, avoid duplication, ensure coherent action in a range of crucial areas, such as security, privacy protection, and to provide the framework and capacity for adequate service delivery to people in public sector. The need for coordination among government agencies becomes more pressing as Asia governments increasingly move to implement more complex transaction services. There is a central-dilemma for e-government success. A generic problem is how agencies' responsibility for effective results and autonomous operation can be retained while at the same time ensuring the interests of government administration at large in question pertaining to interoperable systems and shared use of information resources. While this reflects a broader issue for government on question of coordination versus devolved management responsibility if e-government is to succeed, it is crucial to get the balance right.

Lack of proper coordination may jeopardise innovation and initiatives, even leading to forgone opportunities in e-government application. However, an effective coordination approach can generate efficiencies, reduce risk and facilitate a faster and broader rollout of e-government initiatives. In addition, whole-government structures can play an important role in steering e-government applications by providing a framework for collaboration across agencies and by keeping e-government activity aligned on broader public sector agendas. An approach that can be adopted may include setting up committee of agency heads and chief information officers. Their roles may range from purely advisory and information sharing to policy development and implementation oversight. Also, the involvement of non-governmental representatives from industries, academia and civil society organisations are crucial.

The Need for Public-Private Partnership as Continuum of E-Government Application

It is obvious that engagement with private sector suppliers has been an integral feature of government use of ICT in public sector. Hence, private-public relationships have broadened from the acquisition of products and service such as computer mainframe, which governments themselves could not provide, to services such as the operation of computing facilities and direct provision to end users of government services. Partnership may involve arrangements whereby work, risk and rewards are shared. However, accountability, scrutiny and proper audit are requirements that need to be on sound foundation of such relationship. Retaining the public sector's capacity to manage the relationship with the private partner is of crucial concern. Therefore, managerial awareness and commitment is essential to ensure that the required skills are developed and maintained in public sector.

Respect for Accepted Privacy Principles

The moral challenge facing e-government implementers in public sector is to respect accepted privacy principles while allowing the benefits of e-government to flow to citizens. This balance is of particular importance when considering service delivery involving data sharing among agencies

and government institutional bodies. Government has a responsibility to provide leadership in developing a culture of privacy protection and security. This leadership role must be provided rightly from development of public policy, as owner and operator of systems and networks, and as a user of such systems and networks themselves. As a user of information systems and networks, government shares a role with business, other organisations and individuals for ensuring secured use of the systems.

The Need for Appropriate Legislations on E-Government

The success of e-government application in public sector is highly dependent on government's role in ensuring a proper legal framework for the operation. The application and uptake of e-government services and processes will remain minimal without a legal equivalence between digital and paper processes. For example, the legal recognition of digital signatures is necessary if they are to be used in e-government for the submission of electronic forms containing sensitive personal or financial information.

Additionally, complexity of regulations and requirements on agencies can be another barrier. If agencies are unable to determine what is required of them, they may be unwilling to invest in a project that may not conform with requirements. Also, privacy and security concerns need to be addressed through appropriate legislation and regulations before e-government initiatives can advance in Asia and any part of the world. Hence, it would be a relevant value to regularly undertake a review of the overall regulations and requirements that govern e-government application in public sector particularly, those that govern ICT acquisitions and uses. Identifying these areas would help reveal where redundant or overlapping regulations were existing. An agreed process of regular examination would provide an opportunity to get rid of requirements that have outlived their usefulness.

The Need for Harmonising Technical Framework and Infrastructure

Today, governments continue to make considerable ICT investments and at any point in time will have a wide range in place. All these investments need to be well harmonised. Harmonisation is a particular element in e-government application, as ineffectiveness of strategies may be in part due to failures to harmonise systems and standards. For example, investment of legacy systems can be inflexible and incompatible, which make it hard to deploy new applications that involve the need for data sharing or other interactions between disparate systems. In fact, the difficulty of integrating legacy systems with new initiatives can be a major barrier to the success of e-government application. Establishing common technical standards and infrastructure can pave way for greater efficiency within government agencies. In addition, shared infrastructure for authentication of key customer groups can facilitate individual agency initiatives that would otherwise lack a business function requirement. Therefore, the promotion of 'whole-of-government' framework, standards and data definitions by e-government coordinators will further facilitate proposal to develop across agency integrated services.

The Need for Effective Monitoring and Evaluation of E-Government Application

It is of great importance to monitor and evaluate e-government application in public sector to understand demand, assess the benefits to users from time to time and evaluate the effectiveness of proposed approaches in meeting their objectives. In fact, evaluation is needed to argue the case for new projects and expenditure; to justify continuing

with initiatives; to allocate additional ICT funds; to assess progress towards programme goals and to understand impact of e-government activities. Therefore, in an era of increasingly tight public spending, governments need to show concrete benefits of ICT investments in order to gain and maintain political support of the people whom the programme is meant for.

It is quite understandable that monitoring and evaluation of e-government is generally difficult. For example, given the frequent lack of clarity of objectives owing to the different and often competing views held by different stakeholders. More importantly, overlapping initiatives and policies of continuous fine-tuning of initiatives complicate the efforts of monitoring and/or evaluation. This, in part, may be due to the pervasive nature of ICTs, the integration of ICT goals with policy goals and the organisational changes that necessarily accompany e-government initiatives. Hence, effective evaluation requires good metrics and devices.

To overcome these problems, a successful e-government evaluation effort would need to address the following issues: a framework for assessment which must be prepared prior to initiation; e-government indicators should be designed to reflect programme goals; results need to be available to decision makers at the right time; evaluation process should be unbiased and independent; evaluation should be based on a mixture of qualitative and quantitative indicators; direct and indirect costs-benefits must be taken into account; and e-government application should be repeatedly evaluated from time to time.

CHAPTER SUMMARY

The chapter has shown that e-government application in public sector provides interactive access of people to social services, employment assistance, tax and revenue services, corporate registration, licenses and permits renewals are possible through a common entry point and shared portal services provided by government agencies. Therefore, it is an effective means of building the interface between government-to-government, government-to-business and government-to-citizens. In addition, it helps generate efficiency, improve administrative reforms and improve services delivery of government agencies to people at large. So, by improving connectivity between employees and departments, and with citizens and business, e-government application in public sector offers more convenient government services and greater public access to information. This ultimately creates an administration that is more accountable to those who vote it to power.

Several factors are driving the application of e-government in various government entities in Asia and anywhere else in the world. These include technology development, such as growing of computing power and telecommunications bandwidth; business investment in adoption of technology and competitive pressures. However, e-government application in public sector is associated with many issues, especially privacy and security of masses' data information and many other related problems as highlighted in the paper. It is therefore argued that e-government application in public sector should be value-driven and not technology-driven. The promised benefits of e-government do not take place simply by digitising information and placing it online by government agencies. Instead, the challenge is to understand how the use of new ICT tools in public sector can be used to leverage a transformation in the culture and structure of government institutional bodies or agencies in order to provide better services to citizens. Finally, it is highly hoped that some of the suggestions raised in this chapter would be adopted by governments to address various challenging issues that emerged in applying e-government approach to administrative managements of government bodies.

REFERENCES

Ambali, A. R. (2010). Determinants of e-government satisfaction: The case study of E-procurement. In R. Hakikur (Ed.), Handbook of Research on E-Government Readiness for Information and Service Exchange: Utilizing Progressive Information Communication Technologies (pp. 465-479). Hershey, PA: IGI Global.

Andersen, T. B., & Rand, J. (2006). *Does e-government reduce corruption?* University of Copenhagen, Department of Economics Working Paper.

Asgarkhani, M. (2005). The effectiveness of e-ervice in local government: A case study. *Electronic. Journal of E-Government, 3*(4), 157–166.

Atkinson, D. R. & Ulevich, J. (2000). *Digital government: The next step to reengineering the federal government.* Technology & New Economy Project, Progressive Policy Institute, March.

Bertot, J. C. (2003). The multiple dimensions of the digital divide: More than the technology 'haves' and 'have nots..' *Government Information Quarterly, 20*(2), 185–191. doi:10.1016/S0740-624X(03)00036-4

Bertot, J. C., Jaeger, P. T., & McClure, C. R (2008). Citizen-centered e-covernment services: Benefits, costs, and research needs. In *Proceedings of the 9th Annual International Digital Government Research Conference.* Montreal, Canada: Academic Press.

Bhatnagar, S. (2009). *Unlocking e-government potential concepts, cases and practical insights.* New Delhi: Sage Publication.

Bhatnagar, S. (2014). *Public service delivery: Role of information and communication technology in improving governance and development impact.* Asian Development Bank (ADB), Working Paper Series, No. 391.

Breen, J. (2000). At the dawn of e-government: The citizen as customer. *Government Finance Review, 15*(3), 15–20.

Brian, D., & Finn, K. (2002). Towards a framework for government portal design: The government, citizen and portal perspectives. In A. Gronlund (Ed.), Electronic Government: Design, Application & Management. Hershey, PA: Idea Group Publishing.

Buyers.gov. (n.d.). Retrieved from http://www.buyers.gov

Byungtaa, K. (2000). *Anti-corruption measures in the public procurement service sector.* Paper presented at Conference of Asia Pacific Forum on Combating Corruption. Seoul, Korea.

Economist (2000, June 24). A survey of government and the Internet. *The Next Revolution.*

FirstGov Website. (n.d.). Retrieved from http://www.firstgov.gov

Fred, B. S. (Ed.). (1999). *Trust in cyberspace.* Washington, DC: National Academy of Science.

Gartner Group. (2000). *Key issues in e-government strategy and management.* Research Notes, Key Issues. Stamford, CT: Gartner Group, Inc.

General Accounting Office (GAO). (1999). *Information security: Weaknesses at 22 agencies.* GAO/AIMED-00-32R. Author.

Gilbert, A. (2001, April 6). President Bush backs e-government, digital signatures. *Information Week,* p. 24.

Government Services Administration Auctions (GSAA). (n.d.). Retrieved from http://www.gsaauctions.gov

Gronlund, A. (2002). *Electronic government: Design, application and management.* Hershey, PA: Idea Group Publishing.

Harris, F. J., & Schwartz, J. (2000, June 22). Anti-drug web site tracks visitors. *Washington Post,* p. 23.

Hasson, J. (2001, March 19). Treasury CIO Promotes expand fed portal. *Federal Computer Week,* p. 14.

Ho In Kang. (2012). E-procurement experience in Korea: Implementation and impact. Public Procurement Services, 1-19.

Hung, W., Chang, I., Li, Y., & Hung, H. (2005). An empirical study on the impact of quality antecedents on taxpayers' acceptance of internet tax filing systems. *Government Information Quarterly, 22*(3), 389–410. doi:10.1016/j.giq.2005.05.002

Iglesias, G. (2010). *E-government initiatives of four Philippine cities.* APEC Study Center Network (PASCN), Discussion Paper Series No.22.

Kaboolian, L. Administration Debate. (1988). The new public management: Challenging the boundaries of the management vs. administration debate. *Public Administration Review, 58*(3), 189–193. doi:10.2307/976558

Kieley, B. (2002). *E-government in Canada: Services online or public service renewal? In Electronic Government: Design, Application & Management.* Hershey, PA: Idea Group Publishing.

Kunakornpaiboonsiri, T. (2013). *SMS service for health launched in Indonesian province.* Retrieved from http://www.futuregov.asia/articles/2013

Landsbergen, D. Jr, & Wolken, G. Jr. (2001). Realizing the promise: Government information systems and the fourth generation of information technology. *Public Administration Review, 61*(2), 206–220. doi:10.1111/0033-3352.00023

Langlois, G. (2001, May 14). An equal slice of success. *Federal Computer Week,* p. 44.

Malaysian Administrative Modernization and Management Planning Unit (MAMPU). (n.d.). *Electronic government flagship application*, No: MAMPU/EG/1/97. Author.

Maqbool, M. (2000). *A strategy for Combating Corruption in Pakistan*. Paper presented at Conference of Asia Pacific Forum on Combating Corruption. Seoul, Korea. Retrieved from http://www.oecd.org/daf/ASIAcom/Seoul.htm

Matavire, R., Chigona, W., Roode, D., Sewchurran, E., Davids, Z., Alfred Mukudu, A., & Charles Boamah-Abu, C. (2010). Challenges of egovernment project implementation in a South African context. *Electronic Journal Information Systems Evaluation*, *13*(2), 153–164.

National Institute of Justice (NIJ). (2000). Selected summaries. *Research Review*, *1*(4), 1-6.

Office of the e-Envoy. (2000). *International Benchmarking Report: Summary-Hong Kong Special Administrative Region*. London: Office of the e-Envoy. Retrieved from http://www.eenvoy.gov.uk/publications/reports/benchmarkingV2/summary_hkong.htm

Olson, M. (2000). *Power and prosperity: Outgrowing communist and capitalist dictatorships*. New York: Basic Book.

Paek, K. (2000). *Combating corruption: The role of the ministry of justice and the prosecutor's office in Korea*. Paper presented at Conference of Asia Pacific Forum on Combating Corruption. Seoul, Korea.

Parayno, L. G. (1999). Reforming the Philippines customs service through electronic governance. In Combating Corruption in Asian and Pacific Economies, (pp. 61-69). Manila: ADB.

Parks, T. (2003). Expanding access to information in Cambodia: Community information centers project. *IT in Developing Countries*, *13*(1), 19.

Parry, M. (1997). *Training workshop on government budgeting in developing countries*. Retrieved from http://www.mcgl.co.uk/l-tp.htm

Rais, M. A. K., & Mohd Khalid, N. (2003). *E-government in Malaysia: Improving responsiveness and capacity to serve*. Selangor: Pelanduk Publications.

Rashid, A. A., Jusoh, H., & Abdul Malek, J. (2010). Enhancing urban governance efficiency through the egovernment of Malaysian local authorities – The Case of Subang Jaya. *GEOGRAFIA OnlineTM Malaysian Journal of Society and Space*, *6*(1), 1–12.

Rehman, M., Esichaikul, V., & Kamal, M. (2012). Factors influencing e-government adoption in Pakistan. *Transforming Government: People, Process and Policy*, *6*(3), 256–282.

Relyea, C. H. (2001). *Paperwork reduction act: Reauthorization and government information management issues*. Congressional Research Service (CRS) RL30590.

Republic of Korea. (2003). Innovation in procurement through digitalization. Public Procurement Services, 1-13.

Republic of the Philippines. (2000). *General appropriation act, January1-December31, R.A. No. 8760*. Retrieved from: http://www.dbm.gov.ph/dbm_publications/gaa/gaa2000.htm

Sang-Yool, H. (2000). *Recent reform of Korean tax administration – focused on measures for prevention of corruption*. Paper presented at Conference of Asia Pacific Forum on Combating Corruption. Seoul, Korea. Retrieved from http://www.oecd.org/daf/ASIAcom/Seoul.htm

Smith, M. S.; Moteff, J. D.; Kruger, L.G.; McLouglin, G.J.; & Seifert, J. W (2004). *Internet: An overview of technology policy issues affecting its use and growth*. Congress Research Service, (CRS-98-67), 1-39.

Sprehe, T. (2001, April 30). States show feds the way. *Federal Computer Week*, p. 48.

Stephen, B. (2001, August 10). President searching for a few good e-government ideas. *Washington Post*, p. 2.

Trattner, J. (2000, November 29). E-government revolution transforms federal operations. *Government Executive Magazine*.

William, M. (2000, December 11). Setting a course for e-government. *Federal Computer Week*, p. 13.

World Bank. (2012). *E-Government*. Retrieved from: http://www1.worldbank.org/publicsector/egov/index.htm

KEY TERMS AND DEFINITIONS

Administration: Management of the affairs of an organization, especially government's small and large institutions.

Cost-Effective: Something that produces good value, benefits, results, and efficient outputs.

E-Government: Application of information technology such as networking and electronic devices by government agencies for public services delivery.

Expertise: Special knowledge, skill, and technical know-how possessed by a person for better delivering of the assigned tasks.

Information Technology: A set of tools such as computer systems, networks, and software that can be used for data processing and distribution with the aim of improving and maintaining better records and accurate information.

Internet: A network of computers for sending and receiving information around the world via dedicated routers and servers. Hence, it is an electronic communication network of computers.

Resources: Productive factor needed to accomplish certain activities. Therefore, they are means of undertaken a desired outcome in public sector.

ENDNOTES

[1] Cookies are small text files usually placed on a user's computer by a Web site so that one can track the user's movement through a Web site. Originally, it is designed to allow user-side customization of Web information. The expanded use of cookies has raised concerns about the privacy of user's Web browsing habits. For more details on "cookies," see Marcia S. Smith: *CRS Report RL30784, Internet Privacy: An Analysis of Technology and Policy Issues.*

[2] General Accounting Office, Information Security: Weaknesses at 22 Agencies, GAO/AIMED-00-32R, 10 November 1999, p.1.

Chapter 2
The Wave of Digital Convergence on ICT Adoption and Application in Malaysia

ABSTRACT

How much Malaysian convergence policy has achieved in response to global reform since 1990 is intriguing. The chapter discusses policy and regulatory implications as well as the nature of new mode of governance with particular focus on policy networks. The analysis draws on the scope of collective action that has been compared with the widening of policy participation. Main sources include Malaysian government policy documents and semi-structured interviews with key policymakers, regulators, and experts of Malaysian ICT and convergence initiatives. It is found that those policy network structures are clearly reflected in the design of the current ICT framework. In view of recent institutional and regulatory reforms, the political process toward the removal of analogues laws also exhibits the weaknesses of policy in the networked governance. In sum, both the National IT Council (NITC) and the Malaysia Communication and Multimedia Commission (MCMC) remain vulnerable to pressures from politicians and other ministries.

INTRODUCTION

One of the fundamental questions concerning the future of Malaysia's national "e-agenda" is how to reform the regulatory framework and achieve good governance. It is acknowledged that good governance depends critically on the ability of state actors—be it public, private or civil communities to utilise information and communications technologies (ICTs) by making use of regulatory networks and engaging in multiple levels of interactions. The concept of 'policy community' involves the process which allows members to share resources and experience through the 'complex web of interactions as well as participate in the process of policy making and refinements' (Humphreys, 1994). In light of this concept, the issue is whether this could be applied to Malaysia's case or not.

The major lines of the debate in general commentaries are whether the development of Malaysia digital convergence policy is viewed as

DOI: 10.4018/978-1-4666-6579-8.ch002

successful in promoting a new mode of governance or not. Most previous studies seldom went beyond legal texts and policy practices, drawing little attention to wider institutional or socio-political circumstances. The notion of 'command and control' or 'top-down' approach in policy making among Malaysian administrators and politicians is widely mentioned, rapidly became an object of criticism without any substantive examinations, thus obscuring its success stories.

Aiming to become a post-industrial society (Saloma, 2008; Haslinda et al, 2011) and leveraging on the global march for Information Age agenda, Malaysia is compelled to make efforts towards a more open and integrated policy environment. There is an atmosphere for a cooperative partnership between public, private and community sectors to achieve the Vision 2020 developed through a national-scale policy framework, or the so-called 'National IT Agenda'-NITA- (Azzman, 1998). It is widely believed that digital convergence will be an increasingly important policy avenue in the years to come as the industry has sustained very rapid volume of growth rates over the last decade and its share of total ICT sector continues to climb.

A good deal of debate exists between those who see those changes as significant and those who were skeptical about the development, especially amid the worst financial and political crisis which struck the region in 1997/8, when the MSC was still in its formative stage. For example, Kamarulzaman and Aliza (2001, p. 6) commented that: "since 1997, it has passed a number of acts and legislatures aimed to create the right environment for the development of the communications and multimedia (C&M) industry and to position Malaysia as a major hub for the C&M information and content services." From the viewpoint that Multimedia Super Corridor (MSC) needs to be supported by a high-capacity, digital telecommunications infrastructure designed to the highest standards in capacity and reliability, Hishamudi and Khatibi (2004, p. 309) contended

that multimedia environment and telecommunication industry will play an important role to ensure the success of the MSC.

Yet, Alvin Toffler, an influential member of the MSC's International Advisory Panel had openly criticised Dr Mahathir's style (ex-Prime Minister) in dealing with the crisis, arguing that the viability of the project would be at stake under a "climate of political repression" (Matthew, 1998). To clear any doubt, rather than retreating from such high-priced ventures, it is worth noting that Malaysia has opened its market much earlier than most countries in Asia and today it has one of the most competitive telecommunication markets of any developing nation (Minges & Gray, 2002). This meant that Mahathir's administration viewed that the growth in the IT and C&M industry as critical for future development of the country.

Against this background, this chapter aims at discussing how successful was the development of Malaysian ICT and digital convergence policy since the middle of 1990s with particular focus on the networked governance structures in the policy process. Our analysis is directed to the NITA - based on the motto 'turning the ripples into tidal waves' in Malaysian ICT policy (NITC, 2000; Fariza, et al., 2011) since it was conceived to be 'a major milestone' towards digital convergence. Eventually, there were numerous public and private sector initiatives taken (Ramasamy, 2010). More importantly, various policy, regulatory and institutional reforms were initiated, such as the creation of the Communication and Multimedia Act (CMA,1998) and the Malaysian Communication and Multimedia Commission Act (MCMCA,1998) to promote the development of the new digital convergence industry, and the introduction of industry forums to promote self-regulatory environment (MAIT, 2002; COMNET-IT, 2004). It is argued that digital convergence is a rapidly growing sector which is unprecedented in the Malaysian economic history, extending the penchant for information society rhetoric launched particularly during the middle of 1990s. We argue that such issues that have marked the expansion of the industry include coherent regulatory framework, uncertainty surrounding the roles of Industry Forums (IFs) and their impact on governing the new regime, perceived weaknesses of Industry Codes to facilitate industry growth, allegations on the weak position of the MCMC to resolve persistent conflicts regarding broadcasting media and a host of others related issues need to be carefully examined.

Attempts are made to look at this from different angles. The first section briefly sketches the concept of networked governance structures. Following this, the second section describes major reforms undertaken by the Malaysian Government in the old regime, towards the new regime. Specific areas of focus are political legislative structure, key policy making bureaucrats, and the birth of new regulatory regime. Next, the third section discusses the relationship between digital convergence policy authority and other actors in the Government. Some of the issues include the actual practice of convergence policy and the process impacted by legislative reform. In section four, discussion draws out policy and regulatory implications as well as the nature of new mode of governance. The concluding section aims to provide a basis for further dialogue by bringing together earlier observations on the development of Malaysian ICT and new communication.

THEORETICAL FRAMEWORK FOR ANALYSIS

The new ICTs have opened up the potential for a shift from rigid hierarchical forms of organisation, towards more flexible, adaptive, and interactive systems and networks (Castells, 1996; 2005). The 'new regulatory regime' (NRR) which is 'technologically driven' aspect of digital convergence adds yet another dimension to the concept of network governance, in that it extends governance beyond the old regime of ICT into the less formal arenas of network partnership. Voluntary compliance and mechanisms for governing digital convergence has always been part and parcel of the very notion of a new regulatory environment. Significantly, like industry players or community associations, they are recognised by, or even incorporated into, the more formal structures of policy processes. In more glaring evidence, as in the case of IFs, and in the implementation of the industry codes, the role of non-State actors are expected to be more dominant. In others, as in the existence of the traditional legislations, there may be complications of many sorts, in spite of the more coherent practices. The governance of digital convergence and NRR thus implies not only closer integration within and between the different constituent of the policy actors, but also engagement with the traditional legal systems and frameworks.

Traditionally, the relationships between different constituents of policy actors were essentially seen as hierarchical and mainly unilateral with the central Government at the helm. Each constituent has clear delineated roles and areas of policy manouevre. The new mode of governing has challenged this traditional metaphors of organised pyramids and a new model now have to be pictured in terms of inter-connected networks, and complex procedures in decision making procedures (Hendriks, 2009; Ahmad & Dai, 2007). In other words, the NRR equates the credentials of new theories of governance in which governments attempt to steer network of actors in a desired direction rather than manage the sector through traditional policy instruments (Rhodes, 1996).

However, this is far from straightforward. Network governance structures are harder to model. So, within the organisations, there are glimpses of important features of effective policy networks but are still some way to a more theorised understanding of the often fluctuating and

Table 1. Situating self-regulation

Mode of Regulation	Regulatory Goals and Principles Set by:	Rules and Standards	
		Set by:	Enforced by:
Government intervention	Government	Government	Courts, agencies, Markets
Self-Regulation	Government, industry	Industry	Courts, agencies, industry associations
Market Regulation	Consumer demand	Firms	Markets

Source: Newman and Bach, 2004, p. 390.

ambiguous relationships at the core. In this sort of situation, governments need the chance to learn by experimentation within the new paradigm, before designing the best approach to policy process, or moving to new regulatory framework. According to Klijn and Koppenjan (2000, p.136), the term 'governance' is reserved for theories and cases that take into account the interdependencies of public, private and semi-private actors, in which they refer to as 'self-organising networks.' More specifically, for Newman and Bach (2004, p.387), "private sector self regulation carves out a regulatory middle ground between government intervention and pure market mechanism... often more flexible and less intrusive than formal regulation by governments; at the same time, they reduce uncertainty and enhance consumers' confidence beyond levels attainable by the market alone." Proponents of self-regulation hail it as more flexible, adaptive, and less intrusive than formal government regulation, while delivering many of the same benefits.

Major forms of self-regulation include industry codes of conduct, which largely focus on rules and standard setting by industry, largely enforced by the market or - in some instances - by public bodies. Although there are different forms of self-regulations, Newman and Bach (2004, p.390) in their recent empirical research suggest that there are three basic categories of self-regulation situations: first, government intervention, second, self-regulation, and, third, market regulation (see Table 1).

THE MALAYSIAN DIGITAL CONVERGENCE: THE OLD REGIME

The Malaysian approach to digital convergence, typical to almost every other sectoral policy is deeply affected by Malaysian political federalism. The Constitution of Malaysia, the throne of all legal statutes, legitimised the power of the federal government to intervene directly on jurisdiction over policy development and implementation. Federal jurisdiction is also derived from Ministerial power in the area of policy activities such as formulation, regulation and governance, commonly prescribed under the notion of promoting national interest and development. Regulatory jurisdiction, on the other hand, is based on constitutionally authorised jurisdiction over sectoral policy, i.e. digital convergence and its related numerous policy activities entered into by the federal Government through relevant Ministries/agencies. While the Constitution recognises a shared jurisdiction over sectoral policies, the national policy framework, i.e., NITA has no legal backing thereby the latter deriving its sustainability from political patronage or leadership passion in it.

In consequence, jurisdictional idiosyncrasies have proved to be a considerable obstacle to the sustainable development of the convergence industry. As the Malaysian economy becomes more globalised, the search for a new mode of governing in the digital age continues to press policy makers for much needed reforms. The process of governance cannot be understood simply as a function of state actions as key regulatory processes are increasingly being encroached by non-bureaucratic policy actors from outside. For instance, whilst the NITC was responsible for the NITA, the Institute of Strategic and International Studies (ISIS) was required to prepare the concept paper for the K-Economy Master Plan in 2001. Significantly, this demonstrates that the scope of collective action has been widened significantly. Perhaps, the most symbolic of this was the Global Knowledge Partnership (GKP) which was fully endorsed by the NITC as the model of comprehensive partnership in ICT for the country.

This is not to suggest that the traditional strong policy making authority of the Government has now disappeared. While there are some concerns regarding the inefficiency of regulatory overlap and duplication, due in part to the federalism structure, government manages to escape from the political dilemma in addressing the potential calamity of the regulatory design. As a matter of fact, some political and economic issues were tackled within the prevailing model of intergovernmental federalism through widening up the scope of policy participation. NITC Strategic Five Thrust Areas was jointly administered by NITC, designated Ministries, and Central Agencies under close supervision by the Office of the Prime Minister. The five thrust areas are a comprehensive programme of national ICT. Again, the regime is of the typical traditional command and control type. Under NITA dating back to 1996, the programmes were closely coordinated with those of the Secretariat of the NITC, the Malaysian Institute of Microelectronic System (MIMOS).

Some issues have surfaced with respect to thrust areas. The first centres on the wide impact of the MSC in light of policy development into areas particularly connectivity and digital divide across society. The Government has responded to these concerns by emphasising bridging the digital divide in rural areas through eGovernment and smart schools, but there has also been interest in private-public partnership to extend the reach

of the programme. Second, equally important, were series of hiccups during the implementation when some of the efforts were dampened by many issues such as inability for the contractor to deliver, failure of PC ownership campaign, and limited impact of eGovernment. Thirdly, in the face of revolutionary change in technology, there is the larger issue of the appropriateness of this traditional regime as a means of realising the larger objective of improving governance and new economy. In 2003, Malaysia's global competitive ranking was lowered despite its rigorous effort to be on top of the scale.

From the beginning, the traditional regulatory regime was fundamentally based on Government incentives or subsidy. These included the development and continuing support of the MSC project, funding capacity in NITC and relevant Ministries, a variety of federal tax incentives and guarantees for MSC entrepreneurs and small medium enterprises (SMEs), the extension of ICT grants and facilities to digital connectivity programmes, and various targeted budget allocations through federal and state agencies. Nonetheless, based on a strategic study conducted by McKinsey and Co., in 1995, it was found that, with rising costs, Malaysia was losing its manufacturing edge to lower cost countries in the region. The study indicates that the Malaysian Government was aware of the logical path it should undertake at that stage. Nuraizah (2003) highlighted the rapid progresses the country has witnessed during the period. She explained an important factor that contributed to the interest in convergence that was evident:

To maintain our high-growth momentum, we had to move into value-added ICTs and multimedia. It was estimated that the opportunites these would provide could propel our economy to exceed the Vision 2020 projection, hitting a possible high of USD572 billion instead of the projected USD374 billion in GDP growth.

As the Government realised that the future would continue to be powerfully shaped by digital convergence, those projections clearly indicate significant pressures that will continue to encourage new mode of governing that had already been established since NITA was first mooted. One of the development concerns identified was that public policy may not be able to respond quickly enough to the changes brought on by the Information age. According to Azzman (2000, p.11), "they all stem from our natural selection of a series of institutions that, historically, were progressively fined-tuned to the dictates of an industrial economy and society." This means that Malaysia as a whole did not want to abruptly demand a shift and sharing of traditional power from the state towards the corporation and the community, but rather in the process of experimenting the "viewpoints and possible solutions to the issues of governance in an 'Internetworked' world" (Abdul Halim, 2000, p. xvi). As such, the major concern therefore relates to the emergence of flattery and more transparent framework for governance, which he argued "we do not know how to deal with the situation yet, but we are trying and learning" (Abdul Halim, 11). Unsurprisingly, public officials themselves had been less enthusiastic to prospect of the new mode of governance based on people as conceptualised in NITA[1]

Early regulatory groundwork was largely driven by the need for suitable legislations. A series of cyber laws were initiated in the middle 1990s but did not specifically address the need for a more coherent regulatory framework. Some business and political leaders started calls for the removal of some analogue laws, this time with the idea of digital convergence. In 1996, Government sought the help from a consultant, arguing for the removal of traditional laws for the sake of global convergence claiming that analogue laws should be revised for the sake of digital convergence. The Convergence Bill was introduced immediately after that, even referring to the deadline for NRR to be operationalised. The Ministry of Energy, Telecommunication and Post (METP) acted in concert with Cabinet Ministries. The reform issue was discussed at the Government's most influential council, the NITC. Nevertheless, the agenda for convergence had not immediately led to pervasive change, as the NITC held no direct or formal control over convergence policy. Meanwhile, before 1998, broadcasting activities were regulated by the Broadcasting Act and its accompanying subsidiary legislations.

Immediately after the enactment of the CMA1998, promotion of digital convergence became the responsibility of the Ministry of Energy, Communication and Multimedia (MECM) (later Ministry of Energy, Water and Communication or MEWC) and MCMC, which was designated as the super-regulator body for the convergence industry. The Act consolidated legislation concerning broadcasting and telecommunication, and abrogated the traditional Broadcasting and Telecommunications Act previously under Ministry of Information (MoI). The Act not only facilitates the requirements to migrate to the new regime, but also effectively promotes digital convergence as an industry subject to ICT growth. Regulations relative to the convergence industry include the Ministerial determinations, decisions, MCMC's requirement and order. The MCMC, appeared to be confident of the significance of the new regulation just after the launch of the CMA1998. The majority of convergence policy officials persistently considered digital convergence as the only way forward for the country. In 1998, for instance, the Chairman of the MCMC publicly argued in his speech:

The Commission will work closely with all role players - Ministry, the industry players and the consumer groups towards developing and promoting policies that enhance orderly growth and development for the benefit of all. The success of the Commission shall be measured by the pace of growth and development and by the extent to which it meets the objects of the legislation and the policy objective.[2]

The Chairman was clearly confident about the benefit of digital convergence in this respect. The Government included the revision of MIMOS in the list of the major structural reform since ICT was in the mainstream agenda in 1990s. Further evidence of Government willingness to widen industrial participation was the launch of new regime in 1998. For instance, the Industry Forums have been created and managed to come out with Industry Codes of Practices which is involuntarily accepted by industry players. As opined by the former Chairman of the MCMC, self-regulation is about good governance operating on an industry-wide basis (Nuraizah, 2002). Similarly, there were numerous policy papers and consultations as well as industry dialogues initiated by the MCMC in correspondence with a motive for more transparent governance.

While the general intent of these governing mechanisms is understandable, the necessity for some civic organisations actually is often overlooked. Prior to NITA, the Prime Minister first mooted Vision 2020, in the 1980s regarding a statement of intent of national goals and principles of developed country its aspires to be. This sparked numerous debates that attempted to provide the strategic approach to be pursued in tandem with the mantra of technological change. Through NITA, their connections slowly appear to have been strengthened in a number of ways. First, Government seems to widen the policy avenues due to the underlying philosophy of governance of NITA, which is based on 'people-focus' (NITA's triangle model of governance). Traditionally, in terms of organisational structure, the old world paradigm was based upon power, command and control (Azzman in NITC, 2000, p.7). In 1994, the Government designated the NITC as the top most think-tank for national ICT.

However, the recent move which clarified the position of MIMOS and lines of reporting to the NITC was not without some drawbacks. It has made such connections much less attractive to the policy side, and eventually many of them have got out of the process. As key regulatory processes are increasingly being undertaken by private sector actors, particularly in areas requiring specialist knowledge, it is becoming more difficult for the Government to listen to the civic organisations. Furthermore, the general sentiment was that NGOs is rather distant from the Government, while quite significant scores of them have been linked with opposition parties. In addition, there appears to be somewhat divided public concern of whether the Internet can be governed at all. As a result, Government has become reluctant to adopt a more liberal attitude, no matter how much this policy sector may be clamouring for greater space.

Besides a strong bureaucratic tradition, Government seeks to develop a favourable tie with key officials by honorary award and hereditary titles. It is widely known that Malaysian key public officials will be expected to abide by the aspirations of the Government in relation to the honorary titles they carry with. Adding to this convention, two significant changes seem to have indicated the apparent reluctance of the Government to reduce the scope of state political influence. The first was the abandonment of collective political collaborations vis-à-vis NITA, as mentioned above. Consequently, civic organisations and groups will no longer get their views heard automatically, but they must instead exhaust other avenues, for instance through mass-media or Internet. In recent years, naturally, bloggers gain prominence to champion issues on the ground and somewhat more critical than politicians. The Internet is an important determinant in this regard.

The second significant change was the change of premiership in the 2003, which saw Abdullah replacing Dr Mahathir as the Prime Minister. The expectation that the new Prime Minister would make substantial reform turned out to be true. In retrospective, it is widely acknowledged that Dr Mahathir himself took personal stance of many

ICT initiatives, inside or outside the countries. Even though the ICT agenda remained important, many structural reforms have happened eventually. Currently, the NITC remained as the highest think-tank body for ICT and is expected to continue the NITA's agenda. This is often more challenging with the size of its member having been reduced to half of the previous. Before 2004, for example, the NITC members were comprised of varied backgrounds, thus were able to come out with rather comprehensive views on policy recommendations. Under these circumstances, it is not surprising that many observers relate the changes in the policy interest and orientation on the changing of the country's Prime Minister.

Regardless of the legitimate concern over the current mechanisms developed in the new regime, the key bureaucrats thus have significant ability to deny or require modification of proposals for new or amended regulatory framework, given the above scenario. Together with the generous provision of Ministerial and federalist power under the law, where a "change" may pose a significant threat to political status-quo, the ability of key bureaucrats to foreclose the debate for change has frequently been a significant critique to the industry development. Of course, this has also effectively undermined calls for change of a radical nature.

At the operational level, the potential for some digital convergence activities to fall under traditional and convergence laws, and the regulatory regimes surrounding the issue of Government broadcasting particularly, have caused problems. As contained in Malaysian Constitution, the Federal Administrative power of the Minister allows extensive administrative discretion and the lack of transparency in the exercise of this discretion is potentially an issue. Of course, the extent to which such intensification of digital convergence may compensate for the overall reduction of the scope of collective action varies across different new ICT policy issues. Nonetheless, even though the Government may be the nominal architects of new

mode of governance and celebrates views remaining in the traditional network, their interests have been further undermined by forces from "above."

Such caveats have proved no barrier to the development and increasing influence of the evolving discourse of good governance. Most of the companies and industries were initially not as enthusiastic about convergence policy as to use their own resources, for instance in the universal service obligations projects. But they often come around once the new policy framework is put on the agenda. In this context, it should be noted that the idea of governance promoted in the new regulatory regime while becoming increasingly sophisticated and "less narrowly economic", it continues to set the nature of convergence policy. For industry players, it is not because they were compelled to do so, but rather because it has its interests at stake if they refuse to do so. The new consensus seeks to extend and complement the former emphasis on governance reform based on NITA, even though it no longer has the function of collective participation, may well formalise the social side of the policy position of the whole ICT agenda.

RELATIONSHIP BETWEEN CONVERGENCE REGULATOR AND OTHER GOVERNMENT ACTORS

One of the striking qualities of the status of the convergence policy authority, the MCMC vis-à-vis other Government actors, is its status as the 'semi-independent regulatory commission.' As the key regulatory body charged with the duty of promoting digital convergence in the country, the MCMC is rather independent in several ways. For example, the MCMCA establishes a MCMC Fund, which is to be administered and controlled by the MCMC. Money for the fund may be amounts provided by Parliament, from licence fees, administration charges, levies and other charges imposed by the MCMC, income from the investments, monies derived from the sale, disposal, lease or hire of property, mortgage or changes acquired by the MCMC, money earned from consultancy and advisory services provided by its borrowings (Surin, 2003). The MCMC formally belongs to the MEWC (MECM before 2005), and not to the Ministry of Science, Technology and Innovation (MoSTI), MoI, Ministry of Finance (MoF) or Ministry of International Trade and Industry (MITI), which obviously has similar if not more, interest in convergence policy. Due to this design, like other jurisdictions, legislations, and regulations concerning ICT, the role of MCMC still remains smattered across other departments and agencies under Ministries.

One important issue is that it is true that the MCMC often finds itself isolated within the Government due to its status. The MCMCA1998 as well as the CMA1998 had given some sorts of generous provisions, which made the MCMC appears as part of the family of judicial bodies. Also, the departmental re-structuring happened in 2005 in line with the rebranding of the MEWC. The reforms are believed to put the MCMC staff on better position to embrace the new reality of convergence. However, this change is rather cosmetic. There is, for instance, concern with regard to the working with the Minister. According to the CMA1998, the MEWC (or now MCMM) Minister may give directions to the MCMC regarding the performance of the functions and powers of the MCMC, and the MCMC is obliged to give effect to such directions (Surin, 2003). Besides, the Minister also can issue determination in any matter specified in the CMA1998 without consultation with any of the licencess or other person, in which every Ministerial direction shall be registered by MCMC as soon as it is practical (Surin, 2004).

Isolation often turns to vulnerability. Since the MCMC is a tiny agency regardless of its formal legal position, it is very difficult to withstand outside pressure without any considerable support from policy makers and other ministries. As a matter of fact, it is often the case of which MCMC is caught in the middle of political battles between different Ministries. There is only the MEWC that deals directly with convergence policy. In retrospective, the NITC previously accommodates numerous groups supporting 'people-based agenda,' but convergence policy has to face the issue of how and why they are best suited, and in which ways they can be improved. After all, the new convergence sector generally appeals to business interests, which are often seen as peripheral to ICT-wide policy.

Until now, the absence of direct support from the NITC was compensated by private involvement, notably the industry players. The MCMC, together with the MCMM (previously MEWC), often promotes various advisory and consultative initiatives for the new regime to materialise, for instance, through Industry Forums. As convergence unfolds, the network collaborations have been greatly enhanced since 1998. The NITC scaled down and seemed not to have proceeded as robust as it used to and the more robust role of MCMC gaining ground for closing the digital divide. Consequently, the original philosophy of NITA's governance is seemingly no longer enjoying the same rigour. Due to predominantly traditional regulatory mechanisms, the MCMC seems to be challenged by a mature sector of ICT characterised by a few incumbents with a long history of interactions with Government, while promoting a relatively new and technologically sophisticated sector dominated by industry players.

To some extent, arguably, the MCMC has special relationship with Government. The former staffs of Department of Broadcasting and Telecommunication were transferred to the MCMC upon its abrogation. This was initially one of the reasons why the MCMC had a relatively high number of posts for staff who came from the previous agency under MoI. According to the MCMCA1998, the MCMC shall consist of a Chairman, one member representing the Government and two to five other members who will be appointed for a period of two to five years. The provision for the appointment of who shall be appointed as the Chairman and the Commissioners are actually open to wide interpretation. Indeed, for all the three appointed Chairmen so far, the post was allocated to retirees from senior civil servant who had served at various Ministries, including the MOSTI and then MEWC itself. As this is becoming norms, many see the Chairmanship post of the MCMC just as one exclusively reserved for a figure that shall hold favourable view of the Government.

As transpired, despite being an agency under the purview of MCMM sharing the link with the Ministry's website, the MCMC naturally has arm length relationship with the MEWC. This is not surprising given that it had long been considered important to keep the MCMC away from the MoI, MEWC, MoSTI, or even MCMM in order to avoid their political control over the convergence industry. In the past, when MoSTI was most active and enthusiastic, the MEWC was the only Ministry that could hold out against MoSTI. The MoSTI had the ICT sector under its domain, but the convergence sector had often been peripheral to new ICT regime. In consequence, now, the chairman of MCMC works closely with the Minister of MCMM. Indeed, the Minister can use his Ministerial determinations to urge the Chairman to comply with any decision made by the Government. The Chairman was not necessarily loyal to the Government. Yet, it could well be argued that the Government managed to minimise the political friction or rift due to this position in view of their past services.

While the MCMC was left with the authority of regulating the convergence sector, the MEWC apparently increased its interest in keeping a close connection with MCMC. After all, the convergence sector was more exposed to market competition as a result of digital technology, and hence put under the supervision of the MCMC. On top of that, the MEWC developed its ambition to utilise the MCMC as a tool of its control over digital economy. In fact, a former Minister of MECM opined that:

The Government has therefore taken the bold pre-emptive step to position Malaysia strategically in the information millennium. The formation of the NITC and the MSC has set the strategic direction. The formation of the Communications and Multimedia Ministry and the Communications and Multimedia Commission is a natural development. No one should underestimate their important roles in achieving the strategic national objectives. We must understand that there are critical tasks ahead. A new integrated policy has to be developed in the light of convergence and the network media.[3]

The MCMC's vulnerability also seems to be magnified by the concentration of decision-making power on the Minister. It is true that the Minister's view weighs no more than Commissioners but since the functions of individual Minister is vital, they had placed at particular division of the MCMC, the Minister to hold an almost exclusive authority over MCMC and with external parties. This had, in substance, made the MCMC subject to the control of the Minister. Of course, strong leadership would be a merit when the Chairman has so much vigour and enthusiasm. On the other hand, the stand-off of the Chairman might increase the MCMC's vulnerability in which one single person is exposed to political pressure.

DIGITAL CONVERGENCE: THE NEW MODE OF GOVERNANCE?

In retrospection, one of the particularities of the NITA was to disseminate the idea that new mode of governance is desirable, or even critical for Malaysian information age agenda. NITA was successful in opening up the path to NRR with a view to creating "a public policy environment that encourages the growth of the C&M industry and facilitates the development of an electronic marketplace where the possibilities for trade and investments are limitless."[4] The idea remained even after the NITA and related reforms were over. A number of specific reforms were motivated and were subsequently achieved as efforts for promoting NRR. The abrogation of Broadcasting and Telecommunications Acts (replaced by the CMA1998) was perhaps the most important achievement in terms of infrastructure and institutional building.

Just as the NITA's model of governance has been controversial, CMA1998, which provided the per se provision for NRR based on self-regulation and voluntary compliance, had caused intense debate until now. The purpose of this law is to promote a new form of governing in the digital age, since the country is committed to becoming the global hub for C&M industry. The concept of new governance has been transformed into a new dimension - from ICT to digital convergence governance. The CMA requires Minister's approval before commencing with the development of any convergence related policies. It spells out where an invitation for public consultations must be carried out along with the criteria for a positive assessment. Indeed, this was not a mandatory practices; that before 1998, there was no act which directly specifies that a policy development must have a proper procedures as such in order to be approved. Dialogues or consultations if any were on choice, not obligation.

While NITC actually formed smart collaboration through NITA framework, bureaucrats had long kept a persistent concern over the role of MIMOS as the secretariat of NITC.[5] Furthermore, the k-society or k-economy concept generally received a lukewarm response from the bureaucrats despite the fact it was originated from NITC - the highest governing council for ICT in the country. Some politicians have even openly criticised the provision of the philosophy of 'k-economy' or 'k-society.' Similar feelings were repeated thereafter, most notably towards the end of Mahathir's reign as the Prime Minister. By the early 2000s, however, there was a persistent feeling that the reorganisation of various IT entities, with NITC

is no exception would lead to the emergence of a more conducive environment for the digital technology. Moreover, while being impacted by the proliferation of global digital convergence, most Malaysian industries had not been seriously interested in the need for change, at least before 1998. This is in most cases when Government-Link-Companies (GLCs) were unenthusiastic about the change.

In hindsight, the NITC has spoken about the benefit of new forms of policy integration. In 2000, NITC:

The NITC recognises that Malaysia's migration into the eWorld or ICT-based world requires a new model of decision-making, a model where the state, the corporation and the community form a smart partnership that hinges upon the collective wisdom, cooperation and responsible action of all stakeholders in development. This model of decision-making currently serves as the pillar of the NITC's Governance Agenda.

It should be noted that the above statement was made when NITC was representing the Government of Malaysia (since 1998) and co-host the GKII together with the World Bank. This was obviously among the first formal attempts to represent the view of the NITC.

Interestingly, the Government suddenly changed in its attitude before the governance model fully materialised. In 2004, the Government formed a high-level Government Advisory Committee headed by the Chief Secretary to the Government in early 2003, and tasked with recommendation to the NITC (MEWC, 2003). As governance takes a new shape, to organise a dialogue itself was not necessarily a sign of change, but an obvious response was that there were some disagreements about the revolutionary concept of governance proposed by NITC. The discussion was not made open to the public and the Committee quickly recommended some provisions for change in the NITC.

In the meantime, the sudden change of the industry players was most widely explained by persistent pressure from either the Government, through the MECM or the MCMC. By that time, the Government had consistently urged industry players to prepare themselves to embrace a new regime or risk losing out in their competitiveness. Restructuring of the financial and banking sector seemed to have consequent impact on the convergence sector as well. It was also suspected that the industry players changed its attitude because the Government suggested that the planned organisational reform would also mean that incumbents will not forever be the dominant players (Raslan, 2003). Of course, organisational reform did not completely remove the bureaucratic conflicts and competition between the related Ministries and the Government that might not change its position for pure political reasons. However, it should be noted that those speculations was too simplistic to be taken into account.

Regarding the role of MCMC in governing the industry beyond "regulating", two programmes are of interest in that they indicate the apparent willingness to expand the industry through new mode of governing. First, the CMA1998 specifies that subject to the approval of MCMC, and Industry Forums will be established and is eligible for financial and administrative assistance for a start-up as well as continuing activities. Second, in conjunction with the new emphasis on self-governing and voluntary compliance, the IFs are required to establish and promote the use of industry codes of practices amongst its members. Additionally, the MCMC does not limit its option for policy inputs as policy consultations are also open wide for any interested parties or individual in the public to express their opinions.

With respect to regulatory implementation, MCMC had to face the vertical integration issues between different levels of governing institutions. It has been put under the purview of not less than two Ministries in less than a decade. Problems were caused by mixing old "command and control" stat-

ute administered by various Ministries/agencies with "convergence" legislation or the CMA1998. Similarly, regulatory complications carried on through the MCMC has been complemented with various formal and informal mechanisms created within each regulatory domain, such as dialogues with industry leaders, industry forums, working groups such as the IPV6 Committee, Digital TV Committee and various technical committees. Despite making steady progress, the MCMC's weakness in dealing with issues particularly regarding content regulation was clear at the next stage (see for instance Ahmad & Dai, 2007). Until now, the Government does not intend to remove the clear demarcation between content regulation, content development and content enforcement which is spread across various Ministries and agencies.

Furthermore, exceptions are given to RTM, arguing that Government broadcasters are governed by their in-house codes. Nonetheless, the MoI could not keep even that position when controversies arose regarding the broadcasting content. Politicians and other consumer groups complained about the MCMC's reluctance to take a more coherent approach. Often the MoI managed to escape the political dilemma, but this is not without the MoI putting further pressure on reinstating its power over the content and broadcasting. As a result of this, and after an intense debate in the Parliament, the Government agreed to form a special committee headed by the Deputy Prime Minister to suggest an amicable solution to this issue. Ironically, the discussion was neither made open to public nor within the NITC forum, and political reason clouted the whole scenario.

Because of strong opposition from the MEWC, which has already formed a coalition with the MCMC and convergence industries at that time, the situation remained unchanged. The Government only initiated a special liason Monitoring Committee for Public and Private Broadcasting. It could be interestingly argued that the political decision to maintain the CMA1998 status-quo is to compensate the loss of the NITC for MEWC to MoSTI. The MoI accepted the reform eventually, perhaps not because it supported the original position of the MCMC, but rather because it has no sufficient resources to accomplish another big structural reform - the split between the 'hard' and 'soft' aspect of ICT development policy for the MEWC and the MoSTI. This reform was achieved in 2005. Meanwhile, for the NITC, the provision of people-based agenda remained as it was initially, but seemed to loose its vigour afterwards, due to lack of substantial discussion. The irrelevance of the NITC was even clearer in the policy discussion about digital convergence. In fact, during interviews by the author, the general impression is that 'digital convergence affairs are under the authority of the MEWC/MCMC, and 'everyone else is not supposed to touch on it.'[6] However, this did not last long. The latest rebranding of the Information, Communication and Culture Ministry in 2013 to the Communication and Multimedia Ministry, given the dynamism and vibrancy of the latter's landscape, where consumers are hungry for broadband access, video, audio, graphics, images and animation the elements of content and innovation. The creation of this ministry is highly relevant because Malaysia is leveraging as a developed nation in which a digital platform is critical. Besides, it also wants to be the creative and innovation hub in the region. Overall, it is difficult to be exempted from such criticisms that: although the reform may have a large impact on the Malaysian economy and society, there is an obvious lack of policy discussion about it within the NITC. Ironically, regardless of this fact, as its status specifies that most aspect of ICT policy will still be governed by the federal government under the term national ICT development, in which the NITC's role will still be critical.

CHAPTER SUMMARY

The chapter examines how much Malaysian digital convergence policy changed during the recent years, particularly focusing on the networked governance structures between relevant domestic actors. Alongside with the relationship between civil society and the Government, the scope of 'people-based' policy agenda has been transformed as a result of digital convergence, but an eventual process seems to serve in part as compensation to the lack of consistent approach to the NITA's search of new mode of governance. The experience of the MCMC, in trying to define a digital convergence strategy, appropriate for the industry players, suggests that much effort is still needed at the regulatory level in terms of utilising ICTs for achieving good governance.

Those network reforms represent recognition of the development impacted by Malaysian digital convergence policy. The relevant institutions, mainly the MEWC (now MCMM), MoSTI and MCMC organised its staff and dealt with the 'hard' and the 'soft' aspect of ICT policy in facing the new reality. However, the overall reform was somewhat intriguing. Ironically, the policy process towards the curtailment of NITC members (and subsequently the loosing of NITA's vigoureness), almost in relevance to these changes exhibits the weaknesses of the NITC in shaping the trends in the policy network.

Of course, this is not to suggest that the current framework is a casualty. Since digital technologies are most pervasive and unprecedented, the general trend would be driven towards new mode of governance. Furthermore, it is appropriate to restrict the NITC's role in the policy making rather than policy implementation. Moreover, the NITC is merely an advisory Council without any control by legal accord. Neither is it argued here that all the institutional reforms are politically unreasonable. As a matter of fact, the status of the NITC under the ambit of MIMOS is controversial from an economic or political point of view (interview with some insiders).

Nevertheless, it should be remembered that the ideas and interests of policy makers really matter in the process of digital convergence development. Likewise, it is also risky that the regulator or policy making body is brought under total control of the State. To a great extent, the success of further, continued digital convergence development will depend on the ability of government to expand the network activities and capacity of the industry players in the sector as well as upon the planning and participatory consultation exercises required to gain sectoral and national support for rigourous convergence activities. They have thus become 'critical network' in the sense that their outcomes are vital determinants of licensing and other provisions surrounding convergence operations. Furthermore, whatever is the final decision, it is important to ensure sufficient and holistic discussion for policy-making, but it seems difficult to do so until the NITC or MCMC become more representative.

The promotion of digital convergence and the reinforcement of governance policy appeared on the political agenda once again under the premiership of Prime Minister Abdullah Badawi. Against this background, the NITC will gain more bureaucratic control in the near future, but it is not clear whether this will lead to a real reminiscent or development of the 'NITC's people-based governance policy' without dismantling the current elitist framework between relevant actors to meet political agenda of the State. NRR is a remarkable example in Malaysia as the desired goal of government to become the hub for C&M activities. This not only involves fine tuning the existing policies and better coordination between different regulatory bodies but has also introduced new actors, particular new methods of regulating mechanism. But the existing regulatory style has encountered many constraints, considering the widely employed metaphor of government seeking new governance through "steering" complex networks of public and private actors. This is often stymied with rather unilateral traditional approach possibly through ineffective bureaucracy.

Finally, it is noted that the 10th Malaysia Plan has further leveraged the primary role of ICT as a foundation for the nation to vault forward toward a high value economy. With the changing of country's premiership from Abdullah to Najib, there has been significant reforms to the Ministry that is primarily responsible for e-agenda. The MWEC was renamed Ministry of Energy effective April 2009. Later, it has been renamed as the Ministry of Information, Communication and Culture. In May 2013, it has renamed yet again as the Ministry of Communication and Multimedia Malaysia (MCMM) following the restructuring of the cabinet. 'Communication' function continue to fall under the ambit of MCMM along with the MCMC as the regulatory body. In order to assess whether there is a particular impact on the scale and prospect for new mode of governance, further research is vital to examine the evolution of the digital convergence and new communication policy in the Malaysia context.

REFERENCES

Abdul Halim, A. (2000). Toward Malaysia's knowledge empowerment in the 21st century. In *NITC, Access, Empowerment and Governance in the Information Age* (pp. xii–xvi). Kuala Lumpur: NITC Malaysia Publication.

Ahmad, N. B., & Dai, X. (2007). *The politics of digital convergence in Malaysia: A search for a New mode of governance*. Paper presented at the International Conference of Communication Technologies and Empowerment. Leeds, UK.

Azzman, T. M. S. (1988). *Microelectronics, information technology and society*. Paper presented at First Raja Tan Sri Zainal Lecture, IEM/MIMOS. Kuala Lumpur, Malaysia.

Azzman, T. M. S. (2000). The changing world: ICT and governance. In *NITC, Access, Empowerment and Governance in the Information Age* (pp. 1–13). Kuala Lumpur: NITC Malaysia Publication.

Castells, M. (1996). *The rise of the network society.* Cambridge, MA: Blackwell Publishers.

Castells, M. (2005). Global governance and global politics. *Political Science and Politics, 38*(01), 9–16. doi:10.1017/S1049096505055678

COMNET-IT UNESCO. (2004). *Country profiles of eGovernance – Malaysia.* Retrieved from http://www.dirap.uqam.ca/ahp03e.htm

Fariza, N. M., Norizan, A. R., Abdullah, M. Y., Salman, A., Abdul Malek, J., & Hussin, S. (2011, October). Empowering the community through ICT innovation. In *Proceedings of Communications (MICC),* (pp. 13-17). IEEE.

Haslinda, S. A. N., Azizah, A. R., & Othman, I. (2011, November). Government's ICT project failure factors: A revisit. In *Proceedings of Research and Innovation in Information Systems (ICRIIS).* IEEE.

Hendriks, C. M. (2009). The democratic soup: Mixed meanings of political representation in governance networks. *Governance: An International Journal of Policy, Administration and Institutions, 22*(4), 689–715. doi:10.1111/j.1468-0491.2009.01459.x

Herrera, G. L. (2002). The politics of bandwidth: International political implications of a global digital information network. *Review of International Studies, 28*(01), 93–122. doi:10.1017/S0260210502000931

Hishamudi, I., & Ali, K. (2004, March). Study of relationship between perception of value and price and customer satisfaction: The case of Malaysian telecommunication industry. *The Journal of American Academy of Business,* 309-313.

Humphreys, P. (1994). *Media and media policy in Germany: The press and broadcasting since 1945.* Oxford, UK: Berg.

Humphreys, P. (2006). Globalization, regulatory competition, and EU policy transfer in the telecoms and broadcasting sectors. *International Journal of Public Administration, 29*(4-6), 305–334. doi:10.1080/01900690500437055

Kamarulzaman, A. A., & Aliza Akmar, O. (2001, September). The multimedia super corridor: a physical manifestation of the Malaysian National System of Innovation. In *Proceedings of the Future of Innovation Studies Conference,* (pp. 20-23). Eindhoven University of Technology.

Klijn, E. H., & Koppenjan, J. F. (2000). Public management and policy networks: Foundations of a network approach to governance. *Public Management an International Journal of Research and Theory, 2*(2), 135–158.

MAIT. (2002). *Country Intelligence Report – Malaysia.* Retrieved from http://www.mait.com/

Matthews, J. (1998). *Toffler raises furore over Malaysia's high-Tech future.* Retrieved from http://www.geocities.com/ResearchTriangle/Lab/3937/news.htm

MEWC. (2003). *Press Release: Work to strengthen MIMOS gets underway: Advisory committee to table report in 6 months.* Retrieved from http://www.ktak.gov.my

Minges, M., & Gray, V. (2002). *Multimedia Malaysia: Internet case study.* Retrieved from http://www.itu.int/ITU-D/ict/cs/malaysia/material/MYS%20CS.pdf

Newman, A. L., & Bach, D. (2004). Self-Regulatory Trajectories in the Shadow of Public Power: Resolving Digital Dilemmas in Europe and the United States. *Governance: An International Journal of Policy, Administration and Institutions, 17*(3), 387–413. doi:10.1111/j.0952-1895.2004.00251.x

NITC. (2000). *Access, empowerment and governance in the information age*. Kuala Lumpur: NITC Malaysia Publication.

Nuraizah, A. H. (2002). *Opening Remarks at the Annual Asia Pacific Telecom CFO Roundtable*. Kuala Lumpur, Malaysia: Academic Press.

Ramasamy, R. (2010). Benchmarking Malaysia in the global information society: Regressing or progressing? *Journal of CENTRUM Cathedra*, *3*(1), 67–83. doi:10.7835/jcc-berj-2010-0039

Raslan, S. (2003). MCMC to 'stand firm' on opening up access, Telekom objects. *The Star*, *1*(December), 9.

Rhodes, R. A. W. (1996). The new governance: Governing without government. *Political Studies*, *44*(4), 652–667. doi:10.1111/j.1467-9248.1996.tb01747.x

Saloma-Akpedonu, C. (2008). Malaysian technological elite: Specifics of a knowledge society in a developing country. *Perspectives on Global Development and Technology*, *7*(1), 1–14. doi:10.1163/156914907X253233

Schoof, H., & Watson, B. A. (1995). Information highways and media policies in the European Union. *Telecommunications Policy*, *19*(4), 325–338. doi:10.1016/0308-5961(95)00006-R

Surin, A. J. (2003). The Power to Effect ICT Change. *The Star*, *9*(December), 11–12.

Surin, A. J. (2004). Act Gives MCMC Wide Powers. *The Star*, *6*(January), 8–9.

KEY TERMS AND DEFINITIONS

Digital Convergence: The digitizing of traditional media and the blurring of content, mixing personal (user generated) content with professional (copyright protected) content using Information Communication Technologies (ICTs) as platform.

ICT Governance: Exercise of authority or method to control and manage information and communication technology.

Infrastructure: All types of public systems or resources in the country, state required to for activity.

Institutional Reforms: All changes made for improving, correcting, and removing all kinds of defects within the institutional agencies of the state.

Integrated Policy Environment: A situation in which all efforts are taken to ensure the processes of policy making; minmises any sorts of political division due to sectoral differences or interests.

Network: System of information or service sharing among different group of people or individuals having common interests on certain things.

New Regime: The post 1998 ICT era when Communication and Multimedia Act came into being; characterized by the policy environment governed by the Government and other non-state actors.

Policy Actors: All entities or bodies that involved in enacting certain policy action aimed for resolving certain issues in the country.

Policy Framework: A set of long-term goals and principles that serve as basis for overall direction to rules, planning, and development of the organization.

Self-Regulatory: The private sectors take measures to regulate themselves and thereby minimizing the role of the government or its authorities to ensure compliance with agreed policies, and provides for corrective action.

ENDNOTES

1   Interview with President/CEO of MIMOS, former Secretary of NITC, Kuala Lumpur, 05-Jun-05.

2   Excerpts from the speech by the Chairman of MCMC at the Industry Briefing and Workshop on the CMA1998, PWTC, Kuala Lumpur, 22 Feb 1999.

3   Excerpt from the speech by the Minister of MECM, Leo Moggie, at the launching of Malaysian Communications and Multimedia Commission Logo and Website, 11 May 1999.

4   Excerpt from the speech by Abdullah Badawi, the ex- Deputy Prime Minister, at the 20th Anniversary Celebration of the MECM and the launch of the CMA1998, 31 March 1999.

5   Interviews with key officials of MEWC and MoSTI who remained to be anonymous.

6   Interviews with the key figure of the former NITC members as well as insiders from the MoSTI and MEWC who remain to be anonymous.

Chapter 3
Model of Digital Convergence of ICT Adoption within the Framework of Network Governance Policy

ABSTRACT

This chapter considers the literature relevant to a study of the impact of digital convergence upon governance that impinges the overall manifestation of ICTs in the public sector today. In addressing the issue, the discussion is made within the conceptual evolution and the changing paradigm of ICT and convergence, policy networks, and the related issues, locating them at the centre of network governance literature. The central theme of this chapter is to highlight the proliferation of ICT agenda, in particular reference to digital convergence and eventually how the mode of ICT governance is affected by three important factors: first, policy network; second, new legal or regulatory environment; and third, institutional reforms. Thus, to put things into perspective and as an indication of the genuine contribution of the study of knowledge in the field, these three important domains of analysis in line with the research questions are considered to be most relevant.

INTRODUCTION

The first section reviews the theoretical background of digital convergence, network governance and its relationships to the context underlying the practice of policy network. Section two clarifies digital convergence and its interfaces with industry or private self-regulation. Section three provides systematic explanations of interactions and outcomes of policy processes by which, that

institutional convergence has affected the state and society relations and new mode of governance. Following this, the discussion tries to strengthen the framework on these three dimensions, analysing them in the context of policy network to link the analytical, empirical and normative consideration of network governance. The review, using an interdisciplinary analytical framework, will provide a comprehensive understanding of how a range of

DOI: 10.4018/978-1-4666-6579-8.ch003

scholarly debates from contending backgrounds perceive and interpret the same issues.

For the purpose of establishing the perspective in this chapter, our evaluation of framework is based on two crucial questions stated as follows:

- In what ways and to what extent does digital convergence promote new forms of governance?
- What are the ideal conditions needed to suit digital convergence with a system of network governance?

Following discussion of these two broad issues, the analysis will then consider the notion of a new self-regulatory regime which is already in existence in Malaysia as the most appropriate model towards an ideal form of ICT governance policy.

POLICY NETWORKS AND NEW MODE OF GOVERNANCE

How exactly do technological innovations, in particular digital convergence, enhance the governance process? In order to respond to this question, it is worth examining the various categorical domains of technology itself. Digital convergence can be generally classified as the synchronisation of "voice, data, text, and images, and transmitted in vastly greater volume and at far higher speed" (Humphreys, et al., 1992, pp.3-4). The means of delivering public interest content must be defined in regulatory terms which do not unduly restrict the competitive communications environment operating on a global scale (Jacobs, 2000). In other words, this simply means that through the sophistication of new technology, users will have access to a wide ranging information, entertainment, communications, and transaction services in a single interface point. Policy network is one of the most important features in determining whether a new mode of governance can be successfully achieved by a nation-state, or by supranational bodies. In

this section, various elements concerning policy network and its implications for the search for a new mode governance are highlighted from a variety of academic perspectives.

The Perspective of Policy Networks

It is contended by an increasing number of scholars in media policy that the concept of network governance has emerged in recent decades (Triantafillou, 2004, p.489). These include, for instance, Castells (1996) who points to the grand narratives of network society, Anthony (1990) who gives an account of reflexive modernity, and Rhodes (1998) who provides specific accounts of the formation and functioning of networks of public agencies, private organisations and diverse groups and citizens. The very influential work of Scharpf et al. (1978) used the networks concept to map relationship patterns between organisations and to assess the influence of these patterns for policy processes. Citizens are regarded as "principals" exercising their power by voting their representatives or "agents" (Pavan & Lemme, 2011). In many cases, these are quite complex as they do not only originate from public actors (Kooiman, 1993; Kickert et al., 1997), but also link to private, as well as non-profit elements. Sorenson (2003, p.693) observed that scores of social scientists (e.g. Bogason, 2000; Heinrich & Lynn, 2000; Jessop, 1998; Kickert, et al., 1997; Kooiman, 1993, 2000; Mayntz, 1999; Pierre, 2001; Pierre & Peters, 2000; Rhodes, 1997; Scharpf, 1994; Stoker, 1998) imply that the "political systems slowly and gradually change from hierarchically organised, unitary systems of government that govern by means of law, rule and order, to more horizontally organised and relatively fragmented systems of governance that govern through the regulation of self-regulating networks." It is worth noting, however, that the ultimate target of a network model or approach should not be to control others, but to establish a good policy environment for all parties to cooperate with each other (Hendriks, 2009).

Coinciding with the emerging key words such as "deregulation," "new technologies," and "internationalisation" in more and more sectors of policy (Humphreys, et al., 1992; Katsikas, 2010; Johnston, 2010), the theoretical debates in the 1970s and 1980s about the nature of governance and the properties of state-civil society relations provided roots for the concept of policy network. While such accounts were useful to bring a general understanding of the contextual development to the area, however, it was not until the end of the 1990s that a few formal studies were conducted into the relationship between policy network and the new public governance (Coleman & Perl, 1999).

The causes for this development are numerous: the increased importance of international political institutions; new administrative techniques promoting institutional self-regulation within the political systems; and intensified cooperation between public authorities and private actors, be it market actor or actors within civil society (Sorenson, 2002, p.693) or with the use of local political online fora to support participatory and deliberative democracy (Dunne, 2009). Discussion on this will appear in the next chapter.

In Power/Knowledge: Selected Interviews and Other Writings (1980, originally published in 1972, p.121), Foucault formulated his well-known theory which delineates between "governance" from that of "citizen participation." The former involves "a network of relationship among the governed and the governing, rather than a hierarchical relationship between the governed and the governing" (Beresford, 2003, p.83). Foucault suggests that the process of citizen participation tends to perpetuate the role of the citizen as 'subject to' the control of government, dependent on the protection of government, and bound by an identity that is defined by a position in a social hierarchy. Governance, therefore requires that we "cut off the King's head", and pay attention to the ways in which we direct conduct through the systems

of the body of society, which, in essence, requires government participation in citizen activities rather than citizen participation in government activities. Foucault's theory of governance consists of three basic elements:

- Relations (or interconnections) between individuals and groups;
- Communication and information "by means of language, a system of signs, or any other symbolic medium" (Foucalt, 1983, p.217); and
- Capacities to modify action.

For the period beginning in the 1990s, the growing interest in the use of ICT is having a considerable impact on the way the nation state functions. Nation states, in consequent response to the challenges of the network society and globalisation, are becoming both 'supranational' and 'devolved' by positioning themselves as 'international, supranational and co-national institutions to explore 'shared sovereignty' (Dai, 2003, p.195). This is followed by the nation state's attempts to 'regain legitimacy through the process of decentralisation and devolution of power and resources to sub-national government (Carnoy & Castells, 2001, pp.195-6). Technologies are fast becoming tools that must be used in a transformative way to be transformative (Boyd, 2008). This is also the age in which networking and eGovernance "coalesce around a politics perspective that thrives on a shared interest in digitised communication and decentralised authority" (Calista & Melitski, 2007). Eventually, this forces the state of the information age into a 'Network State.'

The publication of The Rise of the Network Society by Castells in 1996 was widely regarded as the beginning of a new era for studies on policy network and its implication for the new governance mode. Castells perpetuated the notions that a 'network' is a set of inter-connected nodes (Castells,1996, p. 501), that 'networks' constitute the new social morphology of our societies, and that the diffusion of networking logic substantially modifies the operation and outcomes in processes of production, experience, power, and culture (Castells, 1996, p.500). In essence, these networks are characterised by open structures, ability to expand without limits, integrating new nodes and, as they are associated with the social structure, they are "highly dynamic, open system(s), susceptible to innovating without threatening their balance" (Castells, 1996, pp. 501-2).

Following this line of thought, Castells (1991; Castells & Caradoso, 2006) believes there is a decisive shift away from industrial capitalism to a postindustrial conception of economic relations that represent a new form of activity, depicting a striking revolution among techno-industrial elites that ultimately renders the globe a single market, across national borders. These activities are inextricably linked, specialised and globally integrated.

The enrichment of the debates on the legitimate position of the nation-state indeed proved that there is general understanding and recognition about the nature of forms and discourses of what really shapes democratic relations. The Internet affects governance by shifting the power structure in information provision and distribution away from government's traditional policy makers. Governance should no longer be viewed as "the greater exertion of government influence over the affairs of a country"; instead, it must be seen as "the enhancement of the middle ground in the interplay between the three components of governance, namely government, the private sector and what is termed as civil society" (Muhammad Rais, 1999, p. 31). Despite the fact that a major shift of focus is taking place from hierarchical, unitary government to horizontal, fragmented network governance, there seems to be a common agreement that the political system of the world today is a mixture of the two forms of governing. Scharpf (1994, p.37), for instance, describes the mix in the Western countries as networking "in the shadow of hierarchy."

Network theoreticians like Levine and White (1961), Negandhi (1975) and Aldrich (1979) all focused on the dynamism of interaction processes between interdependent actors and the consequence of that interaction in the institutional context. Levine and White (1961), Cook (1977), Aldrich and Whetten (1981) and Benson (1982) have given an extensive account of interorganisational theory, which describes the exchange relations. Also the debate of "whether or to what extent ICT implementation is likely to positively correlate with traditional issues such as democracy, government-citizens relationships, disclosure of financial information, accountability and NPM's legacy" (Pavan & Lemme, 2011). The analysis and practice of governance has obviously been the subject of numerous scholarly debates, despite the main implementation of ICTs, namely as eGovernment and eGovernance, has not been systematically differentiated (Calista & Melitski, 2007). These sorts of issues will be the main focus in the empirical chapter.

Most recently, scholars have recognised the wave of globalisation, which has become a more prominent part both of academic analysis and of public discourse (e.g. Loughlin, 2004; Held, 1995; Johnston, 2010). Following Held, we understand globalisation to refer to 'the stretching and deepening of social relations and institutions across space and time such that, on the one hand, day-to-day activities are increasingly influenced by events happening on the other side of the globe and, on the other, the practices and decisions of local groups or communities can have significant global reverberations' (Held, 1995, p. 20). The process started in the middle of the 1980s, as observed by Loughlin (2004, p.19) and included privatisation, deregulation, regional pacts which lowered them (as with North American Free Trade Agreement or NAFTA) or abolished frontiers (as in the Schengen group of the European Union or EU) and reforms of public administration, which was opened up to internal competition and in effect adopted a new operating culture. The "Third Wave" of change, as he observed, may have happened under the rubric of the "new governance." In fact, a governance infrastructure as an eventual output, "conceptualizes governance as one part of a responsive system, managing information to facilitate interaction between diverse people" (Johnston, 2010) – from "antiquity to modern times, the nation has always been a product of information management" (The Economist, 2010, p.11).

Loughlin (2004) contends that at this stage, it is still too early to give a definite answer to the question whether all of these constitute a new paradigm shift from the period of neo-liberal hegemony. Despite the widespread attempts to refound Western political and administrative systems, there were obviously, uneven development and debates across local, regional and supranational levels, for example, EU in defining the meaning of "new governance."

While many proponents of a new mode of governance believe that governments around the world are confronted with a rapidly evolving and challenging environment in which to try and construct public policy, the positions of these scholars are somewhat contradictory. On the one hand, there are those who see process of globalisation as irrevocably reducing the authority and power of states (Ohmae, 1995; Strange, 1996); on the other, some who claim that, not only is there nothing especially new about globalisation (Hirst, et al., 2009), but the idea that it has reduced state capacities is a "myth" (Weiss, 1998). The major lines of the debate in general commentaries are increasingly polarised between those who contend that the new technology undermines, or at least weakens, state authority, and on the contrary, are those who believe that it strengthens liberal democracy, and thereby the liberal state (Sassen, 2000, p.19). Directly related to these two positions is the more technical debate between those who advocate the idea of a separation between politicians and administrators, and those who maintain that there must be ways and means for public administrators to be granted greater autonomy so that they can

efficiently manage the governing task in the new regime (Lessig, 1999; Reinderberg, 1998). Also, there is research theme on the way individual and group resistance emerges and evolves during prior stages of projects (Meissonier & Houze, 2010). Indeed, the philosophy behind the New Public Management (NPM) is to delineate between the overall political and financial goals or framework and the concrete governing of specific public tasks (see for instance, Pavan & Lemme, 2011; Sorenson, 2002; Caperchione, 2006; Groot & Budding, 2008; Lapsley, 2008).

Following the theoretical roots of the policy network above, we can observe that initially, the theme was to map out patterns of relations between organisations and to assess the influence of these patterns for the policy process (see for instance, Hjern & Porter, 1981; Scharpf, et. al., 1978; Hobson, 2010). The pivotal requirements of a new mode of governance involve complex interaction processes among a large number of actors taking place within networks of interdependent actors, which mutually engage or are dependent on each other resources. However, the lack of a consensus over the nature of policy network and its impact on the role of the State, as well as civil society relations, as indicated above, does not suggest that the study of network governance is worthless, but is a reflection of the reality in which there is no single way for countries to approach the future.

As far as terminology is concerned, the term policy network is commonly associated with other equivalents. For instance, in Public Management and Policy Networks, Klijn and Koppenjan, (2000) use terms, such as network management process management and network constitution (Klijn et al. 1995; Kickert, et al., 1997 for extensive discussions).

New Mode of Governance and Policy Networks

Foucault's famous theory, as mentioned above, is that horizontal, coordinating governing arrangements occur frequently in contemporary policy making and this analytical approach focuses on the distinctions between traditional governmental action and governance, including the manner, or methods, of directing individual and group conduct (Foucault, 1983). Foucault even suggests the idea of seeking and enhancing cooperation outside the circle of government whilst removing the need for traditional control and punitive action through the means of institutions and laws. The role of the state is not an issue, rather how polities function–that is, "how specific rationales are brought into being and enacted, and the diverse mechanisms that attempt to enroll a wide array of actors into attaining particular outcomes," (Hobson, 2010).

The preceding discussion has shown that the notion of network governance essentially calls for a regular and non-hierarchical form of interaction, essentially portrayed by a network. In a similar vein, Rhodes's model of policy networks a "set of resource-dependent organisations linked through their interest in a specific policy sector" (Bache, 2000, p.576). Network itself is a vague concept, understood as a cluster of relationships which spans indefinite ranges of space and time (Jackson, et al., 2000, p.11), and transcends boundaries capitalising on the continuous collaboration with external sources of knowledge and expertise. Variations in the degree of influence over decision making are a product of the goals and the relative power potential of each organisation, of the rules of the game, and of the process of exchange between organisations. As a result of digital convergence, there is general skepticism whether it still makes sense to talk about the top-down, hierarchical nature of interaction.

At the outset, there seems to be a common optimistic understanding among scholars about the significant impact that new technology brings to the act of governing, mostly in the area of management and exercise of governance (Jorgensen, 2002, p.15). The overriding dominance and emphasis on commercial and marketplace interests, however, may undermine the process of governance, especially when the incumbent remonopolises the situation.

At the extreme, scholars even contend that the networks of interested parties would be capable of managing and deciding for the policy areas in which they are involved (Peters, 2003, p.6). Having remained in the shadow of government, there is a progressive evolution from "a more or less well-defined hierarchy or authority encapsulated by the state apparatus", to "a dispersal of authority to a wide array of mobile networks of actors, resources and institutions that precipitate around rapidly waxing and waning issues of public concern" (Triantafillon, 2004, p.489). As Triantafillou (2004) observes, "power is exercised through networks, and individuals do not simply circulate in those networks; they are in the position to both submit to and exercise this power (quoting Foucault, 2003, p.29). Triantafillou has analysed that, "the new thing about network governance is not that the state is losing out as a fixed point of hierarchical forms of power…, rather, we are witnessing the rise of a whole range of norms and governmental technologies that seek to promote agency, efficiency, and accountability by urging us to be active, participate and be responsible for oneself and for organisational goals" (cf. section 4 below). Analytical study of the concepts of power and freedom in this thesis also demonstrates a long-lasting problem faced by governments in facing the new reality.

Viewed from the historical perspective, an initial model of governance was in a sense, highly bureaucratic, in which the state is the principal source of governance for the society. This form of governing encapsulates the Weberian conception in which the public sector is perceived as an autonomous actor, utilising its own expertise, laws and authority, in a hierarchical "top-down" manner (Peters, 2003, p.5). In the early 1980s, reforms were initiated by scores of countries around the world, partly motivated by budget deficits. Since then, other challenges that commonly influenced the reform agenda consisted of a mixture of external factors such as the ageing society, the information society and the tabloid society; and internal factors such as the consequences, both planned and unplanned, arising from the 'first generation' of public sector reforms (Bovaird & Loeffler, 2003, p.13). Towards the end of the last decade, the culmination of a process that made appeal to the transformative potential of information technology began to sweep across the globe, pioneered mostly by the US (Chadwick & May, 2003, p.282).

Accordingly, looking at the governance perspective (in the early 1980s), this mode of governing later came under practical and academic attack, mainly for its elitist character, which did not provide sufficient opportunities for public involvement (Chadwick & May, p.6). It seems that, empirically, the proliferation and overarching impact of new communication technologies and the growing concern with global governance has aggressively swept through the globe. This has put the heavy onus on the part of governments, all over the world, to leverage their NII, and convergence agenda in particular, to bolster the governance issues. Subsequently, an extended version of the above concept, namely, network governance, emerged.

Given this picture, the nature of interaction cannot be viewed in isolation from policy network practices. As the public sector becomes more fragmented and the boundaries between different parties become more blurred, policy networks are concerned about cooperation as well as competition and conflict management (Löffler, 2003, p.170). An apparently broad consensus has developed around the idea that network governance, the state and the society is concerned principally with structure, that is mechanism, rules, norms, institutional arrangements and so on which mediate the process of policy network. To illustrate this point, Osborne (2010) pointed out that such networks, by nature, are 'rarely alliances of equals but rather driven with power inequalities that must be navigated successfully for their effective working.' The connections are actually the shared

values which transcend hierarchy because they are based upon informal mutuality of shared norms, and not on a formal authority relationship. Thus, what will eventually emerge are networks of state and non-state actors in an increasingly complex set of relationships of mutuality (Jackson, et al, 2000, p.11).

There are a number of theoretical propositions of new liberal democracy that have subscribed to the normative values of policy network. They share the common view that policy network remains a complicated subject, but still claims that it has much to offer in the new governing age (Rhodes, 1997; Peters, 2003). Public actors do not play the dominant role often ascribed to them in traditional public administration perspectives. This has evoked criticism. The network approach is accused of considering government merely as 'an actor among actors.' which can lead to problems of democratic legitimacy or accountability (Hirst 2013; Rhodes 1997). Most argue that without policy networks; there can be no such thing as real governance. Policy networks, thus, can be seen as an indispensable element in enhancing the capacity for a new governance mode.

However, though some actors are more powerful or endowed with more control over resources and legitimate decisions, actors are still the subjects of 'network force.' namely, the pressure upon actors to conform to rules, norms and expectations implicated in the network context. Meanwhile, the domestic politics have become even more integrated between government, the market and civil society/consumers, in correspondence with the constant pressure from global convergence. As such, rather than being trapped in discussing the dilemma of the 'hollowing out of the state.' the issue at stake which is more important, for some scholars, is "which set of formal (legal) and informal rules, structures and processes will be needed so that the state, the private and voluntary sector, citizens and other important stakeholders can exercise power over the decisions by other stakeholders so as to create win-win situations for all parties concerned" (Bovaird & Loeffler, 2003, p.20). It is worth noting that government capacity is "not only for adjusting governance structures to new requirements, but also for disposing of important powers and resources that are not available to other actors" (Knill & Lehmkuhl, 2002, p.43). The empirical studies in this study also demonstrate comparable policy, regulatory, and institutional issues faced by Malaysia in coming up with its ICT and convergence initiatives, although within its peculiar features (e.g., predominantly hierarchical society).

With the coming of digital convergence, governance values, such as issues of accountability, autonomy, and transparency, are getting more obvious, and provide a constant interface between network actors. Empirically, in its own right and juxtaposed to the role and behaviour of networked actors, convergence can potentially enhance certain styles of interaction. This is particularly possible as the actors are granted a legitimate status by state, through the regulator, and begin to have influence in the sphere of public policy. This was not the case in the previous traditional regime which was limited mostly by the Government. In the meantime, however, the lack of conflict-regulating mechanisms and trust will potentially lead to violation of social and ethical dimensions of governance. Without doubt, rules are one of the most important pillars of trust. Violation of rules, whether formal or informal, always occurs. In this sense, rules regulate but do not determine and they can be changed. Each analysis of decision making in networks must take this into account. A classic example of the formidable challenge faced by the independent regulator caught at the centre of turf battles is the loss of accountability that characterises the relationship between the MCMC and other stakeholders of the industry. More detailed discussion on this relationship is presented in the empirical chapters of this study.

As far as the network perspective is concerned, in Media and Media Policy in Germany, Humphreys (1994, p.9) puts forward two specific key

concepts. First, is the concept of 'policy community.' to denote "the complex web of interactions and resource dependencies between the various groups and actors closely involved in the policy process." The concept of 'policy network' on the other hand, applies in three ways: firstly, the kind of relationship between groups and actors which may often be "less official, less formalised and perhaps less durable than would merit the description of 'policy community.'" Secondly, a policy network may occur, for example, as the result of a destabilisation of an established 'policy community' by a new issue (e.g. the attempt to introduce commercial broadcasting, or the introduction of new technologies). Humphreys coined the phrases 'conspiracy of interest' to illustrate the emergence of new circle of relationships within the existing policy community when actors are seeking new partnerships. Thirdly, in a similar way, the term 'policy network' might refer to the processing of an issue by an 'inner circle' within the formal and broader 'policy community' to the exclusion of certain members of the latter (Humphreys (1994, p.10).

Based on the assumption that the structural and legal framework of the network can influence strategies and relationships of actors, attempts can somehow be made to change one or more of these relationships. New modes of governance draw a sharp distinction between the network games, network management and network constitution as a prerequisite for ensuring that policy outcomes always promote democratic values. As explained above, the policy process, is, in effect, the reflection of games between actors, and the outcomes of the games are a consequence of the interaction of strategies of different players in the game (Klijn & Koppenjan, 2000, 140). In reality, one could well expect that clashes, tension or conflict may eventually arise as a result of political dependency and the diversity of goals and interest (Klijn & Koppenjan, 2000 p.140). In order to contain this, network theorists advocate the principles of network management and network constitutions

(O'Toole, 1988; Klijn, et al., 1995; Kickert, et al., 1997). They seek to draw the general guidelines with the aim of 'harmonising' the relations between actors so that the environment for policy processes would be conducive and productive to all. We shall return to this point later in the empirical chapter.

To further the discussion, scholars argue that the salient feature of the dynamic, autonomous and productive nature of interaction enhances the new image of democratic policy network. In addition to the impact of convergence, one can identify two different forms of digital space that emerge: public versus private digital space (Sassen, 2000, p.25; see also Coleman and Perl, 1999—they coined the term "private regimes"). Private digital space serves the interest of private and financial actors, whilst, at the same time being constrained by the action of governments and citizens, through the complex interaction between conventional communications infrastructure and digitalisation. The appreciation of the dynamic and productive outcomes of policy network reconstructs the notion of both digital spaces as it authorised and legitimised the will and interests of policy actors, regardless of who they are. In this context, policy networks do not merely symbolise the interest of an exclusive party or actor; rather, they entail the constructive shaping to that interest. Again, parallel to the earlier argument, the interplay between various actors in the process is undergoing a constant process of perfection which happens of its own accord, and is not being intended or decided at the outset by any actor. Defining the context of the relations and interactions is in fact what politics is all about.

No matter what kind of political system a country has inherited from the past, the 1990s seemed to be a new era of challenge faced by all states. Neticians and media scholars who consistently attempt to extend the analysis of diverse forms of rule and authority, may not find it easy to explain the fluctuating and turbulent digital world of the 1990s. Taking into account the spectacular reform and approaches of many countries, at national, supranational and global levels, there are numerous literatures which cast doubt on the assumption that state hierarchies are getting weaker (e.g. Peters, 2001; Harding, 1997). If anything, states are becoming stronger more than ever as they are influential in determining the ways in which cities and regions respond to the challenge of globalisation (Harding, 1997, p.308).

STATE AUTHORITIES AND POLICY NETWORKS

It is without doubt that, in the long run, digital convergence promotes the new conception of collaboration in the policy processes due to its autonomous and dynamic features of the interactions. The multiplicity of policy and issues escalate a series of interactions within which the networks operate, and this is synonymous with what are known as 'games' (see for instance Rhodes, 1981; Scharpf, 1997). In a similar tone, policy processes in the network governance perspective can thus be seen as a 'political game' between actors. In these games, each of the various actors has its own perceptions of the nature of the problem, the desired solutions and of the other actors in the network. On the basis of these perceptions, actors select strategies. Lying at the heart of this is the issue of information and how it is accessed and distributed throughout the system through an avenue of policy networks. Networks enable a sharing of information and knowledge bases (Jackson, et. al., 2000, p.12), which inherently, encapsulates the 'interactive' identity of policy networks.

The process of convergence has dissolved the borderline between what is being long perceived as a dichotomy between politics and administration. As a result of this, the administrative capacity to manouevre has been enhanced considerably. It is worth noting, however, that the network theory never presumes that governments are on an equal footing with other actors. This is because government occupies a unique position, unlike others in the network, due to sizeable control over resources like budgets and personnel, special powers, access to mass media, a monopoly on the use of force and democratic legitimisation (Klijn, et al., 2000, p.151). Within this uniqueness, however, governments encounter various factors that limit their manoeuvring tasks in network situations (Klijn, et al., 2000, p.152). To overcome this, government needs to be politically connected and to a certain extent, control the channels of communication between the network actors, while still maintaining its horizontal position as the co-ordinator or facilitator in the process. In another instance, for some countries, administrators or a Government-armed body begin to take a renewed responsibility, normally in the role of 'regulator.' with increased autonomy and legitimate influence in the new mode of governance. Jessop (1998) coined the term 'meta-governance' to imply the typical autonomous public and semi-public institutions, which according to him, means, governance through self-regulation. In the meantime, more informal meanings of representation are emerging as collective decision making shifts to multiple sites and as constituencies become more plural and cross-territorial (Urbinati & Warren, 2008).

Although interaction happens within this new differentiated polity, it is important to note that, "Government confronts self-steering interorganisational networks. The relationships is asymmetric, but centralisation must co-exist with interdependence" (Urbinati & Warren, 2008, p.4). For instance, in the case of Malaysia, MCMC's efforts to promote self-regulation through policy network practices have enabled the country to lead the convergence activities in a number of areas including public consultations, policy forums etc. One particular aspect of great importance here is the authority and interaction power of the MCMC. As Klijn & Koppenjan (2000, et. al., p.140) argues: "... the outcomes of the game are consequences of the interactions of strategies of different players in the game."

This development has posed several other related issues to the new regime such as: to what degree can Government exert its influence, once the regulatory tasks have been relinquished to a supposedly independent regulatory body? Would it be possible to establish a strict division of roles and responsibilities between politicians, and regulators? While scholars like Dwight Waldo (2006) and Friedrich (1963) advocate the impossibility of separation between politics and administration, there seem to be many contemporary writers who share the idea that it is still possible to develop ethical guidelines for public officials by transforming them into watchdogs of democracy, with the objective of promoting the Common Good (Fox and Miller, 1995; Lundquist, 2000; Wamsley, 1996). By doing this, the creation of an independent and autonomous regulatory body is not only possible, but also enhances the interest of the people, different from the roles performed by the politicians. In other words, the new regime is far better at championing the interest of the general public.

The convergence of the C&M sector, which impinges upon the readily available different forms and layers of political apparatuses in the state, has further intensified the political struggle between contending actors - state and non-state alike, i.e., self-authorised groups such as NGOs (Rehfeld, 2006; Johnston, 2010; Hobson, 2010) and "citizen representatives who participate in citizen's forums and committees on behalf of the broader public" (Brown, 2006 in Hendriks, 2009). It is somewhat strange but undeniably interesting to observe that the interests of the public, which for a long time, were the exclusive concern of government affairs, are now championed by various self-governing bodies, and even voluntary and corporate organisations too (e.g. universal service provision, etc.).

CHAPTER SUMMARY

The chapter not only addressed the rise of the policy network perspectives of ICT governance but it also showed that the representation is not just about representation, rather, it is about innovation and participation. This multifaceted character of policy network holds significant implications for network governance. Policy network aimed at, either creating or stimulating political dynamics, tends to be inspired by political representation theories mainly (in line with the network theoretician perspective of technology) are still embedded in the political-cultural system with conventional norms (Hendriks, 2009), thus neglecting important epistemological factors influencing network governance emergence and growth. The development from a traditional representation to electoral accountability and epistemological perspective of network governance parallels the development of the field of democratic theory and practice.

The parallel with representation, as discussed earlier in this chapter, shows us that, when dealing with purpose of developing and implementing public policy in general, it eventually gives rise to the issue of how to achieve democratic legitimacy. When striving for interactions that exhibit a network dynamic characterised by knowledge sharing and innovation, policymakers need to realise the potential danger of governing network based on formal economic factors only. "Contemporary representation," within the "constellations of interdependent but autonomous actors from public, private, and societal sectors that come together for the purposes of developing and implementing public policy" (Kickert, et. al. 1997; Kooiman, 1993; Hobson, 2010), involves at the very least understanding the rich network dynamics to which the concept of liberal democracy is subject to. Policy designed at influencing formal conventional representation (e.g., principal-agent model) needs to take into account the lessons learned from the field of digital convergence, and thus should be aimed at respecting the policy dynamics unique to every cluster. A solid understanding of the policy dynamics is critical in the context of how it influences and challenges conventional notions of representative democracy. The emergence and development of digital convergence will enrich governance beyond technological factors only. Thus, it is important to suggest that the digital convergence that is believed to influence policy network and growth do not occur in a vacuum.

REFERENCES

Aldrich, H., & Whetten, D. A. (1981). Organization-sets, action-sets, and networks: Making the most of simplicity. In Handbook of organizational design, (vol. 1, pp. 385-408). Oxford, UK: Oxford University Press.

Aldrich, H. A. (1979). *Organisations and environments*. Englewood Cliffs, NJ: Prentice-Hall.

Anthony, G. (1990). *The consequences of modernity*. Cambridge, UK: Polity.

Bache, I. (2000). Government within governance: Network steering in Yorkshire and the Humber. *Public Administration*, *78*(3), 575–592. doi:10.1111/1467-9299.00219

Benson, J. K. (1982). A framework for policy analysis. In D. L. Rogers & D. A. Whetten (Eds.), *Interorganisational Coordination: Theory, Research, and Implementation* (pp. 137–176). Ames, IA: Iowa State University Press.

Beresford, A. D. (2003). Foucault's Theory Of Governance And The Deterrence Of Internet Fraud. *Administration & Society*, *35*(1), 82–103. doi:10.1177/0095399702250347

Bogason, P. (2000). Public policy and local governance: institutions in postmodern society. Edward Elgar Publishing, Incorporated.

Bovaird, T., & Loeffler, E. (2007). Assessing the quality of local governance: A case study of public services. *Public Money and Management, 27*(4), 293–300. doi:10.1111/j.1467-9302.2007.00597.x

Boyd, O. P. (2008). Differences in eDemocracy parties' eParticipation systems. *Information Polity, 13*(3), 167–188.

Brown, M. B. (2006). Survey article: Citizen panels and the concept of representation. *Journal of Political Philosophy, 14*(2), 203–225. doi:10.1111/j.1467-9760.2006.00245.x

Calista, D. J., & Melitski, J. (2007). E-government and e-governance: Converging constructs of public sector information and communications technologies. *Public Administration Quarterly*, 87–120.

Caperchione, E. (2006). *The new public management: A perspective for finance practitioners. Paper presented at the Federation of Europcan Accountants. Debating International Developments in New Public Financial Management.* Oslo: Cappelen.

Carnoy, M., & Castells, M. (2001). Globalization, the knowledge society, and the Network State: Poulantzas at the millennium. *Global Networks, 1*(1), 1–18. doi:10.1111/1471-0374.00002

Castells, M. (1991). The informational city, information technology, economic restructuring, and the urban-regional process. *Environment & Planning A, 23*, 458–459.

Castells, M. (1996). *The rise of the network society.* Cambridge, MA: Blackwell Publishers.

Castells, M. (2005). Global governance and global politics. *Political Science and Politics, 38*(01), 9–16. doi:10.1017/S1049096505055678

Chadwick, A., & May, C. (2003). Interaction between states and citizens in the age of the Internet: "e-Government" in the United States, Britain, and the European Union. *Governance: An International Journal of Policy, Administration and Institutions, 16*(2), 271–300. doi:10.1111/1468-0491.00216

Cohen, M. D., March, J. G., & Olsen, J. P. (1972). A garbage can model of organizational choice. *Administrative Science Quarterly, 17*(1), 1–25. doi:10.2307/2392088

Coleman, W. D., & Perl, A. (1999). Internationalized policy environments and policy network analysis. *Political Studies, 47*(4), 691–709. doi:10.1111/1467-9248.00225

Cook, K. S. (1977). Exchange and power in networks of interorganizational relations. *The Sociological Quarterly, 18*(1), 62–82. doi:10.1111/j.1533-8525.1977.tb02162.x

Dai, X. (2003). A new mode of governance? Transnationalisation of European regions and cities in the information age. *Telematics and Informatics, 20*(3), 193–213. doi:10.1016/S0736-5853(03)00014-5

Dunne, K. (2009). Cross Cutting Discussion: A form of online discussion discovered within local political online forums. *Information Polity, 14*(3), 219–232.

Foucault, M. (1980). *Power/knowledge: Selected interviews and other writings, 1972-1977.* Random House LLC.

Foucault, M. (1982). The subject and power. In Michel Foucault, beyond structuralism and hermeneutics. Chicago: University of Chicago Press.

Foucault, M., & Ewald, F. (2003). Society Must Be Defended: Lectures at the Collège de France, 1975-1976. Administrative Theory & Praxis, 26(4), 489-508.

Fox, C. J., & Miller, H. T. (1995). *Postmodern public administration*. ME Sharpe.

Friedrich, C. J. (1963). *Man and his government: An empirical theory of politics*. New York: McGraw-Hill.

Groot, T., & Budding, T. (2008). New public management's current issues and future prospects. *Financial Accountability & Management, 24*(1), 1–13. doi:10.1111/j.1468-0408.2008.00440.x

Harding, A. (1997). Urban Regimes in a Europe of the Cities? *European Urban and Regional Studies, 4*(4), 291–314. doi:10.1177/096977649700400401

Heinrich, C. J., & Lynn, L. E., Jr. (2000). Governance and performance. Washington DC: Georgetown University Press. Administrative Theory & Praxis, 24(4), 693-720.

Held, D. (1995). *Democracy and the global order* (Vol. 232). Cambridge, MA: Polity Press.

Hendriks, C. M. (2009). The democratic soup: Mixed meanings of political representation in governance networks. *Governance: An International Journal of Policy, Administration and Institutions, 22*(4), 689–715. doi:10.1111/j.1468-0491.2009.01459.x

Hirst, P. (2013). *Associative democracy: new forms of economic and social governance*. John Wiley & Sons.

Hirst, P. Q., Thompson, G., & Bromley, S. (2009). *Globalization in question*. Polity.

Hjern, B., & Porter, D. O. (1981). Implementation structures: A new unit of administrative analysis. *Organization Studies, 2*(3), 211–227. doi:10.1177/017084068100200301

Hobson, K. (2010). Beyond the Control Society. *Administrative Theory & Praxis, 32*(2), 252–261. doi:10.2753/ATP1084-1806320207

Humphreys, P. (1994). *Media and media policy in Germany: The press and broadcasting since 1945*. Oxford, UK: Berg.

Humphreys, P., Dyson, K., Negrine, R., & Simon, J.-P. (1992). *Broadcasting and new media policies in Western Europe: A comparative study of technological change and public policy*. London: Routledge.

Jackson, P. M., & Stainsby, L. (2000). The public manager in 2010: Managing public sector networked organizations. *Public Money and Management, 20*(1), 11–16. doi:10.1111/1467-9302.00196

Jacobs, J. (2000). Interaction in the public interest: Regulating new communications technologies to deliver public interest information services. In M. Sheehan, S. Ramsay, & J. Patrick (Eds.), *Transcending boundaries: Integrating people, processes and systems: Proceedings of the 2000 Conference*. Brisbane, Australia: Academic Press.

Jessop, B. (1998). The rise of governance and the risks of failure: the case of economic development. International Social Science Journal, 50(155), 29-45.

Johnston, E. (2010). Governance infrastructures in 2020. *Public Administration Review, 70*(s1), s122–s128. doi:10.1111/j.1540-6210.2010.02254.x

Jorgensen, D. J., & Cable, S. (2002). Facing the challenges of e-government: A case study of the city of Corpus Christi, Texas. *SAM Advanced Management Journal, 67*(3), 15–21.

Katsikas, D. (2010). Non-state authority and global governance. *Review of International Studies, 36*(S1), 113–135. doi:10.1017/S0260210510000793

Kickert, W. J., Klijn, E. H., & Koppenjan, J. F. M. (Eds.). (1997). *Managing complex networks: strategies for the public sector*. London: Sage.

Klijn, E. H., Koppenjan, J., & Termeer, K. (1995). Managing networks in the public sector: A theoretical study of management strategies in policy networks. *Public Administration, 73*(3), 437–454. doi:10.1111/j.1467-9299.1995.tb00837.x

Klijn, E. H., & Koppenjan, J. F. (2000). Public management and policy networks: Foundations of a network approach to governance. *Public Management an International Journal of Research and Theory, 2*(2), 135–158.

Knill, C., & Lehmkuhl, D. (2002). Private actors and the state: Internationalization and changing patterns of governance. *Governance: An International Journal of Policy, Administration and Institutions, 15*(1), 41–63. doi:10.1111/1468-0491.00179

Kooiman, J. (Ed.). (1993). Modern governance: New government-society interactions. Administrative Theory & Praxis, 24(4), 693-720.

Kooiman, J. (2000). Societal governance: levels, models and orders of social-political interaction. In Debating governance: Authority, steering, and democracy. Oxford University Press.

Lapsley, I. (2008). The NPM agenda: Back to the future. *Financial Accountability & Management, 24*(1), 77–96. doi:10.1111/j.1468-0408.2008.00444.x

Lessig, L. (1999). *Code and other Laws of Cyberspace*. New York.

Levine, S., & White, P. E. (1961). Exchange as a conceptual framework for the study of interorganisational relationships. *Administrative Science Quarterly, 5*(4), 583–601. doi:10.2307/2390622

Lindblom, C. E., & Cohen, D. K. (1979). *Usable knowledge: social science and social problem solving*. New Haven, CT: Yale University Press.

Lőffler, E. (2003) Governance and government. *Public Management and Governance*, 163.

Loughlin, J. (2004). The "transformation" of governance: New directions in policy and politics. *The Australian Journal of Politics and History, 50*(1), 1, 8–22. doi:10.1111/j.1467-8497.2004.00317.x

Lundquist, L. (2000). Demokratiens väktere I ekonomiens samhälle. In Etik til debat. Værdier og etik I den offentlige forvaltning, (pp. 13-36). Jurist- og Økonomforbundets Forlag.

Mayntz, R. (1999). *New Challenges to Governance Theory*. Paper presented at Max-Planck Institut für Gessellshaftsforschung (from Sorenson).

Meissonier, R., & Houze, E. (2010). Toward an 'IT-conflict-resistance theory': Action research during it pre-implementation. *European Journal of Information Systems, 15*(5), 540–561. doi:10.1057/ejis.2010.35

Muhammad Rais, A. K. (Ed.). (1999). *Reengineering the public service: Leadership and change in an electronic age*. Malaysia: Pelanduk Publications.

Negandhi, A. R. (Ed.). (1975). *Interorganisation Theory*. Kansas University Press.

O'Toole, L. J. Jr. (1988). Strategies for intergovernmental management: Implementing programs in interorganizational networks. *International Journal of Public Administration, 11*(4), 417–441. doi:10.1080/01900698808524596

Ōmae, K. (1995). *The end of the nation state: The rise of regional economies*. Simon and Schuster.

Osborne, S. P. (Ed.). (2010). *The new public governance?: emerging perspectives on the theory and practice of public governance*. London: Routledge.

Pavan, A., & Lemme, F. (2011). Communication processes and the 'New Public Space' in Italy and the USA: A Longitudinal Approach. *Financial Accountability & Management, 27*(2), 166–194. doi:10.1111/j.1468-0408.2011.00521.x

Peters, B. G. (2001). *The future of governing (revised)*. Lawrence, KS: University Press of Kansas.

Peters, B. G. (2003, October). The capacity to govern: moving back to the center. In *Proceedings of VIII Congreso Internacional del CLAD sebre la Reforma del Estado y de la Administracion Publica*. Retrieved from http//www.clad.org.ve/congreso/peters.pdf

Pierre, J. (Ed.). (2001). Debating governance: Authority, steering and democracy. Oxford, UK: Oxford University Press.

Pierre, J., & Peters, G. B. (2000). *Governance, politics and the state*. Houndsmill, UK: MacMillan.

Pollitt, C. (1990). *Managerialism and the public services: The Anglo-American experience*. Oxford, UK: Blackwell.

Rehfeld, A. (2006). Towards a general theory of political representation. *The Journal of Politics*, *68*(1), 1–21. doi:10.1111/j.1468-2508.2006.00365.x

Rhodes, R. A. (1997). Understanding governance: Policy networks, governance, reflexivity and accountability. Open University Press.

Rhodes, R. A. (1998). Different roads to unfamiliar places: UK experience in comparative perspective. *Australian Journal of Public Administration*, *57*(4), 19–31. doi:10.1111/j.1467-8500.1998.tb01558.x

Rhodes, R. A. W. (1981). *Control and power in central-local government relations. Brookfield, VT*: Ashgate.

Rhodes, R. A. W. (1996). The new governance: Governing without government1. *Political Studies*, *44*(4), 652–667. doi:10.1111/j.1467-9248.1996.tb01747.x

Sassen, S. (2000). Digital networks and the state, some governance questions. *Theory, Culture & Society*, *17*(4), 19–33. doi:10.1177/02632760022051293

Scharpf, F. W. (1994). Community and autonomy: Multi-level policy-making in the European Union. *Journal of European Public Policy*, *1*(2), 219–242.

Scharpf, F. W. (1997). *Games real actors play: Actor-centered institutionalism in policy research*. Boulder, CO: Westview Press.

Scharpf, F. W., Reissert, B., & Schabel, F. (1978). Policy effectiveness and conflict avoidance in intergovernmental policy formation. In K. Hanf., & F. W. Scharpf (Ed.), Interorganisational Policy Making. London: Sage.

Scharpf, F. W., Reissert, B., & Schnabel, F. (1977). Policy effectiveness and conflict avoidance in intergovernmental policy formation. In K. Hanf & F. W. Scharpf (Eds.), *Interorganizational policy making: limits to coordination and central control*. Sage Publications.

Sørensen, E. (2002). Democratic theory and network governance. *Administrative Theory & Praxis*, *24*(4), 693–720.

Stoker, G. (1998). Governance as theory: Five propositions. *International Social Science Journal*, *50*(155), 17–28. doi:10.1111/1468-2451.00106

Strange, S. (1996). *The retreat of the state: The diffusion of power in the world economy*. Cambridge University Press. doi:10.1017/CBO9780511559143

The Economist. (2010, February 27). Data, data everywhere. *The Economist*.

Triantafillou, P. (2004). Addressing network governance through the concepts of governmentality and normalization. *Administrative Theory & Praxis*, *26*(4), 489–508.

Urbinati, N., & Warren, M. E. (2008). The concept of representation in contemporary democratic theory. *Annual Review of Political Science*, *11*(1), 387–412. doi:10.1146/annurev.polisci.11.053006.190533

Waldo, D. (2006). *The administrative state: A study of the political theory of American public administration*. Transaction Publishers.

Wamsley, G. L. (1996). A public philosophy and ontological disclosure as the basis for normatively grounded theorizing in public administration. In J. F. Wolf (Ed.), Refounding democratic public administration: Modern paradoxes, postmodern challenges. Sage Publications.

Weiss, L. (1998). *The myth of the powerless state*. Cornell University Press.

KEY TERMS AND DEFINITIONS

Civil Society: Independent group of society be it organizations or institutions that advocate for rights, health and general welfare of the people.

Deregulation: Removing or reducing state regulations. That is reducing of government's interventions in certain activities of the state for achieving cost effectiveness and efficiency in service delivery.

Interaction: Sharing and/or engaging in any kind of action that involves the two or more agencies, personnel and even people.

National Information Infrastructure: A national agenda promoting the ICT for all.

Neo-Liberal Hegemony: A new paradigm shift towards a new economy.

Network Governance: Mode of working together by the network members over time as a sequence of exchanges which is facilitated by the network structure. It is a dynamic process that highlights, coordinates, and safeguards exchanges that are not bonded by legal contacts.

Policy Network Model: Stability; demonstrating similarities across nations or sectors where different formal institutional processes exist but poor at explaining policy change or fundamental political processes.

Policy Network: Policy-making and power in different policy sectors. It suggests that informal pressure group activities are more important than constitutional or institutional approaches to policy making and implementation.

Political Game: A political bargaining among contested parties toward achieving common good to ensure compliance with agreed policies.

Regulation: Rule employed with or without coercive power to control or direct and manage the activities of public agencies or organizations.

Techno-Industrial Elites: ICT based industrial key actors.

Technological Innovation: Creation of new technological ideas and thoughts resulting from studies and experiments.

Chapter 4
New Society and ICT Adoption:
A Link between Policy Network and Network Management

ABSTRACT

Academic ideas for network society have been articulated by diverse societal groups and communities. The emerging civil society in many parts of the globe is reflected through the power struggles of old and new political constellations and actions. Within this setting, the coalition of old regime and new regime of digital society is one of the most striking phenomena that can be observed that eventually give rise to the New Regulatory Regime (NRR). This chapter addresses the question of theoretical parameters that can be applied to analyse the critical juncture at which nation-states have arrived at the turn of the century in the march towards a networked society. The approach used in the chapter is to analyse the interplay of domestic and international influence factors in order to explain the current political discourse in digitalized technology.

INTRODUCTION

Researchers argued that the traditional approaches towards people's engagement need to be changed to achieve success from governance reform initiatives (Jones et al., 2007; O'Flynn, 2007; Kanat and Ozkan, 2009). Throughout the 1990s, government intervention has been widely seen as a matter of survival, and with the growing convergence of the ICT sectors, the necessity for a new overall policy framework in the context of the establishment of the information society is generally recognised. Following the proliferation of the new multimedia and ICTs, a new metaphor emerged that impinged

on modern societies – the network society (Castells, 1996; 2005). In their discussion about public actors and policy networks relationships, Klijn and Koppenjan (2000, 151-2), assert that network theory, by no means, presumes that governments are like other actors. Governments, according to them, have access to considerable resources, e.g. sizeable budgets and personnel, special powers, access to mass media, a monopoly on the use of force and democratic legitimisation, which in turn, gives them more power. However, these are not without limitations as and when they enter the network games with other network actors. Despite many problems with the aggregation of

DOI: 10.4018/978-1-4666-6579-8.ch004

the multiple interests in the bargaining process, the proper deliberations of the negotiation process with private and semi-private partners can contribute to more meaningful interaction in policy networks. This Chapter is mainly concerned with the discussion of various issues related to the substance of the multiple intervention in the ICT sector. These include initiatives to encourage self-regulatory mechanisms and institutional regulatory reforms, etc., to promote the industry within the context of new governance.

THE NEW SOCIETY AND THE CHANGING ROLE OF GOVERNMENT

The role of national government is highly debated, but many agree that it is critical to ensure the success of the governance framework. It is proposed that the role of national government is the outcome rather than the process in which new social forms emerged. Castells and Cardoso (2006) conceptualised the network society whereby:

Governance is operated in a network of political institutions that shares sovereignty in various degrees an reconfigurates itself in a variable political geometry... it is not the result of technological change, but the response to the structural contradiction between global system and national state.

In the context of network society, ICT has been thought to be the fundamental feature to help bridging the gap between government and social actors. The new phenomenon of ICT has redefined the meaning of a "new society." Bang & Esmark (2009) argue that nation-states are being replaced by network states, which are "states embedded in local, regional, and global networks of governance hailed as necessary to meet the challenges of increased complexity, connectedness, and globalisation." For Castells and Cardoso (2006), new information technologies allow the formation of new forms of social organisation

and social interaction along electronically based information networks. Next, dimension of social change, affected by ICT, has a profound impact on economy – something that has never been possible to be handled by past forms of pre-ICT times. The pervasive impact of the ICT has created a dominant cultural manifestation which for Castells (2000), is characterised by an interactive, electronic hypertext, that "virtuality becomes a fundamental component of our symbolic environment, and thus of our experience as communication beings." Another important axis of change is the demise of the sovereign nation-state. In this regard, the society is not losing the current feature of nation-states in their institutional existence. Rather, "their existence as power apparatuses is profoundly transformed, as they are either bypassed or rearranged in networks of shared sovereignty formed by national governments, supranational institutions, co-national institutions, e.g., European Union, NATO or NAFTA, regional governments, local governments, and NGOs" (ibid, 694). Last but not least, the culmination of scientific knowledge and the use of science are redefining the relationship between culture and nature. This is then "coincide in time: the revolution in information technology; the socio-economic restructuring of both capitalism and statism (with different fates for these antagonistic mode of production); and the cultural movements that emerged in the 1960s in the United States and Western Europe (ibid)."

The network society may retain its traditional forms but with newly emerging and rigorous techniques of intervention. Bang and Esmark (2009) argue that the shift has reoriented the political system from a focus that is principally one of politics to one of policy. When confronted with a network-like situation, governments may have few options (Klijn and Koppenjan, 2000, 153-4). Firstly, they may choose not to join in network games; instead, to unilaterally impose their ideas and goals on other social actors. Certainly, this is not without some constraints, e.g. political support, effectiveness and efficiency of policy decisions.

Secondly, governments may decide to cooperate with other public, semi-public and private actors. Even this is not without constraint as, for instance, hierarchical supervisory relations between public actors may limit the possibilities for horizontal cooperation. Thirdly, the government can assume the role of a more active and dynamic network manager in mediating the process. Again, there is always a conflict between its role to be neutral while safeguarding common interests and democratic values, and being publicly accountable for its actions. Fourthly, governments may choose to take up the role of network builder, which means collaborative of efforts with other network actors aimed at 'changing network features.' Clearly, this is not an easy task as these changes cannot happen instantaneously.

Pavan and Lemme (2011, 167) sees the critical roles of ICTs in providing the opportunities for strategic choice and interaction:

... the online provision of information is an essential precondition of more evolved forms of citizens' engagement in public life, such as consultation and participation. At present, thus, ICT may be implemented with multi-purpose and multi-faceted functions covering one-way information provision as well as two-way forms of consultation, participation and deliberation. Such forms of citizens' involvement could enable public entities to perceive neatly the actual will of the people.

However, Pavan and Lemme (ibid) has cautioned that even in the information age, engaging citizens in public affairs is neither easy nor straightforward. To be sure, 'the current governance infrastructure is not a scale-free network (Johnston, 2010, S124). As nation grows, voices become proportionally diminished, and additional layers are added to the hierarchies o representation so that individuals are increasingly separated from the feeling that they have an influence on government decisions' (ibid).

Based on their empirical studies about the distinct self-regulatory trajectories in Europe and the US, Newman and Bach (2004) conclude that the differences in both continents give rise to distinct, regional economies. Digital technologies have, undoubtedly, involved a process of one-way relationships (government-citizen relationships) but when implemented with various other thereotical constructs will then be used to gauge a more integrated understanding of the kind of relationships within a new public landscape that is based on a subjective evaluation of benefits and costs. It is argued that governments may feel that the benefits for new governance offset the risk of their supremacy being compromised. In this regard, a new mode of governance is seen as compensating the risk of losing political supremacy.

In the meantime, government's role in the institutional policy reforms is facing various complicated regulatory challenges. As noted by Xavier and Ypsilanti (2010), the speed of technological and market change is an element of this challenge because despite legislation, policy and regulatory reform, there is still question lingers whether public (consumer) have in fact benefited or become more empowered.

The practice of network society and various arguments, either in favour of or against it, are initially related to different perspectives of the so-called 'technical context' that are fast and remarkably superseded by 'relational features' of power dependence, as discussed in the following section.

THE CONCEPT OF POWER-DEPENDENCE AND NETWORK SOCIETY

The central theme of theory proposed by Scharpf (1997) is that horizontal coordinating governing arrangements occur frequently in contemporary policy making and this analytical approach focuses on improving understanding of the strategic interactions that they foster. To be sure, scholarly study has focused on the extent to which relationships among actors vary in the degree and pattern of integration, and in the manner in which public power is shared between state and civil society actors (Coleman and Perl, 1999, 694; Pavan & Lemme, 2011).

The influence of power-dependence on the management of new media policies has been and is proved by public and private relations throughout the world. In particular, the development of the convergence sector is a typical case. In his writing, Bache (2000) summarises the key aspects of the model of policy networks, in which the principle of power-dependence between the regulator and the industry stakeholders, to a great extent, determines the policy's success or failure. This will be shown in greater details in the following empirical chapters, particularly, chapters Five, Six and Seven.

The Rhodes (1986; 1997) and Marsh and Rhodes (1992)'s model refers to a policy network as a set of resource-dependent organisations linked through their interest in a specific policy sector. In explaining this model, the nature of linkages between organisations ranges from tightly integrated policy communities to loosely coupled issue networks. Policy communities are characterised by "restricted membership, high interdependence between organisations and stability overtime", whereas, "issue networks have wide membership, limited interdependence between organisations and a tendency to disperse once issues are dealt with" (Bache, 2000, 576).

In between the extreme ends of the ideal types of policy communities and issue networks, the power-dependence framework is employed to explore linkages between organisations within a network. This framework rests on five propositions (Rhodes, 1981, 88):

- *Any organisation is dependent upon other organisations for resources;*

- *In order to achieve their goals, organisations have to exchange resources;*
- *Decision-making within organisations is constrained by the existence of other organisations within the network;*
- *Organisations employ strategies to secure favoured policy outcomes within known rules of the game;*
- *Variations in the degree of influence over decision making are a product of the goals and the relative power potential of each organisation, of the rules of the game, and of the process of exchange between organisations.*

From a policy network point of view, Bache (2000) asserts that differences in the distribution of resources - financial, informational, political, organisational or constitutional-legal, within a network, explain why some members are more powerful than others. Similarly, from an institutional point of view, one of the most critical advantages for policy manoeuvre has always been to maintain and enhance the organisational capabilities to integrate the institutional resources into a collaborative network. Pertaining to the advantage of this, Joinson and Paine (2007) argue that the benefits are garnered through trust building; mutual empathy and reciprocation, often outweigh the costs associated with increased vulnerability.

Digital Convergence and Policy Networks

It is at first impossible to separate the development of digital convergence from the context of policy networks. In explaining this, three aspects of convergence are worth mentioning. First, digital technology is the driving force for the convergence process. Digital convergence which is 'technology-hunger' cuts across wide ranging of communications, multimedia and broadcasting areas, thereby increasing the pressure for new service capabilities among the concerned bodies. Consequently, this enhances the integration of related component of policy sectors, including 'information policy' and 'telecommunications policy' (Xavier, 1997; Xavier & Ypsilanti, 2010). Second, this leads to the regulatory concern over industry or market convergence which is closely intertwined as it has the most immediate effect on the growth and well-being of the industry. Thirdly, there is a political concern over the degree of distinctiveness of policy impact across previously separate industries or service sectors with social goals, i.e., affordability and accessibility, in particular.

Jane Fountain (2001) further provides a powerful theoretical lens for understanding how technology, organisations and institutions interact. According to her, "technology enactment" has three key elements: first, that objective forms of information technology are adjusted and manipulated once they are applied within some given organisational form; second, that existing institutional arrangements both affect and are affected by those organisational forms; and, third, the result adopted and implemented form of information technology, although a result of the first two processes, can send feedback that directly creates changes in the organisation and indirectly in institutions through the organisation.

Bretschneider (2003, 739) however asserts that the reinvention effort to utilise the power of information technology to enhance operational efficiency is grossly misunderstood, as it assumes that organisations and institutions are essentially "acted upon, being completely malleable and inert." He noted how Fountain contends that computing affects organisations and shows how information technology is not a "simple lever or knob" for reengineering organisations or institutions; for example how information technology can simultaneously bring about "centralised control and decentralised actions," which consequently can have "unanticipated impacts and even contradictory effects" (Ibid., p. 739). Bretschneider noted that most discussions of reinvention, however, are not focused on this area, but rather more on core

assumptions such as centralisation, control, and the empowerment of workers (ibid., 739).

Learning from this phenomenon, the emergence of convergence has, in effect, reinterpreted the nature of interactions between the States vis-a-vis various internal and/or external autonomous societal actors. The new self-regulatory environment, thus, enhanced the sphere of 'shared sovereignty' so that the principles and context of interactions should be amongst relatively autonomous political actors of societal governance. Unlike in the previous traditional regime, as noted above, government's pre-determined attempt to negotiate the nature of relations that has been compromised or even challenged. This calls for appropriate standards that spell out clearly the dynamic forms of interaction processes for good governance to be a reality. The culmination of several models of convergence across nation-states that is happening elsewhere currently, can be understood as a relentless effort to come in terms with such standards. Learning from this, in contrast, convergence initiatives utilise information technology that emphasise horizontal or networked, models of communication and interaction. This has significant impact over the move from vertical hierarchy to a more open horizontal structure and nature of political processes. The case study on Malaysia's ICT and convergence presented in the chapter five will provide better insights on the complexity and challenges faced by the predominantly hierarchical society in implementing this agenda.

Policy Networks and Network Management

Generally speaking, the concepts of communication and control have been altered by the networked approach to governance, which in part, is due to ICTs and digital convergence. In particular, to successfully manage the process of network management is one of the most important aspects of policy network. Under this theme, some issues in connection with network management and the factors relating to its success and failure will be examined.

First of all, one pertinent issue of concern here is that these ideas have been made complex with the influence of convergence, particularly when there is scarcity of empirical evidence, at the moment. It demonstrates remoteness between the reality of practice and ideals in new democracies. This further complicates the debate about the roles and implications of networks in the new governance environment. As Peters (2003, 1) cautioned:

The discussion to this point should make it abundantly clear that the analysis of governance must be both empirical and normative.... That empirical evidence is necessary in order to consider how governments perform their tasks and do, or do not, govern their societies. On the other hand, governance is inherently a normative concern Even without the usual adjectives such as "good" or "democratic" in front of the noun governance does have a pronounced normative dimension. Underlying the concern with governing is the sense that citizens deserve some form of effective governance for their societies, and that one important contribution that the social sciences can make is to think through elements of designing of governing systems.

Closely related to this, the scope, constraints and legitimate roles of Government, in particular the administrators should be delineated with the 'watchdog roles' of regulators in the new regime. In this regard, administrators are merit political actors similar to other social actors. However, their roles are now increasingly and constantly being checked and balanced, in particular, by the watchdog body, the regulator, besides, of course, other private and civil communities. This emerging but significant trend of new regime has given rise to intense debates among researchers about how the politically fragmented roles of administrator and regulator of societal governance can be con-

ceptualised and institutionalised. However, unlike the roles of administrators, the role of the regulator has found less concern in the new regime, due to the seemingly incomplete and rather indeterminate nature of technological change. Thus, one could expect that the relationships between politicians and citizens are far more definite or obvious whereas, on the contrary, those between politicians and regulators still remain to be seen, as the technology continues in its process of maturity.

In correspondence with the above situation, there is an issue whether the 'meta-governor' would be capable of ethically performing its duties, without fear or favour. To be sure, there have been intense debates on the neutrality and impartiality of the governor in this aspect, or to what extent could they be superior or sovereign compared to the other network actors. In an attempt to reconcile this, it seems that both traditional and new governance theories would have to conform to the equilibrium of identity; that they are as sovereign as equally vulnerable, despite of their autonomous positions. Accordingly, in particular, a network manager is not a central actor or director, but rather a mediator and stimulator (Forester 1989, in Klijn and Koppenjan, 2000, 142).

Being aware of these kinds of issues surrounding the concept of governance, Klijn and Koppenjan (2000) have reiterated criticism of the network approach. Putting together the various observations made by scholars, (e.g. Borzel, 1998; Dowding, 1995; Salancik, 1995, etc.), they listed five important criticisms of the network approach:

- Lack of theoretical foundations and clear concepts;
- Lack of explanatory power;
- Neglect of the role of power;
- Lack of clear evaluation criteria; and
- Normative objections against networks and the role of public actors within them.

Second, and more importantly, what are some of the criteria that can be used to determine the

Table 1. Explanations for success and failure from the perspective of the network management approach

	Explanation for Success and Failure
At interaction level	The degree to which actors are aware of their mutual dependencies The degree to which actors succeed in redefining diverging and conflicting interests into a common interest The degree to which interaction costs are balanced favourably or unfavourably with perceived outcomes of the interaction The degree to which risks of the interaction within the game as a consequence of strategies of other actors are limited The degree to which game management is foreseen (mutual perception development; arrangements; game and conflict management)
At network level	The degree to which actors possess veto power because their resources are indispensable The degree to which actors with veto power are actually involved in the process The degree to which actors in a game belong to the same network, so that they also interact with each other elsewhere and have developed mutual rules The degree to which defined problems and solutions, and the way these are handled, fit within the rules developed in the network

extent of policy networks? According to Klijn and Koppenjan (2000, 146), the success or failure of a policy network can be summarised as shown in Table 1.

The differences in socio-economic organisations of domestic interest vis-à-vis forces of globalisation, as well as the peculiarities of a country, will influence the policy network. These elements are key factors shaping capabilities of actors in policy networks and will affect both the types of distributional demands that societal actors place on governments and the macroeconomic constraints under which governments operate (Coleman and Perl, 1999, 699). As governance infrastructures allow for more direct and informed involvement in some government activities, power is returned to the people such that values are articulated through their actions rather than by a one-off vote of state preferences (Johnston, 2010).

In the process of network management, Klijn and Koppenjan (2000, 140-1) have argued that there are two essential network management strategies: process management and network constitution (for extensive discussion, see Klijn et al., 1995; Kickert et al. 1997):

Process management intends to improve the interaction between actors in policy games. In essence, this concerns steering strategies that seek to unite the various perceptions of actors and solve the organisational problem that various organisations, in having autonomously developed their own strategies, are not automatically in concert with one another. In doing so, actors cannot unilaterally determine each other's strategy. What is important, is that strategies of process management assume the structure and composition of the network as given. So, rules (formal and informal), resources divisions and existing actors are treated as given starting point for the management strategies… Network constitution is focused on realising changes in the network. Based on the assumption that the institutional characteristics of the network also influence strategies and co-operation opportunities of actors, attempts can be made to change one or more of these characteristics. In general, these strategies are time-consuming since they seek institutional change. As a result, they are usually unsuitable for influencing policy games that are already underway.

The literature of the network approach explicitly warns that network management is not a simple matter. As such, Klijn and Koppenjan argue that, "knowledge of network" and "numerous skills" including negotiation skills of the network actors are critical in situations of mutual dependency (ibid., 142). For Rhodes (2000, p. xiv), trust is the key element in which the challenge confronting governments is 'diplomacy'; that is, negotiations and agreement about aims and objectives. Arguably, it can be suggested that actors do account for trust when they decide to engage network members while relying on their ability to control information.

Despite all the conceptual confusions about policy network, the hierarchical dominance by a central government no longer works effectively and digital technology continues to provide the sense of urgency for more collaborative forms of governance.[1] This issue will continue to shape the thinking and practice about governance and the changing nature of state-society relations suitable in the digital age.

INDUSTRY SELF-REGULATION AND CAPACITY OF NEW REGIME

Compared to the situation several decades ago, the digital information revolution has become a global phenomenon since the 1980s. Pooling the observations made by many scholars, Herrera, (2002, 93) observed that, on the one hand, optimists (e.g. Toffler, 1980; Wriston, 1992; and Negroponte, 1995) "think the information revolution promises harmony, freedom and prosperity"; on the other hand, pessimists (e.g. Kling, 1996; Slouka, 1995; and Stoll, 1995) see "totalitarianism, a permanent underclass, the debasement of the individual and citizen, and end to art and reason." Thus far, Herrera concluded, the former outnumbered the latter (Ibid). Changes in the transnational ICT networks spark an important debate about the role and nature of State vis-à-vis non-State actors in the new age of governance. More specifically, coinciding with the march towards a new regulatory regime (NRR) and when it comes to regulating new industries, "political battles frequently erupt about whether government intervention is necessary, or whether the market should be allowed to run its course" (Newman and Bach, 2004, 389).

In view of the changing pattern of governance, it is beyond the capacity of a single state to successfully promote a new mode of governance. Instead, self-regulation and widening of policy participation have become the most adopted means to face challenges of new governance and form the most critical components of network governance in the information age.

This section discusses issues related to NRR, in particular, self-regulation and how new modes of governance have been propagated by states through policy participation at the industry level, as well as their involvement with more diverse arrays of network actors. This section also offers some clarifications to assist in integrating the knowledge of the various issues relating to an attempt to promote widening of policy participation initiatives.

NEW AGE OF GOVERNANCE: THE RISE OF INDUSTRY OR PRIVATE SELF-REGULATION

In contrast to formal government regulation, industries develop their own set of rules and implementation processes to achieve socially desirable ends. The focus on industry-level rules and self-policing differs from the market mode of self-regulation, where rules are supplied on the level of the firm and enforced solely through market competition (Ibid., 390). No matter which form they take, however, self regulation always assumes participants have good intentions, but the constant threat of defection frequently undermines necessary collective action (Olson, 1965). This is one of the major reasons why they are hotly debated.

Self-regulation and widening of political participation itself is not a new phenomenon; on the contrary, it has been a long-standing feature in certain areas of economic and social activity engendered private systems of authority (Coleman and Perl, 1999, 705).[2] However, the power of digital technologies has made it one of the most widespread trends (e.g. joint ventures, strategic alliances or partnerships) of recent years that the value of self-regulation has reached a high point with the emergence of a NRR. Before the middle 1990s, industry players were not given much opportunity to decide the course of policy action. It is interesting to note that self-regulation substantially recognises the possibility of industry groups having the chance to participate in the policy process almost in a tentative embrace with digital convergence, which also forms the critical networked component of a new regime.[3]

Purposes of Self-Regulation

There are a number of reasons why industry groups and other network actors have joined forces through self-regulation, which forms a critical component of NRR.

First of all, the existence or absence of competing institutional constelations among which private actors can choose may have important repercussions for the potential for private coordination and self-regulation (Knill and Lehmkuhl, 2002, 48). This is particularly the case of technical standardisation, for instance, with different bodies and organisations at varying levels simultaneously developing standards for similar technological problems. Consequently, "the existence of new exit options in the context of competing instistions weakens the strategic position of potential veto players within single arenas and thus increases incentives for cooperation coordination" (Benz, 1998; Genschel, 1995; Knill and Lehmkuhl, 1998, in ibid., 49). To put it in another way, it is technological or industrial convergence that has made cross-sectoral competition and collaboration necessary; to bring about a new form of partnership which involves several industry groups and needs joint effort for promoting their particular standards.

Secondly, due to the exacerbation of "internationalisation of markets and the emergence of

transnationalisation of information and communication networks" - a term coined by Knill and Lehmkuhl (2002, 41), various kinds of industry groups collaborations are being made to steer the society to attain industry growth. As noted by Humphreys (2006, 306):

It is herein contended that globalisation pressures of an economic and technological kind have stimulated the dynamics of regulatory competition in the 'communication' sectors, which has contributed to a paradigmatic change in regulatory policies for broadcasting and telecommunications.

The conventional means of governance has been for the public sector to use regulation, direct provision and subsidies (among other policy instruments) to achieve the goals. As patterns of governance change, however, the instruments employed have been changing to include a number that involve private sector actors (Salamon, 2002).

Thirdly, as digital technology is increasingly becoming pervasive, and generating revolutionary changes in social, economic and political life of all societies, the emergence of a network society, which in itself requires new forms of governance, is commonly advocated by some influential scholars (Castells, 1996). Peters (2003, 6) suggests that the traditional mode of governance came under practical and academic attack as an appropriate means of providing steering for the economy and society. Against such a background, the critics of the traditional model argued that this form of governance "did not provide a great deal of capacity in the society; especially in modern societies in which the public is reasonably well-educated and in which there are a wealth of civil society organisations that can participate in governance, the continuation of a top-down, hierarchical model of governing is unlikely to produce the best outcomes for society" (ibid., 6).

Fourthly, as Nickel (2007, 216) observed, network governance has proved to constitute the "perception" for government in governance through which a consensus on a set of priorities and goals for society can be agreed upon by that society:

The network is no more something that we must live with than was the supposed hierarchical, state-centered approach that preceded it. There is of course no form of governance that we must live with and make the best of; there is only our perception of permanence or alterability, the latter being the democratic of the two. The fact that governance networks no longer represent something new and exotic is a resigned stance and should be read as evidence of the need to re-imagine possibility.

Fifthly, some authors (e.g. Klijn and Koppenjan, 2000) have suggested that network collaboration, including industry groups, is often an effective and efficient way for network actors to gain recognition over certain resources that are relevant or even necessary to the realisation of policy outcomes. It is also argued that the greater the veto power of an actor, the more indispensable the actor is to the policy games as the resources enable them to veto interaction processes and they thus acquire a privileged position in the network (ibid., 144). Although, the context in which networks may be "conceived of as strategic alliances recursively reconstituted through the process and practice of networking" (Hay, 1998, 44), the policy actors actively seek to change the environment within which they operate. In this cyclical changed policy environment, according to Hay, there is always a two-way relationship between strategic learning by policy actors and network change. Without participating in the self-regulatory regime, even the most resourceful group or incumbent may lose their leadership position.

Sixthly, it is evident that the emergence of a political situation characterised by network governance challenges the traditional perception of representation (monopolised by the national parliament and politicians) because it unveils the autonomous and productive characacter of democratic representation. In some countries, the right of representation is obtained over and over again in ongoing competition with others. Political representation in a system of network governance can therefore best be understood as a process in which an actor, through political battles, obtains the legitimate right to construct the identity of the represented, and make political decisions with reference to this identity (Sorenson, 2002, 698). In the last three decades, the core objective in the debate about governing in the new age was to find the right balance between state, market, and civil society.[4] Despite all these, self-regulation is fast becoming the general trend of convergence today.

Finally, at the core of the convergence thesis lies the concept of regulatory competition. Competing in the increasingly convergence economy and market, governments have had to develop 'governance' policies on a whole range of new approaches (self-regulation, industry codes of practices, public dialogues etc.) to promote industry growth. It seems that industry self-regulatory regimes and widening of policy participations are among the most effective ways for new mode of governance to be realised. While many scholars claim that governments in some countries, particularly developing ones, are too keen to protect the status-quo of the government agencies, examples of successful models of convergence practised by Western models are worthy of emulation. Industry groups may not have the enforcement power of a regulatory body; they have a legitimate share by the teaming up of many partners. Indeed, it is common to see that industry groups have actually become mini policy avenue, and entered formal network relations with multiple stakeholders in the industry, and hence directly recognise the concerns of the consumers and public at large.

In summarising the ideal types of governance, based on the distinctive level of private and public governance capacities, Knill and Lehmkuhl,

(2002, 49-52) put them into four situational types. Briefly, the first is the interventionist regulation, which basically reflects the classical scenario of limited governance whereby the overall responsibility for the provision of public goods lies with the state, even though this does not exclude the involvement of private actors. Second, within the scenario of regulated self-regulation, the relationship between public and private actors can be considered high, notwithstanding the fact that the state still plays a central and active role should there be governance failures for any reason. Third, private self-regulation in which, unlike the regulated self regulation, the state actually has no capacity to directly intervene in private regulation, except in providing complementary governance contributions through mediation or moderation between conflicting interests between different actors. Finally, interfering regulation denotes a constellations of situations in which public actors are no longer able to compensate for the low potential for private governance contributions. Interestingly, governments in this context, can still use their hierarchical powers to interfere in private activities, e.g. through national court rulings; however, this will hardly be sufficient to provide effective solutions to the governance problem.

Katsikas (2010) contend that the formal state authority is still a viable actor in the governance of public social and economic space - a fact that is generally underestimated by many. Notwithstanding this fact, although there are various constellations of governance for private actors or industry groups, empirical examples show that public assistance - usually national assistance - is primarily required when it comes to implementing private solutions (Ibid., 58). In most cases, however, as contended by Hendriks (2009), these modern political representatives are self-authorised (Hendriks, 2009).

Apart from all sorts of reasons or motives for industry groups to collaborate together as mentioned above, some commentators have also stressed that while governments frequently intervene to motivate and steer industry self-regulation, private institutions are the principal agents that monitor firm-level activity and act as clearing houses for consumer concerns. And in contrast to the market mode of regulation, firms participating in industry self-regulation are seen as deliberately and purposefully cooperating with one another (Ibid., 390).

At the other extreme, scholars such as Marsh and Rhodes (1992), Kooiman (1993) and Kickert, Klijn, and Koopenjan (1997), have argued that the network of interested parties would be capable of pursuing the "governance without government." Peters (2003, 6) opined that these networks would be capable of providing the steering for the policy areas in which they are involved, and "capable of making collective decisions and of controlling the manner in which policies are designed and delivered."

The competition between technological standards within the convergence sector is so fierce that at the national level, no single country seems to be able to stay effectively in isolation without some form of commitment with international agencies.[5] In other words, to succeed in the new age of governance, a state would have to get the support of as many industry groups support as possible through their roles. It is also true that, for this reason, these private systems emerged due to fact that the specialised, technical knowledge needed for governance often lay completely within private organisations.

In his assertion about the effect of globalised economy on the new governance, some scholars (see for instance Cutler, 1999, 2; Katsikas, 2010) pointed out that in order to organise global economic exchange while trying to minimise intervention by nation-states, societal actors on the international level are setting up 'private regimes': intergrated complexes of formal and informal institutions that serve as a source of governance for an area of economic, social, or cultural activity.

CHAPTER SUMMARY

Overall, the chapter has reviewed the theoretical literature about the way in which the successful promotion of ICT and digital convergence, and most crucially, the new mode of governance in the digital age, are affected by some specific factors, with varying degrees of influence. As contended by Castells and Cardoso (2006, 16), "we are in the network society, although not everything or everybody is included in its networks." Digital convergence, has been instrumental in bringing some notable changes, even achievements in numbers of areas such as policy orientation, market flexibility, industry initiatives, as well as the general attitudes and responses of the public or consumers at large and eventually to facilitate the formation of a networked society. Whilst acknowledging this, the multifaceted yet intrinsically related factors are established as the major conceptual frameworks to help analyse the process of digital convergence in the Malaysia ICT agenda. The linkages of all these factors are critically examined in the conceptual framework which may prove relevant in explaining network theory.

It is important to bear in mind that the choice of ICT strategies, regulatory reform and institutional design corresponding to the networked society should not be treated as exclusive. On the contrary, other factors, such as market forces to consumer choice, national and global environment, etc., are all relevant to the success or failure of a new mode of governance. The findings explicitly relating to the relationship between these factors are nevertheless, limited and are mostly of a qualitative nature particularly in the context of digital technological change and the progress in the Malaysian ICT policy sector. Siddique argued (2008, 211) that at least in Malaysia, the commitment for engagement is "at both political and administrative levels is fairly high." As a matter of fact, each of the empirical chapters presented in this study demonstrates these two broad analytical frameworks, in one way or another.

REFERENCES

Bache, I. (2000). Government within governance: Network steering in Yorkshire and the Humber. *Public Administration*, 78(3), 575–592. doi:10.1111/1467-9299.00219

Bang, H., & Esmark, A. (2009, March). Good governance in network society: Reconfiguring the political from politics to policy. *Administrative Theory & Praxis*, 31(1), 7–37. doi:10.2753/ATP1084-1806310101

Benz, A. (1998). Politikverflechtung ohne politikverflechtungsfalle: koordination und strukturdynamik im europäischen mehrebenensystem [joint policy-making without joint decision trap: Coordination and structural dynamics in Europe's multilayered polity]. *Politische Vierteljahresschrift* [*Political Science Quarterly*], 39, 558-589.

Börzel, T. A. (1998). Organizing Babylon-On the Different Conceptions of Policy Networks. Public Administration, 76(2), 253-273.

Bretschneider, S. (2003). Information technology, e-overnment, and institutional change. *Public Administration Review*, 63(6), 738–741. doi:10.1111/1540-6210.00337

Castells, M. (1996). *The rise of the network society*. Cambridge, MA: Blackwell Publishers.

Castells, M. (2000). Materials for an exploratory theory of the network society. *The British Journal of Sociology*, 51(1), 5–24. doi:10.1080/000713100358408

Castells, M. (2000). Toward a sociology of the network society. *Contemporary Sociology*, 29(5), 693–699. doi:10.2307/2655234

Castells, M., & Cardoso, G. (Eds.). (2006). The network society: From knowledge to policy. Center for Transatlantic Relations, Paul H. Nitze School of Advanced International Studies, Johns Hopkins University.

Coleman, W. D., & Perl, A. (1999). Internationalized policy environments and policy network analysis. *Political Studies*, *47*(4), 691–709. doi:10.1111/1467-9248.00225

Cutler, A. C., Haufler, V., & Porter, T. (Eds.). (1999). *Private authority and international affairs*. Suny Press.

Dowding, K. (1995). Model or metaphor? A critical review of the policy network approach. Political studies, 43(1), 136-158.

Forestor, J. (1989). Planning in the phase of power. Berkeley, CA: University of California Press.

Fountain, J. E. (2001). *Building the Virtual State: Information Technology and Institutional Change*. Washington, DC: Brookings Institution.

Genschel, P. 1995. Dynamische Verflechtung in der internationalen Standardisierung [Dynamic Joint Decision-Making in International Standarisation]. In Gesellschaftliche Selbstregulierung und politische Steuerung [Societal Self-Regulation and Governance]. Frankfurt/M.: Campus.

Hay, C. (1998). The tangled webs we weave: The discourse, strategy and practice of networking. In Comparing policy networks. Open University Press.

Hendriks, C. M. (2009). The democratic soup: Mixed meanings of political representation in governance networks. *Governance: An International Journal of Policy, Administration and Institutions*, *22*(4), 689–715. doi:10.1111/j.1468-0491.2009.01459.x

Herrera, G. L. (2002). The politics of bandwidth: International political implications of a global digital information network. *Review of International Studies*, *28*(01), 93–122. doi:10.1017/S0260210502000931

Hobson, K. (2010). Beyond the Control Society. *Administrative Theory & Praxis*, *32*(2), 252–261. doi:10.2753/ATP1084-1806320207

Humphreys, P. (2006). Globalisation, Regulatory Competition, and EU Policy Transfer in the Telecoms and Broadcasting Sectors. *International Journal of Public Administration*, *29*(4-6), 305–334. doi:10.1080/01900690500437055

Ioinson, A. N., & Paine, C. B. (2007). Self-disclosure, privacy and the Internet. The Oxford handbook of internet psychology, (pp. 237-252). Oxford, UK: Oxford University Press.

Jackson, P. M., & Stainsby, L. (2000). The public manager in 2010: Managing public sector networked organizations. *Public Money and Management*, *20*(1), 11–16. doi:10.1111/1467-9302.00196

Johnston, E. (2010). Governance infrastructures in 2020. *Public Administration Review*, *70*(s1), s122–s128. doi:10.1111/j.1540-6210.2010.02254.x

Jones, S., Hackney, R., & Irani, Z. (2007). Towards e-government transformation: conceptualising "citizen engagement": A research note. *Transforming Government: People, Process and Policy*, *1*(2), 145–152.

Kanat, I. E., & Özkan, S. (2009). Exploring citizens' perception of government to citizen services: A model based on theory of planned behaviour (TPB). *Transforming Government: People, Process and Policy*, *3*(4), 406–419.

Katsikas, D. (2010). Non-state authority and global governance. *Review of International Studies*, *36*(S1), 113–135. doi:10.1017/S0260210510000793

Kickert, W. J., Klijn, E. H., & Koppenjan, J. F. M. (Eds.). (1997). *Managing complex networks: Strategies for the public sector*. Sage.

Klijn, E. H., Koppenjan, J., & Termeer, K. (1995). Managing networks in the public sector: A theoretical study of management strategies in policy networks. *Public Administration*, *73*(3), 437–454. doi:10.1111/j.1467-9299.1995.tb00837.x

Klijn, E. H., & Koppenjan, J. F. (2000). Public management and policy networks: Foundations of a network approach to governance. *Public Management an International Journal of Research and Theory, 2*(2), 135–158.

Klijn, E. H., & Koppenjan, J. F. (2000). Public management and policy networks: Foundations of a network approach to governance. *Public Management an International Journal of Research and Theory, 2*(2), 135–158.

Kling, R. (Ed.). (1996). *Computerisation and Controversy: Value Conflicts and Social Choices.* San Diego, CA: Academic Press.

Knill, C. (1999). Explaining cross-national variance in administrative reform: Autonomous versus instrumental bureaucracies. *Journal of Public Policy, 19*(02), 113–139. doi:10.1017/S0143814X99000203

Knill, C., & Lehmkuhl, D. (1998). Integration by Globalisation: The European Interest Representation of the Consumer Electronics Industry. *Current Politics and Economics in Europe, 8,* 131–153.

Knill, C., & Lehmkuhl, D. (2002). Private actors and the state: Internationalization and changing patterns of governance. *Governance: An International Journal of Policy, Administration and Institutions, 15*(1), 41–63. doi:10.1111/1468-0491.00179

Kooiman, J. (Ed.). (1993). *Modern governance: New government-society interactions.* Sage.

Marsh, D., & Rhodes, R. A. W. (1992). *Policy networks in British government.* Clarendon Press. doi:10.1093/acprof:oso/9780198278528.001.0001

Negroponte, N. (1996). *Being digital.* Random House LLC.

Newman, A. L., & Bach, D. (2004). Self-regulatory trajectories in the shadow of public power: Resolving digital dilemmas in Europe and the United States. *Governance: An International Journal of Policy, Administration and Institutions, 17*(3), 387–413. doi:10.1111/j.0952-1895.2004.00251.x

Nickel, P. M. (2007). Network governance and the new constitutionalism. *Administrative Theory & Praxis, 29*(2), 198–224.

O'Flynn, J. (2007). From new public management to public value: Paradigmatic change and managerial implications. *Australian Journal of Public Administration, 66*(3), 353-366.

Olson, M. (2002). The logic of collective action. In *Public goods and the theory of groups.* Cambridge University Press.

Pavan, A., & Lemme, F. (2011). Communication processes and the 'new public space' in Italy and the USA: A longitudinal approach. *Financial Accountability & Management, 27*(2), 166–194. doi:10.1111/j.1468-0408.2011.00521.x

Peters, B. G. (1998). Globalisation, institutions, and governance. The Robert Schuman Centre at the European University Institute.

Peters, B. G. (2003, October). The capacity to govern: moving back to the center. In *Proceedings of VIII Congreso Internacional del CLAD sebre la Reforma del Estado y de la Administracion Publica.* Retrieved from http//www.clad.org.ve/congreso/peters.pdf

Rhodes, R. A. (1997). Understanding governance: Policy networks, governance, reflexivity and accountability. Open University Press.

Rhodes, R. A. W. (1981). *Control and power in central-local government relations.* Ashgate.

Rhodes, R. A. W. (1986). *The national world of local government.* Allen & Unwin.

Rhodes, R. A. W. (2000). *Transforming British government: Changing roles and relationships* (vol. 2). Palgrave Macmillan.

Salamon, L. M. (Ed.). (2002). *The tools of government: A guide to the new governance.* Oxford University Press.

Salancik, G. R. (1995). Wanted: A good network theory of organization. *Administrative Science Quarterly, 40*, 345-9). doi:10.1111/j.1467-9299.1995. tb00837.x

Scharpf, F. W. (1997). *Games real actors play: Actor-centered institutionalism in policy research* (Vol. 1997). Boulder, CO: Westview Press.

Siddiquee, N. A. (2008). Service delivery innovations and governance: the Malaysian experience. *Transforming Government: People, Process and Policy, 2*(3), 194-213.

Slouka, M. (1996). *War of the worlds: Cyberspace and the high-tech assault on reality.* Basic Books.

Sørensen, E. (2002). Democratic theory and network governance. *Administrative Theory & Praxis, 24*(4), 693–720.

Stoll, C. (1996). *Silicon snake oil: Second thoughts on the information highway.* Random House LLC.

Toffler, A. (1980). *The third wave.* New York: Bantam books.

Waldo, D. (1948). *The administrative state.* New York: Roland Press.

Wriston, W. B. (1992). *The twilight of sovereignty: How the information revolution is transforming our world* (Vol. 92). New York: Scribner.

Xavier, P. (1997). Universal service and public access in the networked society. *Telecommunications Policy, 21*(9), 829–843. doi:10.1016/S0308-5961(97)00050-5

Xavier, P., & Ypsilanti, D. (2010). Behavioral economics and telecommunications policy. In Regulation and the evolution of the global telecommunications industry. Edward Elgar Publishing.

Ypsilanti, D., & Xavier, P. (1998). Towards next generation regulation. *Telecommunications Policy, 22*(8), 643–659. doi:10.1016/S0308-5961(98)00044-5

KEY TERMS AND DEFINITIONS

Collective Decisions: Common ground for decision processes maximising public participation and exploring alternative dispute resolutions as part of the process.

Digital Technologies: Opposite of manual technologies with Internet as the main conduit for ICT expansion.

Legitimate Right: Constitutional perspective of governing.

Network Theory: A set of ideas that explain the ties and edges between different actors, individuals, groups, and organizations. The ties may be between individual-to-individual or individual-to-group ties. Hence the nature of ties range from exchange of communications, information, advices and reports to work flows.

New Public Landscape: The realisation of a new scenario of policy making process relating to ICT sector.

Political Supremacy: The dominant role of centralised authority and political elites.

Self-Regulatory: State apparatuses which minimises the centralised governing authority by encouraging industry's more proactive as well as voluntary role in policy process.

Telecommunications Policy: Policy related to promoting the proliferation of the telecommunication sector.

ENDNOTES

[1]   The debate about the ability of networks and other social actors to perform some of the functions now performed by government; for example, conflict resolution among competing social interests, will not disappear overnight, and if anything, is something that is unacceptable to the functionalist viewpoint (Peters, 1998, p. 409).

[2]   Common examples are stock exchanges, advertising authorities, the certification and licensing of physicians, and insurance (Ibid., p. 705). Other areas of networks within the public-private sector in sectoral areas also include such as primary and social care in the health service, joint boards; action zones in employment, education and health and the Private Finance Initiatives (PFI).

[3]   In describing this networked form of organisation, Jackson and Stainsby (2000, p. 12) states that, they "are an effective means of achieving improved social outcomes, greater public participation and social inclusions." Elements in the civil society can facilitate governance can be active participants in what Lester Salamon (2002) has deemed to be "New Governance."

[4]   This has become a politically sensitive issue (e.g. a common concern is that self-regulation often lamented as "face saving" tool for industry to benefits firm image, while actually permitting the "wolf to guard the sheep").

[5]   Since the middle of the 1990s, the world has witnessed series of national and international regulatory arrangements over technological standards on a global scale, under scores of various international and regional bodies (such as World Trade Organisation or WTO, International Telecommunication Union or ITU, Internet Corporation for Assigned Names and Numbers or ICANN and Government Advisory Council or GAC) as information technologies become increasingly digitalised. Time and again, these bodies became the avenue for policy debates and battles for the new regime, which certainly will have profound implications for the development of global markets, trade flows, technology transfer, and capital investment.

Chapter 5
Models of Political Representation for ICT Adoption in a Networked Society

ABSTRACT

The Internet, a global network of digital technologies, is arguably the largest and most democratic system that human beings have ever created. It is often proposed that ICT revolution, particularly the Internet, could be well utilised by the parliamentarians to improve the responsiveness and efficiency of transactions between government and elected politicians, elected politicians and their constituents, public services and the citizen. Models of political representation in a networked society and the technological and the constitutional are addressed in this chapter. The former sees the transformative opportunities of the Internet, whereas the latter model sees the Internet as a support to existing relationships between parliamentarians and their constituents. To illustrate this, the chapter examines the role of parliament within contemporary democratic governance and political online communication. Different models of political representation and parliament as a symbol of political representation in the networked society is addressed.

INTRODUCTION

More and more people are joining the information society worldwide. According to Norris (2005), the main influence of this development, as it is theorized in a market model, will be determined by the "supply" and "demand" for electronic information and communications about government and politics. Demand, in turn, is assumed to be heavily dependent upon the social characteristics of Internet users and their prior political orientations. Given this understanding, the study predicts that the primary impact of knowledge societies in democratic societies will be upon facilitating cause-oriented and civic forms of political activism, thereby strengthening social movements and interest groups, more than upon conventional channels of political participation exemplified by

DOI: 10.4018/978-1-4666-6579-8.ch005

voting, parties, and election campaigning. Even though both the number of fixed- and mobile-broadband subscriptions in developing countries surpassed those in developed countries, penetration rates lag seriously behind plus other challenges such as major disparities remain in the coverage, price and quality of broadband services (United Nations, 2013).

With the general growth of research work to investigate the impact of new information and communication technologies (ICTs), in particular the Internet, upon parliamentary democracy in Western countries, it is hardly surprising that the relationship between the role of digital technologies and politics has attracted considerable attention in recent years. In an attempt to go beyond the conventional assumptions about how technological change pertaining to communication since the telegraph, telephone, radio and television, studies have focused on anything from the evolutionary phases of political communication, right through the arrival of the Internet technologies which its exponential growth that open wide the door to electronic democracy (eDemocracy). While some research has focused only on the description of differences (e-voting, e-polling, e-consultation and e-petitions which could stimulate greater political participation (Ward & Vedel., 2006), other work has sought to show how Internet has both strengthen and transform party organizations and the institutional legislative authorities (Vedel, 2006; Coleman, et. al., 1999, Ward & Vedel, 2006). Accordingly Zittel (2003), in his study of the use the Internet by parliamentarians, proposes two models of political representation in a networked society: the technological and the constitutional. The former sees the transformative opportunities of the Internet, whereas the latter model sees the Internet as not to redefine but to support existing relationships between parliamentarians and their constituents (Norton, 2007).

Much of the theoretical aspects of the debate revolve around several key characteristics of new

ICTs, which look to broaden the debate solely from a technological one-to-one concerned with the nature of democracy and democratic activity (Feebenrg, 1999 & Graham, 1999). Thus, Shahin and Neuhold (2008) contend that this can "invoked in different stages of the decision-making process, from agenda setting right the way through the monitoring process." While there are clearly some problems with this contention such questions about the validity of these instruments for enhancing meaningful political participation, or even, problems related to access and representation. Studies has shown that the Internet so far has failed to attract more citizens into the political process, and instead is repeating a 'virtuous circle' of political activism in which the already engaged and politically active are the ones using the new technologies in a political way (Norris, 2002). It is clear that the emphasis on the usage of ICT remained at the centre of much of this debate. Research also has shown how Internet-based political participation is largely applicable to the well-educated and wealthy men, so far as the UK experience is concerned (Gibson, et al., 2005). This is somewhat similar to the finding by Di Gennaro and Dutton, who argued that online political participation was reinforcing or even exacerbating existing inequalities in offline political participation by increasing the involvement online among those who are already politically active, thus disadvantaging those from the less educated and lower socio-economic groups. The chief focus of this approach, then, has been to show how patterns of interaction and usage between MPs and constituents reflect the specific rules and principles theme in it.

Clearly, the use of ICTs as 'an integral tool of strategies to revitalize governance and renew democratic culture' (Lawson, 1998) is somewhat undeniable. Much of these researches have invited optimistic view much to the pessimistic views. The former argue that the interactive nature of Internet technologies has the potential to reinvigorate the democratic process and re-engage citizens in politics against the background of growing voter apathy, including the possibility of creating new political processes (Allan, 2006), whereas, the latter, obviously suggest a rather dismal picture of the potential the technologies could bring (see for instance Davis, 2009; Di Gennaro & Dutton, 2006; Gibson, et. al., 2005). To be sure, the transformative nature of tools of technologies must be used in transformative ways to be transformative – as the simple presence of information and communication technologies will not automatically transform an organisation (Boyd, 2008).

While Malaysia is compelled to make synergistic efforts toward a more open and integrated policy environment, the emphasis on digital convergence policy has been prevailing with respect to the change in policy orientation was an essential feature which shaped the overall emphasis in governance (Ahmad 2008; 2009). This supports the new vision of the Prime Minister, today, that there is a move towards greater transparency to a Malaysian roadmap for the future; but 'this cannot be an old-style political debate' (Najib, 2010). The new economic model has wide ranging implications for the people of Malaysia, and therefore information should be made available to the general public to gather their input and provide them with an opportunity to be part of the decision-making process. Whether in the budget or the recent Government Transformation Programme (GTP), where thousands of public citizens were involved in the process, 'it is only through consultation with the *Rakyat (masses)* and all the other stakeholders that we can achieve a strong, convincing and effective plan to implement our New Economic Model' (Najib, 2010). Obviously, legislative body could be the ideal place to begin with.

Although Zittel (2003) distinction is clearly a useful one, it also seems evident that these two approaches in understanding two models of political representation in a networked society are by no means mutually exclusive. While it is important on the one hand, therefore, not to operate with a simplistic version of technology and to consider communication and politics will automatically create better government or ideal democratic political process, it is also important not to treat the impact of the Internet as if it existed outside political communications. As Graham offers a challenging suggestion saying, "if the availability and efficiency of the means of communication and expression are important elements in the realization of democracy, and if in the Internet we have an unprecedented good means of communication and expression, we may infer that the Internet puts within our grasp an unprecedentedly good form of democracy." In the existing academic literature, comparative data on the impact of the Internet upon parliamentary democracy in Malaysia are scarce. Clearly, there is scope here for a great deal more research that:

- Is based on conceptual and empirical data of ICTs and political legislature;
- Operates with a complex understanding of Internet and political communication (so that digital technologies, for example, can be seen both as a site of strengthen or weaken representative democracy);
- Looks specifically at the contexts of Internet use, rather than assuming broad ICT-engineered communication;
- Involves more work in deepening and widening of the understanding about the relationship between the Internet and the most important institution in a liberal democracy, namely, the Parliament, in a Malaysian context;
- Aims not only to describe and explain but also to interpret pattern of communication in political relationships.

It is argued that democratic political participation must involve both the means to be informed and the mechanisms to take part in the decision making (Macintosh, 2002). The joint perspectives of "informing and participating" are the two principles on which the Internet technology facilitate and enable citizens to express views directly to legislators. Likewise, the Internet offers the potential to link parliamentarian with electors in a direct and relatively inexpensive nature (Norton, 2007). However, Barber (1984) warn of the use of technology in that it could diminish the sense of face-to-face communication and increase the dangers of elite participation; thereby raises concern about the extent to which a single most important symbol of democracy at its best form – Parliament, can be truly representative. In the extensive contemporary literature on the impact of the Internet in parliaments as institutions and on the new media strategies of individual MPs, Chadwick (2006) notes, such an online presence:

If implemented properly can improve current government services, increase accountability result in more accurate and efficient delivery of service, reduce administrative costs and time spent on repetitive tasks for government employees, facilitate greater transparency in the administration of government, and allow greater access to services due to around the clock availability of the Internet.

While there is the potential to transmit vast quantities of information and parliamentary rationales, conduct and on-going business, it is proposed to argue in this Chapter that it is important for parliamentary institutions to sustain public trust if they are to survive in their current forms or, alternatively, to allow their constituent members to push for institutional or constitutional reform, believing that ICTs could 'increase the administrative efficiency of the institution, improve information access and dissemination, and finally enhance MPs' and assemblies' interaction with citizens' (Lusoli, et al., 2006).

POLITICAL REPRESENTATION: ONLINE PRESENCE

The Internet is providing new opportunities for direct and interactive communication through its online features. According to Chadwick (2006):

... if implemented properly, can improve current government services, increase accountability, result in more accurate and efficient delivery of services, reduce administrative costs and time spent on repetitive tasks for government employees, facilitate greater transparency in the administration of government, and allow greater access to services due to around the clock availability of the Internet.

Apart from simply posting personally identifiable information, Internet as new technological means, enables discussion forums and bulletin boards to deliberate with citizens; electronic opinion polls allow parliaments to learn about their particular policy interests in a timely manner; and websites, electronic newsletters, and webcams provide new opportunities to communicate information about the political process and public policies in a comprehensive manner (Zittel, 2003).

The theoretical foundations of online political representation go back to traditional comparative theories, which posit that the relationship between parliaments and citizens are based on a distinction between collectivist and individualist systems (Zittel, 2003). This logic has formed the basis for theories of legislative behavior which argues that 'the type of electoral system' and the 'type of government' have been singled out as institutional factors that pattern legislative behavior in major ways (Mayhew, 1974; Mitchell, 2000; Strom, 2000). In this sense, the institutional structures make the support from party elites and fellow party members a crucial prerequisite for electoral success; thereby MPs will perceive themselves as part of a team rather than as individual player (Zittel, 2003).

Addressing the score points in using the Internet as a means to facilitate access to public information and to increase transparency within the existing institutional framework, Norris (2001) found in mid 2000, national parliaments in 98 countries with websites (out of 189 UN member states) whereas, today, this number has increased significantly to 188 countries (Zittel, 2008). In the context of the Portuguese Parliament for instance, Viegas d'Abreu (2008) find that the Assembly of Republic (AR) has been making a major effort to modernize itself through three key dimensions; first, equipping MPs with IT resources that allow them to be mobile and to work at a distance, I,e, wireless network, free laptops when MPs are on official mission abroad, Virtual Private Network (VPN), wireless technology, palmtops, Internet access via GPRS/3FG, access to a Unified messaging system, SMS, Fax, Voicemail, and a text-to-speech etc.; second, simplifying procedures and making them more flexible; i.e., the AR's official journal–the *Diario da Assembleia da Republica* is published exclusively electronically since 2003; the Parliamentary TV Channel – *Canal Parlamento* is made online; and the database with a dedicated network equipped with digital signatures which is intended to allow the legislative process to circulate between the four bodies, and *third*, improving the interactions with citizens, i.e., a formation of a number of online discussion forums in order to promote active citizen user. Although very minimum study to date has systematically studied the benefits of eParticipation between MPs and the public, initial insights suggest by van Rijn (2008) in his case study of the Netherlands House of Representative Website found that the functionality, content, form and technicality are critical components of design of Parliamentary website which can potentially contribute to user participation (van Rijn, 2008).

TECHNOLOGICAL APPROACH OF REPRESENTATION MODEL

The new digital world matters to political representation because there was a new opportunity for individual representatives – MPs, and parliament, as a representative institution, in their dealings with citizens in dramatic ways with a more open and direct relationship with citizens. The premise was based on three assumptions.

First, the traditional media platforms, i.e. phones, printed bulletins, raised general problems of access and control of the message which could be overcome more easily by way of collective action (Blumler & Gurevitch, 1995). In this regard, political parties were organizational means to pool resources in order to utilize these types of media in the most efficient ways (Zittel, 2003). With the advent of Internet, asynchronous co-presence communication based is made possible, that has the capacity to transcend at some of the traditional barriers of distance and time which have prevented citizens from having a more direct relationship with their elected representatives (Coleman, 2006). Zittel (2003) further explained:

Standard hardware and software for a few thousand dollars, along with broadband Internet access, allows representatives to advertise policies, to deliberate with citizens, and to take polls on policy matters.

As a result, a second assumption is that this shift from traditional to transformative potential of the Internet technologies eventually lead to a scenario in which political parties will become less relevant as a conduit for political communication and computer networks will establish a more direct flow of communication between MPs and particular constituents (Zittel, 2003). Third assumption is that, the marriage between individual types of representation with the institutional basis of political representation can be accelerated with technological convergence. While this might have been a problem in the past, the diffusion of the Internet, especially in established democracies, is now well advanced and has surpassed a critical mass (Norris 2001), thereby lead to a more "activism" mode of relationship (Coleman, 2006; Norris, 2005). Furthermore, with the process of generational change, younger MPs will be able to acclimatize easily to the demand of a new technology. Also, with the generational change, people are getting more indulge into the political discussion, thereby 'widening the sphere of deliberation beyond the insulated portals of parliament (Norris, 2005). These three assumptions heralded the democratic potential of the Internet on the most important institution in a liberal democracy – the parliament, to the point that this marks the beginning of a process for creating a 'virtual parliament,' 'online parliament' and 'virtual parties' (Norris, 2001). Toffler (1981) argued that spectacular advances in communications technology have undermined old political assumptions: the old objections to direct democracy are growing weaker at precisely the same time that the objections to representative democracy are growing stronger. Naisbitt (1982) was so optimist that he has gone even further contending that whether there is the need for representative democracy in a time when ICT can flow so freely.

In the context of the quality of eCommunication, the usability of websites does not indicate anything about the exact relationship between the MPs and optimum usage of the website. Even though more and more MPs publish position papers, newsletters or information on their parliamentary activities on their personal websites, majority of them still publish or use the net for the narrow purposes of political advertisement or public relations; i.e. press releases, general text messages and photos remain the main pieces of content (Zittel, 2008). On the one hand, research on British MPs by Ward and Lusoli (2005) found a negative relationship between rebelliousness and having a website. On the other hand, the use of online consultation can just be

hype when they could be just "project-based," less extensive (16 online consultations in seven years in the UK between 1998 and 2005); and poor feedback to users (Zittel, 2008; Coleman, 2006). However, this is only case-specific evidence which need to be validated against more comparative evidences. Studies conducted in the context of parliamentary online communication emphasise the need to increase office efficiency (Francoli, 2008) as it may eventually impact on political activity within the legislature. In the context of the models of political representation, four models have been proposed – traditional, party, representative and tribune models (Norton, 2007). These models can be used for the structured analysis of Internet communication adoption in parliamentarian works.

The Traditional Model

The traditional model posits a rejection of the use of ICT as a means of reinforcing or changing existing modes of representation. The context emphasis relates to there are emerging opportunities, particularly afforded by the interactive communication technologies, such as the Internet, to make representative institutions more transparently accessible and open to interactive discussion (Coleman, 2006). In a move towards the direction of ubiquitous access to digital ICTs, parliaments remain much the same as they are now, utilizing the Internet as a means of telling the public they exist, but resisting the interactive opportunities that could create a spaces of common deliberations involving both politicians and citizens. Politicians might continue to complain that too much contact with the people they represent constitutes an intractable problem and is making it impossible for them to do their jobs. Citizens might continue to feel estranged and unheard (Coleman, 2006). Although the use of the Internet has been expanded, i.e. proliferation of websites, email databases etc., there could all be utilized in ways that enable the old political game to be played according to the rules of remote and indirect representation (Coleman, 2006). Political communication would remain top-down rather than collaborative, message transmitting rather than interactive rather than deliberative.

The Party Model

The party model posits the dominance of party and that ICT will be employed in order to bolster the position of party in the political system. Where political parties already are dominant in the system, in correspondence to the democratic potential of the Internet has concentrated on the capacity of political institutions to adapt to the consequences of digital interactivity (Blumbler & Coleman, 2001; Zittel, 2004). In his analysis of political party theory, Boyd (2008) has described the evolution of political parties since the early age, thanks to the earlier studies done by Lofgren and Smith (2003) and Krouwel, (2006), started off with elite parties (the earliest form of political parties made up of coalitions of representatives who agreed to share agenda; existed at a time that few people had the franchise, generally only the wealthy male elite. These parties were not accountable to a membership or a wide electorate, but emerged from and were essentially solely made up of legislators. These parties were often informally organized and did not exist beyond the legislative body); replaced by mass parties (spin-off the franchise activities that dominated Europe in the middle of the 20ᵗʰ Century; represented a particular group, i.e. the working class, and focused on furthering the group's interests while enabling active participation of that group in the party through large-scale party membership. Members volunteered and paid dues in order to spread the ideology for a better world the party promoted); which eventually evolved into becoming catch-all parties (as the working class became a middle class and mass media provided new opportunities for contact with voters without the need of a large membership), before being transformed into cartel parties (the focus is beyond a specific group, attempted to appeal to a much more wider swath of the electorate. Instead of volunteers, they depended on paid professionals to run media-based campaigns, dominate especially in North America; have limited memberships, and do not depend on donations or members' volunteered time, but instead the party gives itself state resources. They use these resources to hire professionals to target many voters in generalized electoral campaigns) today in Europe. As noted above, Boyd (2008) argues that simple presence of ICT will not automatically transform an organization, including political parties. The Internet nevertheless, has been deployed to reinforce the party position, regardless of the type of the political party. The aim for wide-scale deliberative or direct citizen participation is nevertheless is driven mainly by the parties; while the role of citizen, as Norton (2007) has coined as "essentially passive" and "communication is primarily, though not exclusively, mono-directional."

The Representative Model

The representative model derives from the distinction drawn between the MP as a representative and as a delegate. Dryzek (2007) favours the idea of discursive representation, where "networks can play a role in the production of public opinion in the public sphere, and not simply act as an arm of government." In this conception of representation, it was in order to justify that participants of networks should be "proper representatives" that provide functional representation and act as accountability holders to their constituents (Es-mark, 2007). This means that, within governance networks, meanings of representation have little to do with conventional democratic understandings, i.e. electoral accountability, authorization, and responsiveness; but more of as a "process of getting the right knowledge into discussions, promoting the network, or fostering problem solving," (Hendriks, 2009). In this model, the

Internet communication has two important implications. First, decision makers should better "adequately or comprehensively" reflect and embody the experiences of those they represent (Phillips, 1995; Williams 1998; Young, 2000); and second, it is also reflected in the actions and settings of policy interactions (Hendriks, 2009). Here, as Pitkin (1967) argues, "what makes it (political representation) is not any single action by one participant, but the overall-structure and functioning of the system, the pattern emerging from the multiple activities of many people." In it, the role of participation "is not gives rise to greater knowledge about democratic politics, but also that it enables people to recognize differences among players in democratic politics."

The Tribune Model

The tribune model sees the MP as acting as the voice of the people (Pitkin, 1967). This is the model that most closely parallel to school of deliberative or participative democracy, for it posits the use of Internet would make possible the free and equal participation of citizens in the debates preceding decision making (Kersten, 2003). According to Coleman (2006), the effectiveness of parliament, "is judged not in terms of its ability to initiate or shape policies and laws, but as a forum in which public aspirations, anxieties and complaints can be aired and addressed, and the public voice can be heard in all of its pluralistic diversity." Also, it equates the advocates of the evolutionary theory, which argues that the ideal citizen is a participating citizen – thereby, participation is considered as exerting social responsibility (Samiei & Jalilvand, 2011). The Internet offers the opportunity for the development of the good citizens as an active and well informed member of the community (Hacker & van Dijk, 2000). However, Wu and Du (2012) have cautioned that to further validate this, scholars should consider and examine both actual usage and assessed usage in every single study that they conduct.

PARLIAMENT AS A SYMBOL OF A POLITICAL REPRESENTATION IN THE NETWORKED SOCIETY

Parliament encapsulates the new meaning of political relationship between policy makers and citizens. Bang and Earmark (2009) call for re-evaluation of the relationship between government and its stakeholders in response to the reconfiguration of the political system according to the ethos of good governance based on the network paradigm:

The only reasonable approach to the rise of network ethos and network organisation in public governance is a clear refusal of the idea of the network state as a helpless victim of network society. The reorientation of steering and coordination from programmes of conventional democratic polity to the stakeholder and partnership programmes of governance intrinsic to network governance is not simply a necessary or functional response to economic globalisation, technological innovation, complexity, and wicked policy problems... Rather it is to be regarded as the core of a more fundamental transformation from a disciplinary society to a control society in which states, or at least governments, are key innovators and benefactors.

In deliberative democracy, Elstub (2006) the four general principles: the making of collective decisions; involving the participation of relevant actors (the more equal this participation the more democratic), through the consideration and exchange of reasons; and aimed at the transformation of preferences. In practice, however, the existing literature can be divided into two broad categories; the first focuses on primarily on modernization and the notion of eGovernment; while the second looks at the new method for engagement or eDemocracy (Francoli, 2008). Internet technologies have played a critical role in leveraging the role of democracy and the role of Parliamentarians.

Malloy (2003) highlighted the score point of digital technologies as follows:

... the advantages of rapid communication, and particularly for the secure and rapid transfer of complex information and documents between constituents, legislators and public servants, could create a dramatically increased role for legislators in the delivery of public services.

The Internet brought an implication on parliamentary sphere which in turn forms normative concepts of democracy. The concept of eDemocracy proposed by Zittel (2008) firstly suggests that the Internet will be able to intensify the quantity and quality of communication between parliament and constituents within a given institutional frame; eDemocracy, secondly suggests that eCommunication will affect parliament as an institution, eDemocracy, thirdly suggests that a more responsive and transparent parliamentary process will eventually increase the political engagement of citizens (Zittel, 2008). In this regard, two important elements to foster a more participatory type of democracy is by increasing the "responsiveness" of parliamentary decision making and the "transparency" of the parliamentary process (Ibid, 2008). Coleman and Gotze (2001) however cautioned that the use of public involvement in policy-making in order to push a particular policy agenda is one that representatives generally wish to resist. He further suggests (Gotze (2001, p. 17):

... the solution here is not for elected representatives to reject public engagement as a challenge to their legitimacy, but to use public engagement themselves as a way of strengthening the quality of their representative mandate and developing more informed, publicly supported policy options as counterweights to executive monopolies on policy formation. In short, public engagement exercises need not only be the tools of the executive, but can become a key tool for legislatures in their role of holding governments to account, scrutinising policies more effectively and serving as democratic conduits for informed public views. Arguably, online engagement with the public could offer a major opportunity for elected representatives to enhance their legitimacy as political mediators of the public voice.

The central normative claim that unites and guide the theory, is that political decision-making should be 'talk-centric' rather than vote-centric' (Bohman & Rehg, 1997). Deliberative democrats believe that traditional notions of democratic legitimation needs to be reconceptualised, so that the outcomes of a political process are only viewed as legitimate where all affected by the decision have had the opportunity to participate in its formative deliberations (see Dryzek, 2001). Norton and Wood (1993) in their analysis of the relationship between the British MPs and their constituents argued that:

There is little research on the extent to which parliamentarians – outside the context of engagement – are able independently to use the Internet as a resource in fulfilling their 'legislative' as opposed to their 'constituency' roles.

In this sense, the potential of ICT to increase electoral turnout and political participation and to address other "democratic deficits" in representative democracy is envisioned. In this regard, the Internet has become the preferred source for political information for Internet users and thus leaves television and other traditional news sources behind (ARDF/ZDF, 2009). The consequences of ICT for representative democracy can be seen from at least two optimistic perspectives, first, as a tool to "reinvigorate civil society as an integral tool to revitalize governance and renew democratic culture" (Lawson, 1998); second, ICT would contribute to the development of the good citizen as an active and well-informed member of the community (Hacker & van Djik, 2000). These two optimistic beliefs in the ICT on democracy have given rise to rather skeptical view which suggests that "politics will normalize the Internet into its established structures, having limited impact (Pautz, 2010), so that there could be just insignificant change or impact to the existing representative system.

While there were quite a number of studies have detailed the rise of eGovernment (Chadwick, 2006, Johnston, 2010), much of the literature focuses on primarily on the bureaucracy with a cursory mention of parliament (Francoli, 2008). Furthermore, there is a lack of comparative studies in this area, partly due to the infancy of this area of research, and/or 'biased' towards typically Anglo-Saxon countries and Northern Europe (Leston-Bandeira and Ward, 2007). However, according to Johnston (2010):

As governance infrastructure allow for more direct and informed involvement in some government activities, power is returned to the people such that values are articulated through their actions rather than by a one-off vote of stated preferences.

Nasim, et al (2010) have summarized some of the significant forces driving change towards eGovernment, pointing out globalization, new opportunities, pressure of good governance, stakeholders' needs and expectations, new technology, the ePlatform, government policies and legislation, public-private partnership, identifying forces of continuity in eGovernment, target number of customer base, well-established physical infrastructure, existing process of delivering services, manual records or legacy databases, core competence in manual systems and existing culture. In surveys conducted by Norris (2002), the validity of ICT instruments (i.e., online political consultation, digital surveys or online message boards) for enhancing meaningful political participation, two issues were raised. First, there are the problems associated with access and representativeness. Norris (2002) found that the Internet so far has failed to attract more citizens into the political processes, and instead is repeating a 'virtuous cycle' of political activism in which the already engaged and politically active are the ones using the new technologies in a political way. Second, Vicente-Merino (2008), points out the possibilities for real deliberation taking place in online format such as the anonymity will lead to depersonalize the discussion and "allows some individuals to use abusive or plain insulting language; others the speed at which communication takes place within them, which neglects the chance of reflection before forming an opinion."

It is proposed that the systems of collectivist representation emphasize the role of political parties as an important linkage between parliaments and citizens (Zittel, 2003). Political parties are assumed to dominate the role perception of MPs, and to affect their legislative behavior as well as the process of political representation (Zittel, 2003). However, research has shown, the mechanisms for coping with such communication have not changed significantly over the past century in which an assumption is that communication needs to be handled individually, even though most correspondents are contacting their MPs about collective policy issues rather than personal problems (Coleman, 2006).

CHAPTER SUMMARY

Overall, theoretical literature provides a number of important insights into the factors behind online political representation. In particular, we find that the online political representation should not be understood in a limited nature of political process such as electoral or referendum purposes but must be "outcome" based, for example, getting the "right" information into the space of discussions, promoting the Internet communication as the innovative conduit for quality participation towards a solid democracy. However, despite many similarities to the already investigated settings, online political representation depicts environments with significantly distinctive characteristics, which may prove relevant to enhance eDemocracy. For example, by focusing on "governance of the affected" (Dryzek, 2007), inclusion moves to centre stage, and democratic legitimacy becomes a matter of whether those potentially affected by a decision have had the right and opportunity to participate in and influence policy deliberations (Benhabib 1996; Dryzek, 2001). To date, findings explicitly related to online participation dynamics remain limited and are mostly skewed towards Western developed countries (see for instance Leston-Bandeira and Ward, 2007). Moreover, different conceptualizations and operational of system usage – whereby a usage construct of one study may significantly differ from that in another study in terms of thereozing about system usage and its idea of construct validity (Wu & Du, 2012; Venkatesh et. al, 2008). Aiming to fill this gap, we adopt a two-stage approach; first, we highlighted an overall conceptual framework of political representation models. Second, we integrate our theoretical framework with our quantitative findings based on the evidences that we found in the context of Malaysia's parliamentarians, later in our empirical Chapter. This is with the hope that it could expand our theoretical understanding of political representation beyond specific scope of activities such as eVoting or eReferendum, but the impact overall to eDemocracy.

REFERENCES

Ahmad, N. B. (2008). *Towards a new mode of governance in Malaysia: Policy, regulatory and institutional challenges of digital convergence.* (PhD Thesis Unpublished). University of Hull.

Ahmad, N. B. (2009). Malaysian new ICT policy: Regulatory reform and the new mode of governance. *The Journal of Administrative Science, 6*(1), 117–141.

Allan, R. (2006). Parliament elected representatives and technology 1997–2005—Good in Parts? *Parliamentary Affairs, 59*(2), 360–365. doi:10.1093/pa/gsl007

ARD/ZDF. (2009). *Online Studies 2009.* Retrieved from www.ard-zdf-onlinestudie.de/fileadmin/Online09/Eimeren1_7_09.pdf

Bang, H., & Esmark, A. (2009). Good governance in network society: Reconfiguring the political from politics to policy. *Administrative Theory & Praxis, 31*(1), 7–37. doi:10.2753/ATP1084-1806310101

Barber, B. R. (2003). *Strong democracy: Participatory politics for a new age.* University of California Press.

Benhabib, S. (Ed.). (1996). *Democracy and difference: Contesting the boundaries of the political.* Princeton, NJ: Princeton University Press.

Blumler, J. G., & Gurevitch, M. (1995). *The crisis of political communication.* London: Academic Press.

Bohman, J. (Ed.). (1997). *Deliberative democracy: Essays on reason and politics.* MIT Press.

Boyd, O. P. (2008). Differences in eDemocracy parties' eParticipation systems. *Information Polity, 13*(3), 167–188.

Chadwick, A. (2006). *Internet politics: States, citizens, and new communication technologies.* Oxford University Press.

Coleman, S. (2006, September). Parliamentary communication in an age of digital interactivity. *Aslib Proceedings, 58*(5), 371–388. doi:10.1108/00012530610692339

Coleman, S. (2007). e-Democracy: The history and future of an idea. In The Oxford handbook of information and communication technologies. Oxford University Press.

Coleman, S., & Gotze, J. (2001). Bowling together: Online public engagement in policy deliberation. London: Hansard Society.

Coleman, S., & Norris, D. F. (2005). *A new agenda for e-democracy*. OII Forum Discussion Paper.

Coleman, S., Taylor, J., & van de Donk, W. (Eds.). (1999). *Parliament in the Age of the Internet*. Oxford, UK: Oxford University Press.

Dai, X., & Norton, P. (2007). The Internet and parliamentary democracy in Europe. *Journal of Legislative Studies*, *13*(3), 342–353. doi:10.1080/13572330701500763

Davis, A. (2009). New media and fat democracy: The paradox of online participation. *New Media & Society*.

Di Gennaro, C., & Dutton, W. (2006). The Internet and the public: Online and offline political participation in the United Kingdom. *Parliamentary Affairs*, *59*(2), 299–313. doi:10.1093/pa/gsl004

Dryzek, J. S. (2001). Legitimacy and economy in deliberative democracy. *Political Theory*, *29*(5), 651–669. doi:10.1177/0090591701029005003

Dryzek, J. S. (2007). Networks and democratic ideals: Equality, freedom, and communication. In *Theories of democratic network governance*, (pp. 262-273). Academic Press.

Elstub, S. (2006). A double-edged sword: The increasing diversity of deliberative democracy. *Contemporary Politics*, *12*(3-4), 301–319. doi:10.1080/13569770601086204

Esmark, A. (2007). Democratic accountability and network governance–problems and potentials. In *Theories of democratic network governance*, (pp. 274-296). Academic Press.

Feenberg, A. (1999). *Questioning technology*. London: Routledge.

Fishkin, J. S. (1997). *The voice of the people: Public opinion and democracy*. Yale University Press.

Francoli, M. (2008). Parliaments Online: Modernizing and engaging? Parliaments in the Digital Age: Forum Discussion Paper, 13, 4-8.

Freeman, L. R., & Freeman, R. (1997). *Democracy in the digital age*. Demos.

Gibson, R. K., Lusoli, W., & Ward, S. (2005). Online participation in the UK: Testing a 'contextualised' model of Internet effects1. *British Journal of Politics and International Relations*, *7*(4), 561–583. doi:10.1111/j.1467-856X.2005.00209.x

Gibson, R. K., Lusoli, W., & Ward, S. (2005). Online Participation in the UK: Testing a 'Contextualised' Model of Internet Effects1. *British Journal of Politics and International Relations*, *7*(4), 561–583. doi:10.1111/j.1467-856X.2005.00209.x

Graham, G. (1999). *The Internet: A philosophical inquiry*. Psychology Press.

Hacker, K. L., & van Dijk, J. (Eds.). (2000). *Digital democracy: Issues of theory and practice*. UK: Sage. doi:10.4135/9781446218891.n1

Heeley, M., & Damodaran, L. (2009). *Digital inclusion: A review of international policy and practice*. Loughborough University.

Held, D. (2006). *Models of democracy*. Stanford University Press.

Hendriks, C. M. (2009). The democratic soup: Mixed meanings of political representation in governance networks. *Governance: An International Journal of Policy, Administration and Institutions*, *22*(4), 689–715. doi:10.1111/j.1468-0491.2009.01459.x

Johnston, E. (2010). Governance infrastructures in 2020. *Public Administration Review*, *70*(1), 122–128. doi:10.1111/j.1540-6210.2010.02254.x

Kersten, G. E. (2003). E-democracy and participatory decision processes: Lessons from e-negotiation experiments. *Journal of Multi-Criteria Decision Analysis, 12*(2-3), 127–143. doi:10.1002/mcda.352

Krouwel, A. (2006). Party models. In R. S. Katz & W. Crotty (Eds.), *Handbook of party politics* (pp. 249–269). London: Sage. doi:10.4135/9781848608047.n22

Lawson, G. (1998). *NetState: Creating electronic government, 18. Demos (Mexico City, Mexico)*, 55.

Leston-Bandeira, C., & Ward, S. (2008). Parliaments in the Digital Age. Oxford Internet Institute, Forum Discussion Report, 13, 2-3.

Lindh, M., & Miles, L. (2007). Becoming electronic parliamentarians? ICT usage in the Swedish Riksdag. *Journal of Legislative Studies, 13*(3), 422–440. doi:10.1080/13572330701500896

Löfgren, K., & Smith, C. (2003). Political parties and democracy in the information age. In Political parties and the internet: Net gain, (pp. 39-52). London: Routledge.

Lusoli, W., Ward, S., & Gibson, R. (2006). (Re)Connecting Politics? Parliament, the Public and the Internet. *Parliamentary Affairs, 59*(1), 28.

Macintosh, A., & Smith, F. (2002). Citizen Participation in Public Affairs. In R. Traunmuller & K. Lenk (Eds.), FGOV, (LNCS), (vol. 2456, pp. 256-63). Berlin: Springer.

Malloy, J. (2003). High discipline, low cohesion? The uncertain patterns of Canadian parliamentary party groups. *Journal of Legislative Studies, 9*(4), 116–129. doi:10.1080/1357233042000306290

Masters, Z., Mactintosh, A., & Smith, E. (2004). Young People and eDemocracy: Creating a Culture of Participation. In R. Traunmuller (Ed.), EGPV (LNCS), (vol. 3183, pp. 15-22). Berlin: Springer.

Mayhew, D. R. (1974). *Congress: The electoral connection.* Yale University Press.

Mitchell, P. (2000). Voters and their representatives: Electoral institutions and delegation in parliamentary democracies. *European Journal of Political Research, 37*(3), 335–351. doi:10.1111/1475-6765.00516

Naisbitt, J. (1982). *Megatrends: Ten New Directions Transforming Our Lives.* New York: Warner Books.

Najib, A.R. (2010). *Keynote Address.* Paper presented at INVEST Malaysia. Kuala Lumpur, Malaysia.

Nasim, & Sushil. (2010). Managing continuity and change: A new approach for strategizing in e-government. *Transforming Government: People, Process and Policy, 4*(4), 338-364.

Norris, P. (2001). *Digital divide: Civic engagement, information poverty, and the Internet worldwide.* Cambridge University Press. doi:10.1017/CBO9781139164887

Norris, P. (2002). *Digital Divide, Civic Engagement, Information Poverty, and the Internet Political Activism.* Cambridge University Press.

Norris, P. (2005). The Impact of the Internet on Political Activism: Evidence from Europe. *International Journal of Electronic Government Research, 1*(1), 19–39. doi:10.4018/jegr.2005010102

Norton, P. (2007). Four models of political representation: British MPs and the use of ICT. *Journal of Legislative Studies, 13*(3), 354–369. doi:10.1080/13572330701500771

Norton, P., & Wood, D. M. (1993). *Back from westminster: British members of parliament and their constituents.* Lexington, KY: University Press of Kentucky.

Pautz, H. (2010). The internet, political participation and election turnout: A case study of Germany's. *German Politics & Society, 28*(3), 156-175.

Phillips, A. (1995). *The politics of presence.* Oxford University Press.

Pitkin, H. F. (1967). *The concept of representation.* University of California Press.

Samiei, N., & Jalilvand, M. R. (2011). The political participation and government size. *Canadian Social Science, 7*(2), 224–235.

Shahin, J., & Neuhold, C. (2007). 'Connecting Europe': The use of 'new' information and communication technologies within European parliament standing committees. *Journal of Legislative Studies, 13*(3), 388–402. doi:10.1080/13572330701500854

Strøm, K. (2000). *Parties at the gore of Government 2000.* New York: Oxford University Press.

Toffler, A. (1981). *The third wave.* New York: Bantam books.

United Nations. (2013). *The Millennium Development Goals Report.* Author.

van Dijk, J. (2000). Models of democracy and concepts of communication. In Digital democracy: Issues of theory and practice. London: Sage. doi:10.4135/9781446218891.n3

Vedel, T. (2006). The idea of electronic democracy: Origins, visions and questions. *Parliamentary Affairs, 59*(2), 226–235. doi:10.1093/pa/gsl005

Venkatesh, V., Brown, S. A., Maruping, L. M., & Bala, H. (2008). Predicting different conceptualizations of system use: The competing roles of behavioral intention, facilitating conditions, and behavioral expectation. *Management Information Systems Quarterly*, 483–502.

Vicente-Merino, M. R. (2007). Websites of parliamentarians across Europe. *Journal of Legislative Studies, 13*(3), 441–457. doi:10.1080/13572330701500912

Viegas d'Abreu, J. (2008). The Portuguese Parliaments in the digital age. Oxford Internet Institute, Forum Discussion Report, 13, 33-7.

Ward, S., & Lusoli, W. (2005). 'From weird to wired': MPs, the Internet and representative politics in the UK. *Journal of Legislative Studies, 11*(1), 57–81. doi:10.1080/13572330500158276

Ward, S., & Vedel, T. (2006). Introduction: The potential of the internet revisited. *Parliamentary Affairs, 59*(2), 210–225. doi:10.1093/pa/gsl014

Wilhelm, A. G. (1998). Virtual sounding boards: How deliberative is on-line political discussion? *Information Communication and Society, 1*(3), 313–338. doi:10.1080/13691189809358972

Wu, J., & Du, H. (2012). Toward a better understanding of behavioral intention and system usage constructs. *European Journal of Information Systems, 21*(6), 680–698. doi:10.1057/ejis.2012.15

Xue, S. (2005). Internet policy and diffusion in China, Malaysia and Singapore. *Journal of Information Science, 31*(3), 238–250. doi:10.1177/0165551505052472

Young, I. M. (2000). *Inclusion and democracy.* Oxford University Press.

Zittel, T. (2003). Political representation in the networked society: The Americanisation of European systems of responsible party government? *Journal of Legislative Studies, 9*(3), 32–53. doi:10.1080/1357233042000246855

Zittel, T. (2004). Digital parliaments and electronic democracy: A comparison between the US House, the Swedish Riksdag and the German Bundestag. In Electronic democracy: Mobilisation, organisation and participation via new ICTs. London: Routledge.

Zittel, T. (2008). Parliaments and the Internet: A Perspective on the State of Research. Parliaments in the Digital Age: Forum Discussion Paper, 13, 11-15.

KEY TERMS AND DEFINITIONS

Constitutional Reform: Agenda for transformation affecting organisations/institutional apparatuses and/or backed by legal framework.

Direct Citizen Participation: People's participation in policy processes without intermediaries.

E-Voting: An election process that allows people to choose their representative elected candidates via encryption whereby voters can transmit their secret ballot over the Internet.

Information Dissemination: The initiative to enhance political participation through information sharing.

Information Access: Opportunity provided for individuals to gain and access information they want regardless of the societal classes.

Internet-Based Political Participation: Motivation of ICT engagement among stakeholders based on Internet technologies.

Virtual Parliament: ICT-enabled parliamentary communication among the MPs and constituent members.

Section 2
Theoretical Explanation of People's Reactions to ICT in the Public Sector

Chapter 6
Theory of Reasoned Actions (TRA) and its Relation to ICT Adoption

ABSTRACT

The Theory of Reasoned Action (TRA) sheds light on the attitudinal behaviour related to acceptance, use, and adoption of technology in organisations. The TRA was developed by both Fishbein and Ajzen way back in 1975 and 1980 from previous studies on attitude and behaviour in organizations towards performing certain actions. The theory argues that intention to perform certain behavioural action is a function of both attitude and subjective norm. Subsequently, when a positive intention is developed, a person tends to really involve in performing the actual action. However, according to the findings of this chapter, one of the weaknesses of this theory is its inability to be applied to non-volitional acts such as those that become obligatory. When a public organization has endorsed the adoption of ICT as new way of performing tasks, it becomes a non-volitional act that everybody must follow to carry out tasks.

INTRODUCTION

One of the potential challenges in public sector is the acceptance of technological innovation. The challenge lies in the fact that application of technology devices brings a different way on how employees or civil servants used to work in the past. Technology, therefore, needs to be accepted by employees and must be fully used to actualise its purposes. As such, Dias (2002) argues that electronic way of executing works reflects a new model in the dissemination of the information in an organisation and must be fully explored. However,

such acceptance and full adoption of technology is a function of users' attitudinal behaviour towards information systems and/or technological devices.

There are some existing theories, such as, TRA that sheds light on the attitudinal behaviour related to acceptance, use and adoption of technology in organisations. The TRA was developed by both Fishbein and Ajzen way back in 1975, and 1980 from previous studies on attitude and behaviour. According to Hale et al. (2003), it was derived out of "frustration with traditional attitude-behaviour research, much of which found weak correlations between attitude measures and performance of

DOI: 10.4018/978-1-4666-6579-8.ch006

Figure 1. Theory of reasoned action (TRA)
Source: Icek Ajzen, (1991, p.4).

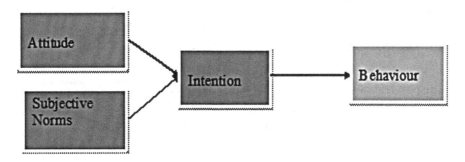

volitional behaviors" (p. 259). The theory of reasoned action (TRA) focuses on how a person's intention depends on his or her attitude towards behaviour and subjective norms. In other words, the theory suggests that if a person intends to perform certain behaviour, it is likely that he or she does it based on his or her attitude towards such behaviour. Hence, behavioural intention in attitude measures a person's relative strength of intention to perform such behaviour.

Basically, there are four components or elements in the TRA that need to be explained clearly in relation to ICT applications. They are attitude, subjective norms, intention, and behaviour as shown in Figure 1. The TRA is of the assumption that every individual human being will always consider the behavioural consequences of intention to do anything before engaging in such behaviour. As such, intention to perform certain act becomes an important element that determines behaviour. Ajzen and Fishbein (1975) opined that intentions are developed from individual's perception of a particular behaviour as either positive or negative depending on one's interpretation of the way the society perceives the behaviour. In other words, the theory contends that personal attitude and social pressure from the surrounding have influence on intention, which is essential to the performance of one's behaviour. To put the relationship simple, the theory holds to a fact that a person's volitional (voluntary) behaviour is predicted by his or her attitude towards that behaviour and how he or

she thinks other people around him will view the behaviour if he finally performed the behaviour.

Thus, a person's attitude always combines with subjective norms to form the person's behavioural intention towards an action. In this theory, Fishbein and Ajzen (1980) also concord that the presence of an unequal weightage for consideration between attitudes and subject norms in predicting behaviour of human beings towards certain acts. In the same vein, Miller (2005) equally expressed the view that "Indeed, depending on the individual and the situation, these factors might *[carry]...* different effects on behavioral intention; thus a weight is associated with each of these factors in the predictive formula of the theory. For example, you might be the kind of a person who cares little for what others think. If this is the case, the subjective norms would carry little weight in predicting your behavior," (p.127). With regard to the fact that behavioural intention is associated with attitudes and subjective norms, Miller (2005) illustrated by explaining that your attitude combined with the subjective norms and each with its own weight, will lead you to your intention to exercise (or not), which will then lead to your actual behavior. According to Oliveira (2006), the people choose to perform certain behaviour, even though they are not in agreement with it and its consequences, simply because they want to please that person.

STRUCTURAL COMPONENTS IN TRA AND ITS RELATIONS TO ICT APPLICATION

The TRA was based on the assumption that people are rational beings that can make use of information within their disposals about certain behaviour and/or action from which decisions are made. As a rational human being, he or she considers the implications of his or her action before deciding to perform a particular behaviour or not to perform it. This is practically in line with the assumption used in explaining people's attitude and behaviour towards acceptance or rejection of ICT application, particularly in the public organisations. As a result, ICT applications in public sector, in a more details, are central to structural assumptions in the TRA elements. The details of these elements in relations to ICT adoption and usage are discussed in the next sections of the chapter.

Attitude

Attitude, literally, is an evaluative statement, either favorable or unfavorable, concerning objects, people, or events (Ajzen, 1991). Attitudes are literally mental postures and guides for conduct to which each new experience is referred before a response is made. In other words, attitudes are evaluation of a psychological object in relations to how good or bad, likeable or dislikeable, harmful or beneficial, pleasant and/or unpleasant an object is (Ajzen & Fishbein 2000). It is resulted from the individuals' feelings about something they like or dislike. A broader understanding from the work of Droba (1974) shows that attitude is a mental disposition of individual human being to act for or against a definite object. It means attitude is a mental state of preparation for certain action or reaction towards something. As such, Siragusa and Dixon (2008) asserted that attitude "represent the way in which we view the world and organise our relationships [with it]" (p.942). According to Krech, Critchfield, and Livson (1958), attitude has

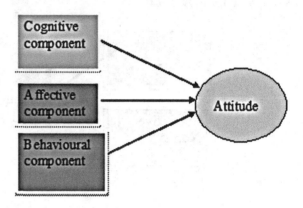

Figure 2. Components of attitude

three main components, which are the cognitive, the affective and the behavioural (see Figure 2). The cognitive part is based on the individual's ideas and beliefs about an object of attention. With this cognitive component, a person may develop certain behavioural pattern with the object in question. Perhaps, this implies a preparation, or readiness for response based on experiences with the object in question.

In other words, similar behavioural pattern might have been developed in relation to interaction of the person with technology as an object in the context of this work. Affective aspect refers to the emotional part of attitude, particularly the feelings of a person over outcomes of something. This feeling will later lead to behavioural component on how a person responds to the given object (McShane & Glinow, 2008).

In addition, the behavioural component of an attitude captures one's intention to behave in a certain way towards something based on the feeling, information, knowledge or the belief about it. In other words, attitude involves conscious reasoning; it is mainly based on people rational logic reason about something, especially devices like ICT which may be challenging the traditional practices. Therefore, we can infer that attitude consists of beliefs about the consequences of performing the behaviour, multiplied by a person's valuation of those consequences especially in the context of adopting or using ICT as an alternative choice to traditional method. Indeed, this happens when people establish perceptions about the object (ICT) and/or what people believe to be true outcomes of it. For example, in adopting technology to aid one's work performance in an organisation as opposed to the traditional way, would mean people believe that with more knowledge of ICT in carrying out works, it can enhance or yield high productivity. So, such beliefs are a perceived fact that comes from the past experience or other forms of learning. Feeling aspect of an attitude represents people's positive or negative evaluation of the attitude object or adopting and using of ICT to enhance their works. Hence, this aspect will reflect people's feeling as to either they like or dislike the new way of accomplishing works with the use of technology. In fact, since attitude refers to the degree to which a person has a favourable or unfavourable evaluation or appraisal of the behaviour (Ajzen, 1991), it is usually evaluated by asking individuals about their feelings towards performing a behaviour, for example, whether the behaviour in question is good, rewarding, useful, responsible, etc. (Tonglet, et al., 2004).

Hence, on the basis of the above understanding, attitude towards adoption of ICT can be explained from two perspectives, which are instrumental (based on knowledge) and experiential (relating to feelings) which is usually known or accomplished by asking individuals about their feeling toward performing certain behaviour (ibid). One important point worthy of notice is the fact that attitude of a person towards adopting ICT can also form the basis of direct experience, which tends to have stronger influence on behaviour than those formed through word of mouth (Ferguson & Mellow, 2004).

In the TRA, attitudes are one predictor of behavioural intentions and the overall evaluations of the behaviour by the individual towards accepting or rejecting performance of works through technology. Applying the principle of compatibility, the relevant attitudes are those towards performance of the behaviour, assessed at a similar level of specificity to that used in the assessment of behaviour itself. Therefore, it is worthwhile to know that the attitude component is a function of a person's salient behavioural beliefs, which represents perceived outcomes and/or the likely attributes of the ICT to be used in performing one's assigned tasks to achieve the outcomes of the organisation.

Following expectancy-value and its conceptualisations (Peak, 1955), the model quantifies outcomes as the multiplicative combination of the perceived likelihood that performance of the behaviour will lead to a particular outcome and evaluation of that outcome. Hence, the TRA assumed that a person's behaviour towards an attitudinal object (i.e., ICT in this context) is a function of an attitude towards it rather than towards the behaviour in achieving or maximizing certain expected outcomes. In other words, a person's attitude towards using or not using ICT is a perception about it, while the user's attitude towards using ICT is the actual behavioural beliefs about advantages and disadvantages of using it (outcomes). At this juncture, a user's attitude towards ICT as an object may be totally different from his or her attitude towards using it as a tool, which eventually determines the intention to use or not to use it. In the literature, very little, if there is any; study investigates the effect or impact of attitude towards the target or object (ICT) instead of towards using ICT to complete one's works.

Theoretically speaking, this line of distinction between target and actual behaviour is of practical significance to body of knowledge because it might shed lights onto why there may be inconsistencies in the findings of empirical studies and the lack of correspondence between the attitude construct and the behavioural criteria. In other words, we may come to a conclusion that the attitude and perceptions about ICT will affect people's beliefs about the consequences of using ICT (behaviour beliefs), which will eventually bear impacts on a nature of policy decision to be adopted regarding the use of ICT in the organisations for accomplishing works with the aim of achieving the organisation's prescribed objectives and goals.

Behavioural Intention

According to Ajzen (1991), behavioural intention refers to person's decision or willingness to perform or not to perform certain behaviour when the behaviour is under volitional control. Behavioural intention in TRA and the choice to use ICT in carrying out works is theoretically assumed that "all behaviour involves a choice, be it a choice between performing and not performing a given action or a choice among several qualitatively or quantitatively different action alternatives" (Ajzen & Fishbein, 1980, p.41). In other words, using a person's intention to predict his or her choice will depend on the availability of different alternatives for a person's preference in doing or delivering works in the organisations. Therefore, in TRA assumption, the intention reflects a decision that the person makes about whether to use ICT or not via his or her mental thinking of method of accomplishing tasks. Hence, a person's intention to use ICT refers to the concept of performing or not performing a particular behaviour. In TRA structural assumption, Ajzen and Fishbein (1980) contended that behaviour intention to predict a particular behaviour is a measure that corresponds to behavioural criterion because the intention has not changed prior to the performance of the behaviour. However, whether intention to use ICT will change when people actually use or experience it need a practical investigation of the theory, which will attempted in part II of the book to see reality.

It worth noting that while behavioural intention is a function of both attitudes towards a behaviour and subjective norms, behavioural intention represents people's motivation to engage in a particular behaviour with respect to the attitude object. Since, intention can be understood as a person's readiness or ambition to perform a given behaviour (Ajzen, 2006), one can confidently say

that with strong attitude but low intention, it may not be possible to build certain behavioural action towards adopting or using ICT in accomplishing works in organisations. People with low intention and negative attitudes towards technology as a new method of doing things may still prefer their manual ways. Hence, without high intention, it is difficult for people to take action based on their attitude. Hence, the use of technology and/or its rejection is the result of an intention in establishing behaviour; and this intention is influenced conjointly by the individual attitudes.

However, according to the theory, attitude towards certain act or behaviour is practically influenced by beliefs in relation to behavioural intention of a person. Thus, strong elements that form the attitudes are the beliefs. The beliefs of person here refer the information that he or she has about importance of ICT and the perception of an external evaluation about adopting such behaviour. Fishbein and Ajzen (1979) contend that intention determines the effective behaviour which results to the observable acts towards something. The TRA suggests that the proximal determinant of volitional behaviour is one's intention to engage in that behaviour.

Intentions represent a person's motivation in the sense of a person's conscious plan or decision to exert effort to enact the behaviour. Intentions and behaviour are held to be strongly related when measured at the same level of specificity in relation to the action, target, context, and time frame (Fishbein & Ajzen, 1975). In suggesting that behaviour is solely under the control of intention, the TRA restricts itself to volitional behaviours towards adoption and acceptance of ICT by individuals in an organisation. It means to say that behaviours requiring skills, resources, or opportunities not freely available are not considered to be within the domain of applicability of the TRA, or that they are likely to be poorly predicted by the TRA as far as ICT adoption, acceptance and its usage is concerned (Fishbein, 1993).

To sum up, according to (Ajzen & Fishbein, 1980) "attitude toward the behaviour and subjective norm determine intention to perform a certain behaviour, and intention is the immediate determinant of the action." The claim that attitudes function to evaluate psychological objects would appear to imply that individuals hold only one attitude towards a given object at any one time. Recent research has indicated that when certain attitudes change, the new attitude may override but not completely replace the old attitude. Wilson et al. (2000) suggests that a model of dual attitudes is a more realistic conceptualisation in that people can hold two different attitudes towards an object at any given time. The TRA makes it clear that any attempt to influence the action of an individual to change his or her attitude, norm, and behavioural intention towards technology must be directed at one's beliefs. Therefore, to change a person's attitude, it is necessary to know the primary beliefs on which the attitude is based with regards to ICT adoption and usage. Only then a message that provides information to change those beliefs will be appropriately constructed. In the same vein, a subjective norm can also be changed by attacking either the specific normative beliefs or the motivation to comply. Therefore, by changing the beliefs underlying either attitudes or subjective norms, behaviours can be changed towards technology acceptance and adoption (Petty & Cacioppo, 1986).

Subjective Norm

Subjective norms are seen as a combination of perceived expectations from relevant individuals or groups along with intentions to comply with these expectations. In other words, "the person's perception that most people who are important to him or her think he should or should not perform the behaviour in question," (Ajzen & Fishbein, 1975). Thus, social norm is significant in the model of behaviour. It usually occurs if a person believes that important people or others around

him, such as peers, family or society at large, support the behaviour. That is, if they have no negative attitude towards the behaviour or if they perceive the relevant action within their control.

So it can be said that people may be influenced to use or adopt ICT by the norms of or behaviour of others and sometimes in contrary to their individual personal attitudes towards technology (Collins, et al., 2003). Thus, attitude towards usage and adoption of technology to deliver works in organisation can be acquired through social learning, social comparison, or genetic factor. According to Miller (2005), subjective norms are the influence of people on one's perception of social environmental surroundings and how it affects or changes his or her behavioural intentions.

Therefore, "The beliefs of people, weighted by the importance one attributes to each of their opinions, will influence one's behavioural intention," (Miller, 2005). In other words, people's propensity to adopt, accept and use technology in an organisation might be influenced by their social environment and beliefs of others. On a practical ground, a person in an organisation may observe other colleagues who are avid ICT users and always encourages him or her to use it. The beliefs of these colleagues about the use or acceptance of ICT, weighted by the importance one attributes to each of their opinions, will influence his or her behavioural intention to adopt, accept and use ICT devices, which will lead to behaviour towards technology at large.

Actual Behaviour

Actual behaviour in TRA structural assumption refers to a single action of actual use of ICT to carry out works. The assumption here is that most of the time, people make a choice on performing certain action. In the TRA, behaviour theoretically contains four components complementing one another. For example, Ajzen & Fishbein (1980) expressed the view that behaviour contains "the action, the target at which the action is directed, the context in which it occurs, and the time at which it is performed" (p.39). Explaining this assumption in the context of ICT application in the public sector means that adoption of ICT is the behaviour target, using it is the action, accomplishing the managerial and professional works or tasks assigned through ICT is the context in which behaviour occurs and the period taken by the user to accomplish such work is the time element therein.

However, the actual use of ICT is a function of behavioural intention of the person who may be affected by one's interaction with it. Thus, over a period of time and/or following a series of experiences, the civil servants or employees in public sectors develop either favourable or unfavourable feelings associated with certain ICT interactions. These situational feelings or states in which he or she found him or herself may well form the basis of their behaviours towards their own self conceptualisation of the use of ICT as a means of enhancing their works or tasks and finally use it. Public servants may, therefore, experience a positive reaction or attitude towards ICT components that assist in the attainment of their personal goals, and/or negative reactions and attitudes towards the ICT components that in some way hinder the attainment of desirable outcomes. Thus, people evaluate ICT components as objects in relation to currently active goals. However, the life cycles of these goals are functions of beliefs and values and the influence of significant others. Hence, employees' attitudinal behaviours towards ICT usage which emerge through the interaction may have started through collaborating with peers, the administration of the project, and the influence of colleagues towards its conceptualisation.

DEFICIENCY OF THEORY OF REASONED ACTIONS

One's experiences lead to the formation of many different beliefs about ICT applications in accom-

plishing works. These beliefs may be the result of direct observation or one's own inference during applications. Some attitudes may be stable over time, others may exhibit frequent shifts. According to Fishbein and Ajzen (1975), a person's attitude towards an object is primarily determined by no more than five to seven beliefs that are salient at any given time. If Fishbein and Ajzen are very correct, the critics argue that there is no single precise measure of the beliefs that can determine an individual's attitudes, since number of salient beliefs will vary from person to person. However, Ajzen and Fishbein (2000) defended their stance by saying that an evaluative meaning of attitudes towards objects arises spontaneously and inevitably as we form beliefs about the given objects. Each belief associates the object with a certain attribute which is embedded in context, culture and one's memory. As earlier as 1980, Zajonc had argued that attitudes may be controlled by affective processes. This view has been supported by other research works conducted in 1998 (Verplanken, et al., 1998). The results of their work had shown that evaluative response times were less for those participants being asked how they *felt* as opposed to how they *thought* about attitudinal objects. It implied that the affective aspects underlying attitudes are more easily accessible in memory and play a larger role in the formation of attitudes than previously thought. Thus, to alter a person's belief system will happen over time.

Critical evaluation of the TRA structural components has raised some issues on inadequacy and insufficiency of these components in predicting directly behavioural intention in the model framework and the actual behaviour. One potential observation is that since the TRA was designed to focus on the voliational behaviour, other behaviours that are equally essential to human life are not addressed. For example, behaviours which are spontaneous, impulsive and habitual are excluded from the scope of the TRA (Bentler & Speckart, 1979; Langer, 1989). According to Hale et al. (2003), such behaviours are excluded their performance might not be voluntary or because engaging in the behaviours might not involve a conscious decision on the part of the action. In addition, Liska (1984) explicated that the TRA component structure does not cover the behaviours that might require special skills, unique opportunities or resources or the cooperation of others before they can be performed. For example, a person may not perform certain behaviour simply because he or she doesn't possess an adequate skill to do so or because of lack of opportunity to perform it. This point or observation is of significant value to policy inputs in the context of adoption and application of ICT in public sector. A person may choose not to use ICT to complete tasks or demand certain needs from authority due to lack of skills to handle the technology or because he was not given the opportunity to do so.

Other critical observations have also reflected that the TRA model assumed that attitudes and subjective norms are by no means having relationship with one another and that each will separately influence behavioural intentions. However, empirical studies have shown that both attitudes and subjectives are correlated both positively and negatively (Bearden & Crokett, 1981; Greene, et al, 1979; Park, 2000). This reflection is academically important to caution because it is possible that a person with positive subjective norms towards a volitional behaviour may also possess a positive attitude towards the volitional behaviour and likewise the negative as well.

In relation to technology adoption and application, a person with positive or negative attitude towards ICT will also develop positive or negative subjective norms towards using ICT. For instance, a person may hold a belief that "increasing his or her ICT usage in carrying out tasks will give his or her boss a good impression about him or her." Such a cognitive thinking is a behavioural belief that combines both positive attitude and subjective norms tied with performance of a volitional behaviour. Hence, beyond doubt, there is an element of correlation between subjective

norms and attitudes to behaviour but the strength of such correlation or relationship would need a step further from theoretical underpinning to a practical significance or reality. This poses TRA model components to some criticisms.

Similarly, Miniard and Cohen (1981) found that it is difficult to conceptually demarcate between attitudes and subjective norms because of the natures of beliefs that underlying human line of thoughts. They argue that the beliefs that produce one's attitude equally produce one's subjective norms leading to high correlation among them. One proposes remedy to treat the preferences of others as behavioural beliefs rather than normative. That is, using normative belief as a determinant of attitude rather than a separate factor that bears direct impact on intention (Eagly & Chaiken 1993; Park, 2000). In addition, some studies have also found that attitudes better predict intentions than does the subjective norms indicating a potential argument for indirect effect of norms on intention. However, the proponent of the TRA (Ajzen & Fisbehin, 1981b) still maintained the treating of normative and attitudinal components of the TRA model separately by arguing that even though empirical studies might have shown a correlation between the two variables, yet each of them is strongly related to intentions than to one another.

In another development, the deficiency of the TRA model was pointed out for lack of focus on target object by the works of some scholars such as Eagly and Chaiken (1993). For example, their study focused on voting behaviour using attitudes and subjective norms as determinants. They have used the TRA to address whether one votes or not without taking political parties, or candidates themselves into consideration. Political parties and candidates are the target objects which are not usually addressed by the TRA. However, it plays significant roles in the performance of actual behaviour. For example, a person's attitude towards the candidates and his or her affiliated party may make him to vote or not to vote (actual behaviour). Contextually, it would mean that nature of ICT features and its configurations might influence a person's attitude towards using it or not to use it. Although, Ajzen and Fishbein asserted that any other variables not explicitly mentioned in the TRA model or framework are external variables, which can only influence volitional behaviour indirectly through attitudes and subjective norms of the original conceptual model yet, the critics argued that attitudes and subjective norms are not sufficient to predict behavioural intention nor enough to indirectly predict actual behaviour (Hale et al, 2003).

From the perspective of behavioural intention in the TRA structural model, four additional distinct variables have been suggested to be included for appropriate and maximum prediction of intention. These include: moral obligations, self-identity, affect and previous behaviour. Moral obligations, by definition, refer to what one believes to be right or wrong in relations to certain volitional behaviour. Warbuton and Terry (2000) had investigated the impact of moral obligations on behavioural intentions along with the TRA components and found out that it significantly related to behavioural intention. The works of other scholars, such as Presthold et al, (1987) and Conner and Armitage (1998), had earlier confirmed such relationship. The implication here worth mentioning with regards to ICT application is that the belief of a person with feeling that adopting ICT is a moral obligation can influence his or her behavioural intention towards using it. Another predictor of behavioural intention lacking in the TRA is self-identity variable or construct. It has been recognised and illustrated by some scholars such as, Hogg and Vaughan (2002); Terry and White (1999) that a person might involve or tend to involve in certain volitional behaviour simply because he or she was known with such behaviour. Empirical studies' results have a significant contribution of self-identity additional to the TRA variables for predicting behavioural intentions. Relating this to ICT applications in any given public organisation, the implication lies on the

needs to recognise the role played by self-identity as an added value to be considered to increase propensity of each individuals towards using ICT.

The previous behaviour has equally been introduced as additional variable to the TRA framework to predict behavioural intentions towards volitional behaviour. Previous interaction with the technology should match the eventual development of the attitudes a person holds regarding ICT components. Analogically, a person who interacts with elements of ICT applications to accomplish works in organisation may have based his or her attitudes towards the experience in the past interactions. These may include formal learning situations which incorporate information communication technology (ICT) as well as the abundance of such technologies available on a daily basis through mass media. The results have shown a positive and direct relationship between them (Bagozi, 1981; Bakar, Morrison, Carter & Verdon 1996; Mullen, et al. 1987). For example, Mullen, et al. (1987) found that previous behaviour such as consumption of unhealthy food, smoking and exercise were significantly predicted in behavioural intentions to engage in similar behaviours at another point in time. Similarly, a person that has previously used ICT to accomplish certain tasks before will tend to use it in another work, later. Thus, the significant implication of this prior behaviour to ICT application in practice is to encourage and/or convince a person to have the taste of using ICT for carrying out works. However, first impression carries a huge weightage in order to convince the person's intention to continue to use it further. In other words, ICT devices have to be made simple and users friendly for accomplishing tasks much more than expectations. If a person has a bad experience or taste of using ICT components previously to do work, then intention to use it again will be very weak, if not totally rejected, no matter how strong the power of the push factors such attitude and subjective norms are! However, it has been argued that past behaviour might be a residue of both subjective norms and attitudes by Ajzen (1991) and Conner and Amitage (1998).

In addition, other eminent scholars have also refuted and lamented that past behaviour might be influenced by a person's perceived moral obligation and self-identity due to close or proximity relationship between them. Relating this view to ICT adoption and application in public sector, it means if a person has used ICT to accomplish his or her tasks for the first time on the basis of the feeling of moral obligation; using ICT in the second time might be as a result of moral obligation as well. Although, this line of thought seems genuine too, however, the standing point of the argument in relation to moral obligation is very weak. Therefore, previous behaviour as a push factor to reuse ICT in completing one's tasks in any given public organisations is still held because such intention to repeat the behaviour highly depends on the experience he or she has encountered in the first place rather than moral obligation.

At another point in time, the TRA has been criticised of non-inclusion of affect variable in its structural model components. By affect, scholars referred to some anticipated affective outcomes that drag one's behavioural intention to do something (van der Pligt & Vries, 1998). A person that anticipates or has feeling of regret related a particular behaviour is less likely to perform the behaviour. For example, Hale et al (2003) expressed the view that "if a person anticipates feeling of regret over consuming alcohol, then he or she is less likely to intend to do so than a person who does not anticipate feelings of regret over the behaviour" (p.273). Similarly, in the public sector organisations, if a person anticipates feelings of regret over using ICT to accomplishing works such as eyes problems, neck pain of long standing or sitting in front of the PC, he or she is less likely to intend to use ICT devices to carry out the tasks. The policy input and implication here for both policy-makers and ICT developers is that a precautionary measure is needed to make users less anticipates regrets. This could be done and achieved at an early stage of design and feature configuration of the ICT devices especially PC, Laptop etc to be coated with strong screen-saver that has zero effect reflection of lights on people sights. Taking this theoretical argument further, Hale et al (2003) asserted that "the impact of the anticipated affect may depend on the perceived salience of the anticipated negative affect" (p.273). For the policy-makers, the implication of the salience of an anticipated negative impact is to make the cost of violation or non-compliance with the use of ICT in carrying out works higher (feelings of regret) than the cost of compliance. For example, a person should be made to realise the severe negative impact of not using ICT to accomplish works such as less productivity, propensity of errors through manual approach and time consuming, etc. Thinking along this line of thoughts, policy-makers might put in place policy of pay according to quantity and quality of the work. The civil servants or employees who attain high quality productivities through the use of ICT are rewarded with more pays (i.e., less costs), while those with low productivities and poor qualities due to non-use of ICT are less paid (i.e., costs to them despite their vigorous efforts).

CHAPTER SUMMARY

The theory of reasoned actions (TRA) has resulted in a useful conceptual framework which has, at its centre, the roles of beliefs, attitudes, norms, and intentions as crucial indicators of particular behaviours. Reasoned action is best described as a process by which an individual arrives at a behavioural intention as well as actual behaviour towards certain act. We noted in the theory that behavioural intentions are thought to result from beliefs about performing the behaviour. However, behavioural intention and norms that people hold about performing certain behaviour are influenced by a range of background factors such as personality, mood, values, education, ethnicity, and gender.

The central premise of this theory concerns the group of effects that start with the development of behavioural elements of attitude and evaluative beliefs, which eventually influence the formation of an attitude towards the behaviour as well as the subjective norm that influences intention (to behave) and the actual behaviour itself. Individuals who undergo these processes in tendam with performing a given behaviour are said to have engaged in reasoned actions (Ajzen & Fishbein, 2005). While it is understood that shortcuts can be made in the process, it is also ascertained that over certain periods of time, attitudes, norms, perceptions of control and intentions are rehearsed and therefore become readily accessible to each individual. In this context, a previously formed attitude towards interacting with any technology such as ICT components for example, can be readily accessed without the need to debate on the perceived advantages and disadvantages of using it.

Thus, the TRA has helped us to understand a set of relationships between people's beliefs about application of information and communication technology (ICT) in relations to attitude, norms, intention and behaviour. In the context of ICT application in public sector, an individual behaviour refers to choice to accept or reject or choice to use and not to use ICT to accomplish his or her work, which is determined by a person's intention. However, such intention is a function of the person's attitude towards the use of ICT as well as perceived social influence of the people who are important to him or her. However, it should be noted that other key external variables not explicitly represented in the theoretical model of TRA are demographic factors or personal traits, the characteristics of the behavioural target itself as discussed earlier, which may also influence a person's formational beliefs about ICT application in carrying out works in organisations. As such, the originators (Fishbein & Ajzen, 1981) of the theory assert that these external variables can only impact behavioural intention towards a given behaviour (i.e., acceptance, and use of ICT in accomplishing works) indirectly.

So the sole objective of TRA lies in helping us to predict and understand an individual's actual behaviour towards ICT application by taking into consideration the effect of personal feelings or attitude and perceived social pressure or subjective norm. As such, this theory reflects why people could use ICT or not to use and what likely determines their choice and how external factors could influence their decision as to adopt, accept or reject and use ICT in public organisations. It is therefore appropriate to conclude that TRA is a generalised model that helps to understand the determinants of people's behaviour, especially under a circumstance where they can exert their own choices that are driven by intentions that emerge through certain beliefs about the attitudinal objects. Finally, although the TRA has significantly contributed to understanding of attitude-behaviour issues in human daily activities, yet it has some limitations especially in behaviours that are non-volitional in nature. This paves way for other theories (i.e., extension of the TRA) that would be addressed in the next few chapters of the book.

REFERENCES

Ajzen, I. (1991). The theory of planned behavior. *Organizational Behavior and Human Decision Processes*, *50*(2), 179–211. doi:10.1016/0749-5978(91)90020-T

Ajzen, I., & Fishbein, M. (1980). *Understanding attitudes and predicting social behavior*. Englewood Cliffs, NJ: Prentice-Hall.

Ajzen, I., & Fishbein, M. (2005). The influence of attitudes on behaviour. In D. Albarracin., B.T. Johnson & M.P. Zanna (Eds.), The Handbook of Attitudes (pp. 173-221). Mahwah, NJ: Erlbaum.

Bagozi, R. P. (1981). Attitudes, intention and behaviour: A test of some key hyphotheses. *Journal of Personality and Social Psychology, 41*(4), 607–627. doi:10.1037/0022-3514.41.4.607

Baker, S. A., Morrison, D. M., Carter, W. B., & Verdon, M. S. (1996). Using the theory of reasoned action (TRA) to understand the decision to use condoms in an STD clinic population. *Health Education Quarterly, 23*(4), 528–542. doi:10.1177/109019819602300411 PMID:8910029

Bearden, W. O., & Crokett, M. (1981). Self-monitoring, norms and attitudes as influences on consumer complaining. *Journal of Business Research, 9*(3), 255–266. doi:10.1016/0148-2963(81)90020-5

Bentler, P. M., & Speckart, G. (1979). Models of attitude-behaviour relations. *Psychological Review, 86*(5), 425–464. doi:10.1037/0033-295X.86.5.452

Collins, C., Buhalis, D., & Peters, M. (2003). Enhancing SMTEs business performance through the Internet and eLearning Platforms. Centre for eTourism Research (CeTR): School of Management, University of Surrey.

Conner, M., & Armitage, C. J. (1998). Extending the theory of planned behaviour: A review and avenues for further research. *Journal of Applied Social Psychology, 28*(15), 1429–1464. doi:10.1111/j.1559-1816.1998.tb01685.x

Dias, G. A. (2002). Periódicos eletrônicos: Considerações relativas à aceitação desterecurso pelos usuários. *Ciência da Informação, Brasília, 31*(3), 18–25.

Droba, D. D. (1974). The nature of attitudes. *The Journal of Social Psychology, 4*(4), 444–463. doi:10.1080/00224545.1933.9919338

Eagly, A. H., & Chaiken, S. (1993). *The Pscyhology of Attitudes*. Fort Worth, TX: Harcourt Brace Jovanovich.

Ferguson, S., & Mellow, P. (2004). Whakahihiko te hinengaro: Lessons from a preshool te reo e-learning resource. *Computers in New Zealand Schools, 16*(2), 41–44.

Fishbein, M. (1993). Introduction. In D. J. Terry, C. Gallois, & M. McCamish (Eds.), *The Theory of Reasoned Action: Its Application to AIDS-Preventive Behaviour* (pp. xv–xxv). Pergamon.

Fishbein, M., & Ajzen, I. (1975). *Belief, attitude, intention, and behavior: An introduction to theory and research*. Reading, MA: Addison-Wesley.

Fishbein, M., & Ajzen, I. (1979). *Belief, attitude, intention, and behaviour: an introduction to theory and research*. Boston, MA: Addison-Wesley.

Fishbein, M., & Ajzen, I. (1981). Attitudes and voting behavior: An application of the theory of reasoned action. In G. M. Stephenson & J. M. Davis (Eds.), *Progress in Applied Social Psychology*. London: Wiley.

Greene, K., Hale, J. L., & Rubin, D. L. (1979). A test of theory of reasoned action in the context of use and AIDS. *Communication Reports, 10*(1), 21–33. doi:10.1080/08934219709367656

Hale, J. L., Householder, B. J., & Greene, K. L. (2003). The theory of reasoned action. In J. P. Dillard & M. Pfau (Eds.), *The persuasion handbook: Developments in theory and practice*. Sage.

Hogg, M., & Vaughan, G. (2002). *Social Psychology* (3rd ed.). London: Person-Prentice Hall.

Langer, E. J. (1989). *Mindfulness reading*. Reading, MA: Merloyd Lawrence Books.

Liska, A. E. (1984). A critical examination of the causal structure of the Fishbein-Ajzen model. *Social Psychology Quarterly, 47*, 61–74. doi:10.2307/3033889

McShane, S., & Glinow, M. V. (2008). *Organizational behaviour: Emerging realities for the workplace revolution* (4th ed.). New York: McGraw-Hill/Irwin.

Miller, K. (2005). *Communications theories: Perspectives, processes, and contexts.* New York: McGraw-Hill.

Miniard, P. W., & Cohen, J. B. (1981). An examination of the Fishbein-Ajzen behavioural intentions model's concepts and measures. *Journal of Experimental Social Psychology, 17*(3), 309–399. doi:10.1016/0022-1031(81)90031-7

Mullen, P. H., Hersey, J. C., & Iverson, D. C. (1987). Health behaviour models compared. *Social Science & Medicine, 24*(11), 973–983. doi:10.1016/0277-9536(87)90291-7 PMID:3616691

Oliveira, R. S. Jr. (2006). Utilização do modelo TAM na avaliação da aceitaçãode sistemas ERP. Rio de Janeiro. *IBMEC, 2006,* 119f.

Park, S. H. (2000). Relationship among attitudes and subjective norms: Testing the theory of reasoned action across cultures. *Communication Studies, 51*(2), 162–175. doi:10.1080/10510970009388516

Peak, H. (1955). Attitude and motivation. In M. R., Jones (Ed.), Nebraska symposium on motivation. Lincoln, NE: University of Nebraska Press.

Petty, R. E., & Cacioppo, J. T. (1986). In L. Berkowitz (Ed.), *The elaboration likelihood model of persuasion.* New York: Academic Press.

Prestholdt, P. H., Lane, I. M., & Mathews, R. C. (1987). Nurse turnover as reasoned action: Development of a process model. *The Journal of Applied Psychology, 72*(2), 221–227. doi:10.1037/0021-9010.72.2.221 PMID:3583978

Sheppard, B. H., Hartwick, J., & Warshaw, P. R. (1988). The theory of reasoned action: A meta-analysis of past research with recommendations for modifications and future research. *The Journal of Consumer Research, 15*(3), 325–343. doi:10.1086/209170

Terry, D. J., Hogg, M. A., & White, K. M. (1999). The theory of planned Behaviour: Self-identity, social identity and group norms. *The British Journal of Social Psychology, 38*(3), 225–244. doi:10.1348/014466699164149 PMID:10520477

Tonglet, M., Phillips, P. S., & Bates, M. P. (2004). Determining the drivers for householder pro-environmental behaviour: Waste minimisation compared to recycling. *Resources, Conservation and Recycling, 42*(1), 27–48. doi:10.1016/j.resconrec.2004.02.001

van der Pligt, J., & de Vries, N. K. (1998). Expectancy-value models of health behaviours: The role of salience and anticipated affect. *Psychology & Health, 13*(2), 289–305. doi:10.1080/08870449808406752

Verplanken, B., Hofstee, G., & Janssen, H. J. W. (1998). Effects of introspecting about reasons: Inferring attitudes from accessible thoughts. *European Journal of Social Psychology, 28,* 23–35. doi:10.1002/(SICI)1099-0992(199801/02)28:1<23::AID-EJSP843>3.0.CO;2-Z

Warbuton, J., & Terry, D. J. (2000). Volunteer decision making by older people: A test of a revised theory of planned behaviour. *Basic and Applied Social Psychology, 22*(3), 245–257. doi:10.1207/S15324834BASP2203_11

Wilson, T. D., Lindsey, S., & Schooler, T. Y. (2000). A model of dual attitudes. *Psychological Review, 107*(1), 101–126. doi:10.1037/0033-295X.107.1.101 PMID:10687404

Zajonc, R. B. (1980). Feeling and thinking: Preferences need no inferences. *The American Psychologist, 35*(2), 151–175. doi:10.1037/0003-066X.35.2.151

KEY TERMS AND DEFINITIONS

Action: What a person consciously does or will do and/or may be characterized by physical or mental activity.

Attitude: Tendency to respond towards something or situation positively or negatively. In other words, it influences individual choice about something or certain act.

Behaviour: Reaction or response made by person or any organism to situations and/or circumstances.

Norms: Standards of acceptable behaviour or guideline about what is considered as normal behaviour in society.

Technology Use: The use of a system to perform certain specific function for the users.

Technology: A tool or branch of knowledge and skill that can be used as means to get something done or used to achieve certain objective pertinent to human life, society, and environment at large.

Volitional Act: Something done by one's will or voluntarily done without force.

Chapter 7
The Theory of Planned Behaviour and its Relation to ICT Adoption

ABSTRACT

Due to practical limitation found in the Theory of Reasoned Action (TRA) such as an inability to cater to non-volitional behaviour towards performing certain actions, the Theory of Planned Behaviour (TPB) was developed in 1985. The main purpose of TPB was to improve the predictive power of TRA to be more applicable to any kinds of behavioural attitude and intention to involve in all type behavioural acts. Findings reflect the needs to carry out some elicitation study on antecedents of attitude, subjective norms, and even perceived behavioural control of the model. This chapter addresses the external influence such as self-efficacy and facilitating condition used as the determinants of perceive behavioural control. As such, attempts were made to pragmatically utilise the theory in research settings by many scholars as well as in this present book.

INTRODUCTION

Theory of Planned Behaviour (TPB) was developed by Icek Ajzen (1985) to improve the predictive power of the earlier theory known as Theory of Reasoned Action (TRA) discussed in Chapter six of this book. Just like TRA, the central focus of discussion in the theory of planned behaviour is on the relationship between attitudes and human behaviour. Theory of planned behaviour is considered to be one of the most predictive theories of actual behaviour available in academic literatures today. Its predictive capacity lies in the addition of perceived behavioural control introduced by Ajzen as compared to TRA. The theory has been applied to many empirical studies on the relationship between beliefs, attitudes, behavioural intentions and the actual behaviour in different fields and disciplines, which widely include, among others, public relations, campaigns, health care and voting behaviour in politics. In the current literature, application of TPB had just begun to appear on the literature about the link between human attitudes and intentions towards usage or interaction with information communication technology (ICT) to accomplish tasks in the public sector.

DOI: 10.4018/978-1-4666-6579-8.ch007

LIMITATION OF TRA AND DEVELOPMENT OF TPB

According to Fishbein and Ajzen (1975), the TRA was grounded in many other vital theories of attitudes such as learning theories, consistency theories, attribution theories and expectancy value theories. The TRA, as explained earlier Chapter one, holds that when a person positively evaluates a behaviour (i.e., attitude) and also thinks that the significant others expect him or her to perform such behaviour (i.e., subjective norm), it will result to his or her higher intention or motivation to do so. Based on this theoretical underpinning amongst the TRA's component constructs, attitudes, subjective norms, intentions and subsequence behaviour, many empirical studies have been conducted to establish and confirm a set of relationships among them (Sheppard, 1998).

However, the results of some empirical studies have also shown a contrary argument against the relationship between behavioural intention and the actual behaviour claimed in TRA's underlined philosophy. This contradictory argument marks a new turning point of reference to re-examine the component variables in TRA. It was later discovered that behavioural intention does not always influence actual behaviour, especially behaviour that a person has no complete control over it.

On the basis of this circumstantial limitation, Ajzen (1985) introduced the Theory of Planned Behaviour (TPB) by adding another component variable known as "perceived behavioural control" (PBC). Ajzen (1985, p.36) has clearly pointed out the difference between the TRA and TPB in his own word by saying: "the two theories are identical when the subjective probability of success and the degree of control of internal and external factors reach their maximum values: When subjective probabilities of success and actual control are less than perfect, however, we enter the domain of Planned Behaviour." Hence, the theory of planned behaviour is an extension of the original theory of reasoned action purposively designed to overcome the deficiency in the predictive capacity of attitudes, subjective norm, and behavioural intention on actual non-volitional behaviour as shown in Figure 1.

Figure 1. Theory of planned behaviour
Ajzen (1991, p.182).

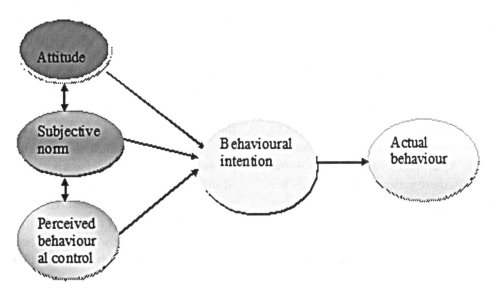

ASSUMPTION, CONCEPTUAL COMPONENTS IN TPB, AND RELATIONS TO ICT ADOPTION

Behavioural Beliefs

By definition, behavioural beliefs in TPB refer to an individual's belief in outcomes of a particular behaviour. Thus, behavioural beliefs are based on the subjective probability that a given behaviour will produce a given outcome. It means that behavioural beliefs link the behaviour of interest (usage of ICT) to expected outcomes (accomplishing one's task more successfully). In other words, a person can hold many behavioural beliefs with respect to any given behaviour in question. However, only a relatively small number are readily accessible at a given moment. Thus, it is assumed that these minimal accessible beliefs in conjunctions with the subjective values of the expected outcomes will determine the prevailing one's attitude towards such behaviour. In other words, the evaluation of each outcome of the behaviour contributes to the attitude in direct proportion to the person's subjective probability that the behaviour produces the outcome.

Behavioural beliefs encompass a wide range of salient beliefs relating to normative beliefs, which held up in subjective norms of the TPB theory such as beliefs in the views of significant others surrounding you (their beliefs in using ICT to complete works). It also embraces salient control beliefs which focus on a belief held by a person in certain factors that may facilitate or object the performance of a given behaviour in relations to perceived control of the TPB's component model. According to Ajzen and Fishbein, (2000) and Higgins (1996), these various salient beliefs are called accessible beliefs. Thus, the TPB holds that individuals' salient behavioural beliefs determine their attitudes towards a given behaviour such as using ICT to do jobs. However, in practice, it is pertinent to identify the set of beliefs that are salient in a given population (Ajzen & Fishbein, 1980, p.68). This will be addressed in the part two of this book.

Normative Beliefs

Normative beliefs in TPB focus on the extent to which important people around a person think he or she should or should not perform a particular behaviour. However, it has to do with level of one's compliance to the wish of others as well. In other words, the influence of others on the extent to which people or colleagues think a civil servant should adopt, use or should not use ICT or adopt it to accomplish a given task will also depend on the level of the willingness of the person to comply or wish to behave consistently with other people's thinking. Hence, dealing with normative beliefs component of TPB is indirectly called for measuring motivation to comply with the prescriptions of important others as well.

Therefore, it worthy to note that normative belief variable in TPB is conditioned by a combined force between the influence of important others and the person's motivation to comply with such important people's prescription, which generally results to a measure that predicts subjective norms. At this juncture, a reader might notice that normative beliefs perform two distinctive functions. The first part is the prediction of other variables such as subjective norms, intention to use ICT to accomplish works, and the actual usage of the ICT itself (actual behaviour). The second function, it sheds light on where intervention should be focused. Hence, effort should be focused on normative beliefs about ICT as a potential predictor of subjective norms rather than beliefs which are not widely spread among the civil servants about the significance of ICT application in public sector for accomplishing works. Evidence has been drawn from social psychology about importance of normative variables. For example, a research conducted by LeBon (1995) has shown that people in a crowd were strongly affected by the beliefs they hold, emotions as well as the behaviours of others around them.

However, there exists a controversy as to whether normative beliefs are really different from behavioural beliefs, which measures the consequences of a particular behaviour as mentioned earlier. The nexus of the argument emerges from level of demarcation between attitudes and subjective norms. This is because normative beliefs component in the TPB are assumed to predict subjective norms, while behavioural beliefs are presumed to determine the attitudes. As such, some argue that normative beliefs and behavioural beliefs are more or less same construct with different names (Miniard & Cohen, 1981). For example, let us consider the following two beliefs in relation to ICT adoption and usage in public sector: "my boss thinks I should use ICT to accomplish a given task" and "if I do not use ICT to accomplish, my task my boss will disagree with me." According to the theory of reasoned action, the former belief is a normative belief (it is a belief about what my boss thinks I should do) whereas the latter belief is a behavioural belief (it is a belief about a consequence arising from my boss's likely reaction to my behaviour). Yet, it could be argued that the difference between the two beliefs is more on the issue of the wording and sentence structure than about the content. If this is so, then the distinction between the two types of beliefs seems to be artificial and should be discarded according to Miniard and Cohen (1981). If the argument of Miniard and Cohen (1981) about normative beliefs and behavioural beliefs are really correct and can be proved to be just ordinary different names for the same construct, it would be a strong allegation against the distinction between attitudes and subjective norm components in the theories of behaviour, particularly the theory of reasoned action. In fact such argument has a big implication as a pathway

to undermine the theory of reasoned action (TRA). But recent research works and written articles have empirically demonstrated the line of distinction between the two constructs. In fact, the distinction is widely accepted and normative beliefs have an important place in theories of behaviour and behaviour change (Trafimow 1994; Trafimow & Duran, 1998; Trafimow, 2000; Trafimow & Fishbein, 1994; 1995).

Subjective Norms

According to Ajzen (1985), subjective norms component in the TPB model refers to a perceived social pressure exerted on a person to either perform or not to perform certain behaviour. Ajzen (1991) has analogously used expectancy-value model of attitude to illustrate subjective norms in relations to the total set of accessible normative beliefs in relations to expectations of important referents that we have explained earlier. He concluded that the strength of each normative belief is weighted by the amount of motivating elements to comply with the referent others.

In other word, subjective norms are directly proportional to both normative beliefs held by a person and the motivation to comply. Mathematically, Ajzen contends that:

$$SN \alpha \ \Sigma n_i m_i$$

where SN denotes subjective norms, n_i refers to strength of normative beliefs and m_i refers to motivation to comply (Ajzen, 1991; Hale et al, 2003) as in Figure 2. In relation to the use of ICT to performance a given task, it means that the normative beliefs of a person must be very strong with supporting facilities needed and technical know-how that can motivate the officer to comply.

The fact is that when a person forms an intention to use ICT to accomplish his or her works, constraints such as limited ability, environmental limits and perhaps unconscious habits might

Figure 2. Full model of theory of planned behaviour

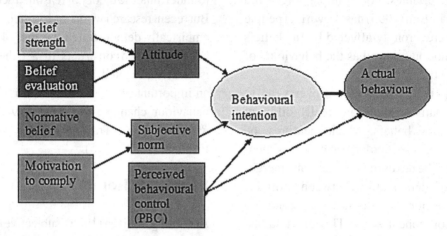

limit the propensity to act or perform the actual behaviour. This point has been seen as fundamental limitation in TRA and the TPB was used to resolve the issue via the introduction of perceived behavioural control (PBC) discussed in the next section.

ORIGIN OF PERCEIVED BEHAVIOURAL CONTROL

The concept of perceived behavioural control was originally derived from self-efficacy theory. Earlier, Bandura (1977) had proposed the concept of self-efficacy in social cognitive theory. Bandura believes that some expectations such as motivation, performance and/or feelings of frustration about certain objects determine the effect and behavioural reaction towards the object. Bandura (1986) categorises expectations into two distinctive perspectives, which are: self-efficacy and outcome expectancy. According to Bandura (1986), self-efficacy is a conviction that a person will be able to execute certain behaviour required to produce a given outcome successfully. In his explanation, outcomes expectancy is driven by the notion that a given behaviour will produce a

certain outcome based one's own self-efficacy. Hence, self-efficacy becomes a prerequisite for behavioural change.

With this theoretical understanding put forward by Bandura (1986) thesis, some empirical studies have been conducted to confirm the hypothetical assumptions of the theory and the results have shown that a person's behaviour was strongly influenced by his or her confidence in the ability to perform such behaviour (Bandura, et al. 1980). From this understanding, it becomes obvious that perceived behavioural control (PBC) component in TPB model is a derivative of self-efficacy and outcome expectancy since the major focus of PBC is a perception on one's ability to perform a given behaviour in question. The next section discusses the PBC in details.

Perceived Behavioural Control and Its Controversy in Literature

Perceived behavioural control is defined as "one's perception of how easy or difficult it is to perform a behaviour" (see Eagly & chaiken 1993, p.185). Perceived behavioural control variable in TPB captures a person's perception on his or her ability to perform a given behaviour. According to

Ajzen (1991), perceived behavioural control is a product of all accessible control beliefs. Therefore, the strength of each control beliefs is directly related to the perceived power of the control factor. Mathematically, this set of relationships has been represented by Ajzen (1991) through the following equation for better understanding:

$$PBC \ \alpha \ \Sigma c_i p_i$$

where c_i denotes the strength of each control belief and p_i refers to perceived power of the control factor in the equation. Relating this significant elements of perceive control beliefs and control factor to adoption of ICT applications in public sector indicates that even though a person may think that using of IT component devices to do work will produce positively valued outcomes, yet he or she will only be motivated to use them in relations to the extent that he or she is confident in his or her ability to operate it successfully.

In a research conducted by Eagly and Chaiken (1993, p.189), the authors had conclusively pointed out that TPB has successfully addressed, "the domains in which TRA is less appropriate." However, there exist some controversial issues relating to clear distinctions between the underlined meaning of PBC and self-efficacy discussed by Bandura et al. (1980). The line of argument lies in both conceptual definition and operationalization issues. For example, Ajzen and Madden (1986) had defined PBC as "a person's belief as to how easy or difficult performance of the behaviour is likely to be." Relating this issue to ICT adoption, PBC was aimed at reflecting perception of an officer or staff who is supposed to complete a task through the use of ICT devices on factors that are both internal such as knowledge, skills, will-power as well as external factors such as time, availability and the cooperation from other individual colleagues that will affect performance of the given behaviour. It seems there was a mixed up of understanding about the aim of PBC in this

context when Sparks, Guthrie, and Sheperd (1997) lamented that Ajzen's earlier definition of PBC included items that measure perceived control over the behaviour or included items that measure the behaviour assumed to be under the control of the actor (Ajzen, 2002a).

The above raises the question of whether PBC should be measured as a uni-dimensional or multi-dimensional construct. Although, most of the recent studies on attitude-behaviour theories have conclusively established the multidimensional construct of PBC (Trafimnow, et al, 2002), however researchers such as Leach, Hennesy, and Fishbein (2001) have sceptically asked if PBC is not a complementary part of attitude in terms of its operational definition of perceived difficulty. Other researchers even doubt the possibility of differentiating PBC from intention especially when measured in terms of its conceptual proximity to self-efficacy (see: Rhodes & Courneya, 2003b). However, both Ajzen (2002a) and Trafimow et al (2002) have concluded from a review of several studies that PBC has been ideally understood as unitary, higher order concept that consists of two interrelated components of self-efficacy and control over behaviour.

On the issues of causal relationship between PBC and intention to perform a given behaviour, Hale et al (2003) had argued that the TPB assumes a positive relation between PBC and intentions. However, the assumption may not be necessarily materialised in reality, especially for behaviours which are negative in nature. They have related this argument with a scenario where "if a male is negatively disposed towards condom use, then even if he believes that condom use is completely under his control, the individual might not intend to use a condom during sex" (p. 280). Analogically, if a person is negatively disposed towards ICT use in accomplishing a task, even though if he or she believes that ICT use is under his control, he might not intend to use ICT to carry out works perhaps due to other reasons best known to him or her. In the same line of argument here,

Hale et al (2003) asserted that there could be other interacting variables with perceived behavioural control such as moral obligations, self-identity, habit, and previous behaviour, which can influence intentions but not addressed by PBC. Although Fishbein and Ajzen considered them to be residues to TRA, however, their implications might be more serious for PBC in the TPB model than TRA attitude-behaviour model.

RESPONSE TO CLARIFY CONTROVERSIES BETWEEN PBC AND SELF-EFFICACY

While Bandura (1982, p.122) has defined self-efficacy as "judgments of how well one can execute courses of action required to deal with prospective situations," he contended that perceived self-efficacy refers to "people's beliefs about their capabilities to exercise control over their own level of functioning and over events that affect their lives" (Bandura, 1991, p.257). However, perceived self-efficacy differs greatly from perceived behavioural control, with focus on the ability to perform a given behaviour. Although, efficacy expectation according to Bandura (1998, p.624), is defined as "the conviction that one can successfully execute the behaviour required to produce certain outcomes" and, consistent with this definition, perceived self-efficacy is said to refer to "beliefs in one's capabilities to organise and execute the courses of action required to produce given levels of attainments." From this definition, the concern is clearly with control over the behaviour itself, not with control over outcomes or events. Hence, the major focus of self-efficacy is pivoted on coping behaviour in the context of behaviour modification (see: Bandura, 1977, Ajzen, 2002a). In other words, perceived behavioural control in the model captures a person's perceived ease or difficulty of performing the particular behaviour (Ajzen, 1988). According to Ajzen (2002a), perceived behavioural control

and self-efficacy are quite similar in that both are concerned with perceived ability to perform a behaviour or sequence of behaviours. Ajzen (2002a) admitted that the decision to use the perceived behavioural control in the theory of planned behaviour may have been misleading because PBC has sometimes been taken to refer to "the belief that performance of a behavior affords control over attainment of an outcome." However, Ajzen refuted that this is not the intended meaning of PBC. Perceived al control simply denotes "subjective degree of control over performance of the behavior itself." The distinction here is the same as that between efficacy expectations such as the perceived ability to perform a behavior as well as the outcome expectation in relations to the perceived likelihood that performing the behaviour will produce a given outcome as argued by Bandura, (1977). To avoid misunderstandings of this kind, the term perceived behavioural control should be read as perceived control over performance of behaviour. Ajzen (2002a) clearly refuted the argument further as quoted saying:

It is also shown that perceived control over performance of a behavior, though comprised of separable components that reflect beliefs about self-efficacy and about controllability, can nevertheless be considered a unitary latent variable in a hierarchical factor model.

It is further argued that there is no necessary correspondence between self-efficacy and internal control factors, or between controllability and external control factors. Self-efficacy and controllability can reflect internal as well as external factors and the extent to which they reflect one or the other is an empirical question. Finally, a case is made that measures of perceived behavioral control need to incorporate self-efficacy as well as controllability items that are carefully selected to ensure high internal consistency.

A deep reflection from the above quotation shows that if perceived behavioural control is understood as control over a given behaviour. It can help us account for variance in both intentions and actions. In addition, it means that while self-efficacy expectations are not necessarily referred to as beliefs about internal control factors, controllability expectations have no basis in perceived external factors. Rather, self-efficacy and controllability do reflect a belief about existence of internal and external factors in perceived behavioural control if measured correctly.

A CALLED FOR EXTENSION OF TPB'S COMPONENT VARIABLES

Just like in TRA previously discussed in Chapter six of this book, additional distinct variables have been suggested to be included in TPB for appropriate and maximum prediction of intention in lieu of its close proximity to TRA. These include: moral obligations, self-identity, affect, and previous behaviour. Moral obligations, by definition, refer to what one believes to be right or wrong in relations to certain volitional behaviour. Warbuton and Terry (2000) had investigated the impact of moral obligations on behavioural intentions along with the TPB components and found out that it significantly related to behavioural intention. The works of other scholars such as Presthold et al way back in 1987; Conner and Armitage (1998); Armitage and Conner (2001) had earlier confirmed such relationship. The implication here worth mentioning with regards to ICT application is that the belief of a person with feeling that adopting ICT is a moral obligation can influence his or her behavioural intention towards using it. Another predictor of behavioural intention lacking in the TPB is self-identity variable or construct. It has been recognised and illustrated by some scholars such as, Hogg and Vaughan (2002); Terry and White (1999) that a person might involve or tend to get involved in certain volitional behaviour simply because he or she was known with such behaviour. Empirical studies' results have a sig-

nificant contribution of self-identity additional to the TPB variables for predicting behavioural intentions. Relating this to ICT applications in any given public organisation, the implication lies on the needs to recognise the role played by self-identity as an added value to be considered to increase propensity of each individuals towards using ICT.

The previous behaviour has equally been introduced as additional variable to the TPB framework to predict behavioural intentions towards volitional behaviour. Previous interaction with the technology should match the eventual development of the attitudes a person holds regarding ICT components. Analogically, a person who interacts with elements of ICT applications to accomplish works in organisation may have based his or her attitudes towards the experience in the past interactions. These may include formal learning situations which incorporate information communication technology (ICT) as well as the abundance of such technologies available on a daily basis through mass media. The results have shown a positive and direct relationship between them (Bagozi, 1981; Baker, et al. 1996; Mullen, et al. 1987). For example, Mullen, et al (1987) found that previous behaviour such as consumption of unhealthy food, smoking and exercise were significantly predicted behavioural intentions to engage in similar behaviours at another point in time. Similarly, a person that has previously used ICT to accomplish certain tasks before will tend to use it in another works later. Thus, the significant implication of this prior behaviour to ICT application in practice is to encourage and/or convince a person to have the taste of using ICT for carrying out works.

However, first impression carries a huge weight in order to convince the person's intention to continue to use it further. In other words, ICT devices have to be made simple and users friendly for accomplishing tasks much more than expectations. If a person has a bad experience or taste of using ICT components previously to do work, then intention to use it again will be very weak, if not totally rejected, no matter how strong the power of the push factors such attitude and subjective norms are! However, it has been argued that past behaviour might be a residue of both subjective norms and attitudes by Ajzen (1991) and Conner and Armitage (1998). In addition, other eminent scholars have also refuted and lamented that past behaviour might be influenced by a person's perceived moral obligation and self-identity due to close or proximity relationship between them. Relating this view to ICT adoption and application in public sector, it means if a person has used ICT to accomplish his or her tasks for the first time on the basis of the feeling of moral obligation; using ICT in the second time might be as a result of moral obligation as well. Although, this line of thought seems genuine too, however, the standing point of the argument in relation to moral obligation is very weak. Therefore, previous behaviour, as a push factor to reuse ICT in completing one's tasks in any given public organisations, is still held because such intention to repeat the behaviour highly depends on the experience he or she has encountered in the first place rather than moral obligation.

Additionally, the TPB has also been criticised of non-inclusion of affect variable in its structural model. According to scholars, affect refers to some anticipated affective outcomes that inspire a person's behavioural intention to do something (van der Pligt & Vries, 1998). When a person anticipates or expects certain form of regret relating to a particular behaviour, he or she is less likely to perform the behaviour. For example, Hale et al (2003) expressed that "if a person anticipates feeling of regret over consuming alcohol, then he or she is less likely to intend to do so than a person who does not anticipate feelings of regret over the behaviour" (p.273). Similarly, in the public sector organisations, if a person anticipates feelings of regret over using ICT to accomplishing works such as eyes problems, neck pain of long standing

or sitting in front of computer, the person is less likely to convince his mind to use ICT devices to carry out the tasks.

At this juncture, the policy implications for both policy-makers and ICT developers is that a precautionary measure is needed to make users less anticipate any form of regrets related to injury in using ICT. This could be done and achieved at an early stage of design and feature configuration of the ICT devices especially PC, Laptop etc to be coated with strong screen-saver that has zero effect reflection of lights on people's sights. Interestingly, Hale et al (2003) have taken this theoretical argument further, saying "the impact of the anticipated affect may depend on the perceived salience of the anticipated negative effect" (p.273). In this context, the policy-makers in public sector should make the cost of violation or non-compliance (feelings of regret) with the use of ICT in carrying out works higher than the cost of compliance. For example, a person should be made realise the severe negative impact of not using ICT to accomplish works in relations to less productivity, propensity of errors through manual approach and time consuming. Thinking along this line of thoughts, policy-makers might put in place policy of pay according to quantity and quality of the work. The civil servants or employees who attain high quality productivities through the use of ICT are rewarded with more pays as mentioned in Chapter 6.

Extension of TPB for Optimising Behavioural Prediction towards the Use of ICT

Recently, some researchers have seen avenues for extension in TPB components with additional variables to optimise attitude-behaviour prediction. Ajzen (2002a) himself has also admitted a possible extension of the TPB component variables. Researchers, such as Pedersen and Nysveen (2002), contend that attitude formation process "is believed to be similar for usefulness, ease of use, enjoyment and expressiveness in that the users perceive a service as instrumental in fulfilling intrinsic, extrinsic, and derived gratifications, and consequently develop a positive attitude towards using it" (p.15). In the light of this, additional variables, such as perceived expressiveness, perceived enjoyment, perceived ease of use and perceived usefulness have added to TPB as determinants of attitude to optimise its prediction of intention.

In addition, while external influence and interpersonal influence have been added to the original TPB framework as determinants of subjective norm, self-efficacy and facilitating conditions have been used as determinants of perceived behavioural control (PBC) of the original TPB in the literature (Pedersen & Nysveen, 2002). Amongst the rationales for inclusion of ease of use to the model is the work of Taylor and Harper (2001) that showed how younger users of mobile phone had perceived ease of using technology differently. The addition of perceived usefulness to the model followed the work of Thompson, et al (1999) to capture efficiency and effectiveness in relations to extrinsic motivation to do work through ICT devices. The rationales for inclusion of perceived enjoyment in the TPB model was based on a conception that the use of many ICT devices, such as mobile games, mobile video, chat, flirt services, are instrumentality for entertainments which are far more than just ease of use (Leung & Wei 1998, 2000; Venkatesh 2000).

Also, it has been argued that element of expressiveness is a condition to get access to symbolic and social capital using a service provided, especially to demonstrate participation in social networks. Boneva, et al (2001), have argued that expressiveness is a demonstration of emotional intimacy and sharing in communication, especially among female participants. Hence, ICT services that communicate expressiveness in this form are more likely to be appreciated by female users than male users. Thus, Pedersen and Nysveen (2002) asserted that "expressiveness is an instrumental

attribute of a communication service partly influencing usefulness and partly influencing attitudes directly," (p.15). Additionally, Leung and Wei (2000) have suggested that external influence in determining subjective norms is extremely important to convince young users of ICT because their subjective norms are developing and changing from time to time in relations to their frequent exposure to media or being directly approached by terminal vendors and operators.

Furthermore, it is believed that interpersonal influence plays a significant role in adoption of ICT and equally serves as a key element of developing norms in relations to expected use of ICT for accomplishing works. For example, Ling and Yttri (2002) concluded in their research work that interpersonal influence on subjective norms is an important element that explicates the adoption of messaging services among young users of mobile phone. It is more important than norm based alone and needs to be seen as determinant of subjective norms for predicting intention to use or adopt ICT. For example, Pedersen and Nysveen (2002) asserted that "young users may find text messaging instrumental in social coordination because all other members of their social network uses it, but still feel little social pressure towards using text messaging services as a norm," (p.17).

In the same vein, perceived behavioural control PBC has been seen to be a function of both self-efficacy and facilitating conditions in adoption of ICT. Self-efficacy needs to be included in the TPB model to capture the user's confidence that adoption of ICT will lead to expected outcome of accomplishing one's work based on the prior experience, skills and/or perhaps training on the technical know-how. Hence, users of ICT to accomplish tasks are believed to be among the more experienced and skillful ones (Ling 2001; Skog, 2002). More so, several conditions can affect, either negatively or positively, the avenue for using and adopting ICT in public sector to accomplish tasks. Thus, lack of effective facilitating conditions might negatively affect behavioural control on using ICT devices or at least reduce such control. These include, among other things, support, price, security issues, interconnectability, and compatibility that can affect continuity of the initial adoption and use of ICT to carry out one's works (Ambali, 2009; Carroll et al. 2002). Hence, on the basis of various observations about the TPB model, there is a need for re-specifications and extensions to optimise the attitude-behaviours of users towards ICT whether in private or public sectors at large.

CHAPTER SUMMARY

As has been earlier mentioned in the beginning of this chapter, the theory of planned behaviour (TPB) is a further extension of the theory of reasoned action (TRA) discussed in Chapter 1 of this book. The component variables in TPB are similar to TPB except with addition of perceived behavioural control (PBC). Just like the case in TRA, TPB further buttresses the explanations on how individual persons make behavioural decisions based on careful consideration of available information relating to a given behaviour. Basically, TPB model accounts for how attitudes cause behaviour which may be volitional or non-volitional in nature. Thus, while the TRA holds that the proximal determinant of volitional behaviour is one's intention to engage in a volitional behaviour, the TPB takes the case further to the performance of certain behaviours which are non-volitional. Non-volitional behaviours are those behaviours which may require skills, resources, and/or prerequisites before a person can perform them. Hence, performance of these types of behaviour is beyond the domain of applicability of the TRA model. The results of many studies have even shown poor predictions or impacts of the TRA on performance of non-volitional behaviours.

As reflected in the chapter, the power of TPB for predicting non-volitional behaviours lies in its addition of PBC variable to the other compo-

nents. The introduction of this variable serves as a turning point for dealing with uneasily perform or complex behaviours which may even require a person's capacity to handle several other behaviours before the *actual* behaviour in question. According to the TPB model, performance of any or actual behaviour is a function of both behavioural intention as well as perceived behavioural control. The chapter shows that PBC is the individual's perception of the extent to which performance of the behaviour is easy or difficult in accordance with Ajzen's view. Although the conceptual understanding of PBC in the theory of planned behaviour is similar to Bandura's concept of self-efficacy, control is seen as a continuum with easily executed behaviours at one end and behavioural goals demanding resources, opportunities, and specialised skills at the other.

As far as adoption and use of ICT in public sector to accomplish a given tasks is concerned, this issue of capability, skills, resources are paramount points for consideration. The fact is that a person's attitude may be positive to influence his or her intention to carry out the compulsory work using ICT but lack of necessary requirements to do so may become an impediment to using it. Therefore, perceived behavioural control suggests that in adopting and utilising of ICT to perform one's duties, is a crucial condition to be fulfilled. It means that inability to have control over the technology in performing the given tasks can prevent a person from using ICT. In addition, it also suggests that if intentions are held constant, usage of ICT to carry out tasks is more likely to take place as the gravity of PBC increases.

Applying the principle of compatibility, the relevant attitudes are those towards performance of the behaviour, assessed at a similar level of specificity to that used in the assessment of behaviour. The TPB also specifies subjective norms as the other determinant of intentions. As we had discussed in the chapter, subjective norms is a person's beliefs about whether others who are important to him or her think he or she should engage in the behaviour. Significant others are individuals whose preferences about a person's behaviour in this domain are important to him or her. Just like in TRA, subjective norms are assumed to address the social pressures on individuals to perform or not to perform a given behaviour.

Finally, the main message of TPB lies in the fact that PBC and intentions would have to interactively predict a behaviour whereby intentions would become stronger predictors of behaviour as PBC increased. However, the discussions in the chapter have shown some arguments where PBC is assumed to unilaterally influence a particular behaviour. According the chapter's findings, many other researchers have also called for extension and expansion of TPB with additional variables to further improve its predictive power on behaviour.

REFERENCES

Ajzen, I. (1985). From intentions to action: A theory of planned behaviour. In J. Kuhl & J. Beckman (Eds.), *Action control: From cognitions to behaviour*. New York: Springer. doi:10.1007/978-3-642-69746-3_2

Ajzen, I. (1988). *Attitudes, personality and behaviour*. Milton Keynes, UK: Open University Press.

Ajzen, I. (1991). The theory of planned behavior. *Organizational Behavior and Human Decision Processes*, *50*(2), 179–211. doi:10.1016/0749-5978(91)90020-T

Ajzen, I. (2002a). Perceived behavioural control, self-efficacy, locus of control, and the theory of planned behaviour. *Journal of Applied Social Psychology*, *32*(4), 665–683. doi:10.1111/j.1559-1816.2002.tb00236.x

Ajzen, I., & Fishbein, M. (1980). *Understanding attitudes and predicting social behaviour*. Englewood Cliffs, NJ: Prentice-Hall.

Ajzen, I., & Fishbein, M. (2000). Attitudes and the attitude-behaviour relation: Reasoned and automatic processes. *European Review of Social Psychology*, *11*(1), 1–33. doi:10.1080/14792779943000116

Ajzen, I., & Madden, T. J. (1986). Prediction of goal-directed behaviour: Attitudes, intention, and perceived behavioural control. *Journal of Experimental Social Psychology*, *22*(5), 453–474. doi:10.1016/0022-1031(86)90045-4

Ambali, A. R. (2009). E-government policy: Ground issues in e-filling system. *European Journal of Soil Science*, *11*(2), 249–266.

Armitage, C. J., & Conner, M. (2001). Self-efficacy of the theory of planned behaviour: A meta-analytic review. *The British Journal of Social Psychology*, *40*(4), 471–499. doi:10.1348/014466601164939 PMID:11795063

Bagozi, R. P. (1981). Attitudes, intention and behaviour: A test of some key hypotheses. *Journal of Personality and Social Psychology*, *41*(4), 607–627. doi:10.1037/0022-3514.41.4.607

Baker, S. A., Morrison, D. M., Carter, W. B., & Verdon, M. S. (1996). Using the theory of reasoned action (TRA) to understand the decision to use condoms in an STD clinic population. *Health Education Quarterly*, *23*(4), 528–542. doi:10.1177/109019819602300411 PMID:8910029

Bandura, A. (1977). Self-efficacy: Toward a unifying theory of behavioural change. *Psychological Review*, *84*(2), 122–147. doi:10.1037/0033-295X.84.2.191 PMID:847061

Bandura, A. (1986). *Social foundations of thought and action: A social cognitive theory*. Englewood Cliffs, NJ: Prentice-Hall.

Bandura, A. (1991, December). (1 99 1). Social cognitive theory of self-regulation. *Organizational Behavior and Human Decision Processes*, *50*(2), 248–287. doi:10.1016/0749-5978(91)90022-L

Bandura, A. (1998). Health promotion from the perspective of social cognitive theory. *Psychology & Health*, *13*(4), 623–649. doi:10.1080/08870449808407422

Boneva, B., Kraut, R., & Frohlich, D. (2001). Using e-mail for personal relationships: The difference gender makes. *The American Behavioral Scientist*, *45*(3), 530–549. doi:10.1177/00027640121957204

Carroll, J., Howard, S., Vetere, F., Peck, J., & Murphy, J. (2002). Just what do the youth of today want? Technology appropriation by young people. *Paper Presented at HICSS*, *35*(Jan), 7–10.

Conner, M., & Armitage, C. J. (1998). Extending the theory of planned behaviour: A review and avenues for further research. *Journal of Applied Social Psychology*, *28*(15), 1429–1464. doi:10.1111/j.1559-1816.1998.tb01685.x

Eagly, A. H., & Chaiken, S. (1993). *The Pscyhology of Attitudes*. Fort Worth, TX: Harcourt Brace Jovanovich.

Fishbein, M., & Ajzen, I. (1975). *Belief, attitude, intention, and behavior: An introduction to theory and research*. Reading, MA: Addison-Wesley.

Hale, J. L., Householder, B. J., & Greene, K. L. (2003). The theory of reasoned action. In J. P. Dillard & M. Pfau (Eds.), *The Persuasion Handbook: Developments in Theory and Practice*. Thousand Oaks, CA: Sage.

Higgins, D. L., O'Reilly, K., Tashima, N., Crain, C., Beeker, C., & Goldbaum, G. et al. (1996). Using formative research to lay the foundation for community-level HIV prevention efforts: The AIDS Community Demonstration Projects. *Public Health Reports*, *111*(Supplement), 28–35. PMID:8862154

Hogg, M., & Vaughan, G. (2002). *Social Psychology* (3rd ed.). London: Person-Prentice Hall.

LeBon. (1995). *The Crowd*. Ransaction Publishers.

Leung, L. (2001). College student motives for chatting on the ICQ. *New Media & Society*, *3*(4), 483–500. doi:10.1177/14614440122226209

Leung, L., & Wei, R. (1998). The gratifications of pager use: Sociability, information-seeking, entertainment, utility, and fashion and status. *Telematics and Informatics*, *15*(4), 253–264. doi:10.1016/S0736-5853(98)00016-1

Leung, L., & Wei, R. (2000). More than just talk on the move: Uses and gratifications of the cellular phone. *J&MC Quarterly*, *77*(2), 308–320. doi:10.1177/107769900007700206

Ling, R. (2001). *Adolescent girls and young adult men: Two sub-cultures of the mobile telephone*. Paper Presented at the InterMedia workshop on mobility. Oslo, Norway.

Ling, R., & Yttri, B. (2002). Hyper-coordination via mobile phone in Norway. In J. E. Katz & M. Aakhus (Eds.), *Perpetual Contact*. New York: Cambridge University Press.

Miniard, P. W., & Cohen, J. B. (1981). An examination of the Fishbein-Ajzen behavioural intentions model's concepts and measures. *Journal of Experimental Social Psychology*, *17*(3), 309–399. doi:10.1016/0022-1031(81)90031-7

Mullen, P. H., Hersey, J. C., & Iverson, D. C. (1987). Health behaviour models compared. *Social Science & Medicine*, *24*(11), 973–983. doi:10.1016/0277-9536(87)90291-7 PMID:3616691

Pedersen, P. E., & Nysveen, H. (2002). *Using the theory of planned behaviour to explain teenagers' adoption of text messaging services*. Working paper, Agder University College, Norway.

Prestholdt, P. H., Lane, I. M., & Mathews, R. C. (1987). Nurse turnover as reasoned action: Development of a process model. *The Journal of Applied Psychology*, *72*(2), 221–227. doi:10.1037/0021-9010.72.2.221 PMID:3583978

Rhodes, R. E., & Courneya, K. S. (2003b). Self-efficacy, controllability and intention in the theory of planned behaviour: Measurement redundancy or causal independence? *Psychology & Health*, *18*(1), 79–92. doi:10.1080/0887044031000080665

Sheppard, B. H., Hartwick, J., & Warshaw, P. R. (1988). The theory of reasoned action: A meta-analysis of past research with recommendations for modifications and future research. *The Journal of Consumer Research*, *15*(3), 325–343. doi:10.1086/209170

Skog, B. (2002). Mobiles and the Norwegian teen: identity, gender and class. In J. E. Katz & M. Aakhus (Eds.), *Perpetual Contact*. New York: Cambridge University Press.

Sparks, P., Guthrie, C. A., & Shepard, R. (1997). The dimensional structure of the perceived behavioural control construct. *Journal of Applied Social Psychology*, *27*(5), 418–438. doi:10.1111/j.1559-1816.1997.tb00639.x

Taylor, A. S., & Harper, R. (2001). *Talking activity: Young people and mobile phones*. Paper presented at the CHI 2001 Workshop on mobile communications. Seattle, WA.

Terry, D. J., Hogg, M. A., & White, K. M. (1999). The theory of planned Behaviour: Self-identity, social identity and group norms. *The British Journal of Social Psychology*, *38*(3), 225–244. doi:10.1348/014466699164149 PMID:10520477

Thompson, S. H., Lim, V. K. G., & Lai, R. Y. C. (1999). Intrinsic and extrinsic motivation in Internet usage. *Omega*, *27*(1), 25–37. doi:10.1016/S0305-0483(98)00028-0

Trafimow, D. (1994). Predicting intentions to use a condom from perceptions of normative pressure and confidence in those perceptions. *Journal of Applied Social Psychology*, *24*(24), 2151–2163. doi:10.1111/j.1559-1816.1994.tb02377.x

Trafimow, D. (2000). Habit as both a direct cause of intention to use a condom and as a moderator of the attitude-intention and subjective norm-intention relations. *Psychology & Health*, *15*(3), 383–393. doi:10.1080/08870440008402000

Trafimow, D., & Duran, A. (1998). Some tests of the distinction between attitude and perceived behavioural control. *The British Journal of Social Psychology*, *37*(1), 1–14. doi:10.1111/j.2044-8309.1998.tb01154.x PMID:9554085

Trafimow, D., & Fishbein, M. (1994). The moderating effect of behavior type on the subjective norm-behavior relationship. *The Journal of Social Psychology*, *134*(6), 755–763. doi:10.1080/0022 4545.1994.9923010

Trafimow, D., & Fishbein, M. (1995). Do people really distinguish between behavioral and normative beliefs? *The British Journal of Social Psychology*, *34*(3), 257–266. doi:10.1111/j.2044-8309.1995.tb01062.x

Trafimow, D., Sheeran, P., Conner, M., & Finlay, K. A. (2002). Evidence that perceived behavioural control is a multidimensional construct: Perceived control and perceived difficulty. *The British Journal of Social Psychology*, *1*(1), 101–121. doi:10.1348/014466602165081 PMID:11970777

van der Pligt, J., & de Vries, N. K. (1998). Expectancy-value models of health behaviours: The role of salience and anticipated affect. *Psychology & Health*, *13*(2), 289–305. doi:10.1080/08870449808406752

Venkatesh, V., & Morris, M. G. (2000). Why don't men ever stop to ask for directions? Gender, social influence, and their role in technology acceptance and usage behaviour. *Management Information Systems Quarterly, 24*(1), 115–139. doi:10.2307/3250981

Warbuton, J., & Terry, D. J. (2000). Volunteer decision making by older people: A test of a revised theory of planned behaviour. *Basic and Applied Social Psychology, 22*(3), 245–257. doi:10.1207/S15324834BASP2203_11

KEY TERMS AND DEFINITIONS

Adoption: The act of using something new or giving official acceptance or approval to something new.

Control Belief: Beliefs about the presence of factors that may facilitate or impede performance of the behaviour.

Motivation: Condition or reason for doing something or eager to act or do certain work and/or perform work.

Non-Volitional Behaviour: The action which is compulsory to be carried out by person.

Perceived Behavioural Control: People's perceptions of their ability to perform a given behaviour.

Predictive Power: Ability of one thing to influence the status or future state of other things.

Probability: A measure of the likelihood that an event will occur or an action will take place.

Chapter 8
Technology Acceptance Models (TAMS) and their Relations to ICT Adoption

ABSTRACT

The TPB might not be totally fit into technology acceptance in organizations unless certain elements are introduced. In the light of this, additional variables, such as perceived expressiveness, perceived enjoyment, perceived ease of use, and perceived usefulness have been introduced to TPB as determinants of attitude to optimise its prediction of intention-actual use behaviour towards technology to develop TAM. In other words, TAM model posits that if a user perceives that a given technology is useful, the person will hold a positive use-performance and strong intention based on his or her belief about it. Findings show that users are likely to accept application of technology when they perceive it easier for them to use, thereby inducing a positive attitude to their minds. However, some scholars have called for extension of TAM to meet the needs of different research settings, which has been discussed in other chapters of this book.

INTRODUCTION

Technology is changing the way people connect and communicate in the public sphere today. In the public sector today, technology allows people to work and coordinate together outside the traditional meeting and office spaces. Hence, the usual geographical distance constraints are decreasing and leading to a new avenue for progressive and dynamic interpersonal communications among people more particularly in the public sector. In addition, the adoption and use of information technology has gone far to enhance the way people

are teaching and learning. However, curiosity and imagination on user's acceptance of the new technology do catch attentions of policy-makers, researchers and academics in tandem with infiltration of ICT into workplaces, classrooms and homes. As such, ICT developers and software industries are also realising a clear distinction between creating technological devices and usage of them because lack of users' acceptance of these devices would result in huge losses to the industries.

Thus, Technology Acceptance Model (TAM) was developed by Davis to explain the underlined

DOI: 10.4018/978-1-4666-6579-8.ch008

phenomena regarding the technology usage behaviour-beliefs. Hence, TAM can be defined as information systems theory that attempts to model how users in organisations can accept and use technology to carry out certain tasks as opposed to traditional methods. As we shall see in the preceding sections of this chapter, TAM hypothesises that when users are supplied with new technological devices, a number of belief-factors relating to decision on how, when, and benefits that could be gained occupied their minds. The answers to these thoughts could lead to favourable usage of it or otherwise, it depends on the answers which could either be positives or negatives. The positive or negative answers are also based on the perceived usefulness and ease of a specific technology.

Therefore, in the context of ICT application and adoption, the beauty of any given theory or model in predicting and explaining human behaviour can be measured by the extent to which the components in the theory could account for a reasonable proportion of the variance in behavioural intention and actual usage of it. In other words, TAM model posits that if a user perceives that a given technology is useful, the person will hold a positive use-performance relationship based on his or her belief about it. Additionally, it is an obvious fact that users are likely to accept application of technology when they perceive it as easier to use thereby inducing a positive attitude and perception about it. More importantly about the model (TAM), the relationship between PU and PEOU is envisaged where PU mediates the effect of PEOU on attitude and intended use of technology. In other words, while PU has direct impacts on attitude and use, PEOU influences attitude and use indirectly through PU according to Davis. In the original TAM, users' acceptance has been coined along the willingness within the users to employ or adopt certain technology to perform a task. However, further researches and studies have reported the influence, and effect of objective characteristics of technology itself

and users' interactions with other users or people around him/her on the perceptions about information technologies. Such observations have been identified as limitations to original TAM and have given rise to many attempts to extend the model (see: TAM2 and TAM3).

LIMITATION OF THEORY OF PLANNED BEHAVIOUR AND THE EMERGENT OF TAM

The theory of planned behaviour (TPB) has substantially helped academics and practitioners to infer the nature and magnitude of relationship between attitude, intention and behaviour. However, the TPB was later realised by scholars that some additional elements are to be incorporated to its model for better prediction of attitude-behaviour issues. In fact, the originator of the TPB himself has admitted the needs for extension based on several simulation studies. In the context of human behaviour towards ICT adoption and use, one of the major limitations of TPB lies in inability of the theory to address the substantial matter of concerns in technology itself. The focus of TPB lies in human reactions towards an object rather than the object per se, whereas TAM deals with the object in question. It assumes that the nature of the object (ICT) itself would determine or warrant intention of a person to use it or not to use it. Since then, TAM has over the years received huge attention from theorists (Davis, et al, 1989) in information and communications technology to explain the underlined relationship between human intention and adoption or acceptance of ICT than even the theory of planned behaviour (Ajzen, 1985).

Thus, Davis (1996) has theoretically proposed TAM to explain how perceived features of technology itself could serve as major determinant elements that can predict intention to use and actual usage of a given technology. The major argument in TAM is that attitude towards technology affects use of it on the basis of two belief variables that can impact attitude, which are perceived ease of use and perceived usefulness of the technology. The details of these two belief variables regarding the technology would be addressed in the remaining sections of this chapter.

ORIGIN OF TECHNOLOGY ACCEPTANCE MODEL

According to (Louho, et al, 2006), "technology acceptance is about how people accept and adopt some technology to use," (p.15). It becomes obvious that the premise of technology acceptance theory is to examine what could encourage usage and/or impede acceptance and usage of technologies at large (Kripanont, 2007). The origin of TAM can be traced back to IBM Canada contract with the *Massachusetts Institute of Technology* – MIT, in the 1980's to examine the market potential of its new computer brand products to the user. According to (Davis, et al. 1989), the main objective was to ascertain the determinants of computers use. In this context, Davis (1989) carried out a research to examine the reasons why the users accept or reject the information technology at large and how to improve the acceptance. Thus Davis (1989), conducted a survey with a group of 112 users at the Canada IBM and in 40 MBA students of Boston University. The result led to proposition of TAM as a model of reasons for users' acceptance and rejection of technologies. The validation of the TAM as a theoretical model of predicting people attitude towards using or rejecting ICT at large was based on the acceptance of a software text editor (Davis, 1989).

However, TAM as a theoretical model has its root embodied in the Theory of Reasoned Action (TRA) developed by both Fishbein and Ajzen (1975) discussed in Chapter 1 of this book. As we had mentioned earlier, the proponents of the TRA model have suggested the need for eliciting salient beliefs about one's attitude relevant to a

particular behaviour being studied. In line with this suggestion, Davis' (1986) proposed two constructs, perceived usefulness (PU) and perceived ease of use (PEOU) in relations to beliefs in information technology (IT) usage contexts. Thus, Davis' (1986) has largely simplified TRA to be more effective for studying IT adoption and acceptance issues across different research settings.

STRUCTURAL COMPONENTS OF TAM AND ICT ADOPTION/USE

The structural components of TAM by Davis (1989) have received a strong theoretical base and have caught the attention of many scholars and researchers in the field of information technology. In fact, its main specific focus on ICT users' intention to accept and reject the usage of ICT have received a wider empirical support, which conform to Davis claims since 1989 until the present time. The structural components in the model (see Figure 1) comprise of two attitudinal variables such as people perceived usefulness of technology and perceived ease of using technology. These two attitude variables were used as the causal relation to users' intention to use or reject technology. Davis (1989) sought the two attitude variables as utility knowledge that can be used to understand the actual behaviour of users towards technologies.

The two main attitude variables in the model deserve further explanations for more understanding. Davis (1989) lamented that technology of any kind has to be useful in the eyes of people to convince their mind (intention). However, the model denotes that technology being useful may not be enough to convince users to optimum level of acceptance. In fact, the usefulness of a technology device can even be sabotaged if it is perceived to be complicated. Therefore, Davis (1989) included the ease or non-complication of technology itself. In other words, users must be able to use technology with ease or that they must

Figure 1. TAM 2 (Technology Acceptance Model-2)
Venketash and Davis, 2000.

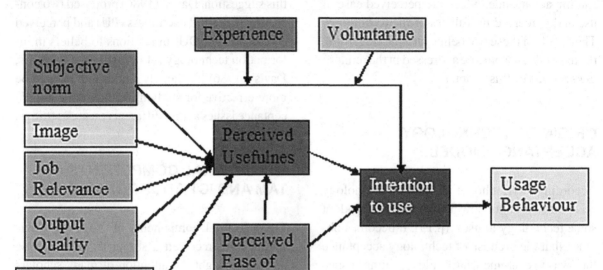

perceive a technology of being simplistic in its compositions and configurations. The implication here for both policy makers and technology designers is a known fact that the end users of technology have the aim to use certain technology in order to improve their performance at work as captured by the perceived ease of use and usefulness in the structural model. Hence, it is worthy to note that as the utility aspect of technology is important in terms of outcomes of using a technology to accomplish one's tasks, yet the ease of using it in terms of perceived facility is equally crucial for the end users. Hence, in the context of public sector adoption and acceptance of ICT, it means effect of some external variables, such as the features of the technology systems, its development process and even training are crucial to address for making the technology usage easy for people.

The ideal in the structural components of TAM lies in holistic understanding that user's intention and attitude are external variables to technology

and can affect its usage both positively and negatively, where its acceptance is considered to be positive effect and rejection as negative effect to both producer and adopter (public sector) of the technology. The main point here is based on the fact that usage of ICT will only be determined by the users' intention towards it. However, such intentions whether positive or negative towards the usage of ICT is turn a function of the two attitudinal variables, which are perceived usefulness and ease as mentioned earlier. Thus, each of the two attitudinal variables relatively exerts certain weightage to convince users' intentions of using the technologies. There is no doubt that people in any given organisations form intention to perform a particular action on the basis of positive feelings towards it. As such, Silva and Dias (2007) came to a conclusion that "the relation between perceived usefulness and use intention, is based on the idea that, inside an organizational context, the people form intentions in relation to behaviours which they believe will increase their performance at work," (p.11). Hence, it is evident from the quotation that perceived saved effort in performing a given tasks in an organisation is a utility outcome of the model which is captured by the perceived usefulness component and the ease of carrying out more or the same works with even less effort when the technology is simply designed for users.

Limitation of Original TAM

Many institutions of public sector have made large investments in technologies but many of these have been underutilised or completely abandoned in tandem with limited users or lack of acceptance (Teo, 2009). The technology acceptance model (TAM), developed by Davis (1989), states that the success of a system can be determined by user's acceptance of the system. Davis has measured this acceptance by three factors which are perceived usefulness (PU), perceived ease of use (PEOU), and attitudes towards usage (ATU) in the model. However, in academic circles and research settings, there has been a growing debate and discussion surrounding the technology acceptance model that was proposed by Davis in 1989. Given that the usages of ICT in public sector vary from one type of application to another, the original technology acceptance model by Davis (1989) may not absolutely fit every acceptance and adoption of ICT situation. This inability to become holistic model for every single situation has been considered as limitation of the model by scholars.

Thus, scholars have come up with various other variables as extensions to the original model in order to fit the context of adoption and acceptance under a particular technological research investigation. Scholars have seen different alternatives to eliciting salient beliefs in each situation relevant to context of ICT usage. As such, Moore (1987) as well as Moore and Benbasat (1996) have proposed a utilisation of more generic set of beliefs that capture perceived characteristics of IT innovations (Moore & Benbasat 1991). More importantly, the

limitation of TAM as a theoretical model, without consideration of other salient variables, has been lamented in a direct expression quoted from Izak Benbasat and Barki (2007) saying "The inability of TAM as a theory to provide a systematic means of expanding and adapting its core model has limited its usefulness in the constantly evolving IT adoption context," p.212). The next sections of the chapter focus on discussions about various extensions of the original TAM.

EXTENSIONS OF TAM

Technology Acceptance Model 2 (TAM 2)

Following the trends and huge changes in technology environment and its wider applications, TAM2 was primarily developed by Venkatesh and Davis (2000) to expand the original TAM framework. The aim was to equip the original TAM (i.e., TAM1) with other eliciting belief variables which are external to the perceived usefulness component of the TAM1. Venkatesh and Davis (2000) had introduced the Social Influence Processes in terms of subjective norm, voluntariness, and image and the Cognitive Instrumental Processes, which include job relevance, output quality, and result demonstrability as determinants of perceived usefulness as depicted in Figure 1.

Social Influence Processes (SIP) in TAM2 is defined as "a person's perception that most people who are important to him think he should or should not perform the behavior in question." It is similar to subjective norms that had been proposed by Ajzen (1991) in the Theory of Planned Behaviour we have discussed in Chapter 7.

Hence, social influence processes in TAM2 is a reflection of subjective norms in TPB and other variables like voluntariness and image. The three variables are considered as influential factors that can determine users' acceptance and adoption of ICT through perceived usefulness of the system.

According to Agarwal and Prasad (1997), voluntariness is defined as "the extent to which potential adopters perceive the adoption decision to be non-mandatory." However, Venkatesh and Davis (2000) noted that there is a need to differentiate between mandatory and voluntary usage of ICT with special reference to adoption and acceptance of any innovative systems. In line with this line of thought, Hartwick and Barki (1994) added that usage intentions can still vary among users even if the organisation makes it compulsory for every individual employee as their level of their compliance with the mandate would be different.

The image component in TAM2 captures the importance of group to an individual on whether certain behaviour should be implemented or not. This is a crucial construct as it can practically affect the quality of ICT usage among users via their social interaction. In fact, in any social settings, people do imitate and copy the ICT image from others who are very important to them. They can easily be influenced by impressions they received from others regarding how the image of ICT to do works is being portrayed. TAM2 also integrated three elements of cognitive instrumental process as influential factors that can have direct statistical impacts on perceived usefulness in the original TAM1. These three components are job relevance, output quality and result demonstrability. In TAM2, job relevance, according to Venkatesh and Davis (2000) is viewed as a process by which a user judges the extent to which the technology can affect his or her job. In other words, it refers to users' perception of the degree to which the IT system introduced by the organisation is applicable to his or her job. This is a crucial policy input to public policy-makers as the type of tasks that can be performed via a given IT system varies in relations to different users. For the output quality in TAM2, it refers to the degree in which individual user judges how the new technology can perform the required tasks. Result demonstrability component captures the positive perception of users on the level of usefulness of the technology most

especially when some positive results of using it are discernible. Perhaps, this is what Moore and Benbasat (1991) termed as "tangibility of the results of using the innovation" in relations to the new way of making public sector works for the benefit of the people at large. The fact to bear in mind is that users will always attribute the level of achievements they had made to their personal work behaviour most especially where the result demonstrability of using certain technological system is very low in the organisation.

In TAM2 framework, Venkatesh and Davis (2000) maintained perceived ease of use just as in TAM1. The judgmental argument is that if a given technology system introduced by organisation can be used with lesser effort; then the probability of usage intention to a greater extent is very high.

A vast number of empirical researches have confirmed this assumption. It was found that perceived ease of use has a significant influence on intention to use a given technology both directly and indirectly through perceived usefulness (see: Venkatesh, 1999; Davis, et al 1989). Furthermore, experience construct has been integrated to TAM2 as a moderating variable.

Venkatesh and Davis (2000) argued that users' acceptance of technology system varies in accordance with the increasing level of their experiences using such system. This argument has been theoretically and empirically supported earlier by other researchers. For example, Hartwick and Barki (1994) have pointed out that subjective norm might have some significant influences on intention to use a technology system in an organisation prior to its implementation. However, such significant effect may not be appreciated or faded away three months after the implementation of the system. Therefore, they have come to a conclusion that users of a given technology must have certain degree of knowledge and beliefs about it based on their experiences.

As we have mentioned earlier, in response to long criticisms against original TAM, most especially on the determinants of perceived usefulness and perceived ease of use, TAM has evolved to both TAM2 and TAM3. As for TAM2 that we have briefly discussed earlier, reader would have noticed that the focus of attention was central to the determinants of perceived usefulness (PU).

In order to further complement the practical significant usage of original TAM in assessing users' acceptance of technology, Venkatesh and Bala (2008) took the pain to develop TAM3 (see Figure 2) with main focus of attention on the determinants of perceived ease of use that was not addressed in TAM2.

TAM3 theoretically assumed that there are more pressing issues from organisational perspective regarding technology acceptance and adoption with special reference to individual differences, system characteristics, social influence and facilitating conditions as the determinants of both perceived usefulness and perceived ease of use. The fundamental variables of TAM3 had relied on anchoring and adjustment in human decision process which believes that users of technology will form early perceptions of ease of use in relations to general individual beliefs

Figure 2. Technology Acceptance Model 3 (TAM3)
Venkatesh and Bala (2008), p.280.

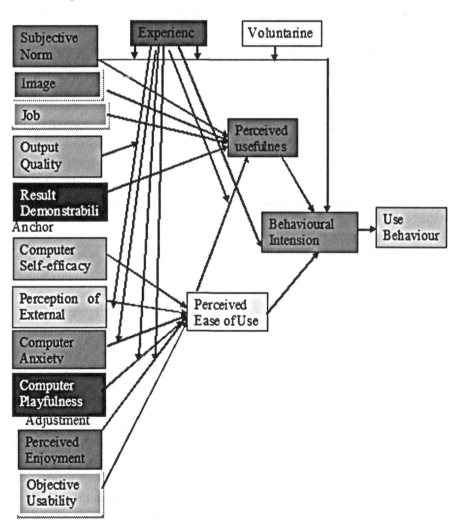

about the technology of interests and its usages. According to Venkatesh and Bala (2008), the early perceptions are usually adjusted after some hands-on experiences being gained during the users' engagement with a particular technology system. In this context, four anchoring elements are identified in the model to be associated with perceived ease of use (PEU).

Three variables of the anchoring frame such as computer self-efficacy, computer anxiety and computer playfulness integrated in the model were meant to capture individual differences with respect to ease of using technology for accomplishing one's work in organisational settings. The last variable- perception of external control of the anchor frame in the model is used to focus on facilitating condition of technology usage. As posited in the model, computer self-efficacy is "the degree to which an individual believes that he or she has the ability to perform a specific task/job using a computer" (Venkatesh and Bala, 2008, 279). It was also defined by Compeau and Higgins (1995) as "a judgment of one's capability to use a computer," p.192). If reader could recall from the chapter 7 of this book, you would notice that these definitions are in line with Bandura's (1978, p.241) definition of self-efficacy concept with a contention that the "outcomes one expects derive largely from judgments as to how well one can execute the requisite behaviour." In the anchoring part of the model, computer self-efficacy captures the impact on individual users' expectation towards using technology. In other words, it focuses on the competency of the users. For example, if a user sees him or herself as a competent computer literate, the tendency of increasing the usability becomes high and if users see him or herself otherwise, the tendency of using it becomes less. In the public sector, this is an important integrated component in the model as it helps to understand how computer self-efficacy can trigger performance and reducing computer anxiety. In other words, the model assumes that high level of computer self-efficacy can lead into increase in performance and

greater achievement in the organisation. It is worth mentioning that computer self-efficacy of a user builds up likeness, knowledge and confidence in handling technology and of course increasing use of it for accomplishing works. Hence, as Wood and Bandura (1989, p.408) put it, it can "mobilize the motivation, cognitive resources and courses of action needed to meet given situational demands" particularly more on computer-based tasks in an organisation.

Computer anxiety in the model is defined, according to (Webster & Martocchio, 1992), as the degree of "an individual's apprehension or fear, when she/he is faced with the possibility of using computers," (p.204). It should be noted that computer anxiety is totally different from negative attitudes towards computer as it indicates certain beliefs and feelings rather than user's emotional reaction towards computer. Hence, computer anxiety in the model is characterised by affective response, emotional fear of any negative outcomes, which may include equipment damage while using technology or getting stacked half-way through. Such feelings of computer-anxiety can detract a user's cognitive resources from task performance (Kanfer & Heggestad, 1997). However, according to the model, the expected effect of computer-anxiety will depend on the level of a user's experience of using technology. In other words, level of experience a user acquired serves as a moderator to minimise the effect of computer anxiety. Thus, we may come to a concrete conclusion that the higher the level of computer experience that a user possessed, the weaker the computer-anxiety. Perhaps, important policy input here for organisation is the urgent need for effective computer training for the civil-servants or public sector users of new emerging technologies to minimise the effect of computer-anxiety and increase performance through their familiarity and experience.

Perception of external control in the model refers to "the degree to which an individual believes that organizational and technical resources exist to support the use of the new system" (Venkatesh et al, 2003). In this context, it is assumed that if a user has a positive perception towards availability of external control such as knowledge, resources and opportunities that required handling a given technology, his or her level of control will increase and of course perceived ease of use will increase too. The implication for policy-makers is to provide consultant support from time to time in order to increase positive perception of control among the users of new technology equipment. In doing so, the knowledge of the users will increase and perceived ease of use will also increase simultaneously.

Another aspect of anchoring frame in TAM3 is computer playfulness. Computer playfulness according to Webster & Martocchio, (1992) is defined as "the degree of cognitive spontaneity in microcomputer interaction," (p.204). The understanding of this concept refers to the desire of the users to perceive using computer for fun rather than for specific outcomes associated with its usage. However, it also conceptually embodies the notion of exploration and discovery as well as curiosity (Venkatesh, 2000). The fact is that when a person uses technology or perceives its usage for fun or playful, he or she does not feel much difficulty using it. In this context, such users enjoy doing works with application of technology devices as compared to those who are less playful. Thus, those who perceive technology somehow playful will likely rate its ease of use higher for them (Venkatesh, 2000). The policy inputs for adoption of ICT in public sector are to make usage of computer applications to accomplish works by civil servants more playful through adequate training in order to override the negative influences that are usually brought by anxiety. According to Hsu and Lu (2004), perceived playfulness was found to influence users' levels of satisfaction with technology system and of course influence usage of it.

The second determinants of ease of use, integrated into TAM2 theoretical framework, was adjustment component which comprises of two elements namely perceived enjoyment and objective usability. By perceived enjoyment, it refers to the extent to which using a new technology system is perceived to be enjoyable in its own right, aside from any performance consequences resulting from its use (Venkatesh, 2000). The introduction of perceived enjoyment in TAM3 serves as an intrinsic motivation that complements the role of perceived usefulness as an extrinsic motivation. Perceived enjoyment was defined as "the extent to which the activity of using the computer is perceived to be enjoyable in its own right, apart from any performance consequences that may be anticipated" (Venkatesh, 2000, p.351). In other words, perceived enjoyment is an intrinsic motivation related to the pleasure and inherent satisfaction a user of technology perceived while doing a specific activity with computer.

The role played by perceived enjoyment in TAM3 has been found to complement the significant effect of perceived usefulness on the intention to adopt a technology for carrying out one's works. Other researchers have also distinguished the effects of extrinsic and intrinsic motivation on the individual's acceptance of various information technologies (Agarwal & Karahanna, 2000; Venkatesh, 2000). It simply means that the more a user experiences enjoyment when doing his or her works in an organisation through the adoption of new technology, the more the positive attitude towards adoption will increase. In other words, users will be more motivated to do and/or repeat an enjoyable activity via a technology device that is perceived enjoyable more as compared to the same activity which is not enjoyable. In this line of thought, a number of studies have confirmed perceived enjoyment to have significantly influenced intention to use computers for accomplishing tasks in the organisation based on the level of perceived enjoyment experienced while doing the work (Burner & Kumar, 2005; Venkatesh, 2000). Analogically to the construct of playfulness or fun, a system perceived to be easy to use will be conceived as more enjoyable leading to a stronger linkage between perceived enjoyment and attitude towards adoption of a system or technology (Bruner & Kumar, 2005). Hence, a user can experience immediate enjoyment from using a specific system, and perceive any active involvement in using new technology to be enjoyable in its own right as contended by Venkatesh, (2000).

Objective usability refers to, "a comparison of the system versus other systems based on the actual level of effort required to complete specific task," (Venkatesh & Bala, 2008, p.279). In this context, it means the extent to which the technology system is compatible with user's cognitive characteristics of achieving a specified goal with effectiveness, efficiency and satisfaction. In the same line of argument, objective usability is crucial in terms of ease of use because there is possibility that a system may be usable but not useful when it is unable to achieve its primary objective of use. In this understanding, usability is considered not only in terms of the ease of use of the users' interface with technology but also in terms of achieving the objectives. Thus, integration of objective usability into the model help captures user's ease of learning the technology while performing his or her tasks. It also helps to assess the efficiency aspect of technology, ease of remembering as well as subjective satisfaction of individual users of the systems (see: Goodwin, 1987).

Other Extensions of TAM on: Perceived Convenience

In relations to adoption and acceptance of ICT usage, perceived convenience can be defined as the extent to which ICT has been able to lower the cognitive, emotional and physical burdens, time saving for its users (see: Chi-Cheng et al. 2012). However, this convenience component was not taken into consideration in the original TAM model. Chi-Cheng et al (2012) have extended the original TAM model with addition of a new variable called perceived convenience to fit into

mobile technology adoption (personal digital assistants or PAD) and English learning for college students in Taiwan. Perceived convenience has been examined in terms of convenience acquisition, execution, time and use by Brown (1990). Along this line of thought, Yoon and Kim (2007) examined the convenience of the wireless LAN based on the perspective of time, place and execution. As such, Yoon and Kim (2007) opined perceived convenience as a level of convenience that a person normally perceives when using the wireless network to complete a given task. The results obtained from their study have shown that perceived convenience was an external factor that affected users' acceptance of a wireless LAN (local area network). In addition, the result of the study has been undertaken by Hossain and Prybutok (2008) also demonstrated that perceived convenience has a significant effect on usage intention with respect to radio frequency identification known as RFID. Given the fact that wireless and RFID frequently used mobile technologies (Wang, Wu & Wang, 2009), the argument on the issue of perceived convenience is well buttressed as an important variable that can predict acceptance of ICT technologies. The main argument is that learning, through wireless networks or e-learning devices, needs to ascertain certain degree of convenience, immediacy and expediency in the mind of users. For example, wireless networks contain features of immediate connection and transmission which enable learners to interact with learning contents and resource materials, peers and instructors especially in a non-face-to-face situation or distance learning mode.

FLOW THEORY AND TAM

Yuan, et al. (2005), have integrated TAM model with flow theory in order to predict user's acceptance behaviour. The researchers aimed to examine how the flow variables integrated into the original TAM model can accurately predict individual's intentions to use the web-based media streaming e-learning system. As has been observed by these groups of researchers, students are usually preoccupied with series of activities during learning to the extent of loosing awareness of time. This phenomenon has been described by Csikszentmihalyi (1990) as "flow" to reflect an optimal psychological state that a person experienced when he or she was entirely concentrated on such activity via technological devices. Hence, full concentration to the extent of losing awareness of time was used to measure "flow" in an online learning behaviour. The underlined assumption is that concentrated users pay little attention to "their limited time and information processing resources" (Yuan, et al. 2005, p.176). In a study conducted by other researchers, concentration was used as proxy for flow and found to positively and significantly affect general experience of ICT users and their intentions (Webster, et al. 1993). In the same vein, Yuan, et al. (2005) also concluded that users' concentration (i.e., users' "flow" state) was positively correlated with their intention to use the technology.

All various extensions to TAM were based on attempts to fit the model into different technological settings. However, one important point to bear in mind in relation to assumption of the first TAM is that all external variables brought to the original model can only have significant effects on technology acceptance and usage through perceived ease of use and perceived usefulness (Burton-Jones & Hubona, 2006). In addition, the development of TAM3 by Venkatesh and Bala (2008) has proved this observation further beyond any reasonable doubt.

CHAPTER SUMMARY

TAM as a theoretical model has its root embodied in the Theory of Reasoned Action (TRA) developed by both Fishbein and Ajzen (1975) discussed in chapter 1 of this book. As we had mentioned earlier the proponents of the TRA model have suggested the need for eliciting salient beliefs about one's attitude relevant to a particular behaviour being studied. In line with this suggestion, Davis' (1986) proposed two constructs, perceived usefulness (PU) and perceived ease of use (PEOU) in relations to beliefs in information technology (IT) usage contexts to form TAM. Thus, Davis' (1986) has largely simplified TRA to be more effective for studying IT adoption and acceptance issues across different research settings. As one can understand in the chapter, the underlined assumptions of TAM by Davis' (1989) are that the actual use of the computer system or ICT in particular is largely determined by a user's behavioural intention to use it or not to use it. This discretionary choice of a user is directly proportional to users' behavioural intention. However, such intention is also determined by attitude toward using ICT as well as how useful a user perceives the ICT (i.e., perceived usefulness).

In addition, users' attitude toward using ICT is determined by both perceived usefulness and perceived ease of use. Finally, perceived ease of use does equally affect perceived usefulness and can also mediate the effect of perceived ease of use on attitude toward using ICT. Furthermore, TAM assumed that some external variables affect perceived usefulness and perceived ease of use, which also mediate the effect of external variables on attitude toward using ICT. However, Davis' (1989) TAM structural components do not specify these external variables that can have effects on both attitude and intention to use ICT. Perhaps, this is what has led to reconfigurations and expansions of the original TAM as a theoretical model for fitting different ICT adoption and acceptance investigations in relation to a growing changing in technology environments and applications.

Following the development of TAM1, Venkatesh and Davis (2000) had introduced the Social Influence Processes in terms of subjective norm, voluntariness, and image and the Cognitive Instrumental Processes, which include job relevance, output quality, and result demonstrability as determinants of perceived usefulness as an extension of TAM1 to form TAM2. With growing applications of TAM2 across various technology acceptance in various parts of the world, yet Venkatesh and Bala (2008) had identified that TAM2 has encountered some limitations with regards to the reasons for which a user will perceive a given technology ease of its use in performing certain tasks. As such, several constructs were integrated to TAM2 as discussed earlier in this chapter. To refresh the readers' memory, these include two main frames namely anchors and adjustments. The anchors focuses on the general beliefs about computer technology and its usages in practice while the adjustment captures the beliefs resulted from direct experience of the users with the adopted technology. In sum, various research settings have tested the model and the results obtained indicated a strong support for the integrated antecedent variables in explaining perceived ease of use for a given technology system being adopted or accepted.

REFERENCES

Agarwal, R., & Karahanna, E. (2000). Time flies when you're having fun: Cognitive absorption and beliefs about information technology usage. *Management Information Systems Quarterly*, *24*(4), 665–695. doi:10.2307/3250951

Agarwal, R., & Prasad, J. (1997). The role of innovation characteristics and perceived voluntariness in the acceptance of information technologies. *Decision Sciences*, *28*(3), 557–582. doi:10.1111/j.1540-5915.1997.tb01322.x

Ajzen, I. (1991). The Theory of Planned Behaviour. *Organizational Behavior and Human Decision Processes*, *50*(2), 179–211. doi:10.1016/0749-5978(91)90020-T

Bandura, A. (1978). The self-sytem in reciprocal determinism. *The American Psychologist*, *33*(4), 344–358. doi:10.1037/0003-066X.33.4.344

Benbasat, I., & Barki, H. (2007). Quo vadis, TAM? *Journal of the Association for Information Systems*, *8*(4), 211–218.

Brown, L. G. (1990). Convenience in services marketing. *Journal of Services Marketing*, *4*(1), 53–59. doi:10.1108/EUM0000000002505

Bruner, G. C. II, & Kumar, A. (2005). Explaining consumer acceptance of handheld internet devices. *Journal of Business Research*, *58*(5), 553–558. doi:10.1016/j.jbusres.2003.08.002

Burton-Jones, A., & Hubona, G. S. (2006). The mediation of external variables in the technology acceptance model. *Information & Management*, *43*(6), 706–717. doi:10.1016/j.im.2006.03.007

Chan, C.-C., Liang, C., Yan, C.-F., & Tseng, J.-S. (2012). The impact of college students' intrinsic and extrinsic motivation on continuance intention to use English mobile learning systems. In Asia-Pacific Education Researcher, (pp. 1-12). Springer.

Compeau, D. R., & Higgins, C. A. (1995). Computer self-efficacy: Development of a measure and initial test. *Management Information Systems Quarterly*, *19*(2), 189–212. doi:10.2307/249688

Csikszentmihalyi, M. (1990). *Flow: The psychology of optimal experience*. Harper & Row.

Davis, F. D. (1989). Perceived usefulness, perceived ease of use, and user acceptance of information technology. *Management Information Systems Quarterly*, *13*(3), 319–340. doi:10.2307/249008

Davis, F. D., Bagozzi, R. P., & Warshaw, P. R. (1989). User Acceptance of Computer Technology: A Comparison of Two Theoretical Models. *Management Science*, *35*(8), 982–1002. doi:10.1287/mnsc.35.8.982

Davis, F. D., Bagozzi, R. P., & Warshaw, P. R. (1992). Extrinsic and intrinsic motivation to use computers in the workplace. *Journal of Applied Social Psychology*, *22*(14), 1111–1132. doi:10.1111/j.1559-1816.1992.tb00945.x

Goodwin, N. (1987). Functionality and usability. *Communications of the ACM*, *30*(March), 229–233. doi:10.1145/214748.214758

Hartwick, J., & Barki, H. (1994). Explaining the role of user participation in information system use. *Management Science*, *40*(4), 440–465. doi:10.1287/mnsc.40.4.440

Hossain, M. M., & Prybutok, V. R. (2008). Consumer acceptance of RFID technology: An exploratory study. *IEEE Transactions on Engineering Management*, *55*(2), 316–328. doi:10.1109/TEM.2008.919728

Hsu, C., & Lu, H. (2004). Why do people play on-line games? An extended TAM with social influences and low experience. *Information & Management*, *41*(7), 853–868. doi:10.1016/j.im.2003.08.014

Kanfer, R., & Heggestad, E. D. (1997). Motivational traits and skills: A person-centred approach to work motivation. *Research in Organizational Behavior*, *19*, 1–56.

Moore, G. C. (1987). End user computing and office automation: A diffusion of innovations perspective. *INFOR*, *25*, 241–235.

Moore, G. C., & Benbasat, I. (1991). Development of an instrument to measure the perceptions of adopting an information technology innovation. *Information Systems Research*, *2*(3), 192–222. doi:10.1287/isre.2.3.192

Teo, T., & van Schalk, P. (2009). Understanding technology acceptance in pre-service teachers: A structural-equation modeling approach. *The Asia-Pacific Education Researcher*, *18*(1), 47–66. doi:10.3860/taper.v18i1.1035

Turel, O., Serenko, A., & Bontis, N. (2007). User acceptance of wireless short messaging services: Deconstructing perceived value. *Information & Management*, *44*(1), 63–73. doi:10.1016/j.im.2006.10.005

Venkatesh, V. (1999). Creation of favourable user perceptions: Exploring the role of intrinsic motivation. *Management Information Systems Quarterly*, *23*(2), 239–260. doi:10.2307/249753

Venkatesh, V. (2000). Determinants of perceived ease of use: Integrating control, intrinsic motivation and emotion into the technology acceptance model. *Information Systems Research*, *11*(4), 342–365. doi:10.1287/isre.11.4.342.11872

Venkatesh, V. (2000). Determinants of perceived ease of use: Integrating control, intrinsic motivation, and emotion into the technology acceptance model. *Information Systems Research*, *11*(4), 342–365. doi:10.1287/isre.11.4.342.11872

Venkatesh, V., & Davis, F. D. (2000). A Theoretical extension of the technology acceptance model: Four longitudinal field studies. *Management Science*, *46*(2), 186–204. doi:10.1287/mnsc.46.2.186.11926

Venkatesh, V., Moris, M. G., Davis, G. B., & Davis, F. D. (2003). User acceptance of information technology: Towards a unified view. *Management Information Systems Quarterly*, *27*(3), 425–478.

Wang, Y.-S., Wu, M.-C., & Wang, H.-Y. (2009). Investigating the determinants and age and gender differences in the acceptance of mobile learning. *British Journal of Educational Technology*, *40*(1), 92–118. doi:10.1111/j.1467-8535.2007.00809.x

Webster, J., & Martocochio, J. J. (1992). Microcomputer playfulness: Development of a measure with workplace implications. *Management Information Systems Quarterly*, *16*(2), 201–226. doi:10.2307/249576

Webster, J., Trevino, L. K., & Ryan, L. (1993). The dimensionality and correlates of flow in human-computer interaction. *Computers in Human Behavior*, *9*(4), 411–426. doi:10.1016/0747-5632(93)90032-N

Wood, R., & Bandura, A. (1989). Impact of conception of ability on self-regulatory mechanism and complex decision making. *Journal of Personality and Social Psychology*, *56*(3), 407–415. doi:10.1037/0022-3514.56.3.407 PMID:2926637

Yoon, C., & Kim, S. (2007). Convenience and TAM in a ubiquitous computing environment: The case of wireless LAN. *Electronic Commerce Research and Applications*, *6*(1), 102–112. doi:10.1016/j.elerap.2006.06.009

Yuan, C., Su, H. L, Yuan, H-L. & Yuan, C-J. P. (2005). Applying the technology acceptance model and flow theory to online e-learning users' acceptance behaviour. *Issues in Information Systems*, *2*, 175–18.

KEY TERMS AND DEFINITIONS

Acceptance: An agreement either expressly or by conduct.

Ease of Using Technology: Lack of difficulty or trouble using a particular technology and/or state of being comfortable using a technology.

Imagination: The ability to form a picture of something in one's mind which is not real or seen.

Usefulness: Ability of something to serve its primary purposes and/or yield good results it is meant for.

User Experience: A person's behaviours, attitudes, and emotions about using a particular system or certain service.

User of System: Those who have used or will use a particular technology such as installers, administrators, and system operators.

Willingness (to Use): Readiness to do something without being persuaded or readiness to use technology without being forced.

Section 3
Application and Practice of ICT in Malaysia:
Empirical Impact of Human Reaction to ICT Adoption in the Public Sector

Chapter 9
Empirical Investigation of ICT Usage in Malaysian Public Sector using Extension of Theory of Reasoned Action

ABSTRACT

The primary aim of this chapter is to examine the TRA in relation to ICT adoption by the Malaysian public sector. Prior experience using ICT was found to be antecedent of attitude towards ICT use among the users. TRA was also extended to find the nature of causal link between subjective norm and attitude itself, and the findings of the chapter show positive relationships between them at alpha level of p < 0.001. The significant contribution to the public sector is that adoption of ICT relies on technical know-how and/or the experience of how to use ICT to accomplish the goal. Experience of ICT and the presence of important individuals would make a user form positive attitude towards using ICT to do work according to the findings. The implication of such findings for policymakers here is to provide adequate ICT training for civil servants to make it more meaningful to them.

INTRODUCTION

In today's indispensable competitive environment between private and public organizations, the success of the any government would largely depend on its ability to adopt Information and Communication Technology (ICT) to confidently meet its increasing demands and stand stout against the various challenges of global scenario. There is no country and its government that is safeguarded from the forces posed by globalization and severe competition of the industrial nations of the world. These challenges have compelled any country to partake in modern mode of service delivery and reform to meet the growing demands of its people through incorporation of ICT to perform tasks. In Malaysia, building knowledge workers (k-workers) with modern technology, creativity and staff innovation are key objectives of the government. These objectives play important role in generating and sustaining not only effective service delivery to the satisfactory level of the

DOI: 10.4018/978-1-4666-6579-8.ch009

citizen but also economic growth of the country. In lieu of this aspiration of the government, a strategic ICT roadmap for Malaysia was mooted by the National IT Council since the period of the 6th Malaysia Plan (1990-1995). In pursuance to this long term vision of the country change in public service delivery system through adoption of ICT, the Malaysia's National ICT Agenda (NITC) was formulated in the 7th Malaysia Plan (1996-2000). The government of Malaysia sought ICT application as a fundamental to transformation of the public sector as whole to a leading industrial player within the Asia continent. Among the crucial steps taken by the government to ensure the integration and adoption of ICT by government agencies was empowerment given to the Malaysian Administrative Modernization and Management Planning Unit (MAMPU) to provide consultation services for work procedures and implementation of ICT with efforts to improve the government service delivery system.

In line with the government of Malaysia's national agenda to reform its traditional way of working and delivering services to its citizens, e-Procurement way back in 1999 under the big umbrella of e-Government or ICT application in public sector through Commerce Dot Com (Ambali, 2010). To implement e-Procurement initiative, the government had launched two modules which are the 'Procurement via Central Contract' and the 'Suppliers Registration' in October 6, 2000. This was followed by 'Direct Purchase module' in May 10th, 2002. The latest modules launched by the government were devoted for both tender and quotation in the e-Procurement system. As part of the government to business (G2B) dimension of the e-Procurement main objective is to enable the suppliers of different products or providers of various services needed by government agencies or even citizens obtained the required information virtually throughout the 24 hours of the day. Thus, both government and citizens become closer to one another as a single entity to collaboratively elevate the economic growth of the country. To

be more specific, the government's objectives also include other pertinent points in its implementation policy worth mentioning here are: ensuring sustainable supply of products and services. The benefit here will enable the government run its operational expenditure more efficiently in the areas of public goods such as health and education, etc. In addition, it can help the government reduce its operational cost. On top of that is to help develop the local small medium companies. Generally is seen as avenue to promote the local industries and allow them to play their roles in the development of the country's economy. With this objective in mind it can help create a resilient Bumiputera Commercial and Industrial Community. The government expects that implementation of the e-Procurement policy will serve as a tool not only to promote transfer of technology or expertise but also enable international tenders through which foreign companies can join venture with the local contractors in businesses.

The government of Malaysia has come with different modalities and flexibilities in implementing e-Procurement system. These include single sourcing (SS), which allows direct purchase from suppliers who have registered with the Ministry of Finance (MOF) in Malaysia. Accordingly, this type of modality for purchasing goods and services is limited to RM20, 000.00. It can also be done through a modality called Central Contact (CC), similar to SS except that there is no restricted amount to be purchased. The government's e-Procurement method also allows quotation from at least five Bumiputera suppliers that have registered with the MOF. However, the amount in this case is ranged from RM50, 000 to RM200, 000 ringgit. The most common modality in the Malaysian e-Procurement is an open tender, especially for government procurements that involve huge sum of money starting from RM200, 000 at least. This is important to facilitate both fair and transparency in government mode of operation. This is done through advertisement in the local news papers for public awareness. If a tender needs direct negotiations, permission must be obtained from MOF prior to the exercise of that practice.

There are many expected outcomes of e-Procurement that pinpoint the rationales for the country's effort to transform Malaysia into a full developed nation by the year 2020. First, it helps government to eliminate time loss due to traditional method of interaction with suppliers. It also lesser the paperwork and make service delivery becomes more efficient (Ambali, 2009). It helps all the government agencies to virtually absorb the latest products and efficient pricing for their operational costs. It can also improve the overall management of government resources allocation and purchasing procedures. Overall, it benefits government in terms of efficient spending and utilising the national endowments for individual citizens, business and promote technology literate workforce as well as the society at large.

STUDY PROBLEM AND EXTENSION OF TRA MODEL

The belief by the Malaysian government that ICT is a strategic driver to support and contribute directly to a fast service delivery system and the growth of Malaysian economy has fuelled its holistic plan of equipping all the government units and service agencies with technology infrastructures according to their needs and types. As such, the Malaysian government had announced its usual Five-Year Plan called 8th Malaysian Plan (2001-2005) incorporated with many initiatives to build vital ICT infrastructure for public sector to make them work smartly just like the private sector. This plan has been focused to increase the usage of computerization and IT infrastructure in all the governmental agencies throughout the country.

However, in a study conducted by Jehangir, et al. (2011) the most common problem and challenge facing ICT application is its usage. In other words, the most important challenge is when people are still not interested to use the created technology.

In addition, even if they tend to use it, the critical issue lies in the level of confidence of using it and assessing its benefits in their daily works. This very complicated based on traditional belief in their usual ways of carrying out the tasks before the advent of technology era.

In addition, using the electronic technology poses some challenges to many business suppliers to fully engage with the system. For the users that are not technologically savvy or with little knowledge of ICT or no prior experience or training on ICT, they portray e-procurement as a new challenge for making progress in their dealing with the government agencies for transactions. Above all are those small scale medium entrepreneurs in the rural area of the country where reception and server are not efficient. In other words using e-procurement system among many of these people is becoming a daunting task when accessing the government website for registrations and transactions.

Given the fact that not all the technologies applied are ease to use or useful for the users, perhaps this could be one of the uncountable reasons why there are so many rejections on the technology applied in many public organisations.

Based on our preliminary interviews among some users, it becomes evidence that rejection of technology is not confined to the government service owned agencies but can also be seen in private organizations due to "lack of experience" using it. In contrast, those with adequate experience of using any form of ICT applications have always eager to use it to accomplish their tasks. Thus, the experience of people with knowledge of how to effectively use technology in service delivery gives them confidence and belief in its benefits as compared to those without knowledge or prior experience. Hence, experience can shape or influence their attitude towards use or not to use ICT. The experience acquired and encountered by users affects their strength and belief about it. In other words having positive experience of using a system leads to positive attitude towards it. In contrast, having negative experience of using it would lead to negative attitude towards using it among the users of the system. That means experience of using technology system has direct effect on mental image of a person's cognitive thinking that control his or her attitude towards use or not to use. Hence, another useful direction of research when applying the Theory of Reasoned Action (TRA), which was established by Ajzen (1991) to usage of ICT for accomplishing public service delivery, is the link or relationship between experience of users and the attitude they form towards the technology system. Thus experience is a new construct for consideration in this chapter. It is used to embed the earlier strength belief in the original TRA. It is obvious that a user cannot hold to any forms of "true belief" that can affect his or her attitude towards ICT without prior experience of using it. Hence experience of using certain technology by users is incorporated to replace belief in this extended model of TRA to suit the research setting and its context based on the information gained from the focus group, which are selected on the basis of their prior experience using e-procurement. The users' experience of ICT deals with evaluative belief in terms of the extent of easiness in using it and/or the benefits they can derive (its usefulness to them) while performing their tasks through it. Another perspective of the model that can have direct effect on users' attitudes according to feedback obtained from the focus group interview is subjective norms as

proposed in the original TRA by Fishbein and Ajzen (1975). Based on the information gathered from the group there is a need to study the effect of subjective norm on attitude rather than only its direct effect on intention as proposed in the original model discussed earlier in Chapter one of this book. This gives us a new perspective of problem based research application of the existing TRA model whereby we are very convinced with answers from the question asked "please explain to us how your colleagues or those who are important to you in this agency influence your (i) attitude and (ii) intention towards use of ICT for your services." To our surprise, majority of the focus group aligned their answers with direct effect of subjective norm on attitude and only a handy few referred its effect on intention. Thus it shows to us that important people or colleagues in the organization can shape other people's attitudinal belief towards use of certain technology. It means that effect of subjective norm on attitude towards technology preceded intention to use a technology or not to use it.

Hence, subjective norms is sought to have direct link to both attitude and intention. In other words, in this new extended model we assumed that there is an indirect effect between subjective norm and intention to use technology through attitude and such effect of subjective norm or its influence could be stronger on attitudes than its direct effect on intention as depicted in Figure 1.

Figure 1. Modified theory of reasoned action

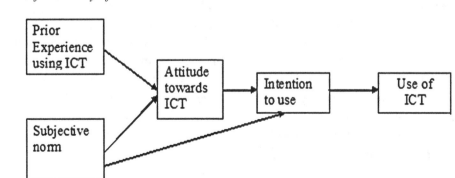

OPERATIONALIZING THE MODEL IN LIEU OF THE LITERATURE

Much attention on the external variables that can influence attitude of a user is not empirically explored in most of the past scholarly works. For example, it has been argued that if users of a technology are well experienced or informed or educated and convinced about the relevance of the technology system, he or she will have belief in its usefulness and hence can have direct influence on the attitude towards that system (Suh & Han, 2002). Having experience of using technology can better evaluate the usefulness of it to the users. Beyond that it can also help user determine how much ICT innovation is compatible with existing organizational work arrangements in the public sector and its visible potential to the users. Experience as antecedent of attitude in this present research setting is obvious where some users are very new and find it hard to accept the system because they have not been using it before, while some are well experienced using it after training yet still encounter problem such as connection error especially when there are too many people accessing the system simultaneously via the same server. Hence, individual experiences could either result to positive or negative attitude towards the system, which could later develop into formation of positive or negative intention to use. Hence, the element of user's convincing belief about technology system lies in his or her experience with it and what is being heard and said by word of mouth from other important people or colleagues about it known as subjective norm (see: Taylor & Todd, 1995). Thus, this provides a new dimension of examining the causal relation between prior experiences of users with technology. The fact is that experience of a user through training, workshop and general knowledge about how to use the technology can shape his or her attitudinal behaviour towards intention to use it. This is very important because subjective norms

alone as in the original model of TRA may not convince a user's intention as this depends on strength of self control individual potential users might possess. Finally, since attitude is the result of what a person believes about the action that is being performed and the expected result, we do not rule out the direct influence of subjective norm on attitude (Pedersen, 2002; Aas & Pedersen, 2012), especially for users with weak self control that can easily be convinced with what people around him or her says about the e-Procurement system. In light of this conceptual explanation, we formulated a three-fold hypothesis as follows:

H1: Experience using technology system will positively influence attitude towards use;

H2: Subjective norms (i.e., pressure from colleagues or important others) has positive influence on attitude of a user towards use; and

H3: Subjective norms (i.e., pressure from colleagues or important others) will positively influence intention to use a system.

A great deal of scholarly works in the literature has shown that actual use of technology, particularly ICT in an organization is significantly influenced by the intention of the users (Davis, 1986; Venkatesh & Bala, 2008). There is a growing attention focusing on the TRA to better understand the relationship between behavioural intention to use and actual use of adopted technology system in public sector as shown in this extended model. This parts or components of the theory have been applied in a number of areas and disciplines to test the universality of the theory or its applicability to different research settings. However, empirical findings of some studies have emphasised the need for its extension with respect to some specific situations or areas of research activity. Some scholarly works since 1960s and 1980s such as Campbell (1963) and Fazio, et al. (1983) had shown that attitude and personality traits do play important role in explaining actual system use. In addition, other works have empirically proved that behavioural intention to use a given system is determined by two-fold factors, especially attitude of the users towards the behavioural intention and subjective norms to facilitate the actual usage, thus as we have assumed in this extended model. In other words, the attitude could develop the intention to use and in turn the intention to use has direct influence on the actual usage (Chen, et al. 2002). In this extended model, the actual usage of technology is conceptualised in terms of how much and how often the system has been employed to accomplish the tasks by the users. At this juncture, we put forward another two hypotheses as follow:

H4: Attitude formed by a user towards use will positively influence intention to use technology system in the organization; and

H5: Intention of a user to use will positively influence the actual usage of a technology system in the organization.

DATA COLLECTION AND METHODOLOGICAL APPROACH

Data collection was done through the design of a survey questionnaire. Information was collected over a period between March and April 2013 at one shot time. Hence it is a cross-sectional design method. The respondents were those citizens that have used e-procurement portal for transacting certain services. The nature of data collection was through a five-point Likert survey questionnaire. A total of 230 (38%) questionnaires were distributed to the total population of 650 in 4 units at the government agency and the returning rate was very interesting where a total of 200 (87%) valid questionnaires were collected back for further analyses. This is more than 52% standard recommended by Baruch and Holton (2008) for response scale of individual respondents in survey analysis

at any given organization research. Hence, the unit of analysis is individual respondent selected based on stratified sampling approach. In this stratified sampling technique, a proportional approach was adopted to ensure that the selected number of respondents is suffice to represent total population in each 5 units participated in the survey. A total of 65 respondents were selected from 185 total population of unit A, while 50 respondents were selected out of 145 total populations at unit B. In addition, 60 respondents out of 165 total populations were selected from unit C and 55 respondents were selected out of total of 155 populations from unit D. As mentioned earlier, the returning rate of 60 from unit A; 45 from unit B; 50 from unit C and 45 from unit D was very interesting. This made up a total of 200 useful questionnaires for further analysis.

Goodness of Measures for Instrumentation

The questionnaire used consists of a five-point Likert scale to obtain data for each of the construct dimension in the extended model of the study (Figure 1). Based on the insights obtained from previous studies by Pedersen and Nysveen, (2012), Lee, et al. (2005), Petrus and Nelson, (2006) and Venketash and Bala, (2008), a questionnaire was reconstructed with some modifications to earn information. In this study, both validity and reliability tests to measure the accuracy of the data were used. Construct validity was used to test how well the instrument developed measures a particular construct (Sekaran & Bougie, 2010), while reliability was used to test how consistently the measuring instruments have measured the constructs. Validity measures in this research were in three folds in terms of construct, convergent and discriminant validities in order to examine how well the questionnaires used could tap the constructs as theorized in the extended model.

Assessing the Inner and Outer Parts of the Model's Constructs

Figure 2 of the extended model displays the outer and inner parts of the model's constructs. This is necessary to confirm the structural links between the variables in the model and the loading of each items used to measure respective variables. An observation shows that the items of each variable really reflect their respective construct intended to measure. The structural links among the variables of interests in the model have yielded positive relations among each of others as expected and predicted. However, there is a need to further test the significances of the relationships among them at another section of the chapter to establish the predicted hypotheses. This is because structural values of the inner model cannot be taken as a proof of the hypotheses until bootstrapping for test of significant is carried out for confirmation.

In addition, there is a need to examine factorial analysis of the constructs in relations to the items used to measure them. This can be explained through rigorous diagnostic of validity of the model with respect to items-relation among all the constructs, which include construct validity itself, discriminant analysis, convergent and divergent validity as well as the measurement model at large.

Construct Validity

Construct validity is assessed by looking at loadings and cross loadings to identify problematic items, if any. Following Hair et al (2010), a significant value of 0.5 loadings is used as a cut-off. As has been depicted in Table 1, items measuring each construct in the study are highly loaded on their particular construct and loaded lower on others, thus construct validity of the instruments is established.

Figure 2. Inner and outer values of the extended model

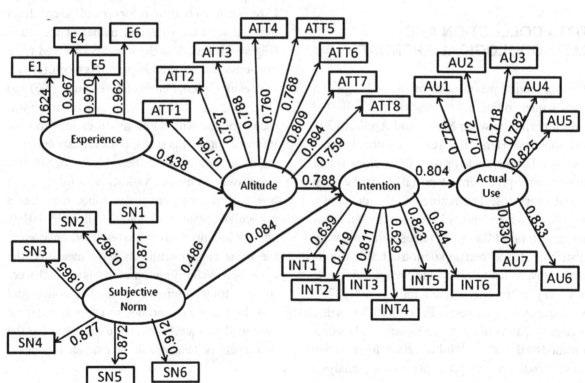

Table 1. Loadings and cross loadings for construct validity

Item Measurements	Actual Use	Attitude	Prior Experience (ICT)	Intention	Subjective Norm
ATUO2	0.494714	0.754052	0.227112	0.263729	0.223825
ATUO3	0.397925	0.736761	0.352824	0.306014	0.493687
ATUO4	0.238738	0.787611	0.310471	0.312245	0.390409
ATUO5	0.265397	0.759869	0.247713	0.432797	0.275721
ATUO6	0.326565	0.788308	0.396557	0.371435	0.383322
ATUO7	0.470308	0.809143	0.382895	0.326942	0.28896
ATUO8	0.281222	0.894409	0.224833	0.284648	0.366056
ATUO1	0.395213	0.758811	0.277467	0.367214	0.322264
AUOI1	0.774915	0.399685	0.480756	0.443073	0.382237
AUOI2	0.771642	0.411703	0.300027	0.247249	0.275876
AUOI3	0.718273	0.269462	0.276078	0.455078	0.251792
AUOI4	0.781531	0.200442	0.400438	0.387501	0.325487
AUOI5	0.82475	0.336572	0.37367	0.223288	0.259331
AUOI6	0.832609	0.45854	0.223245	0.230778	0.301648
AUOI7	0.830394	0.237979	0.341885	0.347539	0.279946
E1	0.352304	0.484773	0.524403	0.342999	0.391173
E4	0.402995	0.256803	0.966907	0.250918	0.245847
E5	0.311759	0.351601	0.97001	0.340511	0.238526
E6	0.23004	0.253606	0.961886	0.443219	0.339304
ITUI1	0.266279	0.32079	0.498482	0.699191	0.455564
ITUI2	0.426857	0.355803	0.334562	0.718986	0.382474
ITUI3	0.355786	0.296768	0.480496	0.766933	0.315499
ITUI4	0.208775	0.497192	0.354501	0.811139	0.237366
ITUI5	0.48235	0.359662	0.240005	0.828588	0.355578
ITUI6	0.36695	0.224157	0.363738	0.823489	0.3397825
ITUI7	0.211663	0.329847	0.402988	0.843961	0.278289
SN1	0.421861	0.441521	0.328398	0.388473	0.870968
SN2	0.321861	0.341521	0.328398	0.288473	0.870968
SN3	0.433429	0.444642	0.378163	0.289854	0.865257
SN4	0.230286	0.314897	0.235973	0.392582	0.877426
SN5	0.341895	0.285386	0.313368	0.360447	0.872061
SN6	0.225177	0.454118	0.470325	0.453114	0.911922

Convergent Validity

The convergent validity of the instrument was also tested to examine the multiple items measuring the same construct of the study and the degree of their agreement with one another. In this respect, the factor loadings alongside both composite reliability and average variance were extracted for proper examination.

$$(\rho c) = (\Sigma \lambda i)2 \ / \ [(\Sigma \lambda i)2 + \Sigma \ Var \ (\varepsilon i)]$$

where λi is the outer factor loading, and $Var \ (\varepsilon i) = 1 - \lambda i$ is the measurement error or the error variance associated with the individual indicator variable(s) for that given factor (see: Fornell & Larcker, 1981).

(AVE)[b]: Average Variance Extracted

$$(AVE) = (\Sigma \lambda 2i) \ / \ [(\Sigma \lambda 2i) + \Sigma \ Var \ (\varepsilon i)]$$

where λi is the outer factor loading, and $Var \ (\varepsilon i) = 1 - \lambda i$ is the measurement error or the error variance associated with the individual indicator variable(s) for that given factor (see: Fornell & Larcker, 1981).

The results of Table 2 show that all items' loadings exceeded the recommended value of 0.5 suggested by Hair et al (2010). In addition, the composite reliability is used to test how far the construct indicators really represent the latent and the values obtained ranging from 0.9187 to 0.9529, which exceeded the recommended value of 0.7 by Hair et al (2010) as shown in Table 2. The average variance extracted (AVE) was used to relatively examine the variance captured by the construct indicators to measurement error. According to Barclay et al (1995), the value must be above 0.5 for justification. In this study, the AVEs for the indicators are within the range of 0.6184 and 0.7713 respectively. Looking at the results

for the parameter estimates and the test of their statistical significance (t-values at p<0.001 alpha levels), it can be concluded that all the variables in the model are valid measures of their respective constructs (see: Chow & Chan, 2008).

Discriminant Validity

The discriminant validity of the measures has equally been tested to examine the degree to which items differentiate among constructs. This is carried out first by looking at correlations between the measures for possible potential overlapping of constructs. Second, whether items are strongly loaded on their own construct in the model were examined. Third, whether the average variance shared between each construct and that its measures are greater than the average variance shared between the constructs and other constructs are also explored, as suggested by Compeau et al, (1999). In this respect, the results of Table 3 shows that the squared correlations for each construct is less than the average squared root of the variance extracted by the indicators measuring that construct. Hence, the measurement model reflects an adequate convergent validity and discriminant validity.

Reliability Analysis

Reliability is an indication of the internal consistency of the instruments measuring the concepts and helps access the "goodness" of measure (Sekaran & Bougie, 2010). There are many different types of reliability estimates (Ambali, 2009). One of the most widely used tests is Cronbach's Alpha that is employed in this study as shown in Table 4. By looking at the results of the Cronbach's Alpha range from 0.879 to 0.941, thus confirming the reliability of the instrument used. It is worth mentioning that the range of reliability test using Cronbach's Alpha ranges from zero to one. The closer to one the higher the level of internal

Table 2. Outer weights (loadings, STDEV, t-values)

	Loadings	Standard Deviation (STDEV)	T Statistics	Composite Reliability (CR)[a]	Average Variance Extract (AVE)[b]
ATUO2 <- Attitude	0.754052	0.005813	28.69017***		
ATUO3 <- Attitude	0.736761	0.005542	22.31055***		
ATUO4 <- Attitude	0.787611	0.005051	28.55902***		
ATUO5 <- Attitude	0.759869	0.005741	29.33914***	0.928646	0.620131
ATUO6 <- Attitude	0.788308	0.005328	31.65042***		
ATUO7 <- Attitude	0.809143	0.005693	36.89839***		
ATUO8 <- Attitude	0.894409	0.007677	66.58977***		
ATUO1 <- Attitude	0.758811	0.005805	29.02792***		
AUOI1 <- Actual use	0.774915	0.010983	20.2513***		
AUOI2 <- Actual use	0.771642	0.011519	19.84435***		
AUOI3 <- Actual use	0.718273	0.011383	18.65076***		
AUOI4 <- Actual use	0.781531	0.008226	26.75138***	0.921351	0.626519
AUOI5 <- Actual use	0.82475	0.008455	28.70509***		
AUOI6 <- Actual use	0.832609	0.00857	39.00346***		
AUOI7 <- Actual use	0.830394	0.009295	36.70255***		
E1 <- Experience ICT	0.524403	0.021719	7.417599***		
E4 <- Experience ICT	0.966907	0.00746	169.8198***	0.926916	0.769013
E5 <- Experience ICT	0.97001	0.007456	207.195***		
E6 <- Experience ICT	0.961886	0.008118	158.2082***		
ITUI1 <- Intention	0.699191	0.00809	19.83217***		
ITUI2 <- Intention	0.718986	0.00718	20.38728***		
ITUI3 <- Intention	0.766933	0.006448	24.96479***		
ITUI4 <- Intention	0.811139	0.007234	38.28817***	0.918654	0.618415
ITUI5 <- Intention	0.828588	0.008215	46.825***		
ITUI6 <- Intention	0.823489	0.008421	34.55934***		
ITUI7 <- Intention	0.843961	0.008464	40.24333***		
SN1 <- Subjective norm	0.870968	0.006586	48.1592***		
SN2 <- Subjective norm	0.870968	0.006586	48.1592***		
SN3 <- Subjective norm	0.865257	0.006837	40.75716***		
SN4 <- Subjective norm	0.877426	0.00533	43.32487***	0.952895	0.771302
SN5 <- Subjective norm	0.872061	0.004726	41.06002***		
SN6 <- Subjective norm	0.911922	0.00667	64.56583***		

***P<0.001, (CR)[a:]: Composite reliability

Table 3. Latent variable correlations

Constructs in the Model	Actual Use	Attitude	Experience ICT	Intention	Subjective Norm
Actual use	0.79153				
Attitude	0.53084	0.78748			
Experience ICT	0.36721	0.45549	0.87693		
Intention	0.41819	0.53631	0.41671	0.78639	
Subjective norm	0.47424	0.47997	0.38552	0.29089	0.87823

Table 4. Reliability tests result

Variable	No. of Items	Cronbach's Alpha
Actual use	7	0.900063
Attitude	8	0.911787
Intention	7	0.896425
Experience ICT	4	0.879622
Subjective norm	6	0.940630

consistency among items and thus the reliability of the instruments are ensured in this study.

The fact that the nature of the data is a self-reported Harman's one-factor test was examined to address any potential common method variance bias that may likely exist. As contended by Podsakoff and Organ (1986), common variance bias is problematic if a single latent factor accounts for the majority of the total explained variance. In this study, the result of the un-rotated factor analysis shows that the first factor only accounted for 26.03% of the total 82.65% variance and thus common method bias is not a problem.

FINDINGS

According to Table 5, majority of the participants are males with 51% as compared to the females. Interestingly, their age ranged from 21-25 years to 36-40 years, which sounds a sense of maturity in engaging with e-Procurement. Hence, it is worth mentioning that most of them are within two major categories of age 21-30 years (29%) followed by 31-35 years (59%). This indicates to us that majority of the business citizens engaging with government's e-Procurement services well matured with adequate experience doing business. However, even though they have business services experience does not really mean that they have been using certain technology to accomplish tasks in their respective businesses. In addition, even if they had ever used technology before, certain technology is different from one another. Majority of them are holding their personal operating business company with 78% while the rest have joint owned company (22%). In addition, many of them have 6-10 years working experience in business services with the government agencies (64%) followed by 1-5 years of experience engaging in business services (31%). Interestingly, some of them have even got 11-15 years business experience (4.5%).

On a separate note, the degree of the e-procurement usage among the respondents for filling applications, downloading related files,

Table 5. Profile of respondents

Variables	Frequency	Percentage
Gender		
Male	102	51%
Female	98	49%
Age		
21-25	10	5%
26-30	58	29%
31-35	118	59%
36-40	14	7%
Organization		
Personal owned company	158	78%
Joint owned company	44	22%
Qualification		
MA/PhD.	3	1.5%
BA	139	69.5%
Diploma/Certificate	29	14.5%
SPM (Secondary Education)	29	14.5%
Work Experience		
1-5	62	31%
6-10	128	64%
11-15	9	4.5%
16-20	1	0.5%

Table 6. Degree of e-procurement usage per week/month

General Use of E-Procurement	Period	Frequency	Percentage
Using of e-Procurement Portal for application; completing requirements, feedback, and approvals, payment, etc.	Less than 1 hour	12	6%
	1 – 5 hours	95	47.5%
	6 hours	35	17.5%
	7 – 8 hours	29	14.5%
	More than 9 hours	29	14.5%

monitoring the feedback and/or approval was assessed and the results have shown that majority of them use it between 1 hour to 5 hours in a week/month. Despite the fact that the users are expected to use the system for at more than 9 hours within a week/month by majority (80%), the duration devoted to its usage for procurement services by majority is far below the expectation (47.5%) as shown in Table 6.

Surprisingly, only about 15% used more than 9 hours per a whole week/month (see Table 6). A critical assessment of this low usage reflects that there could be other means or channel through which procurement activities are being carried out between these business people and the government agencies. Among the alternative channels could be direct phone called, fax and even face-to-face engagement again.

ASSESSING THE STRUCTURAL RELATIONSHIPS OF THE CONSTRUCTS IN THE MODEL

In this section, the researchers address the path coefficients to examine the relationships between the structural latent constructs of the model. The results obtained have shown positive significant relationships among all the constructs in this extended model. As clearly shown in Figure 3, the results indicate a positive significant relationship between the experience of ICT and attitude towards use of e-procurement with beta values of 0.438, p<0.001.

A similar significant positive relationship exists between the causal link of subjective norms and attitude towards use of e-procurement with beta coefficient values of 0.486, p<0.001. In addition, the causal link between subjective norm and the attitude toward use is also positively related with a beta value of 0.084, p<0.05. Furthermore, the path coefficients between attitude toward use and intention of the business people to use e-procurement is positively and significantly related with high beta value of 0.786, p<0.001. The same similar positive causal link and relationship can be inferred between intention to use and the actual usage of e-procurement to facilitate engagement between government agencies and business people to better serve the citizens with a very high beta value of 0.804, p<0.001.

Predictive Capacity of the Extended Model and Hypotheses Testing

As can be seen in the Figure 4 the t-value of the path coefficients are generated to test the significant contribution of each path coefficient of the latent constructs through a bootstrapping procedure in order to validate the predictive capacity of the extended model as well as the hypotheses put forward.

The results show that all hypotheses in the study are supported with t-values ranging from 1.71339* to 22.2079*** at an alpha-value less than 0.05 and 0.001 respectively (see Table 7). As the results depicted in the Figure 3 the R^2 values of the three endogenous latent constructs in the model such as attitude towards use, intention to use e-procurement and the actual use of e-procurement ranged from 0.764, 0.735 to 0.647 respectively (see Table 7). According to Chin, (1998), it is paramount to examine the predictive power of the extended model of the study based on the values of the endogenous constructs obtained. According to Kock (2012, p. 31), this can be done by assess-

Figure 3. Structural coefficient results of the extended model

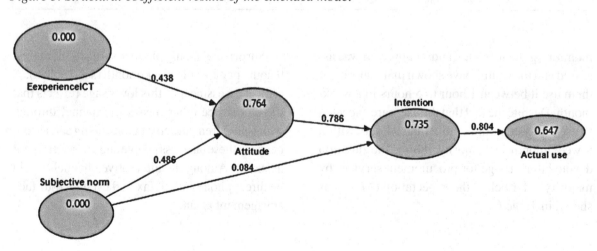

Figure 4. Bootstrapping results of the structural model

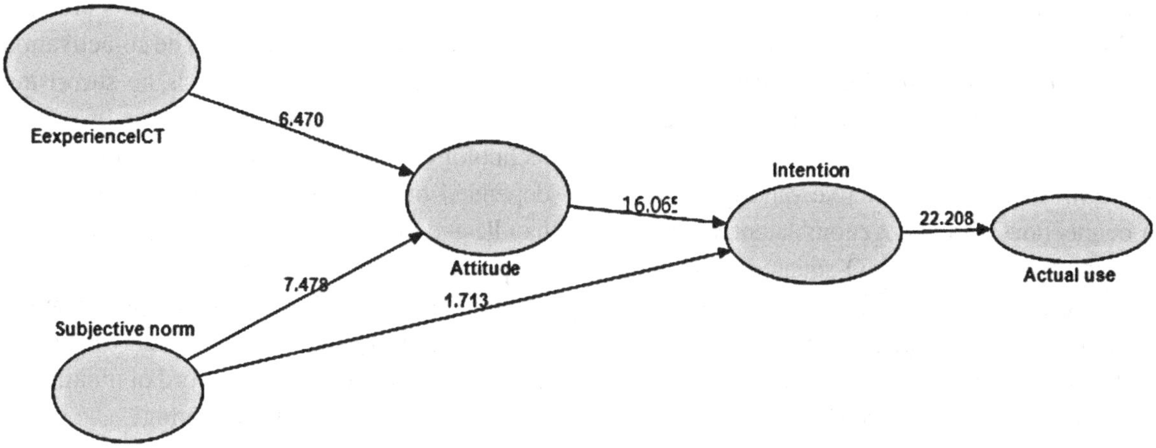

Table 7. Summary of t-statistics of the path coefficients and hypotheses testing

Hypotheses	Construct Causal Relation	Beta (β) Coefficient	Endogenous Latent Variables (R^2)	T -Statistics	Remark
H1	Experience of ICT -> Attitude	0.438	$R^2 = 0.764$ (76.4%)	6.47021**	supported
H2	Subjective norm -> Attitude	0.486		7.47836**	supported
H3	Subjective norm -> Intention	0.084	$R^2 = 0.735$ (73.5%)	1.71339*	supported
H4	Attitude -> Intention	0.786		16.0646***	supported
H5	Intention -> Actual use	0.804	$R^2 = 0.647$ (64.7%)	22.2079***	supported
Predictive Capacity of the Model					
Criteria			**Value**		
AVIF			1.25		
APC			0.5196		
ARS			71.37%		
Q-squared			0.52		

Note: *** P<0.001, **P<0.01; *P<0.05.

ing the average variance inflation factor (AVIF) as a comprehensive analysis of a model's overall capacity and explanatory quality of the latent factors linking to actual use of e-procurement in this study. This is important in order to address the absence of both vertical and lateral collinearities. The result shows a value of 1.25 (see Table 7), which is far below the threshold of 3.3 (Kock, 2012, Ambali, 2013).

Additionally, other indices for the model fit such as average path coefficient (APC), average r-squared (ARS) are addressed in the process of addressing the predictive capacity of the model are very essential. In this respect, the result of both APC and ARS are 0.5196 and 71.37% respectively.

These results indicate a practical significant power of the model (Kock, 2012).

Moreover, Q-squared coefficient was performed through blindfolding in order to assess the predictive validity associated with each latent variable block in the model as well as the strength. Acceptable predictive validity strength in connection with endogenous latent variables as suggested by examine a Q-squared coefficient must be greater than a zero threshold (Kock, 2012; Ambali, 2013). The result of the predictive validity for this extended model is 0.52 indicating good predictive factors that can influence the usage of e-procurement among users.

DISCUSSION OF THE FINDINGS

The findings of the study have shown that the degree of the e-procurement usage among the users for filling applications, downloading feedback information, needed requirements and payment status was not encouraging. The results reflect that majority of the e-procurement usage is between 1 hour to 5 hours in a week/month. Despite the fact that usage of the system is expected to be at least 80% per week/month but the duration the users devoted to it is far below expectation (47%). This smaller time devoted by majority of the users has something to do with interrelationships among all the variables of interests addressed in the extended model.

The results obtained from this extended model have shown that both prior experience of ICT, especially via training and/or the knowledge acquired about how to use a technology as well as subjective norms have positively influenced attitude of the users towards use of e-procurement, with beta values $\beta = 0.438$, t-value of 6.47 and $\beta = 0.486$, t-value of 7.48, p<0.01 respectively. In addition, the results also indicate a weak significant impact of the subjective norm on intention to use e-procurement with $\beta = 0.084$, t-value of 1.71, p<0.05. It is worth mentioning that the results indicate a co-activation between the two antecedences of attitude to use e-procurement system in this extended model. The co-activation between the two antecedences is no surprising because positive attitude towards use of certain technology system like e-procurement is largely depended on the users' ability and capacity to handle and manoeuvre the system. This can only be possible if they have been trained or have prior knowledge on how to use it. Also the positive attitude towards also depends on what other colleagues say about through word of mouth that can be encouraging or discouraging!

However, direct influence of subjective norm on intention to use e-procurement is very weak as compared to the impact of attitude on intention. Critical examination of this point would indicate that direct influence of subjective norm on intention as positioned in the original TRA will depend on mindset that comes from nature of attitude of individual users formed towards use. Those with weak mindset, which may come from negative attitude towards use of e-procurement, can easily be influenced by what their friends say about it. While on those with strong mindset, which is a by-product of positive attitude formed towards use of e-procurement cannot easily be influenced by what their colleagues say about it. In other words, the results indicate that intention to use e-procurement can strongly be influenced by attitude rather than subjective norm. It also means that subjective norm has indirect impact on intention through attitude of the users as posited in this extended model. Usually one aspect of attitude such as cognitive reflection on the e-procurement does occurs based on past experience and previous successful use of the technology to perform certain tasks and can directly influence intention to use it regardless of what important people around the users say about it. Evidently speaking, both attitude and subjective norm have jointly influenced intention to use e-procurement by 73.5%. The major contributing impacts out of this percentage come from the effect of attitude on intention rather than subjective norm.

The result has also shown that actual use of the e-procurement is positively and significantly influenced intention to use the system with a beta value of $\beta = 0.804$, t-values of 22.209, p<0.001. It is evident from the findings intention to use has 64.7% impact on actual use of e-procurement by the users. That implies to us that adopting a technology in a public sector does not indicate automatic usage of it. The users' mindsets and/or intentions must be positively convinced in relations to experience of the technology or training on how it can be used so that they can form a positive towards the system. This would make them have positive belief about it and make up their mind to migrate to the use of the technology system as opposed to their usual manual way of carrying out procurement previously. Otherwise, creating a technology may become useless or neglected by the users if they cannot form positive attitude towards it nor they can have positive intention to use it. However, the formation or development of both positive attitude and intention to use it are only possible when they have certain experience of the technology itself on how to use it. Finally, what other people around the users of the technology say is likely not strongly influence their minds to use it as compared to their personal attitudes. The implications derived from the results are diversified. For policy-makers, it shows that adoption of technology in public sector for achieving a better public service delivery is not the end. First, experience and technical know-how of handling technology devices are crucial to achieve the underlying objectives of IT usage in public sector. Second, the implication for technology designers is that the mindset of the users' needs to be convinced especially on the potential benefits from technology. This can only be possible when technology is designed very friendly to users and help them achieve their primary objectives of using it.

CHAPTER SUMMARY

The focus of this chapter is on the theory of reasoned action (TRA) with an extension of prior experience of ICT as an antecedence of attitude as well as causal link between subjective norm and attitude towards use. A problem based approach was employed to underpin the nature of issue related to use of ICT in public organizations in Malaysia. The results obtained from the preliminary interview conducted have reflected the relative importance of prior experience and subjective norm, which can help form a positive attitude towards the use of ICT to accomplish works. According to the findings, the causal links between prior experience of ICT, subjective norm and attitude of users were found positively and significantly related. There are many implications that can be drawn from these findings. First, most of the users of e-procurement need might effective training especially those are new to technology system as compared to their usual tradition method of carrying transactions. Second, the support from those around them such as colleagues, immediate boss or seniors with certain knowledge of ICT is equally important as this can encourage or discourage their intention to use the system. Finally, it can be concluded that the users' mindsets and/or intentions must be positively convinced in relations to experience of the technology or training on how it can be used so that they can form a positive attitude towards the system. This would make them have positive belief about ICT system and make up their mind to migrate to the use of the technology system as opposed to their usual manual way of carrying out procurement previously. Otherwise, creating a technology may become useless or neglected by the users if they cannot form positive attitude towards it nor have positive intention to use the system.

REFERENCES

Aas, T. H., & Pedersen, P. E. (2012). Open service innovation: A feasibility study. In HuizinghK. R. E.ConnS.TorkkeliM.BitranI., (Eds.), *Proceedings of the 23rd ISPIM Innovation Conference*. Lappeenranta University of Technology Press.

Ajzen, I. (1991). The theory of planned behavior. *Organizational Behavior and Human Decision Processes*, *50*(2), 179–211. doi:10.1016/0749-5978(91)90020-T

Ambali, A. R. (2009). Digital divide and its implication on Malaysian e-government: Policy initiatives. In H. Rahman (Ed.), Social and political implications of data mining: Knowledge management in e-government, (pp. 267-287). New York: IGI Global.

Ambali, A. R. (2009). E-government policy: Ground issues in e-filling system. *European Journal of Soil Science*, *11*(2), 249–266.

Ambali, A. R. (2010). Determinants of E-Government Satisfaction: The case study of E-procurement. In H. Rahman (Ed.), Handbook of Research on E-Government Readiness for Information and Service Exchange: Utilizing Progressive Information Communication Technologies, (pp. 465-479). New York: IGI Global.

Ambali, A. R. (2013). Hala food and products in Malaysia: People's awareness and policy implications. *Intellectual Discourse*, *21*(1), 7–32.

Barclay, D. W., Higgins, C., & Thompson, R. (1995). The partial least square approach to causal modeling: Personal computer adoption use as illustration. *Technology Studies*, *2*(2), 285–309.

Baruch, Y., & Holton, B. C. (2008). Survey response rate levels and trends in organizational research. *Human Relations*, *81*(8), 1139–1160. doi:10.1177/0018726708094863

Campbell, D. T. (1963). Social attitudes and other acquired behavioural dispositions. In S. Koch (Ed.), Psychology: A Study of A Science, (pp. 94-172). New York: McGraw-Hill. doi:10.1037/10590-003

Chen, L., Gillenson, M. L., & Sherrell, D. L. (2002). Enticing online consumers: An extended technology acceptance perspective. *Information & Management*, *39*(8), 705–719. doi:10.1016/S0378-7206(01)00127-6

Chin, W. W. (1998). The partial least squares approach to structural equation modeling. In G.A. Marcoulides (Ed.), Modern Methods for Business Research. Lawrence Erlbaum Associates.

Chow, W. S., & Chan, L. S. (2008). Social network and shared goals in organizational knowledge sharing. *Information & Management*, *45*(7), 24–30. doi:10.1016/j.im.2008.06.007

Compeau, D. R., Higgins, C. A., & Huff, S. (1999). Social cognitive theory and individual reactions to computing technology: A longitudinal-study. *Management Information Systems Quarterly*, *23*(2), 145–158. doi:10.2307/249749

Davis, F. D. (1986). *A technology acceptance model for empirically testing new end-user information systems: Theory and results*. (Doctoral dissertation). MIT Sloan School of Management, Cambridge, MA.

Fazio, R. H., Powell, M. C., & Herr, P. M. (1983). Toward a process model of the attitude–behavior relation: Accessing one's attitude upon mere observation of the attitude object. *Journal of Personality and Social Psychology*, *44*(4), 723–735. doi:10.1037/0022-3514.44.4.723

Fishbein, M., & Ajzen, I. (1975). *Belief, attitude, intention, and behavior: An introduction to theory and research*. Reading, MA: Addison-Wesley.

Fornell, C., & Larcker, D. F. (1981). Evaluating structural equation models with unobservable and measurement error. *JMR, Journal of Marketing Research*, *18*(1), 39–50. doi:10.2307/3151312

Government of Malaysia. (2002). *Eight Malaysia Plan (2001-2005)*. Putrajaya: Economic Planning Unit.

Hair, J. F., Black, W. C., Babin, B. J., & Anderson, R. E. (2010). *Multivariate data analysis*. Upper Saddle River, NJ: Prentice-Hall.

Jehangir, M., & Dominic, P.D.D., Naseebullah, & Khan, A. (2011). Towards digital economy: The development of ICT and e-Commerce in Malaysia. *Modern Apllied Science*, *5*(2), 171–178.

Kock, N. (2012). *WarPLS 3.0, user manual*. Laredo, TX: ScriptWarp System.

Lee, M. K. O., Cheung, C. M. K., & Chen, Z. (2005). Acceptance of Internet-based learning medium: The role of extrinsic and intrinsic motivation. *Information & Management*, *42*(8), 1095–1104. doi:10.1016/j.im.2003.10.007

Pedersen, P. E., & Nysveen, H. (2002). *Using the theory of planned behaviour to explain teenagers' adoption of text messaging services*. Working paper, Agder University College, Norway.

Petrus, G., & Nelson, O. N. (2006). Borneo online banking: Evaluating customer perceptions and behavioural intention. *Management Research News*, *29*(1/2), 6–15. doi:10.1108/01409170610645402

Podsakoff, P. M., & Organ, D. W. (1986). Self-reports in organizational research: Problems and prospects. *Journal of Management*, *12*(4), 531–544. doi:10.1177/014920638601200408

Sekaran, U., & Bougie, R. (2010). *Research methods for business: A skill building approach* (4th ed.). John Wiley & Sons, Inc.

Suh, B., & Han, I. (2002). Effect of trust on consumer acceptance of Internet Banking. *Electronic Commerce Research and Applications*, *1*(3), 247–263. doi:10.1016/S1567-4223(02)00017-0

Taylor, S., & Todd, P. A. (1995). Understanding information technology usage: A test of competing models. *Information Systems Research*, *6*(2), 144–176. doi:10.1287/isre.6.2.144

Venkatesh, V., & Bala, H. (2008). Technology acceptance model 3 and a research agenda on interventions. *Decision Sciences*, *39*(2), 272–315. doi:10.1111/j.1540-5915.2008.00192.x

KEY TERMS AND DEFINITIONS

Better Performance: How effective something or someone is at doing a job or task assigned to him or her.

E-Procurement: The use of electronic system to procure goods and services or conduct business with the government and/or its agencies. It is a good example of G2B and B2G e-government.

ICT Prior-Experience: Past experience in the use of ICT before; it is also known as know-how the works can be done by it.

K-Workers: The civil servants that are equipped and trained with modern technology to perform primary tasks or works assigned to them with the aim of efficiency and improvement.

Service Delivery: Instance of supplying a public need such as transport, communications, or utilities such as electricity and water to the people.

Transaction: The instance of buying and selling goods, services, or money between one person and another.

Work-Procedures: A set of step-by-step guidelines that helps understand complete process of how a particular task must be done.

Chapter 10
Empirical Investigation of ICT Usage in Malaysian Public Sector:
Extension of Theory of Planned Behaviour

ABSTRACT

Information technology has been playing some important roles in expediting service delivery in public organizations to meet the demands of the people in Malaysia and elsewhere in the world. However, some of the civil servants still have pessimistic perceptions of technology devices with negative attitudes towards them. Some even prefer to remain with their traditional ways of doing the obligatory works assigned to them. In this context, this chapter extends the theory of planned behaviour by examining the antecedents of attitude such as perceived usefulness. The findings of the study show that perceived usefulness of technology devices by respondents has a strong and significant influence on attitude towards the use of the system among the civil servants. The practical significant of this finding is that a technology must be very useful to users and meet their expectations in terms of accomplishment of their goals of using it.

INTRODUCTION

The emergence of information and communications technologies (ICTs) has impacted positively many industries and public organizations all over the world. In its effort to transform Malaysia economy from a commodity-based producing nation to being a manufacturer of industrial products and more recently knowledge based economy, the government is putting greater emphasis on ICT. The needs to adopt ICT is in tandem with efforts to support information gathering, processing, distribution and access to services provided by the government for public consumptions. Hence, the significance and essence of ICT adoption in public sector can be envisaged in many forms. These include, among other things, helping the public sector in creating, producing, processing, packaging, distributing, retrieving and transmitting information electronically in a digital form to meeting the ever increasing demands of the public from the government.

DOI: 10.4018/978-1-4666-6579-8.ch010

Malaysian government has currently built the ICT town in Cyberjaya and Multimedia Super Corridor in order to compete with the other leading countries in term of technology and satisfy the need of its people at large. Malaysia Super Corridor (MSC) was a plan that has successfully come into effect and it has been implemented for many years. This is the major plan for Malaysia in order to gain the competitive advantage among the others country. From the launched of MSC, Malaysia had created more and more technology in terms of Information Communications and Technologies (ICT). It was an ideal plan that supposed to help the country in achieving it targets. There are several developmental role played by adoption of ICT and had assisted the government in dealing with enormous amount of jobs, services delivery issues. Thus it has helped the government ensure better service delivery, skills development, and better productivity to meet a high economic growth. Therefore, through adoption and usage, ICT skills in public sector are considered to be means of professional development and an answer to society's requirements.

PROBLEM STATEMENT

The big question mark arising in the adoption and development of the ICT in public sectors around the world is not only pertaining to the technology system itself but also rest on the shoulder of the civil servants who use the technologies provided with special references to their attitude, intention and actual behaviour towards usage of the system in Malaysia. Human behaviour is difficult to forecast, it keeps on changing over time. The changes had created positive and negative effects on the government's targets and achievements. Such behavioural reactions of the civil servants towards adoption and usage of the new technology for service deliveries in Malaysia can be understood and explained via the theory of planned behaviour. As has been earlier discussed in the chapter 7 of

this book, the theory of planned behaviour helps understand the link between attitudes, intention and actual behaviour towards a given object such as technology system. The theory was developed by Icek Ajzen to improve on the predictive power of the theory of reasoned action by including perceived behavioral control. It is one of the most predictive persuasion theories. The theory opines that attitude toward behaviour, subjective norms, and perceived behavioral control, together shape an individual's behavioral intentions and actual behaviours especially when it comes to non-volitional tasks. However, in the course of our preliminary investigation of the underlying antecedents of attitudes among the focus group of civil servants selected from the government agency, user friendly of a given technology system could play an important role in controlling and influencing attitudes. For example, when the focus group respondents was asked on their attitudinal reactions to the use of new technologies provided for delivering services to the public. The selection of the focus group interview was based on the prior experience of those that have applied and used the new installed technologies for accomplishing tasks assigned to them.

For example, 12 focus group members from different departments were asked "when the use of online information (ICT) was introduced into this agency to apply and provide feedbacks to the public demands, can you describe your attitudes towards it and reasons behind it?" The main theme (similarity) found in the various described reasons of positive and/or negative attitude towards the system is the statement "well, it all depends on whether the online technology or ICT introduced is useful or not". This is an important elicitation variable that must be considered as antecedence of attitude because it can shape and/or influence it. Hence, in the context of the agency where the research is conducted, there is a dare need for extending the existing theory of planned behaviour with "perceived usefulness" of technology system as shown in Figure 1.

Figure 1. Extended theory of planned behaviour

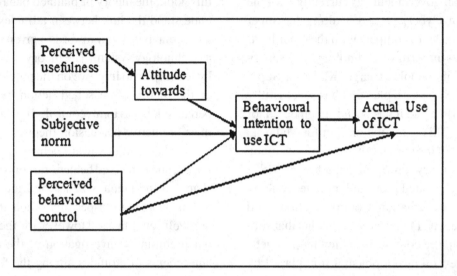

Based on this extended theoretical framework, four fundamental questions are raised in this chapter, which are:

1. To what extent can perceived usefulness influence attitudes of civil servants at the agency towards use of ICT?
2. How do civil servants' attitudes (Att.) towards use of ICT in performing works, the influence of subjective norms (SN) relate to behavioural intention to use ICT?
3. Can perceived behavioural control (PBC) with regard to ICT influence behavioural intention to use ICT and actual use of ICT among the civil servants at the said agency?
4. Overall, to what extent does the extended TPB model provide a basis for predicting and explaining Civil servants' use of ICT in their works?

To provide answers to the questions raised, there is a need to derive different hypotheses pertaining to each of the question, which can only be possible through operationalising the model's constructs in lieu of extensive review of literatures.

OPERATIONALIZING THE MODEL IN LIEU OF THE LITERATURE

Using the theory of planned behavior, it is assumes that rational considerations govern the individuals' behaviour of civil servants as well as their attitudinal intention towards adoption and usage of ICT provided by the government at the agency (Ajzen, 1991; Ajzen & Fishbein, 2005). The first component of the model is perceived usefulness of the introduced technology system in an organization. Perceived usefulness of a system is defined in this work as the degree to which using the technology by civil servants would help them accomplished and achieve or meet the target set. Rogers (2003) lamented that for a technology to be perceived useful to the users it must help them gain certain benefits on a continuous range of time and should be seen with the ability to reach wider populates, able to gather large information within a short time at lower cost of sending disseminating the information to the public. This is in line with technology acceptance model (TAM) by Davis (1989). The model has been widely used in various studies and the conclusions have shown that perceived usefulness of a technology system has a significant and positive influence on attitude of the people toward use. Previous studies showed that usefulness of technology mostly has the greatest association with attitude. For example a very strong correlation between perceived usefulness and attitude was found in studies conducted by Spacey *et al.* (2004a), and Davis, *et al.* (1989). In addition, higher level of correlation between perceived usefulness and attitude was also found in the study conducted by Adnan Riaz (2010), indicating that employees in Iqball Open University have positive attitudinal perception towards ICT, "as they think that it would enable them to accomplish task quickly and effectively, leading towards enhanced performance", (p.8). In other words, perception of the civil servants that using technology will be useful to them in accomplishing the given tasks more efficiently would influence their attitude positively towards adoption of ICT and use. At this juncture, it is hypothesised that:

H1: Perceived usefulness (PU) of ICT among the civil servant has significant influence on their attitudes (Att.).

Behavioural intention to use ICT in the model is posited to be influenced by attitude of the civil servant users. It is useful to highlight that attitude variable has been left out in the technology acceptance research. For example, attitude was earlier theorized not to have a direct influence on behavioural intention in technology acceptance studies by (Venkatesh et al. 2003, p.447). But it has been argued that "attitude should not be eliminated" from technology acceptance study (Zhang, 2007, Zhang & Aikman 2009). However, there is a need to pinpoint that the concept of attitude in this chapter referred to attitude towards behavioural intention rather than towards object. Hence attitude towards behaviour is defined as "an individual's positive or negative feelings (evaluative affect) about performing the target behaviour" (see: Fishbein *et al.* 1975). In other words, this is in line with the underline meaning of attitude towards behaviour in TPB (Ajzen, 1991;

Ajzen et al. 2005). Some attempts were made in the literature to investigate direct effect of attitude on behavioural intention. For example, results of some studies have shown a significant strong correlation between attitudes (as evaluative affect) and behavioural intentions in different situation and cultural settings (see: Zhang, 2007; Zhang & Aikman 2009; Chau, 2001; Shiro, 2008; Dixon, 2009). At this juncture, it is hypothesized that:

H2: Attitude (Att.) has significant influence on behavioural intention (BI) to use ICT among the civil servants at agency.

Subjective norm construct in this chapter is defined as the degree at which a person thinks that people around feel he or she should be using ICT to accomplish works in the organisation. In a recent study conducted using TPB by Delvarani *et al.* (2013), subjective norm, as a perceived social pressure, was found to have a significant positive influence on behavioural intention of the people to use menu provided. Similar result was also found in other studies such as those conducted by Astrom and Rise, (2001) as well as Fila and Smith, (2006). The conclusion of these studies demonstrated that subjective norm plays a significant role in influencing behavioural intention to perform certain actions. In this context, it is hypothesised that:

H3: Subjective norm has a significant influence on behavioural intention to use ICT among the civil servants at the agency.

The concept of perceived behavioural control (PBC) was introduced in the theory of planned behaviour to strengthen the predictive capacity of the original TRA, especially for the non-volitional actions. That is, the performing behaviours which are obligatory in nature such as the adoption and use of ICT in public organisations. Perceived behavioural control is defined as "one's perception of how easy or difficult it is to perform a behaviour"

(Eagly & Chaiken 1993, p. 185). In this chapter, PBC is defined as extent to which a person believes whether he or she has control over performance of a specific behaviour he intends to embark upon. It focuses on situational conditions in which a person found him or her-self and this bear direct influence on intention to do or not do. Empirically, previous studies have formally confirmed the significant impact of perceived behavioural control on behavioural intention and actual use of ICT. For example, perceived behavioural control was found to be significant predictors of teachers' intention to use technology in accomplishing their primary duties (Lumpe & Chambers, 2001). In addition, other studies have similarly reported a direct relationship between PBC and behavioural intention. However, a surprising empirical finding was reported in another study. For example, it was found that a positive and significant relationship exists between PBC and behavioural intention, while a negative relationship exists between PBC and actual use of ICT components such as mobile phone devices in their study. The negative empirical result found between PBC and actual use of mobile phone in their study is not universally confirmed and this needs to be further investigated because it contradicts with many other findings in the literature (Davies, 2008) and more importantly with assumption of the original model (Ajzen, 1991). It worth noting that the nature of relationship is important but it depends on the context and cultural situation in which the research is being conducted. At this juncture, two hypotheses (H4, H5) can be postulated in this chapter as follow:

H4: Perceived behavioural control (PBC) has a significant influence on behavioural intention to use ICT among the civil servants.

H5: Perceived behavioural control (PBC) has a significant influence on actual use of ICT among the civil servants at the agency.

Actual use of ICT refers to performance of the actual behaviour in the TPB model. Thus, in this chapter, it is defined as the degree to which ICT are real used for accomplishing works or tasks among the civil servants at the agency. Empirically, Ajzen (2002b) has demonstrated a significant relationship between behavioural intention and actual behaviour in reality. In other words, Ajzen concluded that behavioural intention is an antecedent of actual action. Some other studies conducted by scholars such as (Rise, et al., 2003) have tested TPB and found a significant influence of behavioural intention on the actual use of ICT in organizations. As such, we hypothesise that:

H6: Behavioural intention has a significant influence on actual use of ICT among the civil servants.

DATA COLLECTION AND METHODOLOGICAL APPROACH

Data collection was carried out using a survey questionnaire. Information was collected over a period between August and September 2013 at one shot time. Hence it is a cross-sectional design method. The respondents were the staff dealing directly with processing and managing services delivery related to (socioeconomic and political matters) to the public at the government agencies in Shah Alam. A total of 400 questionnaires were distributed to the respondents and the returning rate was very interesting where a total of 302 valid questionnaires (i.e., 76%) were collected back for further analyses. Respondents were selected from four agencies namely: A, B, C and D. A total of 70, 74, 78 and 80 questionnaire was collected back from each agency respectively. The question of response bias does not arise and statistical analysis has proven it in the subsequence section of the chapter. Data analysis was done using structural equation model. Other details pertaining to data analysis and adequacy of methodological approach are further discussed in the next sections.

Goodness of Measures of the Instrument: The Structural Model Specification

The questionnaire used consists of a five-point Likert scale to obtain data for each of the construct dimension in the model of the study (Figure 1). Insightful survey scales were adopted from different studies related to perceived usefulness factor which assesses whether a user finds the ICT to be generally helpful, productive, imaginative and interesting in relation to a person's work. Behavioural factor examines approach avoidance or whether computers are used frequently. The measures for behavioural intention and attitude toward objects were adopted from (Wixom et al. 2005) and (Crites et al. 1994) respectively. For attitude toward behaviour, we constructed the measures based on the guideline by (Ajzen et al. 2005, p.199, Zhang, 2007). Perceived behavioural control component which focuses on the extent to which the user is in control of the ICT (see Ajzen, 1991; Davis, 1989; Davis, et al. 1989; Davis & Venkatesh, 1996; Spacey, *et al.*, 2004a; Selwyn, 1987; Soh, 1998; Salleh, & Albion, 2004). All constructs were measured using multiple items on 5-point Likert scales.

Factorial Analysis and Assessment of the Constructs

Factorial analysis of the constructs is usually done in relations to the items used to measure them. This can be explained through rigorous diagnostic of validity of the model with respect to items-relation among all the constructs, which include construct validity itself, discriminant analysis, convergent and/or divergent validity as well as the measurement model at large as discussed in the subsequence sections of the chapter.

Construct Validity

We did address construct validity by looking at loadings and cross loadings to identify problematic items, if any. Following Hair et al (2010), a significant value of 0.5 loadings is used as a cut-off. As has been depicted in Table 1, items measuring each construct in the study are highly loaded on their particular construct and loaded lower on others, thus construct validity of the instruments is established.

Convergent Validity

The convergent validity of the instrument was also tested to examine the multiple items measuring the same construct of the study and the degree of their agreement with one another. In this respect, the factor loadings alongside both composite reliability and average variance were extracted for proper examination.

$$(\rho c) = (\Sigma \ \lambda i)2 \ / \ [(\Sigma \ \lambda i)2 + \ \Sigma \ Var \ (\varepsilon i)]$$

where λi is the outer factor loading, and $Var \ (\varepsilon i) = 1 - \lambda i$ is the measurement error or the error variance associated with the individual indicator variable(s) for that given factor (see: Fornell & Larcker, 1981).

(AVE)[b]: Average Variance Extracted

$$(AVE) = (\Sigma \ \lambda 2i) \ / \ [(\Sigma \ \lambda 2i) + \Sigma \ Var \ (\varepsilon i)]$$

where λi is the outer factor loading, and $Var \ (\varepsilon i) = 1 - \lambda i$ is the measurement error or the error variance associated with the individual indicator variable(s) for that given factor (see: Fornell & Larcker, 1981).

Assessment of the results in Table 2 shows that all items' loadings exceeded the recommended

Table 1. Loadings and cross loadings for construct validity

	Actual Use of ICT (AU)	Attitude (Att.)	Behavioural Intention (BI)	Perceived Behavioural Control (PBC)	Perceived Usefulness (PU)	Subjective Norm (SN)
B1					0.855432	
B2					0.874992	
B3					0.874988	
B4					0.858488	
B5					0.889799	
B6					0.827138	
B7					0.887182	
B8					0.882515	
G1		0.922839				
G2		0.904475				
G3		0.864759				
G4		0.875698				
G5		0.875484				
G6		0.883108				
G7		0.886864				
G8		0.893083				
H1						0.919585
H2						0.916003
H3						0.833408
H4						0.892435
H5						0.905793
H6						0.886594
I1				0.880298		
I2				0.891071		
I3				0.926759		
I4				0.879746		
I5				0.913656		
I6				0.901331		
J1			0.903628			
J2			0.895446			
J3			0.808232			
J4			0.837633			
J5			0.868391			
J6			0.877142			
J7			0.89579			
K1	0.875829					
K2	0.910936					
K3	0.837216					
K4	0.884572					
K5	0.90333					
K6	0.84902					
K7	0.922748					

Table 2. Outer weights (loadings, STDEV, t-values)

Measurement Items	Loadings	Standard Deviation (STDEV)	T -Statistics	Composite Reliability (CR)[a]	Average Variance Extract (AVE)[b]
B1 <- PercievedUseful	0.855432	0.035277	24.24875***		
B2 <- PercievedUseful	0.874992	0.022113	39.56979***		
B3 <- PercievedUseful	0.874988	0.022384	39.09061***		
B4 <- PercievedUseful	0.858488	0.032011	26.81861***		
B5 <- PercievedUseful	0.889799	0.02491	35.72108***	0.9610	0.7552
B6 <- PercievedUseful	0.827138	0.034468	23.99758***		
B7 <- PercievedUseful	0.887182	0.018407	48.19789***		
B8 <- PercievedUseful	0.882515	0.023285	37.90015***		
G1 <- Attitude	0.922839	0.01686	54.73596***		
G2 <- Attitude	0.904475	0.021014	43.04224***		
G3 <- Attitude	0.864759	0.023872	36.22552***		
G4 <- Attitude	0.875698	0.023376	37.46105***		
G5 <- Attitude	0.875484	0.026505	33.03081***	0.9677	0.7893
G6 <- Attitude	0.883108	0.023204	38.05794***		
G7 <- Attitude	0.886864	0.025682	34.53292***		
G8 <- Attitude	0.893083	0.022672	39.39108***		
H1 <- SubjectiveNorm	0.919585	0.012586	73.06212***		
H2 <- SubjectiveNorm	0.916003	0.01342	68.25563***		
H3 <- SubjectiveNorm	0.833408	0.026763	31.13999***	0.9592	0.7970
H4 <- SubjectiveNorm	0.892435	0.017906	49.83896***		
H5 <- SubjectiveNorm	0.905793	0.012874	70.35995***		
H6 <- SubjectiveNorm	0.886594	0.021532	41.17481***		
I1 <- PBC	0.880298	0.0206	42.73225***		
I2 <- PBC	0.891071	0.023888	37.30168***		
I3 <- PBC	0.926759	0.015414	60.12343***	0.9619	0.8082
I4 <- PBC	0.879746	0.022718	38.7238***		
I5 <- PBC	0.913656	0.014665	62.30069***		
I6 <- PBC	0.901331	0.018397	48.99383***		
J1 <- Intention	0.903628	0.017879	50.54239***		
J2 <- Intention	0.895446	0.017778	50.36849***		
J3 <- Intention	0.808232	0.037875	21.33932***		
J4 <- Intention	0.837633	0.028493	29.39803***	0.9561	0.7570
J5 <- Intention	0.868391	0.025569	33.9621***		
J6 <- Intention	0.877142	0.020447	42.89772***		
J7 <- Intention	0.89579	0.015026	59.61591***		

continued on following page

Table 2. Continued

Measurement Items	Loadings	Standard Deviation (STDEV)	T -Statistics	Composite Reliability (CR)[a]	Average Variance Extract (AVE)[b]
K1 <- ActualUse	0.875829	0.019972	43.85343***		
K2 <- ActualUse	0.910936	0.01662	54.81103***		
K3 <- ActualUse	0.837216	0.039486	21.2031***		
K4 <- ActualUse	0.884572	0.021378	41.37729***	0.9615	0.7812
K5 <- ActualUse	0.90333	0.01978	45.66899***		
K6 <- ActualUse	0.84902	0.026315	32.26356***		
K7 <- ActualUse	0.922748	0.014152	65.20307***		

***P<0.001, (CR)[a:] Composite reliability

value of 0.5 suggested by Hair et al (2010) for each of the construct in the extended model. In addition, the composite reliability was used to test how far the construct indicators really represent the latent and the values obtained ranging from 0.9561 to 0.9677, which exceeded the recommended value of 0.7 by Hair et al (2010) as shown in Table 2. In addition, the average variance extracted (AVE) was used to relatively examine the variance captured by the construct indicators to measurement error. According to Barclay et al (1995), the value must be above 0.5 for justification. In this chapter, the AVEs for the indicators are within the range of 0.7552 and 0.8082 respectively. Looking at the results for the parameter estimates and the test of their statistical significance (t-values at p<0.001 alpha levels), it can be concluded that all the variables in the model are valid measures of their respective constructs (see Chow & Chan, 2008).

Discriminant Validity

The discriminant validity of the measures has equally been tested to examine the degree to which items differentiate among constructs. This was carried out first by looking at correlations between the measures for possible potential overlapping of constructs. Second, whether items are strongly loaded on their own construct in the model were examined. Third, whether the average variance shared between each construct and that its measures are greater than the average variance shared between the constructs and other constructs were also explored, as suggested by Compeau et al, (1999). In this respect, the results of Table 3 show that the squared correlations for each construct is less than the average squared root of the variance extracted by the indicators measuring each of the construct. Hence, the measurement model reflects

Table 3. Latent variable correlations

Model Constructs	1	2	3	4	5	6
Actual Use	0.8838					
Attitude	0.5387	0.8884				
Intention to Use	0.6209	0.6014	0.8701			
PBC	0.6285	0.5948	0.6404	0.8989		
Perceived usefulness	0.4352	0.6089	0.5193	0.4637	0.7429	
Subjective Norm	0.3862	0.4461	0.4662	0.4200	0.4107	0.8927

an adequate convergent validity and discriminant validity as results formally confirmed in Table 3.

Reliability Analysis

As has been formally confirmed, reliability is an indication of the internal consistency of the instruments measuring the concepts and it helps access the "goodness" of measure (Sekaran & Bougie, 2010). There are many different ways of estimating reliability of a measure (Ambali, 2009). One of the most widely used tests is Cronbach's Alpha that was employed in this chapter as shown in Table 4. By looking at the results of the Cronbach's Alpha, they are ranged from 0.9462 to 0.9618, thus confirming the reliability of the instrument used. It is worth noting that the range of reliability test using Cronbach's Alpha ranges from zero to one. The closer to one the higher the level of internal consistency among items and thus the reliability of the instruments are ensured in this study.

In this chapter, Harman's one-factor test was examined to address any potential common method variance bias that may likely exist since the data was a self-reported in nature by the respondents. As argued by Podsakoff and Organ (1986), common variance bias is problematic if a single latent factor accounts for the majority of the total explained variance. Thus, the result of the un-rotated factor analysis shows that the

first factor only accounted for 20.6% of the total 73.91% variance and therefore common method bias is not a problem.

FINDINGS

The findings in the Table 5 show that majority of the participants are females with 54% as compared to the male counterparts. Most of the Malay ethnic composition dominates (95.4%) the workforce at the organization. Interestingly, the age of the respondents ranged from 18-28 years to 40-50 years and above, which sounds a sense of maturity in dealing and handling public matters using ICT devices. Hence, it is worth mentioning that most of the civil servants at the organization are within two major categories of age 18-28 years (42.1%) and 29-39 years (45%). However, their high level of maturity does not automatically indicate that all of them are adequately using ICT to accomplish works. There could be variability among them in terms frequency and magnitude of usage for services delivery. In addition, many of the respondents have 6-10 hours in a week using ICT for services delivery with other government agencies or for general public demands as well as retrieving information (42.4%) followed by 11-15 hour of experience engaging in the public over the net (34.8%). Interestingly, some of the old and senior civil servants (2.3) have also adopted ICT

Table 4. Reliability tests result

Model Constructs	No. of Items	Cronbachs Alpha
Actual Use of ICT	7	0.9531
Behavioural Attitude towards ICT	8	0.9618
Behavioural Intention to Use ICT	6	0.9462
Perceived Behavioural Control (PBC)	6	0.9524
Perceived Usefulness (PU)	8	0.9536
Subjective Norm	6	0.9488

Table 5. Profile of respondents

Variables	Frequency	Percentage
Gender		
Male	139	46%
Female	163	54%
Age		
18-28	127	42.1%
29-39	136	45%
40-50	33	10.9%
51-61	6	2%
Qualification		
MA/PhD.	7	2.3%
Degree	69	22.8%
STPM/Diploma	144	41.7%
Certificate (Education)	82	27.2%
Ethnic Group		
Malay	288	95.4%
Chinese	2	0.7%
India	12	4%
Hours of Using ICT for Tasks Per Week		
1-5	62	20.5%
6-10	128	42.4%
11-15	105	34.8%
16-20	7	2.3%

to perform work assigned to them perhaps through shared knowledge of ICT with the younger ones in the organisation.

On a separate note, most of the respondents reported that they have been using ICT among for filling applications, downloading related files, monitoring the feedback and/or approval.

Interestingly, about 43% of the respondents uses ICT for 7-8 hours per day (see Table 6) in accomplishing the tasks assigned to them at the agencies. One would expect the numbers of hours used to be more that this, however a critical assessment of this low expectation reflects that there could be other means or channel through which the staff can to engage with the public masses to meet and attend to their demands. Among the alternative channels could be direct phone called, fax and even face-to-face engagement where necessary.

Table 6. Degree of using ICT per day by the respondents

General Use of ICT	Durations of Use for Any of the Tasks	Frequency	Percentage
-Using of Organization's Portal monitoring application; -Completing requirements or tasks, -Feedback, and approvals, payment, etc.	Less than 1 hour	12	3.9%
	1 – 5 hours	95	31.5%
	6 hours	35	11.6%
	7 – 8 hours	129	42.7%
	More than 9 hours	31	10.3%

ASSESSING THE STRUCTURAL RELATIONSHIPS OF THE CONSTRUCTS IN THE MODEL

In this section, the researchers address the path coefficients to examine the relationships between the structural latent constructs of the model. The results obtained have shown positive significant relationships among all the constructs in this extended model. As clearly shown in Figure 2, the results indicate a positive significant relationship exists between perceived usefulness of ICT in doing works and attitude towards use with beta coefficient values of 0.780, p<0.001. A similar significant positive relationship exists between the causal link of the attitude towards use and the behavioural intention to use with beta coefficient values of 0.311, p<0.001. In addition, the causal link between subjective norm and the behavioural intention to use is also positively related with a beta value of 0.193, p<0.001. Furthermore, the path coefficients between perceived behavioural

control PBC of civil servants and behavioural intention to use ICT for doing tasks is positively and significantly related with a beta value of 0.436, p<0.001. The same similar positive causal relationship can be inferred between behavioural intention to use and the actual usage of ICT to carry out various assigned and obligatory works at the organization with a beta value 0.427, p<0.001. These results have partially established all the causal links in the extended TPB model of this chapter. However, there is a need to further test the predictive capacity and to statistically establish each hypothesis in the model by assessing the t-values.

Predictive Capacity of the Extended Model and Hypotheses Testing

As can be seen in Figure 3 the t-values of the path coefficients are generated to test the significant contribution of each path coefficient of the latent constructs through a bootstrapping procedure in

Figure 2. Structural coefficient results of the extended model

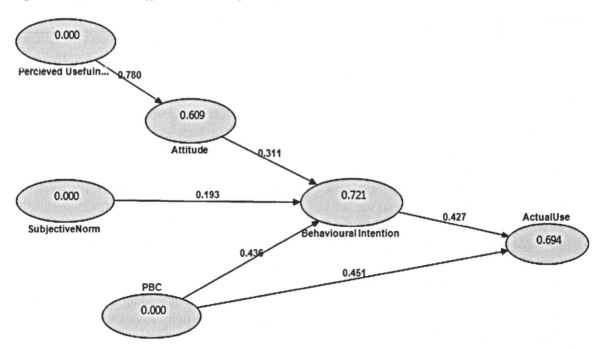

Figure 3. Bootstrapping results of the structural model

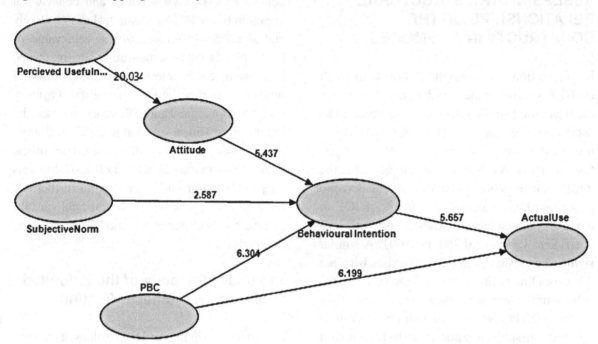

order to validate the predictive capacity of the extended model as well as the hypotheses put forward in this chapter.

The results show that all hypotheses in the study are supported with t-values ranging from 2.587* to 20.034*** at an alpha-value of p<0.001 respectively (see Table 7). As the results depicted in the Table 7, R^2 values of the three endogenous latent constructs in the model such as attitude towards use, behavioural intention to use ICT and the actual use of ICT for performing tasks ranged from 0.609 (attitude), 0.721 (perceived behavioural control) to 0.694 (actual use) respectively (see Table 6). It means that perceived usefulness explained approximately 61% of attitude of staff towards use of ICT. In addition, the three exogenous variables such as attitude, subjective norms and PBC all together explained 72.1% of behavioural intention to use ICT while both intention and PBC accounted for 69.4% of the actual use of ICT by the staff of the organization.

According to Chin, (1998), it is paramount to examine the overall predictive power of the extended model of the study based on the values

of the endogenous constructs obtained. According to Kock (2012, p. 31), this can be done by assessing the average variance inflation factor (AVIF) as a comprehensive analysis of a model's overall capacity and explanatory quality of the latent factors linking to actual use of ICT in this study. This is important in order to address the absence of both vertical and lateral collinearities. The result shows a value of 1.19 (see Table 7), which is far below the threshold of 3.3 (Kock, 2012; Ambali & Ahmad, 2013). Additionally, other indices for the model fit such as average path coefficient (APC), average r-squared (ARS) are addressed in the process of addressing the predictive capacity of the model are very essential. In this respect, the result of both APC and ARS are 0.433 and 67.5% respectively. These results indicate a practical significant power of the extended model of TPB in this chapter (Kock, 2012).

Moreover, Q-squared coefficient was performed through blindfolding in order to assess the predictive validity associated with each latent variable's block in the model as well as the strength. Acceptable predictive validity strength

Table 7. Summary of t-statistics for the path coefficients and hypotheses testing

Hypotheses	Construct Causal Relation	Beta (β) Coefficient	Endogenous Latent Variables (R^2)	T-Statistics	Remark
H1	Perceived usefulness -> Attitude	0.780	$R^2 = 0.609$ (60.9%)	20.034***	supported
H2	Attitude -> Behavioural intention	0.311	$R^2 = 0.721$ (72.1%)	5.437***	supported
H3	Subjective norm -> Intention	0.193		2.587**	supported
H4	PBC -> Intention	0.436		6.304***	supported
H5	PBC -> Actual use	0.451	$R^2 = 0.694$ (69.4%)	6.199***	supported
H6	Behavioural intention -> Actual use	0.427		5.657***	supported
Predictive Capacity of the Model					
Criteria		**Value**			
AVIF		1.19			
APC		0.433			
ARS		67.5%			
Q-squared		0.42			

Note: *** P<0.001, **P<0.01.

in connection with endogenous latent variables as suggested by examine a Q-squared coefficient must be greater than a zero threshold (Kock, 2012; Ambali & Ahmad, 2013). The result of the predictive validity for this extended model is 0.42 indicating good predictive factors that can influence the usage of ICT among users of the organization.

DISCUSSION OF THE FINDINGS

The findings of the study have shown that the degree of the ICT usage among the users of the agencies for filling applications, downloading information, as well as given feedbacks to the public mass, to carry out the needed requirements for tasks assigned to them and payment status was encouraging. The results reflect that the frequency and period spent using ICT to perform tasks per day by majority (42.7%) of the respondents was about 7 to 8 hours. This seems to be encouraging despite the fact that there were other means

of carrying out the tasks such as usage of phone, fax and postage of written materials to the public and/or necessary agencies. This amount of time devoted by majority of the users has something to do with interrelationships among all the variables of interests addressed in the extended model of TPB, which need some valuable explanations.

The results obtained from the extended model have shown that behavioural intention of the staff at agencies is a function of the perceived usefulness of a technology system. A high coefficient beta value (β) = 0.780, p<0.001 indicating a strong relationship between the perceived usefulness and the attitude towards use of technology especially when they have established a convincing belief that use of a technology can help them enhance their works more efficiently. This high significant impact of perceived usefulness added to the TPB as antecedent of attitude suggests two-fold practical importance of the model in reality. First, it shows that users must be convinced of the potential benefits and gains associated with usage of new technology in contrast to their traditional ways of doing things in public sector. Second, it suggests that failure to make users realize such benefits in using a particular technology could negate their attitudes towards using the technology system. If they are really convinced with the gains, the negations developed towards the system for the first time as human being's reactions to change could become positive and this will in turn positively lead to positive intention to use technology. Evidentially speaking, the finding of the study has shown a significant positive relationship between positive attitude towards technology and behavioural intention to use it with beta coefficient value (β) = 0.311, p<0.001. This means that behavioural intention of a user is a function of nature attitude towards the technology system. For example, where a user forms or develops a positive attitude towards a given technology device, his or her behavioural intention would be positive towards using it and vice-versa.

In addition, other variables of interest in the extended model have shown significant positive relationship towards behavioural intention to use ICT for doing works among the staff. The two latent variables such as subjective norm (or social pressures) as well as perceived behavioural control (i.e., ease or extent of difficulty perceived referred to as PCB) have shown significant influences on users' intention to use technology system by the respondents. Evidently, significant correlations were found between subjective norms, PCB and the behavioural intention to use with coefficient beta values (β) = 0.193, t-value of 2.57 and (β) = 0.436, t=value of 6.304, p<0.001 respectively. It means that important people around the users such as their respected colleagues, friends and other reputable or valuable individuals to them can influence their intentions to use the system. However, it is pertinent to highlight in this study that though the relative important individuals around the users has weak correlation value but yet still significantly beard impact on intention. In contrast, the PBC was found in many other studies

to have no impact on behavioural intention but has a strong impact on intention to use ICT among the respondents. Such finding in this study shows that degree of easiness and situational condition at which the users are utilizing ICT are extremely important to develop positive intention towards using it. This result is also supported by similar finding of a strong correlation between PBC and intention by (Davies, 2008).

Furthermore, the results obtained in this study also demonstrate a strong and significant relationship between PBC and actual utilization of ICT among the respondents with a beta coefficient value (β) = 0.451, t-value of 6.199, p<001. It means that situation conditions such as perceived facilitating conditions by users can influence actual use of the technology system. For example, where all things being equal, a person will definitely use technology system with availability of other supporting tools needed in place and vice-versa. It also indicates that having a positive intention to use ICT does not automatically result to actual use of it unless all supporting tools are available. For example stable Internet connection and strong server for easy transmission of messages are very peculiar condition for a person to finally use ICT devices. Ability and competency of the person in terms of computer literacy and technical know-how are crucial for actual usage.

Finally, according to the findings, actual usage of the technology also depends on behavioural intention as well with a beta value (β) = 0.427, t-value of 5.657, p<0.001. It is worth mentioning that such strong relationship reflects the importance of intention and its relative influence on users' choice to eventually use a technology system for doing works in public sector. The main message worth noting is that a user must be convinced to have positive intention to use a particular IT system. This can be easily achieved without the presence of other antecedents of behavioural intention as discussed earlier in this section. In conclusion, it is only when intention has been established through formation of positive attitude, presence of important individuals and perceived ease of technology that ICT system can be finally used.

CHAPTER SUMMARY

This chapter has extended the theory of planned behaviour using a problem based approach of perceived usefulness of ICT among the subjects of the study at selected four public agencies in Selangor. The information obtained through a preliminary interview regarding what normally being the reason for people's reluctant of using a technology system. Most of the respondents unanimously expressed their concerns on the issue of whether technology can really help achieve one's goal of using it or not at first contact. According to results of the interview, most respondents answers, to question on regarding what makes him or her accept the use of technology, are basically on usefulness of it when they use it as well as what they heard from their close friends who had used it. Thus, the study has extended the original TPB model by inclusion of perceived usefulness as antecedent of attitude of the respondents in this chapter. Statistically, the result obtained has reflected the relative importance of the new construct introduced to the original model. In this context, perceived usefulness was found to have highest structural correlation with behavioural attitude in the path-model. In terms of practical significant of this finding, it formally confirmed the call to modify theory of planned behaviour, which was earlier discussed in chapter 7 of this book. In addition, it can be established that perceived usefulness of technology can make users form a positive attitude towards intention to use the system. This finding also indicates that perceived usefulness would strengthen the positive attitude towards use of ICT or can help change negative perception of a user to positively use technology system. In addition, the other findings of the study

have also proven that subjective norm, perceived behavioural control and behavioural attitude towards use are good predictors of intention to use ICT components to perform tasks among civil servants at Selangor government agencies.

REFERENCES

Adnan, R. (2010). *Investigating the strategies to cope with resistance to change in implementing ICT: A case study of Allama Iqbal Open University.* Retrieved Sept. 20 2013 from: http://linc.mit.edu/linc2010/proceedings/session6Riaz.pdf

Ajzen, I. (1991). The theory of planned behaviuor. *Organizational Behavior and Human Decision Processes*, *50*(2), 179–211. doi:10.1016/0749-5978(91)90020-T

Ajzen, I. (2002b). *Construction of a standard questionnaire for the theory of planned behavior.* Retrieved August 8 2013 from http://www-unix.oit.umass.edu/~aizen

Ajzen, I., & Fishbein, M. (1980). *Understanding Attitudes and Predicting Social Behaviuor.* Englewood Cliffs, NJ: Prentice-Hall.

Ajzen, I., & Fishbein, M. (2005). The Influence of Attitudes on Behavior. In D. Albarracin, B. T. Johnson, & M. P. Zanna (Eds.), *Handbook of attitudes and attitude Change*. Mahwah, NJ: Erlbaum.

Ambali, A. R. (2009). E-government policy: Ground issues in e-filling system. *European Journal of Soil Science*, *11*(2), 249–266.

Ambali, A. R. (2013). Hala food and products in Malaysia: People's awareness and policy implications. *Intellectual Discourse*, *21*(1), 7–32.

Astrom, A. N., & Rise, J. (2001). Young adults' intention to eat healthy food: Extending the theory of planned behavior. *Psychology & Health*, *2*, 223–237. doi:10.1080/08870440108405501

Barclay, D. W., Higgins, C., & Thompson, R. (1995). The partial least square approach to causal modeling: Personal computer adoption use as illustration. *Technology Studies, 2*(2), 285–309.

Chau, P. Y. (2001). Influence of computer attitude and self-efficacy on IT usage behaviour. *Journal of End User Computing, 13*(1), 26–33. doi:10.4018/joeuc.2001010103

Chin, W. W. (1998). The partial least squares approach to structural equation modeling. In G. A. Marcoulides (Ed.), *Modern Methods for Business Research,* (pp. 295–358). Mahwah, NJ: Lawrence Erlbaum Associates.

Chow, W. S., & Chan, L. S. (2008). Social network and shared goals in organizational knowledge sharing. *Information & Management, 45*(7), 24–30. doi:10.1016/j.im.2008.06.007

Compeau, D. R., Higgins, C. A., & Huff, S. (1999). Social cognitive theory and individual reactions to computing technology: A longitudinal-study. *Management Information Systems Quarterly, 23*(2), 145–158. doi:10.2307/249749

Crites, S. L. Jr, Fabrigar, L. R., & Petty, R. E. (1994). Measuring the affective and cognitive properties of attitudes: Conceptual and methodological issues. *Personality and Social Psychology Bulletin, 20*(6), 619–634. doi:10.1177/0146167294206001

Davies, C. (2008). The relationship between the theory of planned behaviour, past exercise behaviour and intention in individuals diagnosed with Type 2 Diabetes Studies, *Learning. Innovation and Development, 5*(2), 25–32.

Davis, F. D. (1989). Perceived Usefulness, Perceived Ease of Use and User Acceptance of Technology. *Management Information Systems Quarterly, 13*(3), 319–340. doi:10.2307/249008

Davis, F. D., Bagozzi, R. P., & Warshaw, P. R. (1989). User acceptance of computer technology: A comparison of two theoretical models. *Management Science, 35*(8), 982–1003. doi:10.1287/mnsc.35.8.982

Davis, F. D., & Venkatesh, V. (1996). A theoretical extension of technology acceptance model: Four longitudinal field studies. *Management Science, 46*(2), 186–2004.

Dixon, K. C. (2009). Attitudes towards ICT based interaction: A bachelor of education case studies. Australia: School of Education, Curtin University of Technology Perth. Retrieved from http://www.aare.edu.au/09pap/dix091331.pdf

Eagly, A. H., & Chaiken, S. (1993). *The psychology of attitudes*. Fort Worth, TX: Harcourt Brace Jovanovich.

Fila, S. A., & Smith, C. (2006). Applying the theory of planned behavior to healthy eating behaviors in urban Native American youth. *The International Journal of Behavioral Nutrition and Physical Activity, 3*(1), 11–22. doi:10.1186/1479-5868-3-11 PMID:16734903

Fishbein, M., & Ajzen, I. (1975). *Belief, Attitude, Intention and Behaviour: An Introduction to Theory and Research*. Reading, MA: Addison-Wesley.

Fornell, C., & Larcker, D. F. (1981). Evaluating structural equation models with unobservable and measurement error. *JMR, Journal of Marketing Research, 18*(1), 39–50. doi:10.2307/3151312

Grinter, R. E., & Eldridge, M. (2001). Y do tngrs luv 2 txt msg? In *Proceedings of the Seventh European Conference on Computer-Supported Cooperative Work ECSCW'01,* (pp. 219-238). Kluwer Academic Publishers.

Hair, J. F., Black, W. C., Babin, B. J., & Anderson, R. E. (2010). *Multivariate data analysis*. Upper Saddle River, NJ: Prentice-Hall.

Kock, N. (2012). *WarPLS 3.0, user manual*. Laredo, TX: ScriptWarp System.

Lumpe, A. T., & Chambers, E. (2001). Assessing teacher's context beliefs about technology use. *Journal of Research on Technology in Education, 34*(1), 93–107. doi:10.1080/15391523.2001.10782337

Mahmood, M. A., Burn, J. M., Gemoets, L. A., & Jacquez, C. (2000). Variables affecting information technology end-user satisfaction: A meta-analysis of the empirical literature. *International Journal of Human-Computer Studies, 52*(4), 751–771. doi:10.1006/ijhc.1999.0353

Pedersen, P. E., & Nysveen, H. (2002). *Using the theory of planned behaviour to explain teenagers' adoption of text messaging services*. Norway: Agder University College.

Podsakoff, P. M., & Organ, D. W. (1986). Self-reports in organizational research: Problems and prospects. *Journal of Management, 12*(4), 531–544. doi:10.1177/014920638601200408

Rise, J., Thompson, M., & Verplanken, B. (2003). Measuring implementation intentions in the context of the theory of planned behaviour. *Scandinavian Journal of Psychology, 44*(2), 87–95. doi:10.1111/1467-9450.00325 PMID:12778976

Rogers, E. M. (2003). *Diffusion of Innovations* (5th ed.). New York: The Free Press.

Salleh, S. M., & Albion, P. (2004). Using the theory of planned behaviour to predict Bruneian teachers' intentions to use ICT in teaching. In *Proceedings of the 15th International Conference of the Society for Information Technology & Teacher Education* (SITE 2004). Atlanta, GA: Academic Press.

Sekaran, U., & Bougie, R. (2010). *Research methods for business: A skill building approach* (4th ed.). John Wiley & Sons, Inc.

Selwyn, W. (1997). Students' attitude toward computers: Validation of a computer attitude scale for 16-19 education. *Computers & Education, 28*(1), 35–41. doi:10.1016/S0360-1315(96)00035-8

Soh, K. C. (1998a). *Cross cultural validity of selwyn computer attitude scale*. Unpublished manuscript.

Spacey, R., Goulding, A., & Murray, I. (2004a). Exploring the attitudes of public library staff to the Internet using the TAM. *The Journal of Documentation, 60*(5), 550–564. doi:10.1108/00220410410560618

Venkatesh, V., Morris, M. G., Davis, G. B., & Davis, F. D. (2003). User acceptance of information technology: Toward a unified view. *Management Information Systems Quarterly, 27*(3), 425–478.

Wixom, B. H., & Todd, P. (2005). A theoretical integration of user satisfaction and technology acceptance. *Information Systems Research, 6*(1), 85–102. doi:10.1287/isre.1050.0042

Zhang, P. (2007). Roles of attitudes in initial and continued ICT use: A longitudinal study. In *Proceedings of Americas Conference on Information Systems*. Retrieved Jan 12th 2014 from http://aisel.aisnet.org/cgi/viewcontent.cg

Zhang, P., & Aikman, S. (2009). Attitudes in ICT acceptance and use, *Human-Comput. Interaction. Design Usabil, 4550*, 1021–1030.

KEY TERMS AND DEFINITIONS

Antecedent of Attitude: A thing that existed before or logically precedes another. In this book, it refers to what precedes attitude of users of technology provided or what can influence their attitude towards use of technology.

Behavioural Intention: The tendency of an individual's readiness to perform certain behaviour such as using of technology provided.

Direct Effect: An understanding of mechanistic pathway by which one thing affects or causes another.

Elicitation: Acquiring or getting intelligence information from users of technology about what really brings about the tendency to use the system.

Knowledge (of Technology): Familiarity or understanding of the function of technology devices and how to use them.

Productivity: A measure of the efficiency of a person and/or system, etc., in converting inputs into useful outputs in service delivery.

Skills: Ability and capacity acquired through deliberate learning to carry out a task with predetermined results often within a given amount of time.

System: A set of interacting or interdependent technology components created to carry out a specific activity or perform certain tasks assigned to civil servants.

Chapter 11
Investigation of ICT Usage in Malaysian Public Sector using Extension of TAM:
Case of Higher Learning Institution

ABSTRACT

In terms of student population, Universiti Teknologi MARA is one of the largest universities in Malaysia. It has adopted i-class system through which teaching and learning are facilitated as alternative method of delivering knowledge to students. However, the rate at which the targeted students are using the system is very poor. As such, the chapter revisits technology acceptance from the perspective of a problem-based study and uses the information gathered to extend the original TAM model. The significant contribution of the chapter is the focus on the external variables to perceived usefulness and perceived ease of using i-class. Since the majority of targeted students learning through this mode are adults, perceived computer self-efficacy, perceived convenience, and subjective norm are considered for extension. The results obtained show significant relationships between the causal links among the new constructs.

INTRODUCTION

The adoption of information and communication technology (ICT) in higher learning institutes has dominated education system in Malaysia. Almost every university is changing from absolute traditional method of teaching (i.e., face-to-face) to an online or virtual learning system. In other words, most government owned universities in Malaysia have at least incorporated distance learning and e-learning as part of their curriculum designs for education system. Thus, the Internet has become a strategic education tool being used on daily basis as a resource provider for teaching. Apart from using the technology as a new platform for delivering education and imparting knowledge, it is widely used for registration of new students' intake where course registration is very obvious. Other areas that the use of the ICT has become famous among learning institutes are its uses for electronic examination slips and results, e-billing (bursary) and student's class schedule which

DOI: 10.4018/978-1-4666-6579-8.ch011

enable the education institutes reduce their inefficiencies and avoid errors in the teaching and delivery processes. Therefore, ICT has become the most important tool in the new era of education system, not only in Malaysia but also across varsity education around the globe.

There are many definitions of e-learning, but here, e-learning is defined as learning facilitated and supported through the utilisation of information and communication technologies (ICTs) (see Jenkins and Hanson, 2003). Accordingly, there are various resource options as educational ICT tools which can be divided into three categories: input source such PC, visualised or document camera, slate tablet, application software, student response system. Output sources are projector, interactive whiteboard and display monitor. The third resources will be others such as digital camera, switcher, digital recorder, and other technologies (Elmo Classroom Solution, 2012). A report made by the National Institute of Multimedia Education in Japan proved that exposure of a student to educational ICT, through curriculum integration, has a significant and positive impact on students' achievements, especially in terms of "knowledge-comprehension," "practical skill," and "presentation skill" in subject areas such as mathematics, science, and social studies.

Despite the recognition of the profound benefits in utilisation and adoption of ICT as a new medium of delivering education, there are many potential challenges envisioned. The challenges have been pointed out by many scholars and practitioners. For example, according to Alavi and Leidner (2001):

... while the use of ICT such as online study in education has increased rapidly, key users, particularly students in colleges and university still not grab this opportunity to facilitate the valuable resource of the ICT in their learning thoughts. The benefits of online study cannot be achieved unless students utilize the education website and its associated capabilities such as i-learn (pp.4-5).

Alavi and Leidner (2001) pointed out that e-learning represents one form of technology mediated learning, which is defined as an environment in which the learner's interactions with the e-learning materials peers, and/or instructors is mediated through advanced information technologies (Alavi & Leidner, 2001). In order for e-learning to work, the technology must actually be used (Leidner & Jarvenpaa, 1993).

In Malaysia, the government has encouraged the adoption of e-learning education system as part of curriculum designed for the new generation of students. For example, a recent report from the daily newspaper revealed that a total of 395 students from six secondary schools in the Bagan division have received free notebooks under the 1Malaysia scheme. The government also hoped the students could master ICT knowledge with the notebooks given and improve their academic performance (David Chua, The Star Online, June, 2012). In addition, "the government had provided infrastructure such as school networks, computer labs and software to support the move of introducing creativity and innovation in the curriculum. Thus, ICT was no longer a choice but a necessity, especially for students who could utilise the internet to carry out research and produce reports," said Datuk Fadilah Yusof, Deputy Science, Technology, and Innovation (The Star online, May 27, 2012). However, problem arises when the technology is not fully utilised.

Universiti Teknologi MARA, (UiTM), is the largest university in Malaysia. It has branches all over the states of the country. Currently, its students' population is above 150,000 throughout Malaysia. The university is not only catering for full time students but also for working young and adult students. Many years back, the need to increase k-workers (knowledge based workers), which was one of the government's agenda for transforming the country to a full developed nation by the year 2020 had made the government approved the online learning curriculum system (called ePJJ program) for UiTM. Hence, UiTM has adopted online method as mode of studying and developed both the i-class (for ePJJ students) and i-learn (for full time students) as the main virtual connection between students-students and their facilitators. However, the mode of study that has really and fully integrated online per se in UiTM is ePJJ programme under the jurisdiction of Institute of Neo Education (InED).

STUDY PROBLEM AND EXTENSION OF TAM

The main focus of this chapter is on ePJJ students' response and usage of i-class ICT provided by the university. Most of the ePJJ students are working adults. Therefore, there is a need to find a free time to access i-class. In addition, a longer time is also needed for them to learn how to access the system especially when they are first time users of the system. Experience and preliminary interviews have shown that due to working condition and family commitment, it's hard for them to access i-class frequently. Of course, the adults feel hard and unwilling or reluctant to spend time to learn the i-class with given reasons such as lack of time to focus on system learning.

Therefore, the acceptance of technology between full time and ePJJ students will be different in terms of time consuming, learning effort and social influence. Other problems, ePJJ students which one might face are slow internet connectivity and some of the places or states where they are living or coming from may not even have the Internet coverage. One key point to bear in mind is that Internet is the main channel for the ePJJ students to gain access to their online study. Otherwise, it will be impossible for the students to undergo their learning sessions. The difficulties to launch into the Internet provided by the broadband company will make students to prefer not to use the online study frequently. The issues about system shut down or under maintenance have been complained many times to the UiTM

administrators. The ePJJ students might be facing problems even when they have time to go online and absorb needed important information in i-class. However, more often than none, they are unable to get the access. These problems give rise to perception of difficulty and inconvenience in using ICT for online study.

A simple adoption of the earlier technology acceptance model (Davis, 1986) might not fit into the study of i-class developed by UiTM. In fact, previous detailed review of adoption of earlier TAM has shown that the learner perspective on e-learning systems had been largely overlooked (Sharpe, Benfield *et al.*, 2005). In fact, there was a strong emphasis from Venketash and Davis (2000) on the needs and rationales to extend TAM developed by Davis (1986) in order to suit a particular phenomenon at hand. Davis (1986) has measured this acceptance by only three factors which are perceived usefulness (PU), perceived ease of use (PEOU), and attitudes towards usage (ATU) in the model. To address this issue, we extended the original model of technology acceptance to suit ePJJ students' intention toward the adoption of ICT-based online study applications called i-class in UiTM. As explained earlier in chapter 3 of this book, further researches and studies have reported the influence and effect of objective characteristics of technology itself and users' interactions with other users or people around him/her on the perceptions about information technologies. These observations have been identified as limitations to original TAM and have given rise to many attempts to extend the model. The study aims to collect, verify and analyse students' experiences with the online study via i-class tool in UiTM.

In details, there are nine specific objectives to be achieved in this chapter which are:

1. To examine relationship between computer self-efficacy (SE) and perceived usefulness (PU) of i-class among ePJJ students in UiTM.

2. To examine relationship between perceived convenience (PC) and perceived usefulness of i-class among ePJJ students in UiTM.
3. To examine relationship between perceived convenience and perceived ease of using (PEOU) i-class among ePJJ students in UiTM.
4. To examine relationship between subjective norm (SN) and perceived ease of using i-class among ePJJ students in UiTM.
5. To examine relationship between ease of using i-class and perceived usefulness among ePJJ students in UiTM.
6. To examine relationship between perceived usefulness and attitude towards i-class (ATU) among ePJJ students in UiTM.
7. To examine relationship between perceived ease of use and attitude towards i-class among ePJJ students in UiTM.
8. To examine relationship between attitude towards i-class and intention (INT) to use among ePJJ students in UiTM.
9. To examine relationship between intention to use and actual use (AU) of i-class among ePJJ students in UiTM.

As has been observed by many scholars in the literatures, it is not only that the original TAM model cannot absolutely fit all settings of technology acceptance in the public sector but also it cannot help us achieve those aforementioned specific objectives. It should be borne in mind that those specific objectives have specific observed issues in i-class system which needs to be addressed based on our personal experience of teaching the ePJJ students in UiTM. Hence, there is a need for extending original TAM in the context of the present problems we observed among ePJJ students. It is on this note that we sought a rationale for extending original model. That means the original model of technology acceptance is still useful but needs some additional constructs to be added into its configuration to achieve our objectives in this chapter.

The Extended Model of TAM

Figure 1 displays the extended model and we have made an attempt to operationalise all the given variables in the model with substantive evidence in the literature to justify the links among the variables of interest in the model. For example, all antecedence of both perceived usefulness and ease of use as well as intention which were not considered in the original TAM were incorporated in the extended model. They are highlighted with purple variable box.

Figure 1. Extended model of TAM
Developed for this study, 2013.

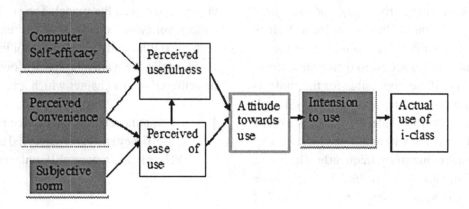

Operationalising the Model

Extension of the original model of TAM (Figure 1) is in line with by Davis (1986) by default. The original model itself obviously shows the need to extend it through the external factors or antecedences of both perceived usefulness and ease of use as well as intention when applying to different situations of technology acceptance. In this model, it is argued that student's perceived usefulness of i-class (i.e., ICT device or tool) can be affected by individual's capacity of handling the system known as computer self-efficacy. Also, the belief in oneself capacity, through self-efficacy, can influence motivational and self-regulatory processes of utilising certain device in several ways. For example, it can influence the choices the students make and the courses of action they pursue as to whether the i-class will be useful to them when they involve and/or engage themselves with it within a given period or will it result to waste of time, not because of the i-class itself but due to their own inferiority complex and capability in computer.

It can be said that most students of ePJJ will frequently engage themselves carrying out assignments or tasks at the i-class portal when they feel competent and confident or otherwise tend to avoid it. As posited in the model, computer self-efficacy is the degree to which an individual student believes that he or she has the ability to perform a specific task/job using a computer (Venkatesh & Bala, 2008, p.279). This valuable observable argument in technology acceptance is supported by Compeau and Higgins that "a judgment of one's capability to use a computer" (1995, p.192), could affect student's perceptive thoughts about usefulness of i-class. Another dimension is that perceived convenience of i-class can also influence perceived usefulness of i-class.

In relations to adoption and acceptance of ICT usage, perceived convenience is defined as the extent to which ICT helps a person lower the cognitive, emotional, physical burdens, and time

saving (see: Chi-Cheng et al. 2012). Here, we refer to a situation where ePJJ students found that i-class is perceived convenience to handle. For example, it is possible for a student to be computer self-efficacy but the i-class system might not be handiness, expedience and/or inconvenience or put extra burdens on the users if it cannot be accessed at any place and/or any time (Yoon & Kim (2007). This situation could immediately lead to a judgment about perceived level of usefulness as well as the ease of using i-class among ePJJ students. On this note, other researchers' works have shown that perceived convenience could be the main drivers for perceiving usefulness of using an online bank (Tan & Teo, 2000; Yoon & Kim, 2007; Chi-Cheng et al. 2012). At this juncture, we hypothesise three distinctive hypotheses as follows:

H1: Computer self-efficacy will positively influence perceived usefulness of i-class among ePJJ students in UiTM.

H2: Perceived convenience will positively influence perceived usefulness of i-class among ePJJ students in UiTM.

H3: Perceived convenience will positively influence perceived ease of using i-class among ePJJ students in UiTM.

Furthermore, in the above model, it is assumed that perceived ease of used by the original TAM does not happen in vacuum but rather through an antecedent variable of interest to be studied such as subjective norm. As we have been informed in the earlier chapter 2 of this book, subjective norms are expectations that valued others about how a person behaves. It refers to a "... perceived social pressure to perform or not to perform the behaviour" in question (Ajzen, 1991, p. 188). Based on this long recognition of the importance of subjective norms, we cannot overlook this variable in the model. The argument is that whatever information a particular student heard, listened and obtained from other students can influence him or her and affect his or her impression about the ease of using the i-class for accomplishing tasks such as assignments, quizzes and other related academic obligatory works. Basically, positive word of mouth about easiness of using i-class from other students can become a driver to make one's mind engage in i-class activities. Thus, encouragement from other peers can attract a student to gain positive intention of using the i-class system. The overall impression of such student is to find the system much ease than how it was imparted to him or her. So, mere hearing about easiness of using i-class from other peers will influence the mind of a particular student to adopt the system. As such, the following hypothesis is proposed:

H4: Subjective norms has positive relationship with perceived ease of using i-class among ePJJ students in UiTM.

The construct, such as perceived usefulness and ease of using i-class system among ePJJ students, can have direct impact on their attitudes Davis (1989). The judgmental argument is that if the i-class system introduced by UiTM can be used with lesser effort to realise students' key objective of using it (i.e., perceived usefulness of i-class), the probability of positive attitude towards intention to use the system will be greater. A vast number of empirical researches have confirmed this assumption. It was found that perceived ease of use has a significant influence on attitude towards use of a given technology both directly and indirectly through perceived usefulness (see Venkatesh, 1999; Davis, et al. 1992). Venkatesh and Davis (2000) argued that users' acceptance of technology system varies in accordance with the increasing level of their experiences using such system with more emphasis on perceived usefulness and ease of using technological device. More importantly is the need to re-examine mutual relation between perceived usefulness and ease of use, which provides a new direction of causal dimension in the model. In the previous studies which have used

original TAM by Davis (1986), due attention to this dimension was lesser. This is despite the fact that the causal direction was emphasised in two distinctive studies conducted by Venkatesh and Davis, (2000), and Venkatesh and Bala, (2008). There is no much work in the literature that pays attention to it. It is high time to incorporate this dimension as shown in this extended model. Thus, in the same line of thoughts, at this juncture, we hypothesise additionally, a three-fold hypothesis as follow:

H5: Perceived ease of using i-class will positively influence perceived usefulness of i-class among ePJJ students in UiTM.

H6: Perceived ease of using i-class will positively influence attitude towards engaging with i-class among ePJJ students in UiTM.

H7: Perceived usefulness of using i-class will positively influence attitude towards engaging with i-class among ePJJ students in UiTM.

According to Siragusa and Dixon (2008) "attitude represents the way in which we view the world and organise our relationships [with it]" (p.942). Similar behavioural pattern might have been developed in relation to interaction of the ePJJ students with i-class as an object in the context of this extended model. An empirical work on relationship between attitude and intention to use i-class among ePJJ students can be inferred from the degree to which individual student has a favourable or unfavourable evaluation or appraisal of the i-class (Ajzen, 1991). Attitude, particularly, the feelings of a student over the outcomes of using i-class will lead to behavioural component on how he or she responds to the given object (see: McShane & Glinow, 2008). On this note, another two fold hypothesis is proposed as follows:

H8: Attitude towards i-class has positive relation with intension to use it among the ePJJ students in UiTM.

H9: Intension to use i-class has positive relation with actual use it among the ePJJ students in UiTM.

DATA COLLECTION METHODOLOGICAL APPROACH

Methodologically, the design of the study was a cross-sectional survey where data was collected at one time only, from April to June 2013. The respondents were from less active students among the ePJJ mode of study in UiTM Shah Alam. Since there is no any other alternative way of harnessing their study other than through effective use of the i-class system, we have observed and extracted their names from the list in the forum as qualified unit of analysis in this chapter. The nature of data collection was through a five-point Likert survey questionnaire. A total of 250 questionnaires were distributed and the response rate was quite encouraging where 200 valid questionnaires (80%) were collected back for further analysis. The questionnaires were distributed to ePJJ students from various filed of and different levels of studies. Other related methodological approach such as goodness of measure and data screening are discussed in the subsequence sections.

Goodness of Measures for Instrumentation

The researchers used a questionnaire with the five-point Likert scale to obtain data for each of the constructs in the model of the study. Based on the insights obtained from previous studies by Pedersen and Nysveen, (2012), Lee, et al (2005), Petrus and Nelson, (2006), Venketash and Bala, (2008), a questionnaire was reconstructed with some modifications to earn information. In this study, both validity and reliability tests to measure the advantages of the data were used. Construct validity was used to test how well the instrument developed measures a particular construct (Sek-

aran & Bougie, 2010), while reliability was used to test how consistently the measuring instruments have measured the constructs. Validity measures in this research were in three folds in terms of construct, convergent and discriminant validities in order to examine how well the questionnaires used could tap the constructs as theorised in the extended model.

Confirmatory Analysis of the Inner and Outer Parts of the Model

Figure 2 of the extended model displays the outer model of each construct. This is necessary to confirm the structural links between the variables in the model and the loading of each items used to measure respective variables. An observation shows that the items of each variable really reflect their respective construct intended to measure. The structure links among the variables of interests in the model have yielded positive relations among each of others as expected and predicted. However, there is a need to further test the significances of the relationships among them at another section of the chapter to establish the predicted hypothesis. This is because structural values of the inner model cannot be taken as a proof of the hypothesis until bootstrapping for test of significance is carried out for confirmation. Prior to that again, there is a need to examine factorial analysis of the constructs in relations to the items used to measure them.

This can be explained through rigorous diagnosis of validity of the model with respect to items-relation among all the constructs, which include construct validity itself, discriminant analysis, convergent and divergent validity as well as the measurement model at large.

Construct Validity

Construct validity is assessed by looking at loadings and cross loadings to identify problematic items, if any. Following Hair et al (2010), a significant value of 0.5 loadings is used as a cut-off.

Figure 2. Displaying of inner and outer values of the extended model

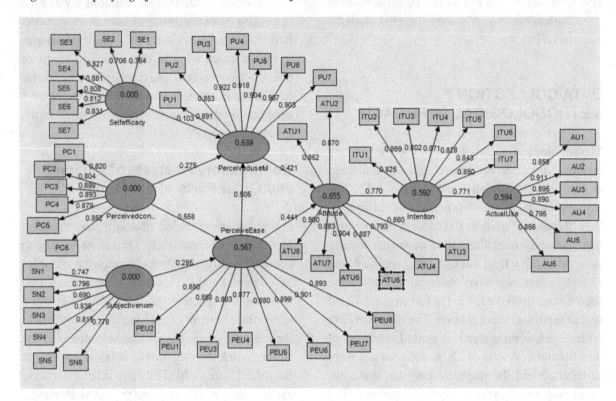

As has been depicted in Table 1, items measuring each construct in the study are highly loaded on their particular construct and loaded lower on others, thus establishing construct validity of the instruments.

Convergent Validity

The convergent validity of the instrument was also tested to examine the multiple items measuring the same construct of the study and the degree of their agreement with one another. In this respect, the factor loadings, alongside both composite reliability and average variance, were extracted for proper examination.

$$(\rho c) = (\Sigma \ \lambda i)2 \ / \ [(\Sigma \ \lambda i)2 + \ \Sigma \ Var \ (\varepsilon i)]$$

where λi is the outer factor loading, and $Var \ (\varepsilon i) = 1 - \lambda i$ is the measurement error or

the error variance associated with the individual indicator variable(s) for that given factor (see: Fornell & Larcker, 1981).

(AVE)[b]: Average Variance Extracted

$$(AVE) = (\Sigma \ \lambda 2i) \ / \ [(\Sigma \ \lambda 2i) + \ \Sigma \ Var \ (\varepsilon i)]$$

where λi is the outer factor loading, and $Var \ (\varepsilon i) = 1 - \lambda i$ is the measurement error or the error variance associated with the individual indicator variable(s) for that given factor (see: Fornell & Larcker, 1981).

The results of Table 2 show that all items' loadings exceeded the recommended value of 0.5 suggested by Hair et al (2010). In addition, the composite reliability is used to test how far the construct indicators really represent the latent and the values obtained ranging from 0.902 to 0.968, which exceeded the recommended value of 0.7 by

Table 1. Loadings and cross loadings for construct validity

Actual Use of i-Class	Attitude	Intention to Use	Perceived Ease	Perceived Convenience	Perceived Useful	Self-Efficacy	Subject-Norm
0.249	0.851	0.147	0.360	0.229	0.510	0.207	0.289
0.109	0.870	0.109	0.245	0.392	0.196	0.196	0.321
0.278	0.859	0.268	0.396	0.297	0.276	0.375	0.149
0.208	0.793	0.207	0.176	0.178	0.351	0.289	0.109
0.196	0.887	0.196	0.251	0.453	0.410	0.321	0.268
0.386	0.903	0.375	0.360	0.369	0.196	0.249	0.207
0.289	0.882	0.189	0.310	0.229	0.207	0.109	0.196
0.322	0.900	0.321	0.229	0.360	0.195	0.368	0.375
0.858	0.249	0.149	0.492	0.410	0.375	0.207	0.229
0.911	0.111	0.108	0.297	0.296	0.289	0.196	0.292
0.895	0.368	0.268	0.178	0.176	0.321	0.375	0.297
0.890	0.207	0.207	0.453	0.351	0.207	0.289	0.178
0.795	0.197	0.296	0.369	0.323	0.196	0.249	0.153
0.856	0.375	0.375	0.229	0.197	0.137	0.109	0.360
0.149	0.289	0.824	0.227	0.375	0.271	0.368	0.210
0.109	0.321	0.868	0.292	0.289	0.385	0.149	0.296
0.259	0.149	0.801	0.297	0.321	0.264	0.148	0.176
0.208	0.248	0.870	0.360	0.149	0.161	0.109	0.251
0.196	0.109	0.827	0.216	0.193	0.314	0.268	0.320
0.275	0.268	0.843	0.197	0.375	0.360	0.207	0.310
0.159	0.207	0.849	0.276	0.259	0.210	0.196	0.191
0.309	0.295	0.360	0.351	0.819	0.196	0.139	0.221
0.369	0.375	0.210	0.323	0.804	0.276	0.149	0.149
0.228	0.289	0.396	0.210	0.897	0.351	0.109	0.186
0.321	0.321	0.178	0.196	0.892	0.320	0.237	0.232
0.349	0.192	0.251	0.276	0.879	0.110	0.171	0.237
0.109	0.353	0.350	0.351	0.851	0.196	0.385	0.171
0.267	0.359	0.360	0.857	0.321	0.353	0.264	0.321
0.207	0.259	0.214	0.879	0.149	0.367	0.361	0.149
0.246	0.396	0.296	0.893	0.192	0.229	0.237	0.194
0.239	0.385	0.276	0.877	0.321	0.229	0.171	0.322
0.229	0.299	0.358	0.880	0.149	0.192	0.385	0.237
0.192	0.352	0.340	0.899	0.191	0.295	0.375	0.175
0.329	0.149	0.110	0.900	0.321	0.253	0.289	0.139
0.248	0.129	0.198	0.893	0.237	0.369	0.321	0.196
0.122	0.288	0.232	0.196	0.171	0.890	0.149	0.321
0.207	0.208	0.364	0.375	0.385	0.852	0.109	0.237

continued on following page

Table 1. Continued

Actual Use of i-Class	Attitude	Intention to Use	Perceived Ease	Perceived Convenience	Perceived Useful	Self-Efficacy	Subject-Norm
0.394	0.396	0.250	0.219	0.264	0.922	0.268	0.171
0.376	0.275	0.396	0.192	0.361	0.918	0.375	0.385
0.322	0.219	0.286	0.297	0.114	0.904	0.351	0.264
0.241	0.321	0.355	0.243	0.105	0.906	0.312	0.149
0.209	0.349	0.380	0.359	0.311	0.903	0.360	0.196
0.268	0.309	0.310	0.229	0.148	0.198	0.763	0.321
0.200	0.268	0.395	0.257	0.109	0.312	0.705	0.207
0.324	0.207	0.318	0.296	0.269	0.362	0.827	0.196
0.310	0.196	0.360	0.345	0.207	0.217	0.881	0.335
0.284	0.375	0.310	0.421	0.312	0.186	0.807	0.321
0.296	0.289	0.199	0.249	0.312	0.312	0.812	0.149
0.351	0.421	0.278	0.227	0.320	0.360	0.831	0.207
0.332	0.149	0.381	0.226	0.128	0.217	0.289	0.746
0.320	0.109	0.368	0.385	0.361	0.196	0.321	0.796
0.240	0.283	0.237	0.331	0.312	0.149	0.149	0.690
0.208	0.307	0.307	0.329	0.360	0.109	0.109	0.837
0.274	0.395	0.191	0.129	0.369	0.267	0.268	0.814
0.248	0.396	0.334	0.227	0.228	0.207	0.207	0.778

Hair et al (2010) as shown in Table 2. The average variance extracted (AVE) was used to relatively examine the variance captured by the construct indicators to measurement error. According to Barclay et al (1995), the value must be above 0.5 for justification. In this study, the AVEs for the indicators are within the range of 0.606 and 0.810 respectively. Looking at the results for the parameter estimates and the test of their statistical significance (t-values at p<0.001 alpha levels), it can be concluded that all the variables in the model are valid measures of their respective constructs (see: Chow & Chan, 2008).

Discriminant Validity

The discriminant validity of the measures has equally been tested to examine the degree to which items differentiate among constructs. This is carried out first by looking at correlations between the measures for possible potential overlapping of constructs. Second, whether items are strongly loaded on their own construct in the model were examined. Third, whether the average variance shared between each construct and that its measures are greater than the average variance shared between the constructs and other constructs are also explored, as suggested by Compeau et al, (1999).

In this respect, the results of Table 3 show that the squared correlations for each construct is less than the average variance extracted by the indicators measuring that construct. Hence, the measurement model reflects an adequate convergent validity and discriminant validity.

Table 2. Results of measurement model

Model Construct	Loading	Standard Deviation (STDEV)	Standard Error (STERR)	T-Statistics	Composite Reliability (CR)[a]	Average Variance Extract (AVE)[b]
ATU1 <- Attitude	0.852	0.009	0.0093	91.3***		
ATU2 <- Attitude	0.870	0.009	0.0092	94.5***		
ATU3 <- Attitude	0.859	0.009	0.0099	86.6***		
ATU4 <- Attitude	0.793	0.021	0.0218	36.3***	0.948	0.754
ATU5 <- Attitude	0.887	0.009	0.0092	96.5***		
ATU6 <- Attitude	0.904	0.007	0.0073	123.1***		
ATU7 <- Attitude	0.882	0.007	0.0077	114.4***		
ATU8 <- Attitude	0.900	0.006	0.0069	129.4***		
AU1 <- Actual Use	0.858	0.009	0.0099	86.0***		
AU2 <- Actual Use	0.911	0.006	0.0064	140.5***		
AU3 <- Actual Use	0.895	0.006	0.0065	135.8***	0.961	0.756
AU4 <- Actual Use	0.890	0.006	0.0069	127.2***		
AU5 <- Actual Use	0.795	0.014	0.0149	53.3***		
AU6 <- Actual Use	0.856	0.013	0.0132	64.7***		
ITU1 <- Intention	0.825	0.014	0.0148	55.8***		
ITU2 <- Intention	0.869	0.008	0.0081	106.8***		
ITU3 <- Intention	0.802	0.016	0.0169	47.2***		
ITU4 <- Intention	0.871	0.009	0.0097	89.3***	0.944	0.708
ITU5 <- Intention	0.828	0.012	0.0122	67.8***		
ITU6 <- Intention	0.843	0.009	0.0092	91.9***		
ITU7 <- Intention	0.849	0.011	0.0111	76.6**		
PC1 <- Perceived convenience	0.819	0.017	0.0177	46.3***		
PC2 <- Perceived convenience	0.804	0.020	0.0202	39.8***		
PC3 <- Perceived convenience	0.898	0.008	0.0089	101.0***		
PC4 <- Perceived convenience	0.893	0.008	0.0083	107.8***	0.943	0.736
PC5 <- Perceived convenience	0.879	0.010	0.0102	86.1***		
PC6 <- Perceived convenience	0.852	0.012	0.0127	66.7***		

continued on following page

Table 2. Continued

Model Construct	Loading	Standard Deviation (STDEV)	Standard Error (STERR)	T- Statistics	Composite Reliability (CR)[a]	Average Variance Extract (AVE)[b]
PEU1 <- Perceived ease	0.858	0.010	0.0107	79.6***		
PEU2 <- Perceived ease	0.879	0.008	0.0088	99.6***		
PEU3 <- Perceived ease	0.893	0.009	0.0098	90.6***		
PEU4 <- Perceived ease	0.877	0.009	0.0097	89.7***		
PEU5 <- Perceived ease	0.880	0.009	0.0097	90.5***	0.966	0.783
PEU6 <- Perceived ease	0.899	0.008	0.0083	107.8***		
PEU7 <- Perceived ease	0.900	0.008	0.0081	110.6***		
PEU8 <- Perceived ease	0.893	0.008	0.0083	107.4***		
PU1 <- Perceived usefulness	0.891	0.007	0.0079	112.3***		
PU2 <- Perceived usefulness	0.853	0.012	0.0121	70.8***		
PU3 <- Perceived usefulness	0.922	0.005	0.0057	162.7***		
PU4 <- Perceived usefulness	0.918	0.007	0.0070	130.4***	0.968	0.810
PU5 <- Perceived usefulness	0.904	0.008	0.0079	114.7***		
PU6 <- Perceived usefulness	0.907	0.006	0.0069	130.8***		
PU7 <- Perceived usefulness	0.903	0.009	0.0096	93.5***		
SE1 <- Self-efficacy	0.764	0.015	0.0153	49.7***		
SE2 <- Self-efficacy	0.706	0.036	0.0367	19.1***		
SE3 <- Self-efficacy	0.827	0.012	0.0117	70.3***		
SE4 <- Self-efficacy	0.881	0.008	0.0085	103.8***	0.928	0.649
SE5 <- Self-efficacy	0.808	0.015	0.0153	52.6***		
SE6 <- Self-efficacy	0.812	0.015	0.0150	53.9***		
SE7 <- Self-efficacy	0.831	0.011	0.0118	70.2***		

continued on following page

Table 2. Continued

Model Construct	Loading	Standard Deviation (STDEV)	Standard Error (STERR)	T-Statistics	Composite Reliability (CR)[a]	Average Variance Extract (AVE)[b]
SN1 <- Subjective norm	0.746	0.017	0.0169	43.9***		
SN2 <- Subjective norm	0.796	0.015	0.0152	52.4***		
SN3 <- Subjective norm	0.690	0.025	0.0250	27.5***		
SN4 <- Subjective norm	0.838	0.011	0.0114	73.4***	0.902	0.606
SN5 <- Subjective norm	0.815	0.011	0.0112	72.4***		
SN6 <- Subjective norm	0.778	0.018	0.0181	42.8***		

***P<0.001, (CR)[a]: Composite reliability

Table 3. Discriminant analysis of the latent variable correlation

Constructs	Actual Use of i-Class	Attitude	Intention	Perceived Ease	Perceived Convenience	Perceived Useful	Self Efficacy	Subjective Norm
Actual use of i-class system	1							
Attitude	0.8759	1						
Intention	0.7706	0.8773	1					
Perceive ease	0.7041	0.7623	0.8743	1				
Perceived convenience	0.7217	0.6969	0.6734	0.8449	1			
Perceived Usefulness	0.6792	0.7575	0.7089	0.7622	0.8397	1		
Self-efficacy	0.6063	0.5593	0.5419	0.5901	0.6732	0.7658	1	
Subjective norm	0.5424	0.5684	0.5815	0.5897	0.5455	0.6080	0.730	1

Reliability Analysis

Reliability is an indication of the internal consistency of the instruments measuring the concepts and helps access the "goodness" of measure (Sekaran & Bougie, 2010). There are many different types of reliability estimates. One of the most widely used tests is Cronbach's Alpha that is employed in this study as shown in Table 4. By looking at the results of the Cronbach's Alpha,

range from 0.869 to 0.961 confirm the reliability of the instrument used. It is worth mentioning that the range of reliability test using Cronbach's Alpha ranges from zero to one. The closer to one, the higher the level of internal consistency among items and thus the reliability of the instruments are ensured in this study.

Given the self-reported nature of the data, Harman's one-factor test was examined to address any potential common method variance bias.

Table 4. Reliability tests result

Variable	No. of Items	Cronbachs Alpha
Actual use of i-class	6	0.934
Attitude	8	0.954
Intention	7	0.931
Perceived ease of use	8	0.961
Perceived convenience	6	0.928
Perceived usefulness	7	0.960
Self-efficacy	7	0.909
Subjective norm	6	0.869

As contended by Podsakoff and Organ (1986), common variance bias is problematic if a single latent factor accounts for the majority of the total explained variance. In this study, the result of the un-rotated factor analysis shows that the first factor only accounted for 20.22% of the total 78.4% variance and thus common method bias is not a problem.

FINDINGS

According to Table 5, majority of the participants are females with 78.5% as compared to the males. Interestingly, their age ranged from 20-25 years to 41 above. Well, it is worth mentioning that most of them are within two categories of 26-30 years (46%) followed by 31-40 years (36.5%). This in-

Table 5. Profile of respondents

Variables	Frequency	Percentage
Gender		
Male	43	21.5%
Female	157	78.5%
Age		
20-25	27	13.5%
26-30	92	46.0%
31-40	73	36.5%
41 Above	08	04.0%
Position		
Senior Management	2	01.0%
Management	19	09.5%
Executive	84	42.0%
Clerical	69	34.5%
Others	26	13.0%
Organisation		
Private	44	22%
Public	158	78%
Year of Service		
1-5	82	41.0%
6-10	77	38.5%
11-15	28	14.0%
16 Above	13	06.5%

dicates to us that majority of students who have registered and pursuing their degree through ePJJ mode are workers or have work experience. In addition, even though they have work experience and likely that some, if not all, must have been using certain technology to accomplish tasks in their respective workplaces does not mean that they know how to use i-class system for studying. Of course, certain technology may be different from another. Many of them are holding different positions in their places of works. Their jobs ranged from senior management to clerical officers. Majority of them are working as executive officers with 42% followed by clerical works (34.5%). In addition, many of them have 5 years working experience (41%) followed by 6-10 years work experience (38.5%). Interestingly, some of them have even got 11-15 years' work experience (14%).

The degree of the i-class usage among the ePJJ students for doing assignment, downloading notes, quizzes and test was assessed and the results have shown that majority of them use it between 1 hour to 5 hours in a week. Despite the fact that ePJJ students are expected to use the i-class system for at least 80% per week, the duration devoted to it by majority of students is far below expectation (45%). Surprisingly, only about 13% used more than 9 hours or a minimal number (17%) per whole week to access the i-class system for their studies (see Table 6).

EXAMINING PATH COEFFICIENT ANALYSIS OF THE MODEL

In this section, the researchers address the path analysis to examine the relationships between the structural latent constructs of the model. The results obtained have shown positive significant relationships among all the constructs in the extended model.

As clearly shown in Figure 3, the results indicate positive significant relationships between the two causal links of self-efficacy and perceived convenience to perceived usefulness with beta values of 0.103 and 0.275, p<0.001 respectively. A similar significant positive relationship exists between the two causal links of perceived convenience and subjective norms to perceived ease of use with beta coefficient values of 0.558 and 0.285, p<0.001 respectively.

In addition, the causal links between perceived ease of using i-class and perceived usefulness are also positively related with Beta value of 0.505, p<0.001. Furthermore, the path coefficients between both perceived ease of use and perceived usefulness to ePJJ students' attitude were also significantly related with Beta values of 0.441 and 0.421, p<0.001 respectively. It is interesting to see a strong positive relationship between the attitude of the students and intention to use i-class with beta value of 0.770, p<0.001. Finally, the result

Table 6. Degree of i-class usage per week

Variable	Period	Frequency	Percentage
Using of i-class for notes completing assignments, quizzes, and tests	Less than 1 hour	14	7%
	1 – 5 hours	90	45%
	6 hours	37	18.5%
	7 – 8 hours	34	17%
	More than 9 hours	25	12.5%

Figure 3. Path coefficient result of the extended model

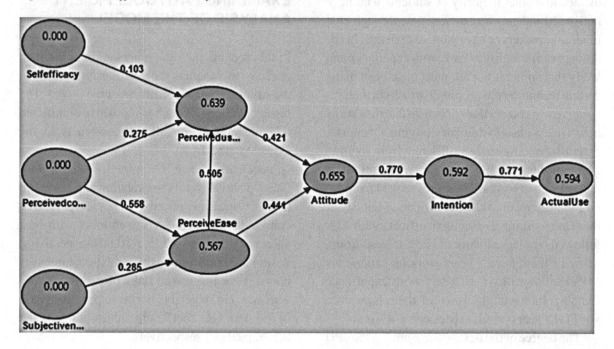

also indicates a very strong causal relation between students' intention to use i-class and actual use of it in reality with beta value of 0.771, p<0.001.

PREDICTIVE CAPACITY OF THE EXTENDED MODEL AND HYPOTHESES TESTING

As can be seen the Figure 4, the t-value of the path coefficients are generated to test the significant contribution of each path coefficient of the latent construct following the bootstrapping approach in order to validate the predictive capacity of the extended model and the hypothesis put forward.

The results show that all hypotheses in the study are supported with t-values ranging from 3.776 to 49.283 at an alpha-value less than 0.001 respectively (see Table 7). As the results depicted in the Figure 4 and Table 6, the R^2 values of the five endogenous latent constructs in the model such as perceived usefulness, perceived ease, attitude intention and actual use of i-class ranged from

0.639, 0.567, 0.655, 0.592, to 0.594 respectively (see Table 6). According to Chin, (1998), it is paramount to examine the predictive power of the extended model of the study.

According to Kock (2012, p.31), this can be done by assessing the average variance inflation factor (AVIF) as a comprehensive analysis of a model's overall capacity and explanatory quality of the latent factors linking to actual use of i-class by ePJJ students. This is important in order to address the absence of both vertical and lateral collinearities. The result shows a value of 1.34, which is below the threshold of 3.3 (Kock, 2012). Additionally, other indices for the model fit such as average path coefficient (APC), average r-squared (ARS) are addressed. The result of both APC and ARS are 0.459 and 60.94% respectively.

Moreover, Q-squared coefficient is performed through blindfolding in order to assess the predictive validity associated with each latent variable block in the model. An acceptable predictive validity in connection with endogenous latent variables is suggested by examine a Q-squared

Figure 4. Bootstrapping results of the structural model

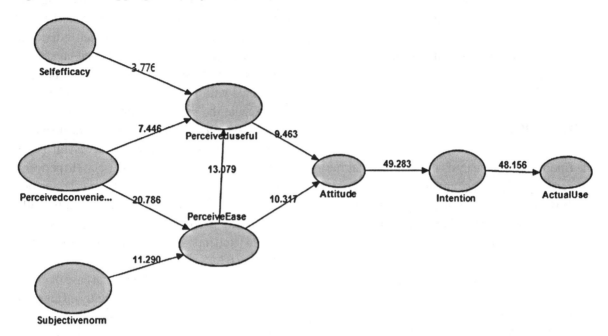

Table 7. Summary of t-statistics of the path coefficients and hypothesis testing

Hypotheses	Construct Causal Relation	Beta (β) Coefficient	Endogenous Latent Variables (R²)	T -Statistics	Remark
H1	Self-efficacy -> Perceived usefulness (PU)	0.103	PU (R² = 0.639) 63.9%	3.776**	supported
H2	Perceived convenience -> Perceived usefulness (PU)	0.275		7.446**	supported
H5	Perceived ease -> Perceived usefulness	0.505		13.079***	supported
H3	Perceived convenience -> Perceived ease of use (PEOU)	0.558	PEOU (R² = 0.567) 56.7%	20.706***	supported
H4	Subjective norm -> Perceived ease of use (PEOU)	0.285		11.290***	supported
H6	Perceived useful -> Attitude (ATU)	0.421	ATU (R² = 0.655) 65.5%	8.463**	supported
H7	Perceived ease -> Attitude	0.441		10.347***	supported
H8	Attitude -> Intention (INT)	0.770	INT (R² = 0.592) 59.2%	49.283***	supported
H9	Intention -> Actual use (AU)	0.771	AU (R² = 0.594) 59.4%	48.166***	supported
Parameters for Predictive Capacity of a Model: AVIF = 1.34; APC = 0.459; ARS = 60.94% (see: Kock, 2012)					

Note: *** P<0.001, **P<0.01.

coefficient that is greater than zero thresholds (Kock, 2012). The result of the predictive validity for this extended model is 0.452 indicating good predictive factors that can influence uses of i-class among ePJJ students.

DISCUSSION OF THE FINDINGS

The findings of the analysis have shown that the degree of the i-class usage among the ePJJ students for doing assignment, downloading notes, quizzes and test was not encouraging. The results reflect that majority of them use it between 1 hour to 5 hours in a week. Despite the fact that ePJJ students are expected to use the i-class system for at least 80% per week but the duration they devoted to it is far below expectation (45%). This small time devoted by majority of these students has something to do with interrelationships among all the variables of interests addressed in the extended model.

The results obtained from this extended model have shown that both computer self-efficacy and perceived convenience have positively influenced the perceived usefulness of i-class system among the ePJJ students. In other words, computer self-efficacy has a positive influence on perceived usefulness whereby $\beta = 0.103$, t-value $= 3.776$, p<0.001. In fact, perceived convenience also shows a significant influence on perceived usefulness of i-class with $\beta = 0.275$, t-value of 7.446, p<0.001. Above all is a profound significant impact of the construct ease of use on perceived convenience with $\beta = 0.505$, t-value of 13.079, p<0.001. The result indicates a co-activation between the three antecedences of perceived usefulness. The co-activation is no surprising because perceived usefulness of any technology system like i-class is largely dependent on student's ability and capacity to handle and manoeuvre the system and how convenient or easy it is for individual students to achieve the purpose of using it.

Perceiving certain technology to be very useful is only when one is able to accomplish a task given through it. Since self-efficacy is an individual belief of each student about personal capability to i-class system, such thought and perception is concerned with judgment of how well a student can execute the required actions via the system. Usually, such cognitive reflections do occur based on past experience and previous successful use of the technology system similar to i-class to perform tasks and how convenient it is when carrying out the task. Evidently speaking, both computer-self-efficacy and perceived convenience have jointly affected students' perceived usefulness of the i-class by 63.9%.

The results have also shown that ease of using i-class by ePJJ students is significantly influenced and affected by both subjective norm and perceived convenience in using the system with beta values of $\beta = 0.285$, t-values of 11.290, p<0.001 and $\beta = 0.558$, t-value of 20.706, P<0.001 respectively. It is evident from the findings that both perceived convenience and subjective norm have 56.7% impact on perceived ease of using i-class. Interestingly, perceived convenience in the model is the feeling of no extra burden while using the i-class by the ePJJ students and it has bigger effect and impact on perceived ease of using the interactive system even relatively more than its effect on perceived usefulness of the i-class as indicated by the coefficient values. This means that both perceived ease of use and the usefulness of any technology devices is largely dependent on the level of its convenience to the users. This implies that the feeling of easiness in using i-class and its perceived usefulness among the students are judged based on the level of it convenience to them when using it. Hence, technology adopted in public sector must not bring extra burden to the users. Failure to design it in a convenient manner would result to useless of it and inability to achieve its purpose. In relation to subjective norm, it means that whatever information each student obtains from other colleagues, through a positive or negative word of mouth about easiness of the i-class, can influence their judgements about it. This may in turn shape their attitude towards the i-class system.

In fact, the findings from the statistical analyses have testified to this significant effect. For example, perception about ease of using i-class has shown a significant impact on attitude with beta value $\beta = 0.441$, t-values of 10.347, $p<0.001$. Likewise, perceived usefulness also has significant effect on attitude with $\beta = 0.421$, t-values of 8.463, $p<0.001$. This indicates that the cognitive judgment or attitudinal reaction towards i-class system among the ePJJ students is shaped by both perceived ease of using it and its level of usefulness to them based on their interaction with the system ($R^2 = 65.5\%$). This can in turn affect their intention to use it or not to use. In fact, the intention is a function of their attitude, which can be positive or negative cognitive reflection of the system. Evidence from the result obtained in this study has shown that attitude significantly affects intention to use i-class with $\beta = 0.770$, t-values of 49.283, $p<0.001$. As such, the magnitude of such effect is about 59% on intention of ePJJ students towards using the i-class system. Finally, the finding has also shown that intention to use i-class system has 59.4% on actual use of the i-class among these students. That implies to us that adopting a technology in a public sector does not indicate automatic usage of it, especially in teaching and learning institution of public higher institutions. Students' mindsets or intentions must be positively convinced in relations to usefulness of the technology, ease of using it as well as the various antecedences discussed as reflected in the findings obtained from the study.

CHAPTER SUMMARY

This chapter has extended the original TAM model of technology acceptance to perform tasks in the public sector. It focuses on the use of technology in higher institute of learning with special reference to ePJJ students. The chapter provides some reflections on the specific issues that are always encountered by different students such as computer self-efficacy, perceived usefulness of the i-class created for them. The main issue addressed lies on poor participation, poor usage and interactions among ePJJ students and lecturers through i-class. The problem statement section of the chapter has shed light on other issues such as failure to contribute to discussion online or not even use the system to submit assignments as required. According to the findings of the chapter, original TAM model cannot be applied to address these specific multifaceted issues and effort was devoted to derive an extended model that can fit the research setting. In doing so, the chapter has shown a new directional links among variables of interests that have bearing on ePJJ students' adoption and usage of the i-class system as a useful tool to carry out their studies and related interaction among them for sharing notes, doing assignments, quizzes, tests, and other works.

According the chapter, ease of using the i-class is relatively different from one student to another. This depends on individual level of technology savvy. In addition, it also depends on how convenient the i-class is; in terms of access to it anywhere, any place and at any time of the day. This is very important because geographical location of each student would affect their access to the system. This relative difference is obvious between students living in remote areas compared to those at the urban areas. According to the findings of the study, perceived computer self-efficacy and perceived convenience have positively influenced students' perceived usefulness of the i-class system based on the students' perceptions.

The same significant impact of perceived convenience was observed on perceived ease of using the i-class. In fact, the findings of the chapter also reflected the important effect of subjective norm through words of mouth on ease of using the system. Other important constructs discussed in the chapter include the issue relating to attitude, which according to the result, has a profound significant effect on intention to use the i-class. Hence, based on the findings of the chapter, it can be concluded that actual usage of i-class to study among the ePJJ students in UiTM is affected by their intention. This implies to us that adopting a technology in a public sector does not indicate automatic usage of it, especially in teaching and learning institution of public institutions. Students' mindsets and intentions must be positively convinced in relations to the usefulness of such technology, ease of using it as well as the various antecedences discussed as reflected in the findings obtained from the study, which include: subjective norms, individual students computer efficacy and perceive convenience of using it. What is paramount to note is that convenience in accessing technology is not definitely related to intention to use technology, but certain connection with ease of using it as well as probability of achieving and accomplishing the purpose of using it (i.e., usefulness of it). This would, no doubt, convince students' mindsets and their intentions to use it and eventually use i-class system.

REFERENCES

Ajzen, I. (1991). The theory of planned behavior. *Organizational Behavior and Human Decision Processes*, 50(2), 179–211. doi:10.1016/0749-5978(91)90020-T

Alavi, M., & Leidner, D. (2001). Technology-mediated learning: A call for greater depth and breadth of research. *Information Systems Research*, (March): 1–10. doi:10.1287/isre.12.1.1.9720

Chan, C.-C., Liang, C., Yan, C.-F., & Tseng, J.-S. (2012). The impact of college students' intrinsic and extrinsic motivation on continuance intention to use English mobile learning systems. In Asia-Pacific Education Researcher, (pp. 1-12). Springer.

Chin, W. W. (1998). The partial least squares approach to structural equation modeling. In G. A. Marcoulides (Ed.), *Modern Methods for Business Research*, (pp. 295–358). Mahwah, NJ: Lawrence Erlbaum Associates.

Chua, D. (2012). E-learning boost for students getting free netbooks. *The Star Online*. Retrieved June 20 2012, from http://www.thestaronline.com.my

Compeau, D. R., Higgins, C. A., & Huff, S. (1999). Social cognitive theory and individual reactions to computing technology: A longitudinal-study. *Management Information Systems Quarterly*, 23(2), 145–158. doi:10.2307/249749

Davis, F. D. (1986). *A technology acceptance model for empirically testing new end-user information systems: Theory and results*. (Doctoral dissertation). MIT Sloan School of Management.

Davis, F. D., Bagozzi, R. P., & Warshaw, P. R. (1989). User acceptance of computer technology: A comparison of two theoretical models. *Management Science*, 35(8), 982–1002. doi:10.1287/mnsc.35.8.982

Davis, F. D., Bagozzi, R. P., & Warshaw, P. R. (1992). Extrinsic and intrinsic motivation to use computers in the workplace. *Journal of Applied Social Psychology*, 22(14), 1111–1132. doi:10.1111/j.1559-1816.1992.tb00945.x

Elmo Classroom Solution. (2012). *What is ICT education*. Retrieved May 19th 2013 from http://www.elmoglobal.com/en/html/ict/01.aspx

Fadilah, D. (2012). ICT a necessity in education. *The Star Online*. Retrieved Feb. 25th 2012 from http://www.thestaronline.com.my

Fornell, C., & Larcker, D. F. (1981). Evaluating structural equation models with unobservable and measurement error. *JMR, Journal of Marketing Research*, *18*(1), 39–50. doi:10.2307/3151312

Hair, J. F., Black, W. C., Babin, B. J., & Anderson, R. E. (2010). *Multivariate data analysis*. Upper Saddle River, NJ: Prentice-Hall.

Jenkins, M., & Hanson, J. (2003). E-learning series: A guide for senior managers, learning and teaching support network (LTSN) generic centre. *Journal of Distance Education*, *9*(3), 162–175.

Lee, J.-S., Cho, H. G., Davidson, B., & Ingraffea, A. (2003). *Technology acceptance and social networking in distance learning*. Retrieved Nov. 16th 2012 from www.ifets info/journals

Lee, M. K. O., Cheung, C. M. K., & Chen, Z. (2005). Acceptance of Internet-based learning medium: The role of extrinsic and intrinsic motivation. *Information & Management*, *42*(8), 1095–1104. doi:10.1016/j.im.2003.10.007

Leidner, D. E., & Jarvenpaa, S. L. (1993). The information age confronts education case studies on electronic classrooms. *Information Systems Research*, *4*(1), 24–54. doi:10.1287/isre.4.1.24

McShane, S., & Glinow, M. V. (2008). *Organizational behaviour: Emerging realities for the workplace revolution* (4th ed.). New York: McGraw-Hill/Irwin.

Pedersen, P. E., & Nysveen, H. (2002). *Using the theory of planned behaviour to explain teenagers' adoption of text messaging services*. Norway: Agder University College.

Petrus, G., & Nelson, O. N. (2006). Borneo online banking: Evaluating customer perceptions and behavioural intention. *Management Research News*, *29*(1/2), 6–15. doi:10.1108/01409170610645402

Podsakoff, P. M., & Organ, D. W. (1986). Self-reports in organizational research: Problems and prospects. *Journal of Management*, *12*(4), 531–544. doi:10.1177/014920638601200408

Sekaran, U., & Bougie, R. (2010). *Research methods for business: A skill building approach* (4th ed.). John Wiley & Sons, Inc.

Sharpe, R., Benfield, G., & Francis, R. (2006). Implementing a university e-learning strategy: Levers for change within academic schools. *ALT-J.*, *14*(2), 135–151. doi:10.1080/09687760600668503

Siragusa, L., & Dixon, K. C. (2008). Planned behaviour: Student attitudes towards the use of ICT interactions in higher education. In *Proceedings of Ascilite 2008*. Retrieved June 11th 2013 from http://www.ascilite.org.au

Tan, M., & Teo, T. S. H. (2000). Factors influencing the adoption of Internet banking. *Journal of the Association for Information Systems*, *1*(5), 1–42.

Teo, T., & van Schalk, P. (2009). Understanding technology acceptance in pre-service teachers: A structural-equation modelling approach. *The Asia-Pacific Education Researcher*, *18*(1), 47–66. doi:10.3860/taper.v18i1.1035

Venkatesh, V. (1999). Creation of Favorable User Perceptions: Exploring the Role of Intrinsic Motivation. *Management Information Systems Quarterly*, *23*(2), 239–260. doi:10.2307/249753

Venkatesh, V., & Bala, H. (2008). Technology Acceptance Model 3 and a Research Agenda on Interventions. *Decision Sciences*, *39*(2), 272–315. doi:10.1111/j.1540-5915.2008.00192.x

Venkatesh, V., & Morris, M. G. (2000). Why don't men ever stop to ask for directions? Gender, social influence, and their role in technology acceptance and usage behaviour. *Management Information Systems Quarterly*, *24*(1), 115–139. doi:10.2307/3250981

Yoon, C., & Kim, S. (2007). Convenience and TAM in a ubiquitous computing environment: The case of wireless LAN. *Electronic Commerce Research and Applications*, *6*(1), 102–112. doi:10.1016/j.elerap.2006.06.009

KEY TERMS AND DEFINITIONS

Access: Means of approaching, entering, and getting near technology systems or a way of being able to use technology systems.

Convenience: The state of being able to proceed with the use of technology system provided without any difficulty.

E-Learning: The use of electronic media, educational technology, and ICT for education system.

i-Class: Virtual classroom where students and lecturers interact for discussions.

Inefficiency: The lack of ability to use technology or accomplishing tasks using technology without wasting materials, time, and energy thereby rendering the purpose of technology to become useless in an organization.

Response: Reaction of a user to the technology provided for accomplishing tasks.

Social Influence: Situations where a person's tendency of using a particular technology or opinion and/or behaviour towards a technology is affected by other people.

Chapter 12

ICT Adoption by Malaysian Parliamentarians for Communication with the Citizens:
Extended TAM with Moderating Effect of Trust in Electronic System

ABSTRACT

The adoption of ICT by MPs as mechanism for socioeconomic and political communications with their representatives in various constituencies has been investigated along side with system factor, social factors, individual factors, and trust in ICT system as moderator. The results show the existence of negative relationship between system factor and MPs e-communication. But when moderated with trust variable, a positive significant effect was obtained. The same moderating effect of trust was envisaged for self-efficacy variable as well as other social factors and individual factors in the model. The inclusion of pertinent variables such as system factors, self-efficacy, and trust make a difference to original Technology Acceptance Model (TAM) in this chapter. Findings show that systems, self-efficacy in an individual, and word of mouth in social situations play important roles in the use of ICT by MPs to engage their electorates when these variables are moderated with trust in ICT.

INTRODUCTION

Nowadays the adoption of ICT is not only peculiar with the private organization but has extensively been used in the public institutions. Public agencies and governmental bodies such as elected officers or politicians have begun to envisage the importance of ICT usage in their related duties and work being assigned to them. In other words, the parliamentarians have seen the needs to embrace the ICT revolution. As a matter of fact, the implementation and adoption of the new technologies in the Malaysian par-

DOI: 10.4018/978-1-4666-6579-8.ch012

liamentary system has become one of the most pressing agenda since 1994 in order to improve the responsiveness and efficiency of transaction between government as whole, the elected politicians or member of parliaments (MPs) and their engagement with their respective constituent members. The main objective of adopting ICT in Parliament is to harness the opportunities for improving the people representation and their engagement with the parliamentary elected officers. In addition, it was sought that adoption and usage of ICT for parliamentary communication would enable the members of parliament either from the house of representative or senate establish a direct contact with the public and their participation in the legislative process will be assured. Hence, with the advent of the Internet, ICTs has become more than just enabling tool but also an efficient and rational internal operational mechanism for effective parliamentary system. The Internet as a new tool of communication to reach out the citizens has a power to transform the relationship between the members of the parliament and the general masses and to enable different parts of a society to be involved in the process of policy formulations as well as to establish a closer rapport between the parliament and the public (Sobaci, 2011). Through the use and adoption of ICT policy in the Malaysian parliament, the basic values envisaged by the government such transparency, accessibility, accountability, and effective representativeness can be achieved. Most of the parliaments around the world are geared towards supporting the entire fundamental and these basic values (Thierry, 2009). The implementation of ICT in the Malaysian parliament can strengthen human and institutional capacity and promote effective democracy through a constant harnessing of ICT as enabling tool. Above all, the ICT adoption can enhance development and inter-parliamentary communications for better service delivery and meeting the challenging demands by electorates in diverse constituencies around Malaysia.

PROBLEM STATEMENT AND DEVELOPMENT OF EXTENDED TAM

Malaysian government had introduced the electronic parliament concept known as eParliament. Since the beginning of the 1994, the Malaysia parliament has built a roadmap for its parliament technology development to roll out for achieving its purpose. The parliament has launched the new project in 2002 called Hansard parliament system. In the Hansard system, all the detail questions and answers in proceedings are to be recorded via an electronic device system. Each question and answer are usually recorded within 10 minutes and transcribed and uploaded or published on the websites. All individuals ranging from the MPs to citizens can download the document and read it. All MPs have their own official email provided by the parliament for example padangbesar@parlimen.gov.my[1]. It is hoped that the citizens can communicate with the MPs by using the e-mail. Besides, according to the parliamentary staff, some of the MPs have their own social networking electronic tools such as blogs, Twitter, and Facebook that are expected to be used for increasing interactions with the citizens. Besides, the public also will be able to participate more directly and collectively in policy input processes in attempt to improve parliamentary democracy in the country. In addition, the government has also established the e-parliamentary library to become a resource centre of excellence for legislative, parliamentary, government and public administrative matters. The e-parliamentary library is used to help and support the research needs and facilitate MPs and staff in the belief that information and knowledge is a lifelong learning process that can help make each elected parliamentarian person perform his or her duties better than expectation. In general, the parliament website was developed to facilitate effective communication and accountability as well as sense of responsiveness among the members of parliament, ministries, various departments, agencies, associations and the public at large. In addition, visitors to this website among the citizens can get information on the proceedings of Parliament in the Dewan Rakyat and Dewan Negara as well as information on the members of parliament for socio-economic and political engagements. Hence, the parliament of Malaysia has provided the infrastructure to open more opportunities for MPs to get more involved with their constituent member utilizing ICT. Likewise the MP themselves especially young ones have begun recognize the importance of ICT and thus taking initiatives on their own as much as possible using ICT in their communication with the citizens.

Although adoption of ICT in public organizations has been seen as another alternative way to reinvigorate new forms of political democracy, the elected political representatives in both western and traditional liberal democracies are often criticized for not being in tune with the digital age or tendency to use ICT for political engagement with citizens is very low (Dai, 2007a; 2007b). There are three unforeseen issues related to intension to use ICT for political communication and engagement with public. These can be compartmentalized into three distinct categories. They are the issues related to the system itself, issues related to individual elected representative and those that related to social factors. All the three categorical issues have a profound implication with intention of MPs to ICT for political engagement with their people and their electorates at large. These issues obviously were not captured by the earlier technology acceptance theory (TAM). First, the only aspect covered by the existing TAM1 or TAM2 is individual factor related to intention to adopting ICT as a medium of communicating in terms of how each MP perceive themselves with the use of ICT to politically communicate with his or her people. In other words, the MPs curiosity and tendency to use it lie in some pertinent issues such as perceived usefulness of

the ICT system, ease of use and self-efficacy of him or herself with respect to the use of ICT for political communication with citizens. Furthermore, in a climate such as Malaysia where the Internet and/or usage of ICT is a new medium for parliamentary communication, it has so far attracted only a small minority of individual MPs. Second, general usage of ICTs in public sector is associated with social factors such as (a) subjective norm where an individual's judgment and intention to use it can be influenced by the people who are important to a person and they can actively encouraged or discouraged him or her to do or not so (see Franzoi, 2003; Ajzen, 1991; Chiasson & Lovato, 2001; Morris & Venkatesh, 2000; Karahann, 1999). This is an existing fact which is based on the feeling of some politicians and bureaucrats who argue that ICT can be disruptive. Thus, it is not surprising that the agenda of ICT adoption as an alternative avenue for political communication and direct engagement with the citizens is not well received or accepted by some parliamentary politicians in Malaysia.

In addition to social factor, (b) our preliminary interview with some MPs has testified to the importance and significant role played by word of mouth in encouraging or discouraging the use of ICT among them. In this context it is believed that word of mouth which is defined in this study as oral information passing from person to person about usage of ICT can easily discourage or encourage others in developing intention to use or not to use ICT among the parliamentarians elected politicians.

Another important construct that emerged during our face-to-face interview with some selected MPs at the inception of this study is the element of trust in electronic information and its significant role of putting socio-economic and political information effectively across the members of the parliament and the citizens themselves at large. Evidence from some researchers such as (Fogg 1999) shows that trust can affect relationships between people's positive belief about the perceived reliability on ICT, its dependability, and the level of confidence a person has for processing or putting information about socio-economic and political matters via electronic system as compared to traditional paper based.

Third, the system factor is equally important for consideration. In this chapter, the concern lies in the types and forms of technologies available for MPs or provided for reaching the citizens in various constituencies. For example, findings from our preliminary interviews have shown that many of the MPs had taken their own initiatives to adopt other forms of technologies or electronic devices other than official website or kiosks provided by the parliament. These include Facebook, Twitter, blogs, etc., used to engage citizens with political communication. In other words, the system factor captures the type computer-mediated communication system that can influence political e-communication between MPs and their people. In light of these associated issues, there is a need to modify and incorporate all the three perspectives into the model as shown in Figure 1.

OPERATIONALIZING THE MODEL IN LIEU OF LITERATURE

The MPs need a well-organized office equipped with modern technologies to work efficiently and communicate effectively with their colleagues and staff, interests and actors, the media, and above all their constituents' electorates. In this chapter we only focus on MPs from *Dewan Rakyat* because they are elected by the voters in various constituencies through the general election. Hence they are accountable to have an interaction and communication with the public. To effectively engage with people they need to use ICT as a medium to hear and listen to their voters' opinion and complaints regarding any issue of concerns that deserved government attention. However, according to Folstad, (2007), the term engagement is a broad concept that comprises of many core features like high involvement, affective energy and self presence in a system. The user perspective of the e-parliament concepts in this chapter covers only user engagement derived from the concept of human computer interaction (Folstad, 2007)

Figure 1. Model of ICT usage for socioeconomic and political communication with citizens (i.e., engaging citizens)

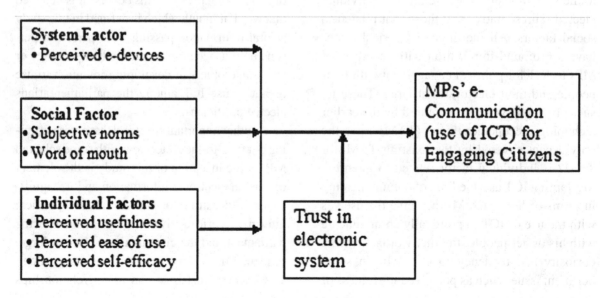

for socioeconomic and political communications among MPs and the general public or citizens.

In this model, the intention to use electronic system by MPs is due to a number of potential factors. The system factor is used to focus on the technical perspective of the processes and the building relationships among both MPs around the parliament and their people in diverse constituency at large through available electronic devices. How all these are coordinated and capture one single system for monitoring the in-and out-flow of socio-political information in the parliament. It is argued that all various types of electronic devices such as face-book, twitters, blogs etc must be encouraged to facilitate and encourage the MPs in engaging their people with vital socio-economic and political information that can meet the need and demand of the public. In the same line of thoughts, Lee and Kanthawong (2007), argued that the integrated information system (IIS) is important for effective and efficient political engagement with citizens via e-communication especially Internet communication. So any form of computer-mediated communications over the Internet as well as over other computer network infrastructures such as support systems and local area network-based communication tools are very essential because the communications enhanced group decision (Knock, 2001). Thus, according to Lee and Kanthawong (2007), in another parts of the world, e-communication as technologies available at the Parliament for the MPs include e-mail, short message service (SMS), web sites, and parliamentary kiosks. Therefore, in this chapter we do not confine the meaning of e-communication within the perspective of the parliamentary website facilities provided alone given that the technology is seamless and also available at any time anywhere. Hence we extend the scope of the system factor for e-communication to cover bigger dimension such as Facebook, twitter, blogs, etc. In other words it covers both the hard and the soft tools used by the MPs for their socio-political communications with the people

in various constituencies in Malaysia, which may or may not significantly affect the behavioural intention to use certain technology. This is because the influence to use e-communication system may not necessarily depend on technology itself but rather on other factors. In this context it can be hypothesized that:

H1: System factor (SF) has no significant influence on intention of MPs to use technology for engaging or communicating (MPeCOM) with their electorates on socioeconomic and political matters.

For social factor variable it is widely defined in a broad sense to include both subjective norms and word of mouth in this chapter. Subjective norm is the perceived social pressure to engage or not to engage in behaviour (Ajzen, 1991). Hence subjective norm means drawing an analogy to the expectancy-value model of attitude. It is assumed that subjective norm is determined by the total set of accessible normative beliefs concerning the expectations of important referents. According to Lee (2003), subjective norm posits that individuals will be more likely to engage in the use of certain technology devices if others who are in their circle such as friends, family members, co-workers, boss or staff members who have influence on them had approved, accepted and encouraged the usage (Carter & Belanger, 2005; Hung et al., 2006). In other words, subjective norm in the context of the MPs' perceptions could be explained along a line of thought that whether using any kind of e-communication technologies is culturally accepted, encouraged, and implemented by the MPs. Hence with subjective norm individual MPs compares him or herself and adjust behaviour more with similar others than with dissimilar others (Miller et al., 1988). Thus, as explained in the earlier chapters of this book, the influence of a person's normative belief that others approve or disapprove a particular behaviour will generate different behavioural intentions among the MPs and would affect tendency to use a given technology. Individuals' intentions to perform a particular action are a function of a subjective norm or their perception that important others think they ought to do so. The second variable of interest for social factor in this chapter is word of mouth. Word of mouth is informal interpersonal messages between the MPs and their people in various constituencies as well as their colleagues. It is an informal, person-to person communication between the perceived natures of technologies available for reaching one another with pertinent information on any matters of concerns. It is an exchange of information between individuals. Therefore, it is an act of telling at least one friend, acquaintance, or family member about the personal experience with a satisfactory or unsatisfactory use of certain technology. These interpersonal communications are evaluated in nature, whereby MPs relate positive or negative information to others in the form of recommending or warning against intention towards using a given technology. Hence, when examining the social factor that contributes to the MPs intention to use technology for political engagement and exchange of ideas, it is necessary to understand the MPs cultural orientation rooted in societal values. The MPs may spend more time online or have the engagement with their people over the Internet because culturally they show a high level of conformity with their peer MPs or electorate and regard the opinions of their people as reference points. Due to the higher level of regard for peers and people at large they tend to share their thoughts, experience with others even family via word of mouth (Cho & Kim, 2001). At this juncture, two distinctive hypotheses can be proposed respectively:

H2: Subjective norm (SN) has a positive influence on intention of MPs to use technology for engaging or communicating with their electorates on socioeconomic and political matters.

H3: Word of mouth (WOM) has a positive influence on intention of MPs to use technology for engaging or communicating with their electorates on socioeconomic and political matters.

Another important component of the framework is individual factors related to the MPs themselves on the basis of perceptual feelings towards a given technology for communication. This consists of three sub-components. The first component in individual factors is usefulness. Perceived usefulness is the extent to which MPs believe that using certain technology system will enhance his or her socioeconomic and political communication and reach to his or her people (Venkatesh & Davis 2000, p. 187). Perceive usefulness is used to determine the MP engagement toward Internet communication as whole. It is assumed that when the usefulness of the system higher the individual MPs tend to engage with the system for communicating with their people. The second component is perceived ease of using the technology devices. Ease of use in this study is the extent to which MPs believe that using ICT technologies for engaging with people would be effortless (Davis, 1989; Venkatesh & Davis, 2000; Hung et al., 2006). Moreover perceive ease of use is a construct tied to an individual assessment of the effort involved in the process of using the system (Pavlou & Fygenson, 2006; Srite & Karahanna, 2006). The third variable considered in this chapter is self-efficacy that can enhance perceived ease or usefulness of the technology by individual MPs. As explained in the earlier theoretical chapter, it is the judgment of a person's capability to perform a particular behaviour (Venkatesh, 2000; Venkatesh & Davis, 2000). Hence, in the context of this chapter it is an individual MPs' belief in his or her ability to successfully use a specific e-device for communication with others. In this respect three distinctive hypotheses are proposed:

H4: Perceived usefulness (PU) has a positive influence on intention of MPs to use technology for engaging or communicating with their electorates on socioeconomic and political matters.

H5: Perceived ease of use (PEOU) has a positive influence on intention of MPs to use technology for engaging or communicating with their electorates on socioeconomic and political matters.

H6: Self-efficacy (SE) has a positive influence on intention of MPs to use technology for engaging or communicating with their electorates on socioeconomic and political matters.

For the model of this chapter, trust is used as a moderating variable. Trust, according to Everard and Galletta, (2005), can be understood as a positive belief about the perceived reliability and/or dependability and confidentiality a person has in an object or other things such as technologies. Trust gives confidence that the trustee will behave ethically and fairly (Gefen et al., 2003, Pavlou & Fygenson, 2006). Hung et al. (2006) found that trust is a significantly important to the determinant of attitude toward online tax filing and payment technology systems in Taiwan. An individual is willing to rely on the performance of the systems because he/she has confidence that the system will behave in accurate and benevolence manner that are expected by the users (Carter & Belanger, 2005; Hung et al., 2006). In another context, trust captures the influence on information disclosure in relations to the belief that their personal particulars are secured and will not leak out to unauthorized third parties. Such trust in the system could moderate the intention to use technology and other influential factors (Jarvenpaa et al., 2000). In addition the trust is central interpersonal communication whereby individual MPs hold to a belief that the rewards in using ICT for political engagement of the citizens outweighs the costs and therefore develop trust in electronic system. Trust is critical to this process

because it is believed to reduce the perceived costs of information disclosure via electronic system. Indeed, several studies of interpersonal communication have confirmed that trust as a precondition for self-disclosure because it reduces the perceived risks involved in revealing private information. Hence, trust is a key condition to engage individual with Internet for political discourse because it reduces the risks associated with online engagement with others. The trust can increase confidence in ICT and Internet communication, which lowers the perceived risk and increases the likelihood of MPs intention to always reach their people through electronic system. Based on these aforementioned precondition roles expected to be played by trust in the model, the following hypotheses are derived:

H7a: Trust will positively moderate the relationship between system factor and intention of MPs to use technology for engaging or communicating with their electorates on socioeconomic and political matters.

H7b: Trust will positively moderate the relationship between subjective norms and intention of MPs to use technology for engaging or communicating with their electorates on socioeconomic and political matters.

H7c: Trust will positively moderate the relationship between word of mouth (MOU) and intention of MPs to use technology for engaging or communicating with their electorates on socioeconomic and political matters.

H7d: Trust will positively moderate the relationship between perceived usefulness (PU) and intention of MPs to use technology for engaging or communicating with their electorates on socioeconomic and political matters.

H7e: Trust will positively moderate the relationship between perceived ease of use (PEOU) and intention of MPs to use technology for engaging or communicating with their electorates on socioeconomic and political matters.

H7f: Trust will positively moderate the relationship between self-efficacy and intention of MPs to use technology for engaging or communicating with their electorates on socioeconomic and political matters.

DATA COLLECTION AND METHODOLOGICAL APPROACH

Data collection was done through the design of a survey questionnaire. Information was collected over a period between May and July 2013 at one shot time. Hence it is a cross-sectional design method. The respondents were those MPs that have used e-Parliament portal and other electronic devices for interacting or communicate with their colleagues and citizens over socioeconomic and political matters. The nature of data collection was through a five-point Likert survey questionnaire. A total of 100 questionnaires were distributed to the MPs and 63% retuning rate of questionnaires was achieved for further analyses. In details, the respondents comprise of both male and female MPs; aged between 38 and 65 years old. The respondents were not discriminated against any criteria but the main criterion is that each of them must have adopted or used ICT tools in their daily chores as MPs to reach their constituent electorates and members. In addition, we have made every attempt to meet the MPs in person at their office, home and even at the Parliamentary lobby to get the questionnaire answered. The MP themselves also have their own initiative to interact with the constituents and the most common ICT tool used by MPs to communicate with the public is personal website, blogs, e-mail, and online social networking. More details on sources of instruments and scales are explained in the subsequence sections.

Goodness of Measures of the Instrument: The Structural Model Specification

The questionnaire used consists of a five-point Likert scale to obtain data for each of the construct dimension in the model of the study (Figure 1 in Chapter 13). Based on the insights obtained from previous studies by Pedersen and Nysveen, (2012); Lee, et al (2005), Petrus and Nelson, (2006), Venketash & Bala, (2008), a questionnaire was reconstructed with some modifications to earn information. In this study, both validity and reliability tests to measure the accuracy of the data were used. Overall, construct validity was used to test how well the instrument developed measures a particular construct (Sekaran & Bougie, 2010), while reliability was used to test how consistently the measuring instruments have measured the constructs. Validity measures in this research were in three folds in terms of construct, convergent and discriminant validities in order to examine how well the questionnaires used could tap the constructs as theorized in the extended model.

Assessing the Structural Model Specification

The Structural Model Specification is necessary to confirm the structural links between the variables in the model and the loading of each items used to measure respective variables. An observation shows that the items of each variable really reflect their respective construct intended to measure. The structural links among the variables of interests in the model have yielded positive relations among each others as expected and predicted. However, there is a need to further test the significances of the relationships among them at another section of the chapter to establish the predicted hypotheses. This is because structural values of the inner model cannot be taken as a proof of the hypotheses until bootstrapping for test of significant is carried out for confirmation. In addition, there is a need to examine factorial analysis of the constructs in relations to the items used to measure them. This can be explained through rigorous diagnostic of validity of the model with respect to items-relation among all the constructs, which include construct validity itself, discriminant analysis, convergent and divergent validity as well as the measurement model at large.

Construct Validity

Construct validity is assessed by looking at loadings and cross loadings to identify problematic items, if any. Following Hair et al (2010), a significant value of 0.5 loadings is used as a cut-off. As has been depicted in Table 1, items measuring each construct in the study are highly loaded on their particular construct and loaded lower on others, thus construct validity of the instruments is established.

Convergent Validity

The convergent validity of the instrument was also tested to examine the multiple items measuring the same construct of the study and the degree of their agreement with one another. In this respect, the factor loadings alongside both composite reliability and average variance were extracted for proper examination.

$$(\rho\, c) = (\Sigma\ \lambda i)2\ /\ [(\Sigma\ \lambda i)2 +\ \Sigma\ Var\ (\varepsilon i)]$$

where λi is the outer factor loading, and $Var\ (\varepsilon i) = 1 - \lambda i$ is the measurement error or the error variance associated with the individual indicator variable(s) for that given factor (see: Fornell & Larcker, 1981).

(AVE)[b]: Average Variance Extracted

$$(AVE) = (\Sigma\ \lambda 2i)\ /\ [(\Sigma\ \lambda 2i) +\ \Sigma\ Var\ (\varepsilon i)]$$

where λi is the outer factor loading, and $Var\ (\varepsilon i) = 1 - \lambda i$ is the measurement error or the error variance associated with the individual indicator variable(s) for that given factor (see: Fornell & Larcker, 1981).

The results of Table 2 show that all items' loadings exceeded the recommended value of 0.5 suggested by Hair et al (2010). In addition, the composite reliability is used to test how far the construct indicators really represent the latent and the values obtained ranging from 0.892 to 0.957, which exceeded the recommended value of 0.7 by Hair et al (2010) as shown in Table 2. The average variance extracted (AVE) was used to relatively examine the variance captured by the construct indicators to measurement error. According to Barclay et al (1995), the value must be above 0.5 for justification. In this study, the AVEs for the indicators are within the range of 0.654 and 0.819 respectively. Looking at the results for the parameter estimates and the test of their statistical significance (t-values at p<0.001 alpha levels), it can be concluded that all the variables in the model are valid measures of their respective constructs (see: Chow & Chan, 2008).

Discriminant Validity

The discriminant validity of the measures has equally been tested to examine the degree to which items differentiate among constructs. This was carried out first by looking at correlations between the measures for possible potential overlapping of constructs. Second, whether items are strongly loaded on their own construct in the model were examined. Third, whether the average variance shared between each construct and that its measures are greater than the average variance shared between the constructs and other constructs are also explored, as suggested by Compeau et al, (1999). In this respect, the results of Table 3 show that the squared correlations for each construct is less than the average squared root of the vari-

Table 1. Loadings and cross loadings for construct validity

Items	Use	MMENG	SNORM	Self-Efficacy	System	TRUST	USEFUL	WOM
E2	0.846							
E5	0.729							
E6	0.902							
E7	0.851							
ENG1		0.880						
ENG4		0.819						
ENG5		0.887						
ENG6		0.820						
ENG9		0.873						
S1					0.839			
S5					0.831			
S6					0.898			
SE3				0.926				
SE4				0.912				
SE6				0.875				
SN1			0.956					
SN4			0.919					
SN5			0.939					
T1						0.886		
T2						0.802		
T3						0.819		
T4						0.791		
T5						0.789		
T6						0.801		
U1							0.845	
U2							0.914	
U5							0.868	
WM1								0.844
WM2								0.873
WM3								0.821
WM4								0.788
WM5								0.708

ance extracted by the indicators measuring that construct. Hence, the measurement model reflects an adequate convergent validity and discriminant validity.

Reliability Analysis

Reliability is an indication of the internal consistency of the instruments measuring the concepts

Table 2. Outer weights (loadings, STDEV, t-values)

	Loadings	Standard Deviation (STDEV)	T-Statistics	Composite Reliability (CR)[a]	Average Variance Extract (AVE)[b]
PE2 <- EOUSE	0.8457	0.0339	24.91***	0.900954	0.6958
PE5 <- EOUSE	0.7286	0.0544	13.377***		
PE6 <- EOUSE	0.9018	0.0248	36.275***		
PE7 <- EOUSE	0.8506	0.0319	26.602***		
eCOM1 <-MPeCOM	0.8796	0.0249	35.250***	0.932066	0.733147
eCOM4 <-MPeCOM	0.8185	0.0338	24.165***		
eCOM5 <-MPeCOM	0.8873	0.0248	35.769***		
eCOM6 <-MPeCOM	0.8204	0.0361	22.712***		
eCOM9 <-MPeCOM	0.8725	0.0243	35.898***		
SF1 <- System factor	0.8394	0.0555	15.118***	0.892096	0.73398
SF5 <- System factor	0.8314	0.0319	25.986***		
SF6 <- System factor	0.8978	0.0324	27.635***		
SE3 <- SelfEfficacy	0.9264	0.0227	40.688***	0.931239	0.818742
SE4 <- SelfEfficacy	0.9124	0.0243	37.515***		
SE6 <- SelfEfficacy	0.8748	0.0285	30.643***		
SN1 <- SNORM	0.9563	0.0116	82.109***	0.956724	0.880542
SN4 <- SNORM	0.9191	0.0227	40.481***		
SN5 <- SNORM	0.9391	0.0159	58.810***		
T1 <- TRUST	0.8864	0.0296	29.851***	0.922376	0.664857
T2 <- TRUST	0.8019	0.0516	15.534***		
T3 <- TRUST	0.8193	0.0298	27.485***		
T4 <- TRUST	0.7905	0.0639	12.360***		
T5 <- TRUST	0.7886	0.0654	12.049***		
T6 <- TRUST	0.8011	0.0653	12.260***		
PU1 <- USEFUL	0.8454	0.0568	14.874***	0.908378	0.767888
PU2 <- USEFUL	0.9136	0.0177	51.561***		
PU5 <- USEFUL	0.8683	0.0451	19.224***		
WM1 <- WOM	0.8442	0.0328	25.698***	0.903965	0.654205
WM2 <- WOM	0.8728	0.0280	31.133***		
WM3 <- WOM	0.8206	0.0343	23.868***		
WM4 <- WOM	0.7886	0.0474	16.612***		
WM5 <- WOM	0.7077	0.0663	10.664***		

***P<0.001, (CR)[æ]: Composite reliability

and helps access the "goodness" of measure (Sekaran & Bougie, 2010). There are many different types of reliability estimates (Ambali, 2009). One of the most widely used tests is Cronbach's Alpha that is employed in this study as shown in Table 4. By looking at the results of the Cronbach's

Table 3. Latent variable correlations

Construct	EUSE	MPeCOM	SUBJECTNORM	Self-Efficacy	System Factor	TRUST	USEFUL	WOM
EUSE	0.834							
MPeCOM	0.586	0.856						
SNORM	0.367	0.424	0.938					
Self-Efficacy	0.441	0.381	0.528	0.905				
System Factor	0.455	0.388	0.478	0.525	0.857			
TRUST	0.432	0.345	0.425	0.567	0.558	0.815		
USEFUL	0.411	0.459	0.466	0.334	0.435	0.665	0.876	
WOM	0.336	0.432	0.367	0.465	0.315	0.628	0.505	0.809

Table 4. Reliability tests result

Variable	No. of Items	Cronbach's Alpha
PE (Perceived Ease of Use)	4	0.85288
MPeCOM (MP e-Communication)	5	0.90885
SNORM (Subjective Norm)	3	0.93243
SE (Self-Efficacy)	3	0.88897
SF (System Factor)	3	0.81813
T (Trust)	6	0.89921
PU (Perceived Usefulness)	3	0.84873
WOM (Word of Mouth)	5	0.86654

Alpha range from 0.818 to 0.932, thus confirming the reliability of the instrument used. It is worth mentioning that the range of reliability test using Cronbach's Alpha ranges from zero to one. The closer to one the higher the level of internal consistency among items and thus the reliability of the instruments are ensured in this study.

The fact that the nature of the data is a self-reported Harman's one-factor test was examined to address any potential common method variance bias that may likely exist. As argued by Podsakoff and Organ (1986), common variance bias is problematic if a single latent factor accounts for the majority of the total explained variance. In this study, the result of the un-rotated factor analysis shows that the first factor only accounted for 13.7% of the total 76.3% variance and thus common method bias is not a problem.

FINDINGS

According to Table 5, majority of the participants are males with 91% as compared to the females. Interestingly, their age ranged from 31-40 years to 51 years and above, which sounds a sense of maturity in engaging others through e-communication. Hence, it is worth mentioning that most of them are within two major categories of age 41-50 years (50.8%) followed by 51 years and above (39.7%). This indicates to us that majority of the MPs are well matured with political experience. However, even though they have political experience does not really mean that they have been using certain technology to accomplish tasks in their respective political careers. In addition, even if they had ever used technology before, certain technology is different from one another. Majority of them (27%) are holding their personal experience as MPs for a number of years not less than 11-15 years. While the MPs belong to different parties, yet most of them (47.6%) were elected from Barisan National party (i.e., a coalition party). This coalition party

comprises of MPs from parties such as UMNO, MCA and MIC. In addition, many of the MPs are drawn from Malay ethnic group with a percentage of 57.1% follow by the Chinese (20%) and the Indian MPs (14.3%). The least number of MPs according to the last general election are those from Bumiputra Sabah and Sarawak with 3.2% and 4.8% respectively. It is interesting to note that some of the Malaysian MPs are highly educated. For example majority are Master degree (MA)

Table 5. Profile of respondents

Variable	Frequency	Percentage (%)
Gender		
Male	57	90.5
Female	6	9.5
Age (Year)		
31-40	6	9.5
41-50	32	50.8
51 and above	25	39.7
Year of Experience as MP		
Less than 5	20	31.7
6-10	11	17.5
11-15	17	27.0
16-20	13	20.6
21 and above	2	3.2
Political Party		
Barisan National (BN)	30	47.6
Party Islam (PAS) Pakatan Rayat (PKR)	8	12.7
DAP	9	14.3
	16	25.4
Ethnic Group		
Malay	36	57.1
Chinese	13	20.6
Indian	9	14.3
Bumiputra Sabah	2	3.2
Bumiputra Sarawak	3	4.8
Level of Education		
PhD	7	11.1
MA	31	49.2
BA	23	36.5
STPM	2	3.2
Religion		
Islam	36	57.1
Buddah	15	23.8
Hindu	6	9.5
Christan	5	8
Sikh	1	1.6

holders with 49.2%. In addition, some of the MPs even possessed highest degree (PhD) of qualification with a percentage of 11.1%. According to the result in Table 5, the second largest (36.5%) level of educational qualification for the majority of the MPs is Bachelor Degree (BA). Religiously, the result also indicates that majority of the MPs are Muslims (57.1%).

Descriptive Statistic Results

The extent to which MPs in Malaysia use the Internet for communications with one another is shown in Table 6. According to the results majority of them use it between 1 hour and 5 hours per day. Most of the MPs (65%) utilize Internet for communication 5 times in a day for engaging and communication with themselves, followed by about 11% have always used it 3 times per day. In addition, 10% of the MPs utilized it for 4 times per day in communicating with their colleagues and

the people they represent in various constituencies. The lowest frequency of using Internet per day among MPs is at least 1 time or 5% approximately according to Table 6.

Surprisingly, only about 10% have always used it 2 times per a whole day just like those who use it 4 times per day. A critical assessment of such usage reflects that there could be other means or channel through which communications are being carried out between the MPs and the government agencies and/or the people they represent. Among the alternative channels could be direct phone called, fax and even face-to-face engagement.

With respect to the type of technology tools use for Internet communications among MPs and their people, the findings in Table 7 show that majority of them utilized smartphone (yes, 82.3%) followed by twitter and facebook with 76.6% yes and 69.8% yes respectively. In addition, about 66.7% of the MPs confirmed that yes they always utilize their blog as Internet tool for

Table 6. Degree of Internet usage per day for communication among MPs

No. of Times for Communication	Frequency	Percentage (%)
1 time	3	4.8
2 times	6	9.5
3 times	7	11.1
4 times	6	9.5
5 times	41	65.1

Table 7. Types of technology tools used for Internet communications

Technology Tools	Frequency of Use		Percentage (%)	
	Yes	No	Yes	No
e-Parliamentary Website	24	39	38.1	61.9
E-mail	40	23	63.5	36.5
Blog	42	21	66.7	33.3
Facebook	44	19	69.8	30.2
Twitter	47	16	76.6	25.4
Smartphone	55	8	82.3	12.7
Others	3	60	4.8	95.2

communications and followed by email (64%). As relatively compared with other tools, it is quite surprising that only little (yes, 38.1%) of the MPs communicated via e-Parliamentary Website provided by the government. The result also indicates that only minimal percentage (yes, 4.8%) of the MPs utilize other means such as face-to-face and/or phone call to engage with others. Higher usage of Internet ICT-tools for communications could be costs saving among MPs as compared to alternative phone calls or costs of face-to-face in moving from one place to another.

The Path Coefficients and Discussions of the Hypotheses in the Model

In this section, the researchers address the path coefficients to examine the relationships between the structural latent constructs of the model with the MP's e-communication (MPeCOM) and to establish the various hypotheses. The results obtained have shown a mix of positive and negative significant relationships of all the independent constructs in this model with MPecom as shown in Table 8.

As clearly shown in Table 8, the results indicate a negative significant relationship between the

system factor (i.e., type of ICT-tools) and MP's e-communications with beta coefficient value of -0.184. It means there is no significant influence of type of ICT tools on the MPs' propensity of communications and engaging their people electronically. In this respect, the hypothesis H1 is rejected with t-value of -1.074, p>0.05. This could happen because of interactive effects among independent variables when using multiple regressions. But when using hierarchical regression with trust as moderator and there is no interactions among independent variables we might arrived at different results. For other variable, the result shows that a significant positive relationship exists between the causal link of perceived usefulness and e-communications among the MPs with beta coefficient values of 0.479, t-value of 2.572, p<0.05. Therefore, the null-hypothesis is rejected in favour of the real hypothesis H2 of the study and established. In addition, the causal link between the ease of using e-system and MP's e-communication is positively related with beta-value of 0.422, t-value of 3.124, p<0.001.

It indicates that ease of using technology is positively and significantly influenced the MPs' e-communications with their people. As such, the hypothesis H3 in the study is accepted and established. According to the results, the self-efficacy

Table 8. Path coefficients of the constructs with MPeCOM

Coefficients[a]					
Model	Unstandardized Coefficients		Standardized Coefficients	t	Sig.
	B	Std. Error	Beta		
1 (Constant)	6.253	2.938		2.129	.037
System factor	-.244	.227	-.184	-1.074	.287
Usefulness	.743	.289	.479	2.572	.013
Ease of use	.492	.158	.422	3.124	.003
Self-efficacy	-.181	.182	-.156	-.991	.325
Subjective norm	.332	.127	.269	2.624	.011
Word of mouth	.132	.136	.106	.969	.336
a. Dependent Variable: MPeCOM					

role in this study is not significantly related to MPs' e-communications with beta-coefficient of minimal value of -0.156, t-value of -0.991, p> 0.05. Hence, the hypothesis H4 is rejected in favour of the null-hypothesis. It means that ICT-tools might be a useful means of communications with high intention to use it for engaging one another; however continuance to use it will highly depend on perceived ability and capacity of the users (MPs) themselves.

No matter how useful or easier is the e-system for communication among the MPs yet, individual MPs must have the capacity and ability to use the system effectively as expected. Furthermore, the path coefficients between subjective norm and intention of the MPs to use e-communication is positively and significantly related with beta value of 0.269, t-value of 2.62, p<0.05. This indicates that the hypothesis H5 of the model is accepted and well established. However, the result shows that there was no significant influence of word of mouth variable on MPs e-communications, with beta-value of 0.106, t-value of 0.969, p>0.05. In this respect, the hypothesis H6 is rejected in favour of the null-hypothesis. It is not surprising that the word of mouth has no significant influence on MPs' e-communication because it is not as powerful as subjective norms. Perhaps, word of mouth's effect has been suppressed by subjective norms. However, we still maintain that the two variables are not the same; in the presence of the two the most dominant and powerful is subjective norm and can overshadow the effect of word of mouth due to their closed resemblance and perceived functional roles in using e-tools. Overall, the statistical power of the model with

respect to the independent variables of the model was assessed via the R-square value of 64.6% as shown in Table 9. It indicates that a unit changed (increase or decrease) in all the various predictor variables will increase or decrease the MP's e-communications by 64.6%.

The Path Coefficients and Discussions of the Moderating Effect of Trust

With regards to hypotheses 7a to 7f that involved the moderating effect of trust in the model, a hierarchical regression analysis was employed to see the significant role played by interaction of trust with individual independent variables in relations to the MPs' e-communication (MPeCOM).

As shown in Table 10, hierarchical regression was employed to examine the moderating effect of trust in the use of ICT for socioeconomic and political communications between MPs and their representatives. The main idea here is to see the impact of trust on the relationships between all the independent variables and the MPs intention to engage the citizens via ICT. It worth noting that two crucial assumptions of regression, (multi-collinearities and autocorrelations), were examined prior to running of the statistics test. First, variance inflation factor (VIF) was examined to see the problem of multi-collinearities that may likely happen due interactions between independent variables and trust construct. The results ranged from 2.67 to 3.89 which are far below the threshold of 10. Thus, indicating the absence of multi-collinearities problem in the study. Perhaps, this is because we had centered the data before

Table 9. Model summary[b]

Model	R	R Square	Adjusted R Square	Std. Error of the Estimate
1	0.798[a]	0.636	0.600	3.22314
a. Predictors: (Constant), word of mouth, system factor, subjective norm, perceived ease of use, self-efficacy, perceived usefulness				
b. Dependent Variable: MPeCOM				

carrying out the interaction procedures. In addition, the results of Durbin Watson also indicate the absence of autocorrelation problems as well with values ranging from 1.61 to 1.90, which are far from threshold of 2.

According to the results in the Table 10, the path coefficient for relationship between system factor and MPs communications before the interaction with trust variable was 0.61 with R^2-value of 0.38, p<0.001. However, when trust was interacted to moderate the relationship, the beta-coefficient (β) increased from 0.61 to 0.71 with a significant changed in R-square from 0.38 to 0.64, p<0.001. The moderating effect of trust is envisaged through a significant R^2 changed of 26% increased. For the individual factors such as perceived ease of using ICT, perceived usefulness and self-efficacy, the results from hierarchical regressions show a significant changed from beta-coefficients of 0.68, 0.69, 0.63 to 0.72, 0.93, and 0.67 due to interactive effect of trust respectively. Hence, this significant moderating effect of trust can be appreciated through a tremendous increase in the values of R-squares by 25%, 19% and 22% respectively (Table 10). The same positive significant effect

of trust can be envisaged for relationship between subjective norms and word of mouth (i.e., social factor) and MPs communications with their electorates through adoption of ICT components. The results show a range of changes in beta-coefficient values of 0.63, 0.59 to 0.66 and 0.65, p<0.001 respectively. Such tremendous changes due to moderating effect of trust can be appreciated via a significant changed in R-square values by 24% and 26% respectively.

CHAPTER SUMMARY

The adoption of ICT is not only peculiar with the private organization but has extensively been embraced in the public institutions. Malaysian government has adopted e-Parliamentary system by taken advantage of new technology for MPs' engagement with their electorates in various constituencies. Public agencies and governmental bodies such as elected officers or politicians have begun to envisage the importance of ICT usage in their related duties and work being assigned to them in Malaysia. In other words, the

Table 10. Hierarchical regression for moderating effect of trust

Variable	Models β	R-square Δ(R²)	T-Statistics	Sig	VIF	Durbin-Watson
System Factor	0.61	0.38	6.26	0.000	2.89	1.73
System Factor * Trust	0.71	0.64	6.76	0.000		
Ease of use	0.68	0.41	7.47	0.000	2.32	1.71
Ease * Trust	0.72	0.66	6.04	0.000		
Usefulness	0.69	0.49	7.86	0.000	2.45	1.81
Usefulness *Trust	0.93	0.68	6.21	0.000		
Self-efficacy	0.63	0.40	6.61	0.000	1.49	1.61
Self-efficacy *Trust	0.67	0.62	5.97	0.000		
Subjective Norm	0.63	0.37	6.25	0.000	2.67	1.89
Subjective norm * Trust	0.66	0.61	6.29	0.000		
Word of mouth	0.59	0.35	5.91	0.000	2.07	1.90
Word of mouth * Trust	0.65	0.61	6.44	0.000		

parliamentarian's officers have seen the needs to embrace the ICT innovations. As a matter of fact, the implementation and adoption of the new technologies in the Malaysian parliamentary system has become one of the most pressing agenda. This is to improve the responsiveness and efficient transaction between government as whole, the elected politicians, or member of parliaments (MPs) and their people in their respective constituencies. The chapter has employed a quantitative approach by extending the existing technology acceptance model (TAM). Additional variables of interests such as self-efficacy as part of individual factors, word of mouth as part of social factors, system factor and trust were used to extend the original TAM. In this chapter, it can be concluded that system factor, self-efficacy in individual factors, word of mouth in social factor play important roles in the use of ICT components by MPs. The result shows that self-efficacy of the individual MPs has negative relation with MPs' e-communication until it was moderated with trust. The same goes to system factor. The results indicate that provision of e-parliament system is not enough until MPs are really trained for appropriate use of ICT otherwise, they might be reluctant due to lack of skills and capability on how to successfully use e-devices. In addition, there is a need to gain people's trust towards ICT in terms of perceived usefulness, ease of using it to achieve their goals. It is also pertinent to note that word of mouth about ICT carries high weightage than subjective norms based on the findings of this chapter. It has been noted that what people say about any given e-device systems (i.e., word of mouth or reputation) is more important than what one thinks people around him or her would like or want the person to do (i.e., subjective norm) especially with regard to usage of ICT in the public sector for discharging designated works.

REFERENCES

Ajzen, I. (1991). The theory of planned behavior. *Organizational Behavior and Human Decision Processes*, *50*(2), 179–211. doi:10.1016/0749-5978(91)90020-T

Ambali, A. R. (2009). E-government policy: Ground issues in e-filling system. *European Journal of Soil Science*, *11*(2), 249–266.

Barclay, D. W., Higgins, C., & Thompson, R. (1995). The partial least square approach to causal modeling: Personal computer adoption use as illustration. *Technology Studies*, *2*(2), 285–309.

Carter, L., & Belanger, F. (2005). The utilization of e-government services: Citizen trust, innovation and acceptance. *Information Systems Journal*, *15*(1), 5–25. doi:10.1111/j.1365-2575.2005.00183.x

Chow, W. S., & Chan, L. S. (2008). Social network and shared goals in organizational knowledge sharing. *Information & Management*, *45*(7), 24–30. doi:10.1016/j.im.2008.06.007

Compeau, D. R., Higgins, C. A., & Huff, S. (1999). Social cognitive theory and individual reactions to computing technology: A longitudinal-study. *Management Information Systems Quarterly*, *23*(2), 145–158. doi:10.2307/249749

Dai, X. (2007b). Prospect and concerns of e-democracy at the European parliament. *Journal of Legislative Studies*, *13*(3), 370–387. doi:10.1080/13572330701500789

Dai, X., & Norton, P. (2007a). The internet and parliamentary democracy in Europe. *Journal of Legislative Studies*, *13*(3), 342–353. doi:10.1080/13572330701500763

Davis, F. D. (1986). *A technology acceptance model for empirically testing new end-user information systems: Theory and results*. (Doctoral dissertation). MIT Sloan School of Management.

Davis, (1989). Perceived usefulness, perceived ease of use, and User Acceptance of Information Technology. *MIS Quarterly*, 319-340.

Everard, A., & Galletta, D. F. (2005). How Presentation Flaws Affect Perceived Site Quality, Trust, and Intention to Purchase from an Online Store. *Journal of Management Information Systems*, 22(3), 55–95.

Fogg, B. (1999). The elements of computer credibility. In *Proceedings of the CHI' 99 (Computer-Human Interaction) Conference on Human Factors in Computing Systems*. ACM.

Fornell, C., & Larcker, D. F. (1981). Evaluating structural equation models with unobservable and measurement error. *JMR, Journal of Marketing Research*, 18(1), 39–50. doi:10.2307/3151312

Gefen, D., Karahanna, E., & Straub, D. (2003). Trust and TAM in online shopping: An integrated model. *Management Information Systems Quarterly*, 27(1), 51–90.

Hair, J. F., Black, W. C., Babin, B. J., & Anderson, R. E. (2010). *Multivariate data analysis*. Upper Saddle River, NJ: Prentice-Hall.

Hung, S. Y., Chang, C. M., & Yu, T. J. (2006). Determinants of user acceptance of the e-government services: The case of online tax filing and payment system. *Government Information Quarterly*, 23(1), 97–122. doi:10.1016/j.giq.2005.11.005

Jarvenpaa, S. L., Tractinsky, N., & Vitale, M. (2000). Consumer trust in and internet store. *Information Technology Management*, 1(2), 45–71. doi:10.1023/A:1019104520776

Kock, N. (2001). The ape that used email: Understand e-communication behavior through evolution theory. *AIS*, 5(3), 1–29.

Lee, M. K. O., Cheung, C. M. K., & Chen, Z. (2005). Acceptance of internet-based learning medium: The role of extrinsic and intrinsic motivation. *Information & Management*, 42(8), 1095–1104. doi:10.1016/j.im.2003.10.007

Lee, (2003). South Korea: From the Land of Morning Calm to ICT Hotbed. *Academy of Management Executive*, 17(2), 7-18.

Pavlou, P. A., & Fygenson, M. (2006). Understanding and predicting electronic commerce adoption: An extension of the theory of planned behaviour. *Management Information Systems Quarterly*, 30(1), 115–144.

Pedersen, P. E., & Nysveen, H. (2002). *Using the theory of planned behaviour to explain teenagers' adoption of text messaging services*. Norway: Agder University College.

Petrus, G., & Nelson, O. N. (2006). Borneo online banking: Evaluating customer perceptions and behavioural intention. *Management Research News*, 29(1/2), 6–15. doi:10.1108/01409170610645402

Podsakoff, P. M., & Organ, D. W. (1986). Self-reports in organizational research: Problems and prospects. *Journal of Management*, 12(4), 531–544. doi:10.1177/014920638601200408

Sekaran, U., & Bougie, R. (2010). *Research methods for business: A skill building approach* (4th ed.). John Wiley & Sons, Inc.

Sobaci, M. Z. (2011). *Parliament and ICT-based legislation: Concept, experiences and lessons*. Premier Reference Source. doi:10.4018/978-1-61350-329-4

Srite, M., & Karahanna, E. (2006). The role of espoused national cultural values in technology acceptance. *Management Information Systems Quarterly*, 30(3), 679–704.

Venkatesh, V. (2000). Determinants of perceived ease of use: Integrating control, intrinsic motivation, and emotion into the technology acceptance model. *Information Systems Research*, *11*(4), 342–365. doi:10.1287/isre.11.4.342.11872

Venkatesh, V., & Bala, H. (2008). Technology acceptance model 3 and a research agenda on interventions. *Decision Sciences*, *39*(2), 272–315. doi:10.1111/j.1540-5915.2008.00192.x

Venkatesh, V., & Davis, F. D. (2000). A theoretical extension of the technology acceptance model: Four longitudinal field studies. *Management Science*, *46*(2), 186–204. doi:10.1287/mnsc.46.2.186.11926

KEY TERMS AND DEFINITIONS

Computer Self-Efficacy: A belief in one's ability to perform a particular task using computer-based systems or other devices.

Constituency: An electoral district, riding, ward, division, and/or electoral area where voting takes place.

E-Communication: Passing of information such as emails or text message from individual parliament members to another or electorates using computer systems.

Electorates: The group of people entitled to vote or expected to vote in an election.

Legislative Process: The process in which bills are considered and laws enacted by the parliament body whether face-to-face or through electronic medium.

Parliamentarian: Elected member of a parliament especially those members who know a lot about the deliberative assembly.

Politicians: Political leader or political figure that can participate and influence public policy and/or decision making.

Representativeness: A person who represents a constituency or community to agitate for the needs, concerns, and demands of the people in a legislative body, especially a member of the parliament and/or assembly body.

ENDNOTE

1. Official portal Malaysia parliament (www.malaysiaparliament.com) retrieved on 23 Jun 2012.

Chapter 13
ICT Adoption in Malaysian Public Sector:
A Modified-Extended Unified Theory of Acceptance and Use of Technology (UTAUT)

ABSTRACT

In this chapter, a modified-extended unified theory of acceptance and use of technology model is applied to one of the government agencies to assess the behavioural intention of the staff and the actual use of ICT. The findings of the study show a positive relationship between performance-expectancy, effort expectancy, facilitating condition, and behavioural intention to use ICT except for social influence, which showed a negative relationship with behavioural intention to use ICT. In addition, the findings show the impact of gender difference on the causal links between the various predictors studied and behavioural intention as well as the actual use of ICT. There were two additional contributions to the theoretical framework in this chapter. Additionally, the moderating effect of gender difference on causal links between facilitating condition (predictor) and the actual use behaviour of ICT among the staff is addressed. Implications of these findings are discussed.

INTRODUCTION

Nowadays, information and communication technologies are widely use in the most government agencies and become very important in organization to improve job performance, productivity, increase knowledge of workers, improve quality of job and improve collaboration and networking among employees by removing the barrier to real – time communication and effective information sharing. Through ICT, the organization can cross geographical and time zone boundaries to meet the demand of a world community and ICT is contributing to environmental responsibility. By using ICT in an organization, it helps the organizations fast respond to their tasks and to their stakeholders by improving quality of services, accountability and efficiency. Knowledge and information are

DOI: 10.4018/978-1-4666-6579-8.ch013

recognized as a two most important strategic resources in any organization. In this chapter, we are investigating factors contributing to usage of ICT using Unified Theory of Acceptance and Use of Technology (UTAUT).

The rapid growth of technology in the developing world has made the agency committed to use of ICT to satisfy the stakeholders on various matters. For example, improve the dissemination technology for weather forecast, weather warning, earthquake information and tsunami warning. Basically the agency provide the forecast information and warning in Malaysia in order to make the people well prepared upon alerted. Hence, the agency is a public organization that communicates to their stakeholders and the government machinery directly. To ensure the satisfaction among the stakeholders, the agency widely uses the ICT in its daily works. For example, Decisions and Dissemination Support System (DDADS) system is reducing the time in delivery of information or warning. DDADS system is a system that uploads all the final information or warning through the Internet and sends the messages to other government related agencies by using SMS Gateway System that provides fastest delivery of information or warning via a Short Sending Messages Service (SSMS) technology.

PROBLEM STATEMENT OF THE STUDY

Agarwal (1999) believes that "acquiring appropriate IT is a necessary but not sufficient condition for utilizing it effectively," (p.85). Therefore, it has been noted that user's interventions attitudes towards and acceptance of a new information system have a critical impact on successful information system adoption (Davis, 1989; Venkatesh & Davis, 1996; Succi & Walter, 1999). Malaysia is still at a developing stage but striving to become a developed country by advancing its service delivery system by harnessing advantage of ICT

usage to achieve its objectives. More importantly, staff of the agency have adopted the use of ICT and believed in its usefulness to the organizations and staffs but admitted that not all the technologies applied in organizations are ease to use for the users. There are various problems regarding the acceptance and use of the technology among agency's staffs (preliminary interview with some officers in July, 2013). Therefore, it is important to determine the factors contributing to usage of ICT using a modified UTAUT among staffs.

There are many problems about contributing factors to the usage of ICT among the staffs. For example, staffs feel that the new human resources management information system (HRMIS) sometimes inconvenient and burden themselves although the technology is good in databases aspect. It was highly pronounced that "People feel the HRMIS technology is inconvenient because the system can't be accessed if too much people are accessing it in the same time due to server limitation of the certain amount of users at one time." Other than that, the technology itself bring problems to staffs when the technologies is not well maintained in terms of too much cookies and bugs in the server that contribute to select false information of the users. For example, it is normally happen at the early and end of the year, the HRMIS system will capture other user databases not the user based on the ID-key-in.

The main focus of attention in this study is about the VSAT (Very Small Aperture Terminal) technology used to transmit data from the sensor equipment at site to PC at the Headquarters through Telekom Malaysia in Cyberjaya. Prior to distribution of real questionnaires, a focus group interview was conducted among six representatives from the agency to pinpoint the most pertinent issues related to VSAT technology used. The result of our interview is line with effort expectancy and performance expectancy. In this study, while performance expectancy is the degree to which a person believes that using a technology system would improve his or her job performance and satisfy the stakeholders. For effort expectancy, it is the degree of simplicity associated with the use of a technology system to perform job. For example, when we interview the participants prior to survey questionnaire, most of them stated that "Ease of use and the useful of the system contributed to improvement on their job performance and satisfaction of the stakeholders." Hence, attitudinally, majority, especially the young ones, hold to the belief that he or she should use the system as it does not demand any calculative efforts from him/her compared to manual procedures. They said for example that "earthquake data can be extract from seismograph using manual whereby a meteorologist needs to calculate manually the epicenter of the earthquake, but since VSAT technologies applied at the agency, the quality, efficiency and effectiveness of the tasks can be appreciated." In addition, in the interview session, it was also revealed by the newly appointed participants at the agency that "the use of VSAT technology by other senior colleagues has influenced us to make use of the system under their supervisions." This is basically in line with influence of social factor. When asked about the maintenance and facilitating conditions of the VSAT, the participant mentioned that "the technical infrastructure is always provided by Telekom Malaysia" to support the use of the system. When asking the participants about gender differences, the participants of our focused group acknowledged that attitudinal view towards the VSAT technology depends on the individual users' sex." However, when asking about age group, experience and voluntariness of the participants, there were no tangible answers. There were variations in the answers given and in this context we did not include them in our conceptual framework.

The main objectives of the chapter are twofold. First, is to examine the relationship between, effort and performance expectancies (EE, PE); social influence (SI) and behavioural intention (IB) to use VSAT system. Second, is to investigate the relationship between facilitating conditions

(FC) and use behaviour (UB) of the staff. Third, is to examine the impact of gender difference of the causal links between the identified factors in the model and IB as well as UB. Such objectives prompted us in this chapter to raise the following research questions are: First, is there any significant relationship between performance expectancy (PE) and behavioural intention (BI) to use VSAT system?

Second, is there any significant relationship between effort expectancy (EE) and behavioural intention (BI) to use the system? Third, is there any significant relationship between social influence (SI) and behavioural intention (BI) to use VSAT system? Fourth, is there any significant relationship between facilitating conditions (FC) and behavioural intention (BI) to use of VSAT system? Fifth, is there any significant relationship between facilitating conditions (FC) and use behaviour (UB) of VSAT system? Sixth, can gender difference significantly affect the relationship between effort, performance expectancies (PE and EE), social influence (SI), facilitating conditions (FC) and behavioural intention (BI) to use *VSAT* system? Seventh, can gender difference significantly impact the relationship between facilitating conditions and behavioural intention (BI) as well as use behaviour (UB) of staff towards the system?

On the basis of the above preliminary information we modified the unified theory of acceptance and use of technology (UTAUT) by excluding non-consensus variables out of the original model and validate the new model. In line with obvious variables of our interests that can be confirmed via focused group interview of the staff, the conceptual framework was developed as in Figure 1.

OPERATIONALIZING THE MODEL IN LIEU OF THE LITERATURE

The unified theory of acceptance and use of technology (UTAUT) was developed by Venkatesh et al. (2003) as a comprehensive model that combined

Figure 1. A modified-extended unified theory of acceptance and use of technology (UTAUT)

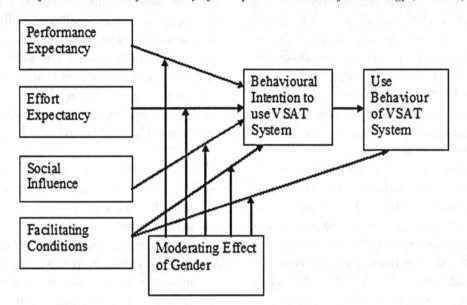

all concepts in the previous models of technology acceptance among people regardless of the type of sectors where it was adopted. In other words, the model has comprehensively integrated the significant elements across eight prominent user acceptance models of technology and formulates a unique measure with core determinants of user behavioral intention and actual use behaviour. In this study, we are replicating the model with modifications to fit our underground interview as in Figure 1. In replicating a model or validating it, Straub and Prasad (1989) argue that study has been very scarce due to lack of attention from researchers. However, Straub and Prasad (1989) lamented that theoretical model may not require the same validation and/or rapid change in technology for different context. This was why we adopted a focus group approach to the organization for interview purpose and pin down the contingent variables that fit their situation. Agarwal and Karahanna, (2000) and Doll et al. (1998) believe that the model replication lies in two directions: exploring new findings and confirming the study by testing the hypothesized measurement model against new gathered data such as the case in the

context of the chosen agency. This justifies our modification-extension of the unified model.

With regards to performance expectancy variable of the model, it refers to the degree to which individual staff believes that the system would help them improve in their job performance. Originally, this concept was derived from five constructs of the past theories which are relative advantages, outcome expectancies, extrinsic motivation, and job fit in relations to perceived gains (Venkatesh et al, 2003) when one intends to use a particular system. An empirical research which tested the model has confirmed a positive influence of the variables on behavioral intention to use certain technologies or systems by performance expectancy factor (Venkatesh et al., 2003). As such we hypothesized that:

H1a: There is a significant relationship between performance expectancy (PE) and behavioural intention (BI) to use VSAT system.

However, the previous study by Wu, Tao, and Yang, (2008) has confirmed the relative significant influence of gender differences on performance expectancy. In their work, it was ascertained that the male workers who pursue performance will be more task-oriented than other group. Earlier work by Venkatech, (2003) has also shown that the relationship between performance expectancy and intention to use a technology system was moderate by gender differences thereby indicated that men tend to be highly task-oriented. In addition, another long overdue work conducted by Minton and Schneider (1980) has proven that a situation where performance expectancy in an organization was focusing on task accomplishment, the outputs are likely to be especially salient to men than women.

H1b: There is a significant impact of gender differences on the relationship between performance expectancy (PE) and behavioural intention (BI) to use VSAT system.

Effort expectancy in this model refers to the degree of ease of using VSAT system. It is expected that before an organization accepts the system, the system provider would have given some training to the users. Thus, during the training of the system, users' pre-usage effort expectancy will undergo a disconfirmation process and in turn influence users' satisfaction with post-usage effort expectancy, which will subsequently lead to a continuance intention to use the system (Venkatesh et al., 2003). Moreover, based on previous research work (Venkatesh et al., 2003) effort expectancy has a positive influence on behavioural intention. This is likely to hold true in a continuance context for the staff at the said agency because human tendency for subconsciously pursuing instrumental behaviors related to the use of VSAT system is independent of the timing or stage of such behaviors (see: Bhattacherjee, 2001). For instance, when users feel easy of using the system it will increase their productivity, performance and quality of services provided to the public at large. Hence, at this juncture, it is hypothesized that:

H2a: There is a significant relationship between effort expectancy (EE) and behavioural intention (BI) to use VSAT system.

However, it is useful to highlight that diligent expectation among gender in using any technology system or device to perform works in public sector is not likely to be the same. This observation has also been confirmed by Venkatech et al. (2003). It was concluded that the diligent expectation of an individual towards the use of system would be somewhat different because of gender with respect to value-differences. As such, another hypothesis put forward here is that:

H2b: There is a significant impact of gender differences on the relationship between effort expectancy (EE) and behavioural intention (BI) to use VSAT system.

In the context of this modified-extended model, social influence is defined as the degree to which individual staff believes that important people such as boss, friends and peers in the organization think he or she should use or not use technology system (i.e., VSAT). In line with the previous tested theories such as TPB, TRA and TAM2/3, social influence has a direct influence on behavioural intention to use technology system and play a significant role in technology acceptance models. Fishbein and Azjen (1975) labeled social influence as 'subjective norm' in their introductory study about beliefs, attitudes and behavior. They defined it as a person's perceptions that most people who are important to him think he should or should not perform the behavior in question. As such, social influence is expected to have a direct effect on behavioural intention to use the VSAT system in this study. This proposition has been tested by many works, including Venkatesh and Davis (2000); and Venkatesh et al., (2003). In short, people around the users may influence them to use certain technologies. In addition, with the help from the experts and more experience in using the technologies, it can encourage the intention to use certain system for work. In this context, Venkatesh et al. (2003) have concluded in their work that there is a positive relationship between social influence and behavioural intention to use certain system. Following the same vein, we hypothesized that:

H3a: There is a significant relationship between social influence (SI) and behavioural intention (BI) to use VSAT system.

Given the fact that gender differences occur in the degree of easiness to convince individuals by peers and friends. Such degree of easiness to convincing others is relatively related to female than male group due to mind set and ability to hold to what one believes about the system. For example, simple convincing explanatory about the usefulness and indispensible use of technology can easily convince female than male counterpart (Ambali, 2009). One important contributing factor here might be because female group tend to be more attentive in listening to what other people say than male group. As such, it is hypothesized that:

H3b: There is a significant impact of gender differences on the relationship between social influence (SI) and behavioural intention (BI) to use VSAT system.

Regarding the facilitating conditions variable, we adopt the same line of thoughts in the work done by Venkatesh et al. (2012) in examining the causal links between both behavioural intention as well as use behaviour of technology among the staff. Originally, Venkatesh et al., (2003) just investigated only direct effect between facilitating conditions and use behaviour. The justification for extending the causal link to behavioural intention is that facilitating conditions can be seen as proxy variable for perceived behavioural control in following the TPB (Ajzen, 1991) discussed earlier in another chapter of this book. In this context,

it has been observed by many researchers that facilitating conditions such as training and support provided are freely across all the staff and who ever among them having favourable access to good conditions tend to develop a higher intention to use the system (i.e., VSAT in this context) and finally use it in actual sense (see: Venkatesh et al. 2012). Thus, given some insights derived from both previous theory of planned behaviour by Ajzen (1991) and a new recently conducted work by Venkatesh et al. (2012), we examine the link between facilitating conditions and behavioural intention as additional value added to the original model (see Figure 1).

H4a: There is a significant relationship between facilitating conditions (FC) and behavioural intention (IB) to use the VSAT system.

Another additional and important concern is the moderating effect of gender differences on facilitating condition variable. This aspect is quiet new in the literature. Other than Venkatesh et al. (2012) recent article in MIS, throughout our readings in the literature, this chapter would be the second work that examine the impact of gender difference on facilitating conditions. The argument put forward is that men tend to be industrious and perseverance by spending more effort to break through any condition in pursuing their desired goals they like to achieve than women. This has been supported by empirical result from the work of Venkatesh et al. (2012). In addition gender differences related to forging through any difficulty conditions to achieve objectives has also been found by other works such Morris and Venkatesh (2000) and Lynott and McCandless (2000). A social cognitive research that examined the roles played by gender differences in society also concluded that women were found more relying on external supports than men at any given situational conditions. Hence, there is a need to examine moderating effect of gender differences in relations to facilitating conditions of using VSAT among the staff and behavioural intention to use VSAT system. Hence, it is hypothesized that:

H4b: There is a significant impact of gender differences on the relationship between facilitating conditions (FC) and behavioural intention (BI) to use VSAT system.

H5: There is a significant impact of gender differences on the relationship between behavioural intention (BI) and the actual use of VSAT system (UB).

DATA COLLECTION AND METHODOLOGICAL APPROACH

Data collection was carried out using a self-administered survey questionnaire. Information was collected over a period between August and September 2013 at one shot time. Hence it is a cross-sectional designed study. The respondents were those citizens that have used VSAT system for providing certain valuable information. The nature of data collection was through a five-point Likert survey. A total of 200 questionnaires were distributed to the respondents and the returning rate very good where 140 valid questionnaires (i.e., 70%) were collected back for further analyses. The items of the questionnaires were drawn from well established different previous studies as explained in the subsequence sections as well as the psychometric properties to fulfill the underlying assumptions of validity involving scale of measurements.

Goodness of Measures and Psychometric Properties

The questionnaire used consists of a five-point Likert scale to obtain data for each of the construct's dimension in the modified-extended model of the study except for moderating variable (Figure 1).

Based on the insights obtained from previous studies by Venkatesh, (2000, 2003), Venkatesh et al. (2012), Pedersen and Nysveen, (2012), Lee, Cheung and Chen (2005), Petrus and Nelson (2006), Venketash and Bala, (2008), and Ajzen, (1991), a questionnaire was reconstructed with some modifications to earn information. In this study, both validity and reliability tests to measure the accuracy of the data were examined. Construct validity was used to test how well the instrument developed measures a particular construct (Sekaran & Bougie, 2010), while reliability was used to test how consistently the measuring instruments have measured the constructs. Validity measures in this research were in three folds in terms of construct, convergent and discriminant validities in order to examine how well the questionnaires used could tap the constructs as theorized in the modified-extended model.

Factorial Analysis of the Constructs and Measurability of Items

Figure 2 of the modified-extended model displays the outer and inner parts of the model's constructs. This is necessary to confirm the structural links between the variables in the model and the loading of each items used to measure respective variables. An observation shows that the items of each variable really reflect their respective construct intended to measure.

Construct Validity

In addition, there is a need to further diagnose the validity of the model with respect to items-relation among all the constructs, which include construct validity itself, convergent validity as well as discriminant analysis of the measurement model at large.

Construct validity is assessed by looking at loadings and cross loadings to identify problematic items, if any. Following Hair et al (2010), a significant value of 0.5 loadings is used as a cut-off. As has been depicted in Table 1, items measuring each construct in the study are highly loaded on

Figure 2. Outer weights of the modified-extended model

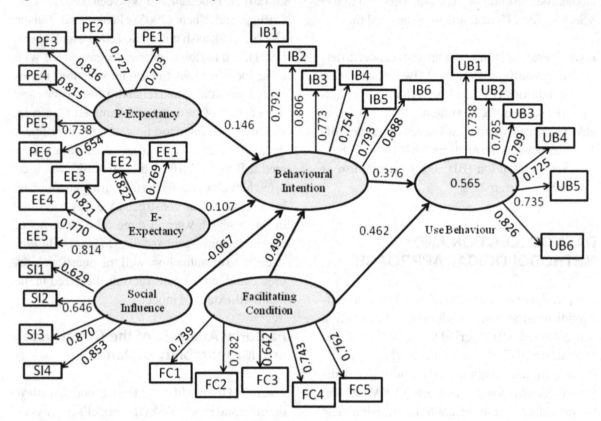

their particular construct and extremely loaded lower on other variables, thus construct validity of the instruments is established.

Convergent Validity

The convergent validity of the instrument was also tested to examine the multiple items measuring the same construct of the study and the degree of their agreement with one another. In this respect, the factor loadings alongside both composite reliability and average variance were extracted for proper examination.

$$(\rho c) = (\Sigma \ \lambda i)2 \ / \ [(\Sigma \ \lambda i)2 + \ \Sigma \ Var \ (\varepsilon i)]$$

where λi is the outer factor loading, and $Var \ (\varepsilon i) = 1 - \lambda i$ is the measurement error or

the error variance associated with the individual indicator variable(s) for that given factor (see: Fornell & Larcker, 1981).

(AVE)[b]: Average Variance Extracted

$$(AVE) = (\Sigma \ \lambda 2i) \ / \ [(\Sigma \ \lambda 2i) + \ \Sigma \ Var \ (\varepsilon i)]$$

where λi is the outer factor loading, and $Var \ (\varepsilon i) = 1 - \lambda i$ is the measurement error or the error variance associated with the individual indicator variable(s) for that given factor (see: Fornell & Larcker, 1981).

The results of Table 2 show that all items' loadings exceeded the recommended value of 0.5 suggested by Hair et al (2010). In addition, the composite reliability was used to test how far the construct indicators really represent the latent

Table 1. Loadings and cross loadings for construct validity

Item	Behaviour Intention (IB)	Effort Expectancy (EE)	Facilitating Condition (FC)	Performance Expectancy (PE)	Social Influence (SI)	Use Behaviour (UB)
EE1	0.22299	0.768814	0.27159	0.33684	0.124587	0.364896
EE2	0.22451	0.822442	0.34123	0.337141	0.281898	0.210848
EE3	0.36092	0.820576	0.12921	0.344754	0.314141	0.156055
EE4	0.32145	0.770234	0.24356	0.310253	0.188012	0.272313
EE5	0.22945	0.8141	0.19805	0.297301	0.3642	0.13165
FC1	0.37777	0.369547	0.73867	0.273935	0.222086	0.200227
FC2	0.13557	0.265907	0.7823	0.267414	0.375869	0.180314
FC3	0.23068	0.100538	0.64228	0.322891	0.385058	0.397203
FC4	0.23536	0.172586	0.74254	0.190012	0.256882	0.61462
FC5	0.34986	0.199794	0.76212	0.10484	0.252053	0.172278
IB1	0.79175	0.281674	0.38171	0.282204	0.082807	0.275484
IB2	0.80609	0.270909	0.37161	0.276809	0.059502	0.155377
IB3	0.77252	0.269822	0.36558	0.296884	0.026972	0.252632
IB4	0.75373	0.368489	0.18262	0.288767	0.255868	0.137867
IB5	0.79309	0.196587	0.20568	0.264192	0.302037	0.182545
IB6	0.68811	0.359703	0.20748	0.277463	0.277439	0.179542
PE1	0.24946	0.267623	0.2852	0.703193	0.158632	0.214112
PE2	0.29881	0.245546	0.10098	0.727153	0.112359	0.39871
PE3	0.29086	0.370979	0.39739	0.816257	0.21341	0.390045
PE4	0.35113	0.282253	0.39283	0.815269	0.161625	0.285059
PE5	0.34335	0.310069	0.2106	0.737645	0.153455	0.229493
PE6	0.31679	0.211837	0.29549	0.653546	0.254161	0.374558
SI1	0.10038	0.114065	0.24984	0.044465	0.628818	0.097682
SI2	0.14162	0.172467	0.26779	0.005739	0.646003	0.094835
SI3	0.19541	0.374945	0.39105	0.247856	0.870376	0.33234
SI4	0.23344	0.290516	0.13858	0.138177	0.853013	0.32134
UB1	0.10350	0.11652	0.24384	0.296327	0.257077	0.737918
UB2	0.28396	0.325809	0.14178	0.110521	0.227215	0.785275
UB3	0.18016	0.332011	0.21433	0.211762	0.248934	0.799337
UB4	0.26140	0.391316	0.15809	0.365285	0.249614	0.724668
UB5	0.20208	0.258277	0.26823	0.331099	0.182879	0.735366
UB6	0.18524	0.169406	0.14802	0.266541	0.272751	0.826137

variables and the values obtained ranging from 0.8408 to 0.8985, which exceeded the recommended value of 0.7 by Hair et al (2010) as shown in Table 2. The average variance extracted (AVE) was also used to relatively examine the variance captured by the construct indicators to measurement error. According to Barclay et al (1995), the value must be above 0.5 for justification. In this

Table 2. Outer weights (loadings, STDEV, t-values)

Measurement Items	Loadings	Standard Deviation (STDEV)	T-Statistics	Composite Reliability (CR)[a]	Average Variance Extract (AVE)[b]
EE1 <- Effort Expectancy	0.7688	0.045177	17.0177***		
EE2 <- Effort Expectancy	0.8224	0.027968	29.4069***		
EE3 <- Effort Expectancy	0.8206	0.031028	26.4462***	0.8985	0.6394
EE4 <- Effort Expectancy	0.7702	0.036011	21.3888***		
EE5 <- Effort Expectancy	0.8141	0.025119	32.4094***		
FC1 <- Facilitating Condition	0.7387	0.052757	14.0014***		
FC2 <- Facilitating Condition	0.7823	0.037382	20.9273***		
FC3 <- Facilitating Condition	0.6423	0.069341	9.2626***	0.8541	0.5405
FC4 <- Facilitating Condition	0.7425	0.033655	22.0632***		
FC5 <- Facilitating Condition	0.7621	0.027138	28.0832***		
IB1 <- Behaviour Intention	0.7918	0.045492	17.4044***		
IB2 <- Behaviour Intention	0.8061	0.043786	18.4097***		
IB3 <- Behaviour Intention	0.7725	0.043186	17.8885***		
IB4 <- Behaviour Intention	0.7537	0.036136	20.8584***	0.8962	0.5907
IB5 <- Behaviour Intention	0.7931	0.024422	32.4752***		
IB6 <- Behaviour Intention	0.6881	0.041879	16.4309***		
PE1 <- Performance Expectancy	0.7032	0.046749	15.0418***		
PE2 <- Performance Expectancy	0.7272	0.040849	17.8009***		
PE3 <- Performance Expectancy	0.8163	0.026263	31.0798***		
PE4 <- Performance Expectancy	0.8153	0.026792	30.4292***	0.8812	0.5542
PE5 <- Performance Expectancy	0.7376	0.041576	17.7419***		
PE6 <- Performance Expectancy	0.6535	0.050309	12.9907***		

continued on following page

Table 2. Continued

Measurement Items	Loadings	Standard Deviation (STDEV)	T-Statistics	Composite Reliability (CR)[a]	Average Variance Extract (AVE)[b]
SI1 <- Social Influence	0.6288	0.202195	3.1099**		
SI2 <- Social Influence	0.6460	0.198283	3.2579**		
SI3 <- Social Influence	0.8704	0.17703	4.9165**	0.8408	0.5745
SI4 <- Social Influence	0.8530	0.188656	4.5215**		
UB1 <- Use Behaviour	0.7379	0.033492	22.0324***		
UB2 <- Use Behaviour	0.7853	0.033398	23.5127***		
UB3 <- Use Behaviour	0.7993	0.032893	24.3009***		
UB4 <- Use Behaviour	0.7247	0.048888	14.8229***	0.8965	0.5914
UB5 <- Use Behaviour	0.7354	0.040994	17.9383***		
UB6 <- Use Behaviour	0.8261	0.023545	35.0878***		

***P<0.001, **P<0.05 (CR)[a]: Composite reliability

study, the AVEs for the indicators are within the range of 0.5405 to 0.6394 respectively. Looking at the results for the parameter estimates and the test of their statistical significance (t-values at p<0.001 and p<0.05 alpha levels), it can be concluded that all the variables in the model are valid measures of their respective constructs (see: Chow & Chan, 2008).

Discriminant Validity

The discriminant validity of the measures has equally been tested to examine the degree to which items are differentiated among constructs. This was carried out first by looking at correlations between the measures for possible potential overlapping of constructs. Second, whether the average variance shared between each construct and that its measures are greater than the average

variance shared between the constructs and other constructs were also explored, as suggested by Compeau et al, (1999). In this respect, the results of Table 3 show that the squared correlations for each construct is less than the average squared root of the variance extracted by the indicators measuring that construct. Hence, the measurement model reflects an adequate convergent validity and discriminant validity.

Reliability Analysis

Reliability is an indication of the internal consistency of the instruments measuring the concepts and helps access the "goodness" of measure (Sekaran & Bougie, 2010). There are many different types of reliability estimates (Ambali, 2009). One of the most widely used tests is Cronbach's Alpha that is employed in this study as shown in Table

Table 3. Latent variable correlations

	Behaviour Intention (IB)	Effort Expectancy (EE)	Facilitating Condition (FC)	Performance Expectancy (PE)	Social Influence (SI)	Use Behaviour (UB)
IB	0.76851					
EE	0.21001	0.79862				
FC	0.36954	0.39819	0.73519			
PE	0.17607	0.16255	0.24330	0.74444		
SI	0.05497	0.11413	0.21308	0.05579	0.75796	
UB	0.43072	0.32014	0.47649	0.31473	0.09706	0.76903

Table 4. Reliability tests result

Variable	No. of Items	Cronbach's Alpha
Effort Expectancy (EE)	5	0.863
Performance Expectancy (PE)	6	0.838
Facilitating Condition (FC)	5	0.791
Social Influence (SI)	4	0.764
Behaviour Intention (IB)	6	0.862
Use Behaviour of *VSAT* (UB)	6	0.871

4. By looking at the results of the Cronbach's Alpha range from 0.764 to 0.871, thus confirming the reliability of the instrument used. It is worth mentioning that the range of reliability test using Cronbach's Alpha is from zero to one. The closer to one the higher the level of internal consistency among items and thus the reliability of the instruments are ensured in this study.

The fact that the nature of the data is a self-reported Harman's one-factor test was examined to address any potential common method variance bias that may likely exist. As contended by Podsakoff and Organ (1986), common variance bias is problematic if a single latent factor accounts for the majority of the total explained variance. In this study, the result of the un-rotated factor analysis shows that the first factor only accounted for 15.5% of the total 74.2% variance and thus common method bias is not a problem.

FINDINGS

According to Table 5, majority of the participants are females with 65% as compared to the males. Interestingly, their age ranged from 21-25 years to 46 years and above, which sounds a sense of maturity in engaging with *VSAT* system for operations and discharging duties. Hence, it is worth mentioning that most of them are within two major categories of age 26-30 years (27.1%) followed by 31-35 years (35%). This indicates to us that majority of the civil servants using *VSAT* system to perform services are well matured with adequate experience. In addition, many of them have 6-10 years (38.6%) working experience using *VSAT* system to disseminate necessary information to the government agencies and people at large. This is followed by the workers with above 21 years of experience (26.4%) using the technology system to discharge services to masses. Interest-

Table 5. Profile of respondents

Variables	Frequency	Percentage
Gender		
Male	49	35%
Female	91	65%
Age		
21-25	8	5.7%
26-30	38	27.1%
31-35	49	35%
36-40	7	5%
41-45	3	2.1%
>46	35	25%
Status		
Single	28	20%
Married	109	77.9%
Divorce	3	2.1
Qualification		
MA/PhD.	8	5.7%
BA	39	27.9%
Diploma/STPM	52	37.1%
SPM (Secondary Education)	40	28.6%
PMR (Primary Education)	1	0.7
Work Experience with Usage of *VSAT*		
1-5	28	20%
6-10	54	38.6%
11-15	17	12.1%
16-20	4	2.9%
>21	37	26.4%

ingly, some of them (5.7%) have even got higher academic qualifications such as MA/PhD that could help leverage the velocity of the services to public using the system.

Descriptive Statistic Results

The level of behavioural intention and use behaviour of the staff towards the *VSAT* technology system was examined using means and standard deviations derived from descriptive statistics as shown in Table 6. According to the results, the means statistical value of the six questions for staff behavioural intention to use *VSAT* system was M=3.91, std. 0.54 out of a five-point Likert scale, while the actual use behaviour of the staff towards *VSAT* system was M=4.11, std., 0.51, both are considered to be very high. It really indicates or

Table 6. Level of behavioural intention and use behaviour of VSAT

Variable	No. of Items	Mean	Standard Deviation (std)	Minimum	Maximum
Behaviour Intention (IB)	6	3.91	0.54	2.00	5.00
Use Behaviour of *VSAT* (UB)	6	4.11	0.51	2.33	5.00

Figure 3. Structural coefficient results of the extended model

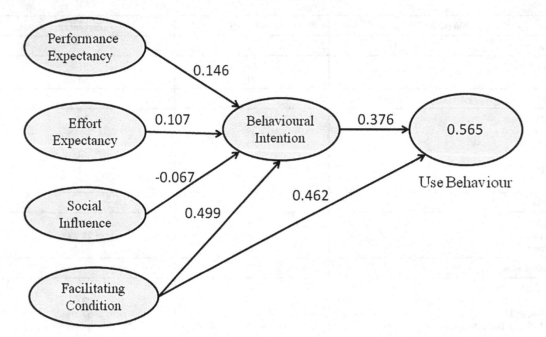

reflects the readiness and intention of the staff to use the system based on certain factors as identified in the model. Hence, there is a need to examine the path coefficients for various identified factors towards such intention and use behaviour, which are addressed in the next section of the chapter.

The Path Coefficient Results of the Model

In this section, the chapter addresses the path coefficients to examine the relationships between the structural latent constructs of the model. The results obtained have shown positive significant relationships among all the constructs in this modified-extended model except for causal link between social influence and behavioural intention towards *VSAT* system among the agency's staff.

As clearly shown in Figure 3, the results indicate a positive significant relationship between the performance expectancy and behavioural intention towards using *VSAT* system with coefficient value of 0.146, p<0.001. A similar significant positive

relationship exists between the causal link of effort expectancy and behavioural intention towards using *VSAT* system with beta coefficient values of 0.107, p<0.001. However, the causal link between social influence and the behavioural intention toward *VSAT* system is negatively related with a coefficient value of -0.067, p>0.05. Furthermore, the path coefficients between facilitating condition and intention towards using *VSAT* system is positively and significantly related with high beta value of 0.499, p<0.001. The same similar positive causal link exists between facilitating condition and actual use behaviour of *VSAT* system among the staff with a high coefficient value of 0.462, p<0.001. Finally, the causal link between behavioural intention and actual use behaviour is also positively and significantly related with a beta value of 0.375, p<0.001. The results reflect a sound structural links among the variables of interests in the model. However, there is a dare need to test the various hypotheses put forward in the chapter based on the model through a bootstrapping approach for each of the coefficient values.

Figure 4. Bootstrapping results of the structural model

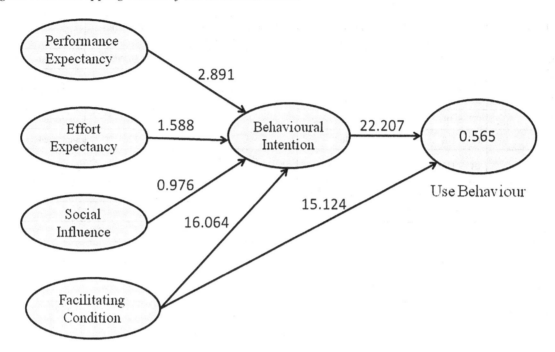

Predictive Capacity of the Extended Model and Hypotheses Testing

As can be inferred in the Figure 4 the t-value of the path coefficients are generated to test the significant contribution of each path coefficient of the latent constructs through a bootstrapping procedure in order to validate the predictive capacity of the extended model as well as the hypotheses put forward.

The results show that all hypotheses in the study are supported with t-values ranging from 1.558* to 8.103*** at an alpha-value less than 0.05 and 0.001 respectively (see Figure 4) except for social influence (i.e., t-value of 0.976, p>0.05. As the results depicted in the Figure 3 the R^2 values of the two endogenous latent constructs in the model such as behavioural intention towards using *VSAT system*, and the actual use of the system ranged from 0.398, to 0.565 respectively indicating the relative important of each predicting factor in the model. However, according to Chin, (1998), it is paramount to examine the predictive power

of the extended model of the study based on the values of the endogenous constructs. According to Kock (2012, p.31), this can be done by assessing the average variance inflation factor (AVIF) as a comprehensive analysis of a model's overall capacity and explanatory quality of the latent factors linking to both behavioural intention and the actual use of the system at the agency.

This is important in order to address the absence of both vertical and lateral collinearities as well as wellness of the model. The result shows a value of 1.82 (see: Table 7), which is far below the threshold of 3.3 (Kock, 2012, Ambali, 2013). Additionally, other indices for the model fit such as average path coefficient (APC), average r-squared (ARS) are addressed in the process of addressing the predictive capacity of the wellness of the model. In this respect, the result of both APC and ARS are 0.254 and 48.15% respectively. These results indicate a practical significant power of the model (Kock, 2012).

Moreover, Q-squared coefficient was performed through blindfolding in order to assess

Table 7. Summary of t-statistics of the path coefficients and hypotheses testing

Hypotheses	Construct Causal Relation	Beta (β) Coefficient	Endogenous Latent Variables (R^2)	T -Statistics	Remark
H1a	PEE -> IB	0.146		2.891**	supported
H2a	EE -> IB	0.107		1.588*	supported
H3a	SI -> IB	0.067	$R^2 = 0.398$ (39.8%)	0.976	rejected
H4a	FC -> IB	0.499		16.064***	supported
H5a	FC-> UB	0.462		15.124***	supported
H5	IB -> UB	0.376	$R^2 = 0.565$ (56.5%)	22.207***	supported
Predictive Capacity of the Model					
Criteria			**Value**		
AVIF			1.82		
APC			0.254		
ARS			48.15%		
Q-squared			0.42		

Note: *** P<0.001, **P<0.01; *P<0.05.

the predictive validity associated with each latent variable block in the model as well as the strength. Acceptable predictive validity strength in connection with endogenous latent variables as suggested by examine a Q-squared coefficient must be greater than a zero threshold (Kock, 2012; Ambali, 2013). The result of the predictive validity for this extended model is 0.42 indicating the overall good predictive factors that can influence the use behaviour of *VSAT system* among the staff of the agency.

The Impact of Gender Difference on Each Causal Link in the Model

Given the fact that type of gender might have a significant interaction with each predicting factor of behavioural intention as well as the actual use of technology system as argued in the literatures, the chapter takes a step further to address such phenomenon as postulated in the model. In this context, hierarchical regression analysis was conducted to evaluate such effect between each predictor and the predicted variables in the model.

A close examination of Table 8, the results indicate a significant effect of gender difference on each predictor with R^2 change value of 0.122, 0.178, 0.188, 0.392 and 0.478 at different significant value of alpha respectively (p<0.05; p<0.001).

A perusal at the R-square changes due to interaction of gender effects on the individual predictors may not really show the effects clearly or may not be able to give the reader a clear picture of the nature of such effect between male and the female. Therefore a step was taken further to graphically display these significant effects. In doing so, a regression equation was estimated for each predictor with the impact of gender parameter values to plot the graphs in Figures 5, 6, 7, 8 and 9 respectively.

Moderating Effect of Gender on Performance-Expectancy and Behavioural Intention

The results display in the Figure 5 (PE) show a clear significant effect of gender difference between male and female with respect to performance

Table 8. Summary of results hierarchical regression with gender impact

Predictor	Without R²	With ΔR²	Unstandardized Coefficients		
			Gender (B)	PE*Gender(B)	Remarks on Hypotheses
PE	0.158	**H1b** = 0.178*	0.206	-0.012	supported
EE	0.111	**H2b** = 0.122*	-7.839	0.315	supported
SI	0.135	**H3b** = 0.188*	-12.237	0.483	supported
FC (BI)	0.286	**H4b** = 0.392**	-4.101	0.169	supported
FC (UB)	0.453	**H5b** = 0.478**	-8.336	0.324	supported

Note: *p<0.05; **p<0.001.

Figure 5. Effect of gender on performance-expectancy and behavioural intention

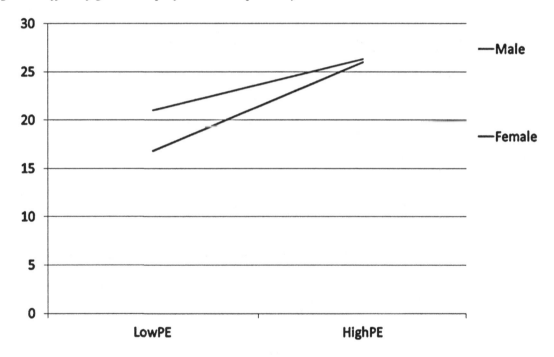

expectancy. According to the graph, the slope for both male and female respondents shows to us that the more the gender perceived the relative important of what they can achieve or get from ICT devices the more their behavioural intention increase to use it. Although the trend of the propensity of their intentions to use the technology upwardly increased for both sexes however, the slope of the male is steeper compared to the female counterpart. For example, at a low level of performance expectancy the female's behavioural intention to use technology was lower than male with an average value of about 4.2 as shown on the graph. However, it is interesting to note that as the perceived expectancy for both sexes increased, the behavioural intentions for them came to a point of interaction. This indicates that at a high level of perceived expectancy of what ICT can help

Figure 6. Effect of gender on effort- expectancy (EE) and behavioural

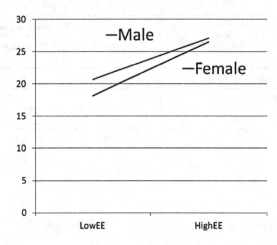

Figure 7. Effect of gender on social influence (SI) and behavioural intention to use ICT

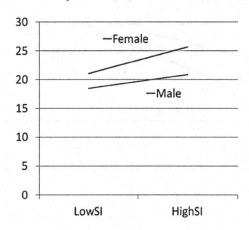

Figure 8. Effect of gender on facilitating condition (FC) and behavioural intention to use ICT

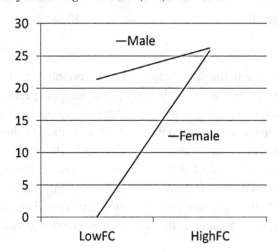

Figure 9. Effect of gender on facilitating condition (FC) and actual use behaviour of ICT

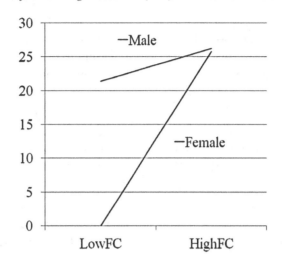

achieved for both sexes in terms of enhancement and accomplishment of their assigned tasks in a more efficient manner, the behavioural intentions of both become the same as shown on the graph (i.e., difference of about 0.31).

Moderating effect of Gender on Effort-Expectancy (EE) and Behavioural Intention

According to the Figure 6 (EE) there is a clear significant effect of gender difference between male and female with respect to effort expectancy. According to the graph, the slope for both male and female participants shows to us that the more the gender perceived the relative ease of using ICT devices to carry their tasks the more their behavioural intention increase to use it. Although the trend of the propensity of their intentions to use the technology upwardly increased for both sexes however, the slope of the male is steeper compared to the female counterpart. For example, at a low level of effort expectancy the female's behavioural intention to use technology was lower than male with an average value of about 2.54 as shown on the graph. However, it is interesting to note that as the effort expectancy for both sexes increased, the behavioural intentions for them came to a point

of interaction. This indicates that at a high level of effort expectancy with respect to easiness in using ICT for both sexes in accomplishing their assigned works in a more efficient manner, the behavioural intentions of both about to intersect (i.e., difference of about 0.54) as shown on the graph.

Moderating Effect of Gender on Social Influence (SI) and Behavioural Intention

As can be seen in the Figure 7 (SI), there is a clear significant effect of gender difference between male and female with respect to social influence. According to the graph, the slope for both male and female participants shows to us that the more the gender is influenced by the relative important people around them on the using ICT devices to carry their tasks the more their behavioural intentions increase to use it. In addition, the trend of the propensity of their intentions to use the technology upwardly increased for both sexes due to social pressures from relative important individuals such as colleagues, boss, senior, etc., however, the slope of the female is steeper compared to the male counterpart. For example, at a low level of social influence the female's behavioural intention to use technology was higher than male with an average value of about 2.5 as shown on the graph. However, it is interesting to note that as the social pressures for both sexes increase, the behavioural intentions for them diverged from one another with a wider gap. This indicates that at a high level of social influence with respect to using ICT for both sexes in accomplishing their assigned works, the behavioural intentions of both cannot intersect. This is an interesting finding to be noted here. Such a finding indicates that the impact of social pressure is high on the female as compared to male counterpart with a huge value of about 4.83 as shown on the graph. In other words, it would mean that female sex can easily be influenced by the relative important people around them by nature compared to male.

This is in line with relative characteristic strength and flexibility of mind sets of male and female respectively. In some society such as Malaysia and/or anywhere, women tend to be more listeners and obedient to what has been instructed to them than men especially on the issues of attentions given by immediate bosses or senior regarding job performance and enhancement using ICT.

Moderating Effect of Gender on Facilitating Condition (FC) and Behavioural Intention

The result in the Figure 8 has shown the relative impact of gender difference on the predictor--facilitating condition and the behavioural intention to use ICT among the staff of the agency. The result shows the relative impact of gender difference on the predictor--facilitating condition and the behavioural intention to use ICT among the staff. According to the result, where the facilitating condition is very low the female respondents have zero behavioural intention to use ICT as compared to their male counterparts. It indicates that even though facilitating is very low the male respondents can still have intentions to use ICT. It is by nature of man to struggle with all efforts

to achieve something regardless of the situational condition in which they are as compared to women.

In addition, the result also shows that as the facilitating condition improved or high, the behavioural intention to use ICT for both sexes sharply increased. In other words, if the trend of the facilitating condition keep on improving further, the intention of both sexes could come to point of interaction as shown on the graph (i.e., about a value of 0.4 difference at high level of facilitating condition).

Moderating Effect of Gender on Facilitating Condition (FC) and Actual Use Behaviour

Again, the result in Figure 9 also shows the relative impact of gender difference on the predictor--facilitating condition and the actual use behaviour of ICT among the staff of the agency. According to the result, where the facilitating condition is very low the female respondents have zero behavioural intention to use ICT as compared to their male counterparts. It indicates that even though facilitating is very low the male respondents can still have intentions to use ICT. It is by nature of man to struggle and utilizes all efforts to achieve something regardless of the situational condition in which they are as compared to women. In addition, the result also shows that as the facilitating condition improved or high, the behavioural intention to use ICT for both sexes sharply increased. In other words, if the trend of the facilitating condition keep on improving further, the intention of both sexes could come to point of interaction as shown on the graph (i.e., about a value of 0.45 difference at high level of facilitating condition).

DISCUSSION

According to the findings, the means statistical value of the six questions for staff behavioural intention to use *VSAT* system was M=3.91, std.

0.54 out of a five-point Likert scale, while the actual use behaviour of the staff towards *VSAT* system was M=4.11, std., 0.51; both are considered to be very high. This indicates the readiness of intention of the staff to use the system based on certain factors as identified in the modified-extended model of this chapter. The finding has shown a positive significant relationship between performance expectancy (PE) and behavioural intention to use *VSAT* system among the staff of the agency with beta value $\beta = 0.146$, t-value 2.891, p<0.001. It means that whenever the users reflect on the importance of ICT device in term of enhancing their works and accomplishing the given tasks more efficiently, their behavioural intention to use technology will increase. However, by looking at the relative impact of gender difference on this predictor (PE), it was found that the slope of the male is steeper compared to the female counterpart. This indicates that at a low level of performance expectancy the female's behavioural intention to use technology was lower than male with an average value of about 4.2 as displayed on the graph. However, it is interesting to note that as the perceived expectancy for both sexes increased, the behavioural intentions for them came to a point of interaction. In other words, it means that lower level of PE the gender behavioural intentions could be different especially when ICT is new to the female users. But as time passes by, female users of ICT may begin to realize the significant benefits behind using ICT and thus resulted to increase in their behavioural intention towards ICT. The implication here for both technology designers and public management officers is that reinforcing the potential benefits of using ICT to perform work can help improve behavioural intention of the users at large. In addition, it is also imperative for designers to ensure that the manufacture technologies are superior and beneficial to users. Hence, users must be the central focal point of technologies being designed.

According to the findings, a similar significant positive relationship exists between the causal link of effort-expectancy and behavioural intention towards using *VSAT* system with beta coefficient values of $\beta = 0.107$, t-value of 1.588, p<0.001. This result indicates that when users are able to appreciate the easiness of using ICT their intention to use it grown up according to such degree of ease and simplicity of using the technology to carry out related works. In this context, it means that technology types must be very friendly with users and there should be no feeling of struggling to navigate through or difficulty using the system. In other words, the more the difficulty encountered by the users the more the decline of their behavioural intentions to use a particular technology system. With respect to the impact of gender difference, the finding here shows that at low level of easiness of using technology (effort-expectancy or EE), female behavioural intention is less compared to the male. However, at a high level of EE both male and female demonstrated a highly significant level of behavioural intention to use *VSAT* system at the agency. The implication here for both technology designers and the management is that users must be able to perceive ICT components to do jobs assigned as simple as possible to motivate their behavioural intention to use them.

Furthermore, one of the findings of this study is the causal link between social influence and the behavioural intention toward *VSAT* system which was found to be negatively related at a coefficient value of $\beta = -0.067$, t-value of 0.976, p>0.05. This negative relationship here indicates that social pressure (important individuals around users) may not necessarily make some users change their minds to use the system was theoretically assumed especially when on the issue of gender difference among the users. Perhaps, this is why the relationship is insignificant (p>0.05). However, probing the result further through examining the impact of gender difference on the influence of social pressure to use ICT, the finding shows that female users were more influenced compared to males as graphically shown. In addition, the statistical regression results for interaction of gender with social pressure variable formally confirmed the impact of gender with R^2-change from 0.135 to 0.188, p<0.05 (Table 14.8). Hence, this result indicates a practical and theoretical contribution of not generalizing an equal effect of social pressure on gender of users of ICT for doing works not only in public sector but also in private organizations as well.

It is interesting to find a positive significant relationship between facilitating condition in using technology system and behavioural intention as well as actual use behaviour in this study as postulated, with beta coefficient value of $\beta = 0.499$, t-value of 16.061, and $\beta = 0.462$, t-value *of 15.124,* p<0.0001 respectively. These findings indicate that facilitating condition is an important predictor of behavioural intention and the actual use behaviour towards ICT as hypothesized in the study. The practical significant of such findings inferred two-fold observation in public sector organizations. First, civil servants' intention to use ICT components to perform tasks may be very high but without other supporting tools or devices, the intention to use might be declined and eventually the actual use behaviour may not be materialized. Second, the findings also indicate that the facilitating condition such as adequate supply of electricity, stable server, just to mention few, to use ICT by the users must be really established in the organization. Otherwise, even if the behavioural intention to use ICT by users is very high; the absence of facilitating condition can jeopardize both intention to use and the actual use of the technology simultaneously. The impact of gender on the relationship between facilitating condition and behavioural intention to use ICT and the actual use has been formally confirmed through one of the findings of the study. For example, the finding shows that a low level of facilitating condition for using ICT, the females' behavioural intention as well as the actual use behaviour was found to be zero compared to male users at the agency. Hence, it means that a conducive-environment, presence

of necessary tools as mentioned earlier are very important conditions that can facilitate high level of behavioural intention as well as actual use of the technology provided to do works in any organizations.

CHAPTER SUMMARY

This chapter focuses on the application of the Unified Theory of Acceptance and Use of Technology (UTAUT) with extension and modification of the original model based on the underlying preliminary investigation about the issues of gender difference in ICT adoption and behavioural intention. Using a problem approach to set the stage for the study, the result of the focus group interview has reflected a wider perception between males and females respondents regarding utilization of ICT components to accomplish their tasks. In this context, we modified the original model to fit the situation with correct data set. Thus, the modified-extended model used in this chapter has statistically examined the relationships between predictors such as performance expectancy, effort expectancy, social influence, facilitating condition and behavioural intention to use ICT at the agency. In addition, it has also examined the relationship between facilitating condition and actual use behaviour as well as moderating effect of gender difference on each predictor and behavioural intention. The findings confirmed a positive and significant relationship between three predictor and behavioural intention as well as actual use behaviour of ICT device among the staff. However, the finding shows an insignificant negative relation between social influence and behavioural intention. Another interesting finding in the chapter is the significant impact of gender on the various predictors and predicted variable as clearly shown on the plotted graphs. Two particular new findings are the impact of gender found on the causal link between facilitating condition and actual use behaviour which was not included in the original model of UTAUT and also the significant causal relationship between facilitating condition and behavioural intention. These findings are the *new* contribution to the theoretical framework. To sum up, the findings have shown the impact of gender difference behavioural intention to use ICT and the actual use behaviour relative to the various predictors examined in this modified-extended model for the study.

REFERENCES

Agarwal, R., & Karahanna, E. (2000). Time flies when you're having fun: Cognitive absorption and beliefs about information technology usage. *Management Information Systems Quarterly*, *24*(4), 665–694. doi:10.2307/3250951

Agarwal, R., & Prasad, J. (1999). Are individual differences germane to the acceptance of new information technologies. *Decision Sciences*, *30*(2), 361–391. doi:10.1111/j.1540-5915.1999.tb01614.x

Ajzen, I. (1991). The theory of planned behavior. *Organizational Behavior and Human Decision Processes*, *50*(2), 179–211. doi:10.1016/0749-5978(91)90020-T

Ambali, A. R. (2009). E-government policy: Ground issues in e-filling system. *European Journal of Soil Science*, *11*(2), 249–266.

Ambali, A. R., & Ahmad, N. B. (2013). Hala food and products in Malaysia: People's awareness and policy implications. *Intellectual Discourse*, *21*(1), 7–32.

Barclay, D. W., Higgins, C., & Thompson, R. (1995). The partial least square approach to causal modeling: Personal computer adoption use as illustration. *Technology Studies*, *2*(2), 285–309.

Bhattacherjee, A. (2001). Understanding information systems continuance: An expectation-confirmation model. *Management Information Systems Quarterly*, *25*(3), 351–370. doi:10.2307/3250921

Chin, W. W. (1998). The partial least squares approach to structural equation modeling. In G. A. Marcoulides (Ed.), *Modern Methods for Business Research* (pp. 295–336). London, UK: Erlbaum Associates.

Chow, W. S., & Chan, L. S. (2008). Social network and shared goals in organizational knowledge sharing. *Information & Management*, *45*(7), 24–30. doi:10.1016/j.im.2008.06.007

Compeau, D. R., Higgins, C. A., & Huff, S. (1999). Social cognitive theory and individual reactions to computing technology: A longitudinal-study. *Management Information Systems Quarterly*, *23*(2), 145–158. doi:10.2307/249749

Davis, F. D. (1989). Perceived Usefulness, Perceived Ease of Use and User Acceptance of Technology. *Management Information Systems Quarterly*, *13*(3), 319–340. doi:10.2307/249008

Doll, W. J., Hendrickson, A. & Xiaodong, D. (1998). Using Davis's perceived usefulness and ease-of-use instruments for decision making: A confirmatory and multigroup invariance analysis. *Decision Sciences*, *29*(4), 839-869.

Fishbein, M., & Ajzen, I. (1975). *Belief, attitude, intention, and behavior: An introduction to theory and research*. Reading, MA: Addison-Wesley.

Fornell, C., & Larcker, D. F. (1981). Evaluating structural equation models with unobservable and measurement error. *JMR, Journal of Marketing Research*, *18*(1), 39–50. doi:10.2307/3151312

Hair, J. F., Black, W. C., Babin, B. J., & Anderson, R. E. (2010). *Multivariate data analysis*. Upper Saddle River, NJ: Prentice-Hall.

Lee, M. K. O., Cheung, C. M. K., & Chen, Z. (2005). Acceptance of Internet-based learning medium: The role of extrinsic and intrinsic motivation. *Information & Management*, 42(8), 1095–1104. doi:10.1016/j.im.2003.10.007

Lynott, P. P., & McCandless, N. J. (2000). The impact of age vs. life experience of the gender role: Attitude of women in different cohorts. *Journal of Women & Aging*, 12(2), 5–21. doi:10.1300/J074v12n01_02 PMID:10986848

Minton, H. L., & Schneider, F. W. (1980). *Differential psychology*. Boston: Waveland Press.

Morris, M. G., & Venkatesh, V. (2000). Age difference in technology adoption decisions: Implications for a changing workforce. *Personnel Psychology*, 53(2), 375–403. doi:10.1111/j.1744-6570.2000.tb00206.x

Pedersen, P. E., & Nysveen, H. (2002). *Using the theory of planned behaviour to explain teenagers' adoption of text messaging services*. Norway: Agder University College.

Petrus, G., & Nelson, O. N. (2006). Borneo online banking: Evaluating customer perceptions and behavioural intention. *Management Research News*, 29(1/2), 6–15. doi:10.1108/01409170610645402

Podsakoff, P. M., & Organ, D. W. (1986). Self-reports in organizational research: Problems and prospects. *Journal of Management*, 12(4), 531–544. doi:10.1177/014920638601200408

Sekaran, U., & Bougie, R. (2010). *Research methods for business: A skill building approach* (4th ed.). John Wiley & Sons, Inc.

Straub, D. W. (1989). Validating instruments in MIS research. *Management Information Systems Quarterly*, 13(2), 147–169. doi:10.2307/248922

Succi, M. J., & Walter, Z. D. (1999). Theory of user acceptance of information technologies: an examination of health care professionals. In *Proceedings of the 32nd Annual Hawaii International Conference on System Sciences* (HICSS-32). doi:10.1109/HICSS.1999.773013

Venkatesh, V. (2000). Determinants of perceived ease of use: Integrating control, intrinsic motivation, and emotion into the technology acceptance model. *Information Systems Research*, 11(4), 342–365. doi:10.1287/isre.11.4.342.11872

Venkatesh, V., & Bala, H. (2008). Technology acceptance model 3 and a research agenda on interventions. *Decision Sciences*, 39(2), 272–315. doi:10.1111/j.1540-5915.2008.00192.x

Venkatesh, V., & Davis, F. D. (1996). A model of the antecedents of perceived ease of use: Development and test. *Decision Sciences*, 27(3), 451–481. doi:10.1111/j.1540-5915.1996.tb01822.x

Venkatesh, V., & Davis, F. D. (2000). A theoretical extension of the technology acceptance model: Four longitudinal field studies. *Management Science*, 45(2), 186–204. doi:10.1287/mnsc.46.2.186.11926

Venkatesh, V., Morris, M. G., Davis, G. B., & Davis, F. D. (2003). User acceptance of information technology: Toward a unified view. *Management Information Systems Quarterly*, 27(3), 425–478.

Venkatesh, V., Thong, J. Y. L., & Xu, X. (2012). Consumer acceptance and use of information technology: Extending the unified theory of acceptance and use of technology. *Management Information Systems Quarterly*, 36(1), 157–178.

Wu, Y. L., Tao, Y. H., & Yang, P. C. (2008). The use of theory of acceptance and use of technology to confer the behavioural model of 3G mobile telecommunication users. *Journal of Statistics & Management Systems*, 11(5), 919–949. doi:10.1080/09720510.2008.10701351

KEY TERMS AND DEFINITIONS

Causal Links: The connection between variables in a model designed to study users behaviour towards a given technology system and an effect or impact of each variable on another.

Effort-Expectancy: A belief that one's own effort of using a particular technology will lead into attainment of the desired purpose.

Facilitating Condition: The extent to which individual users of a particular technology provided believes that an organizational and technical infrastructures are place to support the use of the system.

Gender Differences: Typical differences between sex of the users with reference to a particular technology system provided and its infrastructural supporting system.

Performance-Expectancy: Degree at which an individual believes that using the technology system will help him or her to attain better outputs or productivity.

Quality of Service Delivery: An expression of how well a delivered service conforms to the people or citizen's expectations in the country.

Technology Model: A preliminary framework that serves as a plan from which investigation of the properties of the system and/or prediction of features relationships are determined.

Chapter 14
General Prospects and Contending Issues in Malaysian ICT Policy

ABSTRACT

Malaysia was one of the early adopters of Internet technology to steer innovation policy in a direction that is making the country become a knowledge-based economy. This notion of knowledge-based economy driven by ICT is best exemplified by the borderless connectivity, interactivity, and networking. Since the middle of 1990s, there have been gradual but systematic public and private sector initiatives towards ICT agenda with the prominent role of the state. This chapter aims to unpack ICT developments and examine the implications of the post-MSC formation for Malaysia and its associated issues and challenges. Second, the discussion provides an overview of MSC performance and its importance for enhancing growth, trade, and investment; reducing the digital gap; nurturing innovation; and achieving more inclusive societies. Third, some issues and challenges in MSC development are also highlighted.

INTRODUCTION

Admittedly, as important driver as well as an enabler of national infrastructure, education and human capital development, ICT has become key institution in the knowledge-based economy (Ahmad, 2008), which is continually being scrutinized not only to enhance physical connectivity but also to symbolize policy innovation for addressing the country's growth towards inclusivity and balanced growth as articulated in the New Economic Model (NEM). Thus, in general, ICT projects are designed to support the transformation of the country to

leapfrog into a high-value economy (Haslinda et al., 2011; Xue, 2005), MSC expansion i.e. cyber cities is essential to the realization of Malaysia's innovation goal of technological convergence and is indispensable to Malaysia's future success.

MALAYSIAN ICT CHALLENGES

Amid the advent of digital technologies and convergence, the national ICT in Malaysia has raised some critical questions. One of the purposes of this book is to determine how the process of digi-

DOI: 10.4018/978-1-4666-6579-8.ch014

tal convergence and were facilitated by the ICT development models and to show how they were affected by the three critical factors: the innovative policy, the regulatory, and the institutional reform, within the context of the Malaysian ICT agenda since the middle 1990s.

Section 1, Chapters 1 to 5 of the book, provided an extensive literature review covering a wide range of Asia experiences of ICT and models showing different understanding about the implications of new technologies on the search for new mode of governing ICT tools. This part reflects some significant insights pertaining to the nature of ICT and its convergence policy, industry's self-regulation and institutional forces in pursuing ICT development most importantly in Malaysia. After comprehending the various model underpinnings ICT as well as the interplay between the ICT adoptions, theoretical discussions have been examined in the Section 2—Chapters 6 to 8.

Drawing upon the experience of various ICT policy domains, this book has reported the results of research provided by the convergence model in Malaysia, which lend its root to the proposed NITA with its unprecedented people-based policy, the MSC Flagships and its five strategic thrust areas, the new regulatory regime (NRR) and the relevant initiatives for digital convergence. It was revealed in this book that the global convergence and the industry self-regulation principles as transpired in the new regime were encapsulated in the interplay between the process of digital convergence and ICT policy, embracing new mode of governing ICT. In an attempt to assess to what extent the governance process were impacted by the convergence technology, Chapters 3, 4, and 5 have shown that government policy makers should not preclude the phenomenal growth of digital technologies which requires a restructuring of Government's traditional policymaking roles. The study found that increasing attempts to address the challenge of convergence in the national ICT agenda presented by new technologies were associated with attempts to promote effective model of ICT governance in the Malaysian public sector. In order to provide background knowledge for better understanding of the complicated strategic initiatives and political manoeuvring over these new technologies, the book has also examined the historical origins of Malaysia's national ICT agenda as well as its subsequent progress in corresponding to digital convergence phenomenon and sheds lights on the guiding models for operation.

DIGITAL CONVERGENCE AND POLICY CHANGE

It has been shown that the ICT strategies adopted by the Government are of great significance in determining the extent for new mode of governance. Different ways of understanding the nature of convergence policy partly reflected in unprecedented development in k-economy strategy in correspondence to the global scenario.

The period since the 1990s has witnessed a host of initiatives by the Malaysian Government, as transpired in the preamble section, and empirical chapters that the country had followed a multifaceted strategy characterised by the dominant role of bureaucrat-technocrat in charting the agenda for change. In particular, the Malaysian Government have initiated a series of policy and administrative reform on a national scale. The single most important national ICT agenda for development has been based on the rhetoric of new governance envisaged within the NITA framework. Malaysia had successfully gained international recognition and has since made a remarkable progress as far as an innovative strategy is concerned. Towards the end of 1990s, the country has faced another formidable challenge of new economic growth which is fast shaped by the digital convergence phenomenon. There was a great concern for the country to buck up herself or risk losing its competitiveness. Malaysia's answer to this challenge was to chart a new agenda for convergence.

By the 2000s, the Malaysian ICT agenda had poised to take on the convergence force, and the NRR had been specifically devised as a measure to tap the most of the new paradigm of ICT growth, particularly the digital convergence policy. This newly emerged convergence initiatives was nonetheless, not strategically linked with the original philosophy of NITA, as transpired in Chapter 8. In addition, the innovative agenda seems to experience a lot of constraint when applied in the typically hierarchical society encapsulated by Malaysia.

The fading of NITC's model of governance was due to an extended wide range of concern about the country's long-standing strategy which is now capitalising on the technological convergence. Some commentators believed that Malaysia, seen through a series of regulatory and institutional reforms, have been good at initiating new ideas but poor in sustaining them, and this is regarded as the typical 'Malaysian flaws,' so long as the national policy development is concerned. Governance of digital convergence was not the result of a fundamental restructuring of the sector, but rather the gradual but significant reorientation of policy process in allowing greater participation across policy domains. There is no guarantee digital convergence will facilitate the good governance of national ICT agenda. No doubt, it is implemented with appropriate mechanisms in complementary of a larger package of reforms, which is also critical to determine the extent of good ICT governance. Equally true is the fact that its ultimate success in meeting the governance of ICT objectives will depend heavily on the effectiveness of the other corresponding elements in the reform agenda to befitting the demand of new regime.

This chapter has identified that such challenges are tied with a combination of various social, political and administrative origins of ICT adoption, which could not be justified by looking at Malaysia's own recent effort of digital convergence alone. To be effective in the new search for model of ICT governance, as argued, was a major impetus for Malaysia's growth and success in a number of areas, rather than the reason why the country has failed in its specific sectoral effort of using ICT to accomplish public demands. The setbacks Malaysia suffered have a much more complicated and multifaceted origins, which mainly could be explained by the powerful structured dependence on the central authority of the State. This however does not discourage interest for the country in the further experimentation of new ICT governance model of converging society to one-portal end. The details of some of these issues and prospects for future developments in ICT adoption for Malaysian public sector are further highlighted in the subsequence sections of this chapter.

Policy Networks and Malaysia as a 'Network State'

Governance is not necessarily government as a physical entity, nor is it the act of governing through individuals,' rather 'the process by which institutions, organisations, and citizens 'guide' themselves within the context of 'complementary synergies of conflict management styles' (Meissonier & Houze, 2010). This process sees an interactive wider set of relationships between the public sector and society, organised around transparent mechanisms in every level of decision making[1]. As transpired in our discussion throughout, the value of network interaction using the new media technologies was central that there existed such "network actors" which formed the myriad of a smart partnership between government, private and social sectors. In this context, the 'reform of the public sector commands everything else in the process of productive shaping of the network society' (Castells & Cardoso, 2006). It is opined that such subset of actors will interact and engage strategically by virtue of sharing of information, expertise, and political support (Coleman, et. al., 1999, p. 696) utilising the Web and networked interactions thereby fostering transparency and participation (Calista & Melitski, 2007). Linked to the concept of 'Policy Network,' Malaysia's eVision in general and its new convergence model in particular, is gradually gathering momentum as a 'network forum' for policy affairs, which can be understood from the following perspective issues:

The seven flagships initiated under the MSC are actually being governed by a 'political network' comprises of the National Information Technology Council (NITC), MCMC, Multimedia Development Corporation (MDeC), the Prime Minister's Department which housed many Government's Central Agencies such as the Economic Planning Unit (EPU) and Malaysian Administration Modernisation and Management Planning Unit (MAMPU), as well as the relevant Ministries. This is not a typical bureaucratic government-like structure as it is also being loosely overseen by the International Advisory Panel (IAP)—the highest body comprises of groups of experts providing their policy advice. While Government obviously remains central, its action is often 'highly contingent upon the action of others in the network (John & Cole, 2000, p. 82).

In addition to NITA, the National IT Framework (NITF) is presented as a "strategic and synergistic combination of a number of key components, working in tandem with the situations of what other bodies dictated. However, we sought that the role of information is crucial as a critical node that links between three key elements, namely, people, infrastructure, and application with "people" as the most important of all. Since its inception, apart from attracting a core group of world-class companies into the MSC, Malaysia has put in place a world-leading framework of cyberlaws and established Cyberjaya and Putrajaya as two of the world's leading intelligent cities. In the second phase (2003-2010), the MSC will be linked to other global cybercities to create a web of corridors, set global standard in flagship applications and harmonize global framework of cyberlaws (Anon, 2004). As a matter of fact, the concept of intelligent cities is already becoming a reality in the context of the developed country

and is expected to be necessary in Malaysia in the immediate future. As transpired, the spatial setting for the MSC project consists of several "cybercities." Cybercities development in MSC began with Cyberjaya, can assist in expanding the benefits of the ICT companies and their economic generation activities to wider areas, such as MSC Cyberport at Indah Pura in Kulai Johor to complement the Iskandar Development region at down south Johor and Kulim Hi-Tech Park (KHTP) at far north. It can also become the catalyst in bridging the country's digital divide and enhancing the nation's growth and competitiveness. The ultimate stage of transformation encapsulates the concept of network state as advanced by Castells (1996; Castells, 2005; Castells & Cardoso, 2006).

The CMA 1998, besides detailing MCMC's role as the regulator, more importantly, it also provides the policy and regulatory framework for the convergence of the telecommunications, broadcasting and Internet industries. Because of this, it repealed the Telecommunications Act 1950 and the Broadcasting Act 1988. It should be noted that there are numerous pieces of regulations related to the CMA and in the future, there shall be the creation of more regulations to develop the regulatory framework and to take into account technological innovations as well as changes in the mentioned industries. This clearly reinforces the potential importance and need for flexibility of the new regulatory framework for the integrating industries of telecommunications, broadcasting and online activities through constant engagement by multiple stakeholders facilitated by new technologies.

Different constituents of Malaysian public policies are becoming increasingly inter-linked together driven on the basis of new technologies, which are clearly demonstrated by the promulgation of the 10 National Policy Objectives for Communication and Multimedia." A crucial legal impetus for this policy comes from the CMA 1988, which also sets out the establishment of four Industry Forums (IFs) within the MCMC, in correspondence to the domains of technology, economy, social, and technology.

The governance of digital convergence is based on the interconnectivity of communications networks and interactivity of communications services, which is referring to 'self-organising, inter-organisational networks characterised by interdependence, resource exchange, rules of the game and significant autonomy from the state' (Rhodes 1997, p. 15). In this regard, ICT provides essentially a means to the greater access and enhance deeper participation due to its potential to connect various stakeholders to governance which can never be found in any previous innovation or activity (Rhodes, 1997, p.54). Subsequently, the IFs can create what are known as "voluntary industry codes" (ICs) in line with the 10-point National Policy Objectives for communication and multimedia industry often through considerable exercise of policy networks deliberations within its setting.

The ICs is essentially a unique concept because Malaysia's law (and indeed the common law used by Commonwealth countries) rely substantially on a rule and consequence-based traditional system, where a prohibitive rule is established and a penalty or consequence is created to handle cases where the rule is broken. Thus, this concept of self-regulation with considerable amount of decision processes now occurs within policy networks, i.e. Framework for Industry Development (FID) and Malaysian Information, Communications and Multimedia Services Strategy (MyICMS886), breaks new ground as the private sector together with various civil communities groups or individuals attempt to be its own so-called "policeman" as opposed to the practice in the old regime where Government decides everything and enforces unilaterally. Indeed, eventually it actually recognises that convergence may lead to a less regulation in the new communication and multimedia sectors and should not lead to more regulations to area such as IT.

IMPLICATIONS OF DIGITAL CONVERGENCE FOR MALAYSIAN SOCIETY: NEW BREAK AWAY?

Malaysia is characterised by a typically hierarchical society and has inherited a long-standing and highly bureaucratic political system since independence. One area where the ICT Malaysia raises some critical question is that Malaysia's political and administrative system was one of the major impediments affecting the country's effort towards a new exploration of governance. This problem is made even complicated, often, because of the volatile nature of new technological change; coupled with the dynamism of policy development against the face of the country's own strategies.

On the one hand, it was found that the present notion of 'Kerajaan' implied the traditional Malay royalist administration of the past. This unique political system has been the practice for centuries, resembling the hierarchical society. Today, the political elite groups command wider support and undivided loyalty as much as the King in the past. One more direct case is with regard to a systemic issue of direct political party link the major mass media operators in the country, which means that the ruling coalition has overarching control over most of the mainstream mass media industry in the country. This situation raises valid concern on whether the promises of the fair governance of the mass media content can be realised. However, the proliferation of the Internet has become alternative medium for critical or even disgruntled elements within the political spectrum (Diamond, 2008).

With the ICT transcends borders, hierarchy, and status, conflicts always existed between the various political domains within the Malaysian structure. Often, Ministries act independently and agencies are politically manoeuvred in the policy process. As the empirical studies have shown, these conflicts greatly reduced the accountabilities and create political rivalries between various domains of ICT establishments. In many cases, this partly explained the inability of the Government to be more coherent in policy affairs and implementation. As an important breakthrough to the governance process as well as amidst the controversy, the NITA accorded people-based policy as one of the top priorities in 1994. Indeed, this conception has significantly set the tone for future policy orientation. Though it may not be explicitly related, it is believed that the NITC's principles of governance are embodied in the new regime of convergence. As it turned out, that dramatic technological convergence and a more central role of C&M have been the pervasive causes of the breakdown of the old regime, and, consequently, under the banner of NRR, legitimised the role of networked actors in the policy process quite substantially. In similar vein, some traditional agencies roles as well as their existence were reviewed and vanished in the process. The role of federal government, i.e. Cabinet Ministries and the Central Agencies however, remained pertinent, sometimes taking prominent stance than the regulatory bodies.

On the other hand, Malaysia's multifaceted strategy had enabled the country to move the innovative agenda into a new height of governance. One of the most obvious drawbacks of this strategy however was the fact that the philosophy was not properly communicated or shared with the other political domains. This can partly be explained by the fact that the original governance ideas were not the brainchild of the bureaucrat, rather the technocrat[2] whom is viewed as the 'outsiders' by those within the Government. The arbitrary and integrity of the MIMOS being the Secretariat to the NITC was also became a great concern for many, including the political leaders. To some extent, particularly at the initial development of ICT, some observers regarded the previous NITC as the 'cash cow' for MIMOS, in which its profit and policy capacity has been diluted. Critical

analysis has suggested that, among many other factors, the restructuring of NITC by Government significantly contributed to the eventual limitations of the NITC's model of governance. In this realm, many observers would find it surprising that Government has lost sight on such a noble and idealistic effort faced such a dismal exit before it was fully materialised.

Notwithstanding the above events, as discussed in empirical chapters, the advent of new technology has brought together the new hope and scope for governance. The digital convergence obviously has proposed such a radical exploration on this, in contrast to the centralised, inflexible and concentrated authority at the centre. Clearly then, these approaches however do not easily applied in the Malaysian case. Departing from the general ICT agenda, Malaysia has taken a new route to reform its own regulatory and institutional structure, as a result of digital convergence. Ironically, despite the effort to widening the policy process is done under the banner of NRR, the centralised authority of the Federal Government, through the Cabinet Ministries, Central Agencies, and the Prime Minister's Department are still far too obvious.

A logical conclusion of these changes is that Malaysia's ICT agenda appeared to be much more disaggregated compared to the situation in its early formation. From a commercial viewpoint, the convergence sector seems promising - as indicated in the favourable growth in recent years. From a governance viewpoint, research reported in this book shows that it is Malaysia's long-term strategic target set to be the hub for C&M industry and this would be largely corresponding with the further improvement in the convergence sector. This strategic target may well be realised with the new mode of governance[3]. Given the complication of many sorts across structural boundaries, it is a pressing need to address some of the focal issues pertaining to the regulatory and institutional being first.

THE PARADOX OF DIGITAL CONVERGENCE AND REGULATORY CHANGE

While many Asian countries, including Malaysia, are struggling to experiment the ICT innovative agenda, it has to be borne in mind that there is no one-solution-fit all convergence model offered by any Western industrialised countries. In response to rapid technological change, the new regulatory regime has become a fashionable way for countries to grasp the most potential the convergence model could offer. This book has, on the one hand, discussed some major issues about convergence policy models of ICT adoption (e.g., the perspectives of new technology, the influence of convergence in promoting self-regulation mechanisms) in general terms by presenting a variety of views by many authors in Part I.

First of all, the historical study of Malaysia, in an Introductory section (Part I), showed that the country had been engaged in the innovative agenda since the middle of 1990s. Thanks to digital convergence which dominated the ICT development towards the end 1990s, Malaysia's new ICT strategy was heightened by its pro-active promotion of the new self-regulatory principles which are the important elements of the new regime. This suggests that the NRR was not a new phenomenon altogether, as it was actually an extension to the original motive of information society agenda especially in Malaysia context of ICT adoption. However, it is not until the CMA was introduced in 1998, the NRR has been used as strategic measures to adopt a comprehensive ICT liberalisation policy.

The progressive evolution of the national ICT agenda and eventually convergence, the roles of ICT governing institutions and cyber laws that have been put in place have shown from a different angle the fundamental indicator of new regime of convergence approach towards the process of new ICT governance model in the country.

From the regional as well as global evolution of convergence policy model, examined in the book, it has found that the proliferation of ICT played a significant role in determining the extent of governance implications in many Asia regions. For Malaysia, the success of NRR might not have been possible if the MCMC had not ensured a wide range of strategic partnership with a range of multiple stakeholders to promote the convergence model of ICT adoption on the one hand, and established the necessary institutional mechanism to get the support from the industry players as well as Government agencies on the other. In particular, MCMC's industrial dialogues with the IF and relevant Ministries/agencies had made it possible for the former to successfully perform its super regulator function in promoting self-regulation. In contrast, partly due to the absence of similar support and partly due to its re-structuring, NITC somewhat failed to live up to expectation. Therefore, in spite of its alleged political as well as bureaucratic supremacy to the national ICT agenda, NITC's original model of ICT governance eventually lost its rigour since the beginning of early year 2000.

Having briefly experienced with futile attempt the radicalism NITC's philosophy, the Government now switched the attention to experiment ICT governance model via digital convergence more vigorously in Malaysia. Part 1's Chapters 3 through 5 respectively have examined the convergence strategy adopted by the Government with an emphasis on some regulatory as well as institutional reforms. Firstly, the Government collaborated with external consultants and successfully came out with the CMA1998 - a single most important piece of legislation for convergence agenda. Secondly, following this, the MECM has been tasked to undertake the new agenda under the banner of NRR. Thirdly, with the formation of MCMC, some agencies were abrogated. Fourthly, moving away from the initial phase of convergence model, MCMC made further progress by actively trying to help define the real meaning of k-society with the role of convergence in it. Meantime, embedded in the largely hierarchical system, the NRR began to face formidable challenges from various angles. Apparently, despite some policy complications, MCMC together with MEWC, have continued charting the future growth path by the launching of MyICMS886. In addition to the collaboration with industry players, MCMC has made substantial efforts to establish strategic alliances and partnerships with other stakeholders including establishing contact with its counterpart all over the world. Finally, as a result of Ministerial reform, despite some policy complication facing the NRR, MCMC and MCMM (the then MWEC) have recently entered another phase of industrial development, with the launching of MyICMS886 - ahead of ICT Roadmap led by MOSTI, National Broadband Initiatives and Universal Service Provision. Each side of the two policy domains are hoping to make their own agenda the substantive input for the information society agenda. However, though intended to chart for the future national growth, both Ministries apparently did not significantly communicate with each other regarding their Ministerial agenda.

The emergence of 'two islands' - the soft and the hard aspect - between the MoSTI and the MWEC since the early 2000s discussed in this book is also well illustrated. During the planning stage for ICT Roadmap Blueprint, the two Ministries have not been adequately collaborated, as a result of this segregation. It is found that, for instance, during the 2008 WCIT in Austin, US, the MoSTI was assigned a major role to champion all the Malaysian ICT issues ahead. MoSTI have participated extensively in marketing the Malaysian ICT agendas in the Conference, minus the participation of MWEC, or even the MCMC for that matter. Similarly, the MWEC only collaborated with MCMC to come out with its MyICMS886, without significant involvement from the MOSTI. In similar view, the fragmented and uncoordinated innovation push factor has cost Malaysia through unhealthy competition and ma-

neuvering within the bureaucracy. For example, with UNIK, BioTechCorp, SME Corporation - all focusing on high knowledge innovation, MSC or rather MDeC's unique role is somewhat lost or overshadowed. In the meantime, the ICT agenda did not necessarily become a barrier for Ministries to collaborate for new agenda: at least within the NITC fora. However, inward looking and incoherence kind of relationship can be seen between the two islands of fragmented policy domains. This suggests a significant difference between the Ministerial and the national technology policy: the latter is intended mainly to promote national agenda for development, whilst the former is designed solely to ensure a Ministerial's political agenda for information, communication and new multimedia technologies. As such Ministeries, as in the case of MoSTI and MCMM now, would be devising their own Ministerial strategy under the pretext of national policy. It seems that, as far as the both Ministries are concerned, Ministerial political goals may be given more priority than collaborative of efforts across Ministries in pursuing national agenda for ICT adoption in the country's public sector. From time to time, policy makers either at the Ministerial level or Cabinet Ministries tend to forget about the need for streamlining the effort, thus sharing a more coherent agenda.

The two-island national collaboration seems to be constrained by a specific sectoral ICT area - the soft and the hard ones respectively. Taking the NRR case, as examined earlier, the MWEC was a clear champion in this agenda. With strong political support from MWEC, the MCMC joined forces with industry players to develop NRR, based on the self-regulatory principles. Sharing a common objective to promote convergence model of operation, MCMC together with the four IFs (Content, Consumer, Technical and Access Forum), poised in the new mode of policy processes for the first time in the country. In addition to crafting the framework, the MCMC has also been actively seeking collaboration with relevant

Government agencies. Motivated primarily by the massive opportunities offered by the new lucrative sector, the community of convergence agreed to come into the table to work out how the best the convergence model of governing ICT adoption could offer them. However, the role of MoSTI in this effort is almost unsuccessful.

MCMC's industrial collaboration has also been extended to participation in similar counterparts elsewhere in the world recently. Among many others, the NRR has highlighted the Government's new strategies for tapping the most of new ICT adoption to best practical level. Currently, with strong political backing from the MCMM and industry players, through IF, MCMC joined forces to pursue industry codes, intended to be used at the national level (the first Content Code came out in 2004).

Membership of this forum has been extended to many sectoral players. Sharing a common objective to promote the NRR objectives, all the network actors ended their old style of political manoeuvring and entered a collaborative engagement for the first time in the country. In addition to leading this fora, MCMC and the industry players have been active promoting the self-regulatory mechanisms in collaboration with several Ministries/agencies from the late 2004. Motivated primarily by the favourable progress, the MWEC/MCMC island formed a 'grand alliance' to promote a single framework for the country, at the behest of CMA1998.

The common element in the three important areas of the governance of digital convergence - the industry self-regulation, public consultation and voluntary compliance, was that, firstly, multi-stakeholder partnership proved to be fundamentally important to the coming up of any future policies. In other words, the collaborative stance was in many cases became the forceful factor for the success of NRR. The extent of the success of the industry Code of Practice, for instance, was in part decided by the readiness of each of the parties to get into the table for their common good and resolve any differences. The current ongoing activities in coming out with any convergence-related policies has been largely characterised by the strategic partnership. For instance, the effectiveness of the initial phase of convergence can be explained in part by the MCMC's ability to get industrial as well as the government agencies support, this is in sharp contrast with some complications emerged with regard to the authority over content issues during the initial phase of convergence. In the case of future initiatives for NRR, the force of global convergence has provided a strong push for the Government to review is legal and institutional mechanisms and apparatuses, thus open room for wider political process necessary for the network actors to self-regulate themselves.

Secondly, the governance of digital convergence was closely associated with the availability of industrial dialogues and public consultation processes. The current NITC seems to lack of this, unlike prior to its restructuring mainly due to its new role. The future path of ICT growth including convergence has been centred on the environment which allows greater dialogues among various stakeholders. To some extent, the question of whether or not the NRR can be effective will be determined by the readiness of all parties to engage in industrial dialogues and policy consultations. The same can be true about the policy decision pertaining to newly emergent convergence technologies. In short, it was argued in this book that, to a great extent, the governance of digital convergence is built upon the value of consensus; that is the principle of mutual understanding between all the stakeholders of the industry.

Thirdly, the NRR case was, in one way or another, affected by the policy framework and mechanisms which is conducive for it to operate. The book has argued that the NITA had become a conduit to carry out the Malaysia's search and experimentation for new mode of governance, since 1994. The restructuring of few ICT policy domains involving NITC, MIMOS, and relevant Ministries have caused a demarcation between the soft and the hard aspect of ICT agenda, as well as the reassessment of the NITC's model of governance. Consequently, the Government has been engaged in a process of making new policies and strategies leaning towards digital convergence, as seen since 1998. Despite the lack of collaboration among few ICT establishments, particularly the 'two-ICT-islands,' both Ministries have formed their own strategy in defining the information society agenda. For instance, while the MCMM-MCMC have seemed now emphasising on creating an innovative society, while regulating the C&M sector and services in the hope of pushing the self-regulatory mechanisms to a greater height, the MOSTI-NITC was the driver of the ICT Roadmap Blueprint. Being under the government administrative bodies, the NITC as of current tended to follow political and bureaucratic drummers of MOSTI. MCMC had from the start, tried to nurture the new mode of governance through NRR in collaboration with MCMM; but perhaps the biggest flaw of this strategy adopted by the MCMC management to realise this ambition was the absence of strategic alliances with other Ministries, MOSTI in particular. Nonetheless, the collapse of NITC's model of governance before it was fully materialised, and the proliferation of NRR over recent years has switch the hope for digital convergence as a possible remedy.

Digital Convergence and Institutional Change

Governance of digital convergence, as this research has found, was not a one-way but an interactive and dynamic process as a result of convergence waves which happened at unrelenting pace. To be sure, this has given rise to various complicated political manoeuvring. Convergence policies towards the NRR in Malaysia were not exclusively initiated by policy makers in the first place; rather were in many cases implemented a series of institutional reforms.

As far as the NRR is concerned, it seems that institutional reform and adjustments has become a commonly used method by the Government for the search of a new governance mode. CMA1998 is designed to promote the convergence agenda across to politicians and government bureaucrats in order to influence institutional reform. It has been shown in this book that MCMC, with the strong support from the Ministry as well as the community of convergence, managed to indirectly influence the institutional reforms since the 1998.

Institutional reforms, which are quite radical in the initial phase of convergence, begin with the launched of CMA1998. Partly in response to the strong push of digital technology, and to the successful take up of the initial phase of convergence, major industry players begin to learn and accept the fact that they are now operating in the completely new environment. As argued in Chapter 9, the role of Central Agencies did not prevent the take-up of the convergence industry. On the contrary, the growth of the convergence sector has resulted in the enhanced engagements of the industry stakeholder which have different stake in the industry.

It is believed that the MCMC office in Cyberjaya act as the 'nexus,' whose major task is to maintain good contacts with different policy domains. Empirical research, as reported in the book, suggested that MCMC effectively keep formal communications with the MCMM as they have informed and capable officials concerning the industry. The MCMM's concentration is thereby directed towards mainly on fundamental issues of long-term societal objectives and directions or those matters of compelling policy significance. On the one hand, the MCMC's Chairman, whom are specialised professional policy experts, often in direct relationships with convergence community. In addition, it was found that the Chairman, being the former top official from the Government, had officially neutralised the MCMC to ensure the policy is no conflict with the aspiration of the Government. As such, it eliminates the need for

Government to intervene in the detailed affairs of the MCMC. While it may seem expedient to let the MCMC perform its 'crusade' freely, the complexity of task involved is unsuited to such simple notion as the requirements for convergence extend well beyond telecommunication issues.

The assessment found that MCMC has in particular, adopted a strategy characterised by multi-stakeholder partnerships with various actors since 1998; with the strong backing by the Government. The spirit of NITC as explained, was presented as an impetus to break the pervasive political, bureaucratic and administrative control of the authority, which has quite significantly lead to the creaking down of the old institutional order. In some of the Section 1's chapters, various significant institutional adjustments at both Ministerial level and the convergence sector levels in an effort to improve the ICT governance process of digital convergence have been explained. In the meantime, whilst intended to escalate the growth of the convergence sector, the Government also acknowledges and support any effort to translate the ICT agenda by any Ministries. Instead of encouraging a more coherent agenda across Ministries, however, the MoSTI and the MCMM seems to have been acting independently in defining the national ICT agenda. It appears that there was a wide gap between the Ministerial agenda due to the inward-looking technology policy and exaggerated claims about the strategies adopted since the new regime came into existence, as far as the convergence initiative is concerned. Partly serving the political purposes, it has been projected on a partially commercial footing for some time. The Ministries often consider its ownership of limited sectoral agenda under the prisms of national agenda. The concern is not actually on the collaboration of efforts across Ministries, but political independence at the expense of capital and skills gain.

The governance of digital convergence is contingent upon the standards of accountability to the policy process (e.g. the effectiveness of the policy implementations), the regulatory framework (e.g. the evaluation on the judicial activities such as grievances matters, decisions and appeals) and the institutional mechanisms (e.g., widening of policy access for multiple participation) that are put in place. The institutional convergence development is consistently assessed to determine on the extent to which the industry is meeting the policy objectives that have been decided. Hobson (2010) pointed out the two elements critical to this, first, 'the right attitude' and 'information or policy change' that will bring about the correct behaviour.' In addition, the perceived regulatory procedures and due process and the availability of institutional setting for all to access and involve in the process, all help enhance the governance of digital convergence.

MALAYSIA'S MODEL OF ICT GOVERNANCE FOR DIGITAL CONVERGENCE

Discussions in Section 1—the ICT model chapters—have shown that there are many perspectives on the evolution concept of innovative policy and the new media technology interfaces experienced by many countries. The common agreement is that the adoption of ICT policy and governance experimentation is now fast shaping by the convergence trend. This has been reflected in the vast range of literatures contributed by many authors from different scholarly backgrounds. In particular, conflicting theories of convergence policy have been centred on whether the government, rather than other network actors, should be in the control position. By studying the experience of Malaysia and its convergence policy, this book has analysed the attempts of the Government, in particular the MCMC to get the most of new ICT, thus experimenting the search for new governance mode.

The widening of policy process from the Government to the network actors enabled the latter to intervene over the national policy domain, technology choice and industry wellbeing since 1998. The birth of the NITC's model of governance though had a brief stint, has escalated the concern for further experimentation of new governance on the one hand, and, on the other, this in part promoted the policy makers to use more policy measures to initiate a series of regulatory and institutional reform to promote convergence, despite the wide political challenges and complications across different policy domains.

The NRR case reported in this book have offered some fresh perspectives to assess the effectiveness of Government policies towards the ICT sector, particularly the convergence industry. Firstly, the birth of NRR did have some significant linkages to the original intention of NITA; however, this measure failed to prevent further decline of the NITC's model of governance and its eventual death in the new phase of ICT agenda. As a result, the NRR in practice, could well offer an alternative to the governance process, despite rather sectoral in scope. Secondly, following the decision to reassess the national ICT agenda by giving more focus on the convergence sector, the Government initiated a series of regulatory and institutional reform, and by so doing, given legitimate as well as definitive space for the new regime to operationalise. Within the NRR framework, the notion of voluntary compliance and self-regulatory mechanisms prevailed, and the community of convergence came out with their Industry Code of Practice. This however was widely believed to be rather symbolic gesture devised to contain offensive content spreading on the air, as the disturbing fact remained was that there was such a mess in the content regulatory domain.

Content Code was loosely observed by the Content Forum members as the legitimate authority over the content issues are spread at least across 13 Ministries and regulatory agencies, thus posing a serious risk that this could yield suboptimal, ill-coordinated and potentially incoherent policy outcomes.

The role the previous NITC play in promoting the NITA was most notable in Malaysia during the middle 1990s. Analysis in this book has shown that, initially promoted by the NITC and later endorsed by the Government, NITA was seen as a grand strategy for national ICT development. In response to such political backing and the financial as well as logistic support within the MSC Flagship programmes, MIMOS and MDeC have been championing the agenda, including the radical NITC's model of governance. Following the institutional reform involving the NITC and the few Ministries, the proposed convergence initiative was effectively undertaken by the then MECM, and later the MCMC upon its formal establishment. The scenario of national ICT agenda was further demarcated by the hard and the soft aspect during the reassessment of the role of MoSTI and then MWEC, which has argued in this book, gave birth to the emergence of two ICT island - the MoSTI/NITC versus the MWEC/MCMC. The notion of governance as demonstrated by the NRR regime is now being the industry-driven, and not the community driven as implied in the old regime. This has been compounded by the fact that USP, which generally had not been provided by the private telcos, now has been recognised as an important convergence policy objective of NRR.

Not surprisingly, in consequent to the recent spates of regulatory and institutional reforms involving the NITC and few Ministries, there were mixed political implications to this.

First, NRR was operating against the odd within the political and administrative system which is largely hierarchical and bureaucratic. The philosophy of self-regulatory and voluntary compliance may, arguably, be justified by the strong wave of digital convergence experienced by Malaysia within a period of about few years beginning 1998, compared to about forty years or so (since the independence of the country) unilateral guidance provided by the Government. However, the issue lies is that the Government continued to support convergence agenda in terms of policy coordination by the NITC, whilst letting the MoSTI to initiate its own 'Ministerial' cum 'national' agenda. Even with the absence of NITC, it is argued that the convergence scheme would still be making significant breakthrough in shaping the national ICT agenda. The long-standing political manoeuvring over the national ICT agenda between different institutional domains as well as the rivals between the 'technocrats and bureaucrats' had also triggered the issue of complications of ICT development in Malaysia. The research has found that the need to eliminate restrictions in response to the digital convergence does not imply that Government policy makers should not intervene (see Katsikas, 2010), despite the inefficiency that such interventions imply for the market. Policymakers are likely to intervene as they perceive market failures, or they might be tempted to act in support of the defence of the national interest, e.g. culture, solidarity etc.

Secondly, Government is ever willing to commit across Ministries, to come out with the national agenda, regardless the fact that issue at stake now is actually on streamlining the effort across Ministries. As a matter of fact, the two 'ICT islands' eventually emerged - MoSTI/MDeC/NITC and MCMM(MWEC)/MCMC, did not wholly collaborating themselves to developing the NRR. On the contrary, they were acting rather autonomously in promoting the national ICT agenda through their own understanding and initiatives especially from the 1998. It was argued in this book that commitment to the NRR had enabled MCMC and the Ministry to gauge the support from the industry players, and using the government funds to promote the agenda for convergence and, in the meantime, to further promote the new mode of governance together. The fading of the NITC's model of governance or its changes did not appear to be a major setback to both islands; as both islands were still remained at the forefront of national ICT agenda, as argued in this book, despite impending complications due to the fact that there are seemingly too many areas

of ICT to concentrate upon. In stark contrast, the Government has escaped political dilemma largely due to its exclusive support for the convergence scheme. In the end, the Government did agree to support whatever agenda originating from various Ministries; so long it is made under the name of 'national programme' - a strategy without a focus. As discussed, the mission of the Central Agencies is merely to undertake any directives that come from the Cabinet or Ministries. This seems to be contradictory with another strand of the NITA's k-society philosophy, which is centred on the issues of people-based governance. This suggests that the Malaysian Government will continue to play a dominant role in determining the eventual success or failure of the future ICT path as a whole, no matter what future kind of technology or standard would it be. The national ICT agenda have many issues at the core which must be addressed adequately. The failure to address these issues would simply jeopardise the Government's ability to steer the country forward in the ICT agenda.

The incongruence of policy implementation since NITA until NRR has raised further doubts about whether Government should make it obvious of its governance experiment, and whether bureaucrats are capable of working with the non-State actors. As suggested, the ICT provides a fertile ground towards the governance experiment for many countries with varying degrees and priorities depending on multiple factors such as technological changes, market status and the global economy[4]. The Australian Government has been coordinating and commissioning various efforts related to the convergence initiatives since the early 1990s. The same is applicable to Japan, through MITI and MPT in coordinating various activities and strategies. The difference between the strategies adopted by the Government in relation to NITA and convergence scheme was that, firstly, the Government has relied upon the NITC from the start of ICT development, while the MCMC has became the sole champion for the convergence agenda. Secondly, even though the NITC has been provided with the proper support being under the MIMOS[5], the Government is determined that difficulties of breaking the wall of the bureaucracy are not circumvented by Internet activisim. Further the MIMOS is not directly under the Government's arm, but the MCMC has legal accord to perform its duties as enshrined in the CMA1998. Thirdly, as a result of the institutional changes, the present NITC may not be adequately provided with the input from the non-State actors as they have been excluded (unlike previously), whilst the MCMC, concerning the policy process, allowed for active involvement from all stakeholders within a much more systematic agenda and mechanisms to promote the convergence scheme.

By any measure, NRR has been promoted as the strategic tool of the Government for the search of new governance mode. However, on the ground, different political domains across the Government administrative structure have taken fundamentally different policies and strategies to influence the course of ICT development. Consequently, the effects of these strategies have turned out to be significantly different: the NITA agenda was there, but the NITC's model of governance, have lost its vigour; giving the new hope for convergence, through NRR to be a new experiment for the search of new governance mode. The implications of it on the new governance are certainly overwhelming. In the context of new regime, it has been contended that the reform objectives of digital convergence cannot be possible to be maintained without strong, semi-independent regulator. As such, despite the existence of anti-monopoly provisions, the Government's telcos are still in the control position of the market. As this book has shown, in parallel to experience that has unfolded in many parts of the world, there is a strong need to juggle between the 'highly imperfect markets' with the pressures of good governance (Nasim & Shusil, 2010).

It is emphasised in this book that it is highly inappropriate if Government attempt to make it clear the governance path it choose to follow during the transitional stage of convergence. The consequence of doing so will inevitably forestall any future effort and sometimes suppress further experimental growth. Both the relatively radical people-based governance policy adopted within the NITA framework to manage the ICT agenda and incongruence of efforts to promote NRR have demonstrated that it has sometimes created confusion about what the government priority of ICT agenda really are during rapid technological transition, as under the conditions of convergence, this could lead to inconsistencies or at least the loss of synergies.

Given the above scenario, there is clear evidence that the formation of the policy networks in the case of convergence governance is achieved through culmination of efforts between different constellation of network actors with various resources and power. It exemplifies a provision of seamless and integrated policy avenue for the public and business communities, which will shift the governance agenda in no uncertain terms towards the digital realm.

The remarkable changes in the policy, regulatory and institutional domain of the digital convergence sector in Malaysia has resulted governance in two essential characters. First, deliberate strategic attempt of ICT agenda, principally through NITA's framework of governance in 1996, has facilitated subsequent moves which, for Malaysia, has transformed the governance of the ICT and digital convergence sector centred around the notion of policy network and policy communities, impinged upon a new mode of governance or specifically, network governance. The aims of these measures have been, generally, to capitalise upon radical technological changes, impacted by the recent phenomenon of digital convergence. In effect, a dynamic, mutually reinforcing, dialectical relationship has developed between the process of digital convergence and the political complexities that Malaysia entails. However, as this research has shown, it is vital to understand that such evolution and development of digital convergence policy is deeply embedded in the traditional, largely hierarchical structures of analogue era. Against this really however, the persistent initiatives and detailed policy framework at the sectoral level, represents a unique Malaysian strategic responses to the ever increasing challenges in the digital age. Analysis of the changes - in terms of the critical implications of the policy, regulatory and institutional discourse across Government Ministries and agencies - has also revealed un-uniformity in approach, within a national proclamation of making Malaysia as the hub for C&M.

Second, and in a much more limited extent, there is evidence that within Malaysia, convergence among different parts of the ICT sector, most notably between the historically separated telecommunications and broadcasting sectors, with the Internet has occurred. This calls for policy makers to make necessary adjustments for creating more integrated model of ICT governance frameworks at the institutional levels. Whilst the degree to which this occurred has proved to be limited as it has been mainly riding on political 'push and pull' between the analogues regime and the converging environment, 'bringing in' various network actors, under the auspices of NRR, which is fundamentally based on industry self-regulation and voluntary compliance continue to precipitate further growth.

It is increasingly clear that the further Malaysia's efforts for digital convergence is likely in the future, resulting into further refining, and consequently, recreating of new governance landscape, characterised by the network elements, albeit with at least two challenges:

First, the current framework though supposedly a crucial piece of ICT agenda, is relatively detached with the original philosophy of NITA. The pursuit of the network governance, even when confined exclusively to the country's own national agenda, requires a fundamental reconstruction of the perception of governance, and the mobilisation of a new reality which practices must be reconciled with, if not supersede, bureaucratic, long-established 'command and control' mode of governance embedded from the analogue regime. This is indeed the greatest challenge, as noted throughout the chapters that require the radical reconfiguration among the mindset of policy actors itself. Moreover, this must happen alongside evolving national agendas in a compatible and integrative fashion. The NITA's framework of governance, which subsequently facilitated by the NRR, have merely established the impetus for such a foundation to develop and many impediments lie ahead in terms of the best method to be pursued, not least regarding the specific relationship between different domains of policy network. The long overdue incongruence regarding the content industry illustrates an example of challenges surrounding the effort for creating the suitable approach of governing in the digital age.

Second, and very closely related into the first challenge, the digital convergence, must strive to achieve complete integration with all other policy areas, in promoting the national agenda. Whilst the policy and regulatory initiatives have been substantively accomplished, much of the efforts are dampened by traditional legal systems as well as diversity of institutional capacity to satisfactorily meet with the demand of the governance in the digital age. This situation has left many things to be desired as the process either get delayed or derailed from its original intent, both in direction and scope. To further the argument, the policy, regulatory and institutional elements as found in this book may even require a fundamental re-think of the socio-cultural perceptions to Malaysia's new communications and media policy, in line with the progressive and radical values and practices of network governance which will continue to provide remarkable challenges to the present and future's ICT agenda for the country.

AGENDA FOR FUTURE RESEARCH

Learning from the experience of Malaysia's national ICT agenda and the future development of information infrastructure, this book has argued that, first, the agenda has fast shaping by the convergence phenomenon, and second, the governance of digital convergence had a significant impact on the overall search for better governance. While the empirical analysis derived from the case studies on Malaysia's ICT development, charting its ways towards digital convergence, and the three critical areas, i.e. 'people-based governance' policy, legal and regulatory and institutional framework, remain important to the understanding of such a complicated issue, this book has also opened up avenues for further research.

A closer look at the analysis, in particular the empirical chapters, found that the development of ICT agenda since 1998 has been largely determined by the pervasive change in the digital technology. The rapid technological convergence has also redefined the people-based philosophy underpinning in the NITA. As such, the modes of policy making and processes between the Government and non-State actors have been radically changed. It is now increasingly clear that people based agenda for future k-society and k-economy is not confined to the community-based projects; in effect, it extends to every multifaceted areas of ICT development predominantly determined by the convergence sector.

At the outset, the progressive march towards technological convergence has driven many countries to tap the full potential of this sector. The phenomenal growth of the digital technology coupled with various unprecedented actions taken by many will help realise an integrated ICT sector including information exchange and services, digital communications and digital entertainment. Improving convergence policies and practices to be more responsive to knowledge society is an area with room for new mode of governance. Implicit in most research is the fact that it leads to the

discovery of further research questions and issues. In this regard, one major theme touched on in this book was the vital role of digital convergence to the search for new governance illustrated by the Malaysian ICT agenda. The core strategy of self-regulatory mechanisms and voluntary compliance begins to transcend, and as many other innovations of digital technology expands, these has made the notion of people-based policy a prerequisite for any final output of policy making process. Interestingly, the potential of new convergence technologies cannot be predetermined by a single country case study; there is a need for further research to determine the effectiveness of the Malaysian model.

A comparative study of different models from the part of different countries experiences may help to build a greater understanding of the complex relationship between policies and practices, and indeed, will almost certainly provide compelling reasons for future research.

To recap, with the government's target for making ICT as the driver of economic growth, it can be concluded that addressing the country's current and future demand for innovation policy will be critical and this has, to a large extent, illustrated by the innovative transformation over the years. The 10th Malaysia Plan clearly articulated the central role of ICT to propel the country to a high value economy. The 12 National Key Economic Areas (NKEAs) in the New Economic Model (NEM) concepts and ideas are adopted to translate policy into actions, with renewed commitment by the State to utilize ICT as a key enabler of national infrastructure, which is typical of neo-liberalism strategies in the West. Arguably, while pursuing Malaysia's vision of a developed country, with equitable economic development with reduced digital divide, and becoming a regional hub for C&M industry, MSC is still holding on to the state-centric model of ICT (because of the political reason) but would like also to embrace fashionable American and European models. Intelligent city is a fashionable neo-liberal percept to be included in a innovation agenda for the country, but much remain to be seen when government is taking a dominant stance, particularly when political uncertainty at its extreme. Meantime, high ICT investment in most sectors of the economy has seen substantial benefits, in terms of higher productivity and economic growth, as shown by successful examples of the developed countries are too attractive for Malaysia to ignore. Arguably, "Prime Minister Mahathir has promoted the MSC as a flagship in the state's effort to develop its society and as an alternative model for developing nations. Thus, Malaysia's agenda of ICT through MSC is clearly an attempt to be current and fashionable to face the new challenges in ICT but operationalizing these through the familiar state-centric framework will be an acid test for the whole system, in particular the MSC. This has further resulted in major changes in governmnet policies and legislations including institutional infrastructure and apt legal framework (Yoon & Chae, 2009; Dawes, 2009; Nasim & Shusil, 2010). For instance, the rebranding of the MCMM to refocuss the eAgenda iniatiative particularly digital convergence sector is commendable as it can minimise overlapping of Ministerial functions in dealing with the 'soft' and the 'hard' aspect of ICT.

CHAPTER SUMMARY

In the final analysis, as indicated in the preceding discussion, in the past, the provision of traditional infrastructure facilities have been linked to foreign investments which is no longer sufficient. Now, new age factors such as global connectivity and interactivity technological elements as well as an adequate and steady supply of knowledge workers. Increasingly, new challenges emerged and the intelligent cities are caught up with idea of responsiveness, best practices coupled with a transparent, accountable and corruption-free system. In pursuing this, the ethos of innovation culture is met with these values. To the State, in-

novation policy without top-down initiatives is just not practical. The passing of CMA1998 have provided for wider autonomy for industry players in terms of industry governance and proliferation of the sector but little with respect to flexibility in policy directions. However, it remains to be seen whether this ambitious ICT transformation as well as cutting-edge facilities will also pave way for a more democratic, just and equitable society

Finally, it is appropriate to end this chapter by highlighting the fact that because the States is playing a dominant role as the driver of ICT agenda in Malaysia, it remains that an effective way for it to exert influence (and in some instances interfere with the affairs of the business) is through the use of regulatory mechanisms. Although there were many initiatives to capitalize on ICT, namely, policy and regulatory, none seemed to have the adequate credential to match Mahathir's passion on ICT. If the State is serious to contest its somewhat lack cluster commitment of post-Mahathir era, state has to roll back as a driver of ICT and to act more as enabler and facilitator in this critical sector. This, certainly, will be a challenge for the newly rebranded Ministry of Communication and Multimedia, which was just established. Interestingly, in retrospective, several policy and structural measures have been undertaken since the end of the year 2000, whereby their governance system was revamped to reflect drive towards efficiency, transparency and self-regulation. Prime Minister Najib's latest initiative on Government Transformation Programme (GTP) as well as Economic Transformation Programme (ETP) and the New Economic Model (NEM), reaffirmed the commitment for change (see EPU, 2012). Despite all these, in order to achieve the goal of innovation policies and sustain the country's economic performance, addressing the MSC's current and future demand for growth will continue to be critical. MSC initiative should be built on a shared strategic vision with strong commitment of all relevant actors, bearing a caveat that the continued State-led neo-liberal percepts that this sector has to endure.

REFERENCES

Ahmad, N. B. (2008). *Towards a new mode of governance in Malaysia: Policy, regulatory and institutional challenges of digital convergence.* (PhD Thesis Unpublished). University of Hull.

Anon. (2004). Second phase of MSC to increase income of Malaysian. *BERNAMA.* Retrieved August 8, 2004 from http://www.magazine.jaring.my/

Calista, D. J., & Melitski, J. (2007). E-government and e-governance: Converging constructs of public sector information and communications technologies. *Public Administration Quarterly*, 87–120.

Castells, M. (1996). *The rise of the network society.* Cambridge, MA: Blackwell Publishers.

Castells, M., & Cardoso, G. (Eds.). (2006). The network society: From knowledge to policy. Center for Transatlantic Relations, Paul H. Nitze School of Advanced International Studies, Johns Hopkins University.

Coleman, W. D., & Perl, A. (1999). Internationalized policy environments and policy network analysis. *Political Studies*, *47*(4), 691–709. doi:10.1111/1467-9248.00225

Dai, X. (2003). A new mode of governance: Transnationalisation of European regions and cities in the information age. *Telematics and Informatics*, *20*(3), 193–213. doi:10.1016/S0736-5853(03)00014-5

Dawes, S. S. (2009). Governance in the digital age: A research and action framework for an uncertain future. *Government Information Quarterly*, *26*(2), 257–264. doi:10.1016/j.giq.2008.12.003

Diamond, L. (2008). *How People View Democracy.* Baltimore, MD: Johns Hopkins University Press.

Economic Planning Unit (EPU). (2012, February 25). *RMKE.* Retrieved from http://www.epu.gov.my/html/themes/epu/html/RMKE

Haslinda, S. A. N., Azizah, A. R., & Othman, I. (2011, November). Government's ICT project failure factors: A revisit. In *Proceedings of Research and Innovation in Information Systems (ICRIIS 2011)*, (pp. 1-6). IEEE.

Hobson, K. (2010). Beyond the Control Society. *Administrative Theory & Praxis*, *32*(2), 252–261. doi:10.2753/ATP1084-1806320207

John, P., & Cole, A. (2000). Policy networks and local political leadership in Britain and France. In G. Stoker (Ed.), The new politics of British local governance. Palgrave Macmillan.

Katsikas, D. (2010). Non-state authority and global governance. *Review of International Studies*, *36*(S1), 113–135. doi:10.1017/S0260210510000793

Meissonier, R., & Houzé, E. (2010). Toward an 'IT conflict-resistance theory': Action research during IT pre-implementation. *European Journal of Information Systems*, *19*(5), 540–561. doi:10.1057/ejis.2010.35

Nasim, A., & Sushil, S. (2010). Managing continuity and change: A new approach for strategizing in e-government. *Transforming Government: People. Process and Policy*, *4*(4), 338–364.

Norris, P. (2005). The impact of the Internet on political activism: Evidence from Europe. *International Journal of Electronic Government Research*, *1*(1), 19–39. doi:10.4018/jegr.2005010102

Rhodes, R. A. W. (1997). *Understanding governance: Policy networks, reflexivity and accountability.* Buckingham, UK: Open University Press.

Shahin, J. (2003). *Developing a European polity: The case for governance on the Internet at the European level.* MERIT – Maastricht Economic Research Institute on Innovation and Technology.

Sorenson, E. (2002). Democratic theory and network governance. *Administrative Theory and Praxis*, *24*(4), 693–720.

UN Division for Public Economics and Public Administration-ASPA, (2002). *Benchmarking eGovernment of global perspectives - Assessing the progress of the UN members states.* Author.

Xue, S. (2005). Internet policy and diffusion in China, Malaysia and Singapore. *Journal of Information Science, 31*(3), 238–250. doi:10.1177/0165551505052472

Yoon, J., & Chae, M. (2009). Varying criticality of key success factors of national e-Strategy along the status of economic development of nations. *Government Information Quarterly, 26*(1), 25–34. doi:10.1016/j.giq.2008.08.006

KEY TERMS AND DEFINITIONS

Borderless World: The global connections in the age of the Internet where all the previous barriers to international trade have been removed.

Connectivity: Internet access connecting individual computer terminals, computers, mobile devices, and computer networks together to enhance service delivery.

Delivery System: Any means or technology for administering and providing services to the public.

Digital Divide: The gap or the gulf between those who have access to computers, the Internet and those who do not.

Innovation Policy: Creation of new values, plans, and fresh thinking that encourages better services through advancement in technology.

Institutional Force: Government bodies or agencies including private industrial associations and other social actors that can influence decision-making as well as creating valuable resources.

Issues in ICT: Contending matters in ICT governance model of operations, digital divide, and institutional bodies set for convergence or consolidation.

New Economic Model: A framework that spelled out how the government will bring the country out of its middle-income status and push it into the realm of high-income economy nations in the age of advance technology as enabling tool.

Progress: A development or movement towards an improved or more advanced condition with a goal to attain higher stage.

Technocrat: Government civil servants who make decisions for a governing office based on their technical expertise and background.

Transformation (Malaysia): Change that orients government agencies in a new direction and takes it to a knowledge-base as well as better society with well equipped infrastructural technology.

ENDNOTES

[1]   With these values firmly anchored, it is the phraseology "democratic steering" with no "traditional government" at the European level which reveals many scholars' allegiance to the European model of ICT governance (see for instance, Shahin, 2002; Dai, 2003).

[2]   Especially since the 1980s, Government brought in the expertise from the industry and academic world to provide a fresh perspective of national strategy for growth. Almost half previous members of NITC for instance are not bureaucrats. The move coincides with a dramatic increase in the number of public agencies progressively being assigned to special agencies organised like corporate entity, even the MCMC itself.

[3]   Policymakers hold the view that the multiplier effect for this will generate far outweigh the initial capital costs while enhancing the process of policy process.

[4]   These are illustrated by NII documents from countries such as the US's Global Informa-

tion Infrastructure: Agenda for Cooperation as well as from international bodies such as the European Commission's Bangemann Report which leads to the Conclusion of G-7 Summit 'Information Society Conference.'

5 According to the former NITC Secretariat member, the previous NITC has over 30 officials especially dedicated to do the job, within the Policy Division of MIMOS, compared to very few when it is transferred to MoSTI in 2003.

Chapter 15
Conclusion and Recommendation for Future Enhancement of ICT Adoption in Public Sector

ABSTRACT

This chapter is devoted to recap the key findings in each chapter of the book. It also reflects on the findings with their relevance to technology adoptions and related human factors that could jeopardize the objectives of ICT utilization in the public sector. In addition, the chapter highlights some pertinent issues in adoption and using of ICT to carry out obligatory works ranging from service deliveries to meeting other non-service demands by the public mass at large. Therefore, this chapter touches on different aspects of what has been pointed out in each chapter of the book and lastly provides some crucial suggestions and recommendations that can be used for enhancement of ICT adoption and implementation in the public sector.

FINDINGS ON BACKGROUND SETTING FOR ADOPTION OF ICT IN MALAYSIA

One of the main objectives of the Malaysian government is to expedite the process by which the public organizations in the country work in order to meet the growing demands, needs and expectations of the people in the age of technology advancement. In this context the government of Malaysia sought the need to adopt technology for effective reform of how its bureaucratic machinery operates in all sphere of services delivery. In lieu of such thoughts for change in service delivery in public sector of Malaysia, the government welcomes the idea of capitalizing on the advantage and opportunities in the information communication technology (ICT) to accomplish works. To adopt technology and utilize it effectively for delivery of services, the government has launched Multimedia Supper Corridor (MSC) in 1996 in order to accelerate the country into ICT applications for enhancement of public services. According to the findings of this

DOI: 10.4018/978-1-4666-6579-8.ch015

book, there were some initiatives and attempts before the launch of MSC to meet the public consumptions and to set lay a solid ground for ICT adoption and utilization in public organizations' sphere. These include various services that were introduced such as MAYPAC (Malaysian Packet Switched Network) and MAYCIS (Malaysian Circuit Switched Network), Data Transmission on the Switched Telephone Network (DATEL) which was oriented towards global access at greater speeds of data transmission capability. To exploit the most of information revolution in the Malaysian public sector, Malaysia's own MEASAT-1 (Malaysia East Asia Satellite) launched in January 1996 further marked an exciting journey which supplemented the already improved infrastructure such as a fibre optic cable network nation-wide, optical fibre cables (including laid under the sea bed connecting Sarawak and Sabah), the introduction of the Integrated Services Digital Network (ISDN), the Asynchronous Transfer Mode (ATM), microwave, satellite and other key technologies. The establishment of the National Information Technology Council (NITC) chaired by the former Prime Minister (Dr Mahathir Muhammad) further underscores the importance of the entire IT industry in overall national development and government intent in guiding future directions of delivering public services in the country. NITC, despite has been shrunken in size as well as solely represented by the key bureaucrats (as opposed to its diversified members in its early formation), functions as a think tank and advises government on IT development for efficient public work outputs in the country.

To date, some current policy initiatives eventually emerged include MyICMS886, National Broadband Plan, Critical National Information Infrastructure (CNII), National Cyber-Security Policy (NCSP) to achieve the underpinning objectives of changing the traditional mode of operation in public sector organizations in the country. A number of grass root initiatives were spawned and listed in the NITC's website such as Digital

Malaysia, New Economic Model, MSC Malaysia, MSC Flagship Applications, MSC's Cybercities, MyGovernment Portal, eKuala Lumpur, My Domain Registry, Malaysian Communiaction and Multimedia Commission, Communication Content Infrastructure, Creative Industry, Lifelong Learning Programme, e-Government, and e-Learning system in some higher institutions in the country.

E-government in particular has contributed a lot to the improvement of governmental efficiency and effectiveness in service provision through resilience use of ICT by numerous government agencies and public service organizations. One thing is to adopt ICT devices in public sector; however, it is another thing to utilize them by the bureaucratic bodies and government machineries.

Having shed lights on the background of ICT adoption and utilization in the Malaysian public sector, the overall perspectives of the book can be broadly summarized in three-fold. First, the book examines the governance of adopting ICT in the Malaysian public sector as well as the key players the spearhead its implementation with special references to issues of divergence and convergence. Second, it examines the theoretical framework and/or model that can help explain the impact of the ICT on the people and reactions to new change or mode of working using technology in public sector at large. Third, the book empirically evaluates the extent to which Malaysian civil servants are capable of embracing the opportunity brought by ICT digital revolution and the challenges associated with these new ICTs in light of human factors and reactions to technology. More specifically, the objectives and coverage of the book can be summarised as follows:

- It utilises related models of policy networks as well as the ICT adoption models in analyses of the formation as encapsulated by the overall Malaysian initiatives of ICT and digital convergence;

- It applies and extends all the theoretical frameworks in the context of Malaysian public services' ICT policy adoptions;

- It comprehends the Malaysian ICT agenda in the context of the application and practice of ICT in the country by explaining how such features affect the search of a new mode of ICT governance models;

- It examines the extent to which the policies being adopted are practiced and influenced by the multiple network actors process and how such process is related to digital convergence;

- It identifies and builds a framework explaining the determinants of ICT adoption in Malaysia and empirically evaluates the extent to which values are transpired in the actual practices;

- It evaluates some generic issues pertaining to ICT and challenges from technology and human sides;

- It suggests general policy recommendations that might lead to the improvement in the strategic thinking towards harnessing the potential of ICTs for Malaysia in the digital age for achieving better service delivery and best ICT governance model of combining the roles of ICT players together.

FINDINGS ON SECTION 1: ADOPTION, GOVERNANCE, AND IMPLEMENTATION OF ICT

The successful implementation of ICT agenda and effective governance model is contingent upon many factors. The true value of the digital convergence scheme is viewed not only in the potential the technology offers but equally important also the enabling environments where the technology is operating. In the context of ICT and convergence policy model of adoption, what the country has now are sets of building blocks that do not fit

together very well- if at all, i.e., infrastructure and service competitions. Critiques argue about incongruence between broad policies and implementation on the ground. Furthermore in practice, delivering good ICT governance model has not been easy for public administrators in the country's typical hierarchical and pluralistic society such as Malaysia in that political decision-making has always the need to be sensitive to preserve peace and stability among the multi-players. The challenge for effective ICT governance model in Malaysia therefore is to primarily manage this global age transition whilst reconciling it with such a complex account of the local socio-political reality.

As the findings reflect, it is debatable to say that dilemma of ICT governance models in the era of digital convergence is an obvious issue altogether in the country. The Malaysian Government has become aware of this challenge. The earliest bold effort towards convergence of the telecommunications and broadcasting industries was indeed marked by the enactment of the CMA 1998 which have paved ways for more substantive initiatives thereafter; slowly but significantly emerged itself out of the old regime (i.e., traditional model and laws). This new regime (convergence model) raises the major issue of how the NITC, together with the Ministry of Energy, Water and Communication (MEWC) and the Malaysian Communications and Multimedia Commission (MCMC), as the central ICT policy making body, authority and regulator, should be able to address the new challenges of the ICT adoption to achieve best practices. The change, however, was overshadowed by tremendous regulatory complications as the general framework is still embodied by separate laws which mostly caused the dilemmas between the cyber laws and the traditional laws.

As found in the book, expert in cyber laws argues that there is a challenge the government faced in terms of how to reconcile between the old and the new legislations governing ICT adoption in the Malaysian public sector. Thus the government's awareness of the need to create a new environment for ICT policy process in furtherance to the people-centered agenda of NITA has been reflected by the establishment of a NRR through self-regulatory and voluntary compliance. Of paramount importance is the recreation of the Ministry of Energy, Communication and Multimedia (MECM) to become Ministry of Energy, Water and Communication (MEWC) – now Ministry of Communication and Multimedia Malaysia (MCMM), from previously Ministry of Energy, Telecommunications and Post (METP) as well as the Malaysian Communication and Multimedia Commission (MCMC) is also assigned with the mission of developing and recommending convergence policies to cope with new challenges.

The challenge that arose at the initial stage includes the creation of the NITA's model of ICT governance model based on people. The National IT Framework which subsequently emerged is considered the most instrumental outcome in the ICT governance model development in modern Malaysia history. As we have discussed earlier, the contemporary Malaysian ICT policy framework is expected to fulfill with the spirits of NITA and to make sure its provision are reflected in the convergence policies and procedures, particularly those relevant to ensure the growth of the public sector in meeting the people's expectations from the government. However, the extent of consistency between the current practice and the demands of the new mode of ICT governance model as required by NITA is highly political and requires a close examination.

The findings of the book have also shown that in Malaysia, typical of any modern state, the policy process is constantly being challenged with the unprecedented change in digital technology, compared with much lesser pressure for growth in the early stage of ICT development. One direct result of this pressure for development was that bureaucracy or policy makers were seldom caught off guard and driven by the technological changes without sufficient account of guarantees on what could be the possible outcomes of ICT

adoption. Often the case, the Government would put some breaks when they finally realised that some of decisions were too much politically risk to pursue. For example, during the early years of ICT development and adoption, there was a state of clumsiness in the way the policy and project implementation being organised, particularly by the NITC. To some extent, the failure of some projects (e.g., Smart School, PC Ownership Campaign) were awarded to some individuals/ contractors and they were through their link with political leaders rather than based on their qualities. Favouritism was the direct result of the too much power centralisation at the hand of political masters without formalised or transparent procedures. In Malaysia, as reported in earlier section of the book, the Ministers commonly enjoy greater power by the law and the law itself has many provisional exemptions in the hand of the Minister related to ICT adoption by both ministries and agencies.

The widening of political participation in the past was far less ideal than what it is today, though this is subjected to more debates with special references to ICT adoption in public sector. The nature of digital technology propels new kind of relationship since cyber-spacer is no respecter of any boundaries, and if anything, this is even greater with the `killer applications' afforded by digitalisation. Government may see this as a threat; however, with the impending march towards 'globalisation and the convergence among key ICT players.' Hence, there is always a constant pressure for the Government to secure the principles of effective ICT governance model to ensure that the system works for all regardless of political affiliations, class of status and ethnic belongings. To be sure, digital convergence model has put pressure on Government to explore the most effective mechanism to encourage even more proactive roles of the private sector in overcoming the digital divide issue, particularly the basic connectivity - which was the Government's core business of the past in Malaysian context of ICT adoption in public sector.

Further, as the CMA1998 emerged, the obligation to enhance the value of new mode of ICT governance model is getting ever more prevalent and increasingly formidable. Unlike NITA which has no legal credentials, the CMA1998, by virtue of its existence, demands the review of administrative structures, policies and regulations which should be in conformity with the new mode of governance in ICT system of the country. Hence, combining NITA and CMA together, not only are the Malaysian Government and its political institutions obliged to rule according to the requirements of the model, but the policy framework, regulatory structures, and institutional settings should be in conformity with this two overarching perspectives as well.

Meantime, despite an exponential impact of technology and the Internet, there is very little field investigation to provide evidence on the determinants as well as implications of policy networks and its constituents particularly in the case of Malaysia. Initially, there was a paucity of empirical reports devoted to categorising the influences of the "e" agenda development upon public administration and its services. As of current situation, much more research has been conducted mainly on eGovernment and eCommerce aspect, which falls short of concrete theoretical exposition particularly on the basis of detailed studies of digital convergence. While ad hoc actions have been initiated to adapt public administration with the values of network governance model in correspondence with the eGovernment agenda, there seems to have been patchy effort directed at synthesising views of the implications for digital convergence or developing strategies for dealing with its implications in the country. Almost certainly, this occurred against the midst of the call for better governance between the supporters of pro-governance development of ICT implementation strategies and skeptic views on whether the NRR in Malaysia will `work' to bring about the new image of government in the era of cyberspace.

The chapter on policy network model does not only addressed the rise of the policy network perspectives but also showed that the precipitation of network issues in ICT adoption envisage innovation and participation of the key players in several parts of the world, particularly in Malaysia. The multifaceted character of policy network holds significant implications for network model of ICT governance in Malaysia. Policy network aimed at, either creating or stimulating political dynamics embedded in the political-cultural system. According to the findings, the development from a traditional representation to electoral accountability and epistemological perspective of network governance parallels with the development of the field of democratic theory and practice in ICT adoption by the public agencies. The findings in the chapter also showed that when dealing with purpose of developing and implementing public policy in general, it eventually gives rise to the issue of how to achieve democratic legitimacy in digital age for full participations of all citizens. When striving for interactions that exhibit a network dynamic characterised by knowledge sharing and innovation, Malaysian policymakers need to realise the potential danger of governing network based on formal economic factors only. Rather, it must be within the "constellations of interdependent but autonomous actors from public, private, and societal sectors that come together for the purposes of developing and implementing public policy" related to ICT adoption (Kickert, et. al. 1997; Kooiman, 1993). It should also involve at the very least understanding the rich network dynamics to which the concept of liberal democracy is subjected to. Policy designed at influencing formal conventional representation, such as principal-agent model on ICT adoption in public sector needs to take into account the lessons learned from the field of digital convergence today, and thus should be aimed at respecting the policy dynamics unique to every cluster of society. A solid understanding of the policy dynamics is critical in the context of how it influences and challenges conventional notions of representative democracy via network system especially in Malaysia. Thus, according to the findings, the emergence and development of digital convergence will enrich governance model beyond the technological factors only. Thus, it is important to suggest that the digital convergence that is believed to influence policy network and growth of ICT adoption in public sector do not occur in a vacuum but with political representations from key actors in society both official and none-officials as discussed in the book. This can be better understood in political representation model of ICT adoption.

The findings from chapter on political representation have provided a number of important insights into the factors behind online political representation with respect to ICT adoption perspective in the public sector. In particular, we find that the online political representation should not be understood in a limited nature of political process such as electoral or referendum purposes but must be viewed from the perspective of "outcome" based on ICT adoption. For example, getting the "right" information into the space of discussions, promoting the Internet communication as the innovative conduit for quality participation towards a solid democracy will need a balance online representation from all official and non-official ICT players. Online political representation depicts environments with significantly distinctive characteristics, which may prove relevant to enhance eDemocracy. For example, by focusing on "governance" issues in ICT adoption inclusion moves to centre stage, and democratic legitimacy becomes a matter of whether those potentially affected by a decision have had the right and opportunity to participate in and influence policy deliberations in ICT adoption (Benhabib 1996; Dryzek, 2001). To date, findings explicitly related to online participation dynamics remain limited and are mostly skewed towards certain political representatives and actors not only in Malaysia but elsewhere in the world. In this context, the chapter reflects a two-stage approach; first, it highlighted

an overall conceptual framework of political representation models that could be applied to ICT adoption in public sector. Second, it also integrated our theoretical framework with our quantitative findings based on the evidences that we found in the context of Malaysia's parliamentarians in our empirical chapter. This has helped us expand our theoretical understanding of political representation beyond specific scope of activities such as eVoting or eReferendum, but the overall impact on eDemocracy of reaching electorates directly by member of parliaments (MPs).

Overall, the chapter on network society model has revealed a number of findings related to the successful promotion of ICT and digital convergence, and most crucially, the new mode of governance in the digital age, which are affected by some specific factors, with varying degrees of influence. As contended by Castells (2005), "we are in the network society, although not everything or everybody is included in its networks" (p.16). According to the findings of the chapter, digital convergence has been instrumental in bringing some notable changes, and/or achievements in numbers of areas such as policy orientation, market flexibility, industry initiatives, as well as the general attitudes and responses of the public or consumers at large and could eventually facilitate the formation of a networked society through ICT adoption. Whilst acknowledging this, the findings showed that multifaceted yet intrinsically related factors were established as the major conceptual frameworks to help analyse the process of digital convergence in the Malaysia ICT agenda and adoption. In the chapter, the linkages of all these factors are critically examined in the conceptual framework which may prove relevant in explaining network theory or model of ICT governance. As found in the chapter it is recommended to bear in mind that the choice of ICT strategies, regulatory reforms and institutional designs corresponding to the networked society should not be treated exclusively. On the contrary, other factors, such as market forces to consumer choice in the era of

ICT adoption, national and global environment, etc., are all relevant to the success or failure of a new mode of ICT governance model in public sector in the context of digital technological change and the progress, especially in the Malaysian ICT adoption.

FINDINGS ON SECTION 2: THEORETICAL EXPLANATION OF PEOPLE'S REACTIONS TO ICT

The findings in Chapter 6 of the book on the Theory of Reasoned Action (TRA) have shown some generic issues related to human side of adopting technology system for accomplishing designated works in public sector. These include according to theoretical underpinning of this framework: the attitude, subjective norms and intention are the key elements to utilize the adopted technology system for providing services to the public. It shows that sole intention to use the technology is a function of both attitude and subjective norms or influence of colleagues in the organizational environment. Actual and effective use of such technology may not take place as expected if there is no strong intention and that strong intention can only happen when the bureaucrats develop a positive attitude towards its utilization for accomplishing tasks. However, the chapter highlighted some limitation of TRA, especially on the issues of its applicability to non-volitional behaviours or acts. Basically, the findings show that the theory can only help explain human choice to perform or not to perform volitional behaviours or acts. When it comes to obligatory acts such as in government works and organizations, the use of ICT that has been ratified for performing tasks in a more efficient and effective manner is obligatory on the civil servants. Therefore, according to the findings of the chapter, partially TRA may not be able to explain fully the underpinning reasons behind embracing and utilizing the adopted ICT to do works. Thus,

comparatively, the book further explore alternative theory of planned behaviour (TPB)

As found in the Chapter 7 of the book, the Theory of Planned Behaviour (TPB) was mainly developed to improve the predictive power of the earlier Theory of Reasoned Action (TRA). According to the findings of the book, the main message of TPB is the introduction of perceived behavioural control (PBC) which very is considered critical aspect of technology acceptance among public workers. The chapter highlights that since PBC is the degree of difficulties in performing behaviour (i.e., response perceptual reaction to adopting ICT) would interactively predict a behaviour whereby intentions would become stronger predictors of behaviour as PBC increased favourably. However, the discussions in the chapter have shown some arguments where PBC is assumed to unilaterally influence a particular behaviour, especially in the context of people's reaction towards ICT utilization within the presence of favourable conditions organization settings. However, according the chapter's findings, many other researchers have also called for extension and expansion of TPB with additional variables to further improve its predictive power on behaviour. This is pertinent argument because different research settings and culture will need some specific constructs of interest that match the contingent situation.

The findings of the subsequence chapters are related to technology acceptance model (TAM) of ICT adoption in the public sector. TAM as a theoretical model is rooted in TRA and TPB discussed in Chapters 6 and 7 of the book. TAM and its derivatives has been discussed relatively and comparatively to TRA and TPB in the book. The main significant findings are central to eliciting salient beliefs about about a person's attitude relevant to a particular behaviour being studied. In line with this suggestion, Davis' (1986) proposed two constructs, perceived usefulness (PU) and perceived ease of use (PEOU) in relations to beliefs in information technology (IT) usage as the fundamental root of TAM foundation. Thus, TAM has largely simplified TRA to be more effective for studying IT adoption and acceptance issues across different research settings and different cultural orientations. The argumentative aspect as found and/or understood in the chapter is the underlying assumptions of TAM that the actual use of the computer system or ICT in particular is largely determined by a user's behavioural intention to use it and can be affected by benefits derived from it. In addition, the findings have shown that such discretionary choice of a user is directly proportional to users' behavioural intention. However, the intention is also determined by attitude toward using ICT as well as how useful a user perceives the ICT (i.e., perceived usefulness). Furthermore, TAM assumed that some external variables affect perceived usefulness and perceived ease of use, which also mediate the effect of external variables on attitude toward using ICT. Overall, the hallmark of TAM is that technology of any kind has to be useful in the eyes of people to convince their mind (intention) positively. However, the model denotes that technology being useful may not be enough to convince users to optimum level of acceptance. In fact, the usefulness of a technology device can even be sabotaged if it is perceived to be complicated. Therefore, the theory included the ease or non-complication of technology itself. In other words, users must be able to use technology with ease or that they must perceive a technology of being simplistic in its compositions and configurations. The implication here for both policy makers and technology designers is a known fact that the end users of technology have the aim to use certain technology in order to improve their performance at work as captured by the perceived ease of use and usefulness in the structural model. Hence, it is worthy to note that as the utility aspect of technology is important in terms of outcomes of using a technology to accomplish one's tasks, yet the ease of using it in terms of perceived facility is equally crucial for the end users. Therefore, in the context of public sector adoption and acceptance of ICT, it means

effect of some external variables, such as the features of the technology systems, its development process and even training are crucial to be addressed for making the technology usage easy for people. However, TAM structural components do not specify these external variables that can have effects on both perceived ease of use and usefulness and intention to use ICT. Perhaps, this is what has led to reconfigurations and expansions of the original TAM as a theoretical model for befitting different ICT adoption and acceptance investigations in relation to a growing changing in technology environments and applications in public sector. These deficiencies, according to the book's findings have been comparatively taken care of by both TAM2 and TAM3 of the book. For example, TAM3 theoretically assumed that there are more pressing issues from organisational perspective regarding technology acceptance and adoption with special reference to individual differences, system characteristics, social influence and facilitating conditions as the determinants of both perceived usefulness and perceived ease of use. The fundamental variables of TAM3 had relied on anchoring and adjustment in human decision process which believes that users of technology will form early perceptions of ease of use in relations to general individual beliefs about the technology of their interests and its usages in public sector. According to our findings, the early perceptions are usually adjusted after some hands-on experiences being gained during the users' engagement with a particular technology system. In this context, four anchoring elements are identified in the model to be associated with perceived ease of use (PEU) compared to the TAM1. Three variables of the anchoring frame such as computer self-efficacy, computer anxiety and computer playfulness integrated in the model were meant to capture individual differences with respect to ease of using technology for accomplishing one's work in organisational settings. The last variable- perception of external control of the anchoring frame in the model is used to focus on facilitating condition of technology usage. As posited in the model, For example, if a user sees him or her-self as a competent computer literate, the tendency of increasing the usability becomes high and if users see him or herself otherwise, the tendency of using it becomes less. In the public sector, this is an important integrated component in the model as it helps to understand how computer self-efficacy can trigger performance and reducing computer anxiety among users. In other words, the finding shows that high level of computer self-efficacy can lead into increase in task's performance and greater achievement of staff in public organisations.

FINDINGS ON SECTION 3: EMPIRICAL IMPACT OF HUMAN REACTION TO ICT ADOPTION

The chapters in this section of the book have highlighted a number of crucial findings pertinent to adopting and using ICT to accomplish tasks in public sector. This is in line with applications of the theoretical frameworks of Section 2. First and foremost, chapters in this Section 3 of the book have empirically extended and modified the theories where necessary to fit the fundamental and cultural orientation of ICT adoption in Malaysian public sector. The findings of each chapter for this section are summarized as follows:

Based on the call for extension of theories and models in the Section 2 of this book, the original theory of reasoned action (TRA) has been extended to fit the context of ICT usage in one of the chosen public organisations as a case study. A preliminary focus group interview was used to underpin and identify the most pertinent issues related to usage of ICT in that particular public organization. Based on the result, prior experience was introduced into the original theoretical framework of TRA as antecedent of attitude towards use of ICT in that public organization. As a new variable of interest added to extend the TRA, the causal link

between prior experience and attitude was found to be statistically and positively significant at an alpha level lower than universal acceptable value of 0.05. Additionally, the TRA was also extended to find the nature of causal link between subjective norm and attitude itself and the finding of the chapter has shown a positive relationship between them. According to such findings of this chapter, the practical significant contribution to the public sector is that adoption of ICT is one thing but technical know-how and/or the experience of how to use ICT successfully to accomplish the goal of adoption is the most important. In other words, experience of how to use ICT and the presence of important individuals such as colleagues to give motivation and positive impression would make a user form positive attitude towards using ICT to do work. The implication of such findings for policy-makers in this context is to provide adequate training for users of adopted ICT to make it more meaningful to them in addition to creation of positive environment as well as encouragement from colleagues or leaders. The support from those around users such as immediate boss or senior with certain knowledge of ICT is equally important as this can encourage or discourage their intention to use the system. Finally, it can be concluded that the users' mindsets and/or intentions must be positively convinced in relations to experience of the technology and training on how it can be used so that they can form a positive attitude towards the technology system. This would make them have positive belief about ICT system as opposed to their usual manual way of carrying out transaction previously. The findings showed that creating a technology may otherwise become useless or neglected by the users if they cannot form positive attitude towards it nor have positive intention to use the system effectively.

The empirical chapter on the theory of planned behaviour was extended using a problem based approach of perceived usefulness of ICT among the subjects of the study at one of the government agencies in Malaysia. The information obtained through a preliminary interview regarding what normally being the reason for people's reluctant of using a technology system. According to the findings, most of the respondents unanimously expressed their concerns on the issue of whether technology can really help achieve one's goal of using it or not at first contact. According to the result of the interview on the question regarding what makes him or her accept the use of technology to perform tasks, most of the respondents' answers are basically on usefulness of it when they use it as well as what they heard from their close friends who had used it. Thus, the study has extended the original TPB model by inclusion of perceived usefulness as antecedent of attitude of the respondents in this chapter. Statistically, the result obtained has reflected the relative importance of the new construct introduced to the original model. In this context, perceived usefulness was found to have highest structural correlation with behavioural attitude. In terms of practical significant of this finding, it formally confirmed the call to modify theory of planned behaviour, which was earlier discussed in this book. In addition, it can be established that perceived usefulness of technology can make users form a positive attitude towards intention to use the system. This finding also indicates that perceived usefulness would strengthen the positive attitude towards use of ICT or can help change negative perception of a user to positively use technology system. In addition, the other findings of the study have also proven that subjective norm, perceived behavioural control and behavioural attitude towards use of technologies are good predictors of intention to use ICT and actual use to perform tasks among civil servants. Thus, the practical significant of such findings to both policy-makers and industries is that technologies must be made useful in achieving the purpose of adopting them in organisations.

The chapter on technology acceptance model (TAM) was also extended following a problem-based approach through the results of the interview.

The most important additional contribution of the chapter was the focus on the external variables to perceived usefulness and perceived ease of using i-class. Universiti Teknologi MARA (UiTM) has adopted e-learning using i-class system through which teaching and learning are facilitated as alternative method of delivering knowledge to students face-to-face. However, according to the findings, the rate at which the targeted students are using the system was very poor. Only a minimal number (17%) per whole week devoted their time to access i-class system for their studies among the students. In this context, it seems that the rate of acceptance of the system by the students is very poor. Thus, the main issue addressed was focused on poor participation, poor usage and interactions among students and lecturers through i-class. These led to failure to contribute to discussion online and/or not even use the system to submit assignments as required. Since majority of targeted group of students learning through this mode are adults, thus, perceived computer self-efficacy, perceived convenience and subjective norm were confirmed during the interview section and used to extend the original model. The empirical results obtained have shown significant relationships between the causal links of the new constructs to perceived usefulness, ease of use as well as attitude, intention, and the actual use of the i-class system by the students.

The findings show that ease of using the i-class is relatively different from one student to another and it depends on individual level of technology savvy, how convenient the i-class is; in terms of access to the system anywhere, any place and at any time of the day. This is very important because geographical location of each student would affect their access to the system. This relative difference is obvious between students living in remote areas compared to those at the urban areas. In addition, perceived computer self-efficacy and perceived convenience have positively influenced students' perceived usefulness of the i-class system based on the students' perceptions. The same significant impact of perceived convenience was statistically confirmed on perceived ease of using the i-class. In fact, the findings of the chapter also reflected the important effect of subjective norm through words of mouth on ease of using the system. Other important constructs discussed in the chapter include the issue relating to attitude, which according to the result has a profound significant effect on intention to use the i-class. The practical implications from this findings implies that adopting a technology in a public sector does not indicate automatic usage of it, especially in teaching and learning institution of public institutions. Students' mindsets and intentions must be positively convinced in relations to the usefulness of such technology, ease of using it as well as the various antecedences discussed as reflected in the findings obtained in the chapter. Still on the extension on the extension of TAM, additional variables of interests such as self-efficacy as part of individual factors, word of mouth as part of social factors, system factor and trust were used to extend the original TAM. In this chapter, it was found that system factor, self-efficacy in individual factors, word of mouth in social factor had played important roles in the use of ICT devices by the Malaysian Parliaments members (MPs). The result shows that self-efficacy of the individual MPs has negative relation with e-communication of MPs with electorates until it was moderated with a construct called trust. The same goes to system factor. The findings indicate that provision of e-parliament system is not enough until MPs are really trained for appropriate use of ICT otherwise, they might be reluctant to use the system due to lack of skills and capability on how to successfully use it. In addition, there is a need to gain people's trust towards ICT in terms of perceived usefulness, ease of using it to achieve their goals. It is also pertinent to note that word of mouth about ICT carries high weightage than subjective norms based on the findings of this chapter. In the findings of this chapter, it has been noted that what people say about any

given technology systems (i.e., word of mouth or reputation) is more important than what one thinks people around him or her would likely want the person to do (i.e., subjective norm) especially with regard to using of ICT in the public sector for discharging designated works.

This chapter on the Unified Theory of Acceptance and Use of Technology (UTAUT) sought the importance of extending and modifying the original model based on the underlying preliminary investigation about the issues of gender difference in ICT adoption and behavioural intention. Using a problem-based approach to set the stage for the study, the result of the focus group interview has reflected a wider perception between males and females respondents regarding utilization of ICT components to accomplish tasks. Thus, the modified-extended model used in this chapter has statistically examined the relationships between predictors such as performance expectancy, effort expectancy, social influence, facilitating condition and behavioural intention to use ICT with moderating effect of gender difference at the organization. In addition, it has also examined the relationship between facilitating condition and actual use behaviour as well as moderating effect of gender difference on each predictor and behavioural intention. The findings confirmed a positive and significant relationship between three predictors and behavioural intention as well as actual use behaviour of ICT device among the staff. However, the finding shows a negative insignificant relation between social influence and behavioural intention. Another interesting finding in the chapter is the significant impact of gender on the various predictors and predicted variable as clearly shown on the ploted graphs. Two particular new findings found were the impact of gender on the causal links between facilitating condition and actual use behaviour which was not included in the original model of UTAUT and also the significant causal relationship between facilitating condition and behavioural intention. The findings have shown a new contribution to the theoretical framework. In a nutshell, the findings have shown the impact of gender difference on behavioural intention to use ICT and the actual use behaviour relative to the various predictors examined in this modified-extended model for the original UTAUT. The lesson and implication for both policy-makers and industries is the importance of facilitating condition to use adopted ICT in public organizations. It must be recognised that male staff can pursue goals even though in a very poor condition compared to females. Thus is recommended that facilities and necessary tools needed to ease the usage of ICT to achieve the immediate and long term objectives in public agencies and/or organisations must be always provided to the users.

REFERENCES

Castells, M. (2005). Global governance and global politics. *Political Science and Politics, 38*(1), 9-16.

Davis, F. D. (1986). *A technology acceptance model for empirically testing new end-user information systems: Theory and results.* (Doctoral Dissertation). MIT Sloan School of Management.

Kickert, W. J., Klijn, E. H., & Koppenjan, J. F. M. (Eds.). (1997). *Managing complex networks: Strategies for the public sector.* Sage.

Kooiman, J. (Ed.). (1993). Modern governance: New government-society interactions. London: Sage.

KEY TERMS AND DEFINITIONS

Cyber Security: Policy measures taken to protect access to all computer-based information and services from unintended or unauthorized people.

Future Policy Direction: The possible directions of policy framework that give indications on possible changes for better achievement of ICT adoption in public sector.

Grass-Root Initiatives: Innovative activists that put emphasis on bottom-up solutions for sustainable development of the low income group.

Implementation: The act of putting into effect the policies designed for achieving the objectives of ICT adoption by the government and its agencies.

Integrated Digital Network: Communication standards that can be used for simultaneous digital transmission of voice, video and data, and other services.

National ICT Development Planning: A deliberate plan of action set out to guide the Government for sustainable ICT infrastructure.

Public Services: Services provided by government either directly or indirectly to people living within its governance and control.

Service Expectation: Level of citizen satisfaction reflects and the experiences that he or she has with a product or service received.

Think Tank: A group of experts providing advice and ideas for resolving technological, socioeconomic, and political problems based on intensive research carried out.

Related References

To continue our tradition of advancing academic research, we have compiled a list of recommended IGI Global readings. These references will provide additional information and guidance to further enrich your knowledge and assist you with your own research and future publications.

Adeyemo, O. (2013). The nationwide health information network: A biometric approach to prevent medical identity theft. In *User-driven healthcare: Concepts, methodologies, tools, and applications* (pp. 1636–1649). Hershey, PA: Medical Information Science Reference; doi:10.4018/978-1-4666-2770-3.ch081

Adler, M., & Henman, P. (2009). Justice beyond the courts: The implications of computerisation for procedural justice in social security. In A. Martínez & P. Abat (Eds.), *E-justice: Using information communication technologies in the court system* (pp. 65–86). Hershey, PA: Information Science Reference; doi:10.4018/978-1-59904-998-4.ch005

Aflalo, E., & Gabay, E. (2013). An information system for coping with student dropout. In L. Tomei (Ed.), *Learning tools and teaching approaches through ICT advancements* (pp. 176–187). Hershey, PA: Information Science Reference; doi:10.4018/978-1-4666-2017-9.ch016

Ahmed, M. A., Janssen, M., & van den Hoven, J. (2012). Value sensitive transfer (VST) of systems among countries: Towards a framework. *International Journal of Electronic Government Research*, 8(1), 26–42. doi:10.4018/jegr.2012010102

Aikins, S. K. (2008). Issues and trends in internet-based citizen participation. In G. Garson & M. Khosrow-Pour (Eds.), *Handbook of research on public information technology* (pp. 31–40). Hershey, PA: Information Science Reference; doi:10.4018/978-1-59904-857-4.ch004

Aikins, S. K. (2009). A comparative study of municipal adoption of internet-based citizen participation. In C. Reddick (Ed.), *Handbook of research on strategies for local e-government adoption and implementation: Comparative studies* (pp. 206–230). Hershey, PA: Information Science Reference; doi:10.4018/978-1-60566-282-4.ch011

Aikins, S. K. (2012). Improving e-government project management: Best practices and critical success factors. In *Digital democracy: Concepts, methodologies, tools, and applications* (pp. 1314–1332). Hershey, PA: Information Science Reference; doi:10.4018/978-1-4666-1740-7.ch065

Akabawi, M. S. (2011). Ghabbour group ERP deployment: Learning from past technology failures. In E. Business Research and Case Center (Ed.), Cases on business and management in the MENA region: New trends and opportunities (pp. 177-203). Hershey, PA: Business Science Reference. doi:10.4018/978-1-60960-583-4.ch012

Akabawi, M. S. (2013). Ghabbour group ERP deployment: Learning from past technology failures. In *Industrial engineering: Concepts, methodologies, tools, and applications* (pp. 933–958). Hershey, PA: Engineering Science Reference; doi:10.4018/978-1-4666-1945-6.ch051

Akbulut, A. Y., & Motwani, J. (2008). Integration and information sharing in e-government. In G. Putnik & M. Cruz-Cunha (Eds.), *Encyclopedia of networked and virtual organizations* (pp. 729–734). Hershey, PA: Information Science Reference; doi:10.4018/978-1-59904-885-7.ch096

Akers, E. J. (2008). Technology diffusion in public administration. In G. Garson & M. Khosrow-Pour (Eds.), *Handbook of research on public information technology* (pp. 339–348). Hershey, PA: Information Science Reference; doi:10.4018/978-1-59904-857-4.ch033

Al-Shafi, S. (2008). Free wireless internet park services: An investigation of technology adoption in Qatar from a citizens' perspective. *Journal of Cases on Information Technology*, *10*(3), 21–34. doi:10.4018/jcit.2008070103

Al-Shafi, S., & Weerakkody, V. (2009). Implementing free wi-fi in public parks: An empirical study in Qatar. *International Journal of Electronic Government Research*, *5*(3), 21–35. doi:10.4018/jegr.2009070102

Aladwani, A. M. (2002). Organizational actions, computer attitudes and end-user satisfaction in public organizations: An empirical study. In C. Snodgrass & E. Szewczak (Eds.), *Human factors in information systems* (pp. 153–168). Hershey, PA: IRM Press; doi:10.4018/978-1-931777-10-0.ch012

Aladwani, A. M. (2002). Organizational actions, computer attitudes, and end-user satisfaction in public organizations: An empirical study. *Journal of Organizational and End User Computing*, *14*(1), 42–49. doi:10.4018/joeuc.2002010104

Allen, B., Juillet, L., Paquet, G., & Roy, J. (2005). E-government and private-public partnerships: Relational challenges and strategic directions. In M. Khosrow-Pour (Ed.), *Practicing e-government: A global perspective* (pp. 364–382). Hershey, PA: Idea Group Publishing; doi:10.4018/978-1-59140-637-2.ch016

Alshawaf, A., & Knalil, O. E. (2008). IS success factors and IS organizational impact: Does ownership type matter in Kuwait? *International Journal of Enterprise Information Systems*, *4*(2), 13–33. doi:10.4018/jeis.2008040102

Ambali, A. R. (2009). Digital divide and its implication on Malaysian e-government: Policy initiatives. In H. Rahman (Ed.), *Social and political implications of data mining: Knowledge management in e-government* (pp. 267–287). Hershey, PA: Information Science Reference; doi:10.4018/978-1-60566-230-5.ch016

Amoretti, F. (2007). Digital international governance. In A. Anttiroiko & M. Malkia (Eds.), *Encyclopedia of digital government* (pp. 365–370). Hershey, PA: Information Science Reference; doi:10.4018/978-1-59140-789-8.ch056

Amoretti, F. (2008). Digital international governance. In A. Anttiroiko (Ed.), *Electronic government: Concepts, methodologies, tools, and applications* (pp. 688–696). Hershey, PA: Information Science Reference; doi:10.4018/978-1-59904-947-2.ch058

Amoretti, F. (2008). E-government at supranational level in the European Union. In A. Anttiroiko (Ed.), *Electronic government: Concepts, methodologies, tools, and applications* (pp. 1047–1055). Hershey, PA: Information Science Reference; doi:10.4018/978-1-59904-947-2.ch079

Amoretti, F. (2008). E-government regimes. In A. Anttiroiko (Ed.), *Electronic government: Concepts, methodologies, tools, and applications* (pp. 3846–3856). Hershey, PA: Information Science Reference; doi:10.4018/978-1-59904-947-2.ch280

Amoretti, F. (2009). Electronic constitution: A Braudelian perspective. In F. Amoretti (Ed.), *Electronic constitution: Social, cultural, and political implications* (pp. 1–19). Hershey, PA: Information Science Reference; doi:10.4018/978-1-60566-254-1.ch001

Amoretti, F., & Musella, F. (2009). Institutional isomorphism and new technologies. In M. Khosrow-Pour (Ed.), *Encyclopedia of information science and technology* (2nd ed., pp. 2066–2071). Hershey, PA: Information Science Reference; doi:10.4018/978-1-60566-026-4.ch325

Andersen, K. V., & Henriksen, H. Z. (2007). E-government research: Capabilities, interaction, orientation, and values. In D. Norris (Ed.), *Current issues and trends in e-government research* (pp. 269–288). Hershey, PA: CyberTech Publishing; doi:10.4018/978-1-59904-283-1.ch013

Anderson, K. V., & Henriksen, H. Z. (2005). The first leg of e-government research: Domains and application areas 1998-2003. *International Journal of Electronic Government Research, 1*(4), 26–44. doi:10.4018/jegr.2005100102

Anttiroiko, A. (2009). Democratic e-governance. In M. Khosrow-Pour (Ed.), *Encyclopedia of information science and technology* (2nd ed., pp. 990–995). Hershey, PA: Information Science Reference; doi:10.4018/978-1-60566-026-4.ch158

Association, I. R. (2010). Networking and telecommunications: Concepts, methodologies, tools and applications (Vols. 1–3). Hershey, PA: IGI Global; doi:10.4018/978-1-60566-986-1

Association, I. R. (2010). Web-based education: Concepts, methodologies, tools and applications (Vols. 1–3). Hershey, PA: IGI Global; doi:10.4018/978-1-61520-963-7

Baker, P. M., Bell, A., & Moon, N. W. (2009). Accessibility issues in municipal wireless networks. In C. Reddick (Ed.), *Handbook of research on strategies for local e-government adoption and implementation: Comparative studies* (pp. 569–588). Hershey, PA: Information Science Reference; doi:10.4018/978-1-60566-282-4.ch030

Becker, S. A., Keimer, R., & Muth, T. (2010). A case on university and community collaboration: The sci-tech entrepreneurial training services (ETS) program. In S. Becker & R. Niebuhr (Eds.), *Cases on technology innovation: Entrepreneurial successes and pitfalls* (pp. 68–90). Hershey, PA: Business Science Reference; doi:10.4018/978-1-61520-609-4.ch003

Becker, S. A., Keimer, R., & Muth, T. (2012). A case on university and community collaboration: The sci-tech entrepreneurial training services (ETS) program. In Regional development: Concepts, methodologies, tools, and applications (pp. 947-969). Hershey, PA: Information Science Reference. doi:10.4018/978-1-4666-0882-5.ch507

Bernardi, R. (2012). Information technology and resistance to public sector reforms: A case study in Kenya. In T. Papadopoulos & P. Kanellis (Eds.), *Public sector reform using information technologies: Transforming policy into practice* (pp. 59–78). Hershey, PA: Information Science Reference; doi:10.4018/978-1-60960-839-2.ch004

Bernardi, R. (2013). Information technology and resistance to public sector reforms: A case study in Kenya. In *User-driven healthcare: Concepts, methodologies, tools, and applications* (pp. 14–33). Hershey, PA: Medical Information Science Reference; doi:10.4018/978-1-4666-2770-3.ch002

Bolívar, M. P., Pérez, M. D., & Hernández, A. M. (2012). Municipal e-government services in emerging economies: The Latin-American and Caribbean experiences. In Y. Chen & P. Chu (Eds.), *Electronic governance and cross-boundary collaboration: Innovations and advancing tools* (pp. 198–226). Hershey, PA: Information Science Reference; doi:10.4018/978-1-60960-753-1.ch011

Borycki, E. M., & Kushniruk, A. W. (2010). Use of clinical simulations to evaluate the impact of health information systems and ubiquitous computing devices upon health professional work. In S. Mohammed & J. Fiaidhi (Eds.), *Ubiquitous health and medical informatics: The ubiquity 2.0 trend and beyond* (pp. 552–573). Hershey, PA: Medical Information Science Reference; doi:10.4018/978-1-61520-777-0.ch026

Borycki, E. M., & Kushniruk, A. W. (2011). Use of clinical simulations to evaluate the impact of health information systems and ubiquitous computing devices upon health professional work. In *Clinical technologies: Concepts, methodologies, tools and applications* (pp. 532–553). Hershey, PA: Medical Information Science Reference; doi:10.4018/978-1-60960-561-2.ch220

Buchan, J. (2011). Developing a dynamic and responsive online learning environment: A case study of a large Australian university. In B. Czerkawski (Ed.), *Free and open source software for e-learning: Issues, successes and challenges* (pp. 92–109). Hershey, PA: Information Science Reference; doi:10.4018/978-1-61520-917-0.ch006

Buenger, A. W. (2008). Digital convergence and cybersecurity policy. In G. Garson & M. Khosrow-Pour (Eds.), *Handbook of research on public information technology* (pp. 395–405). Hershey, PA: Information Science Reference; doi:10.4018/978-1-59904-857-4.ch038

Burn, J. M., & Loch, K. D. (2002). The societal impact of world wide web - Key challenges for the 21st century. In A. Salehnia (Ed.), *Ethical issues of information systems* (pp. 88–106). Hershey, PA: IRM Press; doi:10.4018/978-1-931777-15-5.ch007

Burn, J. M., & Loch, K. D. (2003). The societal impact of the world wide web-Key challenges for the 21st century. In M. Khosrow-Pour (Ed.), *Advanced topics in information resources management* (Vol. 2, pp. 32–51). Hershey, PA: Idea Group Publishing; doi:10.4018/978-1-59140-062-2.ch002

Bwalya, K. J., Du Plessis, T., & Rensleigh, C. (2012). The "quicksilver initiatives" as a framework for e-government strategy design in developing economies. In K. Bwalya & S. Zulu (Eds.), *Handbook of research on e-government in emerging economies: Adoption, e-participation, and legal frameworks* (pp. 605–623). Hershey, PA: Information Science Reference; doi:10.4018/978-1-4666-0324-0.ch031

Cabotaje, C. E., & Alampay, E. A. (2013). Social media and citizen engagement: Two cases from the Philippines. In S. Saeed & C. Reddick (Eds.), *Human-centered system design for electronic governance* (pp. 225–238). Hershey, PA: Information Science Reference; doi:10.4018/978-1-4666-3640-8.ch013

Camillo, A., Di Pietro, L., Di Virgilio, F., & Franco, M. (2013). Work-groups conflict at PetroTech-Italy, S.R.L.: The influence of culture on conflict dynamics. In B. Christiansen, E. Turkina, & N. Williams (Eds.), *Cultural and technological influences on global business* (pp. 272–289). Hershey, PA: Business Science Reference; doi:10.4018/978-1-4666-3966-9.ch015

Capra, E., Francalanci, C., & Marinoni, C. (2008). Soft success factors for m-government. In A. Anttiroiko (Ed.), *Electronic government: Concepts, methodologies, tools, and applications* (pp. 1213–1233). Hershey, PA: Information Science Reference; doi:10.4018/978-1-59904-947-2.ch089

Cartelli, A. (2009). The implementation of practices with ICT as a new teaching-learning paradigm. In A. Cartelli & M. Palma (Eds.), *Encyclopedia of information communication technology* (pp. 413–417). Hershey, PA: Information Science Reference; doi:10.4018/978-1-59904-845-1.ch055

Charalabidis, Y., Lampathaki, F., & Askounis, D. (2010). Investigating the landscape in national interoperability frameworks. *International Journal of E-Services and Mobile Applications*, 2(4), 28–41. doi:10.4018/jesma.2010100103

Charalabidis, Y., Lampathaki, F., & Askounis, D. (2012). Investigating the landscape in national interoperability frameworks. In A. Scupola (Ed.), *Innovative mobile platform developments for electronic services design and delivery* (pp. 218–231). Hershey, PA: Business Science Reference; doi:10.4018/978-1-4666-1568-7.ch013

Chen, I. (2005). Distance education associations. In C. Howard, J. Boettcher, L. Justice, K. Schenk, P. Rogers, & G. Berg (Eds.), *Encyclopedia of distance learning* (pp. 599–612). Hershey, PA: Information Science Reference; doi:10.4018/978-1-59140-555-9.ch087

Chen, I. (2008). Distance education associations. In L. Tomei (Ed.), *Online and distance learning: Concepts, methodologies, tools, and applications* (pp. 562–579). Hershey, PA: Information Science Reference; doi:10.4018/978-1-59904-935-9.ch048

Chen, Y. (2008). Managing IT outsourcing for digital government. In A. Anttiroiko (Ed.), *Electronic government: Concepts, methodologies, tools, and applications* (pp. 3107–3114). Hershey, PA: Information Science Reference; doi:10.4018/978-1-59904-947-2.ch229

Chen, Y., & Dimitrova, D. V. (2006). Electronic government and online engagement: Citizen interaction with government via web portals. *International Journal of Electronic Government Research*, 2(1), 54–76. doi:10.4018/jegr.2006010104

Chen, Y., & Knepper, R. (2005). Digital government development strategies: Lessons for policy makers from a comparative perspective. In W. Huang, K. Siau, & K. Wei (Eds.), *Electronic government strategies and implementation* (pp. 394–420). Hershey, PA: Idea Group Publishing; doi:10.4018/978-1-59140-348-7.ch017

Chen, Y., & Knepper, R. (2008). Digital government development strategies: Lessons for policy makers from a comparative perspective. In H. Rahman (Ed.), *Developing successful ICT strategies: Competitive advantages in a global knowledge-driven society* (pp. 334–356). Hershey, PA: Information Science Reference; doi:10.4018/978-1-59904-654-9.ch017

Cherian, E. J., & Ryan, T. W. (2014). Incongruent needs: Why differences in the iron-triangle of priorities make health information technology adoption and use difficult. In C. El Morr (Ed.), *Research perspectives on the role of informatics in health policy and management* (pp. 209–221). Hershey, PA: Medical Information Science Reference; doi:10.4018/978-1-4666-4321-5.ch012

Cho, H. J., & Hwang, S. (2010). Government 2.0 in Korea: Focusing on e-participation services. In C. Reddick (Ed.), *Politics, democracy and e-government: Participation and service delivery* (pp. 94–114). Hershey, PA: Information Science Reference; doi:10.4018/978-1-61520-933-0. ch006

Chorus, C., & Timmermans, H. (2010). Ubiquitous travel environments and travel control strategies: Prospects and challenges. In M. Wachowicz (Ed.), *Movement-aware applications for sustainable mobility: Technologies and approaches* (pp. 30–51). Hershey, PA: Information Science Reference; doi:10.4018/978-1-61520-769-5.ch003

Chuanshen, R. (2007). E-government construction and China's administrative litigation act. In A. Anttiroiko & M. Malkia (Eds.), *Encyclopedia of digital government* (pp. 507–510). Hershey, PA: Information Science Reference; doi:10.4018/978-1-59140-789-8.ch077

Ciaghi, A., & Villafiorita, A. (2012). Law modeling and BPR for public administration improvement. In K. Bwalya & S. Zulu (Eds.), *Handbook of research on e-government in emerging economies: Adoption, e-participation, and legal frameworks* (pp. 391–410). Hershey, PA: Information Science Reference; doi:10.4018/978-1-4666-0324-0. ch019

Ciaramitaro, B. L., & Skrocki, M. (2012). mHealth: Mobile healthcare. In B. Ciaramitaro (Ed.), Mobile technology consumption: Opportunities and challenges (pp. 99-109). Hershey, PA: Information Science Reference. doi:10.4018/978-1-61350-150-4.ch007

Comite, U. (2012). Innovative processes and managerial effectiveness of e-procurement in healthcare. In A. Manoharan & M. Holzer (Eds.), *Active citizen participation in e-government: A global perspective* (pp. 206–229). Hershey, PA: Information Science Reference; doi:10.4018/978-1-4666-0116-1.ch011

Cordella, A. (2013). E-government success: How to account for ICT, administrative rationalization, and institutional change. In J. Gil-Garcia (Ed.), *E-government success factors and measures: Theories, concepts, and methodologies* (pp. 40–51). Hershey, PA: Information Science Reference; doi:10.4018/978-1-4666-4058-0.ch003

Cropf, R. A. (2009). ICT and e-democracy. In M. Khosrow-Pour (Ed.), *Encyclopedia of information science and technology* (2nd ed., pp. 1789–1793). Hershey, PA: Information Science Reference; doi:10.4018/978-1-60566-026-4.ch281

Cropf, R. A. (2009). The virtual public sphere. In M. Pagani (Ed.), *Encyclopedia of multimedia technology and networking* (2nd ed., pp. 1525–1530). Hershey, PA: Information Science Reference; doi:10.4018/978-1-60566-014-1.ch206

D'Abundo, M. L. (2013). Electronic health record implementation in the United States healthcare industry: Making the process of change manageable. In V. Wang (Ed.), *Handbook of research on technologies for improving the 21st century workforce: Tools for lifelong learning* (pp. 272–286). Hershey, PA: Information Science Publishing; doi:10.4018/978-1-4666-2181-7.ch018

Damurski, L. (2012). E-participation in urban planning: Online tools for citizen engagement in Poland and in Germany. *International Journal of E-Planning Research*, *1*(3), 40–67. doi:10.4018/ijepr.2012070103

de Almeida, M. O. (2007). E-government strategy in Brazil: Increasing transparency and efficiency through e-government procurement. In M. Gascó-Hernandez (Ed.), *Latin America online: Cases, successes and pitfalls* (pp. 34–82). Hershey, PA: IRM Press; doi:10.4018/978-1-59140-974-8. ch002 de Juana Espinosa, S. (2008). Empirical study of the municipalitites' motivations for adopting online presence. In A. Anttiroiko (Ed.), *Electronic government: Concepts, methodologies, tools, and applications* (pp. 3593–3608). Hershey, PA: Information Science Reference; doi:10.4018/978-1-59904-947-2.ch262

de Souza Dias, D. (2002). Motivation for using information technology. In C. Snodgrass & E. Szewczak (Eds.), *Human factors in information systems* (pp. 55–60). Hershey, PA: IRM Press; doi:10.4018/978-1-931777-10-0.ch005

Demediuk, P. (2006). Government procurement ICT's impact on the sustainability of SMEs and regional communities. In S. Marshall, W. Taylor, & X. Yu (Eds.), *Encyclopedia of developing regional communities with information and communication technology* (pp. 321–324). Hershey, PA: Information Science Reference; doi:10.4018/978-1-59140-575-7.ch056

Devonshire, E., Forsyth, H., Reid, S., & Simpson, J. M. (2013). The challenges and opportunities of online postgraduate coursework programs in a traditional university context. In B. Tynan, J. Willems, & R. James (Eds.), *Outlooks and opportunities in blended and distance learning* (pp. 353–368). Hershey, PA: Information Science Reference; doi:10.4018/978-1-4666-4205-8.ch026

Di Cerbo, F., Scotto, M., Sillitti, A., Succi, G., & Vernazza, T. (2007). Toward a GNU/Linux distribution for corporate environments. In S. Sowe, I. Stamelos, & I. Samoladas (Eds.), *Emerging free and open source software practices* (pp. 215–236). Hershey, PA: Idea Group Publishing; doi:10.4018/978-1-59904-210-7.ch010

Diesner, J., & Carley, K. M. (2005). Revealing social structure from texts: Meta-matrix text analysis as a novel method for network text analysis. In V. Narayanan & D. Armstrong (Eds.), *Causal mapping for research in information technology* (pp. 81–108). Hershey, PA: Idea Group Publishing; doi:10.4018/978-1-59140-396-8.ch004

Dologite, D. G., Mockler, R. J., Bai, Q., & Viszhanyo, P. F. (2006). IS change agents in practice in a US-Chinese joint venture. In M. Hunter & F. Tan (Eds.), *Advanced topics in global information management* (Vol. 5, pp. 331–352). Hershey, PA: Idea Group Publishing; doi:10.4018/978-1-59140-923-6.ch015

Drnevich, P., Brush, T. H., & Luckock, G. T. (2011). Process and structural implications for IT-enabled outsourcing. *International Journal of Strategic Information Technology and Applications*, 2(4), 30–43. doi:10.4018/jsita.2011100103

Dwivedi, A. N. (2009). Handbook of research on information technology management and clinical data administration in healthcare (Vols. 1–2). Hershey, PA: IGI Global; doi:10.4018/978-1-60566-356-2

Elbeltagi, I., McBride, N., & Hardaker, G. (2006). Evaluating the factors affecting DSS usage by senior managers in local authorities in Egypt. In M. Hunter & F. Tan (Eds.), *Advanced topics in global information management* (Vol. 5, pp. 283–307). Hershey, PA: Idea Group Publishing; doi:10.4018/978-1-59140-923-6.ch013

Eom, S., & Fountain, J. E. (2013). Enhancing information services through public-private partnerships: Information technology knowledge transfer underlying structures to develop shared services in the U.S. and Korea. In J. Gil-Garcia (Ed.), *E-government success around the world: Cases, empirical studies, and practical recommendations* (pp. 15–40). Hershey, PA: Information Science Reference; doi:10.4018/978-1-4666-4173-0.ch002

Esteves, T., Leuenberger, D., & Van Leuven, N. (2012). Reaching citizen 2.0: How government uses social media to send public messages during times of calm and times of crisis. In K. Kloby & M. D'Agostino (Eds.), *Citizen 2.0: Public and governmental interaction through web 2.0 technologies* (pp. 250–268). Hershey, PA: Information Science Reference; doi:10.4018/978-1-4666-0318-9.ch013

Estevez, E., Fillottrani, P., Janowski, T., & Ojo, A. (2012). Government information sharing: A framework for policy formulation. In Y. Chen & P. Chu (Eds.), *Electronic governance and cross-boundary collaboration: Innovations and advancing tools* (pp. 23–55). Hershey, PA: Information Science Reference; doi:10.4018/978-1-60960-753-1.ch002

Ezz, I. E. (2008). E-governement emerging trends: Organizational challenges. In A. Anttiroiko (Ed.), *Electronic government: Concepts, methodologies, tools, and applications* (pp. 3721–3737). Hershey, PA: Information Science Reference; doi:10.4018/978-1-59904-947-2.ch269

Fabri, M. (2009). The Italian style of e-justice in a comparative perspective. In A. Martínez & P. Abat (Eds.), *E-justice: Using information communication technologies in the court system* (pp. 1–19). Hershey, PA: Information Science Reference; doi:10.4018/978-1-59904-998-4.ch001

Fagbe, T., & Adekola, O. D. (2010). Workplace safety and personnel well-being: The impact of information technology. *International Journal of Green Computing*, 1(1), 28–33. doi:10.4018/jgc.2010010103

Fagbe, T., & Adekola, O. D. (2011). Workplace safety and personnel well-being: The impact of information technology. In *Global business: Concepts, methodologies, tools and applications* (pp. 1438–1444). Hershey, PA: Business Science Reference; doi:10.4018/978-1-60960-587-2.ch509

Farmer, L. (2008). Affective collaborative instruction with librarians. In S. Kelsey & K. St.Amant (Eds.), *Handbook of research on computer mediated communication* (pp. 15–24). Hershey, PA: Information Science Reference; doi:10.4018/978-1-59904-863-5.ch002

Favier, L., & Mekhantar, J. (2007). Use of OSS by local e-administration. The French situation. In K. St.Amant & B. Still (Eds.), *Handbook of research on open source software: Technological, economic, and social perspectives* (pp. 428–444). Hershey, PA: Information Science Reference; doi:10.4018/978-1-59140-999-1.ch033

Fernando, S. (2009). Issues of e-learning in third world countries. In M. Khosrow-Pour (Ed.), *Encyclopedia of information science and technology* (2nd ed., pp. 2273–2277). Hershey, PA: Information Science Reference; doi:10.4018/978-1-60566-026-4.ch360

Filho, J. R., & dos Santos Junior, J. R. (2009). Local e-government in Brazil: Poor interaction and local politics as usual. In C. Reddick (Ed.), *Handbook of research on strategies for local e-government adoption and implementation: Comparative studies* (pp. 863–878). Hershey, PA: Information Science Reference; doi:10.4018/978-1-60566-282-4.ch045

Fletcher, P. D. (2004). Portals and policy: Implications of electronic access to U.S. federal government information services. In A. Pavlichev & G. Garson (Eds.), *Digital government: Principles and best practices* (pp. 52–62). Hershey, PA: Idea Group Publishing; doi:10.4018/978-1-59140-122-3.ch004

Fletcher, P. D. (2008). Portals and policy: Implications of electronic access to U.S. federal government information services. In A. Anttiroiko (Ed.), *Electronic government: Concepts, methodologies, tools, and applications* (pp. 3970–3979). Hershey, PA: Information Science Reference; doi:10.4018/978-1-59904-947-2.ch289

Forlano, L. (2004). The emergence of digital government: International perspectives. In A. Pavlichev & G. Garson (Eds.), *Digital government: Principles and best practices* (pp. 34–51). Hershey, PA: Idea Group Publishing; doi:10.4018/978-1-59140-122-3.ch003

Franzel, J. M., & Coursey, D. H. (2004). Government web portals: Management issues and the approaches of five states. In A. Pavlichev & G. Garson (Eds.), *Digital government: Principles and best practices* (pp. 63–77). Hershey, PA: Idea Group Publishing; doi:10.4018/978-1-59140-122-3.ch005

Gaivéo, J. M. (2013). Security of ICTs supporting healthcare activities. In M. Cruz-Cunha, I. Miranda, & P. Gonçalves (Eds.), *Handbook of research on ICTs for human-centered healthcare and social care services* (pp. 208–228). Hershey, PA: Medical Information Science Reference; doi:10.4018/978-1-4666-3986-7.ch011

Garson, G. D. (1999). *Information technology and computer applications in public administration: Issues and trends*. Hershey, PA: IGI Global; doi:10.4018/978-1-878289-52-0

Garson, G. D. (2003). Toward an information technology research agenda for public administration. In G. Garson (Ed.), *Public information technology: Policy and management issues* (pp. 331–357). Hershey, PA: Idea Group Publishing; doi:10.4018/978-1-59140-060-8.ch014

Garson, G. D. (2004). The promise of digital government. In A. Pavlichev & G. Garson (Eds.), *Digital government: Principles and best practices* (pp. 2–15). Hershey, PA: Idea Group Publishing; doi:10.4018/978-1-59140-122-3.ch001

Garson, G. D. (2007). An information technology research agenda for public administration. In G. Garson (Ed.), *Modern public information technology systems: Issues and challenges* (pp. 365–392). Hershey, PA: Idea Group Publishing; doi:10.4018/978-1-59904-051-6.ch018

Gasco, M. (2007). Civil servants' resistance towards e-government development. In A. Anttiroiko & M. Malkia (Eds.), *Encyclopedia of digital government* (pp. 190–195). Hershey, PA: Information Science Reference; doi:10.4018/978-1-59140-789-8.ch028

Gasco, M. (2008). Civil servants' resistance towards e-government development. In A. Anttiroiko (Ed.), *Electronic government: Concepts, methodologies, tools, and applications* (pp. 2580–2588). Hershey, PA: Information Science Reference; doi:10.4018/978-1-59904-947-2.ch190

Ghere, R. K. (2010). Accountability and information technology enactment: Implications for social empowerment. In E. Ferro, Y. Dwivedi, J. Gil-Garcia, & M. Williams (Eds.), *Handbook of research on overcoming digital divides: Constructing an equitable and competitive information society* (pp. 515–532). Hershey, PA: Information Science Reference; doi:10.4018/978-1-60566-699-0.ch028

Gibson, I. W. (2012). Simulation modeling of healthcare delivery. In A. Kolker & P. Story (Eds.), *Management engineering for effective healthcare delivery: Principles and applications* (pp. 69–89). Hershey, PA: Medical Information Science Reference; doi:10.4018/978-1-60960-872-9.ch003

Gil-Garcia, J. R. (2007). Exploring e-government benefits and success factors. In A. Anttiroiko & M. Malkia (Eds.), *Encyclopedia of digital government* (pp. 803–811). Hershey, PA: Information Science Reference; doi:10.4018/978-1-59140-789-8.ch122

Gil-Garcia, J. R., & González Miranda, F. (2010). E-government and opportunities for participation: The case of the Mexican state web portals. In C. Reddick (Ed.), *Politics, democracy and e-government: Participation and service delivery* (pp. 56–74). Hershey, PA: Information Science Reference; doi:10.4018/978-1-61520-933-0.ch004

Goldfinch, S. (2012). Public trust in government, trust in e-government, and use of e-government. In Z. Yan (Ed.), *Encyclopedia of cyber behavior* (pp. 987–995). Hershey, PA: Information Science Reference; doi:10.4018/978-1-4666-0315-8.ch081

Goodyear, M. (2012). Organizational change contributions to e-government project transitions. In S. Aikins (Ed.), *Managing e-government projects: Concepts, issues, and best practices* (pp. 1–21). Hershey, PA: Information Science Reference; doi:10.4018/978-1-4666-0086-7.ch001

Gordon, S., & Mulligan, P. (2003). Strategic models for the delivery of personal financial services: The role of infocracy. In S. Gordon (Ed.), *Computing information technology: The human side* (pp. 220–232). Hershey, PA: IRM Press; doi:10.4018/978-1-93177-752-0.ch014

Gordon, T. F. (2007). Legal knowledge systems. In A. Anttiroiko & M. Malkia (Eds.), *Encyclopedia of digital government* (pp. 1161–1166). Hershey, PA: Information Science Reference; doi:10.4018/978-1-59140-789-8.ch175

Graham, J. E., & Semich, G. W. (2008). Integrating technology to transform pedagogy: Revisiting the progress of the three phase TUI model for faculty development. In L. Tomei (Ed.), *Adapting information and communication technologies for effective education* (pp. 1–12). Hershey, PA: Information Science Reference; doi:10.4018/978-1-59904-922-9.ch001

Grandinetti, L., & Pisacane, O. (2012). Web services for healthcare management. In D. Prakash Vidyarthi (Ed.), *Technologies and protocols for the future of internet design: Reinventing the web* (pp. 60–94). Hershey, PA: Information Science Reference; doi:10.4018/978-1-4666-0203-8.ch004

Groenewegen, P., & Wagenaar, F. P. (2008). VO as an alternative to hierarchy in the Dutch police sector. In G. Putnik & M. Cruz-Cunha (Eds.), *Encyclopedia of networked and virtual organizations* (pp. 1851–1857). Hershey, PA: Information Science Reference; doi:10.4018/978-1-59904-885-7.ch245

Gronlund, A. (2001). Building an infrastructure to manage electronic services. In S. Dasgupta (Ed.), *Managing internet and intranet technologies in organizations: Challenges and opportunities* (pp. 71–103). Hershey, PA: Idea Group Publishing; doi:10.4018/978-1-878289-95-7.ch006

Gronlund, A. (2002). Introduction to electronic government: Design, applications and management. In Å. Grönlund (Ed.), *Electronic government: Design, applications and management* (pp. 1–21). Hershey, PA: Idea Group Publishing; doi:10.4018/978-1-930708-19-8.ch001

Gupta, A., Woosley, R., Crk, I., & Sarnikar, S. (2009). An information technology architecture for drug effectiveness reporting and post-marketing surveillance. In J. Tan (Ed.), *Medical informatics: Concepts, methodologies, tools, and applications* (pp. 631–646). Hershey, PA: Medical Information Science Reference; doi:10.4018/978-1-60566-050-9.ch047

Hallin, A., & Lundevall, K. (2007). mCity: User focused development of mobile services within the city of Stockholm. In I. Kushchu (Ed.), Mobile government: An emerging direction in e-government (pp. 12-29). Hershey, PA: Idea Group Publishing. doi:10.4018/978-1-59140-884-0.ch002

Hallin, A., & Lundevall, K. (2009). mCity: User focused development of mobile services within the city of Stockholm. In S. Clarke (Ed.), Evolutionary concepts in end user productivity and performance: Applications for organizational progress (pp. 268-280). Hershey, PA: Information Science Reference. doi:10.4018/978-1-60566-136-0.ch017

Hallin, A., & Lundevall, K. (2009). mCity: User focused development of mobile services within the city of Stockholm. In D. Taniar (Ed.), Mobile computing: Concepts, methodologies, tools, and applications (pp. 3455-3467). Hershey, PA: Information Science Reference. doi:10.4018/978-1-60566-054-7.ch253

Hanson, A. (2005). Overcoming barriers in the planning of a virtual library. In M. Khosrow-Pour (Ed.), *Encyclopedia of information science and technology* (pp. 2255–2259). Hershey, PA: Information Science Reference; doi:10.4018/978-1-59140-553-5.ch397

Haque, A. (2008). Information technology and surveillance: Implications for public administration in a new word order. In T. Loendorf & G. Garson (Eds.), *Patriotic information systems* (pp. 177–185). Hershey, PA: IGI Publishing; doi:10.4018/978-1-59904-594-8.ch008

Hauck, R. V., Thatcher, S. M., & Weisband, S. P. (2012). Temporal aspects of information technology use: Increasing shift work effectiveness. In J. Wang (Ed.), *Advancing the service sector with evolving technologies: Techniques and principles* (pp. 87–104). Hershey, PA: Business Science Reference; doi:10.4018/978-1-4666-0044-7.ch006

Hawk, S., & Witt, T. (2006). Telecommunications courses in information systems programs. *International Journal of Information and Communication Technology Education, 2*(1), 79–92. doi:10.4018/jicte.2006010107

Helms, M. M., Moore, R., & Ahmadi, M. (2009). Information technology (IT) and the healthcare industry: A SWOT analysis. In J. Tan (Ed.), *Medical informatics: Concepts, methodologies, tools, and applications* (pp. 134–152). Hershey, PA: Medical Information Science Reference; doi:10.4018/978-1-60566-050-9.ch012

Hendrickson, S. M., & Young, M. E. (2014). Electronic records management at a federally funded research and development center. In J. Krueger (Ed.), *Cases on electronic records and resource management implementation in diverse environments* (pp. 334–350). Hershey, PA: Information Science Reference; doi:10.4018/978-1-4666-4466-3.ch020

Henman, P. (2010). Social policy and information communication technologies. In J. Martin & L. Hawkins (Eds.), *Information communication technologies for human services education and delivery: Concepts and cases* (pp. 215–229). Hershey, PA: Information Science Reference; doi:10.4018/978-1-60566-735-5.ch014

Hismanoglu, M. (2011). Important issues in online education: E-pedagogy and marketing. In U. Demiray & S. Sever (Eds.), *Marketing online education programs: Frameworks for promotion and communication* (pp. 184–209). Hershey, PA: Information Science Reference; doi:10.4018/978-1-60960-074-7.ch012

Ho, K. K. (2008). The e-government development, IT strategies, and portals of the Hong Kong SAR government. In A. Anttiroiko (Ed.), *Electronic government: Concepts, methodologies, tools, and applications* (pp. 715–733). Hershey, PA: Information Science Reference; doi:10.4018/978-1-59904-947-2.ch060

Holden, S. H. (2003). The evolution of information technology management at the federal level: Implications for public administration. In G. Garson (Ed.), *Public information technology: Policy and management issues* (pp. 53–73). Hershey, PA: Idea Group Publishing; doi:10.4018/978-1-59140-060-8.ch003

Holden, S. H. (2007). The evolution of federal information technology management literature: Does IT finally matter? In G. Garson (Ed.), *Modern public information technology systems: Issues and challenges* (pp. 17–34). Hershey, PA: Idea Group Publishing; doi:10.4018/978-1-59904-051-6.ch002

Holland, J. W. (2009). Automation of American criminal justice. In M. Khosrow-Pour (Ed.), *Encyclopedia of information science and technology* (2nd ed., pp. 300–302). Hershey, PA: Information Science Reference; doi:10.4018/978-1-60566-026-4.ch051

Holloway, K. (2013). Fair use, copyright, and academic integrity in an online academic environment. In *Digital rights management: Concepts, methodologies, tools, and applications* (pp. 917–928). Hershey, PA: Information Science Reference; doi:10.4018/978-1-4666-2136-7.ch044

Horiuchi, C. (2005). E-government databases. In L. Rivero, J. Doorn, & V. Ferraggine (Eds.), *Encyclopedia of database technologies and applications* (pp. 206–210). Hershey, PA: Information Science Reference; doi:10.4018/978-1-59140-560-3.ch035

Horiuchi, C. (2006). Creating IS quality in government settings. In E. Duggan & J. Reichgelt (Eds.), *Measuring information systems delivery quality* (pp. 311–327). Hershey, PA: Idea Group Publishing; doi:10.4018/978-1-59140-857-4.ch014

Hsiao, N., Chu, P., & Lee, C. (2012). Impact of e-governance on businesses: Model development and case study. In *Digital democracy: Concepts, methodologies, tools, and applications* (pp. 1407–1425). Hershey, PA: Information Science Reference; doi:10.4018/978-1-4666-1740-7.ch070

Huang, T., & Lee, C. (2010). Evaluating the impact of e-government on citizens: Cost-benefit analysis. In C. Reddick (Ed.), *Citizens and e-government: Evaluating policy and management* (pp. 37–52). Hershey, PA: Information Science Reference; doi:10.4018/978-1-61520-931-6.ch003

Hunter, M. G., Diochon, M., Pugsley, D., & Wright, B. (2002). Unique challenges for small business adoption of information technology: The case of the Nova Scotia ten. In S. Burgess (Ed.), *Managing information technology in small business: Challenges and solutions* (pp. 98–117). Hershey, PA: Idea Group Publishing; doi:10.4018/978-1-930708-35-8.ch006

Hurskainen, J. (2003). Integration of business systems and applications in merger and alliance: Case metso automation. In T. Reponen (Ed.), *Information technology enabled global customer service* (pp. 207–225). Hershey, PA: Idea Group Publishing; doi:10.4018/978-1-59140-048-6.ch012

Iazzolino, G., & Pietrantonio, R. (2011). The soveria.it project: A best practice of e-government in southern Italy. In D. Piaggesi, K. Sund, & W. Castelnovo (Eds.), *Global strategy and practice of e-governance: Examples from around the world* (pp. 34–56). Hershey, PA: Information Science Reference; doi:10.4018/978-1-60960-489-9.ch003

Imran, A., & Gregor, S. (2012). A process model for successful e-government adoption in the least developed countries: A case of Bangladesh. In F. Tan (Ed.), *International comparisons of information communication technologies: Advancing applications* (pp. 321–350). Hershey, PA: Information Science Reference; doi:10.4018/978-1-61350-480-2.ch014

Inoue, Y., & Bell, S. T. (2005). Electronic/digital government innovation, and publishing trends with IT. In M. Khosrow-Pour (Ed.), *Encyclopedia of information science and technology* (pp. 1018–1023). Hershey, PA: Information Science Reference; doi:10.4018/978-1-59140-553-5.ch180

Islam, M. M., & Ehsan, M. (2013). Understanding e-governance: A theoretical approach. In M. Islam & M. Ehsan (Eds.), *From government to e-governance: Public administration in the digital age* (pp. 38–49). Hershey, PA: Information Science Reference; doi:10.4018/978-1-4666-1909-8.ch003

Jaeger, B. (2009). E-government and e-democracy in the making. In M. Khosrow-Pour (Ed.), *Encyclopedia of information science and technology* (2nd ed., pp. 1318–1322). Hershey, PA: Information Science Reference; doi:10.4018/978-1-60566-026-4.ch208

Jain, R. B. (2007). Revamping the administrative structure and processes in India for online diplomacy. In A. Anttiroiko & M. Malkia (Eds.), *Encyclopedia of digital government* (pp. 1418–1423). Hershey, PA: Information Science Reference; doi:10.4018/978-1-59140-789-8.ch217

Jain, R. B. (2008). Revamping the administrative structure and processes in India for online diplomacy. In A. Anttiroiko (Ed.), *Electronic government: Concepts, methodologies, tools, and applications* (pp. 3142–3149). Hershey, PA: Information Science Reference; doi:10.4018/978-1-59904-947-2.ch233

Jauhiainen, J. S., & Inkinen, T. (2009). E-governance and the information society in periphery. In C. Reddick (Ed.), *Handbook of research on strategies for local e-government adoption and implementation: Comparative studies* (pp. 497–514). Hershey, PA: Information Science Reference; doi:10.4018/978-1-60566-282-4.ch026

Jensen, M. J. (2009). Electronic democracy and citizen influence in government. In C. Reddick (Ed.), *Handbook of research on strategies for local e-government adoption and implementation: Comparative studies* (pp. 288–305). Hershey, PA: Information Science Reference; doi:10.4018/978-1-60566-282-4.ch015

Jiao, Y., Hurson, A. R., Potok, T. E., & Beckerman, B. G. (2009). Integrating mobile-based systems with healthcare databases. In J. Erickson (Ed.), *Database technologies: Concepts, methodologies, tools, and applications* (pp. 484–504). Hershey, PA: Information Science Reference; doi:10.4018/978-1-60566-058-5.ch031

Joia, L. A. (2002). A systematic model to integrate information technology into metabusinesses: A case study in the engineering realms. In F. Tan (Ed.), *Advanced topics in global information management* (Vol. 1, pp. 250–267). Hershey, PA: Idea Group Publishing; doi:10.4018/978-1-930708-43-3.ch016

Jones, T. H., & Song, I. (2000). Binary equivalents of ternary relationships in entity-relationship modeling: A logical decomposition approach. *Journal of Database Management, 11*(2), 12–19. doi:10.4018/jdm.2000040102

Juana-Espinosa, S. D. (2007). Empirical study of the municipalitites' motivations for adopting online presence. In L. Al-Hakim (Ed.), *Global e-government: Theory, applications and benchmarking* (pp. 261–279). Hershey, PA: Idea Group Publishing; doi:10.4018/978-1-59904-027-1.ch015

Jun, K., & Weare, C. (2012). Bridging from e-government practice to e-government research: Past trends and future directions. In K. Bwalya & S. Zulu (Eds.), *Handbook of research on e-government in emerging economies: Adoption, e-participation, and legal frameworks* (pp. 263–289). Hershey, PA: Information Science Reference; doi:10.4018/978-1-4666-0324-0.ch013

Junqueira, A., Diniz, E. H., & Fernandez, M. (2010). Electronic government implementation projects with multiple agencies: Analysis of the electronic invoice project under PMBOK framework. In J. Cordoba-Pachon & A. Ochoa-Arias (Eds.), *Systems thinking and e-participation: ICT in the governance of society* (pp. 135–153). Hershey, PA: Information Science Reference; doi:10.4018/978-1-60566-860-4.ch009

Juntunen, A. (2009). Joint service development with the local authorities. In C. Reddick (Ed.), *Handbook of research on strategies for local e-government adoption and implementation: Comparative studies* (pp. 902–920). Hershey, PA: Information Science Reference; doi:10.4018/978-1-60566-282-4.ch047

Kamel, S. (2001). *Using DSS for crisis management.* Hershey, PA: IGI Global; doi:10.4018/978-1-87828-961-2.ch020

Kamel, S. (2006). DSS for strategic decision making. In M. Khosrow-Pour (Ed.), *Cases on information technology and organizational politics & culture* (pp. 230–246). Hershey, PA: Idea Group Publishing; doi:10.4018/978-1-59904-411-8.ch015

Kamel, S. (2009). The software industry in Egypt as a potential contributor to economic growth. In M. Khosrow-Pour (Ed.), *Encyclopedia of information science and technology* (2nd ed., pp. 3531–3537). Hershey, PA: Information Science Reference; doi:10.4018/978-1-60566-026-4.ch562

Kamel, S., & Hussein, M. (2008). Xceed: Pioneering the contact center industry in Egypt. *Journal of Cases on Information Technology*, *10*(1), 67–91. doi:10.4018/jcit.2008010105

Kamel, S., & Wahba, K. (2003). The use of a hybrid model in web-based education: "The Global campus project. In A. Aggarwal (Ed.), *Web-based education: Learning from experience* (pp. 331–346). Hershey, PA: Information Science Publishing; doi:10.4018/978-1-59140-102-5.ch020

Kardaras, D. K., & Papathanassiou, E. A. (2008). An exploratory study of the e-government services in Greece. In G. Garson & M. Khosrow-Pour (Eds.), *Handbook of research on public information technology* (pp. 162–174). Hershey, PA: Information Science Reference; doi:10.4018/978-1-59904-857-4.ch016

Kassahun, A. E., Molla, A., & Sarkar, P. (2012). Government process reengineering: What we know and what we need to know. In *Digital democracy: Concepts, methodologies, tools, and applications* (pp. 1730–1752). Hershey, PA: Information Science Reference; doi:10.4018/978-1-4666-1740-7.ch086

Khan, B. (2005). Technological issues. In B. Khan (Ed.), *Managing e-learning strategies: Design, delivery, implementation and evaluation* (pp. 154–180). Hershey, PA: Information Science Publishing; doi:10.4018/978-1-59140-634-1.ch004

Khasawneh, A., Bsoul, M., Obeidat, I., & Al Azzam, I. (2012). Technology fears: A study of e-commerce loyalty perception by Jordanian customers. In J. Wang (Ed.), *Advancing the service sector with evolving technologies: Techniques and principles* (pp. 158–165). Hershey, PA: Business Science Reference; doi:10.4018/978-1-4666-0044-7.ch010

Khatibi, V., & Montazer, G. A. (2012). E-research methodology. In A. Juan, T. Daradoumis, M. Roca, S. Grasman, & J. Faulin (Eds.), *Collaborative and distributed e-research: Innovations in technologies, strategies and applications* (pp. 62–81). Hershey, PA: Information Science Reference; doi:10.4018/978-1-4666-0125-3.ch003

Kidd, T. (2011). The dragon in the school's backyard: A review of literature on the uses of technology in urban schools. In L. Tomei (Ed.), *Online courses and ICT in education: Emerging practices and applications* (pp. 242–257). Hershey, PA: Information Science Reference; doi:10.4018/978-1-60960-150-8.ch019

Kidd, T. T. (2010). My experience tells the story: Exploring technology adoption from a qualitative perspective - A pilot study. In H. Song & T. Kidd (Eds.), *Handbook of research on human performance and instructional technology* (pp. 247–262). Hershey, PA: Information Science Reference; doi:10.4018/978-1-60566-782-9.ch015

Kieley, B., Lane, G., Paquet, G., & Roy, J. (2002). e-Government in Canada: Services online or public service renewal? In Å. Grönlund (Ed.), Electronic government: Design, applications and management (pp. 340-355). Hershey, PA: Idea Group Publishing. doi:10.4018/978-1-930708-19-8.ch016

Kim, P. (2012). "Stay out of the way! My kid is video blogging through a phone!": A lesson learned from math tutoring social media for children in underserved communities. In *Wireless technologies: Concepts, methodologies, tools and applications* (pp. 1415–1428). Hershey, PA: Information Science Reference; doi:10.4018/978-1-61350-101-6.ch517

Kirlidog, M. (2010). Financial aspects of national ICT strategies. In S. Kamel (Ed.), *E-strategies for technological diffusion and adoption: National ICT approaches for socioeconomic development* (pp. 277–292). Hershey, PA: Information Science Reference; doi:10.4018/978-1-60566-388-3.ch016

Kisielnicki, J. (2006). Transfer of information and knowledge in the project management. In E. Coakes & S. Clarke (Eds.), *Encyclopedia of communities of practice in information and knowledge management* (pp. 544–551). Hershey, PA: Information Science Reference; doi:10.4018/978-1-59140-556-6.ch091

Kittner, M., & Van Slyke, C. (2006). Reorganizing information technology services in an academic environment. In M. Khosrow-Pour (Ed.), *Cases on the human side of information technology* (pp. 49–66). Hershey, PA: Idea Group Publishing; doi:10.4018/978-1-59904-405-7.ch004

Knoell, H. D. (2008). Semi virtual workplaces in German financial service enterprises. In P. Zemliansky & K. St.Amant (Eds.), *Handbook of research on virtual workplaces and the new nature of business practices* (pp. 570–581). Hershey, PA: Information Science Reference; doi:10.4018/978-1-59904-893-2.ch041

Koh, S. L., & Maguire, S. (2009). Competing in the age of information technology in a developing economy: Experiences of an Indian bank. In S. Koh & S. Maguire (Eds.), *Information and communication technologies management in turbulent business environments* (pp. 326–350). Hershey, PA: Information Science Reference; doi:10.4018/978-1-60566-424-8.ch018

Kollmann, T., & Häsel, M. (2009). Competence of information technology professionals in internet-based ventures. In I. Lee (Ed.), *Electronic business: Concepts, methodologies, tools, and applications* (pp. 1905–1919). Hershey, PA: Information Science Reference; doi:10.4018/978-1-60566-056-1.ch118

Kollmann, T., & Häsel, M. (2009). Competence of information technology professionals in internet-based ventures. In A. Cater-Steel (Ed.), *Information technology governance and service management: Frameworks and adaptations* (pp. 239–253). Hershey, PA: Information Science Reference; doi:10.4018/978-1-60566-008-0.ch013

Kollmann, T., & Häsel, M. (2010). Competence of information technology professionals in internet-based ventures. In *Electronic services: Concepts, methodologies, tools and applications* (pp. 1551–1565). Hershey, PA: Information Science Reference; doi:10.4018/978-1-61520-967-5.ch094

Kraemer, K., & King, J. L. (2006). Information technology and administrative reform: Will e-government be different? *International Journal of Electronic Government Research, 2*(1), 1–20. doi:10.4018/jegr.2006010101

Kraemer, K., & King, J. L. (2008). Information technology and administrative reform: Will e-government be different? In D. Norris (Ed.), *E-government research: Policy and management* (pp. 1–20). Hershey, PA: IGI Publishing; doi:10.4018/978-1-59904-913-7.ch001

Lampathaki, F., Tsiakaliaris, C., Stasis, A., & Charalabidis, Y. (2011). National interoperability frameworks: The way forward. In Y. Charalabidis (Ed.), *Interoperability in digital public services and administration: Bridging e-government and e-business* (pp. 1–24). Hershey, PA: Information Science Reference; doi:10.4018/978-1-61520-887-6.ch001

Lan, Z., & Scott, C. R. (1996). The relative importance of computer-mediated information versus conventional non-computer-mediated information in public managerial decision making. *Information Resources Management Journal, 9*(1), 27–0. doi:10.4018/irmj.1996010103

Law, W. (2004). *Public sector data management in a developing economy.* Hershey, PA: IGI Global; doi:10.4018/978-1-59140-259-6.ch034

Law, W. K. (2005). Information resources development challenges in a cross-cultural environment. In M. Khosrow-Pour (Ed.), *Encyclopedia of information science and technology* (pp. 1476–1481). Hershey, PA: Information Science Reference; doi:10.4018/978-1-59140-553-5.ch259

Law, W. K. (2009). Cross-cultural challenges for information resources management. In M. Khosrow-Pour (Ed.), *Encyclopedia of information science and technology* (2nd ed., pp. 840–846). Hershey, PA: Information Science Reference; doi:10.4018/978-1-60566-026-4.ch136

Law, W. K. (2011). Cross-cultural challenges for information resources management. In *Global business: Concepts, methodologies, tools and applications* (pp. 1924–1932). Hershey, PA: Business Science Reference; doi:10.4018/978-1-60960-587-2.ch704

Malkia, M., & Savolainen, R. (2004). eTransformation in government, politics and society: Conceptual framework and introduction. In M. Malkia, A. Anttiroiko, & R. Savolainen (Eds.), eTransformation in governance: New directions in government and politics (pp. 1-21). Hershey, PA: Idea Group Publishing. doi:10.4018/978-1-59140-130-8.ch001

Management Association. I. (2010). Information resources management: Concepts, methodologies, tools and applications (4 Volumes). Hershey, PA: IGI Global. doi:10.4018/978-1-61520-965-1

Management Association. I. (2010). Electronic services: Concepts, methodologies, tools and applications (3 Volumes). Hershey, PA: IGI Global. doi:10.4018/978-1-61520-967-5

Mandujano, S. (2011). Network manageability security. In D. Kar & M. Syed (Eds.), *Network security, administration and management: Advancing technology and practice* (pp. 158–181). Hershey, PA: Information Science Reference; doi:10.4018/978-1-60960-777-7.ch009

Marich, M. J., Schooley, B. L., & Horan, T. A. (2012). A normative enterprise architecture for guiding end-to-end emergency response decision support. In M. Jennex (Ed.), *Managing crises and disasters with emerging technologies: Advancements* (pp. 71–87). Hershey, PA: Information Science Reference; doi:10.4018/978-1-4666-0167-3.ch006

Markov, R., & Okujava, S. (2008). Costs, benefits, and risks of e-government portals. In G. Putnik & M. Cruz-Cunha (Eds.), *Encyclopedia of networked and virtual organizations* (pp. 354–363). Hershey, PA: Information Science Reference; doi:10.4018/978-1-59904-885-7.ch047

Martin, N., & Rice, J. (2013). Evaluating and designing electronic government for the future: Observations and insights from Australia. In V. Weerakkody (Ed.), *E-government services design, adoption, and evaluation* (pp. 238–258). Hershey, PA: Information Science Reference; doi:10.4018/978-1-4666-2458-0.ch014

i. Martinez, A. C. (2008). Accessing administration's information via internet in Spain. In F. Tan (Ed.), *Global information technologies: Concepts, methodologies, tools, and applications* (pp. 2558–2573). Hershey, PA: Information Science Reference; doi:10.4018/978-1-59904-939-7.ch186

Mbarika, V. W., Meso, P. N., & Musa, P. F. (2006). A disconnect in stakeholders' perceptions from emerging realities of teledensity growth in Africa's least developed countries. In M. Hunter & F. Tan (Eds.), *Advanced topics in global information management* (Vol. 5, pp. 263–282). Hershey, PA: Idea Group Publishing; doi:10.4018/978-1-59140-923-6.ch012

Mbarika, V. W., Meso, P. N., & Musa, P. F. (2008). A disconnect in stakeholders' perceptions from emerging realities of teledensity growth in Africa's least developed countries. In F. Tan (Ed.), *Global information technologies: Concepts, methodologies, tools, and applications* (pp. 2948–2962). Hershey, PA: Information Science Reference; doi:10.4018/978-1-59904-939-7.ch209

Means, T., Olson, E., & Spooner, J. (2013). Discovering ways that don't work on the road to success: Strengths and weaknesses revealed by an active learning studio classroom project. In A. Benson, J. Moore, & S. Williams van Rooij (Eds.), *Cases on educational technology planning, design, and implementation: A project management perspective* (pp. 94–113). Hershey, PA: Information Science Reference; doi:10.4018/978-1-4666-4237-9.ch006

Melitski, J., Holzer, M., Kim, S., Kim, C., & Rho, S. (2008). Digital government worldwide: An e-government assessment of municipal web sites. In G. Garson & M. Khosrow-Pour (Eds.), *Handbook of research on public information technology* (pp. 790–804). Hershey, PA: Information Science Reference; doi:10.4018/978-1-59904-857-4.ch069

Memmola, M., Palumbo, G., & Rossini, M. (2009). Web & RFID technology: New frontiers in costing and process management for rehabilitation medicine. In L. Al-Hakim & M. Memmola (Eds.), *Business web strategy: Design, alignment, and application* (pp. 145–169). Hershey, PA: Information Science Reference; doi:10.4018/978-1-60566-024-0.ch008

Meng, Z., Fahong, Z., & Lei, L. (2008). Information technology and environment. In Y. Kurihara, S. Takaya, H. Harui, & H. Kamae (Eds.), *Information technology and economic development* (pp. 201–212). Hershey, PA: Information Science Reference; doi:10.4018/978-1-59904-579-5.ch014

Mentzingen de Moraes, A. J., Ferneda, E., Costa, I., & Spinola, M. D. (2011). Practical approach for implementation of governance process in IT: Information technology areas. In N. Shi & G. Silvius (Eds.), *Enterprise IT governance, business value and performance measurement* (pp. 19–40). Hershey, PA: Information Science Reference; doi:10.4018/978-1-60566-346-3.ch002

Merwin, G. A. Jr, McDonald, J. S., & Odera, L. C. (2008). Economic development: Government's cutting edge in IT. In M. Raisinghani (Ed.), *Handbook of research on global information technology management in the digital economy* (pp. 1–37). Hershey, PA: Information Science Reference; doi:10.4018/978-1-59904-875-8.ch001

Meso, P., & Duncan, N. (2002). Can national information infrastructures enhance social development in the least developed countries? An empirical investigation. In M. Dadashzadeh (Ed.), *Information technology management in developing countries* (pp. 23–51). Hershey, PA: IRM Press; doi:10.4018/978-1-931777-03-2.ch002

Meso, P. N., & Duncan, N. B. (2002). Can national information infrastructures enhance social development in the least developed countries? In F. Tan (Ed.), *Advanced topics in global information management* (Vol. 1, pp. 207–226). Hershey, PA: Idea Group Publishing; doi:10.4018/978-1-930708-43-3.ch014

Middleton, M. (2008). Evaluation of e-government web sites. In G. Garson & M. Khosrow-Pour (Eds.), *Handbook of research on public information technology* (pp. 699–710). Hershey, PA: Information Science Reference; doi:10.4018/978-1-59904-857-4.ch063

Mingers, J. (2010). Pluralism, realism, and truth: The keys to knowledge in information systems research. In D. Paradice (Ed.), *Emerging systems approaches in information technologies: Concepts, theories, and applications* (pp. 86–98). Hershey, PA: Information Science Reference; doi:10.4018/978-1-60566-976-2.ch006

Mital, K. M. (2012). ICT, unique identity and inclusive growth: An Indian perspective. In A. Manoharan & M. Holzer (Eds.), *E-governance and civic engagement: Factors and determinants of e-democracy* (pp. 584–612). Hershey, PA: Information Science Reference; doi:10.4018/978-1-61350-083-5.ch029

Mizell, A. P. (2008). Helping close the digital divide for financially disadvantaged seniors. In F. Tan (Ed.), *Global information technologies: Concepts, methodologies, tools, and applications* (pp. 2396–2402). Hershey, PA: Information Science Reference; doi:10.4018/978-1-59904-939-7.ch173

Molinari, F., Wills, C., Koumpis, A., & Moumtzi, V. (2011). A citizen-centric platform to support networking in the area of e-democracy. In H. Rahman (Ed.), *Cases on adoption, diffusion and evaluation of global e-governance systems: Impact at the grass roots* (pp. 282–302). Hershey, PA: Information Science Reference; doi:10.4018/978-1-61692-814-8.ch014

Molinari, F., Wills, C., Koumpis, A., & Moumtzi, V. (2013). A citizen-centric platform to support networking in the area of e-democracy. In H. Rahman (Ed.), *Cases on progressions and challenges in ICT utilization for citizen-centric governance* (pp. 265–297). Hershey, PA: Information Science Reference; doi:10.4018/978-1-4666-2071-1.ch013

Monteverde, F. (2010). The process of e-government public policy inclusion in the governmental agenda: A framework for assessment and case study. In J. Cordoba-Pachon & A. Ochoa-Arias (Eds.), *Systems thinking and e-participation: ICT in the governance of society* (pp. 233–245). Hershey, PA: Information Science Reference; doi:10.4018/978-1-60566-860-4.ch015

Moodley, S. (2008). Deconstructing the South African government's ICT for development discourse. In A. Anttiroiko (Ed.), *Electronic government: Concepts, methodologies, tools, and applications* (pp. 622–631). Hershey, PA: Information Science Reference; doi:10.4018/978-1-59904-947-2.ch053

Moodley, S. (2008). Deconstructing the South African government's ICT for development discourse. In C. Van Slyke (Ed.), *Information communication technologies: Concepts, methodologies, tools, and applications* (pp. 816–825). Hershey, PA: Information Science Reference; doi:10.4018/978-1-59904-949-6.ch052

Mora, M., Cervantes-Perez, F., Gelman-Muravchik, O., Forgionne, G. A., & Mejia-Olvera, M. (2003). DMSS implementation research: A conceptual analysis of the contributions and limitations of the factor-based and stage-based streams. In G. Forgionne, J. Gupta, & M. Mora (Eds.), *Decision-making support systems: Achievements and challenges for the new decade* (pp. 331–356). Hershey, PA: Idea Group Publishing; doi:10.4018/978-1-59140-045-5.ch020

Mörtberg, C., & Elovaara, P. (2010). Attaching people and technology: Between e and government. In S. Booth, S. Goodman, & G. Kirkup (Eds.), *Gender issues in learning and working with information technology: Social constructs and cultural contexts* (pp. 83–98). Hershey, PA: Information Science Reference; doi:10.4018/978-1-61520-813-5.ch005

Murphy, J., Harper, E., Devine, E. C., Burke, L. J., & Hook, M. L. (2011). Case study: Lessons learned when embedding evidence-based knowledge in a nurse care planning and documentation system. In A. Cashin & R. Cook (Eds.), *Evidence-based practice in nursing informatics: Concepts and applications* (pp. 174–190). Hershey, PA: Medical Information Science Reference; doi:10.4018/978-1-60960-034-1.ch014

Mutula, S. M. (2013). E-government's role in poverty alleviation: Case study of South Africa. In H. Rahman (Ed.), *Cases on progressions and challenges in ICT utilization for citizen-centric governance* (pp. 44–68). Hershey, PA: Information Science Reference; doi:10.4018/978-1-4666-2071-1.ch003

Nath, R., & Angeles, R. (2005). Relationships between supply characteristics and buyer-supplier coupling in e-procurement: An empirical analysis. [IJEBR]. *International Journal of E-Business Research, 1*(2), 40–55. doi:10.4018/jebr.2005040103

Nissen, M. E. (2006). Application cases in government. In M. Nissen (Ed.), *Harnessing knowledge dynamics: Principled organizational knowing & learning* (pp. 152–181). Hershey, PA: IRM Press; doi:10.4018/978-1-59140-773-7.ch008

Norris, D. F. (2003). Leading-edge information technologies and American local governments. In G. Garson (Ed.), *Public information technology: Policy and management issues* (pp. 139–169). Hershey, PA: Idea Group Publishing; doi:10.4018/978-1-59140-060-8.ch007

Norris, D. F. (2008). Information technology among U.S. local governments. In G. Garson & M. Khosrow-Pour (Eds.), *Handbook of research on public information technology* (pp. 132–144). Hershey, PA: Information Science Reference; doi:10.4018/978-1-59904-857-4.ch013

Northrop, A. (1999). The challenge of teaching information technology in public administration graduate programs. In G. Garson (Ed.), *Information technology and computer applications in public administration: Issues and trends* (pp. 1–22). Hershey, PA: Information Science Reference; doi:10.4018/978-1-87828-952-0.ch001

Northrop, A. (2003). Information technology and public administration: The view from the profession. In G. Garson (Ed.), *Public information technology: Policy and management issues* (pp. 1–19). Hershey, PA: Idea Group Publishing; doi:10.4018/978-1-59140-060-8.ch001

Northrop, A. (2007). Lip service? How PA journals and textbooks view information technology. In G. Garson (Ed.), *Modern public information technology systems: Issues and challenges* (pp. 1–16). Hershey, PA: Idea Group Publishing; doi:10.4018/978-1-59904-051-6.ch001

Null, E. (2013). Legal and political barriers to municipal networks in the United States. In A. Abdelaal (Ed.), *Social and economic effects of community wireless networks and infrastructures* (pp. 27–56). Hershey, PA: Information Science Reference; doi:10.4018/978-1-4666-2997-4.ch003

Okunoye, A., Frolick, M., & Crable, E. (2006). ERP implementation in higher education: An account of pre-implementation and implementation phases. *Journal of Cases on Information Technology*, *8*(2), 110–132. doi:10.4018/jcit.2006040106

Olasina, G. (2012). A review of egovernment services in Nigeria. In A. Tella & A. Issa (Eds.), *Library and information science in developing countries: Contemporary issues* (pp. 205–221). Hershey, PA: Information Science Reference; doi:10.4018/978-1-61350-335-5.ch015

Orgeron, C. P. (2008). A model for reengineering IT job classes in state government. In G. Garson & M. Khosrow-Pour (Eds.), *Handbook of research on public information technology* (pp. 735–746). Hershey, PA: Information Science Reference; doi:10.4018/978-1-59904-857-4.ch066

Owsinski, J. W., & Pielak, A. M. (2011). Local authority websites in rural areas: Measuring quality and functionality, and assessing the role. In Z. Andreopoulou, B. Manos, N. Polman, & D. Viaggi (Eds.), *Agricultural and environmental informatics, governance and management: Emerging research applications* (pp. 39–60). Hershey, PA: Information Science Reference; doi:10.4018/978-1-60960-621-3.ch003

Owsiński, J. W., Pielak, A. M., Sęp, K., & Stańczak, J. (2014). Local web-based networks in rural municipalities: Extension, density, and meaning. In Z. Andreopoulou, V. Samathrakis, S. Louca, & M. Vlachopoulou (Eds.), *E-innovation for sustainable development of rural resources during global economic crisis* (pp. 126–151). Hershey, PA: Business Science Reference; doi:10.4018/978-1-4666-4550-9.ch011

Pagani, M., & Pasinetti, C. (2008). Technical and functional quality in the development of t-government services. In A. Anttiroiko (Ed.), *Electronic government: Concepts, methodologies, tools, and applications* (pp. 2943–2965). Hershey, PA: Information Science Reference; doi:10.4018/978-1-59904-947-2.ch220

Pani, A. K., & Agrahari, A. (2005). On e-markets in emerging economy: An Indian experience. In M. Khosrow-Pour (Ed.), *Advanced topics in electronic commerce* (Vol. 1, pp. 287–299). Hershey, PA: Idea Group Publishing; doi:10.4018/978-1-59140-819-2.ch015

Papadopoulos, T., Angelopoulos, S., & Kitsios, F. (2011). A strategic approach to e-health interoperability using e-government frameworks. In A. Lazakidou, K. Siassiakos, & K. Ioannou (Eds.), *Wireless technologies for ambient assisted living and healthcare: Systems and applications* (pp. 213–229). Hershey, PA: Medical Information Science Reference; doi:10.4018/978-1-61520-805-0.ch012

Papadopoulos, T., Angelopoulos, S., & Kitsios, F. (2013). A strategic approach to e-health interoperability using e-government frameworks. In *User-driven healthcare: Concepts, methodologies, tools, and applications* (pp. 791–807). Hershey, PA: Medical Information Science Reference; doi:10.4018/978-1-4666-2770-3.ch039

Papaleo, G., Chiarella, D., Aiello, M., & Caviglione, L. (2012). Analysis, development and deployment of statistical anomaly detection techniques for real e-mail traffic. In T. Chou (Ed.), *Information assurance and security technologies for risk assessment and threat management: Advances* (pp. 47–71). Hershey, PA: Information Science Reference; doi:10.4018/978-1-61350-507-6.ch003

Papp, R. (2003). Information technology & FDA compliance in the pharmaceutical industry. In M. Khosrow-Pour (Ed.), *Annals of cases on information technology* (Vol. 5, pp. 262–273). Hershey, PA: Information Science Reference; doi:10.4018/978-1-59140-061-5.ch017

Parsons, T. W. (2007). Developing a knowledge management portal. In A. Tatnall (Ed.), *Encyclopedia of portal technologies and applications* (pp. 223–227). Hershey, PA: Information Science Reference; doi:10.4018/978-1-59140-989-2.ch039

Passaris, C. E. (2007). Immigration and digital government. In A. Anttiroiko & M. Malkia (Eds.), *Encyclopedia of digital government* (pp. 988–994). Hershey, PA: Information Science Reference; doi:10.4018/978-1-59140-789-8.ch148

Pavlichev, A. (2004). The e-government challenge for public administration. In A. Pavlichev & G. Garson (Eds.), *Digital government: Principles and best practices* (pp. 276–290). Hershey, PA: Idea Group Publishing; doi:10.4018/978-1-59140-122-3.ch018

Penrod, J. I., & Harbor, A. F. (2000). Designing and implementing a learning organization-oriented information technology planning and management process. In L. Petrides (Ed.), *Case studies on information technology in higher education: Implications for policy and practice* (pp. 7–19). Hershey, PA: Idea Group Publishing; doi:10.4018/978-1-878289-74-2.ch001

Planas-Silva, M. D., & Joseph, R. C. (2011). Perspectives on the adoption of electronic resources for use in clinical trials. In M. Guah (Ed.), *Healthcare delivery reform and new technologies: Organizational initiatives* (pp. 19–28). Hershey, PA: Information Science Reference; doi:10.4018/978-1-60960-183-6.ch002

Pomazalová, N., & Rejman, S. (2013). The rationale behind implementation of new electronic tools for electronic public procurement. In N. Pomazalová (Ed.), *Public sector transformation processes and internet public procurement: Decision support systems* (pp. 85–117). Hershey, PA: Engineering Science Reference; doi:10.4018/978-1-4666-2665-2.ch006

Postorino, M. N. (2012). City competitiveness and airport: Information science perspective. In M. Bulu (Ed.), *City competitiveness and improving urban subsystems: Technologies and applications* (pp. 61–83). Hershey, PA: Information Science Reference; doi:10.4018/978-1-61350-174-0.ch004

Poupa, C. (2002). Electronic government in Switzerland: Priorities for 2001-2005 - Electronic voting and federal portal. In Å. Grönlund (Ed.), *Electronic government: Design, applications and management* (pp. 356–369). Hershey, PA: Idea Group Publishing; doi:10.4018/978-1-930708-19-8.ch017

Powell, S. R. (2010). Interdisciplinarity in telecommunications and networking. In *Networking and telecommunications: Concepts, methodologies, tools and applications* (pp. 33–40). Hershey, PA: Information Science Reference; doi:10.4018/978-1-60566-986-1.ch004

Priya, P. S., & Mathiyalagan, N. (2011). A study of the implementation status of two e-governance projects in land revenue administration in India. In M. Shareef, V. Kumar, U. Kumar, & Y. Dwivedi (Eds.), *Stakeholder adoption of e-government services: Driving and resisting factors* (pp. 214–230). Hershey, PA: Information Science Reference; doi:10.4018/978-1-60960-601-5.ch011

Prysby, C., & Prysby, N. (2000). Electronic mail, employee privacy and the workplace. In L. Janczewski (Ed.), *Internet and intranet security management: Risks and solutions* (pp. 251–270). Hershey, PA: Idea Group Publishing; doi:10.4018/978-1-878289-71-1.ch009

Prysby, C. L., & Prysby, N. D. (2003). Electronic mail in the public workplace: Issues of privacy and public disclosure. In G. Garson (Ed.), *Public information technology: Policy and management issues* (pp. 271–298). Hershey, PA: Idea Group Publishing; doi:10.4018/978-1-59140-060-8.ch012

Prysby, C. L., & Prysby, N. D. (2007). You have mail, but who is reading it? Issues of e-mail in the public workplace. In G. Garson (Ed.), *Modern public information technology systems: Issues and challenges* (pp. 312–336). Hershey, PA: Idea Group Publishing; doi:10.4018/978-1-59904-051-6.ch016

Radl, A., & Chen, Y. (2005). Computer security in electronic government: A state-local education information system. *International Journal of Electronic Government Research*, *1*(1), 79–99. doi:10.4018/jegr.2005010105

Rahman, H. (2008). Information dynamics in developing countries. In C. Van Slyke (Ed.), *Information communication technologies: Concepts, methodologies, tools, and applications* (pp. 104–114). Hershey, PA: Information Science Reference; doi:10.4018/978-1-59904-949-6.ch008

Ramanathan, J. (2009). Adaptive IT architecture as a catalyst for network capability in government. In P. Saha (Ed.), *Advances in government enterprise architecture* (pp. 149–172). Hershey, PA: Information Science Reference; doi:10.4018/978-1-60566-068-4.ch007

Ramos, I., & Berry, D. M. (2006). Social construction of information technology supporting work. In M. Khosrow-Pour (Ed.), *Cases on information technology: Lessons learned* (Vol. 7, pp. 36–52). Hershey, PA: Idea Group Publishing; doi:10.4018/978-1-59140-673-0.ch003

Ray, D., Gulla, U., Gupta, M. P., & Dash, S. S. (2009). Interoperability and constituents of interoperable systems in public sector. In V. Weerakkody, M. Janssen, & Y. Dwivedi (Eds.), *Handbook of research on ICT-enabled transformational government: A global perspective* (pp. 175–195). Hershey, PA: Information Science Reference; doi:10.4018/978-1-60566-390-6.ch010

Reddick, C. G. (2007). E-government and creating a citizen-centric government: A study of federal government CIOs. In G. Garson (Ed.), *Modern public information technology systems: Issues and challenges* (pp. 143–165). Hershey, PA: Idea Group Publishing; doi:10.4018/978-1-59904-051-6.ch008

Reddick, C. G. (2010). Citizen-centric e-government. In C. Reddick (Ed.), *Homeland security preparedness and information systems: Strategies for managing public policy* (pp. 45–75). Hershey, PA: Information Science Reference; doi:10.4018/978-1-60566-834-5.ch002

Reddick, C. G. (2010). E-government and creating a citizen-centric government: A study of federal government CIOs. In C. Reddick (Ed.), *Homeland security preparedness and information systems: Strategies for managing public policy* (pp. 230–250). Hershey, PA: Information Science Reference; doi:10.4018/978-1-60566-834-5.ch012

Reddick, C. G. (2010). Perceived effectiveness of e-government and its usage in city governments: Survey evidence from information technology directors. In C. Reddick (Ed.), *Homeland security preparedness and information systems: Strategies for managing public policy* (pp. 213–229). Hershey, PA: Information Science Reference; doi:10.4018/978-1-60566-834-5.ch011

Reddick, C. G. (2012). Customer relationship management adoption in local governments in the United States. In S. Chhabra & M. Kumar (Eds.), *Strategic enterprise resource planning models for e-government: Applications and methodologies* (pp. 111–124). Hershey, PA: Information Science Reference; doi:10.4018/978-1-60960-863-7. ch008

Reeder, F. S., & Pandy, S. M. (2008). Identifying effective funding models for e-government. In A. Anttiroiko (Ed.), *Electronic government: Concepts, methodologies, tools, and applications* (pp. 1108–1138). Hershey, PA: Information Science Reference; doi:10.4018/978-1-59904-947-2. ch083

Riesco, D., Acosta, E., & Montejano, G. (2003). An extension to a UML activity graph from workflow. In L. Favre (Ed.), *UML and the unified process* (pp. 294–314). Hershey, PA: IRM Press; doi:10.4018/978-1-93177-744-5.ch015

Ritzhaupt, A. D., & Gill, T. G. (2008). A hybrid and novel approach to teaching computer programming in MIS curriculum. In S. Negash, M. Whitman, A. Woszczynski, K. Hoganson, & H. Mattord (Eds.), *Handbook of distance learning for real-time and asynchronous information technology education* (pp. 259–281). Hershey, PA: Information Science Reference; doi:10.4018/978-1-59904-964-9.ch014

Roche, E. M. (1993). International computing and the international regime. *Journal of Global Information Management*, *1*(2), 33–44. doi:10.4018/jgim.1993040103

Rocheleau, B. (2007). Politics, accountability, and information management. In G. Garson (Ed.), *Modern public information technology systems: Issues and challenges* (pp. 35–71). Hershey, PA: Idea Group Publishing; doi:10.4018/978-1-59904-051-6.ch003

Rodrigues Filho, J. (2010). E-government in Brazil: Reinforcing dominant institutions or reducing citizenship? In C. Reddick (Ed.), *Politics, democracy and e-government: Participation and service delivery* (pp. 347–362). Hershey, PA: Information Science Reference; doi:10.4018/978-1-61520-933-0.ch021

Rodriguez, S. R., & Thorp, D. A. (2013). eLearning for industry: A case study of the project management process. In A. Benson, J. Moore, & S. Williams van Rooij (Eds.), Cases on educational technology planning, design, and implementation: A project management perspective (pp. 319-342). Hershey, PA: Information Science Reference. doi:10.4018/978-1-4666-4237-9.ch017

Roman, A. V. (2013). Delineating three dimensions of e-government success: Security, functionality, and transformation. In J. Gil-Garcia (Ed.), *E-government success factors and measures: Theories, concepts, and methodologies* (pp. 171–192). Hershey, PA: Information Science Reference; doi:10.4018/978-1-4666-4058-0.ch010

Ross, S. C., Tyran, C. K., & Auer, D. J. (2008). Up in smoke: Rebuilding after an IT disaster. In H. Nemati (Ed.), *Information security and ethics: Concepts, methodologies, tools, and applications* (pp. 3659–3675). Hershey, PA: Information Science Reference; doi:10.4018/978-1-59904-937-3.ch248

Ross, S. C., Tyran, C. K., Auer, D. J., Junell, J. M., & Williams, T. G. (2005). Up in smoke: Rebuilding after an IT disaster. *Journal of Cases on Information Technology*, 7(2), 31–49. doi:10.4018/jcit.2005040103

Roy, J. (2008). Security, sovereignty, and continental interoperability: Canada's elusive balance. In T. Loendorf & G. Garson (Eds.), *Patriotic information systems* (pp. 153–176). Hershey, PA: IGI Publishing; doi:10.4018/978-1-59904-594-8.ch007

Rubeck, R. F., & Miller, G. A. (2009). vGOV: Remote video access to government services. In A. Scupola (Ed.), Cases on managing e-services (pp. 253-268). Hershey, PA: Information Science Reference. doi:10.4018/978-1-60566-064-6.ch017

Saekow, A., & Boonmee, C. (2011). The challenges of implementing e-government interoperability in Thailand: Case of official electronic correspondence letters exchange across government departments. In Y. Charalabidis (Ed.), *Interoperability in digital public services and administration: Bridging e-government and e-business* (pp. 40–61). Hershey, PA: Information Science Reference; doi:10.4018/978-1-61520-887-6.ch003

Saekow, A., & Boonmee, C. (2012). The challenges of implementing e-government interoperability in Thailand: Case of official electronic correspondence letters exchange across government departments. In *Digital democracy: Concepts, methodologies, tools, and applications* (pp. 1883–1905). Hershey, PA: Information Science Reference; doi:10.4018/978-1-4666-1740-7.ch094

Sagsan, M., & Medeni, T. (2012). Understanding "knowledge management (KM) paradigms" from social media perspective: An empirical study on discussion group for KM at professional networking site. In M. Cruz-Cunha, P. Gonçalves, N. Lopes, E. Miranda, & G. Putnik (Eds.), *Handbook of research on business social networking: Organizational, managerial, and technological dimensions* (pp. 738–755). Hershey, PA: Business Science Reference; doi:10.4018/978-1-61350-168-9.ch039

Sahi, G., & Madan, S. (2013). Information security threats in ERP enabled e-governance: Challenges and solutions. In *Enterprise resource planning: Concepts, methodologies, tools, and applications* (pp. 825–837). Hershey, PA: Business Science Reference; doi:10.4018/978-1-4666-4153-2.ch048

Sanford, C., & Bhattacherjee, A. (2008). IT implementation in a developing country municipality: A sociocognitive analysis. *International Journal of Technology and Human Interaction*, 4(3), 68–93. doi:10.4018/jthi.2008070104

Schelin, S. H. (2003). E-government: An overview. In G. Garson (Ed.), *Public information technology: Policy and management issues* (pp. 120–138). Hershey, PA: Idea Group Publishing; doi:10.4018/978-1-59140-060-8.ch006

Schelin, S. H. (2004). Training for digital government. In A. Pavlichev & G. Garson (Eds.), *Digital government: Principles and best practices* (pp. 263–275). Hershey, PA: Idea Group Publishing; doi:10.4018/978-1-59140-122-3.ch017

Schelin, S. H. (2007). E-government: An overview. In G. Garson (Ed.), *Modern public information technology systems: Issues and challenges* (pp. 110–126). Hershey, PA: Idea Group Publishing; doi:10.4018/978-1-59904-051-6.ch006

Schelin, S. H., & Garson, G. (2004). Theoretical justification of critical success factors. In G. Garson & S. Schelin (Eds.), *IT solutions series: Humanizing information technology: Advice from experts* (pp. 4–15). Hershey, PA: CyberTech Publishing; doi:10.4018/978-1-59140-245-9.ch002

Scime, A. (2002). Information systems and computer science model curricula: A comparative look. In M. Dadashzadeh, A. Saber, & S. Saber (Eds.), *Information technology education in the new millennium* (pp. 146–158). Hershey, PA: IRM Press; doi:10.4018/978-1-931777-05-6.ch018

Scime, A. (2009). Computing curriculum analysis and development. In M. Khosrow-Pour (Ed.), *Encyclopedia of information science and technology* (2nd ed., pp. 667–671). Hershey, PA: Information Science Reference; doi:10.4018/978-1-60566-026-4.ch108

Scime, A., & Wania, C. (2008). Computing curricula: A comparison of models. In C. Van Slyke (Ed.), *Information communication technologies: Concepts, methodologies, tools, and applications* (pp. 1270–1283). Hershey, PA: Information Science Reference; doi:10.4018/978-1-59904-949-6.ch088

Seidman, S. B. (2009). An international perspective on professional software engineering credentials. In H. Ellis, S. Demurjian, & J. Naveda (Eds.), *Software engineering: Effective teaching and learning approaches and practices* (pp. 351–361). Hershey, PA: Information Science Reference; doi:10.4018/978-1-60566-102-5.ch018

Seifert, J. W. (2007). E-government act of 2002 in the United States. In A. Anttiroiko & M. Malkia (Eds.), *Encyclopedia of digital government* (pp. 476–481). Hershey, PA: Information Science Reference; doi:10.4018/978-1-59140-789-8.ch072

Seifert, J. W., & Relyea, H. C. (2008). E-government act of 2002 in the United States. In A. Anttiroiko (Ed.), *Electronic government: Concepts, methodologies, tools, and applications* (pp. 154–161). Hershey, PA: Information Science Reference; doi:10.4018/978-1-59904-947-2.ch013

Seufert, S. (2002). E-learning business models: Framework and best practice examples. In M. Raisinghani (Ed.), *Cases on worldwide e-commerce: Theory in action* (pp. 70–94). Hershey, PA: Idea Group Publishing; doi:10.4018/978-1-930708-27-3.ch004

Shareef, M. A., & Archer, N. (2012). E-government service development. In M. Shareef, N. Archer, & S. Dutta (Eds.), *E-government service maturity and development: Cultural, organizational and technological perspectives* (pp. 1–14). Hershey, PA: Information Science Reference; doi:10.4018/978-1-60960-848-4.ch001

Shareef, M. A., & Archer, N. (2012). E-government initiatives: Review studies on different countries. In M. Shareef, N. Archer, & S. Dutta (Eds.), *E-government service maturity and development: Cultural, organizational and technological perspectives* (pp. 40–76). Hershey, PA: Information Science Reference; doi:10.4018/978-1-60960-848-4.ch003

Shareef, M. A., Kumar, U., & Kumar, V. (2011). E-government development: Performance evaluation parameters. In M. Shareef, V. Kumar, U. Kumar, & Y. Dwivedi (Eds.), *Stakeholder adoption of e-government services: Driving and resisting factors* (pp. 197–213). Hershey, PA: Information Science Reference; doi:10.4018/978-1-60960-601-5.ch010

Shareef, M. A., Kumar, U., Kumar, V., & Niktash, M. (2012). Electronic-government vision: Case studies for objectives, strategies, and initiatives. In M. Shareef, N. Archer, & S. Dutta (Eds.), *E-government service maturity and development: Cultural, organizational and technological perspectives* (pp. 15–39). Hershey, PA: Information Science Reference; doi:10.4018/978-1-60960-848-4.ch002

Shukla, P., Kumar, A., & Anu Kumar, P. B.Anu Kumar P.B. (2013). Impact of national culture on business continuity management system implementation. *International Journal of Risk and Contingency Management*, 2(3), 23–36. doi:10.4018/ijrcm.2013070102

Shulman, S. W. (2007). The federal docket management system and the prospect for digital democracy in U S rulemaking. In G. Garson (Ed.), *Modern public information technology systems: Issues and challenges* (pp. 166–184). Hershey, PA: Idea Group Publishing; doi:10.4018/978-1-59904-051-6.ch009

Simonovic, S. (2007). Problems of offline government in e-Serbia. In A. Anttiroiko & M. Malkia (Eds.), *Encyclopedia of digital government* (pp. 1342–1351). Hershey, PA: Information Science Reference; doi:10.4018/978-1-59140-789-8.ch205

Simonovic, S. (2008). Problems of offline government in e-Serbia. In A. Anttiroiko (Ed.), *Electronic government: Concepts, methodologies, tools, and applications* (pp. 2929–2942). Hershey, PA: Information Science Reference; doi:10.4018/978-1-59904-947-2.ch219

Singh, A. M. (2005). Information systems and technology in South Africa. In M. Khosrow-Pour (Ed.), *Encyclopedia of information science and technology* (pp. 1497–1502). Hershey, PA: Information Science Reference; doi:10.4018/978-1-59140-553-5.ch263

Singh, S., & Naidoo, G. (2005). Towards an e-government solution: A South African perspective. In W. Huang, K. Siau, & K. Wei (Eds.), *Electronic government strategies and implementation* (pp. 325–353). Hershey, PA: Idea Group Publishing; doi:10.4018/978-1-59140-348-7.ch014

Snoke, R., & Underwood, A. (2002). Generic attributes of IS graduates: An analysis of Australian views. In F. Tan (Ed.), *Advanced topics in global information management* (Vol. 1, pp. 370–384). Hershey, PA: Idea Group Publishing; doi:10.4018/978-1-930708-43-3.ch023

Sommer, L. (2006). Revealing unseen organizations in higher education: A study framework and application example. In A. Metcalfe (Ed.), *Knowledge management and higher education: A critical analysis* (pp. 115–146). Hershey, PA: Information Science Publishing; doi:10.4018/978-1-59140-509-2.ch007

Song, H., Kidd, T., & Owens, E. (2011). Examining technological disparities and instructional practices in English language arts classroom: Implications for school leadership and teacher training. In L. Tomei (Ed.), *Online courses and ICT in education: Emerging practices and applications* (pp. 258–274). Hershey, PA: Information Science Reference; doi:10.4018/978-1-60960-150-8.ch020

Speaker, P. J., & Kleist, V. F. (2003). Using information technology to meet electronic commerce and MIS education demands. In A. Aggarwal (Ed.), *Web-based education: Learning from experience* (pp. 280–291). Hershey, PA: Information Science Publishing; doi:10.4018/978-1-59140-102-5.ch017

Spitler, V. K. (2007). Learning to use IT in the workplace: Mechanisms and masters. In M. Mahmood (Ed.), *Contemporary issues in end user computing* (pp. 292–323). Hershey, PA: Idea Group Publishing; doi:10.4018/978-1-59140-926-7.ch013

Stellefson, M. (2011). Considerations for marketing distance education courses in health education: Five important questions to examine before development. In U. Demiray & S. Sever (Eds.), *Marketing online education programs: Frameworks for promotion and communication* (pp. 222–234). Hershey, PA: Information Science Reference; doi:10.4018/978-1-60960-074-7.ch014

Straub, D. W., & Loch, K. D. (2006). Creating and developing a program of global research. *Journal of Global Information Management, 14*(2), 1–28. doi:10.4018/jgim.2006040101

Straub, D. W., Loch, K. D., & Hill, C. E. (2002). Transfer of information technology to the Arab world: A test of cultural influence modeling. In M. Dadashzadeh (Ed.), *Information technology management in developing countries* (pp. 92–134). Hershey, PA: IRM Press; doi:10.4018/978-1-931777-03-2.ch005

Straub, D. W., Loch, K. D., & Hill, C. E. (2003). Transfer of information technology to the Arab world: A test of cultural influence modeling. In F. Tan (Ed.), *Advanced topics in global information management* (Vol. 2, pp. 141–172). Hershey, PA: Idea Group Publishing; doi:10.4018/978-1-59140-064-6.ch009

Suki, N. M., Ramayah, T., Ming, M. K., & Suki, N. M. (2013). Factors enhancing employed job seekers intentions to use social networking sites as a job search tool. In A. Mesquita (Ed.), *User perception and influencing factors of technology in everyday life* (pp. 265–281). Hershey, PA: Information Science Reference; doi:10.4018/978-1-4666-1954-8.ch018

Suomi, R. (2006). Introducing electronic patient records to hospitals: Innovation adoption paths. In T. Spil & R. Schuring (Eds.), *E-health systems diffusion and use: The innovation, the user and the use IT model* (pp. 128–146). Hershey, PA: Idea Group Publishing; doi:10.4018/978-1-59140-423-1.ch008

Swim, J., & Barker, L. (2012). Pathways into a gendered occupation: Brazilian women in IT. *International Journal of Social and Organizational Dynamics in IT, 2*(4), 34–51. doi:10.4018/ijsodit.2012100103

Tarafdar, M., & Vaidya, S. D. (2006). Adoption and implementation of IT in developing nations: Experiences from two public sector enterprises in India. In M. Khosrow-Pour (Ed.), *Cases on information technology planning, design and implementation* (pp. 208–233). Hershey, PA: Idea Group Publishing; doi:10.4018/978-1-59904-408-8.ch013

Tarafdar, M., & Vaidya, S. D. (2008). Adoption and implementation of IT in developing nations: Experiences from two public sector enterprises in India. In G. Garson & M. Khosrow-Pour (Eds.), *Handbook of research on public information technology* (pp. 905–924). Hershey, PA: Information Science Reference; doi:10.4018/978-1-59904-857-4.ch076

Thesing, Z. (2007). Zarina thesing, pumpkin patch. In M. Hunter (Ed.), *Contemporary chief information officers: Management experiences* (pp. 83–94). Hershey, PA: IGI Publishing; doi:10.4018/978-1-59904-078-3.ch007

Thomas, J. C. (2004). Public involvement in public administration in the information age: Speculations on the effects of technology. In M. Malkia, A. Anttiroiko, & R. Savolainen (Eds.), *eTransformation in governance: New directions in government and politics* (pp. 67–84). Hershey, PA: Idea Group Publishing; doi:10.4018/978-1-59140-130-8.ch004

Treiblmaier, H., & Chong, S. (2013). Trust and perceived risk of personal information as antecedents of online information disclosure: Results from three countries. In F. Tan (Ed.), *Global diffusion and adoption of technologies for knowledge and information sharing* (pp. 341–361). Hershey, PA: Information Science Reference; doi:10.4018/978-1-4666-2142-8.ch015

van Grembergen, W., & de Haes, S. (2008). IT governance in practice: Six case studies. In W. van Grembergen & S. De Haes (Eds.), *Implementing information technology governance: Models, practices and cases* (pp. 125–237). Hershey, PA: IGI Publishing; doi:10.4018/978-1-59904-924-3.ch004

van Os, G., Homburg, V., & Bekkers, V. (2013). Contingencies and convergence in European social security: ICT coordination in the back office of the welfare state. In M. Cruz-Cunha, I. Miranda, & P. Gonçalves (Eds.), *Handbook of research on ICTs and management systems for improving efficiency in healthcare and social care* (pp. 268–287). Hershey, PA: Medical Information Science Reference; doi:10.4018/978-1-4666-3990-4.ch013

Velloso, A. B., Gassenferth, W., & Machado, M. A. (2012). Evaluating IBMEC-RJ's intranet usability using fuzzy logic. In M. Cruz-Cunha, P. Gonçalves, N. Lopes, E. Miranda, & G. Putnik (Eds.), *Handbook of research on business social networking: Organizational, managerial, and technological dimensions* (pp. 185–205). Hershey, PA: Business Science Reference; doi:10.4018/978-1-61350-168-9.ch010

Villablanca, A. C., Baxi, H., & Anderson, K. (2009). Novel data interface for evaluating cardiovascular outcomes in women. In A. Dwivedi (Ed.), *Handbook of research on information technology management and clinical data administration in healthcare* (pp. 34–53). Hershey, PA: Medical Information Science Reference; doi:10.4018/978-1-60566-356-2.ch003

Villablanca, A. C., Baxi, H., & Anderson, K. (2011). Novel data interface for evaluating cardiovascular outcomes in women. In *Clinical technologies: Concepts, methodologies, tools and applications* (pp. 2094–2113). Hershey, PA: Medical Information Science Reference; doi:10.4018/978-1-60960-561-2.ch806

Virkar, S. (2011). Information and communication technologies in administrative reform for development: Exploring the case of property tax systems in Karnataka, India. In J. Steyn, J. Van Belle, & E. Mansilla (Eds.), *ICTs for global development and sustainability: Practice and applications* (pp. 127–149). Hershey, PA: Information Science Reference; doi:10.4018/978-1-61520-997-2.ch006

Virkar, S. (2013). Designing and implementing e-government projects: Actors, influences, and fields of play. In S. Saeed & C. Reddick (Eds.), *Human-centered system design for electronic governance* (pp. 88–110). Hershey, PA: Information Science Reference; doi:10.4018/978-1-4666-3640-8.ch007

Wallace, A. (2009). E-justice: An Australian perspective. In A. Martínez & P. Abat (Eds.), *E-justice: Using information communication technologies in the court system* (pp. 204–228). Hershey, PA: Information Science Reference; doi:10.4018/978-1-59904-998-4.ch014

Wang, G. (2012). E-democratic administration and bureaucratic responsiveness: A primary study of bureaucrats' perceptions of the civil service e-mail box in Taiwan. In K. Kloby & M. D'Agostino (Eds.), *Citizen 2.0: Public and governmental interaction through web 2.0 technologies* (pp. 146–173). Hershey, PA: Information Science Reference; doi:10.4018/978-1-4666-0318-9.ch009

Wangpipatwong, S., Chutimaskul, W., & Papasratorn, B. (2011). Quality enhancing the continued use of e-government web sites: Evidence from e-citizens of Thailand. In V. Weerakkody (Ed.), *Applied technology integration in governmental organizations: New e-government research* (pp. 20–36). Hershey, PA: Information Science Reference; doi:10.4018/978-1-60960-162-1.ch002

Wedemeijer, L. (2006). Long-term evolution of a conceptual schema at a life insurance company. In M. Khosrow-Pour (Ed.), *Cases on database technologies and applications* (pp. 202–226). Hershey, PA: Idea Group Publishing; doi:10.4018/978-1-59904-399-9.ch012

Whybrow, E. (2008). Digital access, ICT fluency, and the economically disadvantages: Approaches to minimize the digital divide. In F. Tan (Ed.), *Global information technologies: Concepts, methodologies, tools, and applications* (pp. 1409–1422). Hershey, PA: Information Science Reference; doi:10.4018/978-1-59904-939-7.ch102

Whybrow, E. (2008). Digital access, ICT fluency, and the economically disadvantages: Approaches to minimize the digital divide. In C. Van Slyke (Ed.), *Information communication technologies: Concepts, methodologies, tools, and applications* (pp. 764–777). Hershey, PA: Information Science Reference; doi:10.4018/978-1-59904-949-6.ch049

Wickramasinghe, N., & Geisler, E. (2010). Key considerations for the adoption and implementation of knowledge management in healthcare operations. In M. Saito, N. Wickramasinghe, M. Fuji, & E. Geisler (Eds.), *Redesigning innovative healthcare operation and the role of knowledge management* (pp. 125–142). Hershey, PA: Medical Information Science Reference; doi:10.4018/978-1-60566-284-8.ch009

Wickramasinghe, N., & Geisler, E. (2012). Key considerations for the adoption and implementation of knowledge management in healthcare operations. In *Organizational learning and knowledge: Concepts, methodologies, tools and applications* (pp. 1316–1328). Hershey, PA: Business Science Reference; doi:10.4018/978-1-60960-783-8.ch405

Wickramasinghe, N., & Goldberg, S. (2007). A framework for delivering m-health excellence. In L. Al-Hakim (Ed.), *Web mobile-based applications for healthcare management* (pp. 36–61). Hershey, PA: IRM Press; doi:10.4018/978-1-59140-658-7.ch002

Wickramasinghe, N., & Goldberg, S. (2008). Critical success factors for delivering m-health excellence. In N. Wickramasinghe & E. Geisler (Eds.), *Encyclopedia of healthcare information systems* (pp. 339–351). Hershey, PA: Medical Information Science Reference; doi:10.4018/978-1-59904-889-5.ch045

Wyld, D. (2009). Radio frequency identification (RFID) technology. In J. Symonds, J. Ayoade, & D. Parry (Eds.), *Auto-identification and ubiquitous computing applications* (pp. 279–293). Hershey, PA: Information Science Reference; doi:10.4018/978-1-60566-298-5.ch017

Yaghmaei, F. (2010). Understanding computerised information systems usage in community health. In J. Rodrigues (Ed.), *Health information systems: Concepts, methodologies, tools, and applications* (pp. 1388–1399). Hershey, PA: Medical Information Science Reference; doi:10.4018/978-1-60566-988-5.ch088

Yee, G., El-Khatib, K., Korba, L., Patrick, A. S., Song, R., & Xu, Y. (2005). Privacy and trust in e-government. In W. Huang, K. Siau, & K. Wei (Eds.), *Electronic government strategies and implementation* (pp. 145–190). Hershey, PA: Idea Group Publishing; doi:10.4018/978-1-59140-348-7.ch007

Yeh, S., & Chu, P. (2010). Evaluation of e-government services: A citizen-centric approach to citizen e-complaint services. In C. Reddick (Ed.), *Citizens and e-government: Evaluating policy and management* (pp. 400–417). Hershey, PA: Information Science Reference; doi:10.4018/978-1-61520-931-6.ch022

Young-Jin, S., & Seang-tae, K. (2008). E-government concepts, measures, and best practices. In A. Anttiroiko (Ed.), *Electronic government: Concepts, methodologies, tools, and applications* (pp. 32–57). Hershey, PA: Information Science Reference; doi:10.4018/978-1-59904-947-2.ch004

Yun, H. J., & Opheim, C. (2012). New technology communication in American state governments: The impact on citizen participation. In K. Bwalya & S. Zulu (Eds.), *Handbook of research on e-government in emerging economies: Adoption, e-participation, and legal frameworks* (pp. 573–590). Hershey, PA: Information Science Reference; doi:10.4018/978-1-4666-0324-0.ch029

Zhang, N., Guo, X., Chen, G., & Chau, P. Y. (2011). User evaluation of e-government systems: A Chinese cultural perspective. In F. Tan (Ed.), *International enterprises and global information technologies: Advancing management practices* (pp. 63–84). Hershey, PA: Information Science Reference; doi:10.4018/978-1-60960-605-3.ch004

Zuo, Y., & Hu, W. (2011). Trust-based information risk management in a supply chain network. In J. Wang (Ed.), *Supply chain optimization, management and integration: Emerging applications* (pp. 181–196). Hershey, PA: Business Science Reference; doi:10.4018/978-1-60960-135-5.ch013

Compilation of References

Aas, T. H., & Pedersen, P. E. (2012). Open service innovation: A feasibility study. In HuizinghK. R. E.ConnS. TorkkeliM.BitranI., (Eds.), *Proceedings of the 23rd ISPIM Innovation Conference*. LappeenrantaUniversity of Technology Press.

Abdul Halim, A. (2000). Toward Malaysia's knowledge empowerment in the 21st century. In *NITC, Access, Empowerment and Governance in the Information Age* (pp. xii–xvi). Kuala Lumpur: NITC Malaysia Publication.

Adnan, R. (2010). *Investigating the strategies to cope with resistance to change in implementing ICT: A case study of Allama Iqbal Open University*. Retrieved Sept. 20 2013 from: http://linc.mit.edu/linc2010/proceedings/session6Riaz.pdf

Agarwal, R., & Karahanna, E. (2000). Time flies when you're having fun: Cognitive absorption and beliefs about information technology usage. *Management Information Systems Quarterly*, 24(4), 665–695. doi:10.2307/3250951

Agarwal, R., & Prasad, J. (1997). The role of innovation characteristics and perceived voluntariness in the acceptance of information technologies. *Decision Sciences*, 28(3), 557–582. doi:10.1111/j.1540-5915.1997.tb01322.x

Agarwal, R., & Prasad, J. (1999). Are individual differences germane to the acceptance of new information technologies. *Decision Sciences*, 30(2), 361–391. doi:10.1111/j.1540-5915.1999.tb01614.x

Ahmad, N. B. (2008). *Towards a new mode of governance in Malaysia: Policy, regulatory and institutional challenges of digital convergence*. (PhD Thesis Unpublished). University of Hull.

Ahmad, N. B., & Dai, X. (2007). *The politics of digital convergence in Malaysia: A search for a New mode of governance*. Paper presented at the International Conference of Communication Technologies and Empowerment. Leeds, UK.

Ahmad, N. B. (2009). Malaysian new ICT policy: Regulatory reform and the new mode of governance. *The Journal of Administrative Science*, 6(1), 117–141.

Ajzen, I. (2002). *Construction of a standard questionnaire for the theory of planned behavior*. Retrieved August 8 2013 from http://www-unix.oit.umass.edu/~aizen

Ajzen, I. (1985). From intentions to action: A theory of planned behaviour. In J. Kuhl & J. Beckman (Eds.), *Action control: From cognitions to behaviour*. New York: Springer. doi:10.1007/978-3-642-69746-3_2

Ajzen, I. (1988). *Attitudes, personality and behaviour*. Milton Keynes, UK: Open University Press.

Ajzen, I. (1991). The theory of planned behavior. *Organizational Behavior and Human Decision Processes*, 50(2), 179–211. doi:10.1016/0749-5978(91)90020-T

Ajzen, I. (2002). Perceived behavioural control, self-efficacy, locus of control, and the theory of planned behaviour. *Journal of Applied Social Psychology*, 32(4), 665–683. doi:10.1111/j.1559-1816.2002.tb00236.x

Ajzen, I., & Fishbein, M. (1980). *Understanding attitudes and predicting social behavior*. Englewood Cliffs, NJ: Prentice-Hall.

Ajzen, I., & Fishbein, M. (2000). Attitudes and the attitude-behaviour relation: Reasoned and automatic processes. *European Review of Social Psychology*, *11*(1), 1–33. doi:10.1080/14792779943000116

Ajzen, I., & Fishbein, M. (2005). The Influence of Attitudes on Behavior. In D. Albarracin, B. T. Johnson, & M. P. Zanna (Eds.), *Handbook of attitudes and attitude Change*. Mahwah, NJ: Erlbaum.

Ajzen, I., & Madden, T. J. (1986). Prediction of goal-directed behaviour: Attitudes, intention, and perceived behavioural control. *Journal of Experimental Social Psychology*, *22*(5), 453–474. doi:10.1016/0022-1031(86)90045-4

Alavi, M., & Leidner, D. (2001). Technology-mediated learning: A call for greater depth and breadth of research. *Information Systems Research*, (March): 1–10. doi:10.1287/isre.12.1.1.9720

Aldrich, H., & Whetten, D. A. (1981). Organization-sets, action-sets, and networks: Making the most of simplicity. In Handbook of organizational design, (vol. 1, pp. 385-408). Oxford, UK: Oxford University Press.

Aldrich, H. A. (1979). *Organisations and environments*. Englewood Cliffs, NJ: Prentice-Hall.

Allan, R. (2006). Parliament elected representatives and technology 1997–2005—Good in Parts? *Parliamentary Affairs*, *59*(2), 360–365. doi:10.1093/pa/gsl007

Ambali, A. R. (2009). Digital divide and its implication on Malaysian e-government: Policy initiatives. In H. Rahman (Ed.), Social and political implications of data mining: Knowledge management in e-government, (pp. 267-287). New York: IGI Global.

Ambali, A. R. (2010). Determinants of E-Government Satisfaction: The case study of E-procurement. In H. Rahman (Ed.), Handbook of Research on E-Government Readiness for Information and Service Exchange: Utilizing Progressive Information Communication Technologies, (pp. 465-479). New York: IGI Global.

Ambali, A. R. (2009). E-government policy: Ground issues in e-filling system. *European Journal of Soil Science*, *11*(2), 249–266.

Ambali, A. R. (2013). Hala food and products in Malaysia: People's awareness and policy implications. *Intellectual Discourse*, *21*(1), 7–32.

Andersen, T. B., & Rand, J. (2006). *Does e-government reduce corruption?* University of Copenhagen, Department of Economics Working Paper.

Anon. (2004). Second phase of MSC to increase income of Malaysian. *BERNAMA*. Retrieved August 8, 2004 from http://www.magazine.jaring.my/

Anthony, G. (1990). *The consequences of modernity*. Cambridge, UK: Polity.

ARD/ZDF. (2009). *Online Studies 2009*. Retrieved from www.ard-zdf-onlinestudie.de/fileadmin/Online09/Eimeren1_7_09.pdf

Armitage, C. J., & Conner, M. (2001). Self-efficacy of the theory of planned behaviour: A meta-analytic review. *The British Journal of Social Psychology*, *40*(4), 471–499. doi:10.1348/014466601164939 PMID:11795063

Asgarkhani, M. (2005). The effectiveness of e-ervice in local government: A case study. *Electronic. Journal of E-Government*, *3*(4), 157–166.

Astrom, A. N., & Rise, J. (2001). Young adults' intention to eat healthy food: Extending the theory of planned behavior. *Psychology & Health*, *2*, 223–237. doi:10.1080/08870440108405501

Atkinson, D. R. & Ulevich, J. (2000). *Digital government: The next step to reengineering the federal government*. Technology & New Economy Project, Progressive Policy Institute, March.

Azzman, T. M. S. (1988). *Microelectronics, information technology and society*. Paper presented at First Raja Tan Sri Zainal Lecture, IEM/MIMOS. Kuala Lumpur, Malaysia.

Azzman, T. M. S. (2000). The changing world: ICT and governance. In *NITC, Access, Empowerment and Governance in the Information Age* (pp. 1–13). Kuala Lumpur: NITC Malaysia Publication.

Bache, I. (2000). Government within governance: Network steering in Yorkshire and the Humber. *Public Administration*, *78*(3), 575–592. doi:10.1111/1467-9299.00219

Bagozi, R. P. (1981). Attitudes, intention and behaviour: A test of some key hyphotheses. *Journal of Personality and Social Psychology*, *41*(4), 607–627. doi:10.1037/0022-3514.41.4.607

Baker, S. A., Morrison, D. M., Carter, W. B., & Verdon, M. S. (1996). Using the theory of reasoned action (TR) to understand the decision to use condoms in an STD clinic population. *Health Education Quarterly*, *23*(4), 528–542. doi:10.1177/109019819602300411 PMID:8910029

Bandura, A. (1977). Self-efficacy: Toward a unifying theory of behavioural change. *Psychological Review*, *84*(2), 122–147. doi:10.1037/0033-295X.84.2.191 PMID:847061

Bandura, A. (1978). The self-sytem in reciprocal determinism. *The American Psychologist*, *33*(4), 344–358. doi:10.1037/0003-066X.33.4.344

Bandura, A. (1986). *Social foundations of thought and action: A social cognitive theory*. Englewood Cliffs, NJ: Prentice-Hall.

Bandura, A. (1991, December). (1 99 1). Social cognitive theory of self-regulation. *Organizational Behavior and Human Decision Processes*, *50*(2), 248–287. doi:10.1016/0749-5978(91)90022-L

Bandura, A. (1998). Health promotion from the perspective of social cognitive theory. *Psychology & Health*, *13*(4), 623–649. doi:10.1080/08870449808407422

Bang, H., & Esmark, A. (2009, March). Good governance in network society: Reconfiguring the political from politics to policy. *Administrative Theory & Praxis*, *31*(1), 7–37. doi:10.2753/ATP1084-1806310101

Barber, B. R. (2003). *Strong democracy: Participatory politics for a new age*. University of California Press.

Barclay, D. W., Higgins, C., & Thompson, R. (1995). The partial least square approach to causal modeling: Personal computer adoption use as illustration. *Technology Studies*, *2*(2), 285–309.

Baruch, Y., & Holton, B. C. (2008). Survey response rate levels and trends in organizational research. *Human Relations*, *81*(8), 1139–1160. doi:10.1177/0018726708094863

Bearden, W. O., & Crokett, M. (1981). Self-monitoring, norms and attitudes as influences on consumer complaining. *Journal of Business Research*, *9*(3), 255–266. doi:10.1016/0148-2963(81)90020-5

Benbasat, I., & Barki, H. (2007). Quo vadis, TAM? *Journal of the Association for Information Systems*, *8*(4), 211–218.

Benhabib, S. (Ed.). (1996). *Democracy and difference: Contesting the boundaries of the political*. Princeton, NJ: Princeton University Press.

Benson, J. K. (1982). A framework for policy analysis. In D. L. Rogers & D. A. Whetten (Eds.), *Interorganisational Coordination: Theory, Research, and Implementation* (pp. 137–176). Ames, IA: Iowa State University Press.

Bentler, P. M., & Speckart, G. (1979). Models of attitude-behaviour relations. *Psychological Review*, *86*(5), 425–464. doi:10.1037/0033-295X.86.5.452

Benz, A. (1998). Politikverflechtung ohne politikverflechtungsfalle: koordination und strukturdynamik im europäischen mehrebenensystem [joint policy-making without joint decision trap: Coordination and structural dynamics in Europe's multilayered polity]. *Politische Vierteljahresschrift* [*Political Science Quarterly*], *39*, 558-589.

Beresford, A. D. (2003). Foucault's Theory Of Governance And The Deterrence Of Internet Fraud. *Administration & Society*, *35*(1), 82–103. doi:10.1177/0095399702250347

Bertot, J. C., Jaeger, P. T., & McClure, C. R. (2008). Citizen-centered e-covernment services: Benefits, costs, and research needs. In *Proceedings of the 9th Annual International Digital Government Research Conference*. Montreal, Canada: Academic Press.

Bertot, J. C. (2003). The multiple dimensions of the digital divide: More than the technology 'haves' and 'have nots..' *Government Information Quarterly*, *20*(2), 185–191. doi:10.1016/S0740-624X(03)00036-4

Bhatnagar, S. (2014). *Public service delivery: Role of information and communication technology in improving governance and development impact*. Asian Development Bank (AD), Working Paper Series, No. 391.

Bhatnagar, S. (2009). *Unlocking e-government potential concepts, cases and practical insights*. New Delhi: Sage Publication.

Bhattacherjee, A. (2001). Understanding information systems continuance: An expectation-confirmation model. *Management Information Systems Quarterly*, *25*(3), 351–370. doi:10.2307/3250921

Blumler, J. G., & Gurevitch, M. (1995). *The crisis of political communication*. London: Academic Press.

Bogason, P. (2000). Public policy and local governance: institutions in postmodern society. Edward Elgar Publishing, Incorporated.

Bohman, J. (Ed.). (1997). *Deliberative democracy: Essays on reason and politics*. MIT Press.

Boneva, B., Kraut, R., & Frohlich, D. (2001). Using e-mail for personal relationships: The difference gender makes. *The American Behavioral Scientist*, *45*(3), 530–549. doi:10.1177/00027640121957204

Börzel, T. A. (1998). Organizing Babylon-On the Different Conceptions of Policy Networks. Public Administration, 76(2), 253-273.

Bovaird, T., & Loeffler, E. (2007). Assessing the quality of local governance: A case study of public services. *Public Money and Management*, *27*(4), 293–300. doi:10.1111/j.1467-9302.2007.00597.x

Boyd, O. P. (2008). Differences in eDemocracy parties' eP-articipation systems. *Information Polity*, *13*(3), 167–188.

Breen, J. (2000). At the dawn of e-government: The citizen as customer. *Government Finance Review*, *15*(3), 15–20.

Bretschneider, S. (2003). Information technology, e-overn-ment, and institutional change. *Public Administration Review*, *63*(6), 738–741. doi:10.1111/1540-6210.00337

Brian, D., & Finn, K. (2002). Towards a framework for government portal design: The government, citizen and portal perspectives. In A. Gronlund (Ed.), Electronic Government: Design, Application & Management. Hershey, PA: Idea Group Publishing.

Brown, L. G. (1990). Convenience in services marketing. *Journal of Services Marketing*, *4*(1), 53–59. doi:10.1108/EUM0000000002505

Brown, M. B. (2006). Survey article: Citizen panels and the concept of representation. *Journal of Political Philosophy*, *14*(2), 203–225. doi:10.1111/j.1467-9760.2006.00245.x

Bruner, G. C. II, & Kumar, A. (2005). Explaining consumer acceptance of handheld internet devices. *Journal of Business Research*, *58*(5), 553–558. doi:10.1016/j.jbusres.2003.08.002

Burton-Jones, A., & Hubona, G. S. (2006). The mediation of external variables in the technology acceptance model. *Information & Management*, *43*(6), 706–717. doi:10.1016/j.im.2006.03.007

Buyers.gov. (n.d.). Retrieved from http://www.buyers.gov

Byungtaa, K. (2000). *Anti-corruption measures in the public procurement service sector*. Paper presented at Conference of Asia Pacific Forum on Combating Corruption. Seoul, Korea.

Calista, D. J., & Melitski, J. (2007). E-government and e-governance: Converging constructs of public sector information and communications technologies. *Public Administration Quarterly*, 87–120.

Campbell, D. T. (1963). Social attitudes and other acquired behavioural dispositions. In S. Koch (Ed.), Psychology: A Study of A Science, (pp. 94-172). New York: McGraw-Hill. doi:10.1037/10590-003

Caperchione, E. (2006). *The new public management: A perspective for finance practitioners. Paper presented at the Federation of European Accountants. Debating International Developments in New Public Financial Management*. Oslo: Cappelen.

Carnoy, M., & Castells, M. (2001). Globalization, the knowledge society, and the Network State: Poulantzas at the millennium. *Global Networks*, *1*(1), 1–18. doi:10.1111/1471-0374.00002

Carroll, J., Howard, S., Vetere, F., Peck, J., & Murphy, J. (2002). Just what do the youth of today want? Technology appropriation by young people. *Paper Presented at HICSS*, *35*(Jan), 7–10.

295

Carter, L., & Belanger, F. (2005). The utilization of e-government services: Citizen trust, innovation and acceptance. *Information Systems Journal, 15*(1), 5–25. doi:10.1111/j.1365-2575.2005.00183.x

Castells, M., & Cardoso, G. (Eds.). (2006). The network society: From knowledge to policy. Center for Transatlantic Relations, Paul H. Nitze School of Advanced International Studies, Johns Hopkins University.

Castells, M. (1991). The informational city, information technology, economic restructuring, and the urban-regional process. *Environment & Planning A, 23*, 458–459.

Castells, M. (1996). *The rise of the network society.* Cambridge, MA: Blackwell Publishers.

Castells, M. (2000). Materials for an exploratory theory of the network society. *The British Journal of Sociology, 51*(1), 5–24. doi:10.1080/000713100358408

Castells, M. (2000). Toward a sociology of the network society. *Contemporary Sociology, 29*(5), 693–699. doi:10.2307/2655234

Chadwick, A. (2006). *Internet politics: States, citizens, and new communication technologies.* Oxford University Press.

Chadwick, A., & May, C. (2003). Interaction between states and citizens in the age of the Internet: "e-Government" in the United States, Britain, and the European Union. *Governance: An International Journal of Policy, Administration and Institutions, 16*(2), 271–300. doi:10.1111/1468-0491.00216

Chan, C.-C., Liang, C., Yan, C.-F., & Tseng, J.-S. (2012). The impact of college students' intrinsic and extrinsic motivation on continuance intention to use English mobile learning systems. In Asia-Pacific Education Researcher, (pp. 1-12). Springer.

Chau, P. Y. (2001). Influence of computer attitude and self-efficacy on IT usage behaviour. *Journal of End User Computing, 13*(1), 26–33. doi:10.4018/joeuc.2001010103

Chen, L., Gillenson, M. L., & Sherrell, D. L. (2002). Enticing online consumers: An extended technology acceptance perspective. *Information & Management, 39*(8), 705–719. doi:10.1016/S0378-7206(01)00127-6

Chin, W. W. (1998). The partial least squares approach to structural equation modeling. In G.A. Marcoulides (Ed.), Modern Methods for Business Research. Lawrence Erlbaum Associates.

Chin, W. W. (1998). The partial least squares approach to structural equation modeling. In G. A. Marcoulides (Ed.), *Modern Methods for Business Research,* (pp. 295–358). Mahwah, NJ: Lawrence Erlbaum Associates.

Chow, W. S., & Chan, L. S. (2008). Social network and shared goals in organizational knowledge sharing. *Information & Management, 45*(7), 24–30. doi:10.1016/j.im.2008.06.007

Chua, D. (2012). E-learning boost for students getting free netbooks. *The Star Online.* Retrieved June 20 2012, from http://www.thestaronline.com.my

Cohen, M. D., March, J. G., & Olsen, J. P. (1972). A garbage can model of organizational choice. *Administrative Science Quarterly, 17*(1), 1–25. doi:10.2307/2392088

Coleman, S. (2007). e-Democracy: The history and future of an idea. In The Oxford handbook of information and communication technologies. Oxford University Press.

Coleman, S., & Gotze, J. (2001). Bowling together: Online public engagement in policy deliberation. London: Hansard Society.

Coleman, S., & Norris, D. F. (2005). *A new agenda for e-democracy.* OII Forum Discussion Paper.

Coleman, S. (2006, September). Parliamentary communication in an age of digital interactivity. *Aslib Proceedings, 58*(5), 371–388. doi:10.1108/00012530610692339

Coleman, S., Taylor, J., & van de Donk, W. (Eds.). (1999). *Parliament in the Age of the Internet.* Oxford, UK: Oxford University Press.

Coleman, W. D., & Perl, A. (1999). Internationalized policy environments and policy network analysis. *Political Studies, 47*(4), 691–709. doi:10.1111/1467-9248.00225

Collins, C., Buhalis, D., & Peters, M. (2003). Enhancing SMTEs business performance through the Internet and eLearning Platforms. Centre for eTourism Research (CeTR): School of Management, University of Surrey.

COMNET-IT UNESCO. (2004). *Country profiles of eGovernance – Malaysia*. Retrieved from http://www.dirap.uqam.ca/ahp03e.htm

Compeau, D. R., & Higgins, C. A. (1995). Computer self-efficacy: Development of a measure and initial test. *Management Information Systems Quarterly, 19*(2), 189–212. doi:10.2307/249688

Compeau, D. R., Higgins, C. A., & Huff, S. (1999). Social cognitive theory and individual reactions to computing technology: A longitudinal-study. *Management Information Systems Quarterly, 23*(2), 145–158. doi:10.2307/249749

Conner, M., & Armitage, C. J. (1998). Extending the theory of planned behaviour: A review and avenues for further research. *Journal of Applied Social Psychology, 28*(15), 1429–1464. doi:10.1111/j.1559-1816.1998.tb01685.x

Cook, K. S. (1977). Exchange and power in networks of interorganizational relations. *The Sociological Quarterly, 18*(1), 62–82. doi:10.1111/j.1533-8525.1977.tb02162.x

Crites, S. L. Jr, Fabrigar, L. R., & Petty, R. E. (1994). Measuring the affective and cognitive properties of attitudes: Conceptual and methodological issues. *Personality and Social Psychology Bulletin, 20*(6), 619–634. doi:10.1177/0146167294206001

Csikszentmihalyi, M. (1990). *Flow: The psychology of optimal experience*. Harper & Row.

Cutler, A. C., Haufler, V., & Porter, T. (Eds.). (1999). *Private authority and international affairs*. Suny Press.

Dai, X. (2003). A new mode of governance? Transnationalisation of European regions and cities in the information age. *Telematics and Informatics, 20*(3), 193–213. doi:10.1016/S0736-5853(03)00014-5

Dai, X. (2007). Prospect and concerns of e-democracy at the European parliament. *Journal of Legislative Studies, 13*(3), 370–387. doi:10.1080/13572330701500789

Dai, X., & Norton, P. (2007). The Internet and parliamentary democracy in Europe. *Journal of Legislative Studies, 13*(3), 342–353. doi:10.1080/13572330701500763

Davies, C. (2008). The relationship between the theory of planned behaviour, past exercise behaviour and intention in individuals diagnosed with Type 2 Diabetes Studies, *Learning. Innovation and Development, 5*(2), 25–32.

Davis, (1989). Perceived usefulness, perceived ease of use, and User Acceptance of Information Technology. *MIS Quarterly*, 319-340.

Davis, F. D. (1986). *A technology acceptance model for empirically testing new end-user information systems: Theory and results*. (Doctoral Dissertation). MIT Sloan School of Management.

Davis, A. (2009). New media and fat democracy: The paradox of online participation. *New Media & Society*.

Davis, F. D., Bagozzi, R. P., & Warshaw, P. R. (1989). User Acceptance of Computer Technology: A Comparison of Two Theoretical Models. *Management Science, 35*(8), 982–1002. doi:10.1287/mnsc.35.8.982

Davis, F. D., Bagozzi, R. P., & Warshaw, P. R. (1992). Extrinsic and intrinsic motivation to use computers in the workplace. *Journal of Applied Social Psychology, 22*(14), 1111–1132. doi:10.1111/j.1559-1816.1992.tb00945.x

Davis, F. D., & Venkatesh, V. (1996). A theoretical extension of technology acceptance model: Four longitudinal field studies. *Management Science, 46*(2), 186–2004.

Dawes, S. S. (2009). Governance in the digital age: A research and action framework for an uncertain future. *Government Information Quarterly, 26*(2), 257–264. doi:10.1016/j.giq.2008.12.003

Di Gennaro, C., & Dutton, W. (2006). The Internet and the public: Online and offline political participation in the United Kingdom. *Parliamentary Affairs, 59*(2), 299–313. doi:10.1093/pa/gsl004

Diamond, L. (2008). *How People View Democracy*. Baltimore, MD: Johns Hopkins University Press.

Dias, G. A. (2002). Periódicos eletrônicos: Considerações relativas à aceitação desterecurso pelos usuários. *Ciência da Informação, Brasília, 31*(3), 18–25.

Dixon, K. C. (2009). Attitudes towards ICT based interaction: A bachelor of education case studies. Australia: School of Education, Curtin University of Technology Perth. Retrieved from http://www.aare.edu.au/09pap/dix091331.pdf

Doll, W. J., Hendrickson, A. & Xiaodong, D. (1998). Using Davis's perceived usefulness and ease-of-use instruments for decision making: A confirmatory and multigroup invariance analysis. *Decision Sciences, 29*(4), 839-869.

Dowding, K. (1995). Model or metaphor? A critical review of the policy network approach. Political studies, 43(1), 136-158.

Droba, D. D. (1974). The nature of attitudes. *The Journal of Social Psychology, 4*(4), 444–463. doi:10.1080/0022 4545.1933.9919338

Dryzek, J. S. (2007). Networks and democratic ideals: Equality, freedom, and communication. In *Theories of democratic network governance*, (pp. 262-273). Academic Press.

Dryzek, J. S. (2001). Legitimacy and economy in deliberative democracy. *Political Theory, 29*(5), 651–669. doi:10.1177/0090591701029005003

Dunne, K. (2009). Cross Cutting Discussion: A form of online discussion discovered within local political online forums. *Information Polity, 14*(3), 219–232.

Eagly, A. H., & Chaiken, S. (1993). *The psychology of attitudes.* Fort Worth, TX: Harcourt Brace Jovanovich.

Economic Planning Unit (EPU). (2012, February 25). *RMKE.* Retrieved from http://www.epu.gov.my/html/themes/epu/html/RMKE

Economist (2000, June 24). A survey of government and the Internet. *The Next Revolution.*

Elmo Classroom Solution. (2012). *What is ICT education.* Retrieved May 19th 2013 from http://www.elmoglobal.com/en/html/ict/01.aspx

Elstub, S. (2006). A double-edged sword: The increasing diversity of deliberative democracy. *Contemporary Politics, 12*(3-4), 301–319. doi:10.1080/13569770601086204

Esmark, A. (2007). Democratic accountability and network governance–problems and potentials. In *Theories of democratic network governance*, (pp. 274-296). Academic Press.

Everard, A., & Galletta, D. F. (2005). How Presentation Flaws Affect Perceived Site Quality, Trust, and Intention to Purchase from an Online Store. *Journal of Management Information Systems, 22*(3), 55–95.

Fadilah, D. (2012). ICT a necessity in education. *The Star Online.* Retrieved Feb. 25th 2012 from http://www.thestaronline.com.my

Fariza, N. M., Norizan, A. R., Abdullah, M. Y., Salman, A., Abdul Malek, J., & Hussin, S. (2011, October). Empowering the community through ICT innovation. In *Proceedings of Communications (MICC)*, (pp. 13-17). IEEE.

Fazio, R. H., Powell, M. C., & Herr, P. M. (1983). Toward a process model of the attitude–behavior relation: Accessing one's attitude upon mere observation of the attitude object. *Journal of Personality and Social Psychology, 44*(4), 723–735. doi:10.1037/0022-3514.44.4.723

Feenberg, A. (1999). *Questioning technology.* London: Routledge.

Ferguson, S., & Mellow, P. (2004). Whakahihiko te hinengaro: Lessons from a preshool te reo e-learning resource. *Computers in New Zealand Schools, 16*(2), 41–44.

Fila, S. A., & Smith, C. (2006). Applying the theory of planned behavior to healthy eating behaviors in urban Native American youth. *The International Journal of Behavioral Nutrition and Physical Activity, 3*(1), 11–22. doi:10.1186/1479-5868-3-11 PMID:16734903

FirstGov Website. (n.d.). Retrieved from http://www.firstgov.gov

Fishbein, M. (1993). Introduction. In D. J. Terry, C. Gallois, & M. McCamish (Eds.), *The Theory of Reasoned Action: Its Application to AIDS-Preventive Behaviour* (pp. xv–xxv). Pergamon.

Fishbein, M., & Ajzen, I. (1979). *Belief, attitude, intention, and behaviour: an introduction to theory and research.* Boston, MA: Addison-Wesley.

Fishbein, M., & Ajzen, I. (1981). Attitudes and voting behavior: An application of the theory of reasoned action. In G. M. Stephenson & J. M. Davis (Eds.), *Progress in Applied Social Psychology*. London: Wiley.

Fishkin, J. S. (1997). *The voice of the people: Public opinion and democracy*. Yale University Press.

Fogg, B. (1999). The elements of computer credibility. In *Proceedings of the CHI' 99 (Computer-Human Interaction) Conference on Human Factors in Computing Systems*. ACM.

Forestor, J. (1989). Planning in the phase of power. Berkeley, CA: University of California Press.

Fornell, C., & Larcker, D. F. (1981). Evaluating structural equation models with unobservable and measurement error. *JMR, Journal of Marketing Research*, *18*(1), 39–50. doi:10.2307/3151312

Foucault, M. (1982). The subject and power. In Michel Foucault, beyond structuralism and hermeneutics. Chicago: University of Chicago Press.

Foucault, M., & Ewald, F. (2003). Society Must Be Defended: Lectures at the Collège de France, 1975-1976. Administrative Theory & Praxis, 26(4), 489-508.

Foucault, M. (1980). *Power/knowledge: Selected interviews and other writings, 1972-1977*. Random House LLC.

Fountain, J. E. (2001). *Building the Virtual State: Information Technology and Institutional Change*. Washington, DC: Brookings Institution.

Fox, C. J., & Miller, H. T. (1995). *Postmodern public administration*. ME Sharpe.

Francoli, M. (2008). Parliaments Online: Modernizing and engaging? Parliaments in the Digital Age: Forum Discussion Paper, 13, 4-8.

Fred, B. S. (Ed.). (1999). *Trust in cyberspace*. Washington, DC: National Academy of Science.

Freeman, L. R., & Freeman, R. (1997). *Democracy in the digital age*. Demos.

Friedrich, C. J. (1963). *Man and his government: An empirical theory of politics*. New York: McGraw-Hill.

Gartner Group. (2000). *Key issues in e-government strategy and management*. Research Notes, Key Issues. Stamford, CT: Gartner Group, Inc.

Gefen, D., Karahanna, E., & Straub, D. (2003). Trust and TAM in online shopping: An integrated model. *Management Information Systems Quarterly*, *27*(1), 51–90.

General Accounting Office (GAO). (1999). *Information security: Weaknesses at 22 agencies*. GAO/AIMED-00-32R. Author.

Genschel, P. 1995. Dynamische Verflechtung in der internationalen Standardisierung [Dynamic Joint Decision-Making in International Standarisation]. In Gesellschaftliche Selbstregulierung und politische Steuerung [Societal Self-Regulation and Governance]. Frankfurt/M.: Campus.

Gibson, R. K., Lusoli, W., & Ward, S. (2005). Online participation in the UK: Testing a 'contextualised' model of Internet effects1. *British Journal of Politics and International Relations*, *7*(4), 561–583. doi:10.1111/j.1467-856X.2005.00209.x

Gilbert, A. (2001, April 6). President Bush backs e-government, digital signatures. *Information Week*, p. 24.

Goodwin, N. (1987). Functionality and usability. *Communications of the ACM*, *30*(March), 229–233. doi:10.1145/214748.214758

Government of Malaysia. (2002). *Eight Malaysia Plan (2001-2005)*. Putrajaya: Economic Planning Unit.

Government Services Administration Auctions (GSA). (n.d.). Retrieved from http://www.gsaauctions.gov

Graham, G. (1999). *The Internet: A philosophical inquiry*. Psychology Press.

Greene, K., Hale, J. L., & Rubin, D. L. (1979). A test of theory of reasoned action in the context of use and AIDS. *Communication Reports*, *10*(1), 21–33. doi:10.1080/08934219709367656

Grinter, R. E., & Eldridge, M. (2001). Y do tngrs luv 2 txt msg? In *Proceedings of the Seventh European Conference on Computer-Supported Cooperative Work ECSCW'01*, (pp. 219-238). Kluwer Academic Publishers.

Gronlund, A. (2002). *Electronic government: Design, application and management*. Hershey, PA: Idea Group Publishing.

Groot, T., & Budding, T. (2008). New public management's current issues and future prospects. *Financial Accountability & Management*, *24*(1), 1–13. doi:10.1111/j.1468-0408.2008.00440.x

Hacker, K. L., & van Dijk, J. (Eds.). (2000). *Digital democracy: Issues of theory and practice*. UK: Sage. doi:10.4135/9781446218891.n1

Hair, J. F., Black, W. C., Babin, B. J., & Anderson, R. E. (2010). *Multivariate data analysis*. Upper Saddle River, NJ: Prentice-Hall.

Hale, J. L., Householder, B. J., & Greene, K. L. (2003). The theory of reasoned action. In J. P. Dillard & M. Pfau (Eds.), *The Persuasion Handbook: Developments in Theory and Practice*. Thousand Oaks, CA: Sage.

Harding, A. (1997). Urban Regimes in a Europe of the Cities? *European Urban and Regional Studies*, *4*(4), 291–314. doi:10.1177/096977649700400401

Harris, F. J., & Schwartz, J. (2000, June 22). Anti-drug web site tracks visitors. *Washington Post*, p. 23.

Hartwick, J., & Barki, H. (1994). Explaining the role of user participation in information system use. *Management Science*, *40*(4), 440–465. doi:10.1287/mnsc.40.4.440

Haslinda, S. A. N., Azizah, A. R., & Othman, I. (2011, November). Government's ICT project failure factors: A revisit. In *Proceedings of Research and Innovation in Information Systems (ICRIIS 2011)*, (pp. 1-6). IEEE.

Hasson, J. (2001, March 19). Treasury CIO Promotes expand fed portal. *Federal Computer Week*, p. 14.

Hay, C. (1998). The tangled webs we weave: The discourse, strategy and practice of networking. In Comparing policy networks. Open University Press.

Heeley, M., & Damodaran, L. (2009). *Digital inclusion: A review of international policy and practice*. Loughborough University.

Heinrich, C. J., & Lynn, L. E., Jr. (2000). Governance and performance. Washington DC: Georgetown University Press. Administrative Theory & Praxis, *24*(4), 693-720.

Held, D. (1995). *Democracy and the global order* (Vol. 232). Cambridge, MA: Polity Press.

Held, D. (2006). *Models of democracy*. Stanford University Press.

Hendriks, C. M. (2009). The democratic soup: Mixed meanings of political representation in governance networks. *Governance: An International Journal of Policy, Administration and Institutions*, *22*(4), 689–715. doi:10.1111/j.1468-0491.2009.01459.x

Herrera, G. L. (2002). The politics of bandwidth: International political implications of a global digital information network. *Review of International Studies*, *28*(01), 93–122. doi:10.1017/S0260210502000931

Higgins, D. L., O'Reilly, K., Tashima, N., Crain, C., Beeker, C., & Goldbaum, G. et al. (1996). Using formative research to lay the foundation for community-level HIV prevention efforts: The AIDS Community Demonstration Projects. *Public Health Reports*, *111*(Supplement), 28–35. PMID:8862154

Hirst, P. Q., Thompson, G., & Bromley, S. (2009). *Globalization in question*. Polity.

Hirst, P. (2013). *Associative democracy: new forms of economic and social governance*. John Wiley & Sons.

Hishamudi, I., & Ali, K. (2004, March). Study of relationship between perception of value and price and customer satisfaction: The case of Malaysian telecommunication industry. *The Journal of American Academy of Business*, 309-313.

Hjern, B., & Porter, D. O. (1981). Implementation structures: A new unit of administrative analysis. *Organization Studies*, *2*(3), 211–227. doi:10.1177/017084068100200301

Ho In Kang. (2012). E-procurement experience in Korea: Implementation and impact. Public Procurement Services, 1-19.

Hobson, K. (2010). Beyond the Control Society. *Administrative Theory & Praxis*, *32*(2), 252–261. doi:10.2753/ATP1084-1806320207

Hogg, M., & Vaughan, G. (2002). *Social Psychology* (3rd ed.). London: Person-Prentice Hall.

Hossain, M. M., & Prybutok, V. R. (2008). Consumer acceptance of RFID technology: An exploratory study. *IEEE Transactions on Engineering Management*, *55*(2), 316–328. doi:10.1109/TEM.2008.919728

Hsu, C., & Lu, H. (2004). Why do people play on-line games? An extended TAM with social influences and low experience. *Information & Management*, *41*(7), 853–868. doi:10.1016/j.im.2003.08.014

Humphreys, P. (1994). *Media and media policy in Germany: The press and broadcasting since 1945*. Oxford, UK: Berg.

Humphreys, P. (2006). Globalization, regulatory competition, and EU policy transfer in the telecoms and broadcasting sectors. *International Journal of Public Administration*, *29*(4-6), 305–334. doi:10.1080/01900690500437055

Humphreys, P., Dyson, K., Negrine, R., & Simon, J.-P. (1992). *Broadcasting and new media policies in Western Europe: A comparative study of technological change and public policy*. London: Routledge.

Hung, S. Y., Chang, C. M., & Yu, T. J. (2006). Determinants of user acceptance of the e-government services: The case of online tax filing and payment system. *Government Information Quarterly*, *23*(1), 97–122. doi:10.1016/j.giq.2005.11.005

Hung, W., Chang, I., Li, Y., & Hung, H. (2005). An empirical study on the impact of quality antecedents on taxpayers' acceptance of internet tax filing systems. *Government Information Quarterly*, *22*(3), 389–410. doi:10.1016/j.giq.2005.05.002

Iglesias, G. (2010). *E-government initiatives of four Philippine cities*. APEC Study Center Network (PASCN), Discussion Paper Series No.22.

Ioinson, A. N., & Paine, C. B. (2007). Self-disclosure, privacy and the Internet. The Oxford handbook of internet psychology, (pp. 237-252). Oxford, UK: Oxford University Press.

Jackson, P. M., & Stainsby, L. (2000). The public manager in 2010: Managing public sector networked organizations. *Public Money and Management*, *20*(1), 11–16. doi:10.1111/1467-9302.00196

Jacobs, J. (2000). Interaction in the public interest: Regulating new communications technologies to deliver public interest information services. In M. Sheehan, S. Ramsay, & J. Patrick (Eds.), *Transcending boundaries: Integrating people, processes and systems:Proceedings of the 2000 Conference*. Brisbane, Australia: Academic Press.

Jarvenpaa, S. L., Tractinsky, N., & Vitale, M. (2000). Consumer trust in and internet store. *Information Technology Management*, *1*(2), 45–71. doi:10.1023/A:1019104520776

Jehangir, M., & Dominic, P.D.D., Naseebullah, & Khan, A. (2011). Towards digital economy: The development of ICT and e-Commerce in Malaysia. *Modern Apllied Science*, *5*(2), 171–178.

Jenkins, M., & Hanson, J. (2003). E-learning series: A guide for senior managers, learning and teaching support network (LTSN) generic centre. *Journal of Distance Education*, *9*(3), 162–175.

Jessop, B. (1998). The rise of governance and the risks of failure: the case of economic development. International Social Science Journal, 50(155), 29-45.

John, P., & Cole, A. (2000). Policy networks and local political leadership in Britain and France. In G. Stoker (Ed.), The new politics of British local governance. Pal grave Macmillan.

Johnston, E. (2010). Governance infrastructures in 2020. *Public Administration Review*, *70*(s1), s122–s128. doi:10.1111/j.1540-6210.2010.02254.x

Jones, S., Hackney, R., & Irani, Z. (2007). Towards e-government transformation: conceptualising "citizen engagement": A research note. *Transforming Government: People, Process and Policy*, *1*(2), 145–152.

Jorgensen, D. J., & Cable, S. (2002). Facing the challenges of e-government: A case study of the city of Corpus Christi, Texas. *SAM Advanced Management Journal*, *67*(3), 15–21.

Kaboolian, L.Administration Debate. (1988). The new public management: Challenging the boundaries of the management vs. administration debate. *Public Administration Review*, *58*(3), 189–193. doi:10.2307/976558

Kamarulzaman, A. A., & Aliza Akmar, O. (2001, September). The multimedia super corridor: a physical manifestation of the Malaysian National System of Innovation. In *Proceedings of the Future of Innovation Studies Conference,* (pp. 20-23). Eindhoven University of Technology.

Kanat, I. E., & Özkan, S. (2009). Exploring citizens' perception of government to citizen services: A model based on theory of planned behaviour (TP). *Transforming Government: People, Process and Policy, 3*(4), 406–419.

Kanfer, R., & Heggestad, E. D. (1997). Motivational traits and skills: A person-centred approach to work motivation. *Research in Organizational Behavior, 19,* 1–56.

Katsikas, D. (2010). Non-state authority and global governance. *Review of International Studies, 36*(S1), 113–135. doi:10.1017/S0260210510000793

Kersten, G. E. (2003). E-democracy and participatory decision processes: Lessons from e-negotiation experiments. *Journal of Multi-Criteria Decision Analysis, 12*(2-3), 127–143. doi:10.1002/mcda.352

Kickert, W. J., Klijn, E. H., & Koppenjan, J. F. M. (Eds.). (1997). *Managing complex networks: strategies for the public sector.* London: Sage.

Kieley, B. (2002). *E-government in Canada: Services online or public service renewal? In Electronic Government: Design, Application & Management.* Hershey, PA: Idea Group Publishing.

Klijn, E. H., & Koppenjan, J. F. (2000). Public management and policy networks: Foundations of a network approach to governance. *Public Management an International Journal of Research and Theory, 2*(2), 135–158.

Klijn, E. H., Koppenjan, J., & Termeer, K. (1995). Managing networks in the public sector: A theoretical study of management strategies in policy networks. *Public Administration, 73*(3), 437–454. doi:10.1111/j.1467-9299.1995.tb00837.x

Kling, R. (Ed.). (1996). *Computerisation and Controversy: Value Conflicts and Social Choices.* San Diego, CA: Academic Press.

Knill, C. (1999). Explaining cross-national variance in administrative reform: Autonomous versus instrumental bureaucracies. *Journal of Public Policy, 19*(02), 113–139. doi:10.1017/S0143814X99000203

Knill, C., & Lehmkuhl, D. (1998). Integration by Globalisation: The European Interest Representation of the Consumer Electronics Industry. *Current Politics and Economics in Europe, 8,* 131–153.

Knill, C., & Lehmkuhl, D. (2002). Private actors and the state: Internationalization and changing patterns of governance. *Governance: An International Journal of Policy, Administration and Institutions, 15*(1), 41–63. doi:10.1111/1468-0491.00179

Kock, N. (2001). The ape that used email: Understand e-communication behavior through evolution theory. *AIS, 5*(3), 1–29.

Kock, N. (2012). *WarPLS 3.0, user manual.* Laredo, TX: ScriptWarp System.

Kooiman, J. (2000). Societal governance: levels, models and orders of social-political interaction. In Debating governance: Authority, steering, and democracy. Oxford University Press.

Kooiman, J. (Ed.). (1993). *Modern governance: New government-society interactions.* Sage.

Krouwel, A. (2006). Party models. In R. S. Katz & W. Crotty (Eds.), *Handbook of party politics* (pp. 249–269). London: Sage. doi:10.4135/9781848608047.n22

Kunakornpaiboonsiri, T. (2013). *SMS service for health launched in Indonesian province.* Retrieved from http://www.futuregov.asia/articles/2013

Landsbergen, D. Jr., & Wolken, G. Jr. (2001). Realizing the promise: Government information systems and the fourth generation of information technology. *Public Administration Review, 61*(2), 206–220. doi:10.1111/0033-3352.00023

Langer, E. J. (1989). *Mindfulness reading.* Reading, MA: Merloyd Lawrence Books.

Langlois, G. (2001, May 14). An equal slice of success. *Federal Computer Week,* p. 44.

Lapsley, I. (2008). The NPM agenda: Back to the future. *Financial Accountability & Management, 24*(1), 77–96. doi:10.1111/j.1468-0408.2008.00444.x

Lawson, G. (1998). *NetState: Creating electronic government, 18. Demos (Mexico City, Mexico)*, 55.

LeBon. (1995). *The Crowd*. Ransaction Publishers.

Lee, (2003). South Korea: From the Land of Morning Calm to ICT Hotbed. *Academy of Management Executive, 17*(2), 7-18.

Lee, J.-S., Cho, H. G., Davidson, B., & Ingraffea, A. (2003). *Technology acceptance and social networking in distance learning*. Retrieved Nov. 16th 2012 from www.ifets.info/journals

Lee, M. K. O., Cheung, C. M. K., & Chen, Z. (2005). Acceptance of Internet-based learning medium: The role of extrinsic and intrinsic motivation. *Information & Management, 42*(8), 1095–1104. doi:10.1016/j.im.2003.10.007

Leidner, D. E., & Jarvenpaa, S. L. (1993). The Information age confronts education case studies on electronic classrooms. *Information Systems Research, 4*(1), 24–54. doi:10.1287/isre.4.1.24

Lessig, L. (1999). *Code and other Laws of Cyberspace*. New York.

Leston-Bandeira, C., & Ward, S. (2008). Parliaments in the Digital Age. Oxford Internet Institute, Forum Discussion Report, 13, 2-3.

Leung, L. (2001). College student motives for chatting on the ICQ. *New Media & Society, 3*(4), 483–500. doi:10.1177/14614440122226209

Leung, L., & Wei, R. (1998). The gratifications of pager use: Sociability, information-seeking, entertainment, utility, and fashion and status. *Telematics and Informatics, 15*(4), 253–264. doi:10.1016/S0736-5853(98)00016-1

Leung, L., & Wei, R. (2000). More than just talk on the move: Uses and gratifications of the cellular phone. *J&MC Quarterly, 77*(2), 308–320. doi:10.1177/107769900007700206

Levine, S., & White, P. E. (1961). Exchange as a conceptual framework for the study of interorganisational relationships. *Administrative Science Quarterly, 5*(4), 583–601. doi:10.2307/2390622

Lindblom, C. E., & Cohen, D. K. (1979). *Usable knowledge: social science and social problem solving*. New Haven, CT: Yale University Press.

Lindh, M., & Miles, L. (2007). Becoming electronic parliamentarians? ICT usage in the Swedish Riksdag. *Journal of Legislative Studies, 13*(3), 422–440. doi:10.1080/13572330701500896

Ling, R. (2001). *Adolescent girls and young adult men: Two sub-cultures of the mobile telephone*. Paper Presented at the InterMedia workshop on mobility. Oslo, Norway.

Ling, R., & Yttri, B. (2002). Hyper-coordination via mobile phone in Norway. In J. E. Katz & M. Aakhus (Eds.), *Perpetual Contact*. New York: Cambridge University Press.

Liska, A. F. (1984). A critical examination of the causal structure of the Fishbein-Ajzen model. *Social Psychology Quarterly, 47*, 61–74. doi:10.2307/3033889

Löffler, E. (2003) Governance and government. *Public Management and Governance*, 163.

Löfgren, K., & Smith, C. (2003). Political parties and democracy in the information age. In Political parties and the internet: Net gain, (pp. 39-52). London: Routledge.

Loughlin, J. (2004). The "transformation" of governance: New directions in policy and politics. *The Australian Journal of Politics and History, 50*(1), 1, 8–22. doi:10.1111/j.1467-8497.2004.00317.x

Lumpe, A. T., & Chambers, E. (2001). Assessing teacher's context beliefs about technology use. *Journal of Research on Technology in Education, 34*(1), 93–107. doi:10.1080/15391523.2001.10782337

Lundquist, L. (2000). Demokratiens väktere I ekonomiens samhälle. In Etik til debat. Værdier og etik I den offentlige forvaltning, (pp. 13-36). Jurist- og Økonomforbundets Forlag.

Lusoli, W., Ward, S., & Gibson, R. (2006). (Re)Connecting Politics? Parliament, the Public and the Internet. *Parliamentary Affairs, 59*(1), 28.

Lynott, P. P., & McCandless, N. J. (2000). The impact of age vs. life experience of the gender role: Attitude of women in different cohorts. *Journal of Women & Aging*, *12*(2), 5–21. doi:10.1300/J074v12n01_02 PMID:10986848

Macintosh, A., & Smith, F. (2002). Citizen Participation in Public Affairs. In R. Traunmuller & K. Lenk (Eds.), FGOV, (LNCS), (vol. 2456, pp. 256-63). Berlin: Springer.

Mahmood, M. A., Burn, J. M., Gemoets, L. A., & Jacquez, C. (2000). Variables affecting information technology end-user satisfaction: A meta-analysis of the empirical literature. *International Journal of Human-Computer Studies*, *52*(4), 751–771. doi:10.1006/ijhc.1999.0353

MAIT. (2002). *Country Intelligence Report – Malaysia*. Retrieved from http://www.mait.com/

Malaysian Administrative Modernization and Management Planning Unit (MAMPU). (n.d.). *Electronic government flagship application*, No: MAMPU/EG/1/97. Author.

Malloy, J. (2003). High discipline, low cohesion? The uncertain patterns of Canadian parliamentary party groups. *Journal of Legislative Studies*, *9*(4), 116–129. doi:10.1080/1357233042000306290

Maqbool, M. (2000). *A strategy for Combating Corruption in Pakistan*. Paper presented at Conference of Asia Pacific Forum on Combating Corruption. Seoul, Korea. Retrieved from http://www.oecd.org/daf/ASIAcom/Seoul.htm

Marsh, D., & Rhodes, R. A. W. (1992). *Policy networks in British government*. Clarendon Press. doi:10.1093/ac prof:oso/9780198278528.001.0001

Masters, Z., Mactintosh, A., & Smith, E. (2004). Young People and eDemocracy: Creating a Culture of Participation. In R. Traunmuller (Ed.), EGPV (LNCS), (vol. 3183, pp. 15-22). Berlin: Springer.

Matavire, R., Chigona, W., Roode, D., Sewchurran, E., Davids, Z., Alfred Mukudu, A., & Charles Boamah-Abu, C. (2010). Challenges of egovernment project implementation in a South African context. *Electronic Journal Information Systems Evaluation*, *13*(2), 153–164.

Matthews, J. (1998). *Toffler raises furore over Malaysia's high-Tech future*. Retrieved from http://www.geocities.com/ResearchTriangle/Lab/3937/news.htm

Mayhew, D. R. (1974). *Congress: The electoral connection*. Yale University Press.

Mayntz, R. (1999). *New Challenges to Governance Theory*. Paper presented at Max-Planck Institut für Gessellshaftsforschung (from Sorenson).

McShane, S., & Glinow, M. V. (2008). *Organizational behaviour: Emerging realities for the workplace revolution* (4th ed.). New York: McGraw-Hill/Irwin.

Meissonier, R., & Houze, E. (2010). Toward an 'IT-conflict-resistance theory': Action research during it pre-implementation. *European Journal of Information Systems*, *15*(5), 540–561. doi:10.1057/ejis.2010.35

MEWC. (2003). *Press Release: Work to strengthen MIMOS gets underway: Advisory committee to table report in 6 months*. Retrieved from http://www.ktak.gov.my

Miller, K. (2005). *Communications theories: Perspectives, processes, and contexts*. New York: McGraw-Hill.

Minges, M., & Gray, V. (2002). *Multimedia Malaysia: Internet case study*. Retrieved from http://www.itu.int/ITU-D/ict/cs/malaysia/material/MYS%20CS.pdf

Miniard, P. W., & Cohen, J. B. (1981). An examination of the Fishbein-Ajzen behavioural intentions model's concepts and measures. *Journal of Experimental Social Psychology*, *17*(3), 309–399. doi:10.1016/0022-1031(81)90031-7

Minton, H. L., & Schneider, F. W. (1980). *Differential psychology*. Boston: Waveland Press.

Mitchell, P. (2000). Voters and their representatives: Electoral institutions and delegation in parliamentary democracies. *European Journal of Political Research*, *37*(3), 335–351. doi:10.1111/1475-6765.00516

Moore, G. C. (1987). End user computing and office automation: A diffusion of innovations perspective. *INFOR*, *25*, 241–235.

Moore, G. C., & Benbasat, I. (1991). Development of an instrument to measure the perceptions of adopting an information technology innovation. *Information Systems Research*, *2*(3), 192–222. doi:10.1287/isre.2.3.192

Morris, M. G., & Venkatesh, V. (2000). Age difference in technology adoption decisions: Implications for a changing workforce. *Personnel Psychology*, *53*(2), 375–403. doi:10.1111/j.1744-6570.2000.tb00206.x

Muhammad Rais, A. K. (Ed.). (1999). *Reengineering the public service: Leadership and change in an electronic age*. Malaysia: Pelanduk Publications.

Mullen, P. H., Hersey, J. C., & Iverson, D. C. (1987). Health behaviour models compared. *Social Science & Medicine*, *24*(11), 973–983. doi:10.1016/0277-9536(87)90291-7 PMID:3616691

Naisbitt, J. (1982). *Megatrends: Ten New Directions Transforming Our Lives*. New York: Warner Books.

Najib, A.R. (2010). *Keynote Address*. Paper presented at INVEST Malaysia. Kuala Lumpur, Malaysia.

Nasim, A., & Sushil, S. (2010). Managing continuity and change: A new approach for strategizing in e-government. *Transforming Government: People. Process and Policy*, *4*(4), 338–364.

National Institute of Justice (NIJ). (2000). Selected summaries. *Research Review*, *1*(4), 1-6.

Negandhi, A. R. (Ed.). (1975). *Interorganisation Theory*. Kansas University Press.

Negroponte, N. (1996). *Being digital*. Random House LLC.

Newman, A. L., & Bach, D. (2004). Self-Regulatory Trajectories in the Shadow of Public Power: Resolving Digital Dilemmas in Europe and the United States. *Governance: An International Journal of Policy, Administration and Institutions*, *17*(3), 387–413. doi:10.1111/j.0952-1895.2004.00251.x

Nickel, P. M. (2007). Network governance and the new constitutionalism. *Administrative Theory & Praxis*, *29*(2), 198–224.

NITC. (2000). *Access, empowerment and governance in the information age*. Kuala Lumpur: NITC Malaysia Publication.

Norris, P. (2002). *Digital Divide, Civic Engagement, Information Poverty, and the Internet Political Activism*. Cambridge University Press.

Norris, P. (2005). The Impact of the Internet on Political Activism: Evidence from Europe. *International Journal of Electronic Government Research*, *1*(1), 19–39. doi:10.4018/jegr.2005010102

Norton, P. (2007). Four models of political representation: British MPs and the use of ICT. *Journal of Legislative Studies*, *13*(3), 354–369. doi:10.1080/13572330701500771

Norton, P., & Wood, D. M. (1993). *Back from westminster: British members of parliament and their constituents*. Lexington, KY: University Press of Kentucky.

Nuraizah, A. H. (2002). *Opening Remarks at the Annual Asia Pacific Telecom CFO Roundtable*. Kuala Lumpur, Malaysia: Academic Press.

Office of the e-Envoy. (2000). *International Benchmarking Report: Summary-Hong Kong Special Administrative Region*. London: Office of the e-Envoy. Retrieved from http://www.eenvoy.gov.uk/publications/reports/benchmarkingV2/summary_hkong.htm

O'Flynn, J. (2007). From new public management to public value: Paradigmatic change and managerial implications. *Australian Journal of Public Administration*, *66*(3), 353-366.

Oliveira, R. S. Jr. (2006). Utilização do modelo TAM na avaliação da aceitaçãode sistemas ERP. Rio de Janeiro. *IBMEC*, *2006*, 119f.

Olson, M. (2000). *Power and prosperity: Outgrowing communist and capitalist dictatorships*. New York: Basic Book.

Olson, M. (2002). The logic of collective action. In *Public goods and the theory of groups*. Cambridge University Press.

Ōmae, K. (1995). *The end of the nation state: The rise of regional economies*. Simon and Schuster.

Osborne, S. P. (Ed.). (2010). *The new public governance?: emerging perspectives on the theory and practice of public governance*. London: Routledge.

O'Toole, L. J. Jr. (1988). Strategies for intergovernmental management: Implementing programs in interorganizational networks. *International Journal of Public Administration*, *11*(4), 417–441. doi:10.1080/01900698808524596

Paek, K. (2000). *Combating corruption: The role of the ministry of justice and the prosecutor's office in Korea.* Paper presented at Conference of Asia Pacific Forum on Combating Corruption. Seoul, Korea.

Parayno, L. G. (1999). Reforming the Philippines customs service through electronic governance. In Combating Corruption in Asian and Pacific Economies, (pp. 61-69). Manila: ADB.

Park, S. H. (2000). Relationship among attitudes and subjective norms: Testing the theory of reasoned action across cultures. *Communication Studies, 51*(2), 162–175. doi:10.1080/10510970009388516

Parks, T. (2003). Expanding access to information in Cambodia: Community information centers project. *IT in Developing Countries, 13*(1), 19.

Parry, M. (1997). *Training workshop on government budgeting in developing countries.* Retrieved from http://www.mcgl.co.uk/l-tp.htm

Pautz, H. (2010). The internet, political participation and election turnout: A case study of Germany's. *German Politics & Society, 28*(3), 156-175.

Pavan, A., & Lemme, F. (2011). Communication processes and the 'New Public Space' in Italy and the USA: A Longitudinal Approach. *Financial Accountability & Management, 27*(2), 166–194. doi:10.1111/j.1468-0408.2011.00521.x

Pavlou, P. A., & Fygenson, M. (2006). Understanding and predicting electronic commerce adoption: An extension of the theory of planned behaviour. *Management Information Systems Quarterly, 30*(1), 115–144.

Peak, H. (1955). Attitude and motivation. In M. R., Jones (Ed.), Nebraska symposium on motivation. Lincoln, NE: University of Nebraska Press.

Pedersen, P. E., & Nysveen, H. (2002). *Using the theory of planned behaviour to explain teenagers' adoption of text messaging services.* Norway: Agder University College.

Peters, B. G. (1998). Globalisation, institutions, and governance. The Robert Schuman Centre at the European University Institute.

Peters, B. G. (2003, October). The capacity to govern: moving back to the center. In *Proceedings of VIII Congreso Internacional del CLAD sebre la Reforma del Estado y de la Administracion Publica.* Retrieved from http//www.clad.org.ve/congreso/peters.pdf

Peters, B. G. (2001). *The future of governing (revised).* Lawrence, KS: University Press of Kansas.

Petrus, G., & Nelson, O. N. (2006). Borneo online banking: Evaluating customer perceptions and behavioural intention. *Management Research News, 29*(1/2), 6–15. doi:10.1108/01409170610645402

Petty, R. E., & Cacioppo, J. T. (1986). In L. Berkowitz (Ed.), *The elaboration likelihood model of persuasion.* New York: Academic Press.

Phillips, A. (1995). *The politics of presence.* Oxford University Press.

Pierre, J. (Ed.). (2001). Debating governance: Authority, steering and democracy. Oxford, UK: Oxford University Press.

Pierre, J., & Peters, G. B. (2000). *Governance, politics and the state.* Houndsmill, UK: MacMillan.

Pitkin, H. F. (1967). *The concept of representation.* University of California Press.

Podsakoff, P. M., & Organ, D. W. (1986). Self-reports in organizational research: Problems and prospects. *Journal of Management, 12*(4), 531–544. doi:10.1177/014920638601200408

Pollitt, C. (1990). *Managerialism and the public services: The Anglo-American experience.* Oxford, UK: Blackwell.

Prestholdt, P. H., Lane, I. M., & Mathews, R. C. (1987). Nurse turnover as reasoned action: Development of a process model. *The Journal of Applied Psychology, 72*(2), 221–227. doi:10.1037/0021-9010.72.2.221 PMID:3583978

Rais, M. A. K., & Mohd Khalid, N. (2003). *E-government in Malaysia: Improving responsiveness and capacity to serve.* Selangor: Pelanduk Publications.

Ramasamy, R. (2010). Benchmarking Malaysia in the global information society: Regressing or progressing? *Journal of CENTRUM Cathedra, 3*(1), 67–83. doi:10.7835/jcc-berj-2010-0039

Rashid, A. A., Jusoh, H., & Abdul Malek, J. (2010). Enhancing urban governance efficiency through the egovernment of Malaysian local authorities – The Case of Subang Jaya. *GEOGRAFIA OnlineTM Malaysian Journal of Society and Space, 6*(1), 1–12.

Raslan, S. (2003). MCMC to 'stand firm' on opening up access, Telekom objects. *The Star, 1*(December), 9.

Rehfeld, A. (2006). Towards a general theory of political representation. *The Journal of Politics, 68*(1), 1–21. doi:10.1111/j.1468-2508.2006.00365.x

Rehman, M., Esichaikul, V., & Kamal, M. (2012). Factors influencing e-government adoption in Pakistan. *Transforming Government: People, Process and Policy, 6*(3), 256–282.

Relyea, C. H. (2001). *Paperwork reduction act: Reauthorization and government information management issues.* Congressional Research Service (CRS) RL30590.

Republic of Korea. (2003). Innovation in procurement through digitalization. Public Procurement Services, 1-13.

Republic of the Philippines. (2000). *General appropriation act, January1-December31, R.A. No. 8760.* Retrieved from: http://www.dbm.gov.ph/dbm_publications/gaa/gaa2000 htm

Rhodes, R. A. W. (2000). *Transforming British government: Changing roles and relationships* (vol. 2). Palgrave Macmillan.

Rhodes, R. A. (1998). Different roads to unfamiliar places: UK experience in comparative perspective. *Australian Journal of Public Administration, 57*(4), 19–31. doi:10.1111/j.1467-8500.1998.tb01558.x

Rhodes, R. A. W. (1981). *Control and power in central-local government relations. Brookfield, VT*: Ashgate.

Rhodes, R. A. W. (1986). *The national world of local government.* Allen & Unwin.

Rhodes, R. A. W. (1996). The new governance: Governing without government. *Political Studies, 44*(4), 652–667. doi:10.1111/j.1467-9248.1996.tb01747.x

Rhodes, R. A. W. (1997). *Understanding governance: Policy networks, reflexivity and accountability.* Buckingham, UK: Open University Press.

Rhodes, R. E., & Courneya, K. S. (2003). Self-efficacy, controllability and intention in the theory of planned behaviour: Measurement redundancy or causal independence? *Psychology & Health, 18*(1), 79–92. doi:10.1080/0887044031000080665

Rise, J., Thompson, M., & Verplanken, B. (2003). Measuring implementation intentions in the context of the theory of planned behaviour. *Scandinavian Journal of Psychology, 44*(2), 87–95. doi:10.1111/1467-9450.00325 PMID:12778976

Rogers, E. M. (2003). *Diffusion of Innovations* (5th ed.). New York: The Free Press.

Salamon, L. M. (Ed.). (2002). *The tools of government: A guide to the new governance.* Oxford University Press.

Salleh, S. M., & Albion, P. (2004). Using the theory of planned behaviour to predict Bruneian teachers' intentions to use ICT in teaching. In *Proceedings of the 15th International Conference of the Society for Information Technology & Teacher Education* (SITE 2004). Atlanta, GA: Academic Press.

Saloma-Akpedonu, C. (2008). Malaysian technological elite: Specifics of a knowledge society in a developing country. *Perspectives on Global Development and Technology, 7*(1), 1–14. doi:10.1163/156914907X253233

Samiei, N., & Jalilvand, M. R. (2011). The political participation and government size. *Canadian Social Science, 7*(2), 224–235.

Sang-Yool, H. (2000). *Recent reform of Korean tax administration – focused on measures for prevention of corruption.* Paper presented at Conference of Asia Pacific Forum on Combating Corruption. Seoul, Korea. Retrieved from http://www.oecd.org/daf/ASIAcom/Seoul.htm

Sassen, S. (2000). Digital networks and the state, some governance questions. *Theory, Culture & Society, 17*(4), 19–33. doi:10.1177/02632760022051293

Scharpf, F. W., Reissert, B., & Schabel, F. (1978). Policy effectiveness and conflict avoidance in intergovernmental policy formation. In K. Hanf., & F. W. Scharpf (Ed.), Interorganisational Policy Making. London: Sage.

Scharpf, F. W. (1994). Community and autonomy: Multi-level policy-making in the European Union. *Journal of European Public Policy, 1*(2), 219–242.

Scharpf, F. W. (1997). *Games real actors play: Actor-centered institutionalism in policy research.* Boulder, CO: Westview Press.

Scharpf, F. W., Reissert, B., & Schnabel, F. (1977). Policy effectiveness and conflict avoidance in intergovernmental policy formation. In K. Hanf & F. W. Scharpf (Eds.), *Interorganizational policy making: limits to coordination and central control.* Sage Publications.

Schoof, H., & Watson, B. A. (1995). Information highways and media policies in the European Union. *Telecommunications Policy, 19*(4), 325–338. doi:10.1016/0308-5961(95)00006-R

Sekaran, U., & Bougie, R. (2010). *Research methods for business: A skill building approach* (4th ed.). John Wiley & Sons, Inc.

Selwyn, W. (1997). Students' attitude toward computers: Validation of a computer attitude scale for 16-19 education. *Computers & Education, 28*(1), 35–41. doi:10.1016/S0360-1315(96)00035-8

Shahin, J. (2003). *Developing a European polity: The case for governance on the Internet at the European level.* MERIT – Maastricht Economic Research Institute on Innovation and Technology.

Shahin, J., & Neuhold, C. (2007). 'Connecting Europe': The use of 'new' information and communication technologies within European parliament standing committees. *Journal of Legislative Studies, 13*(3), 388–402. doi:10.1080/13572330701500854

Sharpe, R., Benfield, G., & Francis, R. (2006). Implementing a university e-learning strategy: Levers for change within academic schools. *ALT-J., 14*(2), 135–151. doi:10.1080/09687760600668503

Sheppard, B. H., Hartwick, J., & Warshaw, P. R. (1988). The theory of reasoned action: A meta-analysis of past research with recommendations for modifications and future research. *The Journal of Consumer Research, 15*(3), 325–343. doi:10.1086/209170

Siddiquee, N. A. (2008). Service delivery innovations and governance: the Malaysian experience. *Transforming Government: People, Process and Policy, 2*(3), 194-213.

Siragusa, L., & Dixon, K. C. (2008). Planned behaviour: Student attitudes towards the use of ICT interactions in higher education. In *Proceedings of Ascilite 2008.* Retrieved June 11th 2013 from http://www.ascilite.org.au

Skog, B. (2002). Mobiles and the Norwegian teen: identity, gender and class. In J. E. Katz & M. Aakhus (Eds.), *Perpetual Contact.* New York: Cambridge University Press.

Slouka, M. (1996). *War of the worlds: Cyberspace and the high-tech assault on reality.* Basic Books.

Smith, M. S.; Moteff, J. D.; Kruger, L.G.; McLouglin, G.J.; & Seifert, J. W (2004). *Internet: An overview of technology policy issues affecting its use and growth.* Congress Research Service, (CRS-98-67), 1-39.

Sobaci, M. Z. (2011). *Parliament and ICT-based legislation: Concept, experiences and lessons.* Premier Reference Source. doi:10.4018/978-1-61350-329-4

Soh, K. C. (1998). *Cross cultural validity of selwyn computer attitude scale.* Unpublished manuscript.

Sorenson, E. (2002). Democratic theory and network governance. *Administrative Theory and Praxis, 24*(4), 693–720.

Spacey, R., Goulding, A., & Murray, I. (2004). Exploring the attitudes of public library staff to the Internet using the TAM. *The Journal of Documentation, 60*(5), 550–564. doi:10.1108/00220410410560618

Sparks, P., Guthrie, C. A., & Shepard, R. (1997). The dimensional structure of the perceived behavioural control construct. *Journal of Applied Social Psychology, 27*(5), 418–438. doi:10.1111/j.1559-1816.1997.tb00639.x

Sprehe, T. (2001, April 30). States show feds the way. *Federal Computer Week*, p. 48.

Srite, M., & Karahanna, E. (2006). The role of espoused national cultural values in technology acceptance. *Management Information Systems Quarterly*, *30*(3), 679–704.

Stephen, B. (2001, August 10). President searching for a few good e-government ideas. *Washington Post*, p. 2.

Stoker, G. (1998). Governance as theory: Five propositions. *International Social Science Journal*, *50*(155), 17–28. doi:10.1111/1468-2451.00106

Stoll, C. (1996). *Silicon snake oil: Second thoughts on the information highway*. Random House LLC.

Strange, S. (1996). *The retreat of the state: The diffusion of power in the world economy*. Cambridge University Press. doi:10.1017/CBO9780511559143

Straub, D. W. (1989). Validating instruments in MIS research. *Management Information Systems Quarterly*, *13*(2), 147–169. doi:10.2307/248922

Strøm, K. (2000). *Parties at the gore of Government 2000*. New York: Oxford University Press.

Succi, M. J., & Walter, Z. D. (1999). Theory of user acceptance of information technologies: an examination of health care professionals. In *Proceedings of the 32nd Annual Hawaii International Conference on System Sciences* (HICSS-32). doi:10.1109/HICSS.1999.773013

Suh, B., & Han, I. (2002). Effect of trust on consumer acceptance of Internet Banking. *Electronic Commerce Research and Applications*, *1*(3), 247–263. doi:10.1016/S1567-4223(02)00017-0

Surin, A. J. (2003). The Power to Effect ICT Change. *The Star*, *9*(December), 11–12.

Surin, A. J. (2004). Act Gives MCMC Wide Powers. *The Star*, *6*(January), 8–9.

Tan, M., & Teo, T. S. H. (2000). Factors influencing the adoption of Internet banking. *Journal of the Association for Information Systems*, *1*(5), 1–42.

Taylor, A. S., & Harper, R. (2001). *Talking activity: Young people and mobile phones*. Paper presented at the CHI 2001 Workshop on mobile communications. Seattle, WA.

Taylor, S., & Todd, P. A. (1995). Understanding information technology usage: A test of competing models. *Information Systems Research*, *6*(2), 144–176. doi:10.1287/isre.6.2.144

Teo, T., & van Schalk, P. (2009). Understanding technology acceptance in pre-service teachers: A structural-equation modeling approach. *The Asia-Pacific Education Researcher*, *18*(1), 47–66. doi:10.3860/taper.v18i1.1035

Terry, D. J., Hogg, M. A., & White, K. M. (1999). The theory of planned Behaviour: Self-identity, social identity and group norms. *The British Journal of Social Psychology*, *38*(3), 225–244. doi:10.1348/014466699164149 PMID:10520477

The Economist. (2010, February 27). Data, data everywhere. *The Economist*.

Thompson, S. H., Lim, V. K. G., & Lai, R. Y. C. (1999). Intrinsic and extrinsic motivation in Internet usage. *Omega*, *27*(1), 25–37. doi:10.1016/S0305-0483(98)00028-0

Toffler, A. (1980). *The third wave*. New York: Bantam books.

Tonglet, M., Phillips, P. S., & Bates, M. P. (2004). Determining the drivers for householder pro-environmental behaviour: Waste minimisation compared to recycling. *Resources, Conservation and Recycling*, *42*(1), 27–48. doi:10.1016/j.resconrec.2004.02.001

Trafimow, D. (1994). Predicting intentions to use a condom from perceptions of normative pressure and confidence in those perceptions. *Journal of Applied Social Psychology*, *24*(24), 2151–2163. doi:10.1111/j.1559-1816.1994.tb02377.x

Trafimow, D. (2000). Habit as both a direct cause of intention to use a condom and as a moderator of the attitude-intention and subjective norm-intention relations. *Psychology & Health*, *15*(3), 383–393. doi:10.1080/08870440008402000

Trafimow, D., & Duran, A. (1998). Some tests of the distinction between attitude and perceived behavioural control. *The British Journal of Social Psychology*, *37*(1), 1–14. doi:10.1111/j.2044-8309.1998.tb01154.x PMID:9554085

Trafimow, D., & Fishbein, M. (1994). The moderating effect of behavior type on the subjective norm-behavior relationship. *The Journal of Social Psychology, 134*(6), 755–763. doi:10.1080/00224545.1994.9923010

Trafimow, D., & Fishbein, M. (1995). Do people really distinguish between behavioral and normative beliefs? *The British Journal of Social Psychology, 34*(3), 257–266. doi:10.1111/j.2044-8309.1995.tb01062.x

Trafimow, D., Sheeran, P., Conner, M., & Finlay, K. A. (2002). Evidence that perceived behavioural control is a multidimensional construct: Perceived control and perceived difficulty. *The British Journal of Social Psychology, 1*(1), 101–121. doi:10.1348/014466602165081 PMID:11970777

Trattner, J. (2000, November 29). E-government revolution transforms federal operations. *Government Executive Magazine.*

Triantafillou, P. (2004). Addressing network governance through the concepts of governmentality and normalization. *Administrative Theory & Praxis, 26*(4), 489–508.

Turel, O., Serenko, A., & Bontis, N. (2007). User acceptance of wireless short messaging services: Deconstructing perceived value. *Information & Management, 44*(1), 63–73. doi:10.1016/j.im.2006.10.005

UN Division for Public Economics and Public Administration-ASPA, (2002). *Benchmarking eGovernment of global perspectives - Assessing the progress of the UN members states.* Author.

United Nations. (2013). *The Millennium Development Goals Report.* Author.

Urbinati, N., & Warren, M. E. (2008). The concept of representation in contemporary democratic theory. *Annual Review of Political Science, 11*(1), 387–412. doi:10.1146/annurev.polisci.11.053006.190533

van der Pligt, J., & de Vries, N. K. (1998). Expectancy-value models of health behaviours: The role of salience and anticipated affect. *Psychology & Health, 13*(2), 289–305. doi:10.1080/08870449808406752

van Dijk, J. (2000). Models of democracy and concepts of communication. In Digital democracy: Issues of theory and practice. London: Sage. doi:10.4135/9781446218891.n3

Vedel, T. (2006). The idea of electronic democracy: Origins, visions and questions. *Parliamentary Affairs, 59*(2), 226–235. doi:10.1093/pa/gsl005

Venkatesh, V. (1999). Creation of favourable user perceptions: Exploring the role of intrinsic motivation. *Management Information Systems Quarterly, 23*(2), 239–260. doi:10.2307/249753

Venkatesh, V. (2000). Determinants of perceived ease of use: Integrating control, intrinsic motivation and emotion into the technology acceptance model. *Information Systems Research, 11*(4), 342–365. doi:10.1287/isre.11.4.342.11872

Venkatesh, V., & Bala, H. (2008). Technology acceptance model 3 and a research agenda on interventions. *Decision Sciences, 39*(2), 272–315. doi:10.1111/j.1540-5915.2008.00192.x

Venkatesh, V., Brown, S. A., Maruping, L. M., & Bala, H. (2008). Predicting different conceptualizations of system use: The competing roles of behavioral intention, facilitating conditions, and behavioral expectation. *Management Information Systems Quarterly*, 483–502.

Venkatesh, V., & Davis, F. D. (1996). A model of the antecedents of perceived ease of use: Development and test. *Decision Sciences, 27*(3), 451–481. doi:10.1111/j.1540-5915.1996.tb01822.x

Venkatesh, V., & Davis, F. D. (2000). A Theoretical extension of the technology acceptance model: Four longitudinal field studies. *Management Science, 46*(2), 186–204. doi:10.1287/mnsc.46.2.186.11926

Venkatesh, V., & Morris, M. G. (2000). Why don't men ever stop to ask for directions? Gender, social influence, and their role in technology acceptance and usage behaviour. *Management Information Systems Quarterly, 24*(1), 115–139. doi:10.2307/3250981

Venkatesh, V., Morris, M. G., Davis, G. B., & Davis, F. D. (2003). User acceptance of information technology: Toward a unified view. *Management Information Systems Quarterly, 27*(3), 425–478.

Venkatesh, V., Thong, J. Y. L., & Xu, X. (2012). Consumer acceptance and use of information technology: Extending the unified theory of acceptance and use of technology. *Management Information Systems Quarterly*, *36*(1), 157–178.

Verplanken, B., Hofstee, G., & Janssen, H. J. W. (1998). Effects of introspecting about reasons: Inferring attitudes from accessible thoughts. *European Journal of Social Psychology*, *28*, 23–35. doi:10.1002/(SICI)1099-0992(199801/02)28:1<23::AID-EJSP843>3.0.CO;2-Z

Vicente-Merino, M. R. (2007). Websites of parliamentarians across Europe. *Journal of Legislative Studies*, *13*(3), 441–457. doi:10.1080/13572330701500912

Viegas d'Abreu, J. (2008). The Portuguese Parliaments in the digital age. Oxford Internet Institute, Forum Discussion Report, 13, 33-7.

Waldo, D. (2006). *The administrative state: A study of the political theory of American public administration*. Transaction Publishers.

Wamsley, G. L. (1996). A public philosophy and ontological disclosure as the basis for normatively grounded theorizing in public administration. In J. F. Wolf (Ed.), Refounding democratic public administration: Modern paradoxes, postmodern challenges. Sage Publications.

Wang, Y.-S., Wu, M.-C., & Wang, H.-Y. (2009). Investigating the determinants and age and gender differences in the acceptance of mobile learning. *British Journal of Educational Technology*, *40*(1), 92–118. doi:10.1111/j.1467-8535.2007.00809.x

Warbuton, J., & Terry, D. J. (2000). Volunteer decision making by older people: A test of a revised theory of planned behaviour. *Basic and Applied Social Psychology*, *22*(3), 245–257. doi:10.1207/S15324834BASP2203_11

Ward, S., & Lusoli, W. (2005). 'From weird to wired': MPs, the Internet and representative politics in the UK. *Journal of Legislative Studies*, *11*(1), 57–81. doi:10.1080/13572330500158276

Ward, S., & Vedel, T. (2006). Introduction: The potential of the internet revisited. *Parliamentary Affairs*, *59*(2), 210–225. doi:10.1093/pa/gsl014

Webster, J., & Martocochio, J. J. (1992). Microcomputer playfulness: Development of a measure with workplace implications. *Management Information Systems Quarterly*, *16*(2), 201–226. doi:10.2307/249576

Webster, J., Trevino, L. K., & Ryan, L. (1993). The dimensionality and correlates of flow in human-computer interaction. *Computers in Human Behavior*, *9*(4), 411–426. doi:10.1016/0747-5632(93)90032-N

Weiss, L. (1998). *The myth of the powerless state*. Cornell University Press.

Wilhelm, A. G. (1998). Virtual sounding boards: How deliberative is on-line political discussion? *Information Communication and Society*, *1*(3), 313–338. doi:10.1080/13691189809358972

William, M. (2000, December 11). Setting a course for e-government. *Federal Computer Week*, p. 13.

Wilson, T. D., Lindsey, S., & Schooler, T. Y. (2000). A model of dual attitudes. *Psychological Review*, *107*(1), 101–126. doi:10.1037/0033-295X.107.1.101 PMID:10687404

Wixom, B. H., & Todd, P. (2005). A theoretical integration of user satisfaction and technology acceptance. *Information Systems Research*, *6*(1), 85–102. doi:10.1287/isre.1050.0042

Wood, R., & Bandura, A. (1989). Impact of conception of ability on self-regulatory mechanism and complex decision making. *Journal of Personality and Social Psychology*, *56*(3), 407–415. doi:10.1037/0022-3514.56.3.407 PMID:2926637

World Bank. (2012). *E-Government*. Retrieved from: http://www1.worldbank.org/publicsector/egov/index.htm

Wriston, W. B. (1992). *The twilight of sovereignty: How the information revolution is transforming our world* (Vol. 92). New York: Scribner.

Wu, J., & Du, H. (2012). Toward a better understanding of behavioral intention and system usage constructs. *European Journal of Information Systems*, *21*(6), 680–698. doi:10.1057/ejis.2012.15

Wu, Y. L., Tao, Y. H., & Yang, P. C. (2008). The use of theory of acceptance and use of technology to confer the behavioural model of 3G mobile telecommunication users. *Journal of Statistics & Management Systems*, *11*(5), 919–949. doi:10.1080/09720510.2008.10701351

Xavier, P., & Ypsilanti, D. (2010). Behavioral economics and telecommunications policy. In Regulation and the evolution of the global telecommunications industry. Edward Elgar Publishing.

Xavier, P. (1997). Universal service and public access in the networked society. *Telecommunications Policy*, *21*(9), 829–843. doi:10.1016/S0308-5961(97)00050-5

Xue, S. (2005). Internet policy and diffusion in China, Malaysia and Singapore. *Journal of Information Science*, *31*(3), 238–250. doi:10.1177/0165551505052472

Yoon, C., & Kim, S. (2007). Convenience and TAM in a ubiquitous computing environment: The case of wireless LAN. *Electronic Commerce Research and Applications*, *6*(1), 102–112. doi:10.1016/j.elerap.2006.06.009

Yoon, J., & Chae, M. (2009). Varying criticality of key success factors of national e-Strategy along the status of economic development of nations. *Government Information Quarterly*, *26*(1), 25–34. doi:10.1016/j.giq.2008.08.006

Young, I. M. (2000). *Inclusion and democracy*. Oxford University Press.

Ypsilanti, D., & Xavier, P. (1998). Towards next generation regulation. *Telecommunications Policy*, *22*(8), 643–659. doi:10.1016/S0308-5961(98)00044-5

Yuan, C., Su, H. L, Yuan, H-L. & Yuan, C-J. P. (2005). Applying the technology acceptance model and flow theory to online e-learning users' acceptance behaviour. *Issues in Information Systems*, *2*, 175–18.

Zajonc, R. B. (1980). Feeling and thinking: Preferences need no inferences. *The American Psychologist*, *35*(2), 151–175. doi:10.1037/0003-066X.35.2.151

Zhang, P. (2007). Roles of attitudes in initial and continued ICT use: A longitudinal study. In *Proceedings of Americas Conference on Information Systems*. Retrieved Jan 12th 2014 from http://aisel.aisnet.org/cgi/viewcontent.cg

Zhang, P., & Aikman, S. (2009). Attitudes in ICT acceptance and use, *Human-Comput. Interaction. Design Usabil*, *4550*, 1021–1030.

Zittel, T. (2004). Digital parliaments and electronic democracy: A comparison between the US House, the Swedish Riksdag and the German Bundestag. In Electronic democracy: Mobilisation, organisation and participation via new ICTs. London: Routledge.

Zittel, T. (2008). Parliaments and the Internet: A Perspective on the State of Research. Parliaments in the Digital Age: Forum Discussion Paper, 13, 11-15.

Zittel, T. (2003). Political representation in the networked society: The Americanisation of European systems of responsible party government? *Journal of Legislative Studies*, *9*(3), 32–53. doi:10.1080/1357233042000246855

About the Authors

Abdul Rauf Ambali received his PhD in Political Science from International Islamic University Malaysia. He is specialized in public policy analysis and public administration. Currently, he is an Assoc. Prof. at Kwara State University (KWASU) Malete, Department of Politics and Governance. Before joining KWASU, he worked as Prof. Madya of Political Science at Universiti Teknologi Mara (UiTM), Shah Alam Malaysia for nearly 10 years with substantive experience and has graduated many Master's and PhD candidates. He has authored a number of textbooks, modules, such as Primer in Public Policy Analysis Techniques and Methods, Seminar in Public Management, Policy Analysis, etc. The author has international refereed indexed articles in SCOPUS, ISI Journals, IEEE, and many other reputable journals. He has published many chapters in international books published by some worldwide leading publishers such as IGI Global, US, and Routledge, UK. He is a member of the Association for Public Policy Analysis and Management (APPAM), Washington, DC, USA. He is also policy analyst and research fellow at Centre for Biodiversity and Sustainable Development (UiTM) Shah Alam. His excellent research has won him a number of research grants from a variety of funding sources such as Excellence Fund, Technology Transfer Fund, the Fundamental Grant Research Scheme (FRGS), and Long Term Research Grant (LRGS) from the Ministry of Education, Malaysia. He is currently the Head of Department Politics and Governance (HOD), member of Panelists for Action Research Grants on Community Development at KWASU, Malete, Nigeria.

Ahmad Naqiyuddin Bakar started his career as a lecturer in the Faculty of Administrative Science and Policy Studies in 1999 at UiTM. He graduated from the International Islamic University Malaysia (IIUM), received his MA in Public Management from University of Exeter, UK, and obtained his PhD in the field of ICT Policy and Governance at the University of Hull, UK. Upon his returned from his PhD studies in 2008, he became the Coordinator of Monitoring Unit at the Centre for Strategic Planning. In 2010, he was the Head for the Institutional Research at the Centre. In 2012, he was appointed as the Research Fellow at the Centre for Bio-Diversity and Sustainable Development, UiTM. Ahmad Naqiyuddin Bakar is currently heading the Institutional Research – one of the Units under the Strategic Planning and Information (CSPI) Centre, at the Office of the Deputy Vice-Chancellor (Research and Innovation) of Universiti Teknologi MARA (UiTM). He has been actively involved in attaining research grants within the last five years and presented numerous papers at national and international levels. The author has also published many journal articles and chapters in edited books both locally and internationally. He served as the member of National Consultative Forum on ISO/CD26000 – Guidance on Social Responsibility (SR26000) representing the National Mirror Committee for Malaysia (2009-2012). He has obtained a number of research grants from a variety of funding sources such as Excellence Fund, Technology Transfer Fund, the Fundamental Grant Research Scheme (FRGS), and Long Term Research Grant (LRGS) from the Ministry of Education, Malaysia.

Index

U

V